Treating Those with Mental Disorders: A Comprehensive Approach to Case Conceptualization and Treatment

You may be experiencing symptoms of . . .

Based on what you are telling me, you seem to be experiencing symptoms consistent with

TREATING THOSE WITH MENTAL DISORDERS: A COMPREHENSIVE APPROACH TO CASE CONCEPTUALIZATION AND TREATMENT

First Edition

Victoria E. Kress
Youngstown State University

Matthew J. Paylo
Youngstown State University

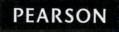

Boston Columbus Indianapolis New York San Francisco Upper Saddle River
Amsterdam Cape Town Dubai London Madrid Milan Munich Paris Montreal Toronto
Delhi Mexico City Sao Paulo Sydney Hong Kong Seoul Singapore Taipei Tokyo

Vice President and Editorial Director:
Jeffery W. Johnston
Vice President and Publisher: Kevin M. Davis
Editorial Assistant: Janelle Criner
Media Development Editor: Hope Madden
Executive Field Marketing Manager: Krista Clark
Senior Product Marketing Manager:
Christopher Barry
Senior Managing Editor: Pamela Bennett
Project Manager: Lauren Carlson
Procurement Specialist: Pat Tonneman

Senior Art Director: Jayne Conte
Text Designer: Aptara®, Inc.
Cover Designer: Karen Salzbach
Cover Art: Shutterstock / Irina_QQQ
Media Producer: Autumn Benson
Full-Service Project Management: Mansi Negi, Aptara®, Inc.
Composition: Aptara®, Inc.
Printer/Binder: Courier/Westford
Cover Printer: Lehigh Phoenix
Text Font: ITC Garamond Std

Credits and acknowledgments for material borrowed from other sources and reproduced, with permission, in this textbook appear on the appropriate page within the text.

Every effort has been made to provide accurate and current Internet information in this book. However, the Internet and information posted on it are constantly changing, so it is inevitable that some of the Internet addresses listed in this textbook will change.

Library of Congress Control Number: 2014933297

10 9 8 7 6 5 4 3 2 1

ISBN 10:   0-13-374072-2
ISBN 13: 978-0-13-374072-1

DEDICATION

To Rob, Isaac, and Ava, whose love, encouragement, and patience were behind every step of this project. ~VK

To Katie ~ MP

ABOUT THE AUTHORS

Victoria E. Kress, Ph.D./LPCC-S (OH), NCC is a professor, counseling clinic director, and the director of the clinical mental health and addictions counseling programs at Youngstown State University. She has over 20 years of clinical experience working in various settings such as community mental health centers, hospitals, residential treatment facilities, private practices, and college counseling centers. She has published over 75 refereed articles, numerous book chapters, and co-authored a book which addressed the ethical and contextual issues associated with applying and using DSM diagnoses. Many of her articles on diagnosing and treating mental disorders have been published in the *Journal of Counseling and Development*. She has been cited as a top contributing author to the *Journal of Mental Health Counseling* as well as the *Journal of College Counseling*, and served as the associate editor of the Theory and Practice Sections of the *Journal of Mental Health Counseling*. She has been teaching treatment planning and DSM-related courses and workshops for almost 20 years. She is passionate about infusing a strength-based, contextual frame into all of her clinical work, and strives to provide counselors with practical ways they can enhance their practices and empower clients. She served two terms as a governor-appointed member of the Ohio Counselor, Social Worker, and Marriage and Family Therapist Board, and served as the chair of the Counselor Professional Standards Committee. She has also served as the ethics liaison for Ohio's state counseling regulatory board, and presently serves as a consultant/expert witness for counselor ethics cases. She was the 2014 recipient of the American Counseling Association's Distinguished Mentor Award, and the 2012 recipient of their Counselor Educator Advocacy Award. She was also the 2008 recipient of the Association for Counselor Education and Supervision's Distinguished Mentor Award, and the 2011 recipient of their Leadership Award. She has also received a number of awards at the university where she teaches (e.g., Distinguished Scholar, Distinguished Public Service). She has received a number of Ohio Counseling Association awards including their Research and Writing Award, Legislative Advocacy Award, and most recently, the Counselor of the Year Award (2011). She is a past president of Chi Sigma Iota International, and she is the president of the Ohio Counseling Association.

Matthew John Paylo, Ph.D./LPCC-S (OH) is an assistant professor, director of the student affairs and college counseling program, and the program director of the counseling program at Youngstown State University. He has over 10 years of clinical experience in various settings including community mental health centers, prisons, hospitals, residential treatment facilities, and college counseling centers. As a former mental health director of a maximum-security female prison, he provided supervision, leadership, and oversight to all mental health treatment including: intakes, assessments, diagnosing, crisis interventions, individual and group treatment, the acute psychiatric unit, and mental health residential units. He has presented and published extensively in the areas of diagnosing and treating mental and emotional disorders. Matthew has also published numerous journal articles and book chapters on trauma, evidence-based treatments, offender treatments, social justice counseling, and the implementation of the DSM. He has received many teaching awards including a prestigious Distinguished Professor of Teaching (2013) award at the university where he teaches.

CHAPTER CONTRIBUTOR BIOS

Nicole Adamson, Ph.D., LPC is a licensed professional counselor and a licensed school counselor in Ohio and North Carolina. She has provided in-home, school-based, and intensive outpatient counseling to children and adolescents. Nicole has published nearly 20 journal articles and book chapters and has delivered over 30 state and national presentations on topics related to counseling and treatment. She was the recipient of the 2013 ACA Courtland C. Lee Multicultural Excellence Scholarship Award and the 2013 CSI Outstanding Doctoral Student Award.

Denise D. Ben-Porath, Ph.D. is a Professor in the Department of Psychology at John Carroll University. She has had extensive experience working with difficult-to-treat, multi-diagnostic individuals. She has worked and consulted in a variety of clinical settings, including university counseling centers, community mental health centers, adolescent residential treatment programs, correctional settings, private practice, and settings. She has consulted at mental health agencies throughout the United States in the treatment of borderline personality disorder, eating disorders, and the implementation of DBT programs. Her research interests include eating disorders, borderline personality disorder, and dialectical behavior therapy. She has published numerous articles in these areas and currently maintains a private practice at Cleveland Center for Eating Disorders where she treats individuals with eating disorders.

Kelly Bhatnagar, Ph.D. is the Assistant Clinical Director and the Director of Research at The Cleveland Center for Eating Disorders. She holds clinical expertise in the treatment of child and adolescent eating disorders, including specialized training in Family Based Treatment, or "The Maudsley Approach," and in the cognitive-behavioral treatment of body image disturbance. She has worked and trained in various settings across the nation including pediatric hospitals, academic institutions, community mental health centers, private practices, and college counseling centers. She has published numerous journal articles and book chapters on the topics of eating disorders and body image.

Emily C. Campbell, Ph.D., LPCA, NCC is a community mental health counselor and a marriage and family therapist. She has clinical experience in college counseling centers, hospitals, and private practice settings. She has counseled couples, families, groups, and individuals of all ages and backgrounds, who experience a variety of different issues which include: relationship issues, adjustment difficulties, mood disorders, anger issues, existential issues, and, trauma. In addition, she has taught graduate courses, and supervised counseling students, at the University of North Carolina at Greensboro.

LaShauna M. Dean, Ph.D., LPC, NCC is an Assistant Professor at William Paterson University in Wayne, NJ. She has worked in the field of mental health counseling, treating people with a wide variety of mental disorders, for nearly a decade. She has worked with clients diagnosed with a variety of mental disorders, as a counselor, case manager, crisis intervention worker, and as an intake/assessment clinician.

Karen M. Decker, Ph.D. is an assistant professor in the Professional Counseling Program at William Paterson University in Wayne, New Jersey. She is a Licensed Professional Counselor

(LPC) and certified school counselor in NJ as well as an Approved Clinical Supervisor (ACS). She has clinical experience in community mental health centers and private practice.

Michelle Gimenez Hinkle, Ph.D. is an assistant professor in the professional counseling program at William Paterson University. She has counseled individuals across the lifespan in community mental health centers and college counseling centers. The majority of her clinical focus has been working with children, adolescents, and families. She has published numerous book chapters and journal articles on a variety of clinical counseling topics.

Holly J. Hartwig Moorhead, Ph.D. is an assistant professor in the Counseling Department at Regent University. Her clinical background includes crisis assessment and counseling children, adolescents, and adults in various settings, including in-patient psychiatric hospitalization, residential treatment, school, and community agency milieus. Formerly, she served as the ethics officer for a professional counseling organization. Her professional publications include journal articles, book chapters, and most recently, a co-edited textbook which addresses relationship between values and ethics.

Brandy L. Kelly Gilea, Ph.D., PCC-S is a core faculty member at Walden University in the Master's in Mental Health Counseling Program. She has over 13 years of clinical, supervisory, and administrative experience in community behavioral health centers and university counseling clinics. In her role as a clinical director of a behavioral health counseling center, she has supervised crisis intervention services, behavioral health counseling, community psychiatric support treatment, inpatient psychiatric stabilization, and pharmacological management services. She has numerous publications and professional presentations on the topics of supervision, ethics, and clinical practice.

Rachel M. Hoffman O'Neill, Ph.D., PCC-S is a core faculty member at Walden University in the Master's in Mental Health Counseling Program. She has also worked as a clinical director at behavioral health organization specializing in addiction and mental health issues. She has over 10 years of experience working in a variety of settings including: addictions treatment, community-based mental health, inpatient psychiatric services, and college counseling. She has published a number of articles and book chapters on topics related to mental health and addictions counseling. She presently serves as the editor of the *Journal of Counselor Practice*.

Amie A. Manis, Ph.D. is a professor in the Department of Counselor Education and Supervision at Capella University. She has a decade of clinical experience in various settings ranging from an elementary school, to a community health center, a private practice, and a college counseling center. Promoting multicultural competence and a social justice advocacy orientation among counselor trainees has been a central focus of her practice and scholarship.

Lisa P. Meyer, M.A., NCC works as an outpatient and crisis stabilization counselor in the Ohio Valley Medical Center. She has worked with children, adolescents, older adults, and families in community mental health centers. She also conducts neuropsychological assessments in outpatient and hospital settings. Her current research is focused on body image and eating disorders.

Casey A. Barrio Minton Ph.D. is an associate professor and the counseling program coordinator at the University of North Texas. Her clinical experiences include serving clients in a range of outpatient, residential, intensive outpatient, and inpatient mental health settings with a focus on crisis intervention and stabilization. She has authored multiple book chapters and journal articles focused on counselor preparation and crisis intervention, and is the co-author a learning companion to the *DSM-5*. She is the editor of the *Journal of Counselor Leadership and Advocacy*, and is a past president of Chi Sigma Iota International and the Association for Assessment and Research in Counseling.

Robin Raniero Norris, Ph.D., LMFT is the founder of Windward Optimal Health, counseling and coaching practice in Sterling, Virginia, and an author for the Zur Institute. She has held a student development chair position for the Northern Virginia Licensed Professional Counselors (NVLPC) and continues to enjoy sharing her passion of wellness with students and clients. Her main research interests are animal assisted therapy, pet loss, giftedness, anxiety in children, positive psychology, the psychology of eating, bariatric psychology, and couples counseling.

Elizabeth A. Prosek, Ph.D. is an assistant professor of counseling at the University of North Texas. Her clinical experience includes community in-home counseling, community outpatient counseling, university supervision, and directing a grant funded in-school program. She has counseled individuals with intellectual disabilities, serious and persistent mental illness, adults with wellness concerns, and at-risk adolescents. She has published journal articles on topics related to diagnosis and assessment, clinical decision-making, vulnerable client populations, and measurement of client outcomes.

Cassandra G. Pusateri, Ph.D., NCC is an assistant professor in the Counseling Program at Youngstown State University. She has experience working in school, hospital, clinic, and community agency settings as well as with grant-funded programs. Her research interests include assessment, rural issues and Appalachian cultural identities, empathy, and gender issues in counseling. Cassandra is an active member of several professional associations and has presented at many local, state, and national conferences, and has co-authored journal articles and book chapters.

Meredith A. Rausch, MS is the Vice President of a non-profit organization that focuses on female victims of abuse; she is passionate about advocacy and empowerment for this population. She also works as a mobile crisis outreach counselor. She has almost a decade of clinical experience in a variety of settings, and has a special interest in mind/body holistic counseling, and, family safety, risk, and permanency counseling and advocacy. She has engaged in neuropsychological research, studying the various effects of traumatic brain injuries, as well as alcohol use disorders in the military veteran population.

Natalie F. Williams, Ph.D. is an Applied Behavior Analysis (ABA) team leader for Autism Concepts, Inc. She has extensive experience providing ABA and working in the field of early childhood mental health. Her research and clinical interests include sexuality education and abuse prevention for children and adults with developmental disabilities. She is an active community advocate for those who have developmental disabilities and has delivered training presentations and television appearances for parents, educators, counselors, and community stakeholders.

Chelsey A. Zoldan, M.S.Ed. has worked in community mental health centers and college counseling clinics, and has been active in university mental health initiatives. She has nearly a decade of experience working with individuals with developmental disabilities in educational, vocational, and residential settings, and has been involved in reviewing rehabilitation programming. She has published articles and presented on topics related to the diagnosis and treatment of mental disorders. She has worked as a research assistant in the Counseling Program at Youngstown State University.

PREFACE

When we were graduate students, we learned the foundations of counseling, including theories and basic techniques for use with clients. We learned about clinical concepts, the *DSM* system of diagnosis, and treatments that could be used to address different disorders and problems in living. However, when faced with actual clients, we struggled to know how to proceed. Like many other counselors-in-training, we felt flooded with information that we needed to digest and determine how to apply. New counselors are challenged to apply years of acquired information to their conceptualization of clients, knowing that information will inform how they proceed in treatment planning, and in the implementation of treatment approaches and interventions. But how does one take years of formal education and apply that information to counseling clients and to helping them to make the changes they require to live optimally? In writing this text, our goal was to develop a resource that would help counselors feel empowered to thoughtfully and deliberately assist their clients in tackling their complex struggles and difficulties.

Throughout our careers, we have repeatedly heard that counselors value strength-based, contextually and culturally sensitive approaches to counseling, yet no one taught us how to integrate this way of thinking with the reality of clinical practice; a reality that requires counselors espouse, to some extent, to a medical-model approach which requires that we diagnose and "treat" mental disorders.

Of fundamental importance to us in developing this text was our desire to create a treatment planning model that incorporated a strength-based and contextually sensitive approach to counseling and treatment planning. What resulted was the formation of our conceptual framework model, ***I CAN START***, which consists of essential case conceptualization components and addresses treatment planning from a strength- and evidence-based, contextually sensitive perspective. This conceptual model is detailed in Chapter 2, and is utilized in conceptualizing each of the case studies presented throughout the text.

Our clients deserve to receive the most efficacious treatments available. As such, this text also provides readers with information on evidence-based approaches that can be used in treating a variety of mental disorders. There is a paucity of research on treating some of the mental disorders described in this text. In these situations, we have made every attempt to provide the reader with the most comprehensive, rigorous assimilation of all of the current treatment literature, along with a summary of any emerging approaches that may warrant further consideration and research.

There are multiple interventions that are associated with the evidence-based approaches discussed in this text. There are also hundreds of different ways these interventions can be applied, illustrated, and woven into the fabric of counseling. We frequently hear our students and supervisees comment that they want to better understand what it "looks" like to apply various theories and/or treatments. The ***Creative Toolbox*** feature found in chapters 4–15 highlights the varied means of applying treatment interventions. These interventions, which include art, play, and movement, are intended to illuminate the treatment concepts, and help readers understand the variety of vehicles that can be used to apply interventions.

To support our goal of creating a practical treatment planning text, Chapter 1 focuses on foundational real-world treatment planning practices, factors that influence counseling and treatment outcomes, and the practical realities of treatment planning.

Chapter 2 presents principles that counselors can use to guide the treatment development process. The ***I CAN START*** case conceptualization and treatment planning model is also presented in chapter 2.

Chapter 3 includes a discussion of select safety-related clinical issues that must be addressed as a part of effective treatment planning. Emphasis is placed on practical steps counselors can take to promote and support their clients' safety. The clinical issues selected, including suicide, homicide, and intimate partner violence, are those that counselors encounter with the greatest frequency, and those that invite the most serious potential for risk to clients, counselors, and/or members of the community.

Chapters 4 through 15 provide a brief discussion of mental disorders (as defined by the *DSM-5*), and counseling considerations and treatment approaches which apply to each disorder. Each chapter has a unified structure and begins with a case study and an overview of information related to the category of disorders discussed in the chapter. Next, more detailed information about the specific disorders, and their associated counseling considerations, treatments, and prognoses is provided. Finally, each chapter concludes with a case treatment application using the ***I CAN START*** treatment model.

ACKNOWLEDGMENTS

Most importantly, we would like to acknowledge our chapter authors and the many people who contributed their voices in the clinical and video features in this text. We are so grateful for the time they invested in sharing their expertise.

We could not have met our tight deadlines without the assistance of Chelsey Zoldan, research assistant extraordinaire, who always stepped up when we most needed her assistance. Her contributions to this text were many and varied, and we are eternally grateful for all of her above-and-beyond hard work. Thanks, too, goes to Alison Zins for her assistance in developing our support materials.

We would also like to thank our publishing team at Pearson. Timing is not everything, but sometimes it sure is important! Thanks goes out to Sybil Geraud for stopping in one beautiful fall morning and setting the wheels of this project in motion; to Meredith Fossel for believing in our vision for this project; to Hope Madden for guiding us through the media development process; to Lauren Carlson for managing our project with care; and to Kevin Davis for his thoughtful feedback and support during the later stages of this project. We would also like to thank Mansi Negi and Munesh Kumar (from Aptara) for their patience and hard work during the production stages of this text.

We would like to acknowledge the following reviewers who offered useful suggestions, which helped us develop this text: Shawn L. Spurgeon, The University of Tennessee at Knoxville; Darcy Granello and Krista Predragovich, The Ohio State University; Sharon K. Anderson, Colorado State University; and Adele Baruch-Runyon, University of Southern Maine.

Special Acknowledgments

Developing a text necessarily requires sacrifice not only from the authors, but also from the people who surround them. My profound thanks go out to my husband, Rob, and my children, Ava and Isaac, who did without my presence for many days as I sat clicking away at my computer.

Matt, thank you for being such a wonderful co-author! There is no one else in the world with whom I would have rather journeyed. Kate, Hudson, Kennedy, and Weston, thank you for your many sacrifices!

Denise, Rob, Paula, and Jake: thank you for always believing in me, and for encouraging me to pursue this project my way, and on my own terms. Denise, per your usual, you were too generous, not only in supporting me, but also this project. Thanks also to Elizabeth Bonness, my very first editor. You have always been—and will always be—my favorite editor!

Thank you to Nathan Woollard and Kimberly Kuhn for helping me to "sit" with this project. You are both exceptionally gifted at your craft, and I quite literally could not have done this without you!

And finally, I also want to acknowledge those who have taught me the most about problems in living and how to overcome them, or what we necessarily had to refer to in this book as mental disorders and their treatment: my clients. When I became a counselor, personal transformation as a result of my work was not something I anticipated. My clients have taught me about the resilience inherent in the human spirit. Their ability to not only endure, but thrive even in the face of adversity, barriers, and injustices has forever changed me, and how I see the world. No book can teach what they have taught me, but I hope that some of the strength-based perspectives and contextually sensitive practices I have developed, because of what my clients have taught me, translates in this text.

Victoria E. Kress

The process of completing a book is time consuming and filled with sacrifice, challenges, and intense deadlines. It is also full of highs and lows and I would not have survived these if it were not for a number of people who would never allow me to quit or second-guess my abilities; to them, I am forever grateful.

I want to thank my co-author, Vicki. I appreciate you more than I can ever put into words. You have taught me so much about being a counselor, an educator, a writer, and a person. I am indebted to you for your supervision, patience, guidance, warmth, and mentorship. I would gladly take this journey again with you!

I want to thank my children, Hudson, Kennedy, and Weston, for tolerating all those early mornings and late nights when I was less than available. You are my joy and inspiration!

I want to thank my family members, who were instrumental in supporting my wife and children throughout this time-consuming process. Thank you Diane, Robert, and Leigh. I appreciate your love and support!

Last, but definitely not least, I want to thank my supportive, loving wife. Katie, what can I say that I have not already said. All of this would never have been possible without you. You kindle a part of me that is authentic, optimistic, driven, confident, and hopeful. You challenged me to envision bigger dreams than I ever thought were possible! I appreciate and delight in you!

Matthew J. Paylo

BRIEF CONTENTS

CONTENTS

The Foundations of Treatment Planning: A Primer

Victoria E. Kress and Matthew J. Paylo

In order to engage in effective treatment planning, counselors must understand the evidence-based factors that influence treatment outcomes. In other words, counselors must understand the foundations of "good" treatment planning. In this chapter we review the essentials of good treatment planning. The first half of the chapter addresses the factors that influence counseling and treatment outcomes. The second half of the chapter focuses on information related to the practical realities of treatment planning, or the common real-world demands placed on counselors. The information provided in this chapter serves as the foundation for the I CAN START treatment model, which will be presented in Chapter 2.

THE FOUNDATIONS OF EFFECTIVE TREATMENT

In order to develop effective treatment plans counselors need to be able to answer the question: Do counseling and psychosocial treatments (i.e., those that involve psychological and/or social factors as the focus of intervention) work, and if so, what makes them work? In this section we will explore these questions and discuss what we know about the foundations of effective treatment planning. More specifically, we will review the literature related to the factors that influence counseling outcomes, or counseling success. This presentation will culminate in suggestions that counselors can use in developing treatment plans.

Factors That Influence Counseling/Treatment Outcomes

If counselors are to understand how to develop "good" or effective treatment plans, they must be mindful of the factors that will impact counseling outcomes (i.e., the end result of counseling). A great deal of research has addressed the topic of factors that influence counseling and treatment outcomes. The factors that influence counseling outcomes can be conceptualized as being related to counselor variables and characteristics, client characteristics, and the relationship between the counselor and client within a treatment setting (i.e., treatment variables). These three clusters of variables influence counseling outcomes and therefore need to be monitored and considered throughout the counseling process. Monitoring these factors will provide clients with the most effective treatment and the best possible conditions to evoke change.

COUNSELOR VARIABLES   Counselor variables are everything seen and unseen that a counselor brings to the counseling relationship and into counseling sessions. These include the counselor's demographics, experience, personality, and way of viewing the world (i.e., worldview). Counselor variables are often grouped by either what is seen (i.e., observable) or unseen (i.e., inferred), and what qualities (i.e., traits) or stances (i.e., states) the counselor possesses (Baldwin & Imel, 2013; Beutler et al., 2004). What follows are four commonly identified categories of counselor variables:

- *Observable traits* of the counselor (i.e., a counselor's age, sex, race/ethnicity)
- *Observable states* of the counselor (i.e., a counselor's professional discipline, training, professional experience, interpersonal style, directiveness, intervention style, and the use of self-disclosure)
- *Inferred traits* of the counselor (i.e., a counselor's general personality, coping style, emotional well-being, values, beliefs, and cultural attitudes)
- *Inferred states* of the counselor (i.e., therapeutic relationship and theoretical orientation)

With regard to a counselor's observable traits, there appears to be little evidence that a counselor's age, sex, or race and ethnicity affect counseling outcomes. In exploring observable states, meta-analytic studies have also indicated no consistent treatment outcome differences among the counseling-related disciplines (i.e., counselor, social worker, marriage and family therapist, psychologist, and psychiatrist), or interestingly, with regard to training or professional experience (Baldwin & Imel, 2013; Beutler et al., 2004).

Inferred traits, such as counselor intervention style (i.e., insight-oriented versus symptom-oriented, emotive versus supportive), counselor directiveness, and counselor self-disclosure, do not equally benefit all clients in all situations (Baldwin & Imel, 2013; Beutler et al., 2004), thus highlighting the importance of tailoring treatments and interventions to a client's unique needs. Inferred states, such as the strength of the therapeutic alliance, are consistently linked with counseling outcomes. The therapeutic alliance is an area that counselors can considerably impact (this topic will be more fully covered later in this chapter).

Counselor theoretical orientation is a much more difficult variable to measure. This may be due to the inherent differences in the ways differing theoretical orientations approach, define, and measure change within their conceptual framework (Baldwin & Imel, 2013; Beutler et al., 2004), and because of the varied ways that counselors actually apply different theories.

CLIENT VARIABLES   Client variables are everything that a client brings into the counseling relationship and into sessions (e.g., experiences, concerns, expectations, mental illness). A counselor must consider that clients are not just the passive recipients of treatment or interventions, but are an active, independent variable in the treatment process (Bohart & Wade, 2013).

Counselors come into treatment with their own lived experiences, strengths, difficulties, expectations, readiness for change, and relationship contexts.

Typically, what brings clients into treatment is some identified difficulty or concern; something is not going the way they want it to or they are unable to do something they hoped or wished to do. These concerns often range in severity and can be situation-related, relationship-oriented, and/or highlight a difficulty due to the direct or indirect effects of a mental health disorder. The severity of a mental disorder, impairment in level of functioning, and/or a problem of a chronic nature all lead to a poorer prognosis and more negatively impact counseling outcomes (Clarkin & Levy, 2004). Clients with more severe issues often require more restrictive settings and more sustained treatment to reach clinically significant, sustained improvements. However, even those individuals who are under the greatest levels of distress can experience considerable change. Clients' initial distress can serve as a positive motivator and promote a desire to actively engage in counseling (Bohart & Wade, 2013).

Client expectations for change have been deemed influential to counseling outcomes; if clients expect change to occur, they have hope and are thus open to change. Frank (1961) contended that clients' confidence in the process and in their counselor was critical for a positive counseling outcome. Counselors need to consider clients' expectations for the consequences of treatment (i.e., outcome expectations) and their expectations about the process, nature, and course of treatment (i.e., treatment expectations; Constantino, Glass, Arnkoff, Ametrano, & Smith, 2011).

A client's outcome expectations are linked to positive counseling outcomes (Constantino et al., 2011). Those who enter treatment with an optimistic and hopeful attitude about the eventual outcomes (e.g., consequences) are more likely to reach their intended goals than those with more negative outcome expectations.

A client's readiness or motivation to change is one of the most important client variables that impact counseling outcomes. For client change to occur, a client must be aware of a problem, open to the consideration of change, and willing to make the needed changes to alter his or her situation. It is not surprising that clients' readiness to change is essential in predicting counseling outcomes. The Stages of Change model (Norcross, Krebs, & Prochaska, 2011) consists of five stages of change that can be utilized as an assessment tool as well as a mechanism to prepare clients for change. These stages are briefly described here:

- *Precontemplation* (i.e., a client may have a lack of awareness that a problem or difficulty is even present and has no intention of changing).
- *Contemplation* (i.e., a client is becoming more aware that a problem exists, may verbalize it and even desire change, but has made no plans to change or act).
- *Preparation* (i.e., a client has moved from a place of increased awareness to the planning of small incremental changes; intention to change is present, but the individual has not begun this process).
- *Action* (i.e., a client is implementing the action plan by modifying his or her behaviors; this is the most active and challenging part of the change process for clients).
- *Maintenance* (i.e., a client continues to maintain his or her stabilization and prepares to thwart relapse opportunities)

Counselors need to be aware of clients' level of motivation to change and continually assess their readiness for change. Resistance to change may arise at any point in the counseling process. This is not necessarily good or bad; just a part of the ebb and flow process of change. Counselors do not necessarily need to directly address this resistance, but can roll with the resistance, attempting to aid clients in understanding their ambivalence, and eventually exploring both sides of the issue or behavior. Utilization of the therapeutic relationship in this way allows the client's ambivalence to be the focus of treatment until the client is able to choose to change. These are essential components of motivational interviewing, a motivational-enhancement approach (Miller & Rollnick, 2012). (See Chapter 8 for a discussion of utilizing motivational interviewing with substance use disorders as well as a case demonstration.) A counselor must consider ways he or she can gently help move clients forward in these stages of change, thus facilitating better counseling outcomes (see Table 1.1 for information about the Stages of Change model). When a client is motivated and ready to change, treatment processes move more quickly and better counseling outcomes are achieved. Most treatments of mental disorders are founded on the assumption that clients are motivated to want to change, thus all clients' motivation to make changes and engage in treatment should be assessed. For example, in order for a client to apply cognitive behavioral therapy to stop self-injuring, the client's motivation to want to change needs to be assessed first as the client will most likely not follow through on using the skills learned in counseling if he or she does not wish to stop self-injuring.

Voices from the Trenches 1.1: In the Pearson etext, click here to watch a video of a counselor providing practice suggestions for using motivational interviewing.

TABLE 1.1   Stages of Change (Based on Norcross et al., 2011)

Stages of Change	Activities for Counselor to Promote	Considerations
Precontemplation	Consciousness raising	Increasing awareness of the advantages of changing
		Increasing awareness of self, disorder/difficulty, and patterns of behaviors
		Dealing with dramatic relief (i.e., the sadness of giving up the behavior/pattern)
Contemplation	Client evaluation of present and future	Questioning self-perception and what client may want to become in the future
		Envisioning a healthier, happier future/self
Preparation	Client empowerment	Increasing client's sense that he or she possesses the power to actually make the needed change
		Providing choices in treatment to aid in client's sense of ownership
Action	Reinforcement of steps towards change	Environmental evaluation: Moving the focus from external reinforcers to internal ones
		Counterconditioning (i.e., replacing less healthy behaviors with healthier ones)
Maintenance	Relapse prevention	Preparing ahead for situations that may induce relapse

One final client variable that requires counselors' consideration is clients' ability to form and maintain social relationships. Since counseling involves an interpersonal interaction between the counselor and the client, the client is required to possess some rudimentary ability to form, interact in, and maintain a social relationship. If clients have significant social impairments, especially a rigid or enmeshed personality, attachment issues, long-standing difficulties in relating to others, and/or deficits in interpreting social interactions, they will not only find the process of building a therapeutic alliance with a counselor to be difficult, but may find it challenging to manage in-session behaviors, thus creating a significant impact on their ability to tolerate sessions, remain in session, complete treatment, and ultimately have positive counseling outcomes (Clarkin & Levy, 2004).

TREATMENT VARIABLES   Not only do counselors and clients impact the counseling outcomes, but so does the structure of treatment as well as the social interaction between the counselor and client within sessions. Counselors need to be mindful of these variables as they will affect counseling outcomes.

Treatment duration is an important treatment planning consideration. Lambert (2013) suggested that most clients will show improvements within seven counseling sessions. Though he also suggested that 75% of clients only show significant changes, under the strictest of rigor, after around 50 sessions thus suggesting that more sessions can be beneficial (Lambert, 2013). The reality of clinical counseling practice is that clients are often only afforded a limited number of sessions annually (e.g., 15–20 sessions). Additionally, most clients expect to be in counseling only until their presenting problems are resolved, with most expecting to attend only eight sessions (Lambert, 2013). Therefore, counselors must have a comprehensive, time-efficient model in place for the diagnosis, case conceptualization, and implementation of treatment approaches if they wish to maximize counseling outcomes.

Another treatment consideration is the social, working interaction between the counselor and the client. This therapeutic alliance (i.e., a counselor's ability to form and maintain a working relationship with the client) is one of the most influential factors in counseling outcomes (Lambert, 2013; Zuroff, Kelly, Leybman, Blatt, & Wampold, 2010). With over 50 years of consistent research, the therapeutic alliance continues to be highly correlated with counseling treatment outcomes across all theoretical treatment approaches (i.e., behavioral, psychodynamic, cognitive behavioral, humanistic) and modalities (i.e., individual, group, couple, and family; Norcross et al., 2011). A therapeutic alliance is strengthened by an active, warm climate of collaboration, in which the counselor attempts to reach a mutually agreeable set of treatment goals, as well as a consensus on the goals and course of treatment (Bordin, 1979). This collaborative relationship often inspires trust and instills a sense of hope and optimism in the process and utility of treatment, thus creating better counseling outcomes. Related to this idea, highly successful counselors consistently ask clients for feedback on the direction, focus, approach, and interventions utilized in treatment, thus reinforcing the importance of the therapeutic alliance and collaboration throughout treatment (Norcross & Wampold, 2011).

All three of the aforementioned clusters of variables (i.e., counselor, client, and treatment) affect the efficiency and effectiveness of counseling outcomes and must be addressed in any effective treatment approach. These sets of variables should be consistently evaluated, monitored, and considered throughout the treatment process. The next section addresses the question: "What is good treatment planning?" Information on counselor, client, and treatment variables are considered in developing our formulation of "good" treatment planning.

What Is "Good" Treatment Planning?

The intention of mental health treatment is to maximize clients' adaptive functioning by developing and building upon their strengths and assets, while concurrently addressing the problems and difficulties that clients bring to counseling. Accurate diagnosing and appropriate treatment planning for individuals with mental disorders promotes health and client empowerment, prevents future problems from developing, and supports productive living.

Without an accurate mental health diagnosis and a thorough understanding of each client's unique situation and circumstances, appropriate treatment approaches cannot be selected. Additionally, when counselors neglect to use evidence-based approaches (i.e., the most up-to-date, relevant research-based approaches and interventions) for treating mental disorders or other client presenting issues, clients are not provided with the quality of care that they deserve.

The process of diagnosing, conceptualizing cases, and treatment planning is a time-limited endeavor. This process is time sensitive because of the limitations of third-party payers (i.e., funding issues), and because of the time expectations of clients (i.e., most clients prefer to attend counseling for a limited amount of time, usually until their presenting problems have been alleviated). In considering the rising costs of health care and the increasing restraints on treatment (i.e., approaches, number of sessions) by managed care agencies (see Chapter 2 for a more detailed discussion of these issues), counselors are charged with adopting an effective and comprehensive approach to client treatment in a limited amount of time. With accountability becoming increasingly more relevant to counselor practice and treatment planning, counselors must adopt a process of "good" treatment planning. A comprehensive, atheoretical approach to treatment planning must incorporate evidence-based approaches, and at a minimum should be composed of the following components (Jongsma, Peterson, & Bruce, 2006):

- Problem selection (i.e., a clearly stated treatment focus)
- Problem definition (i.e., a concrete, operationally defined problem)
- Goal development (i.e., the long-term positive outcomes or consequences of treatment)
- Objective construction (i.e., short-term, behavioral goals that are attainable and measurable, delineating when treatment is completed)
- Interventions (i.e., connecting at least one intervention with each goal)

These components, while not exhaustive, provide a general framework for treatment planning considerations. Counseling processes need to be based on evidence-based research, which provides robustness to external scrutiny and third-party payer questioning. Therefore, "good" treatment planning requires, after an accurate diagnosis, an individualized, culturally- and contextually-sensitive, strength-based framework that implements evidenced-based approaches and interventions with a specific mental health disorder. The following sections address aspects that are important to good treatment planning.

EVIDENCE-BASED   A critically important question that all counselors must ask is: What is known about the overall effectiveness of counseling? Meta-analytic studies conducted over the past three decades (e.g., Lambert, 2013; Lipsey & Wilson, 1993; Smith, Glass, & Miller, 1980) have confirmed that what we do as counselors is effective; counseling is significantly more beneficial for clients than nontreatment or placebo effect conditions. Not only is counseling more beneficial than nontreatment, but it often produces clinically meaningful changes for most individuals who suffer with mental disorders and clinical concerns or issues (Lambert, 2013). Therefore, counselors can safely assert the utility and effectiveness of counseling in aiding and alleviating the distress and discomfort of individuals with mental health disorders. This is great news for counselors: as a profession, we are providing a service that works with most people most of the time! Establishing this foundational cornerstone is critical if we are to move to the next pressing question which is: which approaches within counseling treatment are most effective with which clients, with which mental disorders, and under what conditions? One of the paramount aims of this text is to provide counselors with the most up-to-date, evidenced-based approaches and interventions for use with the mental disorders defined by the fifth edition of the *Diagnostic and Statistical Manual of Mental Disorders* (*DSM-5*; American Psychological Association [APA], 2013).

What does the term *evidence-based practice* (EBP) mean? Simplistically, EBPs are research-based treatments and interventions for use in treating various mental disorders and presenting problems. EPBs and interventions should reduce clients' symptoms, improve their level of functioning, and/or improve their ability to function well within their communities (e.g., create a reduction in their need for more restrictive services such as hospitals, residential treatment, or emergency visits). EPBs have been supported as effective by the gold standard for clinical health care research: randomized controlled trials (RCTs). RCTs are scientific experiments that are controlled (i.e., meaning they have a control group or a nontreatment group that the treatment group is compared to), and are randomized (i.e., meaning that a participant has an equal or random chance of being assigned to any of the treatment groups or the control group). To conduct an RCT is a time consuming and resource intensive undertaking.

Another treatment planning consideration is that many clients have co-occurring disorders (i.e., more than one mental health diagnosis), and as such, choosing an evidence-based approach can be difficult. Typically, to minimize the influence of extraneous variables, established evidence-based approaches have been tested on participants possessing one mental disorder. As such, it is known only that the treatment for the disorder worked for people who had just the one disorder. But would that same treatment work with people who have more than one disorder? And what treatment do you use if someone has more than one disorder? For example, when working with a client who has borderline personality disorder and a substance use disorder, it may be difficult to know how and when to begin applying the most evidence-based treatments that apply to each disorder.

Additionally, there exist what are referred to as "gaps" within the research literature. Gaps refer to a lack of evidence-based approaches and interventions for certain mental health disorders; some have received little research support and may have no known evidence-based treatments at this time. Because of a lack of RCTs as related to the treatment of some disorders, not all of the treatments or treatment research presented in this text are based on RCTs. In the cases where a given disorder lacks a solid treatment research base, the literature was consulted to find emerging treatments that appeared to provide the best, most informed treatment approaches, interventions, and counseling considerations.

INDIVIDUALIZED Knowing that a particular treatment is evidence-based does not neces-sarily mean that it should be used with a given client. Additional factors should be con-sidered before utilizing evidence-based approaches and interventions. Considering each client as a unique person who experiences distinct contextual factors will assist a coun-selor in determining the appropriateness of each treatment approach with each client.

In order for counselors to individualize treatment and be effective, it is important that they receive ongoing client feedback. Clients' voices should be amplified throughout the treatment process so as to increase positive counseling outcomes. Individualized treat-ment involves counselors listening to clients as they continually monitor and evaluate the course and directions of treatment (Bohart & Wade, 2013). Client feedback should be solicited throughout the diagnosis, conceptualization, treatment planning, and treatment implementation processes.

When individualizing treatment, counselors must construct individualized treatment plans that not only highlight clients' goals and objectives, but highlight their strengths, assets, and resources. Additionally, individualized treatment plans should identify strate-gies and methods that will be implemented to address clients' specific issues and con-cerns. Individualized treatment plans should also provide clients with a systematic timeline outlining when each goal and objective will be addressed and by which team member (i.e., counselor, psychiatrist, direct care staff, case manager). By highlighting a client's individualized needs, strengths, and concerns, a counselor can enhance a client's sense of collaboration, reach consensus on therapeutic goals, and reduce the risk of a client's early departure from treatment (Bohart & Wade, 2013).

RELATIONAL When counselors and their clients have a strong relationship, it is mani-fested in an individualized treatment plan that is sensitive to clients' specific goals and objectives, and takes into consideration clients' culture, sexual orientation, gender, spirit-uality, socioeconomic status, and developmental considerations (i.e., physical, psycho-logical, sexual, cognitive, learning styles). A strong therapeutic relationship significantly contributes to treatment outcomes and should be part of any evidenced-based approach (Norcross et al., 2011). Counselors must stay connected to the idea that they are serving complex, unique human beings and that they themselves are unique and complex (Sommers-Flanagan & Sommers-Flanagan, 2009). As such, the counseling relationship must be constantly monitored.

Research supports the idea that for treatment to be the most effective, a strong rela-tionship is required, and in fact, it is one of the most important treatment factors that counselors can influence (Norcross & Lambert, 2011). A strong therapeutic relationship has an effect on clients' satisfaction with counseling services, their level of disclosure, their optimism in the process of counseling, and their sense of hope that their situation can change (Norcross et al., 2011).

A counselor's ability to convey relationship-building characteristics such as empa-thy, congruence, positive regard, and affirmation in the counseling relationship has long been associated with positive counseling outcomes (Norcross et al., 2011). Clients need to feel they are understood by their counselors and that their counselors feels genuine com-passion for them and their situation. Additionally, clients need to perceive counselors as being congruent (i.e., real, authentic) and perceive that they present an accurate sense of self, which is displayed by the counselor's thoughts, behaviors, and emotions. In this affirming stance, the counselor is open, honest, and genuine with the client. Assuming a nonjudgmental stance, viewing clients in a positive light, and attempting to appreciate them without conditions of worth, creates a sense of equality in an otherwise unequal relationship in which the counselor possesses a great deal of power. Empathy, congruence, and positive regard create a climate of collaboration and cooperation in the counseling relationship, thus increasing the probability of goal consensus (i.e., agreement on the direction of change) and change (Bohart & Wade, 2013). If they are congruently counseling clients, counselors should be able to move beyond a pathology-saturated view of their clients and connect with clients' innate strengths and capacities.

STRENGTH-BASED   A lens, in the context of treatment planning, is a way of conceptualizing the client, the client's situation, and the client's treatment plan. A strength-based lens is a paradigm shift from the prescriptive, medical model approach typically taken when treating mental disorders. A traditional medical model approach involves counselors "treating" clients or otherwise doing something to clients to help them change. A traditional medical model approach to treating clients typically assumes an underlying neurological or biochemical cause for client problems and is rooted in a deficit-based narrative or problem conceptualization. It is therefore assumed that mental disorders occur apart from what is happening in the family or in the client's broader social contexts.

A strength-based lens is grounded in the assumption that the development and amplification of strengths and assets within and around the individual provides clients with a greater sense of resiliency against mental illness and future difficulties (Smith, 2006). When counselors work from a strength-based perspective, they actively engage in the process of enhancing, developing, and highlighting clients' resources, strengths, times of resiliency, and their ability to cope and persevere, thus enhancing clients' sense of esteem by increasing their sense of self-determination, mastery of life, and internal fortitude.

 Clinical Toolbox 1.1: In the Pearson etext, click here to review questions that counselors can consider in assessing their value of a strength-based counseling approach.

A strength-based approach is firmly situated in the assumption that counselors should not only explore disease and weakness, but that they should invest equal time and energy in exploring a client's assets and strengths, providing a more holistic and balanced approach to treating each individual. Working from this type of clinical perspective, counselors can instill hope through the building of personal competencies, and they can enhance growth through building upon strengths, all while concurrently addressing aspects of the individual that may be perceived as being deficits of well-being (Smith, 2006). The use of a strength-based lens does not preclude the utilization of evidenced-based approaches; they can be applied concurrently.

A strength-based approach also holds to the idea that in building clients' strengths, counselors provide clients with the resources they need to prevent the development of additional problems, at present and in the future. In this way, a strength-based approach is preventive in that it develops and identifies strengths and can be used not only to address current struggles, but to help insulate clients from developing additional problems. To be more concrete, counselors can work from a strength-based perspective by identifying the unique strengths that an individual has and amplifying those strengths.

Clinical Toolbox 1.2: In the Pearson etext, click here to read about an activity that helps clients connect with gratitude and integrate it into their lives.

Counselors might further focus on any activities or engagements that enhance positive subjective experiences and positive individual traits. Counselors can intervene early with prevention programs that teach cognitive and coping skills in order to decrease the risk of depression, anxiety, and violence. They may also honor and promote such client virtues and character strengths as responsibility, gratitude, nurturance, altruism, civility, moderation, tolerance, and work ethic (Seligman, 2012).

Resilience, or the ability to resist against difficulties, is another essential consideration when working from a strength-based approach. Counselors can attempt to foster resiliency in their clients by enhancing their individual competencies within the following areas (Benard, 2004): (a) social competence, (b) problem solving, (c) autonomy, and (d) sense of purpose. Counselors should not just highlight these strengths, but should also seek to amplify these strengths throughout the counseling process, in an attempt to build a client's resilience against illness and future difficulties.

While a strength-based lens is a part of the orientation and philosophy of some helping professionals (e.g., professional counselors, social workers), there is a paucity of literature describing how clients' strengths can be identified and used in counseling and more specifically, in treatment planning. In fact, we could only find one article in the peer-reviewed literature (written by this text's first author) that explicitly addressed the topic (i.e., White, 2002).

In this text, a strength-based lens is integrated into our treatment planning model, and we challenge all counselors to connect with clients' strengths and use these to help them overcome their struggles. The treatment plans presented in this text incorporate clients' strengths, capacities, and resources. To aid counselors in their identification of client strengths, the following resource material is provided in this chapter's appendices: Appendix 1.1 provides a description of categories of client strengths, capacities, and resources that can be used as a tool in identifying client strengths; Appendix 1.2 provides examples of specific character strengths, capacities, and resources that can be identified and integrated into a client's treatment plan; and Appendix 1.3 provides detailed interview questions that can be used to assess clients' strengths, capacities, and resources.

CULTURALLY AND CONTEXTUALLY SENSITIVE   Professional counselors have an identity that is unique. In the last section, we discussed the value of a strength- and competency-based perspective. Another important aspect of counselors' professional identity is sensitivity to contextual and cultural considerations. A focus on sensitivity to context ties into the importance of individualized treatment, and it relates to what we know from treatment outcomes research: Clients need to be understood in the context of their unique situation if counseling is to be effective.

Context refers to the interrelated conditions in which clients' experiences and behaviors occur, or any factors that surround their experience and throw light on their situation. As previously stated, many traditional understandings of mental disorders focus on a pathology-, deficit-based perspective of mental disorders. In considering clients' situations from a contextual perspective, culture, gender, and various developmental factors are just a few of the important factors that should be considered.

Culture, and as a part of this gender, are exceptionally important contextual considerations; culture defines, expresses, and interprets the beliefs, values, customs, and gender-role expectations of a social group (Bhugra & Kalra, 2010). Multicultural considerations can have a significant impact on counselors' diagnostic decision making and the treatment process. The American Counseling Association's (ACA) *Code of Ethics* (in press) emphasizes that culture influences the way that clients' problems are understood, and this must be considered throughout the counseling and treatment process. Related to this, the ACA's *Code of Ethics* (in press) also indicates that counselors should recognize social prejudices that lead to client misdiagnosis and the overpathologizing of clients from certain populations. Counselors are also encouraged to consider the role that we can play in perpetuating these prejudices through our diagnostic and treatment methods (ACA, in press).

Professional counselors place a premium on understanding culture and its impacts on clients and on our means of helping clients reach their goals. It is impossible to understand clients' unique situations and how to best help them if cultural considerations are not considered. An understanding of clients' culture in relation to treatment planning includes understanding cultural explanations of illness experiences and help-seeking behavior, the cultural framework of clients' identity, cultural meanings of healthy functioning, and cultural aspects that relate to the counselor–client relationship (Eriksen & Kress, 2005).

[handwritten margin note: Sensitive to "normal" for client]

Wide variations exist among people from different cultures in their perspectives about "normal" behavior. For example, clients often present to counseling with relationship problems, and how interpersonal relationships should be navigated is largely based on cultural norms and expectations. Culture may influence what symptoms are permitted as expressions of suffering, and how individuals are allowed or encouraged to manage distress. Culture also determines how one's friends, family, and community respond to distress or problematic behaviors; in particular, deciding the type and severity of the problem that must be evident before intervention is deemed necessary. Culture determines acceptable help-seeking behaviors and interventions, and who may—and may not—intervene. Appendix 1.4 provides detailed interview questions that can be used to assess clients' cultural context.

Socioeconomic status and social position also influence how people manifest and respond to mental health problems both within and across cultures. Counselors must consider not only the interaction of culture, race, ethnicity, and gender when considering the development, maintenance, and treatment of problems, but also the influence of socioeconomic status on problems of language and communication barriers, minority status, experiences of prejudice, and social and economic disadvantages (Kress, Eriksen, Dixon-Rayle, & Ford, 2005).

Gender-sensitive and culturally sensitive counselors are also aware that those with less power in society experience a greater quantity of life's difficulties and are more likely to be vulnerable to mental health struggles than are those from the dominant race, ethnicity, age, sexual orientation, or gender. They also realize that those from nondominant cultural groups garner fewer of society's resources, and thus, often acquire treatment later in their problem cycles; because those with less power are less likely to seek help, they may come to the attention of mental health providers only when the problems have reached a greater intensity.

Overall, culture and gender influence clients in multiple ways, including their experiences of problems, their internal sense of distress, their interpretations of problems after experiencing symptoms, and their presentation of complaints (Eriksen & Kress, 2008). Culture and gender also impact counselors' perceptions of mental disorders, their style of interviewing, and their choice of theoretical perspectives and treatment approaches.

Development is another important aspect of client context. Counselors value a developmental perspective which holds that many people's problems in living are rooted in disruptions to normal developmental processes, the unblocking of which can foster healthy transitions; or in normal developmental transitions that they are presently traversing. For example, a first-generation college student who has just left home to move across the country to attend college may struggle with feelings of sadness and loss secondary to this transition. Considering this situation from a developmental perspective, loss and sadness would be considered a normal reaction, the resolution of which will provide an opportunity for this person to become better connected with his or her sense of resiliency.

A developmental focus depicts people as dynamic, rather than static organisms and highlights people's natural inclinations toward growth and health. Developmental perspectives offer hope because client problems or positions are not permanent; instead people are constantly changing and growing. Inherent in a developmental perspective is the understanding that people have the capacity to move forward, to change, to adapt, to heal, and to attain optimal mental health.

For counselors, fully actualizing relevant knowledge, skills, and awareness with regard to cultural, gender, and developmental issues can be challenging. Contextually sensitive diagnosis, case conceptualization, and treatment in particular, are easier to talk about than to actually do. The case conceptualization model presented in this text will be presented in Chapter 2, and as part of this model, counselors are encouraged to think about the contextual considerations discussed in this section.

Not everyone who pursues counseling has a mental disorder. In fact, some people seek counseling to help enhance their personal development and to live more optimally. However, many who seek counseling services experience challenges within varied developmental and contextual areas. These contextual areas need to be considered in the diagnostic and treatment planning process. In the *DSM-5*, "other conditions that may be a focus of clinical attention" or V-codes (Z-codes in the ICD-10; APA, 2013, p. 715) are suggested as additional issues that may be "encountered in routine clinical practice" (p. 715). These issues consist of difficulties stemming from interpersonal issues (i.e., parent–child, sibling, partner distress), issues with abuse and neglect (e.g., partner abuse, child abuse, maltreatment), issues with education or occupational difficulties, problems with housing and finances, difficulties within their social environment (e.g., phase of life, acculturation, target of discrimination), legal issues, and other personal circumstances (e.g., nonadherence to treatment, obesity, borderline intellectual functioning). While these areas can be the direct focus of clinical attention, they often exacerbate and complicate the diagnosis, prognosis, and treatment of other mental health disorders. Because of space constraints, the treatment of these conditions will not be addressed in this text. However, they should always be considered as important and relevant to the treatment planning and treatment process.

 Clinical Toolbox 1.3: In the Pearson etext, click here to read about contextual and developmental considerations that relate to mental health functioning and treatment.

When developing treatment plans, there are also a number of practical considerations that must be addressed. In a perfect world, counselors would have no external demands placed on them, and clients would have open access to any care they required;

sadly, this is not the case. The next section reviews the practical realities that must be considered when engaging in treatment planning.

THE PRACTICAL REALTIES OF TREATMENT PLANNING: WORKING WITH AND WITHIN SYSTEMS

Chapter 2 of this text presents a treatment planning model for use in addressing clients' mental disorders and problems in living. This presentation, just like other authors' presentations of treatment planning, gives the illusion that treatment planning is a linear process. However, in real-world practice, the development of treatment plans, or what is commonly referred to in counselor practice environments as individualized service plans or ISPs, is quite complex.

Just as clients and their needs are diverse and layered, so are the systems in which counselors practice. The demands of these systems are riddled with regulations and evolving practice expectations. As such, when developing treatment plans with clients a variety of practical issues need to be considered. These practical issues can complicate the treatment process and require counselors to be adaptable and fluid in their case conceptualization and treatment planning processes.

In order for counselors to be effective at treatment planning, they must be aware of the expectations and restrictions of the systems they work not only in, but with. Counselors must learn how to navigate and function within these systems. Not only do counselors need to adapt clients' treatment plans as new needs emerge, they also need to be adaptable and responsive to the constantly changing systems in which they practice.

This section of the chapter addresses the practical realities of treatment planning. This discussion is intended to help counselors develop a greater understanding of the foundational considerations that dictate treatment planning in real-world settings. We spotlight the gray areas that often emerge when creating and implementing treatment plans, and we explore issues associated with various treatment constraints. These include managed care restraints related to issues such as reimbursement policies and their relationship to diagnosis and treatment, and limitations of the settings in which counselors practice.

MANAGED CARE SYSTEMS

Many of the treatment planning restraints discussed in this section are rooted in, or are in response to, managed care initiatives. As such, it is important that readers have a basic understanding of the historical context of managed care, as this informs the present-day context in which most clinical counselors practice.

Over the last two to three decades, significant changes in mental health service reimbursement and administration have had a profound impact on the way counselors practice. The dominance of managed care companies in behavioral health care management and reimbursement has had perhaps the greatest impact on counselors' practice. Since nearly all providers who accept third-party payers operate from a managed care foundation, managed care principles have become the norm in mental health treatment. Counselors' work in private practice settings, residential treatment, crisis stabilization, hospitals, community mental health centers, and increasingly, even college counseling centers, is rooted in managed care principles.

Managed behavioral health care developed in response to the rising costs associated with rapid growth in the utilization of mental health and substance abuse services in the 1970s and 1980s. The impact of managed care systems was further reinforced when mental health parity was granted under the Mental Health Parity Act of 1996 (Moniz & Gorin, 2009). Under this act, the long-held practice of insurance providers providing less insurance coverage for mental disorders than for physical health-related disorders ceased.

More recently, the Patient Protection and Affordable Care Act (ACA) was signed into law (on March 23, 2010; many of the important aspects of the ACA go into effect in 2014) to create a health care system that provides coverage for all Americans. The ACA was designed to expand access to health insurance coverage to all Americans, establish consistent rules and consumer protections for the private health insurance system, and reduce the rate of growth of health care spending. As such, moving into the future, the ACA ensures that a managed care approach to health and behavioral health care is here to stay and foundational to behavioral health treatment in America. Now, more than ever, counselors need to understand how to develop treatment plans based on managed care principles and how to work within managed care systems.

What exactly is managed care? Managed care is an approach to delivering and financing health care that seeks to control costs and ensure the quality and consistency of care provided to clients. To achieve this end, managed care systems use a variety of methods including provider network management, utilization management, and quality assurance. Provider network management is used to determine whether the provider meets the standards set forth by the managed care company and includes standards related to credentialing and practice standards or benchmarks. Utilization management involves monitoring the use of covered services, including how often each service is utilized and whether it is medically necessary. If it is medically necessary, a review is completed at specified intervals to determine the ongoing need for the service. Quality assurance is the process of collecting data related to what and how services are utilized and the performance or effectiveness of services. This includes the use of outcome measures (e.g., progress made in treatment) and client satisfaction surveys.

When a managed care system or organization is established in an area or a network, a predictable series of events typically unfolds (Goodman, Brown, & Deitz, 1996). Service providers often consolidate with other community providers and agree to eliminate overlapping services. Managed care organizations also typically enter into contractual agreements with individual practitioners or agencies who have agreed to offer a specified fee-for-service package. The managed care organization will also try to cut their costs by working with providers to reduce clients' stays in hospitals, increase the utilization of outpatient treatment, and encourage partnering with practice groups, agencies, and hospitals to achieve reduced health care costs. The managed care organization receives bids on contracts from provider agencies (e.g., a bid to provide inpatient acute/crisis psychiatric stabilization to clients as needed). The managed care company typically elects to work with the agencies that provide the most cost-effective services and comply with and support their cost-saving measures.

As previously indicated, the relationships between managed care organizations and service providers are dynamic. Their practices change based on consumers' needs, the needs of payers, governmental bodies, national and regional laws (e.g., the Affordable Care Act and the Mental Health Parity Act), accrediting bodies, other managed care organizations, other service providers, and professional associations' expectations for care.

The Mental Health Parity Act and managed behavioral health care has provided opportunities for counselors as their services are increasingly reimbursable. However, along with these opportunities have come a myriad of new demands with which counselors must comply to be reimbursed. Counselors have been faced with unprecedented demands in terms of documentation and record keeping. Historically, authorizations for mental health treatment sessions, and even treatment reports, either were not required or were completed by individuals not directly involved in the care of health center clients (e.g., office staff members).

In managed care environments, counselors have also been charged with assuming more responsibility for justifying their services and clients' need for intervention. Demonstrating the need for mental health services can be subjective and as such, counselors can find this task to be challenging. As will be discussed later in this chapter, an increased emphasis on the assessment of client impairment and on outcome evaluations has become a necessity as this demonstrates the clients' need for services.

Because managed care companies are involved with reimbursement for mental health services, authorization for mental health services has also become a necessity, with payers wanting to ensure that treatment is necessary and is efficient. Managed care companies have established stricter requirements for the authorization of mental health services and are requesting that counselors report on clients' progress before additional visits are even approved.

The advent of managed care environments has also created dramatic changes in the financing and service provision of mental health treatments, and these changes will continue to evolve. Secondary to the emergence of the aforementioned managed care demands, when planning treatment counselors are challenged to understand and navigate a number of third-party payer expectations, which are couched in a managed care environment. These changes have required counselors to develop the knowledge and practice skills needed to establish economically viable practices.

This discussion is intended to help counselors understand these expectations and how they relate to the development, implementation, and maintenance of treatment plans. The term *agency* will be used to describe the business or organizational setting in which counselors work and render their services. Examples of agencies where counselors practice include hospitals, community mental health centers, private practice counseling centers, college counseling centers, prisons, and residential treatment centers.

As discussed in the previous section, it is important to understand what variables impact client treatment and what makes a good treatment plan. However, the reality of clinical practice is that counselors are required to work within complex, ever-evolving systems that dictate the types of treatment, levels of care, and quantity of care a client can receive. The next section explores these real-world realities in the context of treatment planning.

SYSTEM TREATMENT RESTRAINTS

When developing treatment plans, there are a number of treatment restraints that must be considered. The counseling agency's accrediting body may have requirements that dictate treatment plan specifications. Also, counselors must consider the session and service limits applied by third-party payer sources. Issues associated with a client's diagnosis and its potential for reimbursement are important. Related to this, the level of care and/or services that will be approved by third-party payers are based on the diagnosis. Finally, counselors are often called upon to work as part of a team. In this capacity they will need to adapt their treatment goals to those established by team consensus. All of these considerations impact the types of approaches used, the levels of services that are an option, the number of sessions provided, and subsequently, the types of treatment theories and models that can be applied and considered as part of the client's treatment plan.

Voices from the Trenches 1.2: In the Pearson etext, click here to view a video of a mental health agency director discussing how financial considerations relate to treatment planning.

Accrediting Bodies

When developing treatment plans, accreditation standards and accrediting bodies' requirements are an important consideration. Treatment plans must contain all of the elements required by the agency's accrediting bodies. Most agencies (e.g., community mental health agencies, hospitals, residential treatment facilities) that provide mental health treatment are required to be accredited by a body that oversees and regulates the types of treatments and services provided. There are a number of bodies that accredit agencies. The three primary accrediting bodies for behavioral health organizations include the Commission on Accreditation of Rehabilitation Facilities (CARF), the Joint Commission International (JCO), and the Council on Accreditation (COA). JCO accreditation is primary sought by hospitals and medical treatment facilities (many provide and include behavioral health care services). CARF accreditation is traditionally sought by community-based health and human services organizations. COA accredits child welfare and human services organizations.

All three are nonprofit international organizations that accredit both nonprofit and for-profit organizations with a focus on enhancing the quality of services provided to consumers. All three accreditation bodies' focus is on enhancing the quality of services provided to consumers of services. The overall areas that they focus on are sound business practices; ethical and involved governance; processes for acquiring and utilizing input from consumers, families, and stakeholders; agency leadership; safe facilities; effective information management; and most importantly, performance improvement and performance management processes. Each clinical specialty area, such as substance abuse, outpatient mental health, crisis stabilization, or residential services, has its own standards of care. Agencies pay for accreditation reviews and for the maintenance of the accreditation, but the accreditation enhances the perceived quality of the program and affords the agency with various opportunities and benefits. For example, nonprofit mental health agencies often seek CARF or JCO accreditation because it provides them with a deemed status. This deemed status translates into an assumption by payer sources such as Medicare and Medicaid that the agency meets their requirements, and thus precludes additional layers of review by these payer sources.

Agencies may choose the accreditation (and thus the accrediting body) they prefer to use. Each accrediting organization has unique standards that need to be met. An agency can choose to use whichever accrediting agency they prefer. It is likely that they will choose the organization that is more dominant in their discipline.

Regardless of the accrediting body an agency elects to seek accreditation from, they must fulfill all the standards and pass accreditations and reaccreditations as outlined by the accrediting body. For example, CARF may accredit all the programs at a given community mental health agency, but all programs will also need to undergo periodic review (e.g., every three years) to maintain accreditation. Each accrediting body has its own set of standards that agencies must follow to be in compliance and receive accreditation.

There are also state-level governing bodies (e.g., the Ohio Department of Mental Health [ODMH], Ohio Department of Alcohol and Drug Addiction Services [ODADAS]) that have licensing and certification standards that agency programs must meet in order to receive the credentials they provide. So again, if agencies want to receive funding from a federal program such as Medicaid or Medicare, they need to comply with this state-level certification. This funding is essential to the sustained functioning of agencies that provide various mental health counseling services. The licensing standards are based on state or federal laws with the same intention as the licensing standards for individual practitioners. They are meant to protect the public and ensure certain minimum standards of care are maintained, that the organization has established business and governance practices, and it is a safe environment for consumers.

A given agency may be accredited by two different groups and have different expectations for practice that they need to meet. Each accrediting body has unique requirements related to a variety of treatment considerations, among those being treatment plans. For example, some require a counselor to update the client's treatment plan every 90 days, while others require behavioral health counselors only annually update and modify treatment plans. Should it be found that the agency or certain providers failed to comply with these requirements, it would likely result in the agency having to pay back money provided for services, as the services provided without the up-to-date treatment plan would be considered out of compliance. Failure to comply with the accrediting bodies' standards could also result in the termination of an agency's certification.

Accrediting bodies and governing agencies also specify the criteria that need to be addressed in the treatment plan. For example, most accrediting bodies require that the client's goals and objectives relate to the needs, preferences, and obstacles identified in the preliminary mental health assessment. They also require that the treatment plan reflect the client's involvement in goal development, and that the goals and interventions be tailored to the client's preferences and needs. They typically require that goals be objective, and thus measurable. They usually require that counselors document a time frame for achievement of the goal (e.g., three months), and that the therapeutic interventions, frequency of services, and the provider responsible for service delivery are indicated on the treatment plan. Finally, they also typically require that the treatment plan include a consideration of the client's strengths and resources, and how these can be included in treatment. The I CAN START model presented in this text addresses all of these considerations and more.

Agency Settings and Available Services

Related to agency accreditation, the type of setting (e.g., psychiatric unit, crisis stabilization unit, outpatient behavioral health, private practice) also influences the selection of goals and interventions. The treatment goals selected must take into consideration the available services as well as the nature of the setting. For example, outpatient counseling goals are longer-term and evaluated over a longer duration of time (e.g., three months), and the duration of time between evaluation periods will depend on the agency policy and regulating body standards (e.g., three months, annually). In an acute care setting, crisis or emergency goals are developed to address the current stressor and acute mental health symptoms (e.g., achieve medication compliance). These goals are usually meant to be obtained in three to five days. As such, the services provided focus on helping the client stabilize (e.g., providing a secure setting, medication management, case management services), and any treatment goals will focus on short-term objectives (e.g., 0 episodes of self-harm, cessation of heroin use, 0 episodes of physical aggression), with psychosocial treatments pulling on brief treatment approaches that address behavioral change (e.g., solution-focused brief therapy).

Even if a counselor's agency does not provide services a client needs, ethically counselors have a responsibility to connect the client with needed services. Conversely, just because an agency provides certain services they should not be included in a client's treatment plan unless they are deemed necessary.

The types of services available not only at the agency, but also in the client's community, also factor into treatment planning. For example, a counselor might determine that a client could benefit from medically assisted treatment for an opioid addiction. However, the community may have no such programs or physicians available to provide such treatment. Counselors should also attempt to help clients secure access to treatment resources they need even if they are not available at the counselor's agency.

Diagnosis and Reimbursement

A client's diagnosis directly informs the client's treatment plan and suggests the nature of the treatment the client will require, as well as the likely duration of treatment. As such, an accurate diagnosis is essential to effective treatment planning. However, as with all aspects of client treatment, the interplay of considerations associated with diagnosis and treatment are complex, and there are a number of third-party payer considerations that relate to counselor reimbursement and client diagnosis.

In some situations clients may self-pay for services; but most often, to be reimbursed for services counselors need to apply and present to payer sources a diagnosis based on either the most up-to-date edition of the *DSM*, or the International Classification of Diseases (ICD). This diagnosis communicates to third-party payers (e.g., federal payers such as Medicaid, Tricare, and Medicare; private insurance companies) what types of struggles the client is having and what types of services and/or levels of care are indicated. For example, a diagnosis of an adjustment disorder would likely not be sufficient to justify a third-party payer paying for an acute care hospital stay. However, a diagnosis of major depressive disorder (severe) may warrant an inpatient hospital stay.

As previously mentioned, there are a number of different payer sources that may include, but are not limited to, private insurance, county levy funding, federal programs (e.g., Medicaid, Medicare), and grants. Each payer source has its own standards related to clients' diagnosis and reimbursement, as well as the number of sessions they will provide based on the diagnosis. Payer sources will, however, only reimburse for certain specified diagnoses. The payers also use the diagnosis to determine the treatments, services, and number of sessions for which they will reimburse. For example, for a diagnosis of major depression, a federal program (e.g., Medicaid) may approve 52 hours of counseling in one year, while a private insurance payer may approve only eight hours of counseling in a calendar year. A federal program may reimburse for services provided to people diagnosed with an adjustment disorder while certain private insurance payers may not.

Many third-party payers will not reimburse for services to treat autism spectrum disorders, adjustment disorders, substance-use disorders, personality disorders, and other disorders that may be the focus of clinical attention (i.e., "V-codes" such as childhood sexual abuse). As such, practically speaking, counselors may find that they need to tailor their treatment to co-occurring disorders. For example, when treating a client with borderline personality disorder and major depression, the treatment plan may need to focus on the treatment of depression and not address the personality disorder per se. Despite this, counselors must take care to develop a comprehensive case conceptualization that factors in all relevant issues and co-occurring disorders.

Related to this, not all diagnoses are reimbursed equally by third-party payers. Private insurance companies and government agencies (e.g., Tricare, Medicaid, Medicare, county mental health boards, county substance abuse boards) all accept different diagnoses as billable or reimbursable. For example, a county mental health board that provides financial support to a local mental health agency may not reimburse for a substance abuse diagnosis, while a county substance abuse board may not reimburse for a mental health diagnosis.

This selectivity on behalf of third-party payers puts counselors in a bind: On the one hand, there is an ethical responsibility to provide an accurate, least restive diagnosis and the least restrictive diagnosis, yet on the other hand, depending on the client's diagnosis, this may leave the client unable to receive services because the accurate or least restrictive diagnosis may not be reimbursable.

A severe and persistent mental illness diagnosis designation is required to qualify for more intensive services (e.g., access to health homes), and the qualifications to meet this classification vary by state. This designation is not based on a diagnosis, but rather on identified criteria that relate to the client's functioning. People with more severe disorders may require access to the types of services that these disorders can provide. For example, a person diagnosed with schizophrenia who also has a history of mental health treatment that includes multiple hospitalizations may qualify for Social Security benefits (which provides them with a small income and health insurance access).

Many counselors are taught to ascribe the least restrictive diagnosis for which diagnostic criteria are met. Some even advocate downcoding or avoiding certain diagnoses that may harm the client in some way (e.g., the client is a parent involved in a child custody case; see Kress, Hoffman, Adamson, & Eriksen, 2013, for a discussion of these issues). However, in real-world practice, many counselors feel forced to upcode, or give a more restrictive diagnosis, to ensure service delivery (e.g., adjustment disorder with depressed mood is most accurate, but not reimbursable, so the client is diagnosed with a major depressive disorder, mild, single episode, which is more restrictive, but reimbursable). Ethically, counselors should apply the diagnosis that best describes the client's symptoms (see Eriksen & Kress, 2005, for a discussion of these issues).

In summary, a client's diagnosis is the starting point in determining the types and levels of service that a third-party payer will reimburse. The diagnosis guides the treatment plan, as it is used to determine the level of care and treatment goals. Most payer sources request the client's diagnosis and use it to determine how much (e.g., number of sessions) and what type (e.g., counseling) of services are approved for reimbursement. Counselors need to be aware of these issues and how they will impact the nature and extent of services they provide, as these issues are central to treatment planning.

Payer Source, Session Number, and Service Restraints

Many discussions of treatment planning assume that clients have an unlimited number of counseling sessions, and in a perfect world, clients would be eligible for an unlimited number of mental health services. However, along with the issues associated with diagnosis, the payer source's policies help determine the number of available units (e.g., hours) a client can receive per year, as well as the types of services the client can receive. The allotted amount of services are often fewer than what a counselor would recommend the client receive. A client can elect to self-pay for services that are not reimbursed by the payer source, but for most people, self-pay is not a realistic option. The payer source determines if a client can receive counseling, community psychiatric support (i.e., case management), pharmacological management services, emergency services, crisis stabilization, inpatient treatment, intensive outpatient programming, employment services, education services, and partial hospitalization.

If approved for a type of service, the payer source determines how much of that service a client can receive. For example, Ohio Medicaid reimburses for 52 hours of counseling—annually—per client (interestingly, regardless of diagnosis). This amounts to one hour of counseling services per week, which is likely not enough for someone who needs intensive services (e.g., someone with a severe and persistent mental illness who requires frequent psychiatric hospitalizations), yet it may be more than is necessary for someone with, say, an adjustment disorder. Many private insurance companies will only approve eight hours of counseling at a time, which is not enough time to treat many mental disorders. Another example is the number of days a person may be approved for if admitted to a psychiatric hospital (e.g., a private insurance company may only agree to pay for three days of inpatient hospitalization, and this treatment may also depend on the client having a certain diagnosis). If a longer stay is needed for psychiatric stabilization, then the client will likely be responsible for the payment for additional days.

Payer sources often have "care managers" who (a) follow up with providers to see if clients attended their appointments, (b) make determinations on levels of care that will be reimbursed, and (c) determine if additional services or sessions are warranted. Realistically, the number of sessions a client is approved for, whether eight or 52, must be considered when developing a client's treatment plan. The number of sessions approved for client treatment will impact the development of the treatment plan, including the theory and interventions selected for use by the counselor. For example, if a client is approved for eight sessions, a brief therapy model with refined short-term goals may be most appropriate. The goals will likely address symptoms and circumstances that can be changed in a brief amount of time. If a client is approved for 20 sessions, different theoretical approaches may be appropriate, and long-term goals that address underlying factors contributing to the disorder may be addressed in a client's treatment. Session limits will also impact the goals that are selected to be addressed in treatment, as well as the amount of progress that can be realistically expected. For example, in 52 sessions, a client may be able to overcome all symptoms of depression, reporting a decrease in self-reported symptoms from 10 to 1 on a 10-point scale. The same individual may only realistically be able to achieve 8 out of 10 on a 10-point scale if only eight counseling sessions are approved.

Ethically, clients need to be made aware that if they are relying on payer sources for the cost of their treatment, their treatment will be limited by the regulating standards of the payer. Counselors then have an ethical obligation to communicate to their clients their recommendations and what the third-party payer will cover, and come to an agreement on the treatment plan and on the number of sessions they expect to meet. For example, a counselor may recommend 20 hour-long sessions of counseling using cognitive behavioral therapy to treat depression, but the payer source may only agree to reimburse for eight sessions.

Treatment Teams

Depending on the setting in which counselors work and the behavioral health services provided within that setting, counselors may be required to work in a team environment. The type of behavioral health services provided at the counselor's agency and the members of the treatment team (e.g., psychiatrist, community psychiatric support provider, physician) will impact the services readily available to clients and can impact the clients' treatment goals. For example, if a counselor has a client with borderline personality disorder, and the agency where the counselor works has a dialectical behavior therapy (DBT) program, the client may have an option to receive this treatment, and the counselor may subsequently be called on to be a part of the DBT treatment team for the client.

When working as part of a team, a counselor may not be the person who develops the client's treatment plan; it may be developed by another member of the team with the counselor working with the client to address one aspect of the treatment plan. Counselors also need to be mindful of the treatment plan goals being addressed by various treatment team members. The treatment plans of all treatment team members should be similar, and the team should collaborate with the client to develop an individualized plan. A counselor may need to adapt his or her treatment plan to align with the treatment decisions of the team. Counselors must be aware of their role and function on the treatment team. Counselors should also be mindful of who the team leader is and what his or her role is on the team. Often, a physician or a psychiatrist is deemed to be the team leader and is the final authority on matters related to the client's diagnosis and treatment. For example, if the psychiatrist diagnoses a client with schizophrenia and recommends inpatient hospitalization, the counselor cannot treat the client for depression in an outpatient setting, even if the counselor believes that this is a more appropriate diagnosis and level of care. These discrepancies between provider perceptions of care can place counselors in an awkward situation that needs to be carefully navigated under the guidance of a supervisor or through peer consultation.

Voices from the Trenches 1.3: In the Pearson etext, click here to view a video of a counselor discussing the importance of working effectively as a part of a treatment team.

Summary

This chapter provided information that is foundational to understanding treatment planning, and presented what is known about what works in counseling. Additionally, the chapter discussed what "good" treatment planning looks like, based on the research literature on treatment.

This chapter also addressed the practical treatment restraints counselors need to consider as they develop and maintain clients' treatment plans. These realities are infrequently addressed in academic journals and books, but are important for counselors practicing in real-world settings. These restraints are couched in a managed care context, a context that defines the landscape in which counselors practice. Treatment constraints related to accrediting bodies, session and service limits applied by third-party payer sources, limits related to clients' diagnoses and reimbursement, and the importance of working in a team approach were discussed. These considerations suggest certain practice guidelines that may be useful when developing treatment plans, and these will be explored more in Chapter 2.

References

American Counseling Association. (in press). *2014 ACA code of ethics*. Alexandria, VA: Author.

American Psychiatric Association. (2013). *Diagnostic and statistical manual of mental disorders* (5th ed.). Washington, DC: Author.

Baldwin, S. A., & Imel, Z. E. (2013). Therapist effects. In M. J. Lambert (Ed.), *Bergin and Garfield's handbook of psychotherapy and behavior change* (6th ed., pp. 258–297). New York, NY: Wiley.

Benard, B. (2004). *Resiliency: What do we know?* San Francisco, CA: WestEd.

Beutler, L. E., Malik, M., Alimohamed, S., Harwood, T. M., Talebi, H., Noble, S., . . . Wong, E. (2004). Therapist variables. In M. J. Lambert (Ed.), *Bergin and Garfield's handbook of psychotherapy and behavior change* (5th ed., pp. 227–306). New York, NY: Wiley.

Bhugra, D., & Kalra, G. (2010). Cross cultural psychiatry: Context and issues. *Journal of Pakistan Psychiatric Society, 7*, 51–54.

Bohart, A. C., & Wade, A. G. (2013). The client in psychotherapy. In M. J. Lambert (Ed.), *Bergin and Garfield's handbook of psychotherapy and behavior change* (6th ed., pp. 219–257). New York, NY: Wiley.

Bordin, E. S. (1979). The generalizability of the psychoanalytic concept of working alliance. *Psychotherapy, 16*, 252–260.

Clarkin, J. F., & Levy, K. (2004). The influences of client variables on psychotherapy. In M. J. Lambert (Ed.), *Bergin and Garfield's handbook of psychotherapy and behavior change* (5th ed., pp. 194–226). New York, NY: Wiley.

Constantino, M. J., Glass, C. R., Arnkoff, D. B., Ametrano, R., M., & Smith, J. Z. (2011). Expectations. In J. C. Norcross (Ed.), *Psychotherapy relationships that work: Evidence-based responsiveness* (2nd ed.). New York, NY: Oxford.

Eriksen, K., & Kress, V. E. (2005). *Beyond the DSM story: Ethical quandaries, challenges, and best practices*. Thousand Oaks, CA: Sage.

Eriksen, K., & Kress, V. E. (2008). Gender and diagnosis: Struggles and suggestions for counselors. *Journal of Counseling & Development, 86*, 152–162.

Frank, J. D. (1961). *Persuasion and healing: A comparative study of psychotherapy*. Baltimore, MD: The Johns Hopkins Press.

Goodman, M., Brown, J. A., & Deitz, P. M. (1996). *Managing managed care II: A handbook for mental health professionals* (2nd ed.). Washington, DC: American Psychiatric Press.

Jongsma, A. E., Peterson, L. M., & Bruce, T. J. (2006). *The complete adult psychotherapy treatment planner* (4th ed.). New York, NY: Wiley.

Kress, V. E., Eriksen, K., Dixon-Rayle, A., & Ford, S. (2005). The DSM-IV TR and culture: Considerations for counselors. *Journal of Counseling & Development, 83*, 97–104.

Kress, V. E., Hoffman, R., Adamson, N., & Eriksen, K. (2013). Informed consent, confidentiality, and diagnosing: Ethical guidelines for counselor practice. *Journal of Mental Health Counseling, 35*, 15–28.

Lambert, M. J. (2013). The efficacy and effectiveness of psychotherapy. In M. J. Lambert (Ed.), *Bergin and Garfield's handbook of psychotherapy and behavior change* (6th ed., pp. 169–218). New York, NY: Wiley.

Lipsey, M. W., & Wilson, D. B. (1993). The efficacy of psychological, educational, and behavioral treatment: Confirmation from meta-analysis. *American Psychologist, 48,* 1181–1209.

Miller, W. R., & Rollnick, S. (2012). *Motivational interviewing* (3rd ed.). New York, NY: Guilford.

Moniz, C., & Gorin, S. (2009). *Health and mental health care policy: A biopsychosocial perspective* (3rd ed.). New York, NY: Pearson.

Norcross, J. C., Krebs, P. M., & Prochaska, J. O. (2011). Stages of change. In J. C. Norcross (Ed.), *Psychotherapy relationships that work: Evidence-based responsiveness* (2nd ed., pp. 279–300). New York, NY: Oxford.

Norcross, J. C., & Lambert, M. J. (2011). Evidence-based therapy relationships. In J. C. Norcross (Ed.), *Psychotherapy relationships that work: Evidence-based responsiveness* (2nd ed., pp. 3–24). New York, NY: Oxford.

Norcross, J. C., & Wampold, B. E. (2011). Research conclusions and clinical practices. In J. C. Norcross (Ed.), *Psychotherapy relationships that work: Evidence-based responsiveness* (2nd ed., pp. 423–430). New York, NY: Oxford.

Seligman, M. E. P. (2012). *Flourish: A visionary new understanding of happiness and well-being.* New York, NY: Simon and Schuster.

Smith, E. (2006). The strength-based counselling model. *The Counselling Psychologist, 4*(1), 13–79.

Smith, M., Glass, G., & Miller, T. I. (1980). *The benefits of psychotherapy.* Baltimore, MD: Johns Hopkins Press.

Sommers-Flanagan, J., & Sommers-Flanagan, R. (2009). *Clinical interviewing* (4th ed.). Hoboken, NJ: Wiley.

White, V. E. (2002). Developing counseling objectives and empowering clients: A strength-based intervention. *Journal of Mental Health Counseling, 24,* 270–279.

Zuroff, D. C., Kelly, A. C., Leybman, M. J., Blatt, S. J., & Wampold, B. (2010). Between-therapist and within therapist differences in the quality of the therapeutic relationship: Effects on maladjustment and self-critical perfectionism. *Journal of Clinical Psychology, 66,* 681–697.

Appendix Summary

Appendix 1.1: Categories of Client Strengths, Capacities, and Resources

I. Client Strengths and Resources

    a. Identity—self-image, ability for introspection, set of values and beliefs, sense of meaning, religious and spiritual affiliations, cultural identity, roles (e.g., teacher, mother), self-confidence

    b. Interpersonal Relationships—supportive and healthy relationships with significant others, family members, friends, peers, coworkers, and other members of the community

    c. Social Skills—relationship-building skills, communication skills, manners, listening skills, empathy, sensitivity to other's feelings, conflict management abilities, problem-solving skills, tolerance, ability to connect with people of different cultural backgrounds, leadership abilities

    d. Conflict Management—problem-solving abilities, can effectively regulate emotions, resolves conflicts without use of violence, willing to apologize for wronging others, able to forgive others

    e. Environmental Resources—basic needs (food, water, shelter, clothing), health care, financial support, education, employment opportunities, transportation, other community resources

    f. Good Character—integrity, bravery in standing up for beliefs, advocates for others, honest, can identify strengths and use them to help others

g. **Responsibility**—takes responsibility for actions, able to be responsible for completing tasks or for taking care of something/somebody, internal locus of control, able to plan for future, decision-making skills, sense of social responsibility

h. **Optimistic Outlook**—positive view of own future and life situations

i. **Connectedness with Surroundings**—sense of belonging with peer group/family/community/world, being a part of something greater than oneself, altruistic activities (e.g., volunteerism, social service)

j. **Resistance to Social Pressure**—maintains beliefs and behaves in accordance with values even when they are unpopular, resists participation in dangerous or delinquent activities

k. **Motivation**—motivated to achieve in school/work/hobby, seeks opportunities to better himself/herself in this area

l. **Past Accomplishments and Achievements**

m. **Flexibility**—able to accept life's uncertainties, willing to make changes to plans/actions/beliefs

II. Family Strengths and Resources

a. **Family Relationships**—interactions are healthy, family functioning is adaptive, level of respect between members, members have a sense of belonging

b. **Familial Support**—family members provide each other with encouragement, positive feedback, love, and support

c. **Family Guidelines**—rules and guidelines are established, family is not too controlling in members' lives or too disconnected

d. **Communication**—family communicates feelings and thoughts to each other, regularly converses, feels safe going to each other to solve problems or make decisions

e. **Bonding Time**—regularly spends time together doing particular activities (e.g., going to church, sitting down for dinner each night, playing games), may take time to practice a skill (e.g., baseball) or complete homework together

f. **Family Involvement and Interest**—family encourages individual to perform well and praises accomplishments, attends extracurricular activities, meets with teachers (if a child)

g. **Modeling**—a family member that serves as a role model of adaptive, responsible, appropriate behavior and positive traits

h. **Traditions**—occasions and routine events that the family observes (e.g., dinner with extended family on Sundays), may include religious/ethnic/other cultural observances

III. School Strengths and Resources

a. **Supportive Staff**—teachers and school staff are supportive and interested in helping students to succeed, attentive to unique needs of children, create a caring and inclusive school environment, working relationship with parents

b. **Communication Network**—teachers and school administrators have communication with one another, students' parents, and other professionals as needed (e.g., social workers, counselors)

c. **Academic Interest**—child desires to learn, active during class, engaged in learning, and challenged appropriately

    d. Homework Completion—child demonstrates dedication, responsibility, and accountability by completing homework on time

    e. Rules and Regulations—clear guidelines are established and adhered to

    f. Relationship to School—child feels a sense of belonging at school, cares about the school, has a collective identity with the other students at the school, participates in extracurricular activities at school

    g. Peer Support—child has friendships with others, spend time with friends who model positive behavior

IV. Community Strengths and Resources

    a. Supportive Organizations—organizations that provide help, resources, or support to those with specific needs (i.e., poverty, disabilities, illnesses) or dealing with a specific struggle (e.g., alcoholism, drug addiction, recovery from trauma)

    b. Neighborhood Support—neighborhood is a safe environment, healthy relationships with neighbors, neighbors monitor behavior in neighborhood

    c. Religious Community—supportive members and religious leaders that can be trusted and are supportive, contribute to the community and help others

    d. Cultural Community—derive strength and pride out of a shared cultural identity and shared cultural experiences

    e. Co-workers—have working relationships with others at work who are dependable

    f. Support Groups—groups that provide support for a specific group of people (e.g., those who are alcohol dependent)

    g. Programming and Activities—positive activities in the community (e.g., summer camp, volunteer groups, sports teams, clubs)

Appendix 1.2: Examples of Character Strengths, Capacities, and Resources to Be Identified and Integrated into Treatment Plans

Accepting

Adventurous

Affectionate

Alert

Altruistic

Ambitious

Appreciative

Aspiring

Attractive

Aware

Brave

Calm

Capable

Caring

Cheerful

Committed

Compassionate

Confident

Conscientious

Considerate

Constructive

Cooperative

Courageous

Creative

Curious

Decisive

Dedicated

Determined

Devoted

Disciplined

Educated

Efficient

Empathetic

Empowering

Encouraging

Energetic

Enthusiastic

Ethical

Exercises

Expressive

Flexible

Focused

Forgiving

Friendly

Generous

Gentle

Graceful

Grateful

Handy

Hard-working

Helpful

Honest

Hopeful

Humble

Humorous

Hygienic

Imaginative

Independent

Industrious

Innovative

Insightful

Inspirational

Intelligent

Interested

Intuitive

Knowledgeable

Leadership

Logical

Loving

Loyal

Mastery

Modest

Motivated

Moral

Nurturing

Observant

Open-minded

Optimistic

Organized

Patient

Persistent

Personable

Persuasive

Physically fit

Playful

Positive

Powerful

Practical

Problem solver

Prudent

Punctual

Rational

Relaxed

Reliable

Religious

Resilient

Respectful

Responsible

Self-confident

Self-esteem

Self-regulated

Selfless

Sensitive

Sincere

Skilled

Social

Spiritual

Spontaneous

Strong-willed

Successful

Supportive

Sympathetic

Tactful

Talented

Tenacious

Thoughtful

Thrifty

Tolerant

Trusting

Trustworthy

Wise

Work-oriented

Appendix 1.3: Interview Questions to Assess Clients' Strengths, Capacities, and Resources

INDIVIDUAL STRENGTHS

How do you go about making friends?

With whom do you usually share problems?

How did you usually go about solving problems (e.g., physical, emotional, educational, occupational)?

Talk about a situation in which you took a risk.

Tell me something that you are proud of.

Have you ever won any awards or received any honors? How did this make you feel about yourself?

When you're faced with a challenging situation, what helps you to maintain perspective?

When confronted with a frustrating or disappointing situation, how do you tend to respond?

What enables you to maintain an inner equilibrium when you're faced with difficult circumstances?

Do you have any skills/talents?

What are the most rewarding activities in your life? What other activities do you most enjoy?

Who do you most admire? What is it that you most admire about that person?

What are your short-term goals? How can you use your abilities to achieve them? Who can help you?

What are your long-term goals? How can you use your strengths to achieve them? Who can help you?

Talk about your plans around how to reach your goals.

How do you work well with others?

How do you participate as a part of a team?

Have you ever been a leader?

What are your best traits and abilities?

Talk about your sense of humor.

Do people seek you out for help with tasks or problems?

Do you have any hobbies?

Can you think of a time when you were able to use your abilities to help others?

What academic classes or job activities are you most interested in?

If you could improve an area of your life that you have control over, what would it be?

Are you able to apologize when you have hurt another person?

Are you able to forgive others who have hurt you?

Do you accept responsibility for your actions?

When are you the most relaxed/happy/satisfied?

Do you complete your work on time?

Do you do well on assignments and exams?

Do you try to the best of your abilities in your work/school?

Do you treat others with respect and fairness?

Are you genuine and honest?

What are some of your favorite memories? What made them so special?

Are you supportive of others (i.e., family members, friends, significant other)?

Do you have any special responsibilities (e.g., chores, taking care of sibling/pet)?

What makes you feel good about yourself?

When do you feel the most confident?

What are some things that you are good at?

What makes you special/sets you apart from others?

Do you know how to interact well with others at social events?

Have you ever helped another person who didn't fit in?

Have you ever included a person who was being left out?

Do you enjoy close relationships with others? If so, tell me about those relationships.

Are you creative?

Are you accepting of life's uncertainties?

How do you manage stress?

What do you find fascinating?

What do you enjoy learning about?

Do you find it easy to make decisions? Have you ever helped anybody else make a decision?

How do you solve problems?

Do you finish tasks that you start?

Are you persistent in working toward your goals even when you meet challenges?

What areas interest you?

How do you spend your free time?

If you could spend your free time doing anything you wanted, what would it be?

Have you ever stood up for your beliefs?

Have you ever confronted somebody who you felt was bullying you/somebody else?

Do you ever do favors for others without expecting anything in return?

Do you do any volunteer work?

Do you have any special cause that you identify with?

If you could go back and start your life from the beginning, what would you keep the same?

Have you ever been responsible for the welfare of another (e.g., a pet, a person)?

Are you able to become comfortable in situations where the places, people, and occasions are unfamiliar?

Have you ever been supportive or encouraging to another person?

Talk about how you engage in self-discipline.

Talk about how you control your emotions in stressful situations.

Has there ever been a time when you have treated someone kindly who has not been kind to you?

What are some things for which you are grateful?

What positive things do you expect to happen in the future?

What are your dreams for the future?

Do you thank others when they have helped you?

Do you have relationships that bring meaning to your life?

Do you feel that your life has purpose/purposes?

Do you seek to find meaning and purpose in life?

Can you view challenges as an opportunity to learn and grow?

Do you try new activities, even if they frighten you a bit?

Do you seek opportunities to learn and enhance yourself?

Do you consider other people's feelings when interacting or before making decisions?

Do you notice others' emotions?

What conditions of your life are you the most satisfied with?

What are some things in your life that you wanted and were able to obtain?

Can you think of a situation when you were a good friend to somebody?

FAMILY OF ORIGIN STRENGTHS

Who in your family do you most admire?

What was the role of grandparents in your family?

What role do other close family members play in your family?

How frequently do you have contact with family?

What kinds of values were stressed in your family?

Who are the special people in your life? What makes them special to you?

What are some things you like about your family members?

What are some strengths of your family?

In what ways have your family members positively impacted your life?

What are some important helpful lessons you learned from your family?

Can you look to any family members for support if you want to talk or need help?

How is your family unique? Do you have any special traditions or values?

Do you have a family member whom you trust?

Do you feel that you "belong" in your family?

How have your family members supported you in the past?

How does your family solve problems?

When have you felt encouraged by your family members?

Have you ever collectively worked toward a goal as a family?

How can your family members be helpful to you now?

How has your family successfully dealt with a challenge together?

How do you contribute to your family?

How does your family help you in your daily life?

What have you done to bring pride to your family?

Are you proud of any family members?

What activities does your family enjoy doing together?

COMMUNITY/CULTURAL STRENGTHS

What is valued in your community?

What kinds of social groups existed in your home community?

In what ways does your community support social justice? Work to offset various forms of oppression?

What resources have you used in the community?

How do you contribute to your community?

What are some special or unique traits from your culture?

What are some aspects of your culture that you value?

How have you helped others within your community?

Who are some individuals you admire in the community/from your culture?

What resources are available in the community that might help you to achieve your goals?

How have others in the community helped you to grow and develop?

How can you reach out to others for support in the community?

Can you think of any ways that you can use your talents, abilities, or traits to help others in the community?

What do you value about your community?

SPIRITUAL STRENGTHS

What types of things do you consider of highest importance?

In what ways do you experience meaning in your life?

What role does religion play for you? In what situations might you turn to religion?

What kinds of things help you to feel that you're living your life to the fullest?

In what ways do your religious views provide comfort in times of suffering or sorrow?

How can you use spirituality or religion in helping you to achieve your goals?

Do you have members of your religious community whom you can trust/depend on/talk to in a time of need?

How have members of your religious community helped you or others in the past?

What special memories do you have involving your spirituality/religion?

How have your spiritual/religious beliefs enhanced your life?

What positive traits have you developed from your religious/spiritual beliefs?

Is meditation or prayer a part of your life? If so, how?

Are there any regular religious rituals in which you take part? How often?

If so, are the rituals as part of a community, or are they more personal or within the family?

What religious values do you espouse?

Do you share these values with many other members of your home culture?

Do you incorporate those values into your current beliefs and behavior?

How do you go about making difficult decisions? What values do you rely on to help you in this process?

Do you feel a sense of connectedness with others or the world around you?

What are some strengths of having religious/spiritual beliefs in your life?

How can you use your beliefs to contribute to the world?

How do your beliefs positively impact your interactions with others?

Appendix 1.4: Interview Questions to Assess Clients' Cultural Context

GETTING THE CLIENT'S CULTURAL BACKGROUND

How do you identify yourself (i.e., age, race, ethnicity, culture, SES, sexual orientation, disability/ability)?

What is your country of origin?

Where were your parents born? Where were your children born?

Where do you call home?

Have you always lived in the United States? If not, when did you come to the United States?

What was life like before you came to the United States?

What was it like when you first came to the United States? How is it now?

Why did you leave your country of origin?

What languages do speak? What languages do you prefer to speak? What language is spoken at home/with your family members/in your community?

How would you describe your culture, ethnicity? What are your foundational values and beliefs?

How would you describe your family? Who are the members of your family?

Who raised you? Do you have children? Do you (or does someone else) raise them?

Do you want your family or other important members included in treatment? Would you like me to talk with any of them?

In what ways does your family impact and support you?

How would you describe your community? Do you belong to any groups or organizations?

What do you view as important sources of support?

What activities are you associated with or participate in?

Is religion and/or spirituality important to you?

Are you comfortable talking about values, beliefs, and spirituality with me?

Is religion or spirituality an important aspect of treatment you wish to address?

Is there a religious, spiritual, or healing person who should be part of treatment?

Do you feel that other have discriminated against you because of your culture? Have you seen this at work, in the community, in relationships, or in other settings?

Have you ever felt intolerance due to your religious, spiritual, political, or ethnic worldview?

Have you ever been discriminated against due to your race, social-economic class, sexual orientation, gender, disability, or for any other reason that you would like to talk about and make me aware of?

What is your sexual orientation? How would you describe your gender identity?

What is your political ideology? Is that similar or different from your spouse, family members, friends, or others within your community?

How would you define your social-economic status?

Do you have any customs or practices that you would like to do in here?

UNDERSTANDING THE PROBLEM

How would you describe what is going on with you? How would you define the problem?

How might your spouse, family members, friends, or others within your community define the problem?

What is the most troubling part of the problem?

What would you like to be doing that you are not able to do?

Have you sought help for this problem in the past? If so, from whom? What parts were helpful? What parts were not?

Have you ever had times when you thought you would have the problem, but did not?

How would you name or label what is happing to you?

Are there any beliefs or cultural considerations that you would like to discuss concerning the problem?

Is there anything you are afraid of, or fear?

Does your spouse, family members, friends, or others within your community support your decision to seek help?

What do you think caused or is causing this problem?

What would your spouse, family members, friends, or others within your community say is causing your problem?

Is there any kind or type of support that makes the problem diminish, more tolerable, or better?

Do you feel supported by spouse, family members, friends, and others within the community?

What seems to acerbate or inflame the problem? What stressors make the problem more difficulty to deal with or tolerate?

How have you dealt with the problem in the past?

Has anything been helpful?

How are you currently coping with this problem now?

BARRIERS TO TREATMENT

Has anything ever gotten in your way of seeking help for this problem?

What barriers have prevented you from seeking treatment in the past?

Are you aware of the services here and do you feel they will aid you?

Do you see any potential challenges in your receiving the treatment you desire?

Considering what you know about counseling, is there anything you feel uncomfortable about?

TREATMENT

How have you dealt with the problem in the past?

Has anything been helpful?

How are you currently coping with this problem now?

PREFERENCES OF TREATMENT AND TYPE OF WORKING RELATIONSHIP

What kind or type of help is most useful to you?

What kinds of help would your spouse, family members, friends, or others within your community deem as most useful?

What would you like from me in this relationship?

What expectations do you have for me in this relationship? What expectations do you have for yourself in this relationship?

How do you see treatment progress? What type of pace is ideal?

What would indicate to you that treatment or this counseling relationship is not working?

Do you have any reservation that I will not understand your situation, your culture, or your lived experience?

Do you feel that I will be able to provide you the care and type of help you want/need?

Is there anything I have failed to ask you that would be helpful in facilitating treatment and a working relationship?

Developing Comprehensive Treatment Plans

MATTHEW J. PAYLO AND VICTORIA E. KRESS

CASE STUDY: TERIKA

Terika, a 16-year-old African American female, is brought into a treatment facility by her mother. She reports that she is a Baptist (Christian) and states that she lives in a section of town known for its high crime rate and poverty. She appears slightly disheveled and considerably overweight. Her clothing has noticeable stains and her hair is unkempt. After some silence, she reports that she is here because she is "not doing so well" and it will "get her mother off her back" if she comes to counseling. Terika states she recently attempted suicide when she mixed her mother's antianxiety medication with a significant amount of alcohol; she did not tell anyone about this suicide attempt, and woke up the next morning with a headache. She denied any additional suicide attempts. Additionally, she reports she sometimes uses drugs and alcohol with friends. Slowly, Terika begins to discuss her situation in more depth. She expresses feelings of sadness, rejection, worthlessness, and isolation. Suddenly, she is barely able to talk and breaks into tears. She rubs her eyes, and she then pulls her sweatshirt hood over her head and becomes unresponsive.

The counselor then decides to meet with Terika's mother to garner more detail about Terika's history. She reports that Terika has been unable to care for herself for the last six months and has moved back into her mother's one-bedroom apartment. Prior to moving back into her mother's home, Terika was living in her aunt's home. Terika began living with her aunt secondary to an altercation with her mother over a past boyfriend. Her mother states that Terika has been discussing the option of dropping out of school and obtaining her GED. Her mother, who reports she did not graduate from high school, states that her daughter's grades are mostly Cs this academic year, but she used to get As and Bs. Terika's mother reports that Terika's father has never been involved in Terika's life. Her mother adds that more recently, Terika has been eating more than normal and she seems to be up at all hours of the night.

Terika decides that she wants to continue talking. She reports that she has always been emotional; but more recently, she is finding her emotions difficult to control. She states that she continues to go through what she calls "crying spells", and she recently stopped socializing with friends, and has even started refusing to go to school. Terika indicates she struggles to "fit in" and she "has insecurities" around boys and romantic relationships. She also expresses concerns about her future and what she will do after high school.

Terika loves animals, and prior to the onset of these symptoms, she would volunteer at a local animal shelter where she walked dogs. Historically, she enjoyed spending time with her friends. The counselor also notes that prior to the onset of her symptoms, Terika was very curious and loved to learn. For example, Terika talked about how several years ago—with her saved-up allowance—she had purchased a set of encyclopedias from a local thrift store and would read voraciously.

When discussing the frequency, intensity, and duration of her symptoms, Terika suggests that the onset of these symptoms started about four months ago. She notes the symptoms have increased in severity over time. Terika also reports that she feels "weighted down" and sometimes finds it is impossible to get up from the couch. She states she has no idea why this happened, and she does not feel confident that talking with someone will even help.

PRACTICE SUGGESTIONS FOR DEVELOPING TREATMENT PLANS

Terika's case is layered and complex. When reading a case like this, it is normal for neophyte counselors to wonder where to even begin helping her move forward. However, this complex presentation is not unique to counselors working in the counseling field. Daily, counselors are required to quickly develop a thoughtful clinical picture of a client's situation (i.e., case conceptualization), which leads to the formulation of an accurate diagnosis. This ability to appropriately conceptualize a client's situation and provide a diagnosis is instrumental in developing an appropriate treatment plan. If a counselor has a poor understanding of the client's situation, applies an inaccurate diagnosis, or selects an inappropriate treatment approach, the client will suffer.

To aid counselors in their decision making related to treatment, this first section of the chapter will introduce practical practice principles that counselors can use to guide their treatment development process. In the next section of the chapter, a comprehensive, strength-based treatment planning model (i.e., the I CAN START model) will be presented.

Before exploring suggestions for developing treatment plans, we would like to address the value of using both guided treatment planning principles and a comprehensive treatment planning model when developing treatment plans. There are a variety of resources available to counselors, which can help them readily identify objectives and goals that relate to treating mental disorders (e.g., Jongsma, Peterson, & Bruce, 2006).

For example, the Jongsma et al. (2006) treatment planning series includes numerous treatment planning books, which provide examples of long-term goals, short-term objectives, and therapeutic interventions relating to a number of mental disorders and problems of living. Additionally, there has been a trend towards agencies' use of computer software systems to aid counselors in selecting treatment goals, objectives, and interventions. When using these systems, counselors enter a diagnosis or presenting problem, and the system generates a number of predetermined goals, objectives, and interventions.

While these treatment planning materials are an excellent resource, counselors must have a comprehensive model to guide their case conceptualization and treatment planning process (e.g., the I CAN START model), and they must understand the basic foundations of good treatment planning. It is not enough to cut and paste treatment goals, objectives, and interventions developed by others into a client's treatment plan. Care must be taken to ensure the goals, objectives, and interventions of the treatment plan are tailored to the client's unique needs and strengths, and that they fit into the counselor's— and client's—broader conceptualization of the client's situation and needs. Without a solid understanding of the foundations of good treatment planning, counselors relying exclusively on preestablished treatment goals, objectives, and interventions run the risk of creating treatment plans that are prescriptive, lack individualization, are too generic, and do not best meet clients' needs.

Related to this, in order to engage in effective treatment planning, counselors must also understand what specific treatment models or approaches are useful in treating different disorders. Again, it is reckless to select predetermined treatment objectives that are not rooted in a model or treatment approach that has been articulated, defined, and researched.

Chapter 1 described "good" treatment plans as being evidence-based, individualized, relational, strength-based, and contextually-sensitive. What follows are guiding principles that can be used in the process of developing and maintaining treatment plans. These principles are based on the research and third-party payer guidelines discussed in Chapter 1, and are grounded in the authors' combined 30+ years of experience developing treatment plans in various clinical settings. All of the following principles are also integrated into the I CAN START model, which will be presented later in the chapter. This following list of principles is not exhaustive of all of the principles that are integrated into the I CAN START model; they are intended instead to serve as examples and a starting place for counselors in their treatment plan development process. The suggestions discussed in this following section can assist counselors in selecting and modifying the predetermined goals and objectives provided by others, should they choose to use those.

Voices from the Trenches 2.1: In the Pearson etext, click here to view a counselor discussing his thoughts on what he wishes he had learned more about—in terms of treatment planning—in graduate school.

Be Collaborative with Clients

First, good treatment plans should be individualized to the client's needs and preferences, and be developed in collaboration with the client. This collaborative process in which the client has a voice in his or her treatment complies with ethical standards (e.g., the American Counseling Association's [ACA] *Code of Ethics*, in press; the American Mental Health Counselors Association's *Code of Ethics*, 2010), as well as third-party payers' expectations. This collaborative spirit rests on the assumption that the client is best able to report his or her mental health symptoms, presenting concerns, stressors, needs, and treatment goals.

The idea that clients should be collaborative in their treatment is consistent with the philosophical foundations of professional counseling and with the I CAN START model, which emphasizes clients' strengths and capacities. Counseling and treatment are not things that are *done* to clients. Rather, clients are active participants in the process; clients are experts on themselves and their situations, and their input is crucial to treatment success. A move away from a model that suggests clients are sick or otherwise unable to aid in their own treatment provides clients with a greater sense of resiliency and strength, which may, in turn, lead to a greater belief in their efficacy and enhanced motivation to make life changes (Carney, 2007).

With counselors' assistance, clients should be active in determining their treatment goals and objectives. Counselors should discuss with their clients the advantages and disadvantages of different treatment approaches. The clients' strengths, capacities, and resources that will be integrated into their treatment should also be discussed. Clients who are working on goals they have identified should be more motivated to work towards those changes.

The client, however, will most likely have no knowledge of the system treatment restraints that will impact his or her treatment plan. The counselor must help the client to work collaboratively with the treatment team, agency, regulating bodies, and payer source to develop a treatment plan that meets all standards and expectations, most importantly, those of the client.

There may be times when it is difficult to work collaboratively with a client on a treatment plan, particularly when clients are mandated to counseling and officers of the court are involved. Judges may prescribe treatment through a court order with which clients are mandated to comply to avoid incarceration (e.g., sex offender counseling, substance abuse counseling, domestic violence treatment). The client has a choice to comply, or not, but refusal to comply will typically result in criminal penalties. A situation like this can also arise when a client is placed on an outpatient civil commitment (OPC). The OPC will dictate the client's treatment. For example, if a client with schizophrenia has a history of not taking needed medication and then becoming disruptive in the community, the court may mandate that the person take his or her medication and receive counseling. If the client does not comply with these mandates, then he or she can be forced into a hospital setting for psychiatric treatment. Although the type of treatment is specified by the OPC, the counselor and client still have the option to work collaboratively on the details of the treatment plan and to bring the client's voice into the process. For example, the client may be mandated by the OPC to participate in counseling, but the counselor and client can work together to determine what to address in the treatment plan and in sessions (e.g., identify triggers eliciting outbursts of anger).

Consider the Severity of the Impairment(s)

While a diagnosis provides descriptive information about a disorder, it does not necessarily suggest the level of impairment that the person is experiencing. For example, some clients with narcissistic personality disorder (NPD) function at high levels, often channeling their need for admiration into outlets that are functional (e.g., leadership positions in the workplace). Others with NPD, those who do not have certain strengths or resources such as social skills or greater intelligence, may struggle to function across various domains. Despite the same diagnosis, these two groups of people with the same mental disorder may have grossly different functioning levels.

As such, treatment plans must take into consideration the severity of the client's impairment. Historically, the *Diagnostic and Statistical Manual of Mental Disorders* (American Psychiatric Association [APA], 2000), or the *DSM IV-TR,* had a multiaxial assessment system (indicated on Axis V), which included a Global Assessment of Functioning (GAF) rating scale. This GAF suggested a numeric value that was indicative of clients' level of functional impairment. The GAF assessment combined the assessment of symptom severity, dangerousness to self or others, and decrements in self-care and social functioning into a single score. The latest *Diagnostic and Statistical Manual of Mental Disorders* (*DSM-5*; APA, 2013) does not include the use of a multiaxial assessment and GAF scores. The GAF was used by counselors in determining levels of care and services needed, and it was used by payers—in part—in the determination of necessity for treatment and eligibility for disability compensation.

goals objectives expectations must be realistic + achievable

Despite the removal of GAF scores from the multiaxial assessment system, a client's functioning must still be formally—or informally—assessed, as this will determine the levels and types of care that are required. For example, a person with a severe level of depression may not be able to achieve a goal to alleviate all depressive symptoms. A reasonable goal for someone with severe depression may be the alleviation of three out of 10 depressive symptoms. Conversely, a person diagnosed with mild depression may be able to achieve complete alleviation of all symptoms. A counselor should not set a client up for failure by assisting the client in selecting goals that are unrealistic or unachievable.

In the *DSM-5*, the APA suggested that the World Health Organization's (WHO) Disability Assessment Schedule (WHODAS 2.0) is currently the best measure of disability (2013). The WHODAS 2.0 is applicable to patients with any health condition and is based on the International Classification of Functioning, Disability, and Health (ICF). It was tested in the *DSM-5* field trials and found to be feasible and reliable in routine clinical evaluations (APA, 2013). The WHODAS is a free assessment instrument and can be located on the WHO's website. The WHODAS is a 36-item measure that assesses disability in people 18 years and older. It assesses for disability across six different domains, which include getting around, self-care, understanding and communicating, getting along with people, life activities (e.g., work and/or school activities), and participation in one's community/society. When completing the form, the individual rates these six areas based on his or her functioning over the past 30 days. The respondents are asked to respond as follows: "none" (1 point), "mild" (2 points), "moderate" (3 points), "severe" (4 points), and "extreme or cannot do" (5 points). Scoring of the assessment measure involves either simple scoring (i.e., the scores are simply added up based on the items endorsed with a maximum possible score suggesting extreme disability being 180), or complex scoring (i.e., different items are weighted differently). The computer program that provides complex scoring can be found on the WHO's website. The measure can be used to track changes in the client's level of disability over time, and it can be completed at intervals most relevant to the client's and counselor's needs.

Counselors should also consider the severity of impairment when selecting the interventions to be used in treatment. For example, a reasonable intervention for someone with mild depression may be identifying triggers that elicit a depressed mood. A person with mild depressive symptoms may have the insight and ability to identify triggers, as well as periods of an absence of depressed mood to use as a comparison for when triggers are or are not eliciting depressive symptoms. A person with a more severe and chronic depressed mood may be less able to connect with insights around his or her mood patterns; it may be difficult to identify triggers because he or she may believe that everything is a trigger, and may only remember feeling depressed.

Make Treatment Objectives SMART

Creating a climate of collaboration and adequately assessing a client's level of impairment is essential, yet counselors more often struggle with creating achievable and measurable treatment goals and objectives for clients. Many counselors find selecting and prioritizing treatment goals and objectives and identifying interventions to be the most challenging aspect of the treatment planning process. Some counselors are tempted to identify too many treatment goals, or to have the treatment goals be more complex than is needed. For example, in terms of the quantity of goals, a client with severe depression may realistically only be able to achieve two or three treatment goals in a 2- to 3-month period. An example of an overly complex goal that is difficult to measure might be: "The client will decrease her depression." This goal lacks specificity as to what symptoms will be addressed, and it does not include a measure of evaluation. A better goal would be: "The client will learn and use three positive self-talk strategies to engage with intimate others 50% of the time." With this goal, it is clear what the client will do, when he or she will do it, and how it will be measured (i.e., client self-report, 50% of the time). This goal is also realistic, as a client with severe major depression may not be able to use this skill any more frequently than indicated that early in treatment.

Clients' stated goals are generally very broad (e.g., "to be happy," "to not be depressed," "to get along better with my life partner"), and they often involve other people changing (i.e., "I want my wife to be more engaged and care more about me" or "I want my mother to treat me better"). The counselor's challenge is to take the client's stated goals and help reframe them in a way that is optimally useful to the client and his or her change process. If the restated goals are not meaningful to the client, he or she will not be interested in working toward achieving them, and thus it is important that the counselor's revised goals stay relevant to the client. Solution-focused questioning (e.g., "If a miracle occurred, and you were feeling more happy, what would be different?"; De Shazer, Dolan, Korman, Trepper, & McCollum, 2007) can also be helpful in narrowing the client's focus to more specific areas of change. Again, clients frequently identify things they cannot control, but basic counseling skills can then be used to help clients refocus on what they can and cannot control in terms of their goals.

Related to the aforementioned goal-development principles, simple treatment goals are also generally best. Counselors should develop treatment goals and objectives that are simple and can realistically be achieved by the client. For example, if a client with severe depression is approved for and only plans to attend eight counseling sessions, it is not realistic to develop an overly complex treatment plan and to expect the client to exit counseling with an absence of depressed mood. It is better to expect the client to experience a reduction in the frequency, intensity, and duration of his or her depressive symptoms; an increased level of insight into his or her triggers and patterns of illness; and a variety of applied skills and techniques that can alleviate or moderate his or her depressive symptoms, to develop insight into his or her mood, and to learn skills and techniques he or she can continue to use to help work toward the alleviation of depressive symptoms as he or she moves forward.

Some counselors may also see the treatment plan as an opportunity to lay out a client's map to perfect functioning. Goals that are too ambitious and expansive can be dangerous and can lead to the identification of too many goals and objectives, and result in unrealistic client and counselor expectations and a lack of focus secondary to addressing too much. Treatment plans should be thought of as a first step on a client's journey to improved mental health. Ideally, the foundations that are laid in counseling provide skills and experiences that stay with the client and encourage optimal living long after counseling ends.

Related to the previous section's discussion of assessing impairment and using this to aid in the development of appropriate treatment goals, counselors must also be sure to keep treatment goals specific, measurable, attainable, results-oriented, and timely. The SMART acronym (Substance Abuse and Mental Health Services Administration [SAMHSA], 2006) is a useful tool to use when developing aims and objectives for treatments:

- Specific—Concrete, use action verbs
- Measurable—Numeric or descriptive, quantity, quality
- Attainable—Appropriately limited in scope, feasible
- Results-oriented—Measures outputs or results, includes accomplishments
- Timely—Identifies target dates, includes interim steps to monitor progress

Counselors can also identify short-term and long-term goals that will be addressed simultaneously; not all goals need to have the same achievement/completion date. A client presenting with major depression and issues related to being homeless may need to address the short-term goal of finding shelter, while simultaneously developing the skills needed to help alleviate the depressive symptoms, a potentially longer term goal. Once shelter is secured, the focus of treatment can be refined to address only the client's depressed mood.

When developing treatment plans, counselors must be realistic in their expectations of client change, and these expectations should be reflected in the treatment goals as well as the anticipated dates the goals are expected to be achieved. A number of client factors should be considered when developing treatment goals that are realistic for a given client. These include, but are not limited to, the nature of the disorder, clients' past functioning levels, clients' response to past treatments, various unique internal or external limitations, and unique strengths and resources.

More recently, an increased emphasis has been placed on assessing and measuring client change. Typically, client self-report of symptom reduction is the primary mode of assessment of client change. One useful way to assess for change is to have clients rate their symptoms' severity on a scale from 1 to 10 (with 1 reflecting the worst functioning and 10 reflecting the highest functioning). Informal client self-report assessments can easily be integrated into the client's treatment plan. For example, "the client will self-report an increased ability to manage his anger by moving from a 4 to a 6 on a 10-point anger management scale," or "the client will report fewer sleepless nights, moving from 4 sleepless nights a week to 3—or fewer—a week").

While most third-party payers do not require formal measures of assessment, assessment tools can be a useful way to assess for client change and demonstrate clinical accountability. Should counselors work at an agency that encourages or supports more formal assessment than client self-report, impairment inventories (see Bjorch, Brown, & Goodman, 2000) or disability assessments such as the WHODAS 2.0 (World Health Organization) can be used to rate impairment severity and track clients' changes over time and secondary to specific interventions being applied (Goodman, Brown, & Deitz, 1996). Also, formal assessment measures that assess for the symptom severity of specified disorders can be used to monitor symptom changes (e.g., a depression inventory can be periodically given to the client to assess for changes in depressive symptoms).

Follow the "Golden Thread"

The client's diagnosis is typically the starting place for the development of the treatment plan. The goals and interventions identified in the treatment plan are directly related to the diagnosis. For example, a counselor cannot provide a diagnosis of generalized anxiety disorder and select goals and interventions aimed at treating major depressive disorder. Therefore, the exploration of the presenting problem during the diagnostic assessment interview leads to the provision of a diagnosis that in turn is used to guide the selection of goals and objectives.

The "Golden Thread" refers to the idea that the treatment, and just as importantly, the documentation, progresses in a logical fashion as follows: The diagnosis and the client's goal in seeking treatment leads to the development of aims and objectives of treatment, which leads to counselor-prescribed interventions. Related to this idea of the "Golden Thread," the interventions that are identified in the treatment plan must be the same interventions presented and addressed in the progress notes. Counselors cannot begin to provide interventions that do not relate to the diagnosis, goals, and interventions addressed in the treatment plan without modifying the treatment plan. Finally, treatment summary documentation should also present a unified, cohesive treatment approach that follows the "Golden Thread." A thoughtful, careful presentation in practice and in documentation conveys a cohesive treatment system.

Be Flexible: Treatment Plans Are Not Static

As previously discussed, it is important that counselors understand that treatment plans are not static; rather, they are evolving documents. As mentioned previously, it can be tempting to identify too many counseling goals and objectives. To avoid this, counselors might remind themselves that over time, the treatment plan will be revisited and edited, and additions will be made. When developing a treatment plan, counselors are typically working with a limited amount of information they have been provided at one point in time. It is almost certain that as counseling progresses, counselors will learn new information about the clients, and clients will learn new information about themselves. This information often alters a counselor's understanding of their clients' underlying dynamics and their initial presenting problem; thus altering the formulation and implementation of their diagnosis and treatment plan. The first author had a client she was working with on issues related to anxiety. Despite her best efforts, the client was making no progress. After seven sessions, the client admitted to the counselor that she smoked marijuana on a daily basis and had been doing so for many years. The client had previously denied any substance use, and this new information significantly changed the client's treatment plan.

If there is a change in the client's diagnosis or symptoms, then the treatment plan will need to be updated to reflect these changes. A client may have initially presented with psychosis, but after months of medication compliance, he or she may experience a reprieve from these symptoms. If this occurs, the treatment plan will need to be updated to reflect the current symptoms that the client is presenting. Often, more information will become available in treatment and the provisional diagnosis will become more refined. When that happens, the diagnostic assessment needs to be updated to reflect the current symptoms, and therefore, the current diagnosis. (e.g., a change from severe to mild major depressive disorder)

Related to this discussion of treatment plans being fluid, any time a diagnosis changes, the treatment plan will likely also need to be updated to reflect these changes. This ties back to the idea of the "Golden Thread," or ensuring the diagnosis, treatment goals, objectives, and interventions all relate in a logical fashion.

Counselors must also be fluid in how they approach a treatment plan, understanding that clients will have experiences that change their situations and goals, new issues will emerge, and clients, in fact, may want to change the focus of their treatment. Counselors have an ethical responsibility to be flexible in how they conceptualize clients' treatment planning journey. The first author was once counseling a 25-year-old woman who had a specific phobia and also wanted to address issues related to marital discord and adjusting to having a newborn baby. One hour before a session with the counselor, the client found out that her husband had died in a car accident. This experience obviously changed the focus of her treatment plan. During the first few sessions after this crisis, the counselor provided crisis intervention counseling. Then, instead of addressing her phobia and marital discord, the treatment plan shifted to focus on grief and adjustment to being a single parent.

Related to the idea of being flexible, clients will also present with life crises that may require a counselor to shift a counseling session's focus. All counselors face these detours, and we need to be flexible and skilled enough to know when these detours are appropriate, or not. For example, you may be working with a client on issues associated with a sleep disorder, but if your client has just witnessed a fatal car accident on the way to the session and needs to process that event, you should move with your client. The book's first author had a number of counseling sessions scheduled the day of the 9/11 terrorist attacks. These attacks opened up a variety of issues for her clients, and while not directly related to her clients' treatment plans, she found that with many of her clients, she spent several weeks after the attacks processing clients' reactions and how these reactions related to their struggles. Conversely, clients who routinely have a hard time staying on track and focusing on treatment goals may require frequent redirections to the treatment plan and session goals.

🚗 **Clinical Toolbox 2.1:** In the Pearson etext, click here to read questions counselors might consider when developing treatment plans.

The treatment planning principles discussed in this section can help counselors develop and maintain their treatment plans. In the following section, a model that counselors can use to guide their treatment planning process will be presented.

collaborate, consider severity, SMART objectives, Golden Thread, Be flexible

TABLE 2.1   The I CAN START Treatment Planning Model

The I CAN START Treatment Planning Model	
I	Individual Counselor
C	Contextual Assessment
A	Assessment and Diagnosis
N	Necessary Level of Care
S	Strengths
T	Treatment Approach
A	Aim and Objectives of Treatment
R	Research-Based Interventions
T	Therapeutic Support Services

A CONCEPTUAL FRAMEWORK FOR CASE CONCEPTUALIZATION AND TREATMENT PLANNING

The material presented in Chapter 1 and earlier in this chapter informs the treatment model that will be presented in this section. An understanding of the importance of counselor, client, and treatment variables; the value of evidence-based practices and strength-based, contextual understanding of people's situations; and a knowledge of the practical realities and external constraints related to treatment planning all play an important role in helping people change and in treating mental disorders.

The essential elements needed for a counselor to construct a comprehensive, strength-based treatment plan are organized within the following model. This systematic model is represented by the acronym I CAN START (see Table 2.1). This mnemonic code is intended to assist counselors in the relevant recall of the needed aspects of a comprehensive treatment planning process, a way to fully develop appropriate treatment goals and objectives, and a systematic process to competently move efficiently and quickly through a structured conceptual framework for case conceptualization and treatment planning.

Components of the Conceptual Framework

INDIVIDUAL (I)   It cannot be assumed that all counselors provide the same treatment experience for all clients. Every counselor—just like every client—is unique, and the dynamic interplay between the client and counselor must always be considered when engaging in treatment planning. Therefore our model's first component starts with "I," the counselor as an individual.

Although research suggests that many observable counselor traits appear to have little influence on counseling outcomes (i.e., age, sex, or ethnicity), we do know that counselors who are perceived as empathic, authentic, and accepting of clients form stronger working alliances and have more successful counseling outcomes (Zuroff, Kelly, Leybman, Blatt, & Wampold, 2010). These traits are integrally related to the counselor and his or her personal characteristics. Counselors' interpersonal qualities such as optimism, emotional health, and emotional stability impact treatment. As such, counselors must understand who they are and take steps to ensure that, in the context of the counseling relationship, their strengths are optimized and the potential impacts of their weaknesses are minimized.

The ACA *Code of Ethics* (in press) is clear that counselors are ethically required to be aware of their own biases and prejudices, as well as clients' contexts when diagnosing and treating mental disorders. Counselors bring their own personality, lived experiences, and professional training into each counseling relationship and interaction. Therefore, counselors must be aware of how clients perceive them and how their characteristics impact the counseling relationship. Because some counselor characteristics weaken the therapeutic alliance and impact treatment outcomes, counselors need to monitor their personal reactions and traits. For example, when counselors are overstructuring or understructuring, defensive, overly critical, demanding, or maintain an unsupportive stance, they weaken the therapeutic alliances and risk poorer counseling outcomes for their clients (Sharpless, Muran, & Barber, 2010). Conversely, when counselors are warm, empathetic, interested, open-minded, confident, and display flexibility in practice, they strengthen the working relationship and provide better counseling outcomes for their clients (Sharpless et al., 2010).

Additionally, counselor beliefs and attitudes can either hinder or enhance work with culturally diverse clients (Sue & Sue, 2012). It is important that if they wish to fully understand their clients within their cultural context, counselors be sensitive to their own values, assumptions, and biases. Counselors must not only possess a knowledge of oppression, racism, and discrimination, but also be aware of how their own attitudes, values, and personal reactions impact clients by hindering the counseling relationship and process. Therefore, counselors must seek supervision, consultation, and educational opportunities so that they can move toward a greater level of comfort with diverse clients and recognize their own limitations (Sue & Sue, 2012).

One way for counselors to be better aware of their personal characteristics is to receive their own personal counseling. As counselors, we enhance human development, not just address infirmities or problems. As such, even if one does not have any identified problems to address, counseling is a wonderful way to enhance self-awareness of one's strengths and weaknesses, and facilitate personal development. Personal counseling also provides the added benefit of developing counselors' understanding of what the counseling experience is like for clients.

Another important way for counselors to understand their personal characteristics and how they impact counseling is to engage in regular supervision and/or peer consultation. Regular, open conversation about personal characteristics and how they are impacting the care provided to clients can help facilitate client care. Supervisees and supervisors are both encouraged to introduce this topic into clinical supervision.

CONTEXTUAL ASSESSMENT (C)   When conducting a contextual assessment of a client, counselors must evaluate and consider a client in terms of three specific and interrelated contexts: intrapersonal context or variables within an individual; interpersonal context or relationships with others; and subordinate context or relationships with groups (Wenar & Kerig, 2005). Stated another way, counselors must consider clients as individuals whose perceptions of their problems are rooted in layered experiences and rich social contexts.

The first context to consider when conceptualizing clients' situations is their unique intrapersonal context (i.e., variables within the individual). In particular, counselors need to consider the following areas:

- *Attachment* (e.g., the bonds that people develop with their caregivers and their subsequent ability to trust and develop emotional connections with others)
- *Behaviors or actions* (e.g., principles of learning, or how people have learned to respond to their environments; self-efficacy, or people's learned beliefs about their ability to achieve tasks and reach goals in certain areas of their lives)

- *Biology or organic context* (e.g., genetics, biochemical issues, intelligence)
- *Cognitions or thinking* (e.g., mental processes, which include learning, memory, language, problem-solving, reasoning, attention, and decision making)
- *Developmental considerations*
  - *Cognitive development* (e.g., egocentrism, perspective taking, information processing)
  - *Social and emotional development* (e.g., social skills, self-awareness and ability to self-regulate behaviors and emotions)
  - *Moral development* (e.g., morality, one's connection with concepts like justice and equality)
  - *Physical development* (e.g., physical health and growth)
  - *Educational/occupational development* (e.g., career development)
  - *Sexual development* (e.g., gender identity, sexual orientation)
- *Emotions or feeling* (e.g., ability to identify, understand, regulate, release, and manage feelings)
- *Personality* (e.g., interrelatedness between cognitions, feeling, and behaving, which results in consistent response patterns; temperament, or human characteristics that are often regarded as innate rather than learned; personality traits such as the Big Five personality dimensions [conscientiousness, openness to experience, agreeableness, neuroticism, extraversion])

 Clinical Toolbox 2.2: In the Pearson etext, click here to read about a career development activity that can be used to help enhance clients' career certainty, build their confidence in developing career plans, and promote their goal-oriented thinking related to their educational and occupational future.

The next context to consider when conceptualizing clients is their unique interactions and relationships with others (i.e., interpersonal context). This interpersonal context involves the environment's impact on an individual's growth and development. Bronfenbrenner's (1979) ecological systems theory suggested that five environmental factors impact an individual's development:

small
- *Microsystem* (i.e., the environment in which the person lives; the family siblings, peers, school, work, and neighborhood)
- *Mesosytem* (i.e., the interaction between each microsytem; experiences at home related to experiences at school)
- *Exosystem* (i.e., links between a social setting in which the client does not have an active role and the individual's immediate context; the economic system, political system, educational system, religious system, and government)
- *Macrosystem* (i.e., the overarching beliefs and values of that culture and society; political or religious norms of the culture)

large
- *Chronosystem* (i.e., sociohistorical circumstances or the cumulative experiences a person has over the course of his or her lifetime; divorce, birth of a child)

These environmental factors aid counselors in conceptualizing clients within their interpersonal context. Specifically, counselors need to conceptualize clients within relationships (e.g., the environment where they live), the interactions between these relationships (e.g., family and school; parents and friends), the interactions with societal systems (e.g., educational system, economic), and the culture of the society. For example, a school-age female living in a poor, crime-ridden community may have overprotective parents who have restricted her ability to create and form close peer and community relationships. This may lead to her developing a lack of trust and involvement with her peer groups, school, and community. Because of the conflicted interaction between her parents and the local school system, and feelings of alienation within her school and community, the child may struggle with chronic school truancy. This interaction between systems could lead to a new system becoming involved—the legal system. Bronfenbrenner's model can be applied to clients and help counselors conceptualize clients' contextual circumstances.

In addition to Bronfenbrenner's systems, another context to consider when conceptualizing clients' context is their unique superordinate context (i.e., affiliation with certain groups), which is often generically referred to as a population's demographics. These affiliations are often strengthened and organized by shared worldviews, traditions, situations, and cultures, which significantly impact an individual's personal identity (Sue & Sue, 2012). If a counselor desires to understand clients, their situation, and worldview (i.e., points of view, or perception or orientation to viewing and understanding the world), an understanding of their affiliations is essential. The following superordinate contexts are important in considering clients' context (Sue & Sue, 2012):

- *Age* (e.g., the accumulation of multidimensional [physical, psychological, developmental] change over years)
- *Gender* (e.g., the range of characteristics [behavioral, mental, physical] on the continuum of femininity and masculinity; social gender roles and gender identity)
- *Race* (e.g., a means to classify humans by national, cultural, ethnic, geographic, linguistic, and religious affiliations)
- *Ethnicity* (e.g., the classification of humans based on national or cultural affiliations)
- *Culture* (e.g., the affiliation with a set of values, beliefs, goals, and practices that are often transmitted to future generations)
- *Socioeconomic class* (e.g., a class system based on the affiliation of stratifications or hierarchical categories [lower, middle, upper class] based on economic recourses)
- *Sexual orientation* (e.g., the inclination, attraction, or enduring quality that draws an individual to another person of the opposite gender or sex, the same gender or sex, or to both genders or sexes)
- *Relationship status* (e.g., the classification of human beings based on their interpersonal relationship status [married, single, divorced, widowed, cohabiting, dating])
- *Disability/ability* (e.g., the impairment, limitation, or extreme strengths of a human being, which involves either the physical, mental, emotional, cognitive, sensory, developmental, or some combination of these abilities)
- *Religious Preferences/Spirituality* (e.g., an affiliation with an organized set of beliefs, worldviews, and traditions related to spirituality and humanity)
- *Geographic location* (e.g., the classification of human beings based on their geography)

Clinical Toolbox 2.3: In the Pearson etext, click here to read about an activity that can be used to help clients develop an awareness of sexual orientation–related struggles, and skills that can be used to manage sexual orientation adjustments.

Counselors must be aware of their own assumptions and personal reactions to diverse groups and affiliations, attempt to fully understand individuals within their unique context, and allow these understandings to adequately inform appropriate treatment planning (Sue & Sue, 2012). This meta-theoretical approach to counseling (i.e., multicultural counseling) allows counselors to clarify clients' definition of the problem, perceptions of the cause, the problem's context, factors affecting their self-coping, and their ability to seek help in a culturally sensitive context (Pedersen, 1991). Essentially, this can be done by mindfully attending to the clients' intrapersonal, interpersonal, and superordinate context while allowing clients to engage and share their own past experiences and perceptions of their lived experiences, relationships, and the problem's formation. Appendix 1.4 provides detailed questions that can be used to help in assessing clients' cultural context.

CREATIVE TOOLBOX ACTIVITY 2.1   Community Strengths and Resources Genogram

Victoria E. Kress, PhD, LPCC-S (OH)

Activity Overview

In this activity, to better help themselves and their counselors understand the context in which they live, clients create a visual representation of the relationships in their lives. This activity can help clients to identify strengths and resources within their environment and community. Identifying healthy and supportive relationships can bring attention to the positive aspects of a client's life.

Treatment Goal Addressed

The exercise can be used as an assessment tool to help clients and counselors identify strengths that can be useful in developing their treatment plans. The primary goal of this activity is to encourage the client to examine the ways in which individuals function and develop within a community. Clients explore their support networks and identify strengths and resources with which they had not previously connected. This exercise can also help clients identify strengths within their community.

Directions

1. Instruct the client to choose a piece of paper to represent his or her community.
2. Ask the client to draw himself or herself within the community, represented by any symbol or depiction so wished.
3. Invite the client to draw his or her family, friends, and other people who are important in the client's life (e.g., teachers, coworkers, religious community, social or sports groups). You might use Appendix 1.3, *Interview Questions to Assess Clients' Strengths, Capacities, and Resources,* to help guide you in this assessment process.
4. Instruct the client to draw lines between himself or herself and the other identified individuals. Encourage the client to use different types of lines to depict different types of relationships among the individuals. For example:

positive and supportive relationships: ════════════════

distant relationships: ------------------------------

problematic/conflictual relationships: ∿∿∿∿

Process Questions

1. What is it like for you to see the support and resources you have?
2. Whom can you lean on for support?
3. What other identified individuals or groups might you add to your current support network?
4. Are there any changes you would like to make to your support network?
5. How can you enhance your network to gain more supportive people and resources?

One additional resource that counselors can use in conducting a contextual assessment is the Cultural Formulation Interview (CFI: this measure can be found in the *DSM-5*; APA, 2013). The CFI, a structured, standardized 16-question interview tool, is a resource that can be used to enhance a counselor's understanding of a client's relevant cultural information. This systematic interview is intended to be utilized in the initial sessions of treatment and is broken into four discrete sections (APA, 2013):

1. *Cultural definition of the problem* (e.g., the client's definition of the problem; defining the problem through the perspective of the client's family, friends, or relevant community members)
2. *Cultural perceptions of cause, context, and support* (e.g., personal perceptions of the causes of the problem; problem causes that family, friend, or relevant community members might prescribe; supports and stressors; components of client's background/identity [cultural identity])
3. *Cultural factors affecting self-coping and past help seeking* (e.g., coping skills; past advisement, help, and treatment; barriers to past attempts at help)
4. *Cultural factors affecting current help seeking* (e.g., preferences of counseling style and approach; concerns about the present counseling relationship)

Once a counselor has a richer understanding of who the client is as an individual, within relationships, and within affiliated groups, the counselor is ready to explore the more formal components of the assessment process. The results of this contextual assessment, along with the components of a formal assessment, provide counselors with information that can help them best determine the most accurate and appropriate *DSM-5* diagnosis. An accurate diagnosis and an associated prognosis aids counselors in determining how to move forward in addressing the treatment aspects of the I CAN START model. The next section describes assessment and diagnosis and its role in treatment planning.

ASSESSMENT AND DIAGNOSIS (A)   A formal assessment helps counselors better understand their clients and informs the development of a comprehensive treatment plan. Utilizing formal or informal assessments allows the counselor to not only gain a more thorough understanding of the client's initial concerns, but a more accurate conceptualization of the client's situation, appropriate treatment approaches, and it provides an opportunity to continually monitor the impact of treatment (Whiston, 2012). Formal assessment and the use of formal assessment measures can also be used to help counselors determine if further, more advanced testing is warranted. Sadock and Sadock (2007) outline information that should be gathered during the preliminary assessment process:

- Identifying information (i.e., name, age, sex, marriage status, occupation, language, religion)
- Description of the presenting issues (i.e., in the client's own words, why is the client seeking help?)
- History of the presenting issues (i.e., development of the symptoms, behavioral changes, time of onset, level of impairment)
- Past counseling or medical history (i.e., any emotional disorders, psychosomatic concerns, medical conditions, neurological disorders)
- Family history (i.e., ethnicity, composition of the home, important relationships, illness in the family, community and neighborhood)
- Personal history (i.e., history from childhood, to adolescence, into adulthood; developmental considerations [personality, temperament, social interactions, cognitive, moral, sexuality]; a past history of abuse, neglect, or traumatic experiences; educational history; occupational history)
- Mental status examination data (see below)
- Referrals or further diagnostic considerations (i.e., physical examination, neurological examination, interviews with other family members)

Additionally, counselors may need to collect and review medical records or prior health or mental health treatment information. This information, along with information from collateral reports (i.e., people involved in the client's life, such as family or friends), can aid in the compilation of a complete and comprehensive clinical picture. Collateral reports may be particularly useful when working with clients who are poor historians or lack insight into their situation. Culturally, some clients may expect the counselor to engage friends and family in the counseling process. Counselors may also want to utilize structured interviews, personality inventories, specific symptoms assessments (e.g., Beck Depression Inventory, the State-Trait Anxiety Inventory), and a mental status examination (MSE). An MSE provides counselors with another vehicle for assessing a client's self-presentation and level of functioning. Components of an MSE may have different names or titles, but essentially include an assessment of the following items (Sommers-Flanagan & Sommers-Flanagan, 2009):

- Appearance
- Behaviors/psychomotor activity
- Attitudes
- Affect and mood
- Speech and thought
- Perceptual disturbances
- Orientation and consciousness
- Memory and intelligence
- Reliability, judgment, and insight

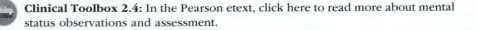 **Clinical Toolbox 2.4:** In the Pearson etext, click here to read more about mental status observations and assessment.

Formal and informal assessments lead to accurate diagnosis and case conceptualization, and comprehensive treatment planning, thus increasing the utility and effectiveness of counseling (Whiston, 2012). The results of the formal assessment will provide counselors with information that can help them best determine the most appropriate *DSM-5* diagnosis. Diagnosing mental disorders is a very complex skill set, which requires counselors to learn about not only the *DSM-5* system and diagnostic criteria, but also the process of diagnostic ascription; it is not enough to just know the diagnostic criteria. A discussion of the *DSM-5* diagnosis process per se and all of its complexities is beyond the scope of this text, and it is assumed that readers have some foundational knowledge of how to use the *DSM-5* to develop and ascribe an appropriate diagnosis. An accurate diagnosis and its associated prognosis aids counselors in determining how to move forward in addressing the next treatment aspects of the I CAN START model.

NECESSARY LEVEL OF CARE (N)   There is a paucity of literature on how to determine the appropriateness of certain levels of care, differing treatment settings (i.e., residential treatment hospitalization, outpatient treatment), types of treatment (i.e., individual, group, couple, family), and pacing of treatment (i.e., daily, weekly, monthly). Some issues that counselors should consider when determining appropriate treatment settings, types of treatments, and pacing are:

- Severity of the mental health symptoms
- Mental health diagnosis (i.e., mental disorder) and its associated prognosis
- Physical limitations or medical conditions
- Suicidal ideation (i.e., threat to self) and homicidal ideation (i.e., harm to others), or a client's ability to be safe in the community
- Ability to care for one's self (i.e., activities of daily living [ADL] like showering, eating, using the toilet, dressing)
- Past treatment settings and responsiveness to those settings
- Aims and goals of treatment
- Social and community support system and resources
- Desired level of care from the client's perspective

When selecting a treatment setting, counselors should utilize the least restrictive setting. Residential treatment, inpatient hospitalization, day treatment (i.e., partial hospitalization), and outpatient treatment are the most common settings for mental health treatment (see Table 2.2, Level of Care Continuum). Counselors, considering the diagnosis and the specific needs of the client, should match the severity of symptoms, specific client situation, and client characteristics with the appropriate level of care. Counselors should provide a balance between optimal safety, potential growth, and autonomy. Cost-effective treatment choices will need to be considered due to increasing limitations in insurance coverage, but these should not be the sole consideration in the decision-making process when determining the necessary level of care.

STRENGTHS (S)   The importance of a strength-based lens was previously discussed. When using a strength-based perspective, clients' strengths and resources are used to help them overcome their struggles. Clients often have a limited understanding of their strengths, and counselors have an important role to play in identifying and connecting clients with these strengths, resources, and competencies. Appendices 1.1, 1.2, and 1.3

Client strengths are integral part

TABLE 2.2 Level of Care Continuum

Inpatient Hospitalization	Residential Treatment (RT)	Day Treatment Partial Hospitalization	Outpatient Treatment
Most restrictive and involves staying at a facility under constant supervision	Temporarily lives in the facility under constant or intermittent supervision	Permitted to live in the community; attends program during the day	Weekly, biweekly, monthly meetings, groups, and/or sessions
Shorter periods of stay than RT (overnight to less than a month)	Extended period of stay (duration is typically not prescribed in advance)	Focused and highly structured treatment during the day	Least restrictive, least structured setting
Highly structured	Highly structured	Leads to step-down treatments, half-day treatment and outpatient treatment	
Stabilization is primary goal (i.e., decrease suicidal behaviors, psychosis)	Leads to day or outpatient treatment		

Level of Personal Restriction

←--→

More   *Less*

provide detailed information that can be used to help in assessing client strengths. Categories of strengths, specific character strengths, and questions that can be used to tap into strengths are provided in these appendices.

Voices from the Trenches 2.2: In the Pearson etext, click here to watch a counselor discuss the importance of counselors retaining a focus on client strengths.

TREATMENT APPROACH (T) This aspect of the model focuses on what specific treatment theory, model, or approach is selected for use with clients (e.g., Cognitive Behavioral Therapy). This theory guides the selection of research-based interventions (addressed later in the model).

When selecting a treatment approach counselors should consider evidence-based practices (which are discussed in a later section in this chapter). However, they must also consider the approaches they are trained to use, client's treatment preferences, the confines of the setting in which they work and a myriad of additional considerations discussed earlier in this chapter and in Chapter 1. When considering the utilization of an evidence-based treatment, theory, or approach, counselors need to consider what is already known in the research literature (e.g., peer-reviewed journals and federal registries). Some helpful guidelines that may assist counselors in evaluating whether a theory, approach, or intervention should be deemed evidenced-based and utilized in clinical practice are (SAMHSA, 2009):

[handwritten margin note: match EBT with client situation]

CREATIVE TOOLBOX ACTIVITY 2.2   Personal Strengths and Resources Collage

Victoria E. Kress, PhD, LPCC-S (OH)

Activity Overview

Clients use collage techniques to identify strengths and resources that can be used in helping them overcome their identified struggles. This activity can help clients to identify strengths and resources within themselves and within their circle of influence.

Treatment Goal Addressed

This exercise can be used as an assessment tool to help clients and counselors identify strengths that can be useful in developing clients' treatment plans. The goal of this activity is to encourage the client to identify his or her personal strengths and resources, and to begin to punctuate and amplify them for use in overcoming struggles.

Directions

1. The counselor and client discuss how all people have strengths and resources. The materials in Appendices 1.1, 1.2, and 1.3 can be used to facilitate this conversation and educate clients on examples of various strengths and resources.
2. The client is then presented with a variety of magazines, catalogues, or any other source that contains different pictures.
3. The client is invited to cut out pictures or words that represent his or her strengths, resources, and competencies across various domains (e.g., his or her personal capacities, resources, personal interests).
4. The client then assembles these words and pictures on a piece of paper in a collage format.

Process Questions

1. What was it like for you to see the strengths/resources/capacities you possess?
2. What most surprised you about this activity?
3. How do you see yourself using these strengths/resources/capacities to overcome the problems with which you have been struggling?
4. What struggles have these strengths/resources/capacities helped you to overcome in the past?
5. What strengths/resources/capacities mean the most to you?
6. How can you use your strengths/resources/capacities to help others or contribute to your community?
7. How do your unique strengths/resources/capacities make you special?
8. How are your strengths/resources/capacities different from others'?
9. How could you use these strengths/resources/capacities to build a more positive future?
10. Are there any other strengths/resources/capacities you want to develop? How can you achieve this?
11. What have you learned from this activity?

- *Guideline 1:* Approaches and interventions need to be based on some documented, clear conceptual model of change.
- *Guideline 2:* Approaches and interventions need to be similar to or found in federal registries and/or the peer-reviewed literature.

- *Guideline 3:* The approaches and interventions are supported by the documentation of multiple scientific enquiries that seem credible, rigorous, and evidence consistent positive effects.
- *Guideline 4:* The approaches and interventions have been reviewed and deemed credible by informed experts in that treatment area.

Additionally, when determining an appropriate treatment approach counselors also need to consider the following (Sommers-Flanagan & Sommers-Flanagan, 2009):

- Does the counselor fully understand the client's issue or concern for entering treatment?
- Does the counselor utilize empirically supported research on the clinical relationship to address the client, counselor, and treatment variables (e.g., therapeutic alliance, collaboration, client feedback)?
- Has the counselor considered how the client's and his or her preferences may intersect (e.g., the counselor's theoretical orientation and the client's desired form/modality of treatment)?
- Has the counselor previously implemented evidence-based treatment approaches for that issue or concern?
- Is the counselor working within or outside of his or her skill or competency level?

Adhering to these considerations enables counselors to select treatment approaches that are consistent with clients' treatment preferences, and adhere to counselors' individual competencies.

AIM AND OBJECTIVES OF TREATMENT (A)   The treatment aims and objectives relate to the selected treatment approach (T aspect of the model) and the research-based interventions (the R aspect of the model discussed in the following section). The aims and objectives of treatment planning must be *tangible*—that is, accessible and useful. Treatment plans need to have clearly defined problems with measurable goals that outline frequency of treatment, and present objectives in behavioral terms to continually evaluate and reevaluate the client's progress. The Joint Commission (i.e., an independent, not-for-profit health care accreditation organization) reported that the most problematic standard (i.e., 38% noncompliance) for behavioral health care organizations in 2010 was the standard on treatment plan writing, which states:

> The organization has a plan for the care, treatment, or services that reflect the assessed needs, strengths, preferences, and goals of the individual served (Joint Commission, 2011, p. 1)

The utilization of a structured model may help assure efficiency when codeveloping clients' aims and objectives for treatment. The SMART model is one example of a model that can be used for writing treatment aims and objectives (SAMHSA, 2006). SMART is an acronym for:

- **Specific**—Concrete, uses action verbs (e.g., *attend, identify, utilize, begin, obtain, transition, report, communicate, process*)
- **Measurable**—Numeric or descriptive, quantity, quality (e.g., client will identify 3 . . . and attempt to implement 1 of them in the midst of personal crisis; client will engage in 20 minutes of . . . on Monday, Wednesday, and Friday after breakfast)
- **Attainable**—Appropriately limited in scope, feasible (e.g., over the next 2 months, the client agrees to attend . . . to increase her or his tolerance of these distressing situations)

- **Results-oriented**—Measures output or results, includes accomplishments (e.g., client will examine thoughts/beliefs 75% of the time each day and will engage in . . . 75% of the time; client will have 0 acts of . . . and document the severity of urges, associated thoughts, and feelings on a nightly basis before bedtime)
- **Timely**—Identifies target dates, includes interim steps to monitor progress (e.g., within 2 months, the client will learn and identify . . . and will gradually tolerate . . . 70% of the time; eventually, through the use of . . . the client will identify, tolerate, and act on an alternative behavior . . . 90% of the time)

Clinical Toolbox 2.5: In the Pearson etext, click here to read about an activity that can be used to empower clients to follow through on reaching their treatment goals.

RESEARCH-BASED INTERVENTIONS (R) Research-based interventions/treatments, or evidence-based interventions/treatments, are interventions that have been researched and found to be efficacious in treating different disorders. These interventions should be grounded in the selected treatment approach (T aspect of this model), and they will inform the aims and objectives (A aspect of this model) of treatment. The importance of using these approaches was discussed in more detail in Chapter 1. Experts in the field have validated these research-based interventions through scientific inquiry, peer-review, and/or consensus. This stage of the I CAN START model does not necessarily follow the identification of the aims and objectives of counseling in a linear fashion. In fact, the two are integrally related with research-based interventions typically informing the aims and objectives. The selected interventions target specific treatment goals (i.e., alleviation of a symptom; increased level of functioning; reducing the need for more restrictive placements).

Although some research gaps do exist in the treatment literature, contemporary literature (e.g., journals) should always be consulted to find the most informed treatment approaches, interventions, and counseling considerations. Counselors should only make recommendations to clients regarding treatment once they have considered the client's unique situation, contextual factors, and personal preferences for counseling. Integrating research-based interventions with an eye to client individuality allows clients to share in the decision-making power with counselors, enabling the client to decide with the counselor what makes the most sense in terms of treatment options.

THERAPEUTIC SUPPORT SERVICES (T) Therapeutic support services complement counseling interventions. These services are intended to support the client through additional education (e.g., nutrition, diet, exercise), training (e.g., parent training, mindfulness, biofeedback), socialization (e.g., support groups, AA), and navigation of difficult processes (e.g., legal issues, governmental services, housing). These support services should always align with treatment goals and reinforce the work that has been done within sessions; these services are most often out-of-session resources. Therapeutic support services can be utilized throughout treatment.

Clients may benefit from different types of support services depending on the severity of their symptoms, the nature of the setting in which they reside (e.g., outpatient, hospital, prison, residential facility, college campus), their diagnosis, their strengths, and their current level of functioning. Support services can complement counseling treatment goals, are unique, and should align with each client, his or her goals, and his or her situation. For example, a client with severe and persistent schizophrenia may benefit from case management, consistent psychiatric evaluation for medication responsiveness, and vocational support services. A college student struggling with adjustment issues may benefit from additional support from student programming, academic advisors, and student success centers (e.g., writing centers, math centers, student progress centers).

I CAN START TREATMENT PLAN APPLICATION: TERIKA

Terika, discussed at the beginning of this chapter, displays a number of characteristics and symptoms consistent with clinical depression. She also displays a number of atypical symptoms that must be considered. A counselor must consider contextual factors, diagnosis, and the necessary levels of care before moving ahead with a comprehensive, strength-based treatment approach. The following I CAN START conceptual framework outlines treatment considerations that may be helpful in working with Terika.

C = Contextual Assessment

Family support (single mother), and small living quarters; African American culture; Baptist (Christian); a low socioeconomic status; educational considerations (i.e., possibly dropping out of school); normal developmental struggles associated with adolescence (identity development, establishing and maintaining healthy friendships, struggles around romantic relationships)

A = Assessment and Diagnosis

Diagnosis = Major Depressive Disorder (single episode, moderate, with atypical features) 296.22 (F32.1); Beck Depression Inventory (given at start of each session); Assessment of Suicidality (on a weekly basis); to rule out drug and alcohol use and its possible role in her struggles: Substance Abuse Subtle Screening Inventory-3 (SASSI-3) and CAGE Assessment (i.e., Have you ever felt you needed to **C**ut down on your drinking?; Have people **A**nnoyed you by criticizing your drinking?; Have you ever felt **G**uilty about drinking?; Have you ever felt you needed a drink first thing in the morning [**E**ye-opener] to steady your nerves or to get rid of a hangover?); physical examination by a physician

N = Necessary Level of Care

Outpatient, individual weekly sessions; mother may be invited to attend some sessions if the idea is acceptable to client; should the client's suicidality escalate, acute care (i.e., a secure hospital setting) may be required

S = Strength-Based Lens

Self: Terika is compassionate and caring. She is curious and has a desire to learn new things. She cares about animals. Despite her depressive symptoms she can still express concerns about her future, and she expresses that she wants to make good decisions to secure a bright future.

Family: Terika cares about her family, especially her mother. She loves her mother. She is invested in having a relationship with her mother and her relatives. She has a supportive aunt. Her mother wants to support Terika in being healthy, and she is able to connect Terika with supportive resources.

School/Community: Terika enjoys volunteering at the local animal shelter where she walks dogs. She loves animals and would love to work with animals in the future. In the past, she has been involved in her church and has participated in a host of church functions. She identifies with her church and values her religion. She reports that people in her church are supportive. Historically, Terika enjoyed going to school, being with friends, and learning new things. She has had a number of past friendships she can build on and friends with whom she can reconnect. Terika noted that she has a good relationship with her school counselor, and she feels she can talk to her when she is feeling badly.

T = Treatment Approach

Behavioral Activation Therapy

A = Aim and Objectives of Treatment (1-month objectives)

Terika will not have any suicide attempts → Terika will have 0 suicide attempts.

Terika will report an improved mood → Terika will report an increase in her positive affective state, moving from 2 to 5 on a 10-point scale.

Terika will increase her positive interactions with others → Terika will plan and participate in one fun activity a week with her mother. Terika will call and talk with one of her friends each evening. She will socialize with a friend at least one time every weekend.

Terika will transition back to school → Terika will attend school 5 days a week.

Terika will volunteer at the animal shelter → Terika will walk a dog at the shelter for 30 minutes after school on her way home on Monday, Wednesday, and Friday.

Terika will reconnect with her church community → Terika will attend church. After completing this goal, she will then attend at least one church-related function every month.

Terika will begin to read and explore → Terika will read a book for 20 minutes each night before bed.

R = Research-Based Interventions (based on Behavioral Activation Therapy)

Counselor will help Terika increase her awareness of her depressive behavior patterns and how they deepen her depression.

Counselor will help Terika make behavior changes by providing skills training (e.g., role plays, mental rehearsal of assigned activities to increase her mastery).

Counselor will assist Terika in changing her depressive behavior patterns.

Counselor will assist Terika in becoming aware of aspects of her strengths and resources and valued experiences that are most important to her (e.g., relationships, school/career, hobbies, spirituality), and activities she can engage in to live in accordance with her expressed values.

> **T = Therapeutic Support Services**
>
> Referral to a psychiatrist to determine if medication is warranted
>
> Consultation with a local teen health center, which uses grant money to help teens increase physical exercise and healthy nutrition in their lives
>
> Teen depression support group after depressive symptoms have been reduced
>
> Terika will speak with her school counselor about her struggles and talk to her about ways she can utilize her as a positive resource

Summary

This chapter provided suggestions and principles that can guide treatment planning efforts. It was emphasized that good treatment plans include certain elements. First, treatment plans must be individualized to the client's needs and preferences, and must be developed collaboratively with the client. The severity of the client's impairments and how these might relate to the treatment plan and outcomes should also be considered when developing a treatment plan. Next, the importance of developing treatment objectives that are SMART (SAMHSA, 2006), or specific, measurable, attainable, results-oriented, and timely was discussed. The concept of the "Golden Thread" was introduced as a way to ensure counselors' treatment plans are developed and flow in a logical fashion. This progression involves the diagnosis and the client's goal in seeking treatment, leading to the development of the aims and objectives of treatment, leading to the treatment interventions. Finally, we discussed the importance of viewing treatment planning as a fluid, evolving process that develops in response to clients' changes and needs.

Next, the I CAN START treatment planning model was presented and applied to a case application. This model is comprehensive in that it addresses multiple layers of factors (e.g., contextual and cultural issues) that impact clients' functioning and treatment needs. The model is strength-based in that it highlights the strengths, competencies, and resources that clients have and integrates these into their treatment. In being strength-based and contextually- and culturally-focused the model is consistent with the theoretical and philosophical foundations of professional counseling. The model also emphasizes the use of evidence-based practices as essential in all client treatment.

In Chapter 3, treatment considerations related to important and high-risk clinical issues will be provided. In particular, Chapter 3 explores suicide, homicide, and interpersonal partner violence, and how these clinical issues should be addressed in relation to clients' treatment.

With the foundations of treatment planning firmly addressed, Chapters 4–15 will address the treatment of the *DSM-5* mental disorders. Where appropriate, some disorders were combined into one category (e.g., oppositional defiant disorder and conduct disorder), but generally, care was taken to keep the disorders discrete so that the treatment literature could be carefully presented with regard to each unique disorder.

Each chapter begins with a case that relates to one of the disorders discussed in the chapter, and ends with an application of the I CAN START model to the case. For each disorder, the following information is addressed: a description of the disorder and typical client characteristics; counselor treatment considerations; treatment models and interventions; and finally, the prognosis for people who have each disorder.

Additionally, each chapter contains two Creative Toolbox activities. These activities are intended to provide readers with an interactive, creative means of applying the evidence-based treatments and interventions discussed in the chapters.

References

American Counseling Association. (in press). *2014 ACA code of ethics*. Alexandria, VA: Author.

American Mental Health Counselors Association. (2010). *Code of ethics*. Alexandria, VA: Author.

American Psychiatric Association. (2000). *Diagnostic and statistical manual of mental disorders* (4th ed., text revision). Washington, DC: Author.

American Psychiatric Association. (2013). *Diagnostic and statistical manual of mental disorders* (5th ed.). Washington DC: Author.

Bjorch, J. P., Brown, J. A., & Goodman, M. (2000). *Casebook for managing managed care: A self-study guide for treatment planning, documentation, and communication*. Washington, DC: American Psychiatric Press.

Bronfenbrenner, U. (1979). *The ecology of human development: Experiments by nature and design*. Cambridge, MA: Harvard University Press.

Carney, J. V. (2007). Humanistic wellness services for community mental health providers. *Journal of Humanistic Counseling, 46*, 154–171.

De Shazer, S., Dolan, Y. M., Korman, H., Trepper, T., & McCollum, E. E. (2007). *More than miracles: The state of the art of Solution-Focused Brief Therapy*. New York, NY: Haworth.

Goodman, M., Brown, J. A., & Deitz, P. M. (1996). *Managing managed care II: A handbook for mental health professionals* (2nd ed.). Washington, DC: American Psychiatric Press.

Joint Commission. (2011). *Top compliance issues for behavioral health care organizations in 2010*. Retrieved from: http://www.jointcommission.org/assets/1/18/BHC_News_2_2011.pdf

Jongsma, A. E., Peterson, L. M., & Bruce, T. J. (2006). *The complete adult psychotherapy treatment planner* (4th ed.). New York, NY: Wiley.

Pedersen, P. B. (1991). Multiculturalism as a generic approach to counseling. *Journal of Counseling and Development, 70*, 6–12.

Sadock, B. J., & Sadock, V. A. (2007). *Kaplan and Sadock's synopsis of psychiatry: Behavioral sciences/clinical psychiatry* (10th ed.). Philadelphia, PA: Lippincott Williams & Wilkins.

Sharpless, B. A., Muran, C. J., & Barber, J. P. (2010). Coda: Recommendations for practice and training. In J. C. Muran & J. P. Barber (Ed.), *The therapeutic alliance: An evidence-based guide to practice* (pp. 341–354). New York, NY: Guilford.

Sommers-Flanagan, J., & Sommers-Flanagan, R. (2009). *Clinical interviewing* (4th ed.). Hoboken, NJ: Wiley.

Substance Abuse and Mental Health Services Administration (SAMHSA). (2006). *S.M.A.R.T. treatment planning*. Retrieved from: http://www.samhsa.gov/samhsa_news/volumexiv_5/article2.htm

Substance Abuse and Mental Health Services Administration (SAMHSA). (2009). *Identifying and selecting evidence-based interventions*. Retrieved from: http://store.samhsa.gov/product/Identifying-and-Selecting-Evidence-Based-Interventions-for-Substance-Abuse-Prevention/SMA09-4205

Sue, D. W., & Sue, D. (2012) (6th ed.). *Counseling the culturally diverse: Theory and practice*. Hoboken, NJ: Wiley.

Wenar, C., & Kerig, P. (2005). *Developmental psychopathology: From infancy through adolescence* (5th ed.). New York, NY: McGraw-Hill.

Whiston, S. C. (2012). *Principles and applications of assessment in counseling* (6th ed.). Belmont, CA: Brooks/Cole.

World Health Organization (WHO). Disability Assessment Schedule (WHODAS 2.0). Retrieved from: http://www.who.int/classifications/icf/whodasii/en/

Zuroff, D. C., Kelly, A. C., Leybman, M. J., Blatt, S. J., & Wampold, B. (2010). Between-therapist and within therapist differences in the quality of the therapeutic relationship: Effects on maladjustment and self-critical perfectionism. *Journal of Clinical Psychology, 66*, 681–697.

Safety-Related Clinical Issues and Treatment Planning

VICTORIA E. KRESS, CHELSEY A. ZOLDAN, AND RACHEL M. HOFFMAN O'NEILL

When counseling clients, counselors have an ethical and legal obligation to do all they can to enhance their safety; safety considerations should always be a top priority. Explicit safety measures, when relevant, should be integrated into all clients' treatment plans. Punctuating safety considerations helps clients to understand their importance while simultaneously protecting counselors from legal liability.

In this chapter, select safety-related clinical issues that are relevant to treatment planning will be discussed, with an emphasis on practical steps counselors can take to promote and support their clients' safety. The clinical issues presented are those that counselors encounter with the greatest frequency, and those that invite the most serious potential for risk to clients, counselors, and/or members of the community.

Suicide assessment and intervention techniques will be discussed in the context of treatment planning. Practical resources that counselors can use in preventing and managing suicide-related risks are also provided.

Next, treatment considerations that relate to homicide risk and intimate partner violence will be discussed. Counselors regularly encounter situations in which their clients are either at risk for experiencing violence, or pose a risk of inflicting violence. Counselors have an ethical obligation to encourage safety, and this chapter will provide practice suggestions and detailed safety planning information that can be integrated into treatment plans and can be used to facilitate safety.

COUNSELING SUICIDAL CLIENTS

In 2010, suicide was the 10th leading cause of death in the United States, accounting for more than 38,000 fatalities (Centers for Disease Control and Prevention, 2010). Data on attempted suicide are not systematically collected, thus it is difficult to assess the frequency of attempts that do not end in death. Various terminology (e.g., suicidal, suicide ideation) can be used to describe an individual's current risk relative to suicide, and it is important that counselors use the correct language in communicating suicidal behaviors.

Clinical Toolbox 3.1: In the Pearson etext, click here to read the definitions of commonly used suicide-related terms.

The risk of suicide can present when working with any client. Clients who are seen in counseling settings and those who have a mental disorder are at a greater risk for suicide attempts and completed suicide. A common misconception is that only those who have depression will experience suicidal ideation. In fact, suicidal ideation, and even suicide attempts, can occur with individuals diagnosed with any variety of diagnoses. Counselors must be prepared to assess suicide with any client who demonstrates the potential for self-harm, regardless of his or her presenting diagnosis.

Counselor Considerations

Working with a suicidal client is often an anxiety-provoking experience for counselors. Counselors must demonstrate the ability to effectively respond to a potential crisis situation in a calm, professional manner. Berman et al. (2004), in conjunction with the American Association of Suicidology, developed a set of 24 core competencies for mental health professionals who work with suicidal clients. These core competencies include the following major elements: (a) managing one's own reactions to suicide, (b) maintaining a sense of collaboration in treatment, (c) understanding the construct of suicide, (d) possessing appropriate risk assessment and intervention skills, (e) developing an effective crisis plan, (f) keeping appropriate documentation related to suicidality, and (g) understanding potential legal and ethical issues in the treatment of suicidality.

In addition to the above-listed competencies, counselors who work with suicidal clients must demonstrate the ability to manage some degree of ambiguity in their clinical practice. Counselors who work with suicidal clients will need to accept the possibility that their assessment could result in false positives (i.e., providing restrictive levels of care to clients not seriously in danger of killing themselves), or false negatives (i.e., failing to hospitalize clients who go on to attempt suicide). Supervision and peer consultation is recommended in all situations involving suicidal clients.

Counselors working with suicidal clients should be aware of the ethical and legal issues associated with counseling this population. An exhaustive review of ethics and legal issues is beyond the scope of this chapter, and readers are encouraged to seek additional information about suicide. As previously stated, it is important that when working with this population, measures are taken to facilitate client safety. These measures should also be integrated into clients' treatment plans with an example of an appropriate objective being "0 suicide attempts."

Related to ethical and legal issues, it is important that counselors document the steps taken to enhance client safety. If counselors' interventions are not documented, it can be argued by external reviewers of records that they did not occur.

Another important ethical/legal issue is the use of safety contracts. These are discussed in greater detail in the interventions section. All counselors should have at least one assessment or decision-making model and one safety planning model that they can use with clients who are suicidal.

Next, counselors need to be aware of community resources and more restrictive settings where clients at risk of suicide can be treated until they are safe. Related to this, counselors should also know their state's guidelines related to involuntary hospitalization. In some states, counselors can have clients admitted to hospitals against their will, and in other states, professionals such as physicians or law enforcement officers must do so.

Client Characteristics

Suicidality is a complex concept and, accordingly, there are many reasons why clients experience suicidal thoughts or behaviors. Van Heeringen (2001) suggested that suicidal behavior results from the interaction of environmental circumstances and factors within the individual. It is often difficult to predict whether an individual will attempt suicide. However, the following factors have been identified as potential indicators of suicidality: (a) past suicide attempts; (b) substance abuse; (c) impulsivity; (d) aggressiveness; (e) thoughts of suicide; (f) hopelessness; (g) loss of control; and (h) presence of a mental health disorder, especially bipolar disorder or depression (Shea, 2002). In addition, counselors must also be aware of any potential recent life stressors, such as a divorce, loss of a job, or financial difficulties (Granello & Granello, 2007). Any abrupt changes in mood (e.g., moving from significant depression to uncharacteristic euphoria) should also be considered a potential warning sign of suicide risk (McGlothlin, 2008). Finally, past suicide attempts are an especially strong predictor of future suicide attempts.

Assessment

Potential suicide risk should be assessed at each of the following points in time: (a) at intake/admission to treatment, (b) at any time suicidal ideation arises or the counselor suspects possible suicidal ideation, (c) when a client experiences a sudden change in mood or behavior, and (d) at the time of discharge from treatment (Shea, 2002). Assessment of clients with suicidal ideation should include the following: (a) identify the presence of psychiatric symptoms (e.g., aggression, impulsiveness, hopelessness, agitation), (b) assess past suicidal behavior, including the presence of self-injurious behaviors, (c) determine past treatment history, treatment relationships, and response to treatment, (d) identify current psychosocial situations and the nature of the crisis, and (e) consider the strengths and resiliencies of the client (Shea, 2002).

The American Association of Suicidology (2013) created a list of behaviors that should be considered an invitation to assess a client's risk of suicide potential. This list is represented by the mnemonic IS PATH WARM (see Table 3.1). This mnemonic is designed to serve as reminder of the potential indicators of suicidality. Once it is determined that the client possesses any number of these indicators, a more detailed risk assessment

---

TABLE 3.1   IS PATH WARM? Suicide Assessment Mnemonic

(American Association of Suicidology, 2013)

I—Ideation. Is suicidal ideation present? Has it been threatened or communicated? Is the client writing or talking about death? How intense and what is the duration of the ideation? Does the client plan to commit suicide at a specific time? Is there a suicide plan? Method?

S—Substance Abuse. Does the client use alcohol or illicit drugs, or abuse prescription drugs? Is the client currently intoxicated? Has the client increased substance use?

P—Purposelessness. Does the client feel that his or her life lacks purpose and meaning? Does the client express that his or her death would not affect others?

A—Anxiety. Is the client experiencing trouble concentrating? Is the client sleeping too much or not enough? Is the client feeling agitated?

T—Trapped. Has the client expressed that he or she feels like "there's no way out" of a situation?

H—Hopelessness. Does the client feel that his or her current situation cannot be changed? Does the client express a dismal view of the future?

W—Withdrawal. Has the client recently been withdrawn from family, friends, and society?

A—Anger. Is the client experiencing uncontrolled rage and a desire for revenge?

R—Recklessness. Has the client been engaging in risky activities?

M—Mood Changes. Has the client experienced dramatic mood changes that deviate from his or her normal behavior (e.g., depression followed by calm or happiness)?

---

should follow. A detailed assessment of risk should generally involve the client, family/ significant others, and any other potential informants (e.g., teacher, physician). An effective risk assessment will include direct questions related to the client's thoughts of death and dying. An effective assessment will also include questions about substance abuse, as there appears to be a strong connection between suicidality and the use of substances.

Signs of acute (i.e., imminent) suicide risk include verbalized threats to harm/kill oneself (e.g., "I'm going to kill myself today"), actively seeking a means to harm/kill oneself (e.g., "I am buying a gun"), and talking or writing about suicide/death (e.g., "Things are going to be so much better once I'm dead"). In the event that these signs are observed, further assessment and immediate intervention (e.g., psychiatric hospitalization) are necessary. Those who display these signs of acute suicidal risk represent a psychiatric crisis, and emergency personnel (e.g., police, paramedics) may need to be contacted to help ensure their entry into a secured setting. Table 3.2 on the next page provides examples of questions that counselors might ask to assess a client's suicide risk.

Intervention

Maltsberger (2006) recommended that counselors who treat potentially suicidal clients must first establish a therapeutic alliance and quickly move to enhancing clients' reasons for living. When attempting to establish a therapeutic alliance with a potentially suicidal client, it may be most important to inquire about how the client is hurting and how the counselor can be helpful (e.g., "Where or how do you hurt?" and "How can I help you?") while simultaneously instilling a sense of hope that the client can feel better.

TABLE 3.2 Questioning Clients about Suicidal Thoughts and Behaviors

---

1. Tell me about a time you've thought life wasn't worth living.
2. When was the most recent time you've thought about killing yourself?
3. On a scale of 1 to 10, with 1 being never and 10 being all the time, how much time do you spend thinking about dying?
4. What methods might you use to kill yourself?
5. Tell me about your plan to kill yourself.
6. On a scale of 1 to 10, with 1 being not likely at all and 10 being 100% likely, how likely are you to kill yourself in the next 2 weeks?
7. Tell me about past times that you've tried to kill yourself.
   a. What happened?
   b. When was the most recent time?
   c. What were you thinking about at the time?
   d. Did someone intervene (i.e., what happened to cause the event not to end in death)?
   e. Did you receive treatment?
8. Who else knows about your thoughts of killing yourself?
9. What are some of your reasons for living?

 Clinical Toolbox 3.2: In the Pearson etext, click here to read about an activity that can be used to help clients with suicidal ideation connect with their reasons for living.

One counselor response to suicidal ideation may be an attempt to *contract for safety*; the client agrees, typically on paper, not to kill him or herself within a specific time frame (e.g., hours, days). Although there may be some benefits to the no-suicide contract (e.g., the contract emphasizes the common goal of treatment, which is client safety; Lee & Bartlett, 2005), there are also a number of potential limitations associated with these documents. The use of no-suicide contracts may lead the client to mistakenly believe that the counselor is only concerned with protecting himself or herself against legal action. Another possible disadvantage is that the contract may serve to inadvertently silence clients; they may feel discouraged, embarrassed, or ashamed if they do experience suicidal ideation (Lee & Bartlett, 2005). The word *contract* may also be problematic, in that it implies the document is a legally binding agreement. Lastly, no-suicide contracts, may inadvertently lead counselors to believe that they are legally protected against malpractice in the event a client does commit suicide; however, in reality, no such protection exists.

An alternative to the no-suicide contract, a Commitment to Treatment Statement, which emphasizes other dimensions of the therapeutic relationship and avoids focusing solely on what the client should *not* do, may be most helpful (Rudd, Mandrusiak, & Joiner, 2006). Commitment to Treatment Statements emphasize positive client coping behaviors (e.g., forms of positive self-soothing behaviors, such as talking or listening to music), focus on what the client is doing well (e.g., commitment to change), and delineate the therapeutic responsibilities of both the client and the counselor. An example of a Commitment to Treatment Statement is provided in Table 3.3.

TABLE 3.3   An Example of a Commitment to Treatment Statement for Suicidal Clients

I agree to commit to counseling, and to be an active participant in the process. I will abide by the various agreed upon aspects of my treatment plan, including:

1. Attending all scheduled sessions, arriving at sessions, on time, and being prepared to actively participate in sessions.

2. Working collaboratively with my counselor to set goals for treatment and taking the steps necessary to work toward achieving these goals.

3. Being open and honest with my counselor about my thoughts and feelings.

4. Using my Crisis Plan when needed to manage any suicidal urges or impulses.

My counselor and I have discussed that it is important that I am an active participant in the counseling process, and that I apply what I have learned in and outside of sessions. I understand that I need to communicate with my counselor about my experiences and express concerns should I believe treatment is not helping me.

Signed: _____ Date:_____ Counselor:_____

Determining the appropriate level of care for the client (i.e., inpatient, partial hospitalization, outpatient) may be the most important element of effective suicide intervention. Containment in an inpatient psychiatric facility is generally necessary when clients present an imminent risk of violence to themselves. Clients with suicidal thoughts who are not at immediate risk of acting on these thoughts can generally be managed in a less restrictive (i.e., partial hospitalization, outpatient) level of care. Counselors may utilize various decision trees to assist in determining an appropriate level of care for a suicidal client. Ultimately, a detailed risk assessment, crisis plan (see Table 3.4 for an example Crisis Plan), and appropriate consultation and supervision will help counselors determine the best course of action with a suicidal client.

Clinical Toolbox 3.3: In the Pearson etext, click here to review a decision-making tree resource that can be used to help counselors assess clients' suicide risk.

TABLE 3.4   An Example of a Crisis Plan for a Suicidal Client

Client Name: Jane Doe   **Crisis Plan Date: 1/18/2014**

If I experience the following triggers:

    1) Feeling Angry at Myself

    2) Feeling Angry at Others

    3) Feeling Hopeless/Helpless

I will attempt to cope with them by:

    1) Counting Backwards from 100

    2) Using my Grounding Exercises

    3) Coloring in my Journal

(Continued)

TABLE 3.4 (Continued)

Client Name: Jane Doe	**Crisis Plan Date: 1/18/2014**

I know that my coping skills aren't working if I experience the following warning signs:

    1) Racing Thoughts

    2) Tingling in My Arms

    3) Stomach Knots

For my own safety, I agree to contact:

    1) My mother: 555-555-5550

    2) My brother: 555-555-5551

    3) My best friend, Sue: 555-555-5552

If I have suicidal or homicidal thoughts, I will call the Emergency Response System using 911, or I will go to the nearest emergency room as indicated below:

Pleasant Valley Hospital, 100 Maple Lane, Anytown, OH. Phone: 555-555-5553.

_____	_____	_____	_____
Client Signature	Date	Counselor Signature	Date

COUNSELING HOMICIDAL CLIENTS

Over 16,000 people in the United States were victims of homicide in 2010 (Centers for Disease Control and Prevention, 2010). Homicides committed by persons unknown to the victim account for under a quarter of total homicides (Bureau of Justice Statistics, 2011). The majority of homicide victims know the perpetrator, who is often a current or former intimate partner, family member, friend, or acquaintance. Homicide is the most serious consequence of intimate partner violence (IPV), with IPV accounting for an estimated 40% of female homicides (Bureau of Justice Statistics, 2011). Violence in the home also affects children. In 2009, homicide was the official cause of death in 57% of child fatalities due to maltreatment (United States Government Accountability Office, 2011). Children also become victims of homicide in 19% of cases involving intimate partner homicide (Websdale, 1999).

Counselor Considerations

Much like suicide, discussing homicidal ideation can be uncomfortable for counselors because of the grave consequences and legal and ethical responsibilities involved. Since client disclosure of homicidal ideation can prevent the loss of life, it is crucial that counselors remain open to encouraging client disclosure and to monitoring for homicide risk. This population is often guarded, thus nonjudgmental responding and neutral body language can be helpful in getting clients to share critical information about their ideation; information that is needed for assessment (i.e., plan, availability of weapon). Counselors should continually monitor their verbal and nonverbal responses for signs of discomfort. Clients at risk for homicidal behavior who are in the midst of a psychotic episode or other disorder with an acute onset may be experiencing feelings of fear and confusion, and counselors should maintain a calm demeanor. Additional considerations for working with this population are adjusting positioning with more distance between the counselor and client, being careful not to startle the client, and repeatedly expressing intentions to help. Clients who suffer from paranoia may be put off by certain counselor behaviors (e.g., writing notes, walking behind client), and attentiveness to these details may help to put clients at ease.

Counselors should be aware that potentially violent clients may be skilled at manipulation and lying, and they must be careful to monitor for signs of these behaviors. Clients mandated by the court to counseling may go to great lengths to deceive the counselor. It is also important for counselors to explore their feelings about working with different populations. Counselors should not underestimate a client's potential for violent behavior because of preconceived stereotypes (e.g., women or children aren't vulnerable to committing homicide). Regular consultation and supervision are recommended when working with this population.

As mentioned with regard to counseling suicidal clients, it is important when working with this population that measures be taken to facilitate safety. Counselors must also document the steps taken to enhance safety. As with suicide, all counselors working with this population should have at least one assessment or decision-making model and one safety plan model that they can use with clients who are homicidal. These measures should also be explicitly integrated into clients' treatment plans. For example, an appropriate objective would be: "0 episodes of aggression toward others."

Again, as with suicide, counselors need to be aware of community resources and more restrictive settings where clients at risk of committing homicide can stay and be treated until they are safe. In addition to knowing the state guidelines related to involuntary hospitalization, counselors should also know their state's guidelines related to the duty to warn others of possible harm as these laws vary by state. Especially when children are involved, counselors must be cautious of risk. Counselors must be aware of their obligation to report concerns about safety to child welfare agencies.

Client Characteristics

Because perpetrators of homicide have diverse motivations for their actions, a single personality profile for a client with homicidal potential is not feasible; however, clusters of violent offenders' personality traits have been identified. Clients who pose a risk to others may display a lack of empathy and understanding of others' emotions. The welfare and needs of others are considered secondary to their own personal needs and goals. They may have a history of harming people or animals beginning during childhood. Destructive behaviors such as fire setting and vandalizing property are also common. These clients may display a marked disregard for social norms and the rights of others, and as such, they may have a history of criminal activity. Clients at risk for homicide may also have a pattern of impulsive behavior with little consideration for consequences and lack remorse for their behavior.

Clients who pose a lethal threat to others are often not likely to enter counseling due to their own discretion. Court-mandated treatment or the presence of a comorbid issue with which the client is struggling may bring this population to counseling. Diagnoses associated with potential violence include conduct disorders, psychotic disorders, cluster B personality disorders, and delirium. Women experiencing homicidal ideation during postpartum depression are also at risk. Clients who are experiencing a psychotic episode or manic episode may act out violently. Those with substance abuse issues in conjunction with mental disorders are at a higher risk for homicidal behavior because of impaired judgment secondary to substance abuse. While particular diagnoses may be associated with homicidal ideation, most clients diagnosed with stable mental disorders are not at an increased risk of committing a violent crime (Rueve & Welton, 2008). Degenerative neurological disorders and medical conditions resulting from severe head trauma have also been associated with an increase in aggression and violent behavior (Rueve & Welton, 2008). Homicidal clients are more likely to harm family members and romantic partners than strangers. While there is no finite set of traits that describes potentially homicidal clients, men from low socioeconomic statuses with cultural backgrounds that encourage male dominance and aggression may be more likely to perpetrate intimate partner homicide. In clients who use drugs or alcohol, homicidal behavior is more likely to occur during intoxication.

Potentially homicidal clients may have previously threatened or perpetrated violence against themselves and others. Past criminal charges and psychiatric illness are often found in perpetrators of intimate partner homicide (Eke, Hilton, Harris, Rice, & Houghton, 2011). The most significant risk factor for intimate partner homicide is a history of intimate partner violence (Campbell, Glass, Sharps, Laughon, & Bloom, 2007). The client may display behaviors such as jealousy, need for control, and aggression, as well as noncompliance with treatment. Intimidating behavior and stalking toward the potential victim may also be seen. Stalking behavior may be triggered by an estrangement between the client and the potential victim. A large age difference between partners and the presence of a nonbiological child living in the home have also been identified as factors in intimate partner homicide (Campbell et al., 2007). Because guns are the most commonly used means for committing an intimate partner homicide (Sorenson, 2006), firearms in the home should be considered a risk factor.

Perpetrators of intimate partner homicide who commit a homicide–suicide fit a different pattern from those who do not harm themselves. Past threats of suicide and bouts of depression are often found in this population. Clients who commit a homicide–suicide are more likely to be employed and less likely to use substances (Campbell et al., 2007), and as such, professionals often underestimate their risk. In cases in which intimate partner violence was not prevalent before the intimate partner homicide occurred, it is common for the act to be triggered by a separation (Koziol-McLain et al., 2006). Clients who commit a homicide–suicide are more likely to be married and of Caucasian, Latino, and Asian backgrounds than perpetrators of intimate partner homicide without suicide (Koziol-McLain et al., 2006).

Assessment

Counselors must use clinical judgment when determining whether an assessment for homicidal ideation is needed. Clients should be asked about homicidal ideation in a clear, direct manner. As with suicide assessment, the counselor should inquire directly if the client has intentions of harming another person, if a plan exists, the method of carrying out the plan, and whether the client has access to the means to fulfill the plan (e.g., access to a firearm). Counselors must be mindful of the ethical duty to notify intended targets and the authorities. In addition, counselors should be alert for reasons that the client may overexaggerate or underexaggerate his or her potential for violence. Within the confines of appropriate ethical boundaries, family members and other possible informants should be consulted to gain richer assessment information.

Counselors can begin to assess the level of risk by determining the client's current level of distress, possible intoxication, recent behavior, and communication of ideation. If the client potentially poses a safety risk to the counselor, the session should take place in a safe environment. The setting should be free of dangerous objects, have alarms or ways to indicate a need for assistance, and have quick access to an exit that is not blocked by the client. Assessments should include questions about ideation and attitudes, current life stressors, past reactions to stressors, client history, mental health status, and protective factors that could prevent homicidal behavior (see Appendix 3.1 for a list of questions to ask clients to assess for risk in each of these areas).

> **Clinical Toolbox 3.4:** In the Pearson etext, click here to review questions that can be asked to establish a client or another person's homicidal behavior risk.

All threats of homicidal behavior should be taken seriously. Additional risk factors for homicidal behavior are listed in Table 3.5. McGlothin's (2008) SIMPLE STEPS mnemonic can be used for assessing risk of homicidal behavior (see Table 3.6 for an overview of this assessment tool). Upon completing an assessment, counselors should then determine the level of risk that the client poses—low, medium, or high—and implement appropriate interventions.

Interventions

No comprehensive interventions exist for treating homicidal ideation. The factors and motivations contributing to homicidal ideation are unique to each client, and treatment must address this issue on an individual basis. In clients with an active mental disorder or substance abuse issue, interventions should focus on treating these issues as a means to diminish homicidal ideation. In compliance with limits of confidentiality, counselors may

---

TABLE 3.5   Homicide Risk Factors

The presence of the following risk factors may indicate an increased risk of homicidal behavior:

- History of threats and/or premeditated violence against others resulting in injury
- History of fire-setting
- Use of drugs or alcohol (higher risk if client is currently intoxicated)
- Recent acute change in mental status
- Access to lethal weapons
- Diagnosis of schizophrenia, cluster B personality disorders, postpartum depression (only if homicidal ideation is present), delirium, conduct disorder (diagnoses are of particular attention if they are unstable)
- Homicidal ideation
  - Past attempt or plan
  - Intended victim and motive
  - Obsessions with potential victim
  - Expressed rage, anger, and desire for revenge
- Command hallucinations (i.e., voices telling the person to do something)
- Noncompliant with past psychiatric treatment
- Pattern of impulsive behavior
- Currently experiencing a psychotic or manic episode
- Social isolation
- Experiencing significant life stressors (e.g., legal, financial, relationship problems)
- Exhibiting stalking behavior
- Expressing feelings of hopelessness
- Escalation in level of violence (if in the context of intimate partner violence)

TABLE 3.6 SIMPLE STEPS Homicide Assessment Mnemonic

(McGlothin, 2008)

S—Suicidal/homicidal ideation. Are you thinking of killing yourself or somebody else?

I—Ideation. How likely are you to kill somebody else in the next 24 hours?

M—Method. How will you kill somebody else?

P—Pain. How much emotional pain are you feeling? What makes this pain worse?

L—Loss. Have you lost a significant other recently? Have you experienced a loss in your past that you have not been able to move on from?

E—Earlier attempts. Have you ever tried to kill somebody else before? When? How? What interfered?

S—Substance use. Do you use drugs or alcohol? Do you take prescription drugs?

T—Troubleshooting. How much of your ideation has to do with work, family, or other stressors? How can you make things easier? If everything was perfect in your life, what would it look like?

E—Emotions/diagnosis. Have you ever been diagnosed with a mental, emotional, or medical disorder? How is the disorder being treated? Are you complying with treatment? How is it affecting you now?

P—Parental/family history. Has anybody in your family thought about or completed suicide or an act of homicide?

S—Stressors and life events. What events and feelings have made you think that killing somebody else will be a solution?

---

be able to contact the client's significant others to provide support for the client and possible supervision. If possible, it may be helpful to include the client's significant others in counseling, or maintain consistent contact, to monitor and implement action to decrease the client's risk to others. Steps may also be taken to limit the client's access to weapons. Working within the confines of ethics and laws, intended victims or structures that the client potentially poses a risk to should be notified, as well as law enforcement.

After careful assessment, if the counselor determines that the client poses a significant risk to others, the client should be placed in a more restrictive level of care. If the client does not voluntarily agree to a greater level of care, the counselor may need to have the client admitted to a secure setting or contact law enforcement to implement an involuntary hospitalization depending on the state's laws. Medical staff may apply pharmacological interventions to immediately reduce the client's level of distress, including antianxiety, fast-acting antipsychotic, and sedative medications. Medication may be integrated into long-term treatment plans, with the likelihood of client compliance with medication management being considered. A deeper exploration into the client's presenting issues will be more useful when the client has stabilized. Counseling sessions with high-risk clients will focus on ascertaining the nature of a client's violent ideation, potential targets, motivations, lethality of plan, and access to weapons. Consistent follow-up contact is highly recommended in the days following release from hospitalization so as to continually assess client risk.

Counseling interventions that involve teaching coping skills and exploring alternatives to violence are appropriate with clients who have stabilized and are not an imminent

TABLE 3.7   Homicide Safety Plan

What I can do if I start feeling that I want to hurt somebody (e.g., practice coping skills, contact crisis line, go to the ER) is . . .

If I start feeling that I want to hurt somebody, I can call the following people for help (include contact information) . . .

These things have helped me to hurt others in the past (e.g., coping skills, protective factors) and include . . .

What my counselor will do to help me is . . .

Family members/friends I can provide with information about warning signs and emergency contact numbers so that they can help me monitor my behavior are . . .

If I am placed in the hospital, contact . . .

My preferences for treatment if I am hospitalized (e.g., health care provider, medications) . . .

Things that may need attention if I am hospitalized (e.g., children, pets) . . .

threat to others. Counselors will at first need to focus on building a working alliance with the client to understand the emotions connected to the homicidal ideation. The counselor can address the emotions that the client is experiencing and help the client to identify more adaptive coping methods. Pointing out emotional triggers and encouraging self-awareness can be helpful in encouraging the development of new coping skills. Working to establish and strengthen social support networks should also be a part of an intervention for homicidal ideation, as it is a protective factor against violent behavior.

Additionally, crisis cards with information about warning signs, a reminder of useful coping skills, and a plan of action to prevent homicidal behavior can be given to clients (James & Gilliland, 2013). A safety plan can be created with clients if they feel that they may act upon their homicidal ideations. Because clients with homicidal ideation pose a threat to others, assessment must be ongoing. A client's level of risk may ebb and flow, and interventions must be adapted accordingly. Table 3.7 provides examples of prompts that can be used when developing a safety plan.

COUNSELING INTERPERSONAL PARTNER VIOLENCE VICTIMS

Intimate partner violence (IPV) is defined as physical, sexual, or threatened abuse that is perpetrated by a current or former romantic partner. IPV most frequently occurs between a male perpetrator and a female victim, and it is estimated that 31% of women and 26% of men experience violence at the hands of a romantic partner over their lifespan (Nelson, Bougatsos, & Blazina, 2012). The risk of serious harm or death is significantly greater though with male perpetrators. Psychological abuse often occurs with physical abuse and may include verbal abuse, isolation, stalking, threatening, financial abuse, breaking items, punching or kicking walls or doors, and wielding a weapon. Individuals of all ethnicities, religions, socioeconomic statuses, educational backgrounds, genders, ages, and sexual orientations are affected by IPV. Intimate partner violence is present in both heterosexual and same-sex relationships. Because of the frequency of IPV and the related development of psychological problems, counselors are likely to encounter clients in violent relationships. The widespread nature of IPV has even prompted the U.S. Department of Health and Human Services to recommend that screening for IPV and referral to mental health counseling services be integrated into all women's health visits. Counselors have a responsibility to assess for IPV and to address these issues in clients' treatment.

Counselor Considerations

Intimate partner violence is a highly emotional and personal topic, and clients may be reluctant to disclose their experiences out of embarrassment, fear, or guilt. Establishing rapport and providing clients with a safe and comfortable environment is crucial in encouraging disclosure of abuse. Counselors should explore their feelings about IPV to ensure that their attitudes and feelings will not hinder the counseling relationship, in particular, through blaming the victim or imposing values on the client (e.g., encouraging a client to take an unwanted action, such as leaving the relationship). A nonjudgmental and empathetic attitude should be conveyed. Questioning about IPV should be conducted privately with the client and is not appropriate within couples counseling due to the risk of perpetrator retaliation. The client should be presented with multiple opportunities to disclose IPV experiences during the session, as many are hesitant to disclose.

Counselors should be prepared to provide the client with information about IPV and community resources (e.g., battered women's shelters, legal aid, crisis hotline). If the client chooses to disclose, counselors should validate the experiences by offering support. Should the client want to report his or her IPV experiences, the counselor should be prepared to help the client contact the police. Because the client's home and cell phones may be monitored by the perpetrator, allowing the client to use an office phone to contact the police, or IPV resources such as shelters, may add another layer of client protection.

Counselors should understand the barriers that clients may face in terminating an abusive relationship and moving forward. Clients may have language, acculturation, financial, educational, racial, and accessibility of service barriers, which make their ability to leave difficult. For example, clients may attempt to become financially independent, but face difficulties finding a job due to low educational attainment, employment history, or disruptive behavior in the workplace caused by the perpetrator. Financial dependence and poverty can limit clients' access to health care, legal services, and child care, further impeding their ability to maintain a job.

Client Characteristics

Victims of IPV enter counseling with a variety of presenting problems. While posttraumatic stress disorder (PTSD) is one of the more common disorders seen in this population, they may also experience any number of disorders including depression, substance use, eating, and anxiety disorders. Perpetrators of IPV often isolate victims from family members and friends, and may forbid employment outside the home. Social interaction and the maintenance of social support networks can be severely reduced as a result. Antisocial behavior, fear of intimacy, low self-esteem, emotional detachment, and inability to trust others may further impair social functioning in IPV survivors.

In addition to psychological problems, several medical issues associated with IPV warrant attention in counseling and may require medical evaluation and intervention. Chronic headaches, gastrointestinal issues (e.g., irritable bowel syndrome), immune disorders, pregnancy difficulties, endocrine system disorders, cardiovascular disorders, and asthma are conditions that may be exacerbated with stress or may appear as clinical manifestations of internalized stress in victims of IPV. Clients may also experience emotional problems related to medical issues such as traumatic brain injury, chronic pain, and sexually transmitted diseases.

Counselors should be aware of risk factors that are associated with the increased likelihood of IPV. Risk factors for experiencing IPV include being young, unemployed, of a low socioeconomic status, having low self-esteem, a history of abuse, and drug or alcohol use. While these characteristics are common in survivors, individuals across all cultural boundaries may experience IPV. Risk factors for becoming a perpetrator of IPV often overlap with those of victims. Common personality and attitudinal traits among perpetrators of IPV include subscription to strict gender roles, anger, being antisocial, hostility, low self-esteem, desire for control and power in relationships, possessiveness, jealousy, and emotional dependence. Perpetrators are often young, from a low socioeconomic status, and may have a history that includes aggressive behavior or delinquency, being a victim of past physical or psychological abuse, witnessing IPV as a child, and experiencing depression. Poor problem-solving skills and use of drugs or alcohol can also increase abusive patterns. Situations in which IPV is more likely to occur in a relationship are those that involve relationship conflict or instability, financial hardships, and relationships dominated by one partner. Individuals living in communities that have poor formal (e.g., legal ramifications) and informal (e.g., responses from bystanders) sanctions against IPV may be more likely to experience violence by a partner.

Assessment

Assessment should begin with the accurate detection of IPV. Clients may not identify their experiences as abuse, and psychoeducation about IPV may be needed to define abuse and violence. Inquiries about IPV should avoid stigmatizing language and be conducted exclusively with the client. In couples counseling settings, counselors should be aware of behavior and signs that may suggest IPV. Submissive, anxious, or fearful behavior of one partner toward the other may indicate IPV. Additionally, a partner who demands to be in all sessions, answers for the other partner, and appears possessive or jealous may also suggest IPV.

Upon disclosure, the immediate safety of the client must be assessed. To gain a greater understanding of a client's IPV experiences, counselors can gather information in the following areas: (a) detailed descriptions of typical IPV experiences, (b) the most severe IPV experience, (c) the most recent IPV experience, and (d) the frequency of IPV. Several formal self-report and clinician-administered assessments are available for use with IPV survivors. Assessments such as the Hurt, Insult, Threaten, and Scream (HITS; Sherin, Sinacore, Li, Zitter, & Skakil, 1998), Woman Abuse Screening Tool (WAST; Brown, Lent, Brett, Sas, & Pederson, 1996), and Abuse Assessment Screen (AAS; McFarlane, Parker, Soeken, & Bullock, 1992) are among the most commonly administered assessments of IPV, and they can be quickly completed due to the limited number of questions on each instrument. The Danger Assessment (DA; Dienemann, Campbell, Landenburger, & Curry, 2002) is administered to survivors of IPV to determine the risk of intimate partner homicide. The Spousal Assault Risk Assessment Guide (SARA; Kropp, Hart, Webster, & Eaves, 1994) is administered to identify clients at risk for becoming abusive toward an intimate partner. Additional assessments to measure for suicide risk and psychological disorders (e.g., depression, PTSD) should also be administered. Counselors may also assess the risk of harm to children involved in homes where IPV occurs. Counselors should not give clients IPV-related assessments to complete outside the office as home-work assignments, as they may be cause for perpetrator retaliatory behavior.

Intervention

Client safety is the first priority in any therapeutic intervention for IPV (Murray & Graves, 2012). Safety plans can be used to monitor and facilitate client safety. Safety plans outline the safest way for clients to make decisions in the management of a variety of violent situations, and a good safety plan should also address the safety of children in the home. An example of safety plan–related questions that can be used when working with adults in a violent relationship can be found in Table 3.8.

When working with children, it is also important that a safety plan be developed.

 Clinical Toolbox 3.5: In the Pearson etext, click here to read suggestions for developing safety plans with children and adolescents who are living in violent homes.

Whenever possible, treatment planning should include a multidisciplinary approach with collaboration among mental health and other health care professionals to ensure the most comprehensive care for the client. Psychoeducation can be used to discuss cycles and patterns of abuse and safety planning, and to explore issues related to IPV such as police protection and community resources. Counselors should empower

---

TABLE 3.8   Safety Plan Considerations for People in Violent Relationships

The development of a safety plan should always be included as an objective when developing a treatment plan for clients in violent or potentially violent relationships. The following are important aspects of safety plans:
- Keeping a purse and car keys in a place that is easy to access for quick escape
- Deciding where the client will go the next time he or she needs to leave the house or go somewhere safe (there should be a backup safe place as well)
- Telling friends or neighbors about the violence and requesting that they call the police if they hear suspicious noises or witness suspicious events
- Identifying the safest rooms in the house, school, and so on where the client can go if she or he fears an argument will develop (i.e., the lowest-risk places)
- Storing an escape kit (e.g., a copy of a protection order, extra keys, money, checks, important phone numbers, medications, Social Security cards, bank documents, birth certificates, change of clothes, bank and house information, address book, school and vaccination records, and valuables) somewhere safe (preferably not in the house)
- Processing the safety plan with children, when appropriate
- Identifying individuals to call in a crisis and safe places to go when leaving (e.g., domestic violence crisis shelters)
- Identifying and practicing escape routes and rooms that are safe and not close to weapons (e.g., what doors, windows, elevators, stairwells, or fire escapes would you use?)
- Identifying safe places to go when leaving

clients to feel confident in making decisions about the future, and help them manage their IPV-related feelings (e.g., guilt and shame). Treatment may address enhancing self-esteem and building social support networks that may have been diminished by the perpetrator. Cautious documentation of the client's IPV experiences is important because it may be requested by the court system should the client seek legal recourse or even in divorce proceedings.

Couples counseling is generally regarded as an inappropriate approach to treating those in actively violent relationships, and as such, it should not be part of a treatment plan with a person actively living in a violent situation. Exposure-based cognitive behavioral therapy has been recommended for use with clients who have experienced IPV and are experiencing trauma symptoms (Iverson et al., 2011). However, exposure-based CBT may not be appropriate for use with clients who are not yet in a stable and safe environment. Motivational interviewing and dialectical behavior therapy have also been supported for use with survivors of IPV (Hughes & Ramussen, 2010; Iverson, Shenk, & Fruzzetti, 2009). Issues of substance abuse must be addressed before accurate assessment and treatment of other mental and emotional disorders can take place.

Summary

This chapter addressed clinical issues that involve client safety. It is recommended that when working with clients with any of these issues, counselors explicitly integrate safety considerations into the client's treatment plan. In addition, regular assessment of the level of risk should occur and be well documented. All of the issues discussed in this chapter may invoke strong emotions for counselors. It is important that all counselors explore and monitor their personal reactions to these issues. Finally, counselors should seek supervision and regular consultation as a means of safeguarding their practice when working with these populations.

References

American Association of Suicidology. (2013). Know the warning signs. *American Association of Suicidology*. Retrieved April 3, 2013 from http://www.suicidology.org/web/guest/statsandtools/warningsigns

Berman, A., Ellis, T. E., Jobes, D., Kaslow, N., King, C., & Linehan, M. (2004). *Core competencies for the assessment and management of individuals at risk for suicide*. Retrieved February 18, 2013 from http://www.suicidology.org/c/document_library/get_file?folderId=233&name=DLFE-33.pdf

Brown, J. B., Lent, B., Brett, P. J., Sas, G., & Pederson, L. L. (1996). Development of the Woman Abuse Screening Tool for use in family practice. *Family Medicine, 28*(6), 422–428.

Bureau of Justice Statistics. (2011). Homicide trends in the United States, 1980–2008. *Bureau of Justice Statistics (BJS)*. Retrieved March 18, 2013 from http://bjs.gov/index.cfm?ty=pbdetail

Campbell, J. C., Glass, N., Sharps, P. W., Laughon, K., & Bloom, T. (2007). Intimate partner homicide. *Trauma, Violence, & Abuse, 8*, 246–269.

Centers for Disease Control and Prevention, National Center for Injury Prevention and Control. *Web-based Injury Statistics Query and Reporting System (WISQARS)* [online]. (2010). [cited 2013 Feb 18] Available from www.cdc.gov/injury/wisqars/index.html.

Dienemann, J., Campbell, J., Landenburger, K., & Curry, M. A. (2002). The domestic violence survivor assessment: A tool for counseling women in intimate partner violence relationships. *Patient Education and Counseling, 46*, 221–228.

Eke, A., Hilton, N., Harris, G., Rice, M., & Houghton, R. (2011). Intimate partner homicide: Risk assessment and prospects for prediction. *Journal of Family Violence, 26*, 211–216.

Granello, D. H., & Granello, P. F. (2007). *Suicide: An essential guide for helping professionals and educators*. Boston, MA: Pearson.

Hughes, M., & Rasmussen, L. (2010). The utility of motivational interviewing in domestic violence shelters: A qualitative exploration. *Journal of Aggression, Maltreatment & Trauma, 19*, 300–322.

Iverson, K. M., Gradus, J. L., Resick, P. A., Suvak, M. K., Smith, K. F., & Monson, C. M. (2011). Cognitive behavioral therapy for PTSD and depression symptoms reduces risk for future intimate partner violence among interpersonal trauma survivors. *Journal of Consulting and Clinical Psychology, 79*, 193–202.

Iverson, K. M., Shenk, C., & Fruzzetti, A. E. (2009). Dialectical behavior therapy for women victims of domestic abuse: A pilot study. *Professional Psychology: Research and Practice, 40*, 242–248.

James, R. K., & Gilliland, B. E. (2013). Crisis of lethality. *Crisis intervention strategies* (7th ed., pp. 209–247). Pacific Grove, CA: Brooks/Cole.

Koziol-McLain, J., Webster, D., McFarlane, J., Block, C. R., Ulrich, Y., Glass, N., . . . Campbell, J. C. (2006). Risk factors for femicide-suicide in abusive relationships: Results from a multi-site case control study. *Violence and Victims, 21*(1), 3–21.

Kropp, P. R., Hart, S. D., Webster, C. W., & Eaves, D. (1994). *Manual for the Spousal Assault Risk Assessment Guide* (2nd ed.). Vancouver, British Columbia: British Columbia Institute on Family Violence.

Lee, J. B., & Bartlett, L. (2005). Suicide prevention: Critical elements for managing suicidal clients and counselor liability without the use of a no-suicide contract. *Death Studies, 29*, 847–865.

Maltsberger, J. T. (2006). Outpatient treatment. In R. I. Simon & R. E. Hales (Eds.), *Textbook of suicide assessment and management* (pp. 367–379). Washington, DC: American Psychiatric Publishing.

McFarlane, J., Parker, B., Soeken, K., & Bullock, L. (1992). Assessing for abuse during pregnancy: Severity and frequency of injuries and associated entry into prenatal care. *The Journal of the American Medical Association, 267*, 3176–3178.

McGlothlin, J. M. (2008). *Developing clinical skills in suicide assessment, prevention, and treatment*. Alexandria, VA: American Counseling Association.

Murray, C. E., & Graves, K. N. (2012). *Responding to family violence: A comprehensive, research-based guide for therapists*. New York, NY: Routledge.

Nelson, H. D., Bougatsos, C., & Blazina, I. (2012). Screening women for intimate partner violence: A systematic review to update the 2004 U.S. Preventive Services Task Force recommendation. *Annals of Internal Medicine, 156*, 796–808.

Rudd, M. D., Mandrusiak, M., & Joiner, T. (2006). The case against no-suicide contracts: The commitment to treatment statement as a practice alternative. *Journal of Clinical Psychology, 62*, 243–251.

Rueve, M. E., & Welton, R. S. (2008). Violence and mental illness. *Psychiatry, 5*, 35–48.

Shea, S. C. (2002). *The practical art of suicide assessment: A guide for mental health professionals and substance abuse counselors*. New York, NY: Wiley.

Sherin, K. M., Sinacore, J. M., Li, X. Q., Zitter, R. E., & Skakil, A. (1998). HITS: A short domestic abuse violence screening tool for use in a family practice settings. *Family Medicine, 30*, 508–12.

Sorenson, S. B. (2006). Firearm use in intimate partner violence: A brief overview. *Evaluation Review, 30*, 229–236.

United States Government Accountability Office. (2011). *Child maltreatment: Strengthening national data on child fatalities could aid in prevention* (Rep. No. GAO-11-599). Retrieved from http://www.gao.gov/products/GAO-11-599

van Heeringen, K. (2001). Towards a psychobiological model of the suicidal process. In K. van Heeringen (Ed.), *Understanding suicidal behavior* (pp. 137–159). New York, NY: Wiley.

Websdale, N. (1999). *Understanding domestic homicide*. Boston, MA: Northeastern University Press.

Appendix 3.1: Questions for Assessing Facets of Homicide Risk

IDEATION AND ATTITUDES

1. Do you have thoughts about hurting yourself or others?
2. Do you have thoughts about hurting your significant other?
3. Would you like to hurt a certain person or group of people?
4. Do you feel that you are a threat to somebody else's safety?
5. Do you think that anybody else views you as a threat to his or her safety?
6. How often do you have these thoughts?
7. How long have you been having these thoughts?
8. Are there any times when these thoughts are more intense? Are there any triggers?
9. Have you told others about your thoughts of harming yourself/others?
10. If you wanted to hurt somebody else, how would you do it?
11. Do you have a plan?
12. Have you ever rehearsed your plan?
13. Do you have access to the means to carry out the plan?
14. Do you have weapons in your home? What are they and where are they located?
15. Do you have access to weapons? What kind? Does it/Do they belong to you or somebody else?
16. When do you feel that it is appropriate to use a weapon?
17. Do you think weapons should be used to solve conflicts?
18. How do you feel about recent violent events reported on the news?
19. Describe the most violent thing you have witnessed in person. How about in a TV show/movie/video game? How did it make you feel?

CURRENT STRESSORS

1. How are things going with your significant other/family/at school/at work?
2. Are you experiencing any conflicts?
3. What would you like to do about this situation?
4. Is there a reason that you want to hurt somebody or yourself?
5. Are you going through any changes right now?
6. Has anything been bothering you recently?
7. Have you experienced any losses lately? Have you experienced any losses that you don't feel you have been able to get over? (May include loss of relationship, death, job.)
8. Have you felt victimized, treated unfairly, or humiliated?
9. Have you felt bullied recently? How did you react? What were your thoughts and feelings? Did you want to seek revenge?
10. Describe the significant relationships in your life.
11. Do you feel jealous of your significant other? Do you think he or she will be unfaithful or leave you? How do you react?
12. What events in your life impacted you the most? How do they still affect you?

PAST REACTIONS TO STRESSORS

1. When somebody or something upsets you, how do you feel? What do you think? How do you react?
2. If you could react the way you would like to when somebody hurt or bothered you, what would you do?
3. Do you ever have thoughts of hurting others? Can you describe those thoughts?
4. How have you reacted in the past when someone or something made you upset?
5. Do you ever feel that you are being treated unfairly? How do you react? What thoughts do you have?
6. When you become upset, what happens to you physically? Do you ever feel out of control?

HISTORY

1. Have you been seen by a mental health professional before? If so, for what?
2. Have you ever been diagnosed with a psychiatric disorder?
3. Were you ever treated with medication? Do you currently take medication?
4. Have you had problems with substance abuse in the past?
5. What is your history with weapons? Have you ever used one? Would you like to?
6. Have you ever been in a physical altercation?
7. Have you ever used violence or threats of violence to solve a conflict?
8. Have you thought of hurting yourself or others in the past?
9. Have you ever tried to hurt yourself or somebody else in the past? What interfered?
10. Have you ever felt that you were not in control of your actions?

ADDITIONAL MENTAL HEALTH QUESTIONS

1. Do you use alcohol or drugs? What and how often?
2. Do you take prescription drugs that are not yours, or in incorrect dosages?
3. Have you ever seen things or heard things that others do not?
4. How do you usually feel?
5. How do you picture your future?
6. Do you feel that your life is getting better or worse?
7. What activities do you enjoy? How often do you engage in them? Have you been enjoying them less recently?
8. Do you have trouble sleeping? Do you sleep too little or too much?
9. Have you done things lately without thinking of the consequences?
10. Have you made any impulsive decisions recently?
11. What is your current level of anxiety? Do you feel this way most of the time?
12. Have you been more easily irritated by things that didn't bother you before?

PROTECTIVE FACTORS

1. What are your religious or spiritual beliefs? How might these help you deal with the problems you are experiencing? Do your religious/spiritual beliefs support your thoughts of hurting others or yourself?
2. What are your core values?
3. What skills have you used to cope with your troubles in the past? Did they work?
4. Do you have supportive family members or friends that you can talk to?
5. Who is the person you are closest to?
6. Do you have a person that you can count on to discuss problems in your life?
7. What or who has helped you to deal with your problems in the past?
8. What has prevented you from hurting yourself or others in the past?
9. Are there safe places you can go or people you can contact if you are having thoughts of hurting yourself or others?
10. How can I (counselor) help you?
11. How can your significant other/family member/friends help you?

Depressive, Bipolar, and Related Disorders

Amie Manis, Robin Norris, Matthew J. Paylo, Victoria E. Kress, and Karen Decker

CASE STUDY: MANUEL

Manuel is a 20-year-old Dominican American male who lives with his parents. He reports that three weeks ago he was released from a psychiatric hospital. He decided to seek out counseling because the hospital recommended he do so and because his mother pressured him to come.

Manuel was friendly, agreeable, and open with the counselor. Manuel reports that he is the oldest of four children. His father works as a school custodian and his mother has never been employed outside the home. He indicates his father is "hard working," but his family struggles financially and they only have enough money to cover basic living expenses. Manuel adds that he had a "good" childhood. He states that he was surrounded by supportive family members and enjoyed solid relationships with his extended family and community friends. He further states that when he was younger he attended church (his family is Catholic), but he stopped going at the age of 14. He explains that at this time, religion is not important to him.

Prior to his recent move back in with his parents, he was living on campus and attending classes at a regional state university. After a "difficult" freshman year Manuel was placed on academic probation. He expresses that he enjoyed his first year of college, but often "partied" and his "grades reflected it." Entering his sophomore year Manuel attempted to do better in school. However, after the start of the school year, he soon became overwhelmed. He could not keep up with the work and reported feeling "exhausted," and he even had days when he "could not get out of bed." When Manuel started missing classes and began to have thoughts of suicide, he decided to seek counseling.

At that time, he went to his university counseling center for help. A university counselor decided to contact Manuel's parents, and she encouraged them to take Manuel to a local hospital emergency room. At that time, Manuel was hospitalized for three days. He was diagnosed with major depressive disorder, and received a prescription for an SSRI antidepressant.

Manuel then returned to the university. However, he was unable to catch up on his course work and he failed three classes. His resulting poor grades caused him to lose his scholarship, and resulted in his needing to leave the university since he could not pay for his courses.

At that point, Manuel returned home to live with his parents. He was eager to reassess his situation and future. Things initially went well after he moved back home. He continued to take the antidepressant medication, and he reported feeling much better than he had prior to his hospitalization.

Within a month of returning home to live with his parents, Manuel became intently focused on the military. He began to consider joining the military secondary to his college difficulties. He spent a great deal of time researching military careers, practicing fitness drills, and playing military-based video games. Manuel began to dress in camouflage, and he constantly talked about his plans to join the Army. Manuel slept for three to four hours per night, and he would do his "drills" at all hours of the night.

Around this time, Manuel began acting erratically and had a physical altercation with his brother. His father called the police. When the police arrived they noted Manuel was highly agitated, and they tried to deescalate him. Manuel became even more upset and threatened the officers. The officers then brought him to the local hospital emergency room. At the emergency room Manuel explained that he was a brilliant military mastermind and that he should be working for the federal government. The hospital staff's reports suggest that in addition to Manuel's grandiose ideas, he spoke quickly and was easily distracted. A physician evaluated Manuel. A toxicology test revealed he had marijuana and alcohol in his system. At that point, Manuel was again admitted to the hospital's psychiatric unit for further treatment and a full diagnostic evaluation.

After a week in the hospital and a medication readjustment, he was stabilized and released from the hospital. He again returned to his family's home. The psychiatrist's discharge recommendations included Manuel seeking out counseling. Manuel decided to follow this recommendation at the insistence of his mother.

Manuel admits to the counselor that he uses alcohol and marijuana in situations where he "needs a confidence boost," and he indicates that he used to use them to help "quiet his mind." He reports he still occasionally uses alcohol and marijuana despite his physician's requests to stop using all substances while taking his psychiatric medication.

Manuel is future-oriented and he expresses that he would like to go back to college and earn enough money to help take care of his family. He feels embarrassed and ashamed that he had to drop out of school. He believes he has "let his family down." Additionally, Manuel discloses that he is facing legal charges following the physical altercation with his brother. Again, he expresses regret and shame that he attacked his brother. Over the past month, since his release from the psychiatric hospital and the accompanying medication adjustment, Manuel has felt stable. He is taking all medication as prescribed by his psychiatrist.

DESCRIPTION OF THE DEPRESSIVE, BIPOLAR, AND RELATED DISORDERS

Over the course of their lifetimes, one in five people will meet the criteria for a depressive or bipolar disorder (National Comorbidity Survey, 2007). These disorders are common, affecting around 9.5% of the general population in a given year (Kessler et al., 2005), and affecting women more often than men (Sadock & Sadock, 2007). This chapter will address major depressive disorder (MDD), persistent depressive disorder (PDD), disruptive mood dysregulation disorder (DMDD), premenstrual dysphoric disorder (PMDD), bipolar I disorder, bipolar II disorder, and cyclothymic disorder.

According to the *DSM-5* (American Psychiatric Association [APA], 2013), depressive disorders are characterized by sadness, hopelessness, irritability, or dysphoria; whereas the bipolar disorders include periods of marked elevation in activity and mood, and may also involve episodes of depression.

The *DSM-5* uses the term *episodes* to classify the symptoms of depressive and bipolar disorders. In order to meet the criteria for major depressive disorder, an individual must meet the criteria for a major depressive *episode*. In order to meet the criteria for bipolar I disorder, an individual must have met (or must currently meet) the criteria for a manic episode at least once, and he or she must have met (or must currently meet) the criteria for a major depressive episode. In order to meet the criteria for bipolar II disorder, an individual must have experienced at least one major depressive and one hypomanic episode, but never have met the criteria for a manic episode.

 Clinical Toolbox 4.1: In the Pearson etext, click here to read about the mood episodes that characterize depressive and bipolar disorders.

People with depressive disorders often have a loss of energy, feel hopeless and worthless, are discouraged, and have a persistent dysthymic or dysphoric mood. Commonly, they have disruptions in their sleep (e.g., insomnia), appetite, motivation, ability to find pleasure in activities (e.g., anhedonia), and overall enjoyment of life. Individual manifestations of the depressive disorders vary, often consisting of anxious distress (e.g., restless, difficulty concentrating, fear of losing control), melancholic features (e.g., absence of pleasure, despair, reduction of food and sleep), atypical features (e.g., mood reactivity, overeating, oversleeping), or catatonic features (APA, 2013).

In addition to these depressive features, periods of elevated activity and energy are associated with bipolar disorders. Manic episodes may involve changes in behavior that include increased impulsivity and risk taking. It is not uncommon for the person in a manic episode to fail to recognize or to minimize the level of impairment due to the changes in mood and energy. This presents challenges with wellness management and can contribute to significant negative consequences in relationships, work, and school. According to the *DSM-5* (APA, 2013), in severe cases, a manic episode may be characterized by abuse or violent behavior and an elevated risk of suicide.

Each of the depressive and bipolar disorders represents a complex clinical phenomenon. Taking care to attend to the biopsychosocial (i.e., biological, psychological, and social aspects of an individual) components of these disorders is critical to forming a clear diagnostic impression and selecting and implementing a treatment plan that will effectively meet clients' needs.

COUNSELOR CONSIDERATIONS

All effective counseling begins with the establishment of a therapeutic alliance. It is universally agreed that the core conditions of unconditional positive regard, empathy, and congruence are foundational to all good counseling. Counselors must not only be adept in the genuine application of essential counseling skills such as active listening, conveying empathy, and reflecting content and feelings, but they must also maintain a culturally alert and sensitive presence.

In many cultures, the clinical presentation and expression of depression may present as emotional or affective symptoms, or as somatic and/or dissociative symptoms (Kirmayer, 2001). For example, those of Chinese descent may experience depression not as a psychological phenomenon (e.g., feelings of intense and prolonged sadness), but as a conglomeration of physical or somatic complaints (e.g., inner pressure, discomfort, pain, fatigue, dizziness; Kleinman, 2004). Many cultures conceptualize depression not as a disease or illness (i.e., such as in Western cultures), but as a social problem, moral issue, or as a reaction to situational stressors (Karasz, 2005). These differing clinical presentations and conceptual models of depression create cross-cultural variability in prevalence, presentation, and how and if people seek treatment (Karasz, 2005).

Engaging clients early in the counseling process is important. Socializing clients to the counselor's treatment approach and anticipated outcomes is an important means of promoting client engagement. Recent studies (e.g., Carter et al., 2011) suggest this may be particularly important in the treatment of depressive disorders.

Attending carefully to client history and symptoms within a biopsychosocial context should begin with the intake paperwork and continue with treatment planning and assessment of treatment outcomes. In terms of psychosocial history, the following information may be particularly important in the accurate diagnosis of a depressive and bipolar disorder and in an initial risk assessment: (a) past and present medical conditions and medications, (b) past diagnosis or treatment of mental health conditions, suicidal or homicidal ideation, and/or hospitalizations, (c) use of substances, (d) legal history, (e) past or current concerns about emotional or physical safety or abuse, (f) current symptoms, onset, frequency, and severity, as well as changes in mood, weight, sleep, appetite, concentration, energy or activity levels, or overall functioning, (g) recent or current changes, stressors, or losses, (h) resources for treatment, and finally, (i) emergency contact information.

Conducting a thorough mental status exam is essential to a thorough assessment of symptoms and functioning. In the case of screening for depressive or bipolar disorders, attending to the potential for significant impairment in functioning, suicidal ideation or behavior, and psychosis is critical not only for an accurate diagnosis, but also in assessing the appropriate level of care and managing the lethality associated with the disorders. Additionally, a careful history and assessment of current symptoms (i.e., frequency, duration, and intensity) should also be conducted during the initial clinical interview. Counselors should be familiar with the diagnostic criteria for the depressive and bipolar disorders. Because depressive and bipolar disorders are complex and differential diagnosis can be difficult, readily available checklists that detail the diagnostic criteria for each disorder and the types of underlying mood episodes may be helpful. Assessing for affect disturbances (e.g., history, type, current symptoms, onset, and patterns) and recent changes in energy or activity levels is the foundation for establishing whether a person meets the criteria for a major depressive episode, a hypomanic episode, or a manic episode.

Clinical Toolbox 4.2: In the Pearson etext, click here to view a form counselors can use in assessing and distinguishing manic and hypomanic episodes.

According to the *DSM-5* (APA, 2013), the diagnosis of depressive and bipolar disorders entails an elevated risk of completed suicide. It is estimated that as many as 15% of those with MDD die by suicide. Notably, this risk is not limited to adults. The age of onset of depressive disorders appears to be decreasing, with an estimated 1–3% of children at the primary school level meeting the criteria for major depressive disorder (Huggins, Davis, Rooney, & Kane, 2008). Additionally, as many as 10–15% of those with bipolar disorders die by suicide. Ongoing attention to risk assessment and ready familiarity with the range of risk factors for suicide is of critical importance when counseling clients with depressive and bipolar disorders (see Chapter 3 for a detailed discussion of these issues as related to treatment planning).

Depending on the results of an initial assessment, referral for a full medical, psychological, or psychiatric assessment may be warranted. Given the possibility that depressive and bipolar disorders may co-occur with a range of other medical, mental, or substance use disorders, differential diagnosis may require referral and interprofessional collaboration. In the case of mild to moderate depression, referral to an individual's physician to rule out a medical condition such as hypothyroidism, and to explore the potential benefit of antidepressant medication may also be warranted.

In cases where the level of affect disturbance or impairment is severe (e.g., psychotic symptoms or suicidal ideation or behaviors), or when differential diagnosis is complicated given the potential for overlapping depressive disorders (e.g., persistent depressive disorder and major depressive disorder) or co-occurring disorders (e.g., anxiety, eating or personality disorders), referral for a psychiatric evaluation (i.e., an assessment for psychiatric medication) is recommended. It may be valuable to explore psychopharmacotherapy options under the care of a psychiatrist to assist with rapid and effective symptom relief. In addition, an established working relationship with a psychiatrist or federally funded community mental health clinic may also be necessary in screening clients for hospitalization and facilitating hospital admissions.

There are a number of considerations when selecting an effective counseling approach for treating depressive/bipolar disorders. These considerations include the etiology of the disorder, differential diagnosis (i.e, the type of depressive or bipolar disorder), biopsychosocial characteristics of clients, symptom severity, and resources for treatment. Counselors should be aware that there are a number of specific evidence-based approaches that can be used to treat these disorders. In addition to being knowledgeable and trained in the most evidence-based treatments for specific disorders, counselors should also remain mindful of emerging and adjunct approaches to counseling. Adjuncts to treatment may range from psychoeducation on wellness strategies related to diet, exercise, and sleep hygiene, to neurotherapies that alter brain functioning.

Counselors are well positioned to foster hope and resiliency among those who may be coming to terms with a depressive or bipolar diagnosis. Educating clients on the causes of mental health disorders could help to combat the negative impact of both externalized and internalized messages related to depression (e.g., "I am lazy").

PROGNOSIS

Symptom management and enhanced adaptive functioning are reasonable goals in the treatment of depressive and bipolar disorders. The nature of these disorders is such that for many of those who experience these disorders, a full remission of symptoms is not achieved; episodes of affect disturbance occur cyclically or episodically recur relative to a psychosocial stressor, or occur chronically. Yet, with the appropriate use of evidence-based treatments for depressive and bipolar disorders, clients' prognoses are favorable (Craighead, Sheets, Brosse, & Ilardi, 2007). Although the prognosis varies by disorder, the recurrence of these disorders and symptoms is fairly common. Therefore, counselors must consider integrating a relapse prevention component into treatment in order for clients' treatment gains to be maintained.

MAJOR DEPRESSIVE DISORDER

Description of the Disorder and Typical Client Characteristics

Major depressive disorder (MDD) is one of the most common disorders counselors will confront in clinical practice. MDD has a lifetime prevalence of 16.9% (National Comorbidity Survey, 2007). MDD is more prevalent in women than men, occurring in about 20.2% of women and about 13.2% of men (National Comorbidity Survey, 2007). While MDD may occur at any age, the average age of onset is 20 (Huggins et al., 2008).

MDD is characterized by one or more major depressive episodes. A major depressive episode entails a period of at least two weeks of depressed mood, or loss of interest or pleasure, accompanied by at least four other symptoms that result in clinically significant distress or impairment in functioning. The additional symptoms may include changes in appetite or weight, insomnia or hypersomnia, psychomotor retardation or agitation, fatigue or loss of energy, feeling worthless or experiencing excessive guilt, difficulty concentrating or indecisiveness, recurrent thoughts of death, suicidal ideation, or suicide attempts.

While the etiology of depression is not fully understood and may vary according to individual biopsychosocial vulnerabilities, MDD often follows a psychosocial stressor (e.g., divorce, job loss). Historically, bereavement following the loss of a loved one precluded the diagnosis of MDD, even if all other criteria were met. In an effort to recognize the possibility of MDD following a death and to improve access to treatment, this exclusion has been eliminated in the *DSM-5* (APA, 2013).

In addition to the likelihood that there will be an identifiable trigger preceding a major depressive episode, those presenting with major depression almost always present with a loss of pleasure or interest in activities and may seem apathetic, have a flat affect, or appear as withdrawn. In addition, the individual may report changes in mood in terms of persistent sadness or hopelessness, frequent tearfulness, or increased irritability. Symptoms may also be reported in terms of somatic complaints, including fatigue or irritability, aches and pains, decreased libido, restlessness, agitation, or conversely, feeling slowed down, or having difficulty concentrating. Clients may also present with inappropriate or excessive guilt manifested as statements about others being better off if they were not around, or they may express feeling that they are a burden. This may be accompanied by reports of passive or active suicidal ideation or behaviors.

An individual's presentation and identification of symptoms is likely to vary relative to age, developmental factors, and culture. For example, children and adolescents frequently report depression in terms of somatic complaints, social withdrawal, and irritability. Depression in children and adolescents is often characterized by initial disruptions in normal functioning, which may include changes in school performance and the desire to attend school, withdrawing from social activities and peers, behavioral changes (e.g., in sleep, eating, aggression), and substance use and abuse. Additionally, children and adolescents with depression can present with sensitivity to rejection, self-deprecatory ideation (i.e., feelings of worthlessness), difficulty concentrating, physical complaints (i.e., headaches, stomachaches), reduced ability to function in school, vocal and crying outbursts, and lower energy levels (Field, Seligman, & Albrecht, 2008). In older adults the prevalence rates of depression increase, yet many go unrecognized and untreated because of difficulties with accurate symptom reporting secondary to cognitive impairment, or depressive symptoms being mistaken for apathy, somatic complaints, or dementia (Sadock & Sadock, 2007).

Cultural variation in the expression and presentation of major depression has been seen across cultures, with many people with depression endorsing insomnia, fatigue, and somatic complaints (APA, 2013). For example, Latinos may be more likely to report "nerve" problems or headaches, whereas Asians may report symptoms in terms of tiredness or imbalance, and Middle Easterners may reference problems of the heart (Sue & Sue, 2012). Some cultures, such as the Hmong, are more likely to conceptualize mental health disorders in terms of the spirit world. Special care must be taken to understand the individual's cultural definition of depression and the differentiating cultural models of conceptualizing depression (Sue & Sue, 2012).

Diagnostically, MDD presentations may vary; therefore, the *DSM-5* (APA, 2013) distinguishes these variations through the use of outlining specifiers. Diagnostic specifiers in the *DSM-5* (APA, 2013) assist in capturing these differences: (a) recurrence (single or recurrent episodes); (b) the severity of symptoms (mild, moderate, severe without psychotic features, and severe with psychotic features); (c) the current clinical status (with psychotic features, in partial remission, in full remission); and (d) the features of the most recent episode (catatonic, melancholic, atypical or peripartum onset, mixed, and with seasonal pattern). Notable among these is the addition in the *DSM-5* of a mixed specifier when symptoms of a hypomanic or manic episode accompany MDD, but are insufficient to meet the full criteria for either type of episode.

Adding to the complexity of accurately assessing MDD and its associated risks, it frequently co-occurs with other mental health or substance use disorders. Comorbidity of depression and alcohol dependence is of particular concern with co-occurrence rates among men at 24% and over 45% for women (Conner, Pinquart, & Gamble, 2009). It is hypothesized that alcohol may produce or contribute to symptoms of depression; life stressors related to substance dependence can promote depression, and self-medication of depression leads to substance dependence.

A number of other disorders commonly co-occur with MDD. These include substance use disorders, panic attacks and panic disorder, obsessive-compulsive disorder, eating disorders, and borderline personality disorder. Underlying medical conditions may also contribute to MDD, particularly diabetes, heart attacks, cancers, and strokes.

Counselor Considerations

Given its prevalence, comorbidity with other disorders, and the risk of completed suicide, counselors must possess a solid knowledge of assessment and diagnosis when working with clients presenting with a possible diagnosis of MDD. In addition, counselors must also be prepared to work collaboratively with a range of other professionals in ruling out underlying or comorbid medical, mental health, or substance use disorders and in developing treatment plans to match the needs and resources of clients. In addition to maintaining currency through research and continuing education, active engagement with other counselors and mental health professionals is critically important when working with this population.

Familiarity and ready access to brief and reliable assessment instruments suited to diverse client populations can help in accurately diagnosing and assessing this population. The Beck Depression Inventory-II (BDI-II), the Hamilton Depression Rating Scale, and the Children's Depression Inventory are among the most widely used and reliable indicators of depression. The Beck Anxiety Inventory is often used in combination with the BDI-II to screen for symptoms of anxiety and their severity. In addition, there are a variety of assessment tools that can be helpful in screening for the possibility of a substance use disorder (National Institute on Alcohol Abuse and Alcoholism, 2013). Please see Chapter 8 for a more detailed discussion of substance-related disorders and their assessment.

Counselors must also attend to ensuring proper training and competence in practicing the most evidence-based treatments for MDD. Historically, identifying with a single theoretical school of thought was the norm. At present, counselor training programs place more of an emphasis on theoretically integrated and eclectic approaches, as they offer greater flexibility in factoring in client needs and treatment efficacy into the treatment approach.

Treatment Models and Interventions

There is consistent empirical evidence to support the use of psychotherapy alone, or in combination with antidepressants, in the effective treatment of MDD. Recent research suggests that a range of psychotherapies are as effective in treating MDD as medication (Imel, Malterer, McKay, & Wampold, 2008). However, when treating severe depression, medication is highly beneficial and is often necessary (Fournier et al., 2010). Furthermore, while antidepressant medication may indeed assist with more rapid symptom relief in the acute phase of treatment (Klein, Jacobs, & Reinecke, 2007), without psychotherapy, symptoms often reoccur when the medication is discontinued (Butler, Chapman, Forman, & Beck, 2006).

Randomized controlled trials (RCTs) have shown that cognitive behavioral therapy, mindfulness-based cognitive therapy, behavioral activation therapy, interpersonal psychotherapy, and psychopharmacotherapy are the most effective therapeutic approaches in treating MDD (Chartier & Provencher, 2013; Craighead et al., 2007; Segal, Williams, & Teasdale, 2013). In addition, some emerging adjunct therapies to consider include mindfulness-based interventions, electroconvulsive therapy, bright light therapy, and neurofeedback. Likewise, holistic approaches geared toward symptom relief and wellness management also merit consideration. Factors to be considered in treatment planning include: the severity of symptoms, the singular or recurrent nature of major depressive episodes, the risks and benefits associated with medication, comorbidity with another mental health or substance use disorder, and client investment and resources for treatment.

COGNITIVE BEHAVIORAL THERAPY (CBT)   CBT therapies are among the most popular therapeutic approaches for treating MDD. This, in addition to their proven efficacy in the treatment of MDD (Butler et al., 2006; Young, Rygh, Weinberger, & Beck, 2008), contributes to their prominence in the literature as the "go to" approach for treating MDD in adults and youth. One study spoke to the definition of CBT aptly as "interventions that promote emotional and behavioral change by teaching youth to change thoughts, thought processes, and behaviors in an overt, active, and problem-oriented manner" (Klein et al., 2007, p. 1404). The central goal of using CBT with clients with MDD is to teach clients to recognize and manage their reactions to depressive symptoms, as well as to apply behavioral strategies in active and adaptive symptom management. In applying CBT, clients are invited to consider a recent situation that produced depressive symptoms, explore the automatic thoughts associated with the situation, consider the emotions tied to those thoughts, and then, after altering the thoughts, reevaluate their emotional reactions.

Clinical Toolbox 4.3: In the Pearson etext, click here to view a cognitive behavioral therapy form that counselors can use to help clients challenge depressive thoughts.

Most evidence-based approaches to treating depression include a combination of cognitive and behavioral strategies (Paradise & Kirby, 2005). Cognitive Therapy, even over CBT and behavior therapy approaches, tends to yield the most significant and enduring effects among adolescents and adults, particularly in severe cases. The efficacy of CBT with a number of co-occurring disorders may be one factor that promotes its consideration. Evidence suggests that those with MDD who also have a comorbid personality disorder may respond better to CBT because of their lower levels of insight into interpersonal problems, and because of CBT's directive and structured nature (Carter et al., 2011). In particular, there is empirical support for CBT's effectiveness in both individual and group modalities for adolescents and adults with MDD (Klein et al., 2007; Oei & Dingle, 2008). Its versatility is a strong consideration for CBT as a cost-effective treatment for MDD.

Clinical Toolbox 4.4: In the Pearson etext, click here to watch a video of a counselor utilizing cognitive behavioral therapy with a client who has depression.

MINDFULNESS-BASED COGNITIVE THERAPY (MBCT)   MBCT is an approach designed to teach those who are susceptible to recurrent episodes of depression the art of mindfulness meditation in a cognitive therapy context (Segal et al., 2013). The aim of this approach is to assist clients with depression away from obsessing and perseverating on thoughts and feelings of depression, and instead, teach them to them to be more present in the here and now. Counselors working from an MBCT approach help clients shift away from these negative thoughts and moods towards a place of personal acceptance. Instead of allowing these thoughts and feelings to direct an individual's behaviors or reactions, in this approach clients are instructed to acknowledge that these thoughts or feelings exist, but alternatively allow them to pass over them and not control them. This approach aids clients in moving from a place where unconscious automatic thought patterns rule their behaviors, and

biological + environmental

towards more conscious thought processing. This conscious thought processing significantly disrupts and disables their traditional, destructive thought patterns. This approach has been manualized for use in an eight-week group treatment (Segal et al., 2013).

BEHAVIORAL ACTIVATION THERAPY (BAT)   BAT is a behavior therapy treatment approach intended to offer positive reinforcement for engagement in pleasurable activities (Cuijpers, van Straten, & Warmerdam, 2007). Essentially, this approach conceptualizes depression as being maintained by the environmental context rather than by internal cognitions. Therefore, counselors utilizing BAT seek to promote their clients' awareness of their environmental sources of depression and attempt to target behaviors that worsen or maintain their depression. Theoretically, those with depressive symptoms have experienced situational stressors and possess a biological predisposition that has adversely led to changes in their behaviors. Behaviorally, they tend to isolate themselves and avoid various situations that could potentiality provide an opportunity for growth and joy (Chartier & Provencher, 2013). By increasing clients' participation in more desirable and pleasurable activities, clients experience a more positive affect, and this change in affect impacts their depressive symptoms.

Using this simple approach, clients are taught to monitor their affect and activity daily, and engage proactively in scheduling more pleasurable activity. The message conveyed to clients about the approach is that acting *as if* one is not depressed is a proven strategy in effective treatment (Chartier & Provencher, 2013). Targeting these avoidance behaviors provides clients the opportunity to reconnect with sources of positive reinforcement, while decreasing aversive conditions (e.g., boredom, complaints, insomnia). In using this approach, the counselor identify a hierarchy of potential activities (e.g., previous activities, social activities, leisure activities, physical activities, or even lifestyle changes) that will be rewarding and pleasurable (Chartier & Provencher, 2013). The counselor then aids the client in problem solving by reviewing the obstacles and challenges to engaging in these tasks. Weekly activities are scheduled and the client monitors his or her affect (e.g., pre-activity, during, and postactivity) during each scheduled activity.

 Clinical Toolbox 4.5: In the Pearson etext, click here to watch a video of a counselor utilizing behavioral activation therapy with a client with depression.

INTERPERSONAL PSYCHOTHERAPY (IPT)   IPT uses the therapeutic alliance as a foundation for facilitating positive counseling outcomes and linking the occurrence of depression to interpersonal disturbances (e.g., loss of a loved one, illness, interpersonal conflict; Markowitz & Weissman, 2004). This is an approach that focuses on the relationship between mood and situational factors in a present, relational context.

IPT has been manualized for individual treatment and consists of 12 to 16 weeks of individual, weekly counseling sessions that are divided into three phases of treatment (Markowitz & Weissman, 2004). The first phase is focused on MDD in an interpersonal context. Assisting the client in forging the connection between mood and interpersonal contexts sets the stage for the second phase of treatment. During the second or middle phase of treatment, the client is engaged in identifying and asserting interpersonal needs.

CREATIVE TOOLBOX ACTIVITY 4.1   Now vs. Future Collage

Lisa P. Meyer, MA, NCC

Activity Overview

This creative intervention invites clients with depressive disorders to increase their awareness of the components, characteristics, or activities they hope to incorporate into their future self via the use of collage techniques.

Treatment Goal(s) of Activity

The primary goals of this activity are to help clients (a) identify the components, characteristics, or activities they hope to have be part of their future self, (b) behaviorally define the changes clients need to make to live more fully; and (c) take the necessary action to facilitate these desired changes.

Directions

1. Ask clients to divide a large piece of construction paper into two equal sides. Additionally, ask the client to write the terms "now" and "future" at the top of each side.
2. After providing art supplies and various magazines, ask the clients to make a collage of his or her current (now) and ideal (future) self. This could include the characteristics they already possess or wish to possess. It may also include hobbies or projects they would like to complete in the future.
3. After completion of the collage, the counselor and client can address each side of the collage. For the components, characteristics, or activities that the client does not already possess/engage in, the client can discuss what is keeping him or her from them. Additionally, the counselor can discuss with the client ways to incorporate these into his or her ideal (future) self.
4. Next, one aspect of the collage can be the focus (the client's choosing), and the client can behaviorally define what this component, characteristic, or activity would look like in practice.
5. A plan can be developed to work toward incorporating this component, characteristic, or activity.

Process Questions

1. Tell me what this exercise was like was for you.
2. After completing the collage, what stands out to you in the "now" side of the collage?
3. What stands out to you in the "future" side of the collage?
4. List the components, the characteristics, or activities that you do not already possess or engage in currently.
5. Identify one of these components, characteristics, or activities that you would like to adopt. What is getting in your way?
6. What was the most and/or least challenging for you?

During this phase, clients' anger and interpersonal disappointments and frustrations are validated, and clients are encouraged to express their emotions and take social risks. In the final phase, the client is prepared for termination, which in itself entails an interpersonal transition. Given the risk of recurrence of symptoms and the efficacy of IPT as a maintenance therapy with MDD, clients may transition to less frequent sessions.

IPT groups can be useful in helping clients work through interpersonal loss or improve social functioning (Bleiberg & Markowitz, 2008). Group IPT can be divided into distinct phases of treatment, which are similar to individual IPT. The first phase of group IPT focuses on aiding clients to develop personal counseling goals, understand how their depression occurs in an interpersonal context, more effectively utilize coping skills, and understand their affect relative to interpersonal problems. The next phase consists of the working phase of treatment and focuses on developing practical solutions to current interpersonal problems and difficulties (e.g., increased problem-solving skills). Finally, the last stage of group IPT treatment involves clients recognizing and consolidating gains as they prepare to identify and counter signs of depression (e.g., relapse prevention, maintenance).

EMERGING ADJUNCT THERAPIES   There are a number of emerging approaches and adjuncts to psychotherapy worthy of consideration in treatment planning for MDD. Chief among these in mental health practice are mindfulness-based interventions, electroconvulsive therapy, and neurotherapies such as neurofeedback, transcranial magnetic stimulation, and vagus nerve stimulation. The value of these approaches in symptom relief and maintenance of wellness should be considered as a part of a comprehensive treatment plan.

Mindfulness-Based Interventions   One approach gaining empirical support in treating a wide range of mental health disorders, in particular depression, is mindfulness-based treatment. The practice of mindfulness involves a purposeful and nonjudgmental focus on the present (Brown, Marquis, & Guiffrida, 2013). This approach can be divided into three steps: (a) making clients aware of the value and empirical support for these interventions use (so as to enhance their commitment to the approach); (b) teaching clients mindfulness-based techniques such as meditation or breathing that promote increased self-awareness and acceptance; and (c) nonreactivity (i.e., an ability to tolerate and accept situations and emotions without becoming emotionally activated; Brown et al., 2013). Clients are encouraged to integrate these practices into their daily lives as a strategy for managing their symptoms. Arguably, as clients experience symptom relief and increased wellness, motivation will be generated to use these techniques more regularly.

Electroconvulsive Therapy (ECT)   ECT is a treatment involving the deliberate initiation of a seizure by passing electric currents through the brain via the use of electrodes (Cusin & Dougherty, 2012). Advances in the field have greatly reduced the risks once associated with ECT such that possible side effects (e.g., short-term memory loss, confusion, headache, or nausea) generally dissipate in a few days. It is administered under general anesthesia and carefully controlled conditions, and is applied in small second and minute increments during a few sessions in up to four weeks in both inpatient and outpatient settings (Cusin & Dougherty, 2012). ECT may be recommended for people suffering from severe depression accompanied by suicidal ideation or psychosis, or treatment-resistant depression. This intervention is usually implemented under the supervision of a psychiatrist and an anesthesiologist.

Bright Light Therapy   Bright light therapy or phototherapy is believed to impact neurochemicals linked to mood and has long been a treatment of choice for depression that is seasonal in nature (i.e., sometimes referred to as seasonal affective disorder or SAD;

Pail et al., 2011). Additionally, there are some preliminary findings that suggest efficacy with regular bright light use in relieving the symptoms associated with other depressive disorders (i.e., PDD, MDD, and bipolar depression; Pail et al., 2011). Bright light therapy used regularly during the premenstrual phase of the menstrual cycle may also help to provide symptom relief and improved quality of life in women with PMDD (Haffmans, Richmond, Landman, & Blom, 2008).

Essentially, bright light therapy shifts an individual's circadian rhythm (i.e., internal clock) and counters the hormone melatonin (i.e., the hormone associated with sleep). Bright light therapy is usually done through a light box that emits 10,000 lux of light (i.e., daylight). An individual then positions himself or herself about 60 to 80 centimeters from the box for at least 30 minutes a day (Pail et al., 2011). This light box is prescribed for certain times of the day, often 8 to 9 hours after the body starts to secrete melatonin (Pail et al., 2011). One concern of this use of treatment is that bright light may affect clients' eyes, although well-constructed light boxes may mitigate these risks. Counselors should seek training and consultation before prescribing this intervention.

Neurofeedback Neurofeedback (e.g., EEG biofeedback) is a means for clients to retrain brainwaves and increase their self-regulation through the use of operant conditioning (Hammond, 2007). Neurofeedback is essentially biofeedback applied directly to an individual's brain. Neurofeedback targets the frontal area of the brain with the goal of stimulating brain wave activity in the left frontal area, which is associated with positive emotions and motivations, and decreasing brain wave activity in the right frontal area, which is associated with fear and depression (Hammond, 2007). Counselors should seek additional training before engaging in this intervention.

Transcranial Magnetic Stimulation (TMS) TMS is an FDA-approved treatment that may be useful for treatment-resistant depression (Cusin & Dougherty, 2012). It entails the placement of an electromagnetic coil against the scalp to stimulate nerve cells in regions of the brain associated with mood and depression. Theoretically, this intervention attempts to increase activity in the left prefrontal cortex (L DLPF), an area often associated with lower levels of activity in people with depression (Cusin & Dougherty, 2012). TMS is considered the least invasive brain stimulation intervention, yet it does involve some risks (e.g., headaches, facial pain, seizures). Sessions typically last for 30 to 60 minutes, five times a week, over a 4- to 5-week period (Cusin & Dougherty, 2012). Time constrains and the cost of treatment are two major obstacles associated with this intervention. TMS is often performed in an outpatient setting under the direction and supervision of a psychiatrist.

Vagus Nerve Stimulation Vagus nerve stimulation involves stimulation of the vagus nerve through electrical impulses (Cusin & Dougherty, 2012). It requires a surgeon to surgically implant the device just below the skin on the left chest wall. The procedure takes about 1 to 2 hours, and the client is placed under local or general anesthesia. Once implanted, the device will send electrical signals to the vagus nerve, which in turn signals other areas of the brain in an attempt to improve affect and depressive symptoms. While its primary use is in treating epilepsy, there are some early findings that suggest this may be a helpful treatment for depression (Cusin & Dougherty, 2012).

PSYCHOPHARMACOTHERAPY There is ample research supporting the use of antidepressants in the treatment of MDD; its utility in quick symptom relief in the acute phase of treatment can be significant (Fournier et al., 2010). Antidepressant medication can be divided into seven distinct categories:

- *Tricyclic antidepressants* (TCAs; e.g., Elavil, Norpramin)
- *Monoamine oxidase inhibitors* (MAOIs; e.g., Marplan, Nardil)
- *Norepinephrine and dopamine reuptake inhibitors* (NDRIs; e.g., Wellbutrin)
- *Selective serotonin reuptake inhibitors* (SSRIs; e.g., Paxil, Prozac, Zoloft, Luvox, Lexapro) effective for severe symptoms
- *Serotonin norepinephrine reuptake inhibitors* (SNRIs; e.g., Cymbalta, Effexor)
- *Serotonin antagonist and reuptake inhibitors* (SARIs; e.g., Serzone)
- *Alpha-2 adrenergic antagonists* (e.g., Remeron)

While all antidepressants pose certain side effects (e.g., nausea, weight gain, loss of sexual desire, constipation, dizziness), these categories of antidepressants vary significantly on the side effects of sedation, hypotension (i.e., decreased blood pressure), anticholinergic side effects (i.e., dry mouth), and cardiac side effects (i.e., slowed heart rate; First & Tasman, 2004). A full medical history and evaluation is required before any of these medications can be prescribed. Physicians typically select the medication that best targets identified symptoms the client experiences, and whose side effects will be the best choice considering the clients' symptoms. For example, if a client has sleep difficulties, a loss of appetite, and weight loss as symptoms, a tricyclic antidepressant (e.g., Elavil) taken at bedtime might be a useful medication to consider as it has weight gain and drowsiness as side effects.

Selective serotonin reuptake inhibitors (SSRIs) and serotonin norepinephrine reuptake inhibitors (SNRIs) have become the most prescribed antidepressants in the treatment of depressive symptoms, while older antidepressants like tricyclic antidepressants (TCAs) and monoamine oxidase inhibitors (MAOIs) are less frequently utilized (Undurraga & Baldessarini, 2012). SSRIs and SNRIs are effective in treating depressive symptoms (i.e., poor sleep, appetite patterns, agitation, anxiety, depressive episodes, low energy), are tolerable for more clients, and are safer (e.g., less toxic in overdose) than the TCA and MAOI antidepressants (Sadock & Sadock, 2007).

Unfortunately, some people with depressive symptoms do not respond to any antidepressant medications. This type of depression is often considered by mental health professionals to be *treatment-resistant depression*. In these cases, many physicians consider augmenting antidepressants with either mood stabilizers (e.g., Depakote) or low-dose antipsychotics (e.g., Risperdal). There is limited and conflicting evidence of the effectiveness of this technique, yet if additional comorbid symptoms exist (e.g., psychotic symptoms, severe personality disorders), then augmenting antidepressants with additional medications may be warranted.

Some clients with MDD have psychotic symptoms. These psychotic symptoms may involve delusions or hallucinations, and their psychotic content is typically mood congruent (Preston, O'Neal, & Talaga, 2013). An example of mood congruent symptoms are when clients, because of the depressive symptoms of low self-worth and guilt, contend that others are conspiring against them because of their moral depravity. These symptoms should be taken seriously, as they suggest a severe level of depression and a possible risk of suicide. The most effective treatments are often multifaceted and may include hospitalization, pharmacotherapy (i.e., antidepressants and antipsychotics), and even ECT in cases where medications are not effective (Preston et al., 2013).

While antidepressants pose a great benefit for many people experiencing severe depressive symptomology, some evidence exists that in the mild to moderate cases, antidepressants are less effective (Fournier et al., 2010). When counseling clients with mild to moderate depression, psychosocial treatments should be tried before making a medication referral.

Prognosis

The prognosis for those with MDD is good; approximately two-thirds of people who experience a major depressive episode will experience a remission of symptoms within a year (Young et al., 2008). Symptom remission may predict the pattern of recovery experienced after subsequent episodes. It is estimated that at least 60% of those who experience a single major depressive episode will experience a second episode. Among those who experience two episodes, 70% are at risk for a third episode, and of those people, 90% are at risk of a fourth episode. An estimated 5–10% of those who experience a single major depressive episode will subsequently experience a manic episode and meet the criteria for bipolar disorders.

Counselors should note that the severity of the initial major depressive episode may predict its course, and that psychosocial stressors are likely to play a role in precipitating a first or second episode of major depression. Chronic medical conditions and substance dependence, specifically to alcohol or cocaine, may contribute to the onset of a major depressive episode, and also place people at higher risk for persistent episodes of depression (APA, 2013). For many people the recurrence of major depressive episodes and depressive symptoms is common. Therefore, counselors must consider integrating a relapse prevention component into treatment in order for clients' treatment gains to be maintained and monitored.

PERSISTENT DEPRESSIVE DISORDER

Description of the Disorder and Typical Client Characteristics

Persistent depressive disorder is estimated to affect anywhere from 1 to 8% of children (Huggins et al., 2008), and the occurrence appears to be similar among boys and girls. Notably, among adults women are twice as likely to develop chronic depression (National Comorbidity Survey, 2007). Early and late onset may be specified with PDD, based on whether symptoms occurred before or after age 21.

First introduced in the *DSM-5*, PDD is a disorder new to the DSM system (APA, 2013). PDD is a combination of the formerly discrete diagnoses of chronic major depressive disorder and dysthymic disorder, and is characterized by the persistence of chronic depressive symptoms and functional impairment (APA, 2013). Those with PDD have chronic depression almost daily for at least two years. In addition, those with PDD may present with sleep disturbance issues (e.g., insomnia or hypersomnia), low energy or fatigue, low self-esteem, poor appetite or overeating, poor concentration or indecisiveness, and feelings of hopelessness.

While the low-grade, persistent malaise associated with PDD may lead to the assumption that it should be less concerning than major depressive disorder with its acute onset, this is far from the case. In fact, according to Schramm et al. (2008), PDD is a "particularly disabling disorder which is associated with higher comorbidity, higher impairments in functioning, increased health care utilization, and more frequent suicide attempts and hospitalizations than acute major depressive episodes" (pp. 65–66). The chronicity and entrenched nature of the symptoms associated with PDD present challenges in both assessment and treatment.

The low-grade and persistent nature of the symptoms of PDD may make this disorder more likely to be under- or unreported. Furthermore, people will often report these symptoms in somatic terms, and thus may risk remaining undiagnosed and untreated. The literature points to the risk of misdiagnosis among cultural minorities due to externalized and behavioral manifestations arguably correlated with unremitting poverty and discrimination (Nguyen, Huang, Arganza, & Liao, 2007; Vontress, Woodland, & Epp, 2007). These externalized and behavioral manifestations may include anger, hostility, or self-injurious behavior, particularly among males, that translate to diagnoses of behavioral disorders rather than PDD in children (Nguyen et al., 2007), or personality disorders among minority adults, particularly African American men (Vontress et al., 2007).

In light of the insidious nature of PDD, careful assessment is necessary in making differential diagnoses. A medical examination or psychological assessment may be needed to rule out disorders such as hypothyroidism and neurocognitive disorder. It is also important to screen for substance use to eliminate the possibility that the symptoms are related to prescribed medications (e.g., hypertensives) or other substance use (e.g., alcohol; APA, 2013). Notably, substance-related disorders among older adults are increasing, yet shame related to substance use is often a barrier to seeking treatment (Sue & Sue, 2012).

Counselor Considerations

Counselors must remain aware that the unrelenting nature of PDD is such that those with the disorder may present with significant internalization of the disorder, and thus symptoms may appear to be personality characteristics. It is not difficult to imagine how this chronic symptomatology contributes to a pervasive sense of hopelessness and helplessness that may be perceived as apathy toward treatment (Preston et al., 2013). It is critical that counselors do not further pathologize or dismiss clients who may appear self-absorbed, negative, or apathetic. In fact, taking care in establishing the therapeutic alliance and socializing the client to the treatment approach may hold extraordinary importance with those with PDD (Carter et al., 2011).

Monitoring the risk for suicide among clients with PDD is as critical, if not more so, than with clients with MDD. In addition, counselors should screen and monitor for problems with intimate partners. There is a correlation between chronic depression and divorce among women (Foran, Klein, Manber, & Thase, 2012). Furthermore, chronic depressive symptoms are correlated with marital dissatisfaction, which is correlated with psychological and physical victimization.

Treatment Models and Interventions

The majority of the randomized controlled trials on treating depressive disorders have focused on major depressive disorder. Appropriate treatment of PDD should be intensive and involve medication and maintenance therapy. As with the treatment of MDD, cognitive behavioral therapy, behavioral activation therapy, interpersonal psychotherapy, and psychopharmacotherapy are the most prominent therapeutic approaches in treating PDD (Craighead et al., 2007). Additionally, the cognitive behavioral analysis system of psychotherapy seems to hold promise for treating those with PDD. The previously mentioned emerging therapies found in the MDD treatment section may also be warranted for use with those who have PDD.

Change of thoughts + behavior allows clients to see progress

COGNITIVE BEHAVIORAL THERAPY (CBT) As noted earlier (see CBT treatment section under MDD), CBT is recognized in the research as a versatile and effective approach in treating a range of mental health disorders, among which is PDD (Hoffman, Asnaani, Vonk, Sawyer, & Fang, 2012). CBT's focus on cognitions and behaviors is well-suited for the treatment of PDD, (Craighead et al., 2007). In order to achieve progress when working with those who have PDD, more frequent (i.e., sessions twice weekly) and intensive treatment is sometimes warranted.

BEHAVIORAL ACTIVATION THERAPY (BAT) BAT is an approach specifically developed to treat depression and its associated disorders. It is founded on the idea that one's context—rather than internal factors (e.g., cognitions)—are a more efficient explanation for the occurrence of depression. According to this approach, to target the depression, clients must focus on changing their activities or behaviors. BAT seeks to help people better understand the environmental sources of their depression (e.g., avoidance of activities that may potentially provide pleasure such as going out with one's friends). BAT encourages clients to engage in actual activities and behaviors that may alleviate depression. Conversely, clients are encouraged to avoid behaviors that might maintain or worsen their depression (e.g., withdrawing from social connections with others). Clients are taught to monitor their affect in relation to daily activities, paying attention to the negative effects of their inactivity, avoidance, and tendencies to withdraw. By scheduling proactive, pleasurable activities, clients will, according to this theory, begin to feel better. This change in behaving reinforces to clients that making deliberate decisions related to their daily activities—decisions that are based upon the clients values, or what is important to them—can positively impact affect (Chartier & Provencher, 2013). Aggressive activity scheduling is encouraged as a means of encouraging clients to approach activities that they have been avoiding (because of the depression). One advantage of BAT over traditional CBT approaches for treating depression is that the training on the use of this approach is less complex than it is for many CBT approaches.

externalize the disorder, see self seperate from symptoms

INTERPERSONAL PSYCHOTHERAPY (IPT) According to IPT, the events surrounding interpersonal relationships (e.g., loss of a loved one, illness, interpersonal conflict) do not cause depression. Rather, depression occurs within an interpersonal context and affects relationships and the roles of people within those relationships (Markowitz & Weissman, 2004). The basic premise of IPT is that this interpersonal distress is connected with the psychological symptoms of depression. By addressing interpersonal issues, IPT puts an emphasis on the way symptoms are related to a person's relationships with others (e.g., family, colleagues, friends). Using this approach, counselors help clients focus on the interaction between interpersonal and situational factors and their mood.

Clients are also taught the skills needed to manage these relationships and events. Treatment may include a focus on grief, interpersonal conflict resolution, life changes (e.g., divorce), and interpersonal deficits (e.g., difficult forming and maintaining social relationships). The essential goals of IPT are symptom reduction, developing social support, and increasing interpersonal functioning. At present, there is some evidence to support the use of IPT in treating depression. Antidepressant medication used in conjunction with IPT may be especially helpful in treating clients who have PDD (Browne et al., 2002; Markowitz, Kocsis, Bleiberg, Christos, & Sacks, 2005; Schramm et al., 2008). Clients who engage in IPT can experience significant symptom relief, and are able to manage relationships more successfully (Browne et al., 2002). Rather than identifying themselves as a list of symptoms or a diagnosis, clients are assisted in conceptualizing themselves as a person in a social, interpersonal context; as people who have a malleable struggle that can be resolved.

COGNITIVE BEHAVIORAL ANALYSIS SYSTEM OF PSYCHOTHERAPY (CBASP) The need to address the maladaptive cognitions and behaviors characteristic of clients with PDD led to the development of CBASP. CBASP is aimed at exposing and challenging maladaptive beliefs and behaviors through situational analyses (McCullough, 2006). By sequentially deconstructing events with the goal of identifying junctures where changes in client cognition or behavior would have led to positive outcomes or exceptions, clients may be empowered and assisted to think, behave, and react differently.

Studies suggest that the combination of antidepressant medication and CBASP is particularly useful in relieving the insomnia that can be problematic in those with PDD. Consistent with research on the treatment of depressive disorders, the combination of CBASP and antidepressant medication is also likely to be more effective in reducing the recurrence of symptoms, as clients translate cognitive behavioral strategies into daily practice, and can thus enjoy enduring change (Thase et al., 2002; Schatzberg et al., 2005).

PSYCHOPHARMACOTHERAPY In light of current practice and research on chronic depression, antidepressant medication should be an integral component of effective treatment for PDD (Preston et al., 2013). The most common antidepressants utilized in the treatment of those with PDD are selective serotonin reuptake inhibitors, bupropion (i.e., an atypical antidepressant), and monoamine oxidase inhibitors (Sadock & Sadock, 2007). Results of a recent meta-analysis on the treatment of chronic depression point to psychopharmacotherapy as more efficacious than psychotherapy (Imel et al., 2008). Yet the researchers suggest the results may have been limited by the brief nature of the psychotherapeutic interventions that were compared to medication. Due to the persistent and chronic nature of this type of depression, the initial symptom reduction usually afforded with the beginning of antidepressants may be less dramatic than with MDD (Imel et al., 2008). Researchers, though, do not discount the value of psychotherapy, and universal evidence supports the additive value of psychotherapy in the treatment of chronic depression (Schramm et al., 2008).

Prognosis

The prognosis for those with PDD appears to be best when antidepressant medication is combined with psychotherapy (Carta et al., 2012). The previously mentioned psychotherapies that challenge and assist clients to cultivate adaptive cognitions and behaviors may contribute to enduring treatment effects.

PREMENSTRUAL DYSPHORIC DISORDER

Description of the Disorder and Typical Client Characteristics

An estimated 75% of premenopausal women report normal and expected mood changes during the premenstrual cycle. In addition, 20–80% of women may meet the criteria for premenstrual syndrome, which includes a range of emotional, behavioral, or physical symptoms. However, only an estimated 2–8% of women meet the criteria for PMDD (APA, 2013). Most women first seek help for premenstrual dysphoric disorder (PMDD) in their 30s (DiGiulio & Reissing, 2006). Recent findings suggest that while many African American women do report premenstrual symptoms, they are significantly less likely than Caucasian women to experience PMDD (Pilver, Kasl, Desai, & Levy, 2011).

The diagnosis of PMDD is reserved for girls and women from menarche up until menopause who meet the criteria for a significant mood disturbance and impairment in functioning. Notably, the symptoms of PMDD are not to be confused with premenstrual syndrome, which affects a large number of women who experience as few as one symptom without significant distress or impairment in functioning. The significant level of mood disturbance and impairment with PMDD distinguishes it from premenstrual syndrome (Pearlstein & Steiner, 2008).

Women with PMDD experience a cyclical pattern of symptoms occurring for most months in a year in the last week of the luteal phase of their menstrual cycle, all of which resolve entirely in early to mid-menses. Women with PMDD will present with a range of symptoms that must include sadness, anxiety, mood or emotional lability with tearfulness, or persistent irritability. Additional symptoms may include decreased interest in usual activities, difficulty concentrating, lack of energy, marked changes in appetite, changes in sleep, feeling overwhelmed, and physical discomfort such as breast tenderness, headaches, or bloating, and even suicidal ideation.

The symptoms and level of impairment of PMDD occur at a severity consistent with those of other mental disorders, such as a major depressive episode or generalized anxiety disorder. Impaired functioning is typically related to affect disturbance, as opposed to somatic symptoms, and may impact all spheres of a woman's life (DiGiulio & Reissing, 2006). During the symptomatic period, women may experience increased conflict in interpersonal relationships and decreased satisfaction with quality of life. Time lost at work and/or school may also be significant.

The cyclical nature of the onset and resolution of symptoms with menses, physiological symptoms (e.g., breast tenderness or bloating), and the anxiety, tension, and affective lability associated with the menstrual cycle is also helpful in distinguishing PMDD from MDD (DiGiulio & Reissing, 2006). Compared to major depressive disorder, PMDD symptoms are more responsive to medications; symptoms are typically relieved quicker, and with lower doses of medication (DiGiulio & Reissing, 2006).

While comorbidity of PMDD with other mental health and medical disorders is not uncommon, counselors should be cautious in diagnosing PMDD when there is a depression or anxiety disorder that may be exacerbating the premenstrual symptoms (DiGuilio & Ressing, 2006; Pearlstein & Steiner, 2008). Noted for their potential for premenstrual exacerbation are PDD, major depressive disorder panic disorder, and generalized anxiety disorder. Some suggest that once symptom management of an underlying depressive or anxiety disorder is achieved, the use of daily prospective ratings of symptoms, abatement of comorbid disorders, and functional impairment specific to mood symptoms, rather than somatic symptoms, aids in this process (DiGuilio & Reissing, 2006).

Counselor Considerations

Counselors must remain mindful of contextual dynamics that may impact women with PMDD and their loved ones. Stereotyping and stigma around menstruation abounds and may inhibit or delay women from seeking help and limit their support. Prevalence rates may rise as societal and cultural stereotypes around menstruation are challenged, awareness increases, and women feel more comfortable seeking PMDD treatment (DiGiulio & Reissing, 2006).

Given the biopsychosocial nature of mental health and PMDD, it is likely that counselors will be engaged in collaborative work in developing a treatment approach that effectively and holistically addresses each client's preferences, needs, and resources. This may entail exploration of nutritional supplements, hormonal treatment, and/or psychotropic medication with physicians and psychiatrists. Finally, because of the increased interpersonal conflict associated with PMDD, there may be a need for marriage or family counseling.

Treatment Models and Interventions

The biopsychosocial etiology of PMDD is hypothesized to involve hormonal, neurotransmitter, neuroendocrine, and neurosteroid abnormalities (Pearlstein & Steiner, 2008), anxiety sensitivity, maladaptive rumination related to the physiological changes associated with menstruation (Sigmon, Schartel, Hermann, Cassel, & Thorpe, 2009), and disempowering internalized cultural expectations and narratives about menstruation (Ussher & Perz, 2006). There is empirical evidence in support of a range of treatments targeting the key biopsychosocial vulnerabilities associated with PMDD, and it is reasonable to anticipate that research focused exclusively on PMDD will develop with its inclusion as a discrete disorder in the *DSM-5*.

Cognitive behavioral interventions and psychopharmacotherapy are consistently supported in the literature for their efficacy, as are self-help and psychoeducational interventions. As with all treatment planning, there are pros and cons to each approach that need to be carefully weighed in light of the severity of symptoms and impairment, the risks and benefits of each approach, and client preferences and resources. Attending to access to community resources may be of particular importance in treatment planning for PMDD, as poverty rates among women in the United States are consistently higher than among men (National Women's Law Center, 2013). Women with PMDD also navigate struggles associated with an increased likelihood of utilizing sick days, thus limiting the time they can get away from work to attend counseling. Many women also struggle to find or be able to afford childcare so that they can attend counseling (Ussher & Perz, 2006).

COGNITIVE BEHAVIORAL THERAPY There is consistent, if not universal, support for cognitive behavioral approaches in treating PMDD. A number of randomized controlled trials support their effectiveness (Christensen & Oei, 1995; DiGiulio & Reissing, 2006; Sigmon et al., 2009).

Cognitive behavioral approaches with this population target beliefs about menstruation and promote efficacy in management of symptoms. Research suggests that negative attitudes toward menstruation, greater physical symptomology, and insufficient preparation for menstruation all predict more negative responses (Stanton, Lobel, Sears, & Stein DeLuca, 2002). As such, a critical examination of cultural messages and stereotyping about menstruation will be a key task in examining and restructuring clients' cognitive schemas (Ussher & Perz, 2006).

One study found that women with high anxiety sensitivity who engaged in depressive rumination experienced higher levels of premenstrual distress (Sigmon et al., 2009). These findings point to the merit of evaluating and addressing anxiety sensitivity and rumination among women with PMDD with the goal of challenging depressive ruminations, and possibly even promoting adaptive rumination. Consistent with cognitive behavioral approaches, it may be helpful to assist women in conceptualizing the premenstrual phase as a stressor to be managed via the application of CBT strategies (Sigmon et al., 2009). More specifically, assisting women to explore and modify their beliefs about their menstrual cycle, utilizing cognitive behavioral strategies to recognize and address negative premenstrual experiences, expectations, and menstrual-related concerns, may be helpful.

Empowering women by assisting them to recognize and develop effective strategies to manage symptoms is another guiding principle in cognitive behavioral approaches to treatment. Behavioral interventions such as assertiveness and relaxation training may also be useful. Other strategies that assist women in anticipating and managing wellness include charting cycles, increased attention to diet, exercise, sleep, and pleasurable activities on a regular basis and at key times in the menstrual cycle.

PSYCHOPHARMACOTHERAPY There is substantial research supporting the effectiveness of low doses of selective serotonin reuptake inhibitors (SSRIs), prescribed either continuously or intermittently, in relieving the emotional and somatic symptoms associated with PMDD (DiGiulio & Reissing, 2006). Xanax (i.e., a benzodiazepine) also yields symptom relief, particularly related to premenstrual anxiety. However, because of their addictive potential, caution is indicated with the use of benzodiazepines. While SSRIs such as Prozac are considered the first-line treatment in terms of medication therapy, and symptom relief may be achieved more quickly with medication, some report symptom recurrence when the SSRIs have been discontinued (Pearlstein & Steiner, 2008). Cost and potential side effects of medication include weight gain and sexual dysfunction (Pearlstein & Steiner, 2008; Ussher & Perz, 2006).

Hormonal treatments such as oral contraceptives or gonadotropin-releasing hormone agonists that suppress ovulation may also be prescribed for symptom relief; however, findings are mixed with respect to their effectiveness (Kroll & Rapkin, 2006). There are also significant side effects associated with gonadotropin-releasing hormone agonists (e.g., hot flashes, headaches).

Prognosis

increased understanding of the biopsychosocial correlates of PMDD has pointed to effective interventions for symptom reduction and management (Christensen & Oei, 1995; Sigmon et al., 2009). While providers must take care to avoid the pitfalls of cultural stereotyping related to women and menstruation, it is clear that symptom validation alone can have a relieving effect for women. Interventions as simple and cost-effective as psychoeducation through pamphlets or with a professional, to counseling and episodic use of a low-dose SSRI, yield positive results for women (Ussher & Perz, 2006). With intervention and treatment, PMDD has a positive prognosis.

DISRUPTIVE MOOD DYSREGULATION DISORDER (DMDD)

Description of the Disorder and Typical Client Characteristics

Disruptive mood dysregulation disorder (DMDD) is a disorder newly added to the *DSM-5* (APA, 2013). Prevalence rates are estimated between 0.8 and 3.3% over a 3-month period (Copeland, Angold, Costello, & Egger, 2013), with one-year rates around 2.5 to 5% (APA, 2013). DMDD often occurs in conjunction with other mood disorders and oppositional defiant disorder (Copeland et al., 2013), and is more prevalent in males than females (APA, 2013). DMDD applies to children with chronically unstable moods, heightened irritability, and intense and disruptive behaviors (e.g., verbal outbursts, temper tantrums, or physical aggression three or more times in a given week over a 12-month period) inappropriate to the child's age and out of proportion to situational stressors.

As compared to their peers, children with DMDD often react negatively to external stressors or stimuli and engage in verbal outbursts, temper tantrums, and aggressive behaviors to get their needs met. They have a low tolerance for delayed gratification, and seem to have significant difficulties dealing with frustration and ambiguity. The intensity and duration of their behaviors poses complications to their functioning, their family, and other social systems within their environments (i.e., school, community).

These children are often demanding and react impulsively toward people in authority positions, struggling with their social judgment and decision-making skills. For example, a child may be asked to comply with a standard set of rules within a classroom and respond with excessive temper tantrums and verbal aggression, eventually becoming destructive toward property within the classroom when the teacher continues to maintain age-appropriate expectations.

When children with DMDD are not acting out verbally or aggressively, they are often perceived as being irritable, angry, or even sad (APA, 2013). Their moods tend to be chronic and consistent with a "low grade" depression (e.g., dysthymic) and would not meet the threshold for other more severe mood disorders (e.g., major depressive disorder and bipolar disorder). This criterion aids in distinguishing oppositional defiant disorder from DMDD and is grounded in studies which suggest that irritability and aggressive behaviors are strongly linked to depressive and anxiety disorders in adulthood (APA, 2010a; Stringaris, Cohen, Pine, & Leibenluft, 2009).

Children with DMDD may also struggle with hyperarousal (e.g., agitation, racing thoughts, pressured speech, insomnia, intrusive thoughts), which is part of other childhood diagnoses (i.e., attention-deficit/hyperactivity disorder and bipolar disorders), yet this symptom is not a specific criterion for DMDD (APA, 2010b). Therefore, if hyperarousal is present, which is often the case, counselors need to distinguish whether these symptoms occur within the context of clearly defined mood episodes, or if they are part of a general, nonepisodic irritability. Children who experience symptoms outside of a defined mood episode will not meet the criteria for major depressive disorder and bipolar disorders. If any of the following appear to be present, counselors should explore a diagnosis other than DMDD (Leibenluft, 2011):

- Manic/hypomanic episodes (e.g., elevated mood, grandiosity, decreased need for sleep);
- Symptoms are contained within discrete periods of times (i.e., more episodic in nature);

- Symptoms of another diagnosis seem to be present (e.g., schizophrenia, bipolar disorder, major depressive disorder, persistent depressive disorder, or posttraumatic stress disorder); or
- The symptoms are possibly due to the physiological effects of substance use, a neurological condition, or a general medical conditions.

Currently, DMDD is designated for children who have experienced these symptoms before the age of 10, but not before the age of six. Children who have displayed distinct manic episodes will be excluded from this diagnosis. Those with DMDD may also have a number of co-occurring disorders including attention-deficit/hyperactivity disorder, conduct disorder, oppositional defiant disorder, and/or substance use disorders. Prevalence rates for DMDD appear to be higher in boys than girls (APA, 2013).

Counselor Considerations

Counselors should realize that it can be challenging to work with children with DMDD. Counselors need to be prepared to work with many systems including the child's family, the school system, and multiple agencies within the community. Additionally, the counselor should be prepared to assess and treat a number of diagnoses frequently comorbid with DMDD (e.g., attention-deficit/hyperactivity disorder, oppositional defiant disorder; see Chapter 12 for the treatment and counseling considerations that apply when working with these populations, as many will overlap).

Furthermore, as is typical of children with oppositional defiant disorder, children with DMDD will often direct their hostility and negative feelings toward authority figures, and this may include the counselor. Counselors should be mindful of their own reactions toward clients' anger, defiance, impulsivity, and irritability. They must be patient with clients and continually monitor their own internal reactions to the child, the child's behaviors, the child's parents (e.g., caregivers), other family members, and other decision-makers within the child's environment. These issues of countertransference will only negatively impact the counselor's conceptualization of the situation and produce poorer treatment outcomes, and therefore need to be monitored and processed.

In addition to monitoring their own internal reactions, counselors must be prepared to work with multiple systems and professionals from other agencies (e.g., parents, family members, teachers, community agencies, legal professionals). Counselors must be willing to work within the family system and possess the knowledge and ability to not only work individually with the child, but also to assess family dynamics, parental structure, and disciplinary issues that may be exacerbating the behaviors and the child's irritability. Counselors are often required to provide and implement decision-making skills training, social skills training, anger management, and parent education. These adjunct treatments can be utilized to complement a thorough approach to treatment that attempts to address the child's behaviors within multiple systems.

Because of the nature of the symptoms associated with DMDD (e.g., outbursts, aggression, impulsivity), some counselors may struggle to connect with this population. However, a therapeutic relationship is essential and critical when working with children with DMDD. Counselors should attempt to strengthen this alliance by being active, warm, and creating a climate of collaboration. This collaborative relationship will inspire trust and a sense of hope in the process and utility of treatment, thus creating more positive treatment outcomes.

Treatment Models and Interventions

At this time, likely because this is a newly identified disorder, there is little research on treating clients with DMDD, and currently no randomized controlled trials are reported in the literature (APA, 2010b). Evidence-based treatments currently utilized for treating oppositional defiant disorder and other mood-related disorders should be considered when warranted and appropriate. Specifically, the treatment approaches that address the symptoms of verbal outbursts, temper tantrums, and irritability should be the primary approaches considered and researched with this emerging population. Cognitive behavioral therapies that address the oppositional behaviors and the irritability (Weersing & Brent, 2010) within the family system appear to have the most clinical potential for those with DMDD.

Only one research study has explored the utility of medication in treating DMDD. This study did not find any treatment efficacy when comparing Lithium to a placebo treatment in addressing DMDD symptoms (Dickstein et al., 2007). Because the behavioral symptoms are similar to the disruptive behavior disorders (see Chapter 12) and depressive/bipolar disorders, medications used to treat these disorders may be used by physicians to treat DMDD.

PARENT MANAGEMENT TRAINING (PMT) PMT is a behavioral approach in which parents are instructed on how to alter their child's behavior within the home, school, and community (Kazdin, 2010). The focus of treatment tends to be on the sequences of parent-child interactions (e.g., how to alter this sequence), and how to foster desired behaviors. The central aim of PMT is to change the way parents interact with their child. Ideally, as a result of PMT, parents learn to consistently use behavioral interventions to decrease the child's outbursts and temper-related behaviors. This approach is grounded in the belief that behavioral problems are formed and maintained by maladaptive parent-child interactions. These interactions, when altered, can change the child's behaviors.

[handwritten margin note: Parents become more prosocial with child]

PMT is rooted in behavioral learning principles, or more specifically, operant conditioning. The context (antecedent) influences behaviors, which results in consequences that increase, decrease, or have no effect on future behaviors. Counselors attempt to reveal this relationship between behaviors and the environment (or the antecedent and consequences) to parents. The counselor aids the parent in a host of areas: becoming more observant and adequately defining the child's behaviors, increasing awareness of positive reinforcements (e.g., attention, praise, points), the use of a token economy, appropriate use of punishment (e.g., loss of privileges, time out from reinforcement, and reprimands), knowing when to attend to behaviors and when to ignore them, implementing learned skills in session through family role-playing, and learning and utilizing the skills of contracting, negotiating, prompting, and fading.

PROBLEM SOLVING SKILLS TRAINING (PSST) PSST is a cognitive behavioral approach that aims to decrease a child's disruptive behaviors by teaching the child to develop effective problem-solving and decision-making skills (Kazdin, 2010). The counselor aids the child in challenging faulty underlying assumptions that maintain problem behaviors, confronting irrational interpretations of others' behaviors, and generating new alternative solutions to problems. The behavioral component of this approach utilizes role-play and coaching techniques to model positive problem-solving, rewards more positive behaviors, and provides corrective feedback on ways to handle situations more appropriately. Kazdin (2010) suggested that parent management training and PSST be used together to optimally enhance treatment effectiveness, and ensure that both the parents and the child develop the skills necessary to experience long-term change.

COGNITIVE BEHAVIORAL THERAPY (CBT)   CBT approaches aimed at treating depression in children and adolescents target cognitive distortions. However, they also have a focus on behavior change which includes teaching clients prosocial activities, and adequate problem-solving skills (Weersing & Brent, 2010). CBT teaches children and adolescents the skills they need to effectively navigate negative life stressors. Often, those who are irritable or depressed have an inaccurate, overly negative view of themselves, their world, and their future (Beck, Rush, Shaw, & Emery, 1979). This negative view, along with the client's propensity to process current events and situations through the lens of past negative experiences, can create errors in how information is processed. Additionally, if an individual has experienced negative, uncontrollable life events, these environmental factors may exacerbate her or his depressive symptoms and faulty cognitions.

A comprehensive CBT approach for treating child and adolescent depression integrates psychoeducation, behavioral activation skills, emotional regulation skills (e.g., distraction, relaxation), cognitive restructuring, problem solving skills, and parental involvement (Weersing & Brent, 2010). The aim of CBT treatment is to alter a client's irrational negative cognitions; cognitions that are at the root of his or her depressive symptoms. Specifically, this process of treatment attempts to assist a client in identifying, labeling, and challenging overly distorted negative thoughts that contribute to depressive symptomology. Additionally, affect regulation (i.e., the ability to maintain and increase positive feelings), and reducing impulsive, risky behaviors is another common focus of treatment. Enhanced mood regulation skills are believed to support one's ability to manage frustrating situations thus alleviating aggressive, impulsive, or risky behaviors.

CREATIVE TOOLBOX ACTIVITY 4.2   The Cool-Down Space

Matthew J. Paylo, PhD, LPCC-S

Activity Overview

This creative intervention invites children with disruptive mood dysregulation disorder (or adults who have anger management struggles) to increase their utilization of problem-solving skills learned in treatment, while attempting to avoid stressful and frustrating situations. Clients are asked to designate a space at home or at school (whichever is most applicable) to utilize during times of intense anger and/or frustration. The client then uses the space and identified distraction techniques in an attempt to problem-solve the current situation.

Treatment Goal(s) of Activity

The primary goals of this activity are to help clients (a) identify emotions in real-life situations; (b) learn and implement distraction techniques; and (c) learn and implement problem-solving skills in real-life settings rather than having a temper outburst or being aggressive toward others.

Directions

1. The counselor and client can process the importance of taking time out to cool down when feeling angry. This discussion establishes the foundation for this activity.
2. Provide the client with a piece of construction paper and art supplies. Ask the client to draw a blueprint of his or her home or school area. Then ask the client to identify a space that he or she can seek in times of anger and frustration. Ask the client to identify the space on the blueprint. Make sure the space is located outside of active living areas where others are located.
3. Ask the clients to discuss situations that have caused temper outbursts or aggression toward others. Place this situation on the piece of construction paper.
4. Ask the client to identify how he or she feels in each of those situations and inquire about the associated feelings, behaviors, and situations.
5. Ask the client to list a number of possessions or activities that he or she utilizes to distract himself or herself in these agitating situations. These possessions can be a notebook, a book, a stress ball, Play-Doh, or any other object or activity that is helpful.
6. The counselor and the client can now collaborate on ways that the client can better handle each of these situations (this is significantly easier for clients to do when they are not in the midst of a stressful situation).
7. The counselor and client can process how the cool-down space can be utilized to remove himself or herself long enough to devise specific strategies for managing anger so that he or she can return to his or her environment with a well-constructed plan.

Process Questions

1. Tell me, what was this exercise like for you?
2. What did it feel like to be utilizing the cool-down space in those situations?
3. Were you able to distract yourself from your overwhelming anger and/or frustration? What did you do in the space?
4. What did you notice about your thoughts, feelings, and behaviors after being in the space?
5. What was most and/or least challenging for you?

Prognosis

Little is known about the prognosis of DMDD. Many factors may be associated with a successful outcome including early intervention, parent involvement, and the use of evidence-based treatment approaches (Kazdin, 2010). Parental involvement in treatment is one of the best predictors of positive treatment outcomes for children with disruptive behaviors, and this is also likely true with DMDD (Carr, 2009).

BIPOLAR AND RELATED DISORDERS

Description of the Disorders and Typical Client Characteristics

The prevalence rates in a given year for bipolar disorders are about 2.6% among the U.S. adult population, with 82.9% of these cases classified as "severe" in terms of symptomology (National Institute of Mental Health [NIMH], 2013). The onset of these disorders typically begins in a person's late teens or twenties, and seems to affect men and women in roughly equal proportions. The prevalence among children and adolescents is between 0 and 3%, although there is much controversy with regard to accurately and reliably diagnosing these disorders in this population (Parens & Johnston, 2010).

Bipolar disorders, historically referred to as manic-depressive disorder, are characterized by dramatic changes in general energy and activity levels, mood, and perception of reality. These changes are so profound that during a symptomatic phase, they can significantly affect an individual's ability to function and carry out even basic day-to-day tasks. Those with bipolar disorders experience cyclical mood swings and prolonged episodes of mania and/or hypomania alternating with a depressed mood. The median duration for these alternating mood episodes (mania or depression) for clients with bipolar disorders is around 13 weeks (Solomon et al., 2010).

During a manic episode an individual may experience a sudden dramatic decrease in the need for sleep, a rush of excessive energy, feelings of euphoria, extreme talkativeness, grandiosity, elevated libido, and an inability to concentrate. These symptoms can lead to poor judgment and impulsivity, resulting in reckless behaviors such as excessive spending, self-injury, substance abuse, or engaging in dangerous sexual activities. This experience is comparable to being under the influence of an amphetamine or cocaine in terms of physiological processes.

During a severe manic or depressive episode, some clients also experience psychotic delusions and hallucinations. A manic episode sometimes occurs spontaneously, but they can be triggered or influenced by outside factors. These outside factors can be as minor as changes in sleeping habits (e.g., staying up a few hours later than usual; Gruber et al., 2011), or changes in caffeine intake. Significant changes such as positive or negative emotional stress or life events can also have significant triggering effects. Medications such as antidepressants also have the potential to trigger manic episodes in people with these disorders. Thus, it is critical that counselors assist clients in monitoring changes in activity, energy, or affect, and ensure that these changes are communicated to the prescribing psychiatrist when antidepressant medication is begun. Additionally, keeping a daily routine and documenting changes in affect that occur in relation to events is crucial to helping clients identify symptom triggers and in enhancing effective symptom management.

During depressive episodes, the symptoms of the individual with bipolar disorder will be the same as those of a person experiencing the depressive disorders discussed earlier in this chapter. It is important to note that people are more likely to seek treatment during the depressive phase as this is the time they feel depressed and unhappy. It is often during the depressive phase that they find themselves faced with the consequences of their behaviors during the manic phase. While in the manic phase they tend to feel "so good" that there is often no intrinsic need to seek help; in fact, many clients value the sense of euphoria and the energy they experience during the manic phase. It is not uncommon in the depressive phase for the individual not to remember some of her or his actions during a manic phase. This is especially true if the manic phase was accompanied by psychotic delusions.

According to the *DSM-5*, bipolar II disorder is characterized by a lifetime history of at least one episode of major depression and one hypomanic episode (APA, 2013). Bipolar I and II disorders share similar characteristics. One the main differences between the two is that in bipolar II disorder, there are no full-blown manic episodes. Instead, there is a pattern of depressive episodes with hypomanic episodes.

A hypomanic episode has similarities to a full-blown manic episode, but it is also distinctively different from it in many ways. Perhaps the most important difference is that during a hypomanic episode, clients do not experience psychotic symptoms, and the symptoms are generally not as severe and do not interfere with everyday functioning as do those of a manic episode. One of the warning signs of entering a hypomanic episode is that there is a remarkable, directly noticeable and sudden change in functioning that is uncharacteristic of the individual. People often become highly social, virtually overnight, and may impulsively become involved in high-risk activities (e.g., sexual indiscretions or excessive buying sprees). It is also common for those in a hypomanic episode to experience a drastically reduced need for sleep, feelings of grandiosity, talkativeness, distraction, and agitation.

In contrast, those with cyclothymia experience moderate to mild fluctuations of thought, mood, and behavior. Cyclothymia can be conceptualized as "subsyndromal" depressive and hypomanic states with symptoms that are too mild to meet formal diagnostic criteria for those conditions (Baldessarini, Vazquez, & Tondo, 2011). Since the symptoms tend to be relatively mild and ambiguous in nature, there has been a long debate about how to best conceptualize the disorder. Some have even posited that cyclothymia should be regarded as a type of temperament and/or personality trait as opposed to an affective disorder. Some believe that it is not a distinct disorder itself, but is more of a prodrome to bipolar II disorder.

Counselor Considerations

For those with bipolar disorders, the ups and downs can be both exciting and lonely. The individual's mood may vacillate from extreme depression to euphoria. It is important that counselors recognize that either mood state is cause for alarm and should be swiftly addressed. The complexity of these disorders and the likelihood that medication will be necessary underscore the need for counselors to engage in regular consultation, and to establish and maintain connections with psychiatrists and facilities that may assist with crisis stabilization.

Counselors must also remain cognizant of the elevated risk for suicide among those with bipolar disorders. Notably, a meta-analysis revealed the prevalence of attempted suicide in those with bipolar I disorder as 36%, and in people with bipolar II disorder it was found to be 32% (Novick, Swartz, & Frank, 2010). Ongoing assessment and risk management with any client diagnosed with bipolar disorders is essential.

In addition to remaining alert to the behavioral risks associated with the bipolar disorders, counselors must be prepared to assist clients with the range of emotions that may accompany being diagnosed with a serious mental illness. People may experience a great sense of loss when diagnosed with bipolar disorders, and it is important for counselors to assist clients in their grieving process (Federman & Thomson, 2010). Upon diagnosis, they may feel anger or helplessness. Counselors must be prepared to validate, while also offering the client hope and adaptive strategies to support healthy and productive functioning.

Counselors should also consider that those with bipolar disorders can struggle to function across a variety of domains. There may be moments of irritability that arise at work, school, or within familiar relationships that hinder functioning. Daily routines will be important to maintaining balance and wellness, but may be more difficult for some clients to manage given their age, occupation, or resources. Counselors may need to emphasize the reality of mental health stigma and the need for those with bipolar disorders to make deliberate decisions about disclosing their disorder (Federman & Thomson, 2010).

Treatment Models and Interventions

Because of the similarities of the treatments for all bipolar disorders, the treatment approaches for these disorders will be presented collectively. Effective treatment for those with bipolar disorders is aimed at establishing and maintaining stabilization of affect and functioning, and it must include ongoing risk assessment and management. Treatment may be conceptualized in terms of three general phases: acute, stabilization, and maintenance. Clients often present during a period of acute symptomology, but this is not always the case. A client in the midst of a manic or hypomanic episode may experience psychosis or express suicidal intent; thus, the counselor's primary role will be crisis management. This is likely to involve collaboration with a psychiatrist or a crisis stabilization facility on an inpatient basis. Once the acute symptoms or crisis has been resolved, the treatment focus shifts to stabilization. Once the client's condition has stabilized and the client is prepared to resume normal functioning, the treatment focus will shift to symptom maintenance. During this phase the counselor and client may shift their attention to establishing a regular rhythm of life which focuses on the regulation of sleeping, eating, and mood.

Treatment for clients with bipolar disorders includes collaboration with a psychiatrist, case managers, and whenever possible, the client's own support system. Randomized controlled trials suggest that psychopharmacotherapy is an essential component of effective treatment of these disorders, which should be complemented with the following psychosocial approaches: cognitive behavioral therapy, family-focused therapy, and interpersonal and social rhythm therapy (Miklowitz et al., 2007; Miklowitz & Otto, 2006; Sachs et al., 2003). Counseling is not only useful in supporting medication compliance, but can also support the individual in establishing a daily routine that promotes wellness and balance, monitoring symptoms, and offering perspective on behaviors that may indicate relapse or elevated risk of negative consequences. In addition, a number of emerging approaches (i.e., those that lack support as evidenced by a lack of randomized controlled trials) may also be considered based on the client's needs, preferences, and resources for treatment. At this time, there is little research on treating those with cyclothymia. Evidence-based treatments such as those employed in the treatment of the bipolar disorders should also be considered for use with this population.

COGNITIVE BEHAVIORAL THERAPY (CBT) A CBT approach to treating bipolar disorders assumes that the mood and conduct of this population is influenced by a pattern of core beliefs as well as by physiological factors (Virgil, 2010). Core beliefs act like mental filters, selectively sorting and interpreting information. Information that is congruent with the individual's preexisting core beliefs tends to be magnified, while information that is not congruent tends to be minimized or ignored. When treating bipolar disorders, CBT is not meant to replace the use of medication, and in fact, CBT counselors acknowledge the significance and powerful influence of the underlying biological processes in the development of the bipolar symptoms. The CBT treatment framework is considered to be complementary to the use of medications and is not intended to be a replacement for medication in treating bipolar disorders.

CBT offers very precise behavioral targets and methods for intervention. Some of the most commonly used CBT interventions for bipolar disorders include core CBT techniques such as the use of cost-benefit analyses, consideration of alternative ways of thinking, behavioral experiments, daily thought records, and activity scheduling. In terms of therapeutic objectives, CBT aims to target the symptoms of bipolar disorders by educating clients about the disorder, teaching CBT skills for managing manic-depressive symptoms, supporting medication compliance, teaching clients to effectively cope with stress, and teaching clients to monitor their symptoms (Virgil, 2010).

Clinical Toolbox 4.6: In the Pearson etext, click here to see an example of a cognitive behavioral therapy form that counselors can use to help clients chart and rate their moods.

FAMILY-FOCUSED THERAPY (FFT)   FFT is a treatment delivered in 21 sessions over nine months to clients and their families, entails three modules (psychoeducation, communication, and problem-solving), and is utilized in conjunction with medication (Miklowitz et al., 2004). In the psychoeducation phase of treatment, the client and family learn about the symptoms of bipolar disorders, possible courses the disorder may take, overall treatment, and management of the disorder (Miklowitz, 2006). Families are engaged in strategies that enable prevention and early detection of warning signs that the client may soon experience a severe mood episode. This module also allows for the client and family to clarify any questions about the etiology of the disorder, and to voice any concerns about medications. During the second module, communication is the primary goal. Studies indicate that clients in an environment which supports active listening, positive feedback and interactions, and constructive criticism may have longer periods without relapse than those who are not in such an environment (Miklowitz et al., 2004). The education and engagement of the client's family or support system is critical to ongoing and adequate support through the maintenance phase of treatment and beyond. During the final stage of treatment, problem-solving skills training becomes the central aim. The client, along with family members, learns to identify specific family stressors and problems, brainstorm possible alternative behaviors, evaluate the advantages and disadvantages of each potential behavior, and implement the best option for all members.

Clinical Toolbox 4.7: In the Pearson etext, click here to read about an activity that can be used to help clients enhance their knowledge and understanding of bipolar disorder, identify costs and benefits of recovery, and enhance motivation for change.

INTERPERSONAL AND SOCIAL RHYTHM THERAPY   IPSRT is a form of behavior therapy that focuses on helping clients to recognize that while medication may be one form of treatment for bipolar disorders, there are actions in the client's everyday life that can enhance or hinder the success of stabilization and relapse prevention (Frank, 2007). To help a client achieve overall stability with routine, this approach involves an examination of a client's circadian rhythm (Hlastala, Kotler, McClellan, & McCauley, 2010) in concurrence with his or her pattern of eating, sleeping, socializing, exercise, and overall mood. This approach appears to be particularly effective in managing the depressive episodes associated with the bipolar disorders (Miklowitz et al., 2007), and holds the potential to assist clients in avoiding even minor disruptions to routine that could trigger a mood episode.

PSYCHOPHARMACOTHERAPY   Because of the neurobiological underpinnings of these disorders, medication is integral to the treatment of bipolar disorders. Bipolar disorders involve many neurotransmitters including norepinephrine, serotonin, GABA (gamma-aminobutyric acid), glutamate, and acetylcholine (Nemade & Dombeck, 2009). Researchers are investigating neuropeptides (e.g., endorphins, somatostatin, vasopressin, and oxytocin) to determine their role in bipolar disorders (Nemade & Dombeck, 2009).

Since the 1950s, lithium, a mood stabilizing medication, has been a key medication for use with those with bipolar disorders (Calkin & Alda, 2012). In recent years, newer medications have come into favor (e.g., the anticonvulsant medications) because they invite fewer side effects. Beyond lithium, there have been three categories of medication examined for use with patients who have a bipolar disorder. The first class of medications are the anticonvulsant medications or mood stabilizers, which include divalproex sodium (e.g., Depakote), lamotrigine (e.g., Lamictal), gabapentin (e.g., Neurontin), Topamax (e.g., topiramate), and oxcarbazepine (e.g., Trileptal); Food and Drug Administration (FDA, 2013). The second class of medications are the antipsychotics such as olanzapine (e.g., Zyprexa), aripiprazole (e.g., Abilify), quetiapine (e.g., Seroquel), risperidone (e.g., Risperdal), and ziprasidone (e.g., Geodon; FDA, 2013). The third class of drugs is the antidepressants such as fluoxetine (e.g., Prozac), paroxetine, (e.g., Paxil), sertraline (e.g., Zoloft), or bupropion (e.g., Wellbutrin; National Institute of Mental Health, 2013).

With the exception of Prozac, sometimes given in a combination with Zyprexa to create Symbyax (Mayo Foundation for Medical Education and Research, 2013), antidepressants are still under investigation for use with the bipolar disorders because of the possible propensity to trigger a manic episode. In a study by Sachs et al. (2007), results suggested that the addition of an antidepressant to a mood stabilizer is no more effective in treating the depression than the use of mood stabilizers alone.

Some people with bipolar disorders exhibit psychotic symptoms as part of their symptomology. These psychotic symptoms involve delusions or hallucinations, and signify severe impairment to an individual's level of functioning (Preston et al., 2013). These symptoms should be taken seriously, especially when combined with racing thoughts, grandiosity, distractibility, and increased engagement in pleasurable activities. All of these symptoms can lead to an increased risk of hospitalization. Similar to the psychopharmacotherapy treatments for those with major depressive disorder and psychotic symptoms, the most effective treatments for those with bipolar and psychotic symptoms are often multifaceted and include hospitalization, psychopharmacotherapy (i.e., mood stabilizers and antipsychotics), milieu therapy (i.e., psychotherapy, psychoeducation, group therapy), and even electroconvulsive therapy in cases where medications are not effective in altering symptoms (Preston et al., 2013).

Generally, the medications used to treat bipolar disorders have a number of side effects. Counselors can play an integral role in assisting clients and their family in monitoring and tracking side effects associated with medication during each phase of treatment. Increased appetite, dizziness, blood pressure changes, changes in heartbeat, constipation, nausea, vomiting, difficulty with speech, and fatigue are among the most commonly reported side effects (AstraZeneca, 2012). Furthermore, counselors may be helpful in ensuring that the treating psychiatrist is informed of any side effects or challenges with medication compliance. Minimizing side effects is not only important to quality of life, but may also impact medication compliance.

Voices from the Trenches 4.1: In the Pearson etext, click here to watch a psychiatrist discuss the use of medications with clients suffering from depressive or bipolar disorders.

EMERGING ADJUNCT APPROACHES   There are a number of emerging approaches and adjuncts to psychotherapy worthy of consideration in treatment planning for bipolar I, II, and cyclothymic disorders. These approaches consist of transcranial magnetic stimulation, electroconvulsive therapy, diet and exercise, and cranial electrotherapy stimulation. These approaches may be helpful in symptom relief and maintenance of wellness.

Transcranial Magnetic Stimulation (TMS)   TMS is an emerging treatment method that involves delivering repetitive magnetic pulses to specific areas of the brain, causing neuronal depolarization (Rado, Down, & Janicak, 2008). At present, TMS is only approved for the treatment of drug-resistant major depression; however, there have been recent promising clinical trials examining TMS in the treatment of bipolar disorders (Bersani et al., 2013). Some of the advantages of TMS are that it can target very specific and localized areas of the brain, it can be performed without sedation, it does not cause seizures or memory loss (Loo, Schweitzer, & Pratt, 2006; Rado et al., 2008), and the overall side effects seem to be minimal (mild headaches were reported at the initial stages of treatment, and in very rare cases, minor seizures; Wasserman et al., 2008). One of its disadvantages is that the long-term side effects of the treatment are not fully understood (Dell'Osso et al., 2009).

Electroconvulsive Therapy (ECT)   ECT, or electroshock therapy, (for more information, see the treatment section under major depressive disorder) is a short-term treatment for clients who are suicidal, psychotic, or dangerous to others and have had limited success with medication treatment either because the length of time for drug absorption was not adequate, medication is too risky, or because the medications simply were not effective for that particular individual. ECT has been reported to be effective in treating many peoples' depressive episodes, yielding remission of symptoms for up to six months before another episode may appear (Amino, Katayama, Iimori, 2011; Sienaert & Peuskens, 2006).

Diet and Exercise   When examining treatment options for the bipolar disorders, attention to diet, nutrition, and exercise merits consideration. There is promising research on the role of genetic patterns relative to vitamin deficiencies that may be related to the bipolar disorders (Ozbek et al., 2008), and overall, clients with bipolar disorders often lack sufficient engagement in exercise and may not eat properly (Kilbourne et al., 2007).

Food plays an integral role in affect regulation, as a lack of food or the incorrect food can drastically affect weight (Fagiolini, Frank, Scott, Turkin, & Kupfer, 2005) and sleep, which can lead to mood management issues. The interplay between nutrition and mood disorders is highlighted in a study (Simona & Hibbeln, 2003) on the consumption of seafood by people living in 10 different countries. The findings pointed to a correlation between the ingestion of omega-3 fatty acids and lower bipolar prevalence rates, and they suggest that there may be an important relationship between diet and the onset and maintenance of bipolar disorders. It may be beneficial for clients to seek a consultation with a health professional about their diet and its possible relationship to their mood states.

Cranial Electrotherapy Stimulation (CES)   CES is an emerging therapy that may be useful in relieving the sadness that can occur with cyclothymia. CES involves increasing the ability of cells to produce serotonin, dopamine, endorphins, and other neurotransmitters that stabilize the neurohormonal system (Gilula & Kirsh, 2005). This procedure involves fitting a machine to the head, placing electrodes around the mastoid area (i.e., behind the ears), and then sending low-intensity electric pulses throughout the brain. Recently, a machine called the Fisher Wallace Cranial Stimulator was developed that can be prescribed for client use in the home (Fisher Wallace Laboratories, 2013). This therapy is still in its early stages of development and more needs to be learned about it before it can be recommended to clients.

Prognosis

People with bipolar disorders experience variable success with treatment (Maj, Akiskal, López-Ibor, & Sartorius, 2002). With treatment intervention and medication compliance, people with bipolar disorders can function quite well. The high rates of comorbidity with other mental disorders can complicate the prognosis (Soreca, Frank, & Kupfer, 2009). Researchers are exploring considerations related to circadian rhythm instability, mood and affect instability, cognitive and executive functioning, and co-occurring mental and medical conditions (e.g., diabetes and obesity) to try and predict the course of this disorder (Soreca et al., 2009).

TREATMENT PLAN FOR MANUEL

This chapter began with a discussion of Manuel, a 20-year-old Dominican American male who was originally diagnosed with major depressive disorder. During his most recent hospitalization it was determined that Manuel met the criteria for bipolar I disorder. The following I CAN START conceptual framework outlines treatment considerations that may be helpful in working with Manuel.

C = Contextual Assessment

Family dynamics to be considered in this case include parental support, expectations of success, limited financial resources, and his parents' concern about their ability to manage Manuel at home after his manic episode and second hospitalization. Manuel is proud of his Dominican heritage and values his cultural identity. Manuel had trouble acclimating to college, and felt that he did "not fit in" when removed from his own community into the larger cultural context of college. Manuel noted that he is not religious and is uncertain about his spiritual beliefs. Manuel strives to be successful and has worked to support his family. Manuel is a male in late adolescence/early adulthood using alcohol and marijuana, which may be considered the norm among his peers; however, his substance use requires further exploration.

A = Assessment and Diagnosis

Diagnosis = Bipolar I Disorder (in partial remission) 296.45 (F31.73); Beck Depression Inventory II at initial session and then as needed to assess for treatment progress or if the onset of major depressive episode is suspected; regular Suicide Assessment (see Chapter 3); SASSI (Miller, 1985) to assess for substance use and its possible role in is bipolar symptomatology; examination by a physician to rule out other health concerns; psychiatric care for outpatient management of psychiatric medications.

N = Necessary Level of Care

Outpatient, individual sessions (once per week).

Acute/hospital care should be readily accessible.

Possible treatment for substance use/abuse.

S = Strength-Based Lens

Self: Manuel appears to be of at least average intelligence and his high school grades indicate that he has the potential to be a strong student. He is motivated to develop a career and has a good work ethic. He takes pride in his Dominican heritage and contributes to a positive community. He is willing to seek and use professional support to feel well.

Family: Manuel describes his parents as loving and supportive. Although he recently had a physical altercation with his brother, he has good relationships with his siblings and extended family members.

Community: Manuel has close ties within his community and describes them as "like family" to him. Manuel has developed close relationships with people within his community and has found many of them to be supportive throughout his lifespan.

T = Treatment Approach

Cognitive Behavioral Therapy (CBT)

Interpersonal and Social Rhythms Therapy (IPSRT)

A = Aim and Objectives of Treatment (3-month objectives)

Manuel will maintain medication compliance → Manuel will have 100% compliance with taking prescribed medications and will miss 0 psychiatric appointments. If issues arise with medications, he will immediately contact his psychiatrist and counselor.

Manuel will increase his awareness of his affective states and possible mood episodes → Every day, Manuel will document his mood experiences in a daily journal/log. He will identify triggers, and look for any patterns concerning fluctuations in his affective state.

Manuel will actively commit to, and engage in, the treatment process → Manuel will attend all individual therapy sessions; he will engage in honest, open communication with his counselor; he will follow up on interventions mutually developed with his counselor; and he will attend a bipolar support group 80% of the time.

Manuel will learn and use skills that can help him regulate his emotions → Manuel will identify and learn 2 CBT skills (e.g., thought stopping, restructuring, coping strategies) to help him examine how his thought patterns are impacting his emotions; he will examine ways to change negative thinking patterns 80% of the times when he feels depressed.

To aid in mood regulation, Manuel will identify and use daily life routines → Manuel will apply social rhythm therapy skills by daily scheduling and documenting his activities. Manuel will learn about the importance of maintaining healthy social rhythms including diet, exercise, nutrition, and sleep in order to keep stable biological rhythms that help to regulate mood.

Manuel will develop his understanding of bipolar disorder and its treatment → Manuel will read *Facing Bipolar: The Young Adult's Guide to Dealing with Bipolar Disorder* (Federman & Thomson, 2010) and he will discuss what he is learning with his counselor.

R = Research-Based Interventions *(based on CBT and IPSRT)*

Counselor will engage Manuel in the therapeutic process by developing a strong therapeutic alliance to help Manuel be successful.

Counselor will help Manuel develop and apply the following skills:
• Mood regulation skills
• Healthy coping strategies
• Lifestyle management skills
• Problem-solving skills

T = Therapeutic Support Services

Medication management by his psychiatrist

Weekly individual therapy based on CBT/IPSRT

Biweekly bipolar support group meetings

Possible substance abuse support program such as Alcoholics Anonymous

Access to a secure setting should he need it

References

American Psychiatric Association (APA). (2010a). *DSM-5 proposed revisions include new diagnostic category of temper dysregulation with dysphoria (TDD).* Retrieved from: http://www.dsm5.org/Newsroom/Documents/TDD%20release%202.05%20(1).pdf

American Psychiatric Association (APA). (2010b). *Justification for temper dysregulation disorder with dysphoria DSM-5 childhood and adolescent disorder work group.* Retrieved from: http://www.dsm5.org/Proposed%20Revision%20Attachments/Justification%20for%20Temper%20Dysregulation%20Disorder%20with%20Dysphoria.pdf

American Psychiatric Association (APA). (2013). *Diagnostic and statistical manual of mental health disorders* (5th ed.). Washington, DC: Author.

Amino, K., Katayama, S., & Iimori, M. (2011). Successful treatment with maintenance electroconvulsive therapy for a patient with medication-resistant rapid cycling bipolar disorder. *Psychiatry & Clinical Neurosciences, 65,* 299–300.

AstraZeneca (2012). Bipolar disorder treatment. Retrieved from: http://www.seroquelxr.com/bipolar-disorder/

Baldessarini, R. J., Vazquez, G., & Tondo, L. (2011). Treatment of cyclothymic disorder: Commentary. *Psychotherapy and Psychosomatics, 80,* 131–135.

Beck, A. T., Rush, A. J., Shaw, B. F., & Emery, G. (1979). Cognitive therapy for depression. New York, NY: Guilford.

Bersani, F. S., Minichino, A., Enticott, P. G., Mazzarini, L., Khan, N., Antonacci, G.,…Biondi, N. (2013). Deep transcranial magnetic stimulation as a treatment for psychiatric disorders: A comprehensive review. *European Psychiatry, 28,* 30–39.

Bleiberg, E., & Markowitz, J. C. (2008). Interpersonal psychotherapy for depression. In D. H. Barlow (Ed.), *Clinical handbook of psychological disorders: A step-by-step treatment manual* (4th ed., pp. 306–327). New York, NY: Guilford.

Brown, A. P., Marquis, A., & Guiffrida, D. A. (2013). Mindfulness-based interventions in counseling. *Journal of Counseling & Development, 91,* 96–104.

Browne, G., Steiner, M., Roberts, J., Gafni, A., Byrne, C., Dunn, E.,…Kraemer, J. (2002). Sertraline and/or interpersonal psychotherapy for patients with dysthymic disorder in primary care: 6-month comparison with longitudinal 2-year follow-up of effectiveness and costs. *Journal of Affective Disorders, 68,* 317–330.

Butler, A. C., Chapman, J. E., Forman, E. M., & Beck, A. T. (2006). The empirical status of cognitive-behavioral therapy: A review of meta-analyses. *Clinical Psychology Review, 26,* 17–31.

Calkin, C., & Alda, M. (2012). Beyond the guidelines for bipolar disorder: Practical issues in long-term treatment with lithium. *Canadian Journal of Psychiatry, 57,* 437–445.

Carr, A. (2009). The effectiveness of family therapy and systematic interventions for child-focused problems. *Journal of Family Therapy, 31,* 3–45.

Carta, M. G., Petretto, D., Adama, S., Bhat, K. M., Lecca, M. E., Mura, G.,…Moror, M. F. (2012). Counseling in primary care improves depression and quality of life. *Clinical Practice and Epidemiology in Mental Health, 8,* 152–157.

Carter, J. D., Luty, S. E., McKenzie, J. M., Mulder, R. T., Frampton, C. M., & Joyce, P. R. (2011). Patient predictors of response to cognitive behaviour therapy and interpersonal psychotherapy in a randomized clinical trial for depression. *Journal of Affective Disorders, 128,* 252–261.

Chartier, I. S., & Provencher, M. D. (2013). Behavioural activation for depression: efficacy, effectiveness and dissemination. *Journal of Affective Disorders 145,* 292–299.

Christensen, A. P., & Oei, T. P. S. (1995). The efficacy of cognitive behavior therapy in treating premenstrual dysphoric changes. *Journal of Affective Disorders, 33,* 57–63.

Conner, K. R., Pinquart, M., & Gamble, S. A. (2009). Meta-analysis of depression and substance use among individuals with alcohol use disorders. *Journal of Substance Abuse Treatment, 37,* 127–137.

Copeland, W. E., Angold, A., Costello, E. J., & Egger, H. (2013). Prevalence, comorbidity, and correlates of DSM-5 proposed disruptive mood dysregulation disorder. *American Journal of Psychiatry, 171,*173–179.

Craighead, W. E., Sheets, E. S., Brosse, A. L., & Ilardi, S. S. (2007). Psychosocial treatments for major depression disorder. In P. E. Nathan & J. M. Gorman (Eds.), *A guide to treatments that work* (3rd ed., pp. 289–307). New York, NY: Oxford University Press.

Cuijpers, P., Driessen, E., Hollon, S. D., van Oppen, P., Barth, J., & Andersson, G. (2012). The efficacy of non-directive supportive therapy for adult depression: A meta-analysis. *Clinical Psychology Review, 32,* 280–291.

Cuijpers, P., van Straten, A., & Warmerdam, L. (2007). Behavioral activation treatments of depression: A meta-analysis. *Clinical Psychology Review, 27,* 318–326.

Cusin, C. & Dougherty, D. D. (2012). Somatic therapies for treatment-resistant depression: ECT, TMS, VNS, DBS. *Biology of Mood & Anxiety Disorders, 2:14.* Retrieved from: http://www.biolmoodanxiety disord.com/content/pdf/2045-5380-2-14.pdf

Dell'Osso, B., Mundo, E., D'Urso, E., Pozzoli, S., Buoli, M., Ciabatti, M.,…Altamura, A. C. (2009). Augmentative repetitive navigated transcranial magnetic stimulation (RTMS) in drug-resistant bipolar depression. *Bipolar Disorders, 11,* 76–81.

Dickstein, D. P., Nelson, E. E., McClure, E. B., Grimley, M. E., Knopf, L.V., Brotman, M. A.,…Leibenluft, E. (2007). Cognitive flexibility in phenotypes of pediatric bipolar disorder. *Journal of American Academy of Child and Adolescent Psychiatry, 46,* 341–355.

DiGiulio, G., & Reissing, E. D. (2006). Premenstrual dysphoric disorder: Prevalence, diagnostic considerations and controversies. *Journal of Psychosomatic Obstetrics & Gynecology, 27,* 201–210.

Fagiolini, A., Frank, E., Scott, J., Turkin, S., & Kupfer, D., (2005). Metabolic syndrome in bipolar disorder: Findings from the Bipolar Disorder Center for Pennsylvanians. *Bipolar Disorder, 7,* 424–430.

Federman, R., & Thomson, J. A. (2010). *Facing bipolar: The young adult's guide to dealing with bipolar disorder.* Oakland, CA: New Harbinger.

Field, L. F., Seligman, L., & Albrecht, A. C. (2008). Mood disorders in children and adolescents. In R. R. Erk (Ed.), *Counseling treatment for children and adolescents with DSM-IV-TR disorders* (2nd ed., pp. 253–293). Columbus, OH: Pearson.

First, M. B., & Tasman, A. (2004). *DSM-IV-TR mental disorders: Diagnosis, etiology, & treatment.* Hoboken, NJ: Wiley.

Fisher Wallace Laboratories. (2013). Current research studies. Retrieved from: http://www.fisherwallace.com/research-current

Food and Drug Administration (FDA). (2013). *Approved drug products with therapeutic equivalence evaluations* (32nd ed.). Retrieved from: http://www.accessdata.fda.gov/scripts/cder/ob/default.cfm.

Foran, H. M., Klein, D. N., Manber, R., & Thase, M. E. (2012). Risk for partner victimization and marital dissatisfaction among chronically depressed patients. *Journal of Family Violence, 27,* 75–85.

Fournier, J. C., DeRubeis, R. J., Hollon, S. D., Dimidjian, S., Amsterdam, J. D., Shelton, R. C., & Fawcett, J. (2010). Antidepressant drug effects and depression severity: A patient-level meta-analysis. *Journal of the American Medical Association, 303,* 47–53.

Frank, E. (2007). *Treating bipolar disorder: A clinician's guide to interpersonal and social rhythm therapy.* New York, NY: Guilford.

Gilula, M., & Kirsch, D. (2005). Cranial electrotherapy stimulation review: A safer alternative to psychopharmaceuticals in the treatment of depression. *Journal of Neurotherapy, 9,* 7–26.

Gruber, J., Miklowitz, D., Harvey, A., Frank, E., Kupfer, D., Thase, M.,…Ketter, T. (2011). Sleep matters: Sleep functioning and course of illness in bipolar disorder. *Journal of Affective Disorders, 134,* 416–420.

Haffmans, J., Richmond, A., Landman, F., & Blom, M. (2008). The effects of light therapy and cognitive behavioral therapy in premenstrual dysphoric disorder (PMDD). *Journal of Affective Disorders, 107,* S86.

Hammond, D. C. (2007). What is neurofeedback? *Journal of Neurotherapy, 10,* 25–36.

Hlastala, S., Kotler, S., McClellan, M., & McCauley, A. (2010). Interpersonal and social rhythm therapy for adolescents with bipolar disorder: Treatment development and results from an open trial. *Depression and Anxiety (1091–4269), 27,* 457–464.

Hoffman, S. G., Asnaani, A., Vonk, I. J., Sawyer, A., & Fang, A. (2012). The efficacy of cognitive behavioral therapy: A review of meta-analyses. *Cognitive Therapy and Research, 36,* 427–440.

Huggins, L., Davis, M. C., Rooney, R., & Kane, R. (2008). Socially prescribed and self-oriented perfectionism as predictors of depressive diagnosis in pre-adolescents. *Australian Journal of Guidance and Counseling, 18,* 182–194.

Imel, Z. E., Malterer, M., McKay, K. M., & Wampold, B. E. (2008). A meta-analysis of psychotherapy and medication in unipolar depression and dysthymia. *Journal of Affective Disorders, 110,* 197–206.

Karasz, A. (2005). Cultural differences in conceptual models of depression. *Social Sciences & Medicine, 60,* 1625–1635.

Kazdin, A. E. (2010). Problem-solving management training for oppositional defiant disorder and conduct disorder. In J. R. Weisz and A. E. Kazdin (Eds.), *Evidence-based psychotherapies for children and adolescents* (2nd ed., pp. 211–242). New York, NY: Guilford.

Kessler, R. C., Berglund, P., Demler, O., Jin, R., Merikangas, K. R., & Walters, E. E. (2005). Lifetime prevalence and age-of-onset distributions of DSM-IV disorders in the National Comorbidity Survey Replication. *Archives of General Psychiatry, 62,* 593–602.

Kilbourne, A., Rofey, D., McCarthy, Post, E., Welsh, D., & Blow, F. (2007). Nutrition and exercise behavior among patients with bipolar disorder. *Bipolar Disorders, 9,* 443–452.

Kirmayer, L. J. (2001). Cultural variation in the clinical presentation of depression and anxiety: Implications for diagnosis and treatment. *Journal of Clinical Psychiatry, 62,* 22–30.

Klein, J. B., Jacobs, R. H., & Reinecke, M. A. (2007). Cognitive-behavioral therapy for adolescent depression: A meta-analytic investigation of changes in effect-size estimates. *Journal of the American Academy of Child and Adolescent Psychiatry, 46,* 1403–1413.

Kleinman, A. (2004). Culture and depression. *The New England Journal of Medicine, 351,* 951–953.

Kroll, R., & Rapkin, A. J. (2006). Treatment of premenstrual disorders. *Journal of Reproductive Medicine, 51,* 359–370.

Leibenluft, E. (2011). Severe mood dysregulation, irritability, and the diagnostic boundaries of bipolar disorder in youths. *American Journal of Psychiatry, 168,* 129–142.

Loo, C., Schweitzer, I., & Pratt, C. (2006). Recent advances in optimizing electroconvulsive therapy. *Australian and New Zealand Journal of Psychiatry, 40,* 632–638.

Maj, M., Akiskal, H., López-Ibor, J., & Sartorius, N. (Eds.). (2002). *Bipolar Disorder* (vol. 5). Hoboken, NJ: Wiley.

Markowitz, J. C., Kocsis, J. H., Bleiberg, K. L., Christos, P. J., & Sacks, M. (2005). A comparative trial of psychotherapy and pharmacotherapy for "pure" dysthymic patients. *Journal of Affective Disorders, 89,* 167–175.

Markowitz, J. C., & Weissman, M. M. (2004). Interpersonal psychotherapy: Principles and applications. *World Psychiatry, 3*(3), 136–139.

Mayo Foundation for Medical Education and Research (MFMER). (2013). Bipolar disorder. Retrieved from: http://www.mayoclinic.com/health/bipolar-disorder/DS00356/DSECTION=treatments-and-drugs

McCullough, J. P. (2006). Treating chronic depression with disciplined personal involvement: Cognitive behavioral analysis system of psychotherapy (CBASP). Richmond, VA: Springer.

Miklowitz, D. (2006). A review of evidence-based psychosocial interventions for bipolar disorder. *Journal of Clinical Psychiatry, 67,* 28–33.

Miklowitz, D., Axelson, D., Birmaher, B., George, E., Taylor, D., Schneck, C.,…Brent, D. (2004). Family-focused treatment for adolescents with bipolar disorder: Results of a 2-year randomized trial. *Journal of Affective Disorder, 82,* 113–128.

Miklowitz, D., & Otto, M. (2006). New psychosocial interventions for bipolar disorder: A review of literature and introduction of the systematic treatment enhancement program. *Journal of Cognitive Psychotherapy, 20,* 215–230.

Miklowitz, D., Otto, M., Frank, E., Reilly-Harrington, N., Kogan, J., Sachs, G.,…Wisniewski, S. (2007). Intensive psychosocial intervention enhances functioning in patients with bipolar depression: Results from a 9-month randomized controlled trial. *American Journal of Psychiatry, 164,* 1340–1347.

Miller, G. A. (1985). *The Substance Abuse Subtle Screening Inventory (SASSI) manual.* Springville, IN: The SASSI Institute.

National Comorbidity Survey. (2007). *Lifetime prevalence estimates.* Retrieved from: http://www.hcp.med.harvard.edu/ncs/ftpdir/NCS-R_Lifetime_Prevalence_Estimates.pdf

National Institute of Mental Health. (2013). Bipolar disorder. Retrieved from: http://www.nimh.nih.gov/health/topics/bipolar-disorder/index.shtml

National Institute on Alcohol Abuse and Alcoholism. (2013). *Screening tests.* Retrieved from: http://pubs.niaaa.nih.gov/publications/arh28-2/78-79.htm

National Women's Law Center. (2013). *Poverty still on the rise for women in 2010; Record numbers lived in extreme poverty.* Retrieved from: http://www.nwlc.org/our-blog/poverty-still-rise-women-2010-record-numbers-lived-extreme-poverty

Nemade, R., & Dombeck, M. (2009). Neurochemistry and endocrinology in bipolar disorder. Retrieved from: http://www.mentalhelp.net/poc/view_doc.php?type=doc&id=11204

Nguyen, L., Huang, L. N., Arganza, G. F., & Liao, Q. (2007). The influence of race and ethnicity on psychiatric diagnoses and clinical characteristics of children and adolescents in children's services. *Cultural Diversity and Ethnic Minority Psychology, 13,* 18–25.

Novick, D. M., Swartz, H. A., & Frank, E. (2010). Suicide attempts in bipolar I and bipolar II disorder: A review and meta-analysis of the evidence. *Bipolar Disorders, 12,* 1–9.

Oei, T. P. S., & Dingle, G. (2008). The effectiveness of group cognitive behaviour therapy for unipolar depressive disorders. *Journal of Affective Disorders, 107,* 5–21.

Ozbek, Z., Kucukali, C., Ozkok, E., Orhan, N., Aydin, M., Kilic, G.,…Kara, I. (2008). Effect of the methylenetetrahydrofolate reductase gene polymorphisms on homocysteine, folate and vitamin B12 in patients with bipolar disorder and relatives. *Neuro-Psychopharmacology & Biological Psychiatry, 32*, 131–1337.

Pail, G., Huf, W., Pjrek, E., Winkler, D., Willeit, M., Praschak-Rieder, N., & Kasper, S. (2011). Bright-light therapy in the treatment of mood disorders. *Neuropsychobiology, 64*, 152–162.

Paradise, L. V., & Kirby, P. C. (2005). The treatment and prevention of depression: Implications for counseling and counselor training. *Journal of Counseling and Development, 83*, 116–119.

Parens, E., & Johnston, J. (2010). Controversies concerning the diagnosis and treatment of bipolar disorder in children. *Child and Adolescent Psychiatry and Mental Health, 4*(9). Retrieved from: http://www.capmh.com/content/pdf/1753-2000-4-9.pdf

Pearlstein, T., & Steiner, M. (2008). Premenstrual dysphoric disorder: Burden of illness and treatment update. *Journal of Psychiatry & Neuroscience, 33*, 291–301.

Pilver, C. E., Kasl, S., Desai, R., & Levy, B. R. (2011). Health advantage for black women: Patterns in premenstrual dysphoric disorder. *Psychological Medicine, 41*, 1741–1750.

Preston, J. D., O'Neal, J. H., & Talaga, M. C. (2013). *Handbook of clinical psychopharmacology for therapists* (7th ed.). Oakland, CA: New Harbinger.

Rado, J., Down, S., & Janicak, P. (2008). The emerging role of transcranial magnetic stimulation (TMS) for treatment of psychiatric disorders. *Directions in Psychiatry, 28*, 315–332.

Sachs, G. S., Nierenberg, A. A., Calabrese, J. R., Marangell, L. B., Wisniewski, S. R., Gyula, L.... Thase, M. E. (2007). Effectiveness of adjunctive antidepressant treatment for bipolar depression. *New England Journal of Medicine, 356*, 1711–1722.

Sachs, G., Thase, M., Otto, M., Bauer, M., Miklowitz, D., Wisniewski, S.,...Rosenbaum, J., (2003). Rationale, design, and methods of the systematic treatment enhancement program for bipolar disorder (STEP-BD). *Biological Psychiatry, 53*, 1028–1042.

Sadock, B. J., & Sadock, V. A. (2007). *Kaplan and Sadock's synopsis of psychiatry: Behavioral sciences/clinical psychiatry* (10th ed.). Philadelphia, PA: Lippincott Williams & Wilkins.

Schatzberg, A. F., Rush, A. J., Arnow, B. A., Banks, P. L., Blalock, J. A., Borian, F. E.,...Keller, M.B. (2005). Chronic depression: Medication (nefazodone) or psychotherapy (CBASP) is effective when other is not. *Archives of General Psychiatry, 62*, 513–520.

Schramm, E., Schneider, D., Zobel, I., van Calker, D.,

Dykierek, P., Kech, S.,...Berger, M. (2008). Efficacy of interpersonal psychotherapy plus pharmacotherapy in chronically depressed inpatients. *Journal of Affective Disorders, 109*, 65–73.

Segal, Z. V., Williams, J. M. G., & Teasdale, J. D. (2013). *Mindfulness-based cognitive therapy for depression* (2nd ed.). New York, NY: Guilford.

Sienaert, P., & Peuskens, J. (2006). Electroconvulsive therapy: An effective therapy of medication-resistant bipolar disorder. *Bipolar Disorders, 8*, 304–306.

Sigmon, S. T., Schartel, J. G., Hermann, B. A., Cassel, A. G., & Thorpe, G. L. (2009). The relationship between premenstrual distress and anxiety sensitivity: The mediating role of rumination. *Journal of Rational Emotive Cognitive Behavioral Therapy, 27*, 188–200.

Simona N., & Hibbeln, J. R. (2003). Cross-national comparisons of seafood consumption and rates of bipolar disorders. *American Journal of Psychiatry, 160*, 2222–2227.

Solomon, D., Leon, A., Coryell, W., Endicott, J., Fiedorowicz, J., Li, C.,...Keller, M. (2010). Longitudinal course of bipolar I disorder: duration of mood episodes. *Archives of General Psychiatry, 67*, 339–47.

Soreca, I., Frank, E., & Kupfer, D. (2009). The phenomenology of bipolar disorder: What drives the high rate of medical burden and determines long-term prognosis? *Depression and Anxiety, 26*, 73–82.

Stanton, A. L., Lobel, M., Sears, S., & Stein DeLuca, R. (2002). Social aspects of selected issues in women's reproductive health: Current status and future directions. *Journal of Consulting and Clinical Psychology, 70*, 751–770.

Stringaris, A., Cohen, P., Pine, D. S., & Leibenluft, E. (2009). Adult outcomes of youth irritability: A 20-year prospective community based study. *American Journal of Psychiatry, 166*, 1048–1054.

Sue, D. W., & Sue, D. (2012). *Counseling the culturally diverse: Theory and practice* (6th ed.). Hoboken, NJ: Wiley.

Thase, M. E., Rush, A. J., Manber, R., Kornstein, S. G., Klein, D. N., Markowitz, J. C.,...Keller, M.B. (2002). Differential effects of nefazodone and cognitive behavioral analysis system of psychotherapy on insomnia associated with chronic forms of major depression. *Journal of Clinical Psychiatry, 63*, 493–500.

Undurraga, J., & Baldessarini, R. J. (2012). Randomized, placebo-controlled trials of antidepressants for acute major depression: Thirty-year meta-analytic review. *Neuropsychopharmacology, 37*, 851–864.

Ussher, J. M., & Perz, J. (2006). Evaluating the relative efficacy of a self-help and minimal psycho-educational intervention for moderate premenstrual distress conducted from a critical realist standpoint. *Journal of Reproductive and Infant Psychology, 24,* 347–362.

Virgil, G. (2010). Cognitive-behavioral therapy for bipolar disorder: Implications for clinical social workers. *Journal of Social Service Research 36,* 460–469.

Vontress, C. E., Woodland, C. E., & Epp, L. (2007). Cultural dysthymia: An unrecognized disorder among African Americans? *Journal of Multicultural Counseling and Development, 35,* 130–141.

Wasserman, E., Epstein, C., Ziemann, U., Walsh, V., Paus, T., & Lisanby, S. (2008). *Oxford handbook of transcranial stimulation.* Oxford: Oxford University Press.

Weersing, V. R., & Brent, D. A. (2010). Treating depression in adolescents using individual cognitive behavioral therapy. In J. R. Weisz and A. E. Kazdin (Eds.), *Evidence-based psychotherapies for children and adolescents* (2nd ed.) New York, NY: Guilford.

Young, J. E., Rygh, J. L., Weinberger, A. D., & Beck, A. T. (2008). Cognitive therapy for depression. In D. H. Barlow (Ed.), *Clinical handbook of psychological disorders: A step-by-step treatment manual* (4th ed., pp. 250–305). New York, NY: Guilford.

CHAPTER 5

Anxiety Disorders

MATTHEW J. PAYLO AND LISA P. MEYER

CASE STUDY: KA-SEAN

Ka-Sean is a 25-year-old African American lesbian who lives with her partner in an apartment outside a large city. She is currently enrolled in a counseling graduate program. Ka-Sean is the youngest of three children, having one older brother and one older sister. She has not talked with her brother for a number of years; this coincided with his verbal opposition to her moving in with her female partner. Her support system is primarily her partner, her older sister, and her father. She regularly attends a local church and has a number of friends who are spread across the country.

Ka-Sean has had longstanding, excessive bouts of anxiety. She worries excessively and uncontrollably about things within and outside of her control. She often expects the worst to happen even if there is no evidence to warrant these extreme concerns. Ka-Sean finds that she can worry about almost anything, and she reports she is consumed by fears and angst about her relationships, daily activities, health, future (e.g., career, partner), and schooling. These worries are extremely time-consuming (e.g., dominating 80% of her awake time) and leave her physically and emotionally drained.

This excessive worrying has contributed to health issues and concerns. Ka-Sean has a history of chronic restlessness, stomach issues, muscle tension, fatigue, and difficulties with sleep. She describes her sleep cycles as "battles" consisting of repetitive "tossing and turning," as the "to-do list" rattles about in her head. Recently, she was diagnosed with a stomach ulcer after she experienced significant heartburn, an upset stomach, fatigue, and bowel changes. Another area of concern is her inability to maintain concentration. She finds that tasks with a number of sequential steps tend to be extremely exhausting and time consuming. This may in part be due to her "overthinking" things. She considers all the ways a given task could be accomplished, does extensive Internet research, evaluates all potential obstacles, and plans the best course of action. This often results in "analysis paralysis" and was one of the reasons she quit her job at a local department store. She felt exhausted and drained by the constant decisions her boss pushed her to make around areas she believed were outside of her expertise. Last year, after leaving her job, she decided to enter a graduate program in counseling.

As a student, Ka-Sean wrestles with completing assignments because of her excessive procrastination. She often finds writing papers to be unmanageable because she believes she needs to retrieve excessive amounts of information on a given topic, and then seeks reassurance from her classmates and professor that her topic is worthy to explore. All this is done before she is able to move ahead with assignments. Her classmates believe she is a perfectionist, and they say she is unwilling to delegate tasks within a group.

She has some insight into the effect of her excessive worrying. Tending to overly compensate for her worrying, Ka-Sean often tries to seek reassurance and guidance from others to help support her decision-making process. Her partner, friends, and family tell her that she worries way too much; yet she is unable to control these worries, especially when, as she says, "the flooding" of questions emerges. A recent example of this was when Ka-Sean thought her partner was cheating on her because she was unavailable on a Friday night. The "flooding" began like this: What if she is cheating on me? What if she doesn't love me? What if she never loved me? What if she has always been using me to get to someone else? What if she is dating someone I know? What if they are talking about me and having a good laugh at how stupid I am? What if they are out together right now? Is that why she is unavailable today? What would my sister say—would she judge me? What would she say about me not being able to keep my partner happy? Am I enough to keep anyone happy? How can I be a counselor if I can't even control my own life? What have I done to deserve all of this? Why does God keep punishing me? These questions berate her, wear on her sense of self, and lead to even more worrying.

In some situations, Ka-Sean can be so filled with anxiety that she begins to experience tightness in her chest, heart palpitations, shaking of her hands, shortness of breath, and thoughts of losing control. She becomes immobile in these situations. The first time this happened (about 2 years ago), her partner took her to the emergency room because she thought she was having a heart attack. Although these situations cannot be predicted, they occur relatively infrequently (once or twice a month), and happen around others as often as when she is alone. Ka-Sean has not attempted to avoid any social situations. She is, however, hypersensitive to these types of attacks and she persistently worries after each of these events.

A few years ago, Ka-Sean lost her mother and describes this time as a "very dark" period. She previously sought treatment after her mother's death due to bereavement, an increased level of anxiety, and the emergence of self-injurious behaviors (e.g., cutting, burning, punching herself). She states that she no longer copes by engaging in these behaviors, but acknowledges that her worrying reaches debilitating levels during times of extreme stress and uncertainty. During such turbulent times, she feels even less in control and has more intense fears of losing control.

Ka-Sean is intelligent, witty, and has a charismatic personality. She is a nurturer who seems to care for others, often more than she does herself. This is the reason why she decided to go back to school and pursue a degree in a helping profession. Ka-Sean is also passionate about reading and writing. She has written two science fiction novels, yet she has not sought publishing outlets because of her fears of rejection.

Ka-Sean's father and sister are supportive and stabilizing figures in her life. Additionally, her partner is a childhood friend who has continually and unconditionally accepted and supported her. Ka-Sean currently takes alprazolam (Xanax) as needed, which is prescribed by her primary care physician, and would like to seek mental health treatment to help her cope more effectively with her worries and fears.

DESCRIPTION OF THE ANXIETY DISORDERS

The National Comorbidity Survey (2007) reports that nearly one in four people will meet the criteria for an anxiety disorder over the course of their lifetime. Anxiety disorders are common, affecting around 19% of the general population in a given year (Kroenke, Spitzer, Williams, Monahan, & Lowe, 2007), and affecting women twice as often as men (Sadock & Sadock, 2007). This section will address the DSM-5 (American Psychiatric Association [APA], 2013) anxiety disorders, which include panic disorder, specific phobia, social anxiety disorder, agoraphobia, separation anxiety disorder, generalized anxiety, and selective mutism.

Anxiety (i.e., distress, uneasiness, or apprehension) is an adaptive and normal reaction to everyday stressors. These vague feelings of apprehension are more fully realized when one experiences automatic, related physical symptoms such as tightness in the chest, stomach discomfort, dizziness, muscle tension, restlessness, perspiration, palpitations, and headaches (Sadock & Sadock, 2007). These physical experiences lead some to believe they are experiencing a medical condition, when in reality, anxiety is at the root of their discomfort. The combination of these physical and emotional reactions causes people with anxiety to evaluate their situation and decide whether to take action or to avoid an anxiety-provoking event. If these reactions persist or increase in duration and intensity, to the point of affecting one's ability to function, then these anticipatory reactions transition into becoming an anxiety disorder.

People with anxiety disorders concurrently experience physiological sensations (e.g., tightness of chest, shortness of breath, stomach discomfort), and the emotional response of apprehension or fear. While feelings of apprehensiveness and fright are most common, feelings such as confusion, avoidance, selective attention, and even impairment in concentration are not uncommon. People may also experience a sense of overwhelming shame (e.g., "Others are aware that I am fearful") and a sense of hypervigilance (i.e., always looking out for potential danger).

Anxiety disorders also affect people's thoughts, perceptions, and interpretations of their surroundings and interactions. People with anxiety disorders often selectively attend to certain aspects of their environment and only pay attention to those interactions that maintain their perceptions that the world is a dangerous place, falsely justifying their individual apprehensions and fears. Not only do people with anxiety disorders have a distorted sense of self-evaluation, they are often unable to control their own critical statements and thoughts. This cycle of distorted perceptions and self-criticism tends to perpetuate their anxiety and overall level of worry.

 Clinical Toolbox 5.1: In the Pearson etext, click here to read about the prevailing psychosocial theories of the causes of anxiety.

According to the *DSM-5* (APA, 2013) each anxiety disorder has different symptoms, but all of the symptoms cluster around excessive, irrational fear and dread. The different anxiety disorders' symptoms cluster around symptoms of anxiety, worry, or fear in response to a specific situation or object, a perceived threat, or general free-floating feelings of anxiety. Furthermore, these individuals will most likely exaggerate their responses to (a) their physical arousal, (b) their cognitive distortions or responses, and (c) their coping strategies to deal with anxiety (Barlow, 2004). While people with anxiety disorders often have high levels of perceived stress and predict they will have negative outcomes (i.e., trait anxiety), they often attempt to protect themselves by overly controlling situations, or outright avoiding situations, because of their fear, tension, and apprehension (i.e., state anxiety).

COUNSELOR CONSIDERATIONS

Anxiety-related symptoms can contribute to suicidal ideation, depressive symptoms, and substance misuse and abuse (i.e., a desire to self-medicate), and they can be comorbid with some personality disorders (Woo & Keatinge, 2008). Therefore, accurate assessment and diagnosis of anxiety symptoms and disorders is essential.

When assessing for anxiety disorders, counselors need to consider relevant cultural factors that may be impacting or exacerbating the clients' anxiety symptoms. In many cultures, the clinical presentation and expression of anxiety may present as primarily affective, or be comprised of somatic and/or dissociative symptoms (Kirmayer, 2001). This clinical presentation, or expression of anxiety, deviates from the normal anxiety descriptors within the context of the *DSM-5*, which has created a "great degree of cross-cultural variability in the prevalence of anxiety disorders" (Lewis-Fernández et al., 2010, p. 225). For example, Asian cultures have significantly lower rates of social anxiety disorder compared to Russian and U.S. sample populations (Hofmann, Asnaani, & Hinton, 2010). One possible explanation for this phenomenon may be the concept of *taijin kyofusho* (TKS). Those with TKS are often fearful of doing something that may embarrass or insult *another* person (e.g., inappropriately staring, giving off an offensive odor, blushing); therefore, they will avoid a variety of social situations. This is in stark contrast to social anxiety disorder in the United States, where people are often more worried about embarrassing *themselves*, as opposed to embarrassing or offending *another*.

Although not entirely insulated from cultural assumptions or biases, one assessment tool that may have utility for counselors in the assessment and diagnosis of anxiety disorders is the Beck Anxiety Inventory (Beck & Steer, 1990). This self-report inventory is composed of factors related to the cognitive and physical elements of anxiety disorders and can lead to a more accurate conceptualization of clients symptoms. Counselors might consider conducting assessments prior to moving forward with treatment selection. Assessment can also be used throughout the treatment process to monitor progress.

As is the case in treating all disorders, a strong therapeutic relationship is essential. Secondary to clients' apprehension, fears, selective attention, and faulty cognitions, a strong relationship that is rooted in patience, encouragement, and reassurance is vital to ensuring that clients feel safe and can be forthcoming in counseling. Although counselors may need to be moderately directive, they should appreciate that anxious clients may perceive themselves as being fragile and may need significant amounts of empathy and encouragement to fully engage and benefit from treatment. Since anxious clients are often experiencing distress and emotional pain, they are generally motivated to work collaboratively to alleviate their symptoms. A counselor should work to aid in symptom relief before probing or doing significant exploration work. This will help to reduce clients' levels of distress and create conditions in which they can tolerate their anxiety enough to engage in self-exploration.

With anxiety disorders, clients feel uncomfortable, often desire immediate symptom relief, and seek medications from their primary care physicians. While benzodiazepines are effective in the temporary relief of anxiety symptoms, these types of medications (e.g., Xanax, Valium) possess the potential for creating physiological dependency and are often ineffective when depressive symptoms are present (Roy-Byrne & Cowley, 2007). Another, safer alternative to benzodiazepines are buspirone (e.g., Buspar) and antidepressants marketed for treating anxiety (i.e., SSRIs), as both have significantly lower rates of dependency and fewer long-term side effects (Roy-Byrne & Cowley, 2007).

While psychopharmacotherapy can provide some immediate symptom relief, the use of psychotropic medication is often more effective when complemented with a multifaceted approach to treatment (Kendall, Furr, & Podell, 2010). Cognitive behavioral and behavior treatments are the most heavily researched and supported treatments for addressing anxiety disorders (Barlow, Allen, & Basden, 2007). More recently, mindfulness-based practices have gained momentum within the literature as effective in treating anxiety (Harris, 2009; Hayes, Strosahl, & Wilson, 2012). Because anxiety has cognitive, physiological, and behavioral components, a multifaceted treatment approach is warranted (Kendall et al., 2010). When considering specific treatments and modalities, cognitive behavioral therapy, behavior therapy (e.g., exposure-based), acceptance-based therapy, group therapy, family therapy, and the use of psychotropic medications all have been evidenced as useful in managing and treating anxiety disorders.

PROGNOSIS

With the appropriate use of evidence-based treatments for anxiety disorders, clients' prognoses are favorable; approximately 75% of those who receive cognitive behavioral therapy show significant improvement of their symptoms (Evans et al., 2005). Although the prognosis varies by disorder, the recurrence of anxiety disorders and symptoms is fairly common. Therefore, counselors must consider integrating a relapse prevention component into treatment in order for clients' treatment gains to be maintained.

PANIC DISORDER

Description of the Disorder and Typical Client Characteristics

Panic disorder (PD) is found in approximately 4% of the population (National Comorbidity Survey, 2007). PD is twice as common in women as in men, occurring in about 6.2% of women and in about 3% of men (National Comorbidity Survey, 2007). Most people who experience panic attacks do so by late adolescence or early adulthood (Barlow, 2008), and approximately three-fourths having their first panic attack by age 40 (Kessler, Berglund, Demler, Jin, & Walters, 2005).

People with PD experience recurrent and unexpected panic attacks that consist of physical symptoms (i.e., accelerated heart rate, sweating, trembling, shortness of breath, feelings of choking, chest pain or discomfort, nausea, dizziness, numbness or tingling sensations [paresthesias], and chills or hot flashes), and cognitive symptoms (i.e., feelings of unreality [derealization] or being detached from oneself [depersonalization], fear of losing control or going crazy, fear of dying; APA, 2013). A panic attack typically has a sudden onset and lasts for 5 to 20 minutes, although this heightened state of anxiety typically lingers long after the attack has abated (Rachman, 2004). People experiencing panic attacks frequently misconstrue their physical symptoms as having a heart attack, losing their mind, or being on the brink of death (National Institute of Mental Health [NIMH], 2009).

 Clinical Toolbox 5.2: In the Pearson etext, click here to read about biological explanations of the interaction between physical symptoms and anxiety.

People who experience panic attacks, in addition to enduring intense anxiety, often experience thought patterns that escalate the panic symptoms. These thoughts revolve around not being able to escape situations or receive aid from others, and they can significantly increase an individual's propensity to avoid situations in which attacks have occurred or could occur (i.e., agoraphobia, or an avoidance of crowded places). Those with PD report situational avoidance (i.e., the refusal to enter anxiety-provoking situations; 98%), experiential avoidance (i.e., strategies to minimize contact with the feared stimulus; 90%), and interoceptive avoidance (i.e., the refusal to take part in anything that may result in the physical symptoms of panic; 80%; Clark & Beck, 2010). For example, an individual who experiences a number of panic attacks at the local grocery store may come to believe that she can no longer go to any crowded places where escaping or receiving help from others would be difficult. She may avoid grocery stores and solicit someone else to do her shopping, or may endure it with significant panic-like symptoms, asking a companion to assist her.

Panic attacks can occur at any time, even during sleep, and are followed by persistent concern about having additional attacks, worry about the implications of the attack, and a significant change in behavior secondary to the attack (APA, 2013). The apprehension about future panic attacks, also known as anticipatory anxiety, is a hallmark of the disorder (Daitch, 2011). This apprehension, in combination with catastrophic cognitions when facing a panic attack, differentiates those with PD from those who have occasional panic attacks but do not meet the criteria for PD (Nathan & Gorman, 2007).

🚗 **Clinical Toolbox 5.3:** In the Pearson etext, click here to review the different categories of panic attacks.

Those with PD are not necessarily more reactive to stressors than those who have occasional panic attacks and do not meet the criteria for the diagnosis (Taylor, 2000), but they do have a greater awareness and sensitivity to their physical symptoms (Kroeze & van den Hout, 2000). They are often influenced by anticipatory anxiety (i.e., self-reporting panic attacks without evidence of any particular physical symptoms; Barlow, 2008). Not everyone who has a panic attack will go on to meet the criteria for the disorder; many have a single attack and never experience another. However, it is common for those with untreated PD to develop subsequent disorders, such as specific phobia and social anxiety disorder, persistent depressive disorder, substance abuse, major depressive disorder, or generalized anxiety disorder (Barlow, 2008).

Voices from the Trenches 5.1: In the Pearson etext, click here to watch a video of a firsthand account of someone who experienced panic attacks and her recovery.

Counselor Considerations

People with this disorder are often unsuccessful at reducing the impact of these attacks. The diagnosis of PD may initially go undetected, as they frequently view their difficulties as being physical in nature (Kroenke et al., 2007). Therefore, it may be a considerable amount of time before treatment commences, and clients may be guarded when initially meeting a counselor. Counselors must reassure clients that their reactions are normal and that counseling is successful in treating panic disorders.

First and foremost, counselors should cultivate a warm and supportive environment in which they demonstrate empathy, positive regard, and genuineness. Clients who perceive their counselor as understanding, respectful, confident, and directive are most likely to improve. The counselor should focus on empathy and information gathering in the early stages of therapy, progressing to a more directive and active role later in treatment (Barlow, 2008). Just as when working with other disorders, the counselor should promote an expectation of change and should clarify any ambiguity about the nature of counseling.

When assessing clients with PD, the counselor should thoroughly evaluate the contextual factors, frequency, severity, and subjective experience of the attacks. This evaluation should include an assessment of partial and full-blown panic episodes, and should focus on the variety of situations, experiences, feelings, and physical symptoms the client avoids.

Counselors should also assess for comorbid conditions, such as major depressive disorder, substance abuse, personality disorders, and other anxiety disorders, as the presence of any of these will impact the course of treatment. Tobacco and alcohol dependence and abuse are especially prevalent in those with PD; daily smoking is three times more likely and, alcohol use is two times more likely in those with a history of panic (Mathew, Norton, Zvolensky, Buckner, & Smits, 2011). Counselors should consider what role substance use plays in exacerbating clients' panic attacks.

There can be cultural variations in how panic attacks are experienced. Some people from certain cultures do not experience panic attacks unexpectedly, and there may also be variability in the time durations of attacks across cultures (Lewis-Fernández et al., 2010). In some cultures, identified causes (e.g., nature, nerves, spirits) are thought to explain panic reactions. There do not appear to be any gender differences in the prevalence rates of panic disorder (APA, 2013).

Even though many people with PD seek medical treatment prior to psychological treatment, medical examinations can provide beneficial information regarding co-occurring medical concerns or conditions that might aggravate symptoms. During the initial period of assessment and treatment, a counselor may need to educate the client on the symptoms and treatments of panic disorders. This, in turn, will aid clients' ability to properly monitor and self-intervene. In addition, counselors must also be aware of clients' past and current negative life events, coping styles, and their overall impairment in functioning. Each of these factors plays a significant role in the progression of the disorder and the clients' response to treatment.

Treatment Models and Interventions

A number of randomized controlled trials (RCTs) have been conducted on treatments for PD. These RCTs suggest that cognitive behavioral therapy and panic control therapy are the most effective in treating PD accompanied by mild agoraphobia (i.e., an intense fear or anxiety triggered by actual or anticipated exposure to different situations which include being in public and engaging in various activities). Situational in vivo exposure therapy is most useful with those who have PD and more significant levels of agoraphobia (Barlow et al., 2007). The similarities between cognitive behavioral therapy and panic control therapy include: education about anxiety and panic symptoms, cognitive therapy, and some blending of exposure therapy with coping skills (Barlow et al., 2007). Cognitive behavioral therapy, panic control therapy, medication, and several emerging approaches (e.g., acceptance and commitment therapy, sensation-focused intensive treatment, exercise) will be discussed in this section. Situational in vivo exposure therapy will be addressed in the agoraphobia and phobia sections of this chapter and should be incorporated into these approaches when warranted.

COGNITIVE BEHAVIORAL THERAPY (CBT)   As applied to treating those with PD, CBT (Beck & Emery, 2005; Koemer, Vorstenbosch, & Antony, 2012) aims to address distorted and dysfunctional thoughts related to panic attacks by identifying, challenging, and modifying these ideas. In applying a CBT approach, counselors must first gather information related to the nature of the panic attacks (e.g., locations, symptoms) and provide a psychoeducational component to teach clients about their natural responses to fear and attacks. Counselors can use Socratic questioning to highlight the fundamental beliefs and ideas related to the attacks (e.g., Why do you believe this thought? Is there reason to doubt this belief? How do these thoughts affect your physical responses?). The validity of irrational and maladaptive thoughts are tested and subsequently replaced with more functional thoughts. For example, an individual may be hesitant about going out to dinner with a friend because he or she thinks, "Restaurants make me anxious and I will probably end up having a panic attack." When the validity of this idea is tested, the individual may realize that he or she has never experienced a full-blown panic attack in a restaurant before.

The client can then adopt a more realistic thought (e.g., "I may become anxious, but that is okay. I have never had a panic attack in a restaurant, and I will be able to manage my anxiety"). CBT can also include in vivo exposure-based components (see the agoraphobia section for more detail on this treatment approach), which involves clients entering feared situations (e.g., driving in traffic) while applying the skills needed to counteract anxiety responses. Homework assignments, which involve clients identifying and challenging negative automatic thoughts when in these situations, are often given. For example, an individual may think, "I feel as if I am dying because I am having a hard time breathing." The homework assignment would involve the client finding evidence against the statement (e.g., "My lungs are inflating with each breath"; "I have been to the doctor and no respiratory issues were found"), and then prompting the client to replace the irrational belief with a more realistic statement (e.g., "I may be having a panic attack. While this is uncomfortable, I am not dying").

 Clinical Toolbox 5.4: In the Pearson etext, click here to view an example of a cognitive behavioral therapy form that can be used by clients to document panic attacks.

Panic control therapy (PCT) PCT is a cognitive behavioral approach that focuses on interoceptive (i.e., physiological) sensations that are similar to the symptoms that are experienced during panic attacks (Craske & Barlow, 2007). When using this approach, the client engages in controlled physical activities to induce panic-type physical symptoms. For example, running in place for 5 minutes would produce rapid heart rate; spinning while standing or sitting in a swivel chair would produce dizziness; and breathing through a slim straw would create the feeling of not getting enough air. Clients endure the induced symptoms without distracting themselves in order to learn that these symptoms are tolerable and will not lead to their worst fears (e.g., death, losing control). PCT also includes a cognitive restructuring component that targets clients' misconceptions about anxiety, panic, and their own overestimations of the threat and danger associated with these attacks. In addition, breathing retraining is incorporated by means of mediation, and calming exercises, which serve to correct the tendency to hyperventilate in panic situations. In utilizing this approach, counselors must be sure to (a) use protective measures to ensure the safety of the client when conducting interoceptive activities, and (b) refrain from allowing a client to over utilize these breathing retraining techniques because this can be a form of avoidance behaviors and thus dilute the intended effects of the interoceptive activities.

Acceptance and Commitment Therapy (ACT) ACT is a cognitive behavioral therapy that incorporates acceptance, mindfulness, and behavior-change strategies (Hayes et al., 2012). It is an emerging treatment (i.e., at this time no randomized controlled trials exist) for panic disorder. It is based on a model that promotes the enhancement of cognitive flexibility and behavior change. The "hexaflex" model is based on the idea that six processes contribute to healthy, flexible living, including (a) attention to the present moment, (b) acceptance, (c) defusion (i.e., the ability to "step back" and separate from thoughts and language), (d) self-as-context (i.e., realization that you are not your thoughts, feelings, and memories; although they are a part of you, they are not the essence of who you are),

accept and seperate self from anxiety; change strategies

(e) values (i.e., what we find meaningful in life), and (f) committed action (i.e., setting goals according to values and carrying them out in a responsible way). When one or more of these aspects of the hexaflex model are absent, people risk psychological rigidity. The premise of ACT is that psychological pain is a natural consequence of living; however, psychological rigidity is the cause of unnecessary suffering and maladaptive functioning.

> **Clinical Toolbox 5.5:** In the Pearson etext, click here to read more about Acceptance and Commitment Therapy treatment goals and phases of treatment.

Sensation-Focused Intensive Treatment (SFIT) SFIT is an 8-day intensive treatment program aimed at treating those with PD and moderate to severe agoraphobia (Britran, Morissette, Spiegel, & Barlow, 2008; Morissette, Spiegel, & Heinrichs, 2005). This program utilizes CBT and exposure therapy (e.g., exposure to the feared situation while using relaxation skills) that is intentionally direct in nature: exposing clients to their fear sensations and agoraphobic avoidance without teaching anxiety-reducing techniques (Morissette et al., 2005). Through the use of exposure therapy, an individual's anxiety peaks and then eventually dissipates, resulting in symptom reduction because of the withstanding of the anxiety-provoking situation. SFIT has been demonstrated to decrease panic symptoms and avoidance behaviors (Britran et al., 2008). SFIT is an intensive, time-consuming treatment intervention that requires a client to dedicate at least 8 hours a day to treatment (i.e., individual sessions, group sessions, and out-of-session homework assignments).

EXERCISE An emerging line of research (e.g., Antony, Roth Ledley, Liss, & Swinson, 2006; Smits, Powers, Berry, & Otto, 2007) suggests that exercise can be used to decrease panic symptoms. People with PD may avoid exercise because the physical effects (e.g., increased heart rate, sweating, changes in breathing) can mimic panic attack symptoms. Exercise may significantly impact clients' perceptions of their physiological sensations by altering their level of association with these symptoms and ultimately diminishing their own fear of these attacks. When considering exercise as an intervention, counselors need to ensure that clients have been medically evaluated (i.e., been cleared to utilize aerobic exercise) and must construct a moderate to intense workout plan (i.e., 2 to 4 times a week for at least 30 minutes each time) that lasts at least 4 weeks in duration, and is approved and monitored by a medical professional (Smits et al., 2007).

PSYCHOPHARMACOTHERAPY Selective serotonin reuptake inhibitors (SSRIs; e.g., paroxetine, sertraline, fluvoxamine, fluoxetine, citalopram, escitalopram), tricyclic antidepressants (e.g., imipramine, clomipramine), and benzodiazepines (e.g., lorazepam, diazepam) have demonstrated effectiveness in the treatment of PD (Ravindran & Stein, 2010; Roy-Byrne & Cowley, 2007). SSRIs alter levels of serotonin and aid cell communication in the brain. They are now considered a first-line agent for the treatment of anxiety disorders over both tricyclic antidepressants and benzodiazepines (Roy-Byrne & Cowley, 2007). Prozac, Paxil, and Zoloft are examples of SSRI medications approved by the FDA to treat PD.

Tricyclic antidepressants are often helpful in the overall reduction of panic attacks, yet are less robust at diminishing anticipatory anxiety and avoidance behaviors. Clients often have a poorer tolerance for these types of medications (over SSRIs) due to the side effects of jitteriness and weight gain (Roy-Byrne & Cowley, 2007).

Benzodiazepines are the most commonly prescribed class of anxiolytics (antianxiety medications) and are usually prescribed for short periods of time secondary to their highly addictive nature. Benzodiazepines slow down the central nervous system and provide fast-acting relief from panic symptoms. Xanax, Valium, and Ativan are all approved by the FDA for use in treating PD. Both SSRIs and benzodiazepines have shown reductions in anticipatory anxiety, avoidance behaviors, and the frequency of panic attacks.

Prognosis

If utilizing evidence-based approaches such as CBT and PCT, the prognosis for people with PD is excellent (Barlow et al., 2007). When counselors incorporate client education about the anxiety and panic symptoms, cognitive therapy, some blending of exposure therapy, and coping skill development, clients' symptomology is significantly reduced (i.e., often with panic-free rates in 70–80% of those with PD; 50–70% for those with PD with mild agoraphobia), and results are often maintained (e.g., at 2-year follow-ups; Barlow, 2008).

SPECIFIC PHOBIA

Description of the Disorder and Typical Client Characteristics

Specific phobias (SP) are found in approximately 8% of the population, with lower prevalence rates in the older adult population (APA, 2013). SPs are twice as likely to be found in women as they are in men (Nathan & Gorman, 2007). Most people who have a SP have either animal (e.g., snake phobia), natural environment (e.g., tornado phobia), situational (e.g., fear of small confined spaces), or the blood-injection-injury phobia subtypes (APA, 2013).

People with SPs experience persistent and unreasonable fears in response to the presence or the anticipation of a particular object, event, or situation (APA, 2013). These fears are dealt with in dysfunctional ways (e.g., avoidance, self-medication, refusal to leave home), which cause significant distress and impairment in relationships and everyday functioning (Nathan & Gorman, 2007). They typically realize their fears are irrational, and they endure anticipatory anxiety, panic attacks, and even fainting when thinking about, or being exposed, to a particular object, event, or situation. Unlike panic disorder, these attacks are associated with a specific trigger and are typically cued directly by the object, event, or situation. The fear and overall level of anxiety is generally related to both the degree of proximity to the stimulus and the degree to which escape from the object or situation is limited. Often, children are less aware of the unreasonable nature of their fears, and their responses may take the form of crying, freezing, clinging, or tantrums.

 Clinical Toolbox 5.6: In the Pearson etext, click here to read about different categories or types of phobias.

People with specific phobias may become easily agitated, irritable, and can experience emotional breakdowns (e.g., become tearful, outraged) when confronted with the feared object, event, or situation. They may experience a number of physical reactions that are often associated with panic attacks (e.g., shortness of breath, palpitations, nausea). This presentation may appear diagnostically unclear and resemble other types of conditions, such as panic disorder, obsessive-compulsive disorder, post-traumatic stress disorder, and illness anxiety disorder (Daitch, 2011).

Those who have specific phobias, social anxiety disorder, and panic disorder all tend to avoid particular situations or endure them under significant distress. Being prone to panic attacks, people with SP will only experience them in anticipation or in the face of the specific object, event, or situation. If a panic attack ensues, it is in response to the feared stimulus, unlike PD in which panic attacks can seem to arise spontaneously.

An individual can acquire a particular phobia in a host of ways: a negative association with the object or situation, unexpected panic attacks in the face of the feared stimulus, observation of others experiencing distress in a situation (e.g., social learning), or by means of information transmission. However, specific phobias typically begin in childhood or early adolescence, occurring at younger ages for women than men (APA, 2013). Early development of a specific phobia has not been found to relate to the development of other psychological disorders (Daitch, 2011). In fact, the diagnosis of SP has lower rates of comorbidity than many other diagnoses (Nathan & Gorman, 2007), even though phobias are sometimes accompanied by anxiety, depressive, and substance-related disorders. The diagnosis of a SP increases the likelihood that another phobia within the same category will develop (Daitch, 2011).

Counselor Considerations

It is usually when the avoidance symptoms begin to significantly interfere with everyday functioning that this population seeks treatment (NIMH, 2009). In fact, most people will only seek treatment for their phobia after getting into treatment for another difficulty (Daitch, 2011). Therefore, many cases of SP may go untreated.

A counselor who is accepting, supportive, and who models a calm demeanor while still encouraging an individual to tolerate distressing experiences, is the most ideal. Counselors must ensure that their clients are safe when engaging in exposure interventions (i.e., treatments that present clients with the objects, events, or situations they fear). This exposure can be gradual, virtual, or all at once (flooding); nonetheless, it requires a counselor to be concurrently supportive and encouraging. For example, blood-injection-injury phobias have the potential to make clients faint when exposed to the feared stimulus, so physical strategies must be put into place in order to ensure that an individual's safety is maintained. Counselors need to be creative, accommodating, and emotionally present, tolerating objects and situations with clients, to complete exposure experiences.

Treatment Models and Interventions

A number of randomized controlled trials (RCTs) exist in the literature on treating SP, and they indicate that exposure therapy, namely in vivo exposure, is an effective treatment (Antony & Barlow, 2002; Barlow et al., 2007). In vivo exposure (i.e., exposure to feared stimulus) is considered to be the most effective and powerful means for addressing SP, and imaginal exposure should only be considered for use in treatment when in vivo exposure is not feasible (Barlow, 2002; Barlow et al., 2007). Therefore, in vivo exposure will be the only treatment covered in this section.

EXPOSURE THERAPY (IN VIVO) Exposure-based treatment approaches are often implemented in the context of behavior or cognitive behavioral treatments and aim to help clients confront the feared stimulus in a gradual and repeated manner until the stimulus no longer evokes anxiety (Barlow et al., 2007). Counselors using exposure therapy encourage clients to enter and remain in situations so they can learn to tolerate their fear, learn that fear will subside without avoiding it, and learn that the outcome will not be as terrible as they imagined. With help from the counselor, a hierarchy is developed, starting with the least anxiety-provoking encounters and building to more feared situations. For example, a person who has a spider phobia may begin by looking at a picture of a spider, work to be in the same room as a spider in a sealed container, and eventually work up to touching a spider. A practical way to help clients rank anxiety-provoking stimuli is to use the subjective units of discomfort scale (SUDS; Wolpe, 1990). Ratings range from 1 to 10, with higher numbers signifying greater distress, and lower numbers indicating little or no distress. Next, clients list distressing situations in order of least to most anxiety-provoking. This hierarchy is utilized to initiate exposure treatment, which involves clients remaining in each of these situations until their SUDS/ distress ratings decrease to acceptable levels. At the point their distress is manageable with a given activity, they move to the next activity on their hierarchy. The goal SUDS/distress rating for mastery would be 0 (i.e., no distress), whereas for appropriate coping, a decrease of a few subjective rating points (e.g., from an 8 to a 5) may be acceptable (Cormier, Nurius, & Osborn, 2013). In addition to clients rating their levels of subjective distress, counselors should explore clients' associated thoughts, feelings, and physical reactions throughout these exposure experiences.

> **Clinical Toolbox 5.7:** In the Pearson etext, click here to review a cognitive behavioral scale, the subjective units of distress scale (SUDS), which can be used by clients with anxiety to record their distress, thoughts, feelings, and physical reactions.

Exposure works best when it occurs frequently (i.e., numerous times per week) and when the duration of sessions is long enough to decrease anxiety (i.e., up to two hours). Guided mastery or participant modeling occurs when the counselor actively models each step in the exposure and teaches the client how to interact with the feared object or situation.

Although exposure treatments seem to be relatively straightforward, there are a number of considerations that should be addressed when utilizing this approach. Such factors include the duration of exposure, counselor directiveness, and other additional components that may need to be incorporated into an exposure treatment approach (Barlow et al., 2007). Prolonged exposure of the anxiety-provoking object or situation appears to be the most significant predictor in positive treatment outcomes. In addition, exposure activities in which the counselor is readily available to direct and coach the client are significantly more useful for decreasing phobic symptomology. Finally, exposure treatments need to be tailored to each client's unique needs. For example, clients suffering from injection phobias often faint (due to the sudden drop of their heart rate) at the sight of needles; therefore, counselors may need to teach *applied tension* (tensing all muscle groups for 15 seconds and continually repeating) to aid in sustained heart rate before, during, and secondary to an injection (Barlow et al., 2007).

> **Clinical Toolbox 5.8:** In the Pearson etext, click here to watch an exposure therapy demonstration.

PSYCHOPHARMACOTHERAPY No psychopharmacotherapy interventions are demonstrated to be effective in treating specific phobia (Roy-Byrne & Cowley, 2007), although some antianxiety medications are used with benzodiazepines being the most common (Ravindran & Stein, 2010). Benzodiazepines provide fast-acting relief from anxiety and promote a more relaxed state. However, medications like anxiolytics and benzodiazepines can sometimes be counterproductive to exposure-based approaches because they reduce the anxiety level required for these approaches to work effectively. These medications are most helpful when used on an as-needed basis. Ativan, Valium, and Xanax are the most commonly prescribed benzodiazepines used to treat SP.

Prognosis

When counselors use exposure therapies, especially in vivo exposure, the prognosis for those with specific phobias is excellent (Barlow et al., 2007). While significant improvements are often experienced, some relapse can occur over time, and relapse prevention should be a part of any treatment plan.

AGORAPHOBIA

Description of the Disorder and Typical Client Characteristics

Agoraphobia affects approximately 2% of the population, and is diagnosed nearly twice as often in women as in men, (APA, 2013). While there is some debate as to whether agoraphobia can exist without panic (Barlow et al., 2007), the *DSM-5* classifies agoraphobia as a separate phobic disorder not requiring that panic attacks be present. Clients may fear panic-like symptoms, and may also fear humiliating and debilitating symptoms (e.g., fear of incontinence, fear of falling; APA, 2013). Therefore, if clients present with both agoraphobia and panic attack symptomology both are diagnosed as separate diagnoses.

Most people who do experience panic attacks do so by late adolescence or early adulthood (Barlow, 2008), with approximately three-fourths of people having their first panic attack by age 40 (Kessler et al., 2005); therefore, agoraphobia often begins to develop in people's twenties or thirties. In some cases, as panic history lengthens, the risk for developing agoraphobia increases; however, some clients may have long panic disorder histories without ever developing agoraphobia (Barlow, 2008).

Agoraphobia refers to the avoidance, or endurance with extreme distress, of situations from which escape may be difficult or embarrassing, or those in which help may be unavailable if a panic attack or panic-like symptoms should occur (APA, 2013). Situations that typically produce agoraphobic responses include shopping malls, crowded restaurants, traveling by car or public transportation, and being alone. These situations often act as a trigger for ensuing emotional and physical anxiety symptoms (i.e., shortness of breath, dizziness, and faintness). There are varying degrees of agoraphobia, including mild, moderate, and severe, and each degree's presentation differs in restrictive and in associated avoidance behaviors (Barlow, 2008).

Those with mild agoraphobia may experience anxiety when going into crowded places or when driving alone. However, they will endure these situations and accommodate as necessary, rather than avoiding them completely (e.g., sitting at the end of a row at a movie theater). Those with moderate agoraphobia are much more restricted in their activities and demonstrate more avoidance than accommodation behaviors (e.g., only going to the grocery store during nonbusy times, only driving a car a certain number of miles from their home). People with severe agoraphobia, however, completely avoid such settings. Places and activities may become so restricted that they become housebound.

This population's apprehension and fear leads to significant restriction of movements, with frequent refusal to enter situations in which escape may be difficult (e.g., cars, planes, elevators, supermarkets). A reliance on safe places (e.g., often their home) and safe individuals (e.g., family member, significant other) may inadvertently contribute to their continued avoidance behaviors. Those with agoraphobia may also avoid any activities that produce similar physical sensations resembling panic attacks such as sex or exercise (White & Barlow, 2002). People with agoraphobia frequently self-medicate in an attempt to reduce anxiety and may consequently develop substance use problems (Mathew et al., 2011). Agoraphobia is often comorbid with other disorders, such as social anxiety disorder, specific phobia, generalized anxiety disorder, major depressive disorder, and some personality disorders (e.g., avoidant, dependent; Barlow, 2008; Meyer & Deitsch, 1996).

Counselor Considerations

As with the treatment of other anxiety disorders, counselors should facilitate a warm and supportive environment. Early on, the expectations for treatment should be outlined and the client should be educated about the discomfort that may result from situational exposure. Empathy and information gathering should be the focus during the early stages of treatment, while a more directive and confronting role is useful in the latter portions of treatment (Barlow, 2008).

A thorough evaluation of the contextual factors, frequency, severity, and subjective experience of the feared situations should be conducted. This assessment should highlight the level of fear related to each situation, as well as the impact of avoidance on the individual's everyday functioning. The counselor should also assess for any comorbid disorders, as these will influence treatment goals. Agoraphobia's presentation and prevalence do not seem to vary significantly between cultures, although males with agoraphobia tend to have higher comorbidity with substance use disorders (APA, 2013). Counselors must be aware of any past or current negative life events and the individual's coping styles, as these will inevitably impact his or her response to treatment.

Agoraphobia treatment induces a great deal of client anxiety, so counselors need to be accepting and supportive, while also encouraging clients' ability to tolerate distressing experiences. Counselors must ensure that clients are safe when engaging in situational exposure interventions and should offer continual support and encouragement throughout the treatment process, recognizing the distress being endured at each stage. Treatment must be fitted to the specific needs of the client. The involvement of significant others should also be considered, as these people can act as supportive coaches, increasing treatment adherence and the likelihood of favorable outcomes (Nathan & Gorman, 2007).

Treatment Models and Interventions

First, there are no psychopharmacotherapy interventions proven to be more effective than exposure and cognitive therapy in the treatment of agoraphobia (Roy-Byrne & Cowley, 2007; White & Barlow, 2002). When medications are utilized, medications like anxiolytics and benzodiazepines can be counterproductive to exposure-based approaches because they reduce the anxiety level required for these approaches to work effectively. Medication for treating agoraphobia may be beneficial in the short term, but it rarely has long-standing benefits, with high relapse rates usually following the discontinuation of medications.

There are a number of randomized controlled trials in the agoraphobia treatment literature, and they suggest that in vivo exposure (e.g., often integrating a cognitive therapy approach) is the most evidence-based treatment approach (Barlow, 2002; Barlow et al., 2007). Imaginal exposure should only be considered when in vivo exposure is not feasible (Barlow, 2002; Barlow et al., 2007). Because imaginal exposure has been shown to be significantly less effective than in vivo exposure, only in vivo exposure will be covered in this section.

SITUATIONAL IN VIVO EXPOSURE This intervention is often implemented in the context of behavior or cognitive behavioral treatment and typically begins with the client determining various feared situations or activities that he or she tends to avoid (Barlow et al., 2007). Examples include eating in a restaurant, driving outside of one's safety zone, or shopping in a crowded store. With help from the counselor, a hierarchy is developed, ranging from least anxiety-provoking situations to highly feared situations. This typically involves identifying about 10 increasingly fearful situations. For example, if an individual wanted to be able to travel by bus from her or his home to the city and back, steps could include the following: travel the bus for one stop during a quiet time; travel for two stops during a quiet time; travel for two stops during a busy time; travel for four stops during a quiet time; travel for four stops during a busy time; and so on, until the individual could travel from his or her home to the city and back during rush hour.

Using coping strategies learned in sessions, clients are encouraged to enter and remain in these situations until their anxiety diminishes. Clients with mild to moderate agoraphobia are generally able to do this alone or with a trusted friend or family member, while those with more severe forms of the disorder may require the counselor to take part in exposure sessions.

Situational in vivo exposure combined with cognitive therapy can be another effective approach (Nathan & Gorman, 2007). A technique such as cognitive restructuring can teach clients to observe their automatic thinking, evaluate its accuracy, and challenge misassumptions. For example, if a client observed the thought, "Something horrible is probably going to happen on this bus ride and I will be trapped," the client could counter it with another thought, such as "Nothing has happened before when I traveled by bus," or "If I become anxious, it will eventually pass and I will be able to make it until my stop." In essence, clients learn to stop their downward, negative thinking when exposed to anxiety-provoking situations.

Flooding is a more prolonged exposure to feared stimuli that involves fewer sessions and longer exposure (e.g., several hours at a time). Through extended exposure, clients become less sensitive to the previously threatening stimuli. Their familiarity with the feared situation evokes progressively less anxiety, and they eventually habituate, or become desensitized to it. While this is a faster approach with superior efficacy at follow-up, dropout rates are significantly higher, and this approach is generally unpopular with those with agoraphobia (Barlow, 2008).

If clients present with mild agoraphobia due to panic attacks, counselors should consider utilizing CBT and panic control therapy. A combination of CBT with situational in vivo exposure therapy should be used with clients who present with more significant levels of agoraphobia (Barlow et al., 2007). When treating both agoraphobia and panic disorder concurrently, treatment should consist of education about the course and impact of anxiety and panic symptoms, cognitive therapy, social skills training, and some blending of exposure therapy with the development of coping skills (Barlow et al., 2007). As previously mentioned in the panic disorder section, the use of CBT, panic control therapy, acceptance and commitment therapy, and sensation-focused intensive treatment should be considered when treating PD in conjunction with agoraphobia.

Prognosis

The prognosis in those with moderate to severe agoraphobia is slightly less favorable than for those with mild agoraphobia; however, approximately 60 to 75% of clients who complete situational in vivo exposure treatments show significant reductions in avoidance behaviors (Nathan & Gorman, 2007). There is evidence of continued improvement over time, particularly when significant others are involved in treatment (Barlow, 2008).

SOCIAL ANXIETY DISORDER

Description of the Disorder and Typical Client Characteristics

Social anxiety disorder is one of the most prevalent anxiety disorders and is the fourth most common of all mental disorders (Clark & Beck, 2010; Kessler et al., 2005). While women are affected slightly more than men, prevalence rates for the US adult population are approximately 7% (APA, 2013).

People with social anxiety disorder experience intense anxiety and excessive self-consciousness in social situations (APA, 2013). This population experiences an extreme and chronic fear of being scrutinized and judged by others, fearing they will inevitably do something that will lead to embarrassment, humiliation, and shame (Beck, Emery, & Greenburgh, 2005). Those with social anxiety disorder maintain high levels of self-consciousness; they wish to make a certain impression on others, but doubt that they will be able to do so (Beck et al., 2005; Hofmann & Barlow, 2002). They are highly inhibited, tend to appear rigid, and find it difficult to articulate points and positions in conversations with others (Clark & Beck, 2010).

The hallmark of social anxiety disorder is the fear of negative evaluation in social situations. Commonly, these social situations include public speaking, interviews, running and facilitating meetings, taking examinations, attending social gatherings, and interacting with powerful, influential people. Performance-specific social anxiety disorder involves all situations in which an individual must speak or perform in front of others and evaluation is possible.

When people with this disorder sense that evaluation is inevitable, they experience physical reactions (e.g., sweating, blushing, trembling, accelerated heart rate) and cognitive symptoms (e.g., feelings of losing control, performance anxiety). These physical symptoms compound the distress, causing them to fear that their anxiety is obvious to others, and reinforces their belief that they may lose control over the symptoms and thus endure further negative evaluation. Inevitably, this increased anxiety and embarrassment translates into a sense of shame, which causes them to attribute rejection or loss of social standing to their own personal qualities and behaviors (Gilbert, 2000).

Those with social anxiety disorder can perseverate for days or weeks before a social situation, which significantly impairs their ability to function in these social situations. They frequently have difficulties with educational attainment, work productivity, career advancement, and overall functioning (Zhang, Ross, & Davidson, 2004). Because of their negative self-concepts and preoccupation with social situations, they may also have difficulty making, maintaining, and keeping friends.

Negative life events, such as physical or sexual abuse, conflict in the family of origin, and lack of a close relationship with an adult, are associated with the development of social anxiety disorder (Chartier, Walker, & Stein, 2001). Parents and caregivers of those with social anxiety disorder are sometimes reported to be emotionally distant and less likely to encourage social engagement with others (Harvey, Ehlers, & Clark, 2005). Therefore, those with social anxiety disorder tend to have fewer relationships throughout their lives and may develop an interpersonal style that can produce negative reactions from others; this pattern can perpetuate the cycle of social anxiety (Alden & Taylor, 2004). Children with social anxiety disorder often exhibit selective mutism, school refusal, and even separation anxiety.

Although people with social anxiety disorder are often considered to be shy (Stravynski, 2007), shyness is a normal personality trait that is more common, less chronic, associated with fewer avoidance behaviors, and is not typically debilitating (Beidel & Turner, 2007). Similar to those with other anxiety disorders, those with social anxiety disorder recognize that their fears are irrational; however, they still have significant trouble tolerating, managing, and overcoming their fear of social situations.

This population often meets the criteria for another mental health diagnosis (i.e., 70–80%), which can include major depressive disorder, persistent depressive disorder, substance abuse, obsessive-compulsive disorder, additional anxiety disorders (Barlow, 2008; Nathan & Gorman, 2007), and avoidant personality disorder (van Velzen, Emmelkamp, & Scholing, 2000).

Counselor Considerations

Despite the unfavorable consequences of social anxiety disorder, many people with this disorder are unlikely to seek treatment because of their self-consciousness and fear of embarrassment (Clark & Beck, 2010). When they do seek treatment, they do not often fully disclose the spectrum of their symptoms and difficulties, usually bringing physical concerns or depressive complaints to the foreground.

Counselors should recognize that people with social anxiety disorder have generally established a pervasive pattern of avoidant behaviors, which are distinct from typical shyness seen in the general population. Counselors need to consider that these clients bring their discomfort and extreme fears into the therapeutic relationship; thus, the building of trust and rapport is paramount if treatment is to progress. Counselors working with this population need to convey empathy, availability, acceptance, and support, and build upon the individual's strengths and the courage that brought them into treatment.

Counselors should also recognize that the process of building rapport and progressing through treatment might be slow. This may be the result of clients' avoidant behaviors (e.g., not attending sessions, coming in late, or not coming prepared for sessions out of fear of completing tasks "wrong" and being embarrassed). Counselors need to utilize these avoidance opportunities and be supportive while also enhancing clients' awareness of the feelings, attitudes, and behaviors which relate to their avoidance. Counselors need to assess the clients' ability to adequately deal with the evaluation inherent in completing homework assignments and consider implementing them gradually (McNeil, 2001). Counselors should monitor their own internal reactions and balance their expectations for treatment with the severity of the symptomology. By having realistic change expectations, highlighting progress at multiple stages of treatment, and facilitating rapport and trust, counselors can help empower clients.

Treatment Models and Interventions

A number of randomized controlled trials exist for the treatment of social anxiety disorder. Although exposure therapy is an effective stand-alone treatment for social anxiety, CBT that incorporates social skills training, relaxation training, and exposure-based methods appears to be the most effective treatment for social anxiety disorder (Barlow et al., 2007; Wong, Gordon, & Heimberg, 2012). This type of CBT approach (i.e., with social skills training, relaxation training, and exposure-based methods) appears to produce greater, more sustained long-term gains than exposure therapy alone (Wong et al., 2012). Additionally, acceptance and commitment therapy and group therapy appear to hold promise in treating social anxiety.

COGNITIVE BEHAVIORAL TREATMENTS (CBT)   CBT approaches for social anxiety disorder aim to address clients' anxiety-provoking thoughts related to social and performance situations (Beck et al., 2005). According to CBT, since thoughts, feelings, and behaviors are interrelated, changing one will then alter another. For example, altering thoughts related to negative evaluation will lead to less distress and a greater likelihood of engaging with others. Therefore, the goal of CBT, as related to social anxiety, is to help clients identify and change catastrophic thinking patterns about being negatively scrutinized by others and feeling embarrassed by performing inadequately. For those with social anxiety, a more gradual approach is needed to make the implementation of adaptive thoughts more automatic. This cognitive restructuring is intended to address clients' maladaptive thought patterns (i.e., examining thoughts/beliefs, evidence-review of accuracy, and behavioral experimentation of alternative and more accurate thoughts/beliefs), and their avoidance behaviors that are continually maintaining their social anxiety. Social effectiveness training, relaxation training, and exposure methods are behavioral treatment interventions that can be integrated into a CBT treatment model when treating social anxiety disorder. Each will be briefly described below.

Social Effectiveness Therapy (SET)   Not all people with social anxiety lack adequate social skills. However, for those with such deficits, SET can teach them how to initiate, maintain, and broaden the range of their interpersonal interactions. SET is a 28-session individual treatment that includes psychoeducation (i.e., nature of social fears and anxiety), social flexibility exercises (i.e., socially oriented tasks that promote the social engagement of the individual), modeling, role-plays, and imaginal and in vivo exposure (Turner, Beidel, Cooley, Woody, & Messer, 1994). In addition, weekly homework assignments are given as a supplement to counseling sessions. The corrective feedback and positive reinforcement from the counselor can enhance the development of each targeted skill. Social skills training works most effectively when it is used in combination with other therapies (e.g., CBT, exposure).

Relaxation Training Relaxation training is rooted in behavior therapy principles and includes any technique or process that aids an individual in reducing his or her anxiety, thus reaching a more relaxed state. This training has not been deemed to be an appropriate stand-alone treatment for social anxiety disorder, but it is an appropriate complement to CBT approaches that utilize social effectiveness therapy and exposure-based interventions (Barlow et al., 2007). For people with social anxiety disorder, this relaxation training usually consists of progressive muscle relaxation, deep breathing, and applied relaxation (i.e., relaxation techniques are utilized in role plays that relate to social situations).

Exposure-Based Interventions Exposure-based interventions are rooted in the behavioral component of CBT, and these methods include decreasing the avoidance behaviors (i.e., not entering a situation or not entering it fully) by encouraging clients to engage and remain in anxiety-provoking social situations. With help from the counselor, a hierarchy is developed, starting with the least anxiety-provoking settings and building up to more feared social situations. These exposure methods can be imaginal (i.e., use of imagery to envision the feared situation), in vivo in session (e.g., directly confronting fearful situations in session), and/or in vivo outside of sessions (e.g., homework assignments to confront fearful situations directly). Exposure is usually done in a gradual, systematic manner until clients can remain in a feared situation with minimal anxiety. This technique is based on classical conditioning principles, which suggest that through the toleration of increased exposure (i.e., anxiety-provoking situations), the process of extinction (i.e., extinguishing of a behavior) and habituation (i.e., a decrease response to a stimulus after repeated exposure) occurs.

CREATIVE TOOLBOX ACTIVITY 5.1 The Confidence Stone

Matthew J. Paylo, PhD, LPCC-S

Activity Overview

This creative intervention is a type of grounding activity in which clients use an object to connect with a sense of calm and safety when in situations in which they are psychologically activated. Clients learn to associate relaxation with an object (e.g., a rock) in the midst of anxiety-provoking situations. This activity can be used with any client who feels overwhelmed (e.g., PTSD symptoms such as flashbacks, social anxiety disorder symptoms, panic attacks).

Treatment Goal(s) Addressed

The primary goals of this activity are to help clients (a) learn and utilize mindfulness behaviors in the midst of an anxiety-provoking situation; (b) learn and utilize deep-breathing exercises in the midst of an anxiety-provoking situation; and, (c) tolerate anxiety-provoking situations in real-life settings rather than avoiding them.

Directions

1. Ascertain client preparedness to engage in this creative intervention. This intervention may be inappropriate for clients who are not grounded in reality.
2. Purchase or otherwise acquire a number of rocks (synthetic gemstones are alternative materials) that are small enough to fit in the palm of a hand.
3. Ask the client to select a rock of his or her liking from the collection. This rock could be painted and decorated by the client to create a more meaningful connection with it.
4. Ask the client to place the rock in his or her pocket.
5. At this time, suggest the client imagine being in the midst of an anxiety-provoking situation. This should be specific to the client's concerns and issues in treatment. Then walk the client through a deep-breathing exercise. Ask the client to breathe in (four counts), hold for a second, and then exhale (four counts) through the nose.
6. Concurrently, ask the client to either (a) bring out the rock and grip it in her or his hand, or (b) put her or his hand in the pocket and grip the rock. Ask the client to mindfully visualize the anxiety being absorbed by this rock.
7. After the client has mastered this process within sessions, ask the client to practice this intervention in a real-life situation. Process this homework assignment in the following session.

Process Questions

1. What was this exercise like for you?
2. What did it feel like to be utilizing deep breathing in those situations?
3. How did it feel to have all of your anxiety absorbed by the rock?
4. What did you notice about how your thoughts changed as the rock absorbed the anxiety?
5. What was the most and/or least challenging aspect of this activity for you?
6. How and when can you use the rock to help you connect with feelings of relaxation and security?

ACCEPTANCE AND COMMITMENT THERAPY (ACT) ACT is an emerging cognitive behavioral treatment for those with social anxiety disorder (Brady & Whitman, 2012; Hayes et al., 2012; Herbert & Cardaciotto, 2005). People with this disorder have a tendency to restrict their engagement in meaningful relationships in order to avoid negative internal experiences. ACT draws on metaphors and mindfulness exercises to change clients' relationships with their internal experiences (Phase 1). It promotes acceptance and being in the present moment (i.e., being a mindful observer) rather than a focus on future-oriented thoughts or concerns. Clients are encouraged to notice their emotional responses, tolerate discomfort, and ultimately engage in valued activities. They learn to see anxiety for what it is, learn the cost of trying to control it, learn to differentiate it from the self, and learn how to act in accordance with their values. This phase involves two primary components: acceptance and distancing (e.g., "I am having an anxious thought related to this interaction" vs. "I am an anxious person who cannot relate to others"), and commitment and change (e.g., engages in relationships that are deemed valuable). Counselors help clients to identify their values and present actions with the goal of reducing the discrepancy (Phases 2 and 3). The client takes part in exposure exercises (e.g., paradoxes, mindfulness practice) to learn how to be in the presence of anxiety so that anxiety is no longer a barrier to valued relationships and living.

COGNITIVE BEHAVIORAL GROUP THERAPY (CBGT)   CBGT is a 12-session treatment that incorporates elements of cognitive restructuring and exposure to feared situations through group therapy, which is, by definition, an experience that forces social interaction and exposures (Heimberg, 1991, 2002). The first two sessions are psychoeducational in nature and teach clients about the basic tenets of cognitive therapy, namely the relationship between irrational thoughts about social situations and anxiety. Clients are provided an opportunity to identify, evaluate, and dispute their own maladaptive thoughts. The remaining 10 sessions focus on the development of concrete behavioral goals, exposure exercises, and the delegation or review of homework assignments. Exposure exercises are tailored to group members based on their individualized hierarchies. The group format allows for ongoing in vivo—real-time exposure, as well as an opportunity to normalize experiences and receive feedback from group members. This approach is promising, yet it needs further validation of its effectiveness.

PSYCHOPHARMACOTHERAPY   Selective serotonin reuptake inhibitors (SSRIs; e.g., fluvoxamine, sertraline, paroxetine), serotonin norepinephrine reuptake inhibitors (SNRIs; e.g., venlafaxine) and benzodiazepines (e.g., clonazepam, alprazolam) have demonstrated effectiveness in the treatment of social anxiety disorder (Roy-Byrne & Cowley, 2007). Paxil, Zoloft, Luvox (i.e., SSRIs) and Effexor (i.e., SNRI) are usually the first medications utilized and are approved by the FDA for the treatment of SAD. Klonopin and Xanax (i.e., benzodiazepines) are also commonly prescribed to help control anxiety in anxiety-provoking social situations. As mentioned previously, the use of benzodiazepines can be addictive for some clients and have been associated with higher rates of comorbid alcohol abuse (Roy-Byrne & Cowley, 2007). This makes SSRIs and SNRIs a more logical medication choice given the side effects of benzodiazepines. Currently, there are no FDA-approved medications for the treatment of social anxiety disorder in children.

Prognosis

The prognosis for social anxiety disorder is good and is most promising when cognitive strategies are combined with exposure methods (Nathan & Gorman, 2007). For some clients, the integration of social skills training and relaxation (i.e., applied relaxation) into treatment can also enhance the long-term prognosis (Nathan & Gorman, 2007).

SEPARATION ANXIETY DISORDER

Description of the Disorder and Typical Client Characteristics

Separation anxiety disorder (SAD) is found in approximately 0.9–1.9% of the US adult population, and in 4% of children (APA, 2013), with lower prevalence rates in older adults. Females are slightly more likely than males to have SAD (National Comorbidity Survey, 2007).

Those diagnosed with SAD experience intense fear and worry related to leaving their home or being removed from their primary attachment figures (APA, 2013). SAD can be diagnosed in adults, although it is more frequently observed in children and adolescents (APA, 2013). While many children experience separation anxiety throughout their development in childhood, those with SAD suffer from a debilitating anxiety that impairs their abilities to function personally, socially, and academically. When these children are separated from attachment figures, they are preoccupied with worry about the figures' whereabouts, long to be reunited, and often entertain reunion fantasies. Their worries are rooted in the assumption that illness, abduction, or accidents will befall these attachment figures. This assumption leads these children to assume they will be left, lost, or separated from these figures, which inevitably causes them to be reluctant to go places, to be left alone, or to go to sleep without these people close to them.

Children with SAD often endure repeated nightmares related to separations, refuse to sleep alone, or attempt to sleep in their parents' (guardians') beds. They also frequently report physical complaints, such as headaches, stomachaches, and nausea, which are the physical manifestations of their worry and anxiety. Older clients with SAD may complain of cardiovascular symptoms, such as dizziness, light-headedness, and even heart palpitations.

Children typically appear to be "clingy" with their caregivers and will forgo experiences with their peers in order to stay in contact with these attachment figures. Children with SAD may come to the school nurse with somatic complaints (i.e., stomachaches, dizziness, and headaches) in an attempt to call home or have their attachment figures intervene. These behaviors and fears often create absenteeism and indirectly affect the children's academic and social success. Additionally, those with SAD often have other coexisting struggles related to mood, conduct, impulse control, and attention; struggles which exacerbate and complicate the symptoms of separation anxiety.

Developmentally, all children wrestle with the issues of separation and individuation. As they attempt to establish their sense of self, they also attempt to distinguish themselves from their attachment figures (Kins, Beyers, & Soenens, 2013; Mahler, Pine, & Bergman, 1975). This happens in early childhood and adolescence and is marked by the balance of decreased psychological dependence from caregivers and a sense of connectedness with those loved ones. If appropriate individuation does not occur, they will inadequately cope with the developmental task of independence, and potentially have additional problems emerge later in life.

Counselor Considerations

As is true in all treatment, counselors need to work hard to create a climate of trust and safety in which the client feels accepted and rapport is cultivated. Validation of clients' experiences is especially important, as this has typically not been provided to them. The counselor must be aware that some children may have difficulties articulating and talking about their fears. They may also feel isolated and shameful if parents, siblings, teachers, and/or peers belittle their anxiety. Therefore, extra care must be taken when asking these children about the nature of their concerns; questions must be developmentally appropriate and reflect a sense of acceptance. Counselors should provide a consistent pattern to treatment and should provide choices in the process, as these will grant some control and indirectly promote a safe therapeutic environment.

Counselors also need to be flexible in the assessment process and they may find it helpful to do separate interviews with family members to evaluate the severity and onset of the anxiety (Kendall et al., 2010). Comprehensive interviews can provide a more complete picture of the course, onset, family dynamics, unintentional reinforcement of fearful thoughts, attempted interventions, and the child's coping skills. Counselors must be particularly attuned to parental overcontrol, criticism and rejection, anxious modeling, very low or very high family cohesion, high levels of conflict, and hostile sibling relationships, as these can all exacerbate the child's level of anxiety (Drake & Ginsburg, 2012). If parents engage in anxious modeling, this may inadvertently teach their child to be avoidant and anxious (Bogels & Brechman-Toussaint, 2006); therefore, inclusion of parent anxiety management may be beneficial in these instances. It is essential that counselors present as confident, directive, and model appropriate social skills and boundaries with the client and his or her family. Family counseling is often a component of treatment, so counselors must be comfortable with this modality. Conversely, counselors need to consider the value some cultures place on interdependence on family members, differentiating this core cultural belief from the conceptualization of separation anxiety disorder.

Treatment Models and Interventions

Little research is available on evidence-based approaches for treating those with SAD. Conceptually, since SAD can be considered a fear or phobic response (e.g., leaving a primary caregiver), such fears may be unlearned through the use of exposure therapy. While this approach is highly useful in the treatment of phobias, exposure therapy should be considered in conjunction with a multifaceted approach that includes CBT and family education (Sadock & Sadock, 2007). Research suggests that a CBT approach called Coping Cat may be useful in treating SAD in children (Kendall & Hedtke, 2006).

CBT (WITH EXPOSURE THERAPY): "COPING CAT"   Coping Cat is a manualized treatment for children ages 7 to 13 with generalized anxiety disorder, social anxiety disorder, or separation anxiety disorder (Kendall, Choudhury, Hudson, & Webb, 2006). This program aims to increase children's awareness of their reactions (i.e., emotional and physical) to anxiety, clarify their thoughts and feelings, develop more effective coping skills, and become more self-governing and reinforcing (Kendall & Hedtke, 2006). This program is highly structured, involving 16 sessions, with the first eight sessions being more psychoeducational, and the next eight sessions being more exposure-based. Games are utilized to help children learn how to identify signs of anxiety (i.e., facial expressions, gestures, body posture) and the various skills (e.g., self-talk, relaxation skills) that can be used to manage their anxiety. Counselors teach children that while it is reasonable to have anxiety, they can control these fears through their thinking and can utilize learned coping skills to tolerate and manage their anxiety, making their avoidance behaviors unnecessary.

In the exposure portion of treatment, children confront their feared situations through a gradual hierarchy. This is developed through their own "FEAR" plan. FEAR is an acronym for:

- "F" (Feeling Frightened?) addresses physiological responses to anxiety
- "E" (Expecting Bad Things to Happen?) helps children identify unhelpful, anxious thoughts

- "A" (Attitudes and Actions That Can Help) focuses on coping skills to utilize when experiencing anxiety (e.g., relaxation, helpful thoughts, problem solving)
- "R" (Results and Rewards) helps clients evaluate their performance in facing their feared situation

In addition to the psychoeducational, cognitive, and behavioral components of this approach, a family counseling approach is integrated into this model. If it appears that family members or a primary caregiver are exacerbating the symptoms or that their own mental illness is contributing to the child's anxiety, then boundary setting (i.e., facilitating the interactions of parents and child) should become another focus of treatment. Parental involvement is especially helpful when treating younger children.

PSYCHOPHARMACOTHERAPY   While there are currently no medications approved by the FDA for the treatment of SAD, SSRIs have historically been cautiously utilized in the treatment of anxiety disorders in children (Sadock & Sadock, 2007). More research is warranted on the usefulness of SSRIs with those diagnosed with SAD.

Prognosis

A large number of clients with SAD (i.e., approximately 70%) see significant symptom relief and remain symptom-free long after being treated with a multifaceted approach (e.g., cognitive behavioral, exposure, family education; Kendall et al., 2010). However, childhood anxiety can sometimes be a precursor for other anxiety disorders (e.g., panic disorder and agoraphobia) and personality disorders (e.g., avoidant, dependent; Evans et al., 2005) that have long-lasting effects on an individual's level of functioning. If left untreated, SAD can persist into adulthood and continue to impair clients' functioning throughout their lifespan (NIMH, 2009).

GENERALIZED ANXIETY DISORDER

Description of the Disorder and Typical Client Characteristics

Generalized anxiety disorder (GAD) is found in approximately 3% of the population (APA, 2013). Women are affected slightly more than men (National Comorbidity Survey, 2007). Prevalence rates for generalized anxiety disorder are lowest in older adults.

People with GAD worry excessively about activities and situations that revolve around everyday life, such as family, money, health, and work, most days without obvious precipitants (APA, 2013). This worry is difficult for clients to control, and they often anticipate disasters occurring within these domains (NIMH, 2009). Despite the realization that their concerns are unwarranted, people with GAD have trouble controlling their fears and excessive worrying. They have difficulty relaxing, concentrating, falling or staying asleep, and often are so hypervigilant that they startle easily. Their extreme anxiety often produces physical symptoms, such as headaches, restlessness, muscle tension, trembling, irritability, nausea, hot flashes, and fatigue, among others (APA, 2013).

The hallmark of this disorder is excessive, unwarranted worry. Worry encourages the avoidance of things and activities through the perseveration of negative emotions, somatic responses, and the reinforcement of mentally represented threats (Sibrava &

Borkovec, 2006). Although worry can have some adaptive functions (Watkins, 2008), it can become pathological and more pervasive, uncontrollable, time-consuming, narrow-focused, and biased to certain threats. The central component of maladaptive worry is the exaggerated anticipation of future events and potentially adverse outcomes (Clark & Beck, 2010). Worry is thought to reinforce and maintain anxiety; it inevitably exacerbates anxiety rather than decreases it.

GAD creates difficulty in three realms: cognitive, physical, and emotional (Daitch, 2011). On the cognitive level, the individual catastrophizes, fearing unfavorable outcomes will occur. In the physical realm, people experience physiological arousal in response to those fears, causing excessive levels of stress hormones to be continually sent throughout the body. These chronic physical symptoms can cause further worry, producing greater physical complaints. This often results in this population seeking medical attention because they believe their issues are physical in nature. GAD also impacts individuals' emotional realm. As people with GAD continue to worry about potentially adverse outcomes and physically maintain a state of being "on edge," they often become emotionally exhausted. When anxiety levels are mild, they can function socially and within their occupation. However, if their anxiety is moderate to severe, they find it difficult to take part in simple aspects of daily life (NIMH, 2009).

Counselor Considerations

As with the treatment of other anxiety disorders, counselors should attempt to create a warm, accepting, and supportive environment. People with GAD often directly attribute their symptoms to some unknown medical condition; therefore, counselors need to help these clients understand the connection between their physical complaints and their current worry and anxiety.

From a cross-cultural perspective, the focus of clients' worries may be related to their culture, with some clients experiencing worry across different domains, depending on their culture. For example, family, social relationships, finances, and health status may be more of a focus of worry for some groups, while work and school are areas of worry for others (Lewis-Fernández et al., 2010). Additionally, those from some cultures experience more somatic symptoms of anxiety (Kirmayer, 2001). While the *DSM-5* (APA, 2013) utilizes the somatic criteria of fatigue, muscle tension, and sleep disturbance, many people from other cultures experience additional somatic symptoms like indigestion, bowel issues, palpitations, and dizziness (Lewis-Fernández et al., 2010). When counselors provide psychoeducation to increase a client's knowledge of how anxiety affects emotional and physical reactions, they need to be mindful of cultural variations; this can have a normalizing effect for clients, which may provide some symptom relief.

People with GAD are often reluctant to engage in treatment; therefore, counselors need to assume a collaborative stance. In doing this, counselors who are confident can attempt to increase the client's investment and hope in treatment. Early in the treatment process, empathy and information gathering should be the main focus, while a more directive and confronting role is required as treatment progresses (Barlow, 2008).

A thorough evaluation of the contextual factors, frequency, severity, and subjective experience of the individual's worry and anxiety should be obtained. Exploration of excessive worries related to minor matters has diagnostic and treatment implications.

Counselors also need to assess for any comorbid disorders that may impact treatment goals and must be aware of any past or current negative life events and the individual's coping styles, all of which may impact the client's response to treatment.

Treatment Models and Interventions

Although no randomized controlled trials (RCTs) have significantly differentiated treatment conditions for those with GAD, recent studies have suggested that a combination of CBT and relaxation exercises appear to be the most promising treatment for GAD (Barlow et al., 2007; Ouimet, Covin, & Dozois, 2012). Additionally, two emerging treatments (i.e., without RCTs) that seem to have some early clinical promise and warrant further research and consideration are (a) the intolerance of uncertainty model (Dugas, Buhr, & Ladouceur, 2004), and (b) acceptance and commitment therapy (Hayes et al., 2012).

CBT: BORKOVEC'S COGNITIVE AVOIDANCE MODEL (CAM) Maladaptive thinking and a tendency to continually worry, rather than problem solve, maintain the excessive, uncontrollable worry that is the hallmark of GAD. Those with GAD have difficulty relaxing and attempt to avoid negative thoughts and feelings. Borkovec's cognitive avoidance model (CAM; Borkovec & Costello, 1993) is a theory that integrates cognitive therapy (i.e., examining thoughts/beliefs, evidence-review of accuracy, and behavioral experimentation of alternative and more accurate thoughts/beliefs), and applied relaxation or relaxation training, which teaches an individual to release his or her tension by tensing and then relaxing the muscles in the midst of imaginal or in vivo anxiety-provoking situations. This type of CBT focuses on altering an individual's catastrophic thinking and the belief that worry is beneficial. The intent is to teach clients how to tolerate feared thoughts and situations and realize that these thoughts do not produce horrible outcomes.

CBT: INTOLERANCE OF UNCERTAINTY MODEL (IUM) Those with GAD are more often susceptible to react negatively to uncertain events, regardless of the likelihood of positive, neutral, or negative consequences of an event. The intolerance of uncertainty model (IUM) postulates that clients frequently consider their worry to be a protective mechanism that either aids in their avoiding of negative events, or better prepares them to endure these future events (Dugas et al., 2004). As with CAM, IUM contends that this worry produces poor problem solving skills and cognitive avoidance, which perpetuates their own anxiety. From the IUM approach, the aim of treatment is to aid clients in grouping their worries into either solvable or unsolvable categories. Problem solving is then applied to solvable worries, while hypothetical situations are dealt with through the use of cognitive exposure.

ACCEPTANCE AND COMMITMENT THERAPY (ACT) Because those with GAD have a tendency to restrict their engagement in meaningful activities in order to avoid negative internal experiences, ACT draws on various metaphors and mindfulness exercises to change clients' relationship with their internal experiences (Hayes et al., 2012). ACT promotes acceptance and being in the present moment rather than focusing on future-oriented thoughts or concerns. Because worry is seen as a form of avoidance of distressing thoughts and situations, clients are encouraged to notice their emotional responses, tolerate discomfort, and ultimately engage in valued activities. They learn to see anxiety for what it is, differentiate it from the self, and act in accordance with their values. It involves acceptance and distancing (i.e., "I am having an anxious thought" vs. "I am an anxious person"), and commitment and change (i.e., engaging in activities that are in accordance with one's values). Counselors help clients to identify their values and what they are doing in the present with the goal of reducing the discrepancy. Clients take part in exposure exercises (e.g., paradoxes, mindfulness practice) to learn how to be in the presence of anxiety so that anxiety is no longer a barrier to valued living, and they can live in accordance with their goals.

CREATIVE TOOLBOX ACTIVITY 5.2   Waves in the Ocean

Lisa P. Meyer, MA, NCC

Activity Overview

This creative mindfulness intervention invites clients to be in the presence of positive, neutral, and distressing thoughts without attempting to change or become stuck in the thoughts.

Treatment Goal(s) Addressed

The primary goals of this activity are to help clients (a) notice when they are looking at their thoughts versus when they are looking *from* their thoughts; (b) distinguish between states of *fusion* and *defusion*; (c) learn how to be aware of distressing thoughts (i.e., worry) without becoming stuck in the content of those thoughts.

Directions

1. Assess the client's readiness to engage in this mindfulness exercise. This intervention may be inappropriate for those clients who are cognitively unable to understand the metaphor and meaning of the activity, or are not grounded in reality.
2. Dim the lights and ask the client to close his or her eyes.
3. Ask the client to imagine he or she is on a shore of a beach, watching the waves rise, fall, and pass. Tell the client to think whatever thoughts come to mind, allowing each to pass just like the waves in the ocean. Tell the client that every passing wave represents a thought and that he or can imagine words, sentences, or images on each wave.
4. Share that this will be a difficult task and that there may be a point when he or she may begin to follow a particular wave. Ask the client to back up and see what he or she was doing right before following any wave.
5. If the client opens his or her eyes or speaks, encourage him or her to focus on the waves.
6. After about 3 minutes, ask the client to let the last few waves pass by and prepare to come back to the room. Allow 2 minutes for the client to reorient before processing.

Process Questions

1. Tell me what this exercise was like for you.
2. What did you notice about the thoughts and images on the waves?

3. What did you notice about the waves you began to follow?
4. What did you find yourself doing right before you began to follow a wave?
5. Were you able to let any waves with distressing thoughts or images pass by? Tell me what that was like, and how you did that.
6. How can these concepts be applied to distressing thoughts and anxiety you have in your everyday life?

PSYCHOPHARMACOTHERAPY Typically, in treating GAD, antidepressants (e.g., tricyclics, SNRIs, SSRIs) and antianxiety medications (e.g., benzodiazepines, buspirone) are used (Ravindran & Stein, 2010). SSRIs (e.g., paroxetine, escitalopram, sertraline), SNRIs (e.g., venlafaxine), benzodiazepines (all have been equally effective), and buspirone have all been used with success in treating generalized anxiety disorder (Roy-Byrne & Cowley, 2007). In comparison studies, benzodiazepines have been equivalent to SSRIs in terms of effectiveness. Xanax is a benzodiazepine currently approved by the FDA for use with those with GAD, but it should be used with caution due to its potential for addiction and abuse.

Prognosis

Throughout their lives, people with GAD often struggle with fear and worry, although many receive significant relief when treated with CBT (Evans et al., 2005). The greatest treatment gains are made when clients are treated with some combination of CBT and relaxation methods, with the worry being brought under the client's control (Barlow et al., 2007). GAD symptoms frequently return; therefore, clients should receive some training and education in the prevention, signs of relapse, and coping strategies needed to manage anxiety when stressful situations arise in the future.

SELECTIVE MUTISM

Description of the Disorder and Typical Client Characteristics

The onset of selective mutism (SM) generally occurs before the age of 5, and it is considered a rare disorder, with an estimated prevalence of only 0.47 to 0.76% in the general population (Viana, Beidel, & Rabian, 2009). The age of onset typically ranges from 2.7 to 4.1 years; however, due to the potential delay between onset and school entry, this may not accurately reflect the true age of onset (Viana et al., 2009).

People with SM consistently fail to speak in social situations where speech is expected (e.g., with playmates, school), even though speaking occurs in other situations (e.g., at home, with family members; APA, 2013). The failure to speak is not due to clients' deficit of knowledge or comfort level with the spoken language used in that particular setting. Instead of using verbalization, they may communicate by gestures, nodding or shaking their heads, pushing or pulling, or by monosyllable utterances (APA, 2013). This absence of standard speech is selectively dependent on the social context and is not considered to be an oppositional behavior. Additionally, this lack of speech is not due to the embarrassment of stuttering or any other communication disorder. Children with SM typically present as excessively shy, have difficulty separating from parents, have fears regarding social embarrassment, may have experienced a traumatizing event, and may exhibit compulsive and oppositional behaviors (Carlson, Mitchell, & Segool, 2008; Yeganeh, Beidel, & Turner, 2006).

School is the most common context where SM symptoms are displayed. As such, this is typically the setting where an individual's impairment is first noticed. Those with this disorder face significant impairments in their educational achievement and social communication. It is unclear what particular stimuli elicit anxiety in children with SM. Their anxiety may be rooted in the presence of those outside of one's family, the presence of others in general, the requirement to speak to others, or having attention directed towards one's self (Shriver, Segool, & Gortmaker, 2011).

SM is viewed as a disorder of anxiety, characterized by avoidance rather than opposition. Environmental and familial factors, such as marital conflict (Elizur & Perednik, 2003) and social modeling of anxiety symptoms (Davis, Munson, & Tarcza, 2009), may also contribute to the development of SM. Family members of those with SM have significantly higher rates of anxiety and other clinical disorders, as compared to those without the disorder (Viana et al., 2009).

Counselor Considerations

Even though children with SM typically exhibit similar behaviors, their presentation can differ and such variations will impact treatment. The situations in which children speak, to whom they speak, their volume and quantity of speech, use of gestures, and presentation of anxiety often varies. Some may appear anxious, while others may not explicitly demonstrate any symptoms of nervousness. Insight into internal experiences when expected to speak also varies, with some endorsing feeling "put on the spot" or unable to get the words out, while others may simply say, "I don't know."

These potential variations should be considered in the assessment and treatment of those with SM. It is important to understand how the child operates in all areas (i.e., school, home, and in public) to determine an accurate baseline and subsequent treatment goals. Counselors should attempt to evaluate these children in the areas where speech is not as lacking. For example, a caregiver might audio record a play interaction with a parent within the child's home (if that is an area where the child is more expressive). This can be utilized for treatment planning and can allow for a diagnostic rule out of a communication disorder or a language delay. Additionally, the treatment goals for a child who is restricted nonverbally may include developing nonverbal communication prior to a focus on verbalization, while goals for a child who is slightly more comfortable with speech may include progressing through a hierarchy of increasingly anxiety-provoking speaking situations.

Understanding the manifestation of anxiety symptoms can be complicated, as some children appear inhibited while others are highly engaged and display positive affect despite remaining mute. For children who have not spoken for a very long time, a lack of speech has likely become a learned behavior and has ceased to be experienced with anxiety. For children who do not exhibit anxiety, as well as for those who have minimal insight into their reasons for not speaking, behavioral exposure and reinforcement may be more effective than treatments that focus on cognitive and affective components (Laptook, 2012).

SM is a difficult disorder to treat (Kehle, Bray, & Theodore, 2006), as the behaviors associated with the disorder are often unintentionally reinforced. Teachers and parents may misinterpret the lack of speech as shyness, and may reduce the burden of talking (Shriver et al., 2011). Likewise, peers and siblings may reinforce the behaviors by speaking on behalf of the child (Shriver et al., 2011). Treatment goals should include a focus on all settings where lack of expected speech occurs and should recruit the help of prominent members in those domains (i.e., parents, family members, and teachers). Considering that a child is part of a family system, it seems intuitive to consider interventions that are directed at the family system.

Treatment Models and Interventions

While there is no single standardized treatment model for treating clients with SM (Reuther, Davis, Moree, & Matson, 2011), a multifaceted approach including behavior, cognitive behavioral, and family interventions seems to hold the most clinical promise (Sadock & Sadock, 2007). Additionally, appropriate approaches for treating SM in children need to include a focus on reducing clients' overall anxiety, increasing their self-esteem, and improving their skills in social settings (Cohan, Chavira, & Stein, 2006). In the following section, behavior, cognitive behavioral, family, and play therapy will be presented as possible treatments of SM.

BEHAVIOR THERAPY Behavioral interventions for SM include the use of the following treatment interventions: contingency management, shaping, stimulus fading, and exposure (Busse & Downey, 2011).

Contingency management is based on operant conditioning principles and involves providing reinforcers for verbalizations. It is based on the assumption that behaviors are controlled by their consequences, so they will increase if a positive reinforcer follows, and will decrease if they are not reinforced. For example, a teacher could give reinforcers such as stickers or candy for verbal participation in class.

Shaping is often used with contingency management and involves applying small steps and working toward changing a broader target behavior. For example, if two full verbalized sentences during a counseling session or class period is the target behavior, then the focus may be on using one word instead of a physical gesture, then using two to three words together, then verbalizing an entire sentence, until the child is eventually able to speak two full sentences during a class period.

Stimulus fading, which is also frequently paired with contingency management, aims to diminish the power a parent or caregiver has on a particular behavior. For example, if a child is only comfortable speaking when a parent is in close proximity, then the treatment focus may be to have the child speak to a person (e.g., counselor, teacher) while the parent is with him or her, and then progressively move the parent away from the interaction (e.g., stand several feet away, stand on the other side of the room, stand outside the room) until the child is able to speak to the person without the parent being present.

Use of exposure techniques is even more effective than contingency management in dealing with the distress associated with speaking (Vecchio & Kearney, 2009). With the help of a counselor, a hierarchy of feared situations is created, starting with the least anxiety-provoking interactions and progressing to more feared speaking situations. With recruitment of the above techniques, the child is systematically desensitized to anxiety-provoking stimuli. For example, once a child gains comfort with one-to-one interactions, she or he may be exposed to speaking with two other persons, then to a small group, and eventually to a larger group (e.g., the class).

MODULAR COGNITIVE BEHAVIORAL THERAPY (M-CBT) M-CBT (Chorpita, 2007) is an adaptation of traditional CBT and is unique in that it accounts for the child's developmental level and individualized needs (Reuther et al., 2011). M-CBT can be divided into four phases of treatment:

1. The initial phase of treatment focuses on psychoeducation about anxiety, development of a fear hierarchy, and then gradual exposure to feared speaking situations.
2. The middle phase focuses on changing cognitions by identifying thoughts and incorporating helpful cognitive strategies into exposure activities, and on practicing conversation skills with the counselor.
3. In the latter portion of treatment, the client practices having conversations with unfamiliar adults (e.g., within the school or clinic).
4. The final sessions address maintenance of newly developing skills and plans for relapse prevention.

M-CBT appears to have significant clinical promise, yet it requires more research to substantiate its utility with this population.

PLAY THERAPY Play therapy is an emerging approach (i.e., that lacks randomized controlled trials to support its use) to treating children with SM (Busse & Downey, 2011). Play therapy is especially useful if the child is not speaking to the counselor; the nonverbal play can be a means for the child to express himself or herself without words. Play therapy may be the most useful when it is combined with behavioral interventions (Busse & Downey, 2011), although only a few case studies have been reported in the literature. While play therapy seems to hold clinical promise, more research is warranted to evaluate its overall effectiveness in treating this disorder.

MUSIC THERAPY Music therapy for SM involves the use of musical instruments to promote emotional expression and connectedness with others (Amir, 2005; Mahns, 2003). Music represents a microcosm of the child's life and uninhibited play creates avenues for communication. It is a here-and-now approach that indirectly explores the child's inner world, highlights his or her interpersonal patterns, uncovers unresolved issues, and exposes blocked emotions. Case studies have shown promise for this modality with significant gains in verbal communication, self-confidence, social relationships, and overall well-being (e.g., Amir, 2005).

 Clinical Toolbox 5.9: In the Pearson etext, click here to read about practical considerations for using music therapy with clients who have selective mutism.

PSYCHOPHARMACOTHERAPY The medications used to treat social anxiety disorder in adults and children are often used in the treatment of SM (Carlson et al., 2008). SSRIs seem to be the most promising medications for those with severe cases of selective mutism (Sadock & Sadock, 2007). However, the FDA has not yet approved any medications for the treatment of SM.

Prognosis

While half of all children diagnosed with SM improve by age 10, those who do not seem to have a poorer overall prognosis (Sadock & Sadock, 2007). Therefore, younger children seem to have a better prognosis, especially if they receive an early diagnosis and are treated with behavior, cognitive behavioral, family, and psychopharmacological interventions. Those who do not improve by age 10, or who go without any treatment, often develop other psychiatric disorders in adolescence and adulthood (Sadock & Sadock, 2007).

TREATMENT PLAN FOR KA-SEAN

This chapter began with a discussion of Ka-Sean, a 25-year-old single African American female with longstanding bouts of anxiety who meets the criteria for generalized anxiety disorder. A counselor must consider a number of factors before moving ahead with a strength-based treatment approach. The following I CAN START conceptual framework outlines treatment considerations that may be helpful in working with Ka-Sean.

C = Contextual Assessment

Ka-Sean has her father's cultural value of hard work and "going after" what she wants. She has a good sense of her values and beliefs as they relate to her culture and ethnicity. She has strong convictions and regular religious involvement. Her spirituality is important to her sense of self. Ka-Sean believes it is more difficult for women within society, yet she is persistent in overcoming double standards. Being a lesbian, she also has to deal with prejudices within her cultural community and within her own family. She regularly seeks the reassurance of others (i.e., father, sister, significant other) and often minimizes her own voice in situations. Additionally, she has had to deal with the death of her mother, which has significantly impacted her sense of worth, attachment, and overall stability.

A = Assessment and Diagnosis

Diagnosis = Generalized Anxiety Disorder 300.02 (F41.1) and Panic Disorder 300.01 (F41.0); The following formal assessments will be conducted: The Beck Anxiety Inventory (at the initial session and then as needed for follow-up), assessment of suicidality (see Chapter 3), and a physical examination by a physician to monitor psychiatric medications.

N = Necessary Level of Care

Outpatient, individual (once per week)

S = Strength-Based Lens

Self: Ka-Sean is an intelligent, insightful, and witty woman. She is passionate about writing and reading and has written two science fiction novels. She is a hard worker who is motivated to be successful. Ka-Sean excels in her graduate program and does well academically. She is nurturing and cares for cares about others and strives to help them.

Family: Ka-Sean frequently sees her father and sister. She cares about her father, brother, and sister. She is close to her sister and desires to be close with her brother again. Her father and sister are social support resources for her and they are willing to help and assist her in all of her endeavors.

Community: Ka-Sean's significant other is supportive and is a positive resource for her. Also, Ka-Sean is actively engaged in her local church and has longstanding relationships with other parishioners. She has maintained relationships with high school and college friends. She appears to have a supportive, positive friend base.

T = Treatment Approach

Cognitive Avoidance Model (CAM)—Cognitive therapy with applied relaxation and

Panic Control Therapy (PCT), which includes a focus on interoceptive sensations (e.g., exercise)

A = Aim and Objectives of Treatment

Ka-Sean will learn to decrease maladaptive and catastrophizing thoughts → Ka-Sean will utilize cognitive restructuring to examine her thoughts/beliefs (i.e., that her worrying is a useful way to deal with her problems), evidence-review of the accuracy of those thoughts/beliefs, and will engage in behavioral experimentation of alternative and more accurate thoughts/beliefs 80% of the time. She will, in session and out of session, learn to be aware of, to confront, and to test her maladaptive and catastrophizing thoughts/beliefs 80% of time, utilizing these cognitive skills.

Ka-Sean will increase her ability to manage her physical tension → Ka-Sean will utilize applied relaxation 80% of the time when feeling physically tense.

Ka-Sean will learn to use interoceptive sensations activities to manage her anxiety → She will actively exercise (e.g., go running) 3 times per week for at least 30 minutes.

Ka-Sean will continue to write → Ka-Sean will utilize writing (as an anxiety management skill) at least 3 times per week.

R = Research-Based Interventions (based on CAM and PCT)

Counselors will use Socratic questioning to help Ka-Sean make guided discoveries and begin to question her maladaptive and catastrophic thinking. The counselor will aid her in generating alternative interpretation, while helping her gather more evidence in the behavioral practice (e.g., imaginal, in vivo) of these anxiety-provoking situations.

Counselor will effectively utilize cognitive restructuring techniques with Ka-Sean. This restructuring will be aimed at her misconceptions about anxiety, panic, and her own overestimations of the threat and danger around her. Ka-Sean will learn how her maladaptive thinking generates overly-negative interpretations of life events, how these thinking patterns create rigid rules and behaviors, and how they can be examined and changed.

Counselor will utilize applied relaxation so Ka-Sean can avoid and learn to manage anxiety-provoking situations.

> Counselor will assist Ka-Sean in learning that anxiety symptoms are tolerable and will not lead to her worst fears (i.e., death, losing control).
>
> She will be invited to exercise 3 times a week for 30 minutes.
>
> ### T = Therapeutic Support Services
>
> Referral to a psychiatrist for consultation regarding anxiety medication currently prescribed by her PCP
>
> Medical consultation before an exercise program is started
>
> Weekly individual counseling
>
> Community-based support group for people with anxiety disorders

References

Alden, L. E., & Taylor, C. T. (2004). Interpersonal processes in social phobia. *Clinical Psychology Review, 24,* 857–882.

American Psychiatric Association (APA). (2013). *Diagnostic and statistical manual of mental disorders* (5th ed.). Washington, DC: Author.

Amir, D. (2005). Re-finding the voice: Music therapy with a girl who has selective mutism. *Nordic Journal of Music Therapy, 14,* 67–77.

Antony, M. M., & Barlow, D. H. (Eds.). (2002). *Handbook of assessment and treatment planning for psychological disorders.* New York, NY: Guilford.

Antony, M. M., Roth Ledley, D. R., Liss, A., & Swinson, R. P. (2006). Response to symptoms induction exercises in panic disorder. *Behavior Research and Therapy, 44,* 85–98.

Barlow, D. H. (2002). *Anxiety and its disorders: The nature and treatment of anxiety and panic* (2nd ed.). New York, NY: Guilford.

Barlow, D. H. (Ed.). (2008). *Clinical handbook of psychological disorder: A step-by-step treatment manual* (4th ed.). New York, NY: Guilford.

Barlow, D. H., Allen, L. B., & Basden, S. (2007). Psychological treatments for panic disorders, phobia, and generalized anxiety disorder. In P. E. Nathan & J. M. Gorman (Eds.), *A guide to treatments that work* (3rd ed., pp. 351–394). New York, NY: Oxford University Press.

Beck, A. T., & Emery, G. (with Greenberg, R. L.). (2005). *Anxiety disorders and phobias: A cognitive perspective* (15 anniversary ed.). New York, NY: Basic Books.

Beck, A. T., & Steer, R. A. (1990). *Manual for the Beck Anxiety Inventory.* San Antonio, TX: Psychological Corporation.

Beidel, D. C., & Turner, S. M. (2007). *Shy children, phobic adults: Nature and treatment of social anxiety disorder* (2nd ed.). Washington, DC: American Psychological Association.

Bogels, S. M., & Brechman-Toussaint, M. L. (2006). Family issues in child anxiety: Attachment, family functioning, parental rearing and beliefs. *Clinical Psychology Review, 26,* 834–856.

Borkovec, T. D., & Costello, E. (1993). Efficacy of applied relation and cognitive-behavioral therapy in the treatment of generalized anxiety disorder. *Journal of Consulting and Clinical Psychology, 61,* 611–619.

Brady, V. P., & Whitman, S. M. (2012). Acceptance and mindfulness-based approach to social phobia: A case study. *Journal of College Counseling, 15,* 81–96.

Britran, S., Morissette, S. B., Spiegel, D. A., & Barlow, D. H. (2008). A pilot study of sensation-focused intensive treatment for panic disorder with moderate to severe agoraphobia: Preliminary outcomes and benchmarking data. *Behavior Modification, 32,* 196–214.

Busse, R. T., & Downey, J. (2011). Selective mutism: A three-tiered approach to prevention and intervention. *Contemporary School Psychology, 15,* 53–63.

Carlson, J. S., Mitchell, A. D., & Segool, N. (2008). The current state of empirical support for the pharmacological treatment of selective mutism. *School Psychology Quarterly, 23,* 354–372.

Chartier, M. J., Walker, J. R., & Stein, M. B. (2001). Social phobia and potential childhood risk factors in a community sample. *Psychological Medicine, 31,* 307–315.

Chorpita, B. F. (2007). *Modular cognitive-behavioral therapy for childhood anxiety disorders*. New York, NY: Guilford.

Clark, D. A., & Beck, A. T. (2010). *Cognitive therapy of anxiety disorders: Science and practice*. New York, NY: Guilford.

Cohan, S. L., Chavira, D. A., & Stein, M. B. (2006). Practitioner review: Psychosocial interventions for children with selective mutism: A critical evaluation of the literature from 1990–2005. *Journal of Child Psychology and Psychiatry, 47,* 1085–1097.

Cormier, S., Nurius, P. S., & Osborn, C. J. (2013). *Interviewing and change strategies for helpers* (7th ed.). Belmont, CA: Cengage.

Craske, M. G., & Barlow, D. H. (2007). *Mastery of your anxiety and panic: Therapist guide* (4th ed.). Oxford, UK: Oxford University Press.

Daitch, C. (2011). *Anxiety disorders: The go-to guide for clients and therapists*. New York, NY: Norton.

Davis III, T. E., Munson, M., & Tarcza, E. (2009). Anxiety disorders and phobias. In J. Matson (Ed.), *Social behavior and social skills in children* (pp. 219–244). New York, NY: Springer.

Drake, K. L., & Ginsburg, G. S. (2012). Family factors in the development, treatment, and prevention of childhood anxiety disorders. *Clinical Child and Family Psychology Review, 15,* 144–162.

Dugas, M. J., Buhr, K., & Ladouceur, R. (2004). The role of intolerance of uncertainty in etiology and maintenance. In R. G. Hemberg, C. L. Turk, & D. S. Mennin (Eds.), *Generalized anxiety disorder: Advances in research and practice* (pp. 143–163). New York, NY: Guilford.

Elizur, Y., & Perednik, R. (2003). Prevalence and description of selective mutism in immigrant and native families: A controlled study. *Journal of the American Academy of Child and Adolescent Psychiatry, 42,* 1451–1459.

Evans, D. L., Foa, E. B., Gur, R. E., Hendin, H., O'Brien, C. P., Seligman, M. E. P., . . . Walsh, B. T. (2005). *Treating and preventing adolescent mental health disorders*. New York, NY: Oxford University Press.

Gilbert, P. (2000). The relationship of shame, social anxiety and depression: The role of the evaluation of social rank. *Clinical Psychology and Psychotherapy, 7,* 174–189.

Harris, R. (2009). *ACT made simple: An easy to read primer on acceptance and commitment therapy*. Oakland, CA: New Harbinger.

Harvey, A. G., Ehlers, A., & Clark, D. M. (2005). Learning history in social phobia. *Behavioural and Cognitive Psychotherapy, 33,* 257–271.

Hayes, S. C., Strosahl, K. D., & Wilson, K. G. (2012). *Acceptance and commitment therapy: The process and practice of mindful change*. New York, NY: Guilford.

Heimberg, R. G. (1991). *Cognitive-behavioral group therapy for social phobia: A treatment manual*. Unpublished manuscript. The University at Albany, State University of New York.

Heimberg, R. G. (2002). Cognitive-behavioral therapy for social anxiety disorder: Current status and future directions. *Biological Psychiatry, 51,* 101–108.

Herbert, J. D., & Cardaciotto, L. (2005). An acceptance and mindfulness-based perspective on social anxiety disorder. In S. M. Orsillo & L. Roemer (Eds.), *Acceptance and mindfulness-based approaches to anxiety* (pp. 189–212). New York, NY: Springer.

Hofmann, S. G., Asnaani, A., & Hinton, D. E. (2010). Cultural aspects in social anxiety and social anxiety disorder. *Depression and Anxiety 27,* 1117–1127.

Hofmann, S. G., & Barlow, D. H. (2002). Social phobia (social anxiety disorder). In D. H. Barlow (Ed.), *Anxiety and its disorders: The nature and treatment of anxiety and panic* (2nd ed., pp. 454–476). New York, NY: Guilford.

Kehle, T. J., Bray, M. A., & Theodore, L. A. (2006). Selective mutism. In G. G. Bear & K. M. Minke (Eds.), *Children's needs III: Development, prevention, and intervention* (pp. 293–302). Bethesda, MD: National Association of School Psychologists.

Kendall, P. C., Choudhury, M., Hudson, J., & Webb, A. (2002). *The C.A.T. project manual for the cognitive behavioral treatment of anxious adolescents*. Ardmore, PA: Workbook Publishing.

Kendall, P. C., Furr, J. M., & Podell, J. L. (2010). Child-focused treatment of anxiety. In J. R. Weisz & A. E. Kazdin (Eds.), *Evidence-based psychotherapies for children and adolescents* (2nd ed., pp. 45–60). New York, NY: Guilford.

Kendall, P. C., & Hedtke, K. A. (2006). *Coping cat workbook* (2nd ed.). Ardmore, PA: Workbook Publishing.

Kessler, R. C., Berglund, P., Demler, O., Jin, R., & Walters, E. E. (1005). Lifetime prevalence and age-of-onset distributions of DSM-IV disorders in the National Comorbidity Survey Replication. *Archives of General Psychiatry, 62*(6), 593–602.

Kins, E., Beyers, W., & Soenens, B. (2013). When the separation-individuation process goes awry: Distinguishing between dysfunctional dependence and dysfunctional independence. *International Journal of Behavioral Development, 37,* 1–12.

Kirmayer, L. J. (2001). Cultural variation in the clinical presentation of depression and anxiety: Implications for diagnosis and treatment. *Journal of Clinical Psychiatry, 62,* 22–30.

Koerner, N., Vorstenbosch, V., & Antony, M. M. (2012). Panic disorder. In P. Sturmey & M. Hersen (Eds.), *Handbook of evidence-based practice in clinical psychology volume 2: Adult disorders* (pp. 285–312). Hoboken, NJ: John Wiley & Sons.

Kroenke, K., Spitzer, R. L., Williams, J. B., Monahan, P. O., & Lowe, B. (2007). Anxiety disorders in primary care: Prevalence, impairment, comorbidity, and detection. *Annals of Internal Medicine, 146,* 317–325.

Kroeze, S., & van den Hout, M. A. (2000). Selective attention for cardiac information in panic patients. *Behaviour Research, 38,* 63–72.

Laptook, R. (2012). Prevalence, assessment, and treatment of selective mutism: Heterogeneity in clinical presentations. *The Brown University Child and Adolescent Behavior Letter, 28,* 3–5.

Lewis-Fernández, R., Hinton, D. E., Laria, A. J., Patterson, E. H., Hofmann, S. G., Craske, M. G., . . . Liao, B. (2010). Culture and the anxiety disorders: Recommendations for DSM-V. *Depression and Anxiety, 27,* 21–229.

Mahler, M. S., Pine, F., & Bergman, A. (1975). *The psychological birth of the human infant: Symbiosis and individuation.* New York, NY: Basic Books.

Mahns, W. (2003). Speaking without talking: Fifty analytic music therapy sessions with a boy with selective mutism. In S. Hadley (Ed.), *Psychodynamic music therapy: Case Studies* (pp. 53–72). Gilsum, NH: Barcelona Publishers.

Mathew, A. R., Norton, P. J., Zvolensky, M. J., Buckner, J. D., & Smits, J. A. J. (2011). Smoking behavior and alcohol consumption in individuals with panic attacks. *Journal of Cognitive Psychotherapy: An International Quarterly, 25,* 61–70.

McNeil, D. W. (2001). Terminology and evolution of the constructs in social anxiety and social phobia. In S. G. Hofmann & P. M. DiBartolo (Eds.), *From social anxiety to social phobia: Multiple perspectives* (pp. 8–19). Boston, MA: Allyn & Bacon.

Meyer, R. G., & Deitsch, S. E. (1996). *The clinician's handbook: Integrated diagnostics, assessment, and intervention in adult and adolescent psychopathology* (5th ed.). Boston, MA: Allyn & Bacon.

Morissette, S. B., Spiegel, D. A., & Heinrichs, N. (2005). Sensation-focused intensive treatment for panic disorders with moderate to severe agoraphobia. *Cognitive and Behavioral Practice 12,* 17–29.

Nathan, P. E., & Gorman, J. M. (2007). *A guide to treatments that work* (3rd ed.). New York, NY: Oxford University Press.

National Comorbidity Survey. (2007). *Lifetime prevalence estimates.* Retrieved from: http://www.hcp.med.harvard.edu/ncs/ftpdir/NCS-R_Lifetime_Prevalence_Estimates.pdf

National Institute of Mental Health. (2009). *Anxiety disorders.* Retrieved from: http://www.nimh.nih.gov/health/publications/anxiety-disorders/nimhanxiety.pdf

Ouimet, A. J., Covin, R., & Dozois, D. J. (2012). Generalized anxiety disorder. In P. Sturmey & M. Hersen (Eds.), *Handbook of evidence-based practice in clinical psychology volume 2: Adult disorders* (pp. 651–680). Hoboken, NJ: John Wiley & Sons.

Rachman, S. J. (2004). *Anxiety* (2nd ed.). East Sussex, UK: Psychology Press.

Ravindran, L. N., & Stein, M. B. (2010). The pharmacological treatment of anxiety disorders: A review of progress. *Journal of Clinical Psychiatry, 71,* 839–854.

Reuther, E. T., Davis III, T. E., Moree, B. N., & Matson, J. L. (2011). Treating selective mutism using modular CBT for child anxiety: A case study. *Journal of Clinical Child & Adolescent Psychology, 40,* 156–163.

Roy-Byrne, P. P., & Cowley, D. S. (2007). Pharmacological treatments for panic disorder, generalized anxiety disorder, specific phobia, and social anxiety disorder. In P. E. Nathan & J. M. Gorman (Eds.), *A guide to treatments that work* (3rd ed., pp. 395–430). New York, NY: Oxford.

Sadock, B. J., & Sadock, V. A. (2007). *Kaplan and Sadock's Synopsis of psychiatry: Behavioral sciences/clinical psychiatry* (10th ed.). Philadelphia, PA: Lippincott Williams & Wilkins.

Shriver, M. D., Segool, N., & Gortmaker, V. (2011). Behavior observations for linking assessment to treatment for selective mutism. *Education and Treatment of Children, 34,* 389–411.

Sibrava, N. J., & Borkovec, T. D. (2006). The cognitive avoidance theory of worry. In G. C. L. Davey & A. Wells (Eds.), *Worry and its psychological disorders: Theory, assessment and treatment* (pp. 239–256). Chichester, UK: Wiley.

Smits, J. A. J., Powers, M. B., Berry, A. C., & Otto, M. W. (2007). Translating empirically supported strategies into accessible interventions: The potential utility of exercise for treatment of panic disorder. *Cognitive and Behavioral Practice, 14,* 364–374.

Stravynski, A. (2007). *Fearing others: The nature and treatment of social phobia.* Cambridge, UK: Cambridge University Press.

Taylor, S. (2000). *Understanding and treating panic disorder: Cognitive-behavioural approaches.* Chichester, UK: Wiley.

Turner, S. M., Beidel, D. C., Cooley, M. R., Woody, S. R., & Messer, S. C. (1994). A multicomponent behavioral treatment for social phobia: Social effectiveness therapy. *Behavioral Research and Therapy, 32,* 381–390.

van Velzen, C. J. M., Emmelkamp, P. M. G., & Scholing, A. (2000). Generalized social phobia versus avoidant personality disorder: Differences in psychopathology, personality traits, and social and occupational functioning. *Journal of Anxiety Disorders, 14,* 395–411.

Vecchio, J., & Kearney, C. A. (2009). Treating youths with selective mutism with an alternating design of exposure-based practice and contingency management. *Behavior Therapy, 40,* 380–392.

Viana, G. A., Beidel, D. C., & Rabian, B. (2009). Selective mutism: A review and integration of the last 15 years. *Clinical Psychology Review, 29,* 57–67.

Watkins, E. R. (2008). Constructive and unconstructive repetitive thought. *Psychological Bulletin, 134,* 163–206.

White, K. S., & Barlow, D. H. (2002). Panic disorder and agoraphobia. In D. H. Barlow (Ed.), *Anxiety and its disorders* (2nd ed., pp. 328–379). New York, NY: Guilford.

Wolpe, J. (1990). *The practice of behavior therapy* (4th ed.). New York, NY: Pergamon.

Wong, J., Gordon, E. A., & Heimberg, R. (2012). Social anxiety disorder. In P. Sturmey & M. Hersen (Eds.), *Handbook of evidence-based practice in clinical psychology volume 2: Adult disorders* (pp. 621–650). Hoboken, NJ: John Wiley & Sons.

Woo, S. M., & Keatinge, C. (2008). *Diagnosis and treatment of mental disorders across the lifespan.* Hoboken, NJ: Wiley.

Yeganeh, R., Beidel, D. C., & Turner, S. M. (2006). Selective mutism: More than social anxiety? *Depression and Anxiety, 23,* 117–123.

Zhang, W., Ross, J., & Davidson, J. R. T. (2004). Social anxiety disorder in callers to the Anxiety Disorders Association of America. *Depression and Anxiety, 20,* 101–106.

Obsessive-Compulsive and Related Disorders

VICTORIA E. KRESS, CHELSEY A. ZOLDAN, NICOLE A. ADAMSON, AND MATTHEW J. PAYLO

CASE STUDY: JOHN

John is an affable 40-year-old Latino male who works as a high school art teacher. He is a well-liked teacher, and even won a district-wide teaching award three years ago; he is known for giving his students "110%." For the past 20–25 years, he has been engaging in repetitive hand washing and checking behaviors (e.g., checking report card grades, for locked doors, the stove). These checking behaviors can take upwards of 2–3 hours each day. He also has intrusive thoughts that he cannot shake. For example, he has a number of rituals he feels compelled to complete, and if he does not do these, he thinks something bad will happen (e.g., he taps his car keys on his steering wheel 10 times before he starts the ignition, and fears that if he does not do this, he will get into a car accident). He attempts to fight these urges, but he becomes excessively anxious and scared if he does not engage in the activities.

John reports that he has been engaging in checking behaviors since middle school. For example, he recalls that he would repeatedly check for his house key and make sure the door was locked (even though he knew he had his key and the door was locked). John expresses some insight, noting, "My dad was a verbally and physically abusive alcoholic who was in and out of our lives, and my checking seemed to get worse when he was around." He indicates that throughout high school and on into college, these types of checking behaviors escalated. It was also during this time that his repetitive hand washing began. He indicates that over the past six months, his hand washing has esca-lated, and at present, he washes his hands about once every hour. He has a sink in his classroom, and he finds it difficult to resist the urges. He fears that his students are notic-ing this behavior and may think him strange. He has developed hand dermatitis, visible red rashes on his hands, from the excessive washing. The rashes are painful and, he reports, embarrassing.

John indicates that he has noticed that as his marital discord has escalated, so have his compulsive behaviors. John has been married to his high school sweetheart for 20 years, and they have two teenage children together. He reports that his wife frequently becomes annoyed with his inability to get things done around the house and to help with child rearing. John loves his wife and children, and generally has a great relationship with them, but his obsessions and compulsive behaviors exhaust him, leaving him with little energy left to support his family. Related to this, John has several close friends whom he has seen progressively less over the past year, secondary to his escalating symptoms. John's wife encouraged him to come to counseling and seek help.

John is active in his church, reporting he "never" misses Sunday services. He is also involved in his church's youth group, and finds a sense of purpose and meaning in this work. In addition to his work with his church, John is active in his local art community. For the last two years, he has rented an exhibit booth at the county's annual art festival, and he has begun to sell some of his artwork. He enjoys displaying and selling his work; it is essentially the reason he studied art and art history. His eldest daughter is also artistic and these exhibits provide an area of bonding and shared interest. Additionally, he has been outspoken in the community about the importance of art in the schools (i.e., creat-ing an outreach organization called Promoting Arts in Schools).

John is an insightful, intelligent, and creative person. He is passionate about his artwork, and his passion is contagious. He desires to live a more "free and relaxed" life, and is very motivated to enter treatment. John currently takes fluoxetine (Prozac), which is prescribed by his primary care physician, and would like to seek mental health treatment to help him cope more effectively with these intrusive thoughts and compul-sive behaviors.

DESCRIPTION OF THE OBSESSIVE-COMPULSIVE AND RELATED DISORDERS

The obsessive-compulsive and related disorders discussed in this chapter include obsessive-compulsive disorder, hoarding disorder, body dysmorphic disorder, trichotillomania (hair pulling), and excoriation (skin picking) disorder as per DSM-5. The disorders in the chapter are identified by either obsessions (recurrent and persistent urges, thoughts, or images that are unwanted) and compulsions (physical or mental repetitive acts or behaviors), or recur-rent body-focused repetitive behaviors (e.g., skin picking, hair pulling), and are accompa-nied by unsuccessful attempts to stop the behaviors.

COUNSELOR CONSIDERATIONS

The disorders in this chapter tend to overlap and are frequently comorbid with anxiety disorders (American Psychiatric Association [APA], 2013). Care should be taken in differ-ential diagnosis as the treatments for each, while sometimes overlapping, are also unique.

Clients' culture and developmental level should also be considered prior to ascribing a diagnosis from this category. While many people engage in rituals and have preoccupations, the disorders discussed in this chapter are unique in that they extend beyond developmentally appropriate stages, cause the individual distress, and cause impairment in functioning (APA, 2013).

People who have these disorders possess varying degrees of insight related to the accuracy of the beliefs that underlie their symptoms. People with these disorders may find some relief in the behaviors in which they engage, and so they may struggle to fully commit to treatment. As such, it is important that counselors assess clients' motivation to change and work to enhance their motivation and commitment so that they can fully engage in treatment. Clients may actually be fearful and experience significant anxiety when faced with making behavioral changes. Care should be taken to develop a strong therapeutic alliance and to constantly assess clients' engagement in treatment, so as to avoid premature counseling termination.

Clients with obsessive-compulsive and related disorders are also at risk for social isolation, which may further exacerbate their symptoms. The compulsive behaviors (i.e., checking, straightening, hoarding, pulling, and picking) cause clients with these disorders to feel self-conscious, often resulting in diminished social functioning. The enhancement of social supports may be an important treatment goal when working with this population.

PROGNOSIS

Efficacious treatments have been identified for the disorders discussed in this chapter. All of the evidence-based approaches used in treating clients with these disorders involve some type of cognitive and behavioral change as their treatment focus.

The prognoses of these disorders vary, with disorders such as obsessive-compulsive disorder having a good prognosis with aggressive treatment, and hoarding disorder having a fair, but less favorable prognosis. For all of the disorders discussed in this chapter, relapse prevention plans should be a part of the treatment plan. All clients with these behaviorally-based disorders are vulnerable to relapsing into old behaviors, especially during times of transition and stress.

OBSESSIVE-COMPULSIVE DISORDER

Description of the Disorder and Typical Client Characteristics

The 12-month prevalence of OCD is estimated to be about 1.2% (APA, 2013), and as many as one in every 200 children suffers from OCD (American Academy of Child and Adolescent Psychiatry, 2011). Those with OCD have unwanted and intrusive thoughts, and engage in repetitive behaviors. Recurrent unwelcome impulses, thoughts, and images that cause significant distress are referred to obsessions. Repeated behaviors in which a person engages to reduce distress are referred to as compulsions. Obsessions and compulsions can occur together or discretely in those who have OCD. Most frequently, compulsive behaviors are engaged in to reduce the anxiety associated with obsessions. Compulsions may serve to temporarily relieve anxiety, but they do not bring long-term gratification to the individual; this is important as the motivation for engaging in behaviors differentiates OCD from other disorders. Obsessions are frequently categorized as follows:

- Contamination (e.g., fear of germs from shaking hands, touching money)
- Recurrent images or impulses to engage in violent or other socially inappropriate behavior (e.g., fear of hurting self or loved ones, urge to shout obscenities in inappropriate situations)
- Repeated self-doubt (e.g., fear of leaving a stove turned on, leaving doors unlocked, harming another by accident)
- Orderliness and symmetry (e.g., organizing objects in a particular manner, intense need for evenness)
- Religious (e.g., overly concerned with behaving in a moral way, fear of committing a blasphemous act)
- Sexual thoughts or images (e.g., repeated unwanted pornographic images, sexual thoughts including an unacceptable partner)

Compulsions are frequently categorized as follows:

- Cleansing (e.g., hand washing, washing household items viewed as contaminated)
- Counting (e.g., counting steps, performing actions based on preference for a particular number)
- Checking (e.g., stove, locks, as a method of self-reassurance)
- Demanding reassurances (e.g., assuaging fears via Internet searches, asking others if they have harmed another by accident)
- Performing behaviors repeatedly (e.g., tapping an object, repeating words silently)
- Orderliness (e.g., arranging objects symmetrically)

Rules and patterns typically govern the compulsions, and people usually do not have insight into why they engage in the behaviors. Compulsions are primarily performed as an effort to suppress or alleviate the obsessions. Most people with OCD recognize that their obsessions and compulsions are unreasonable; when using the *DSM-5* diagnostic system, those who do not have this awareness are labeled with the specifier "with poor insight." These patterns of obsessions and compulsions are time consuming, and to qualify for an OCD diagnosis (according to the *DSM-5*), the cognitions and behaviors must occur for at least one hour a day. Attempts to ignore or resist obsessions and compulsions must also cause great psychological distress and escalate fears of a particular consequence (e.g., a loved one will be harmed if I do not tap the door with my thumb 10 times). Compulsive behaviors can also lead to the development of general medical conditions (e.g., dermatitis caused by excessive hand washing).

Counselor Considerations

Relevant cultural factors should be examined when diagnosing and treating a client's obsessions and compulsions. Many cultures have superstitious behaviors and rituals. The content of one's obsessions and compulsions could be related to beliefs rooted in one's culture. However, the hallmark characteristics of OCD, such as cleaning, symmetry, hoarding, intrusive thoughts, and fear of harming self or others, are consistent across cultures. Variations in presentation exist, though, across cultures, in terms of the content of obsessions and compulsions (APA, 2013).

Children with OCD are less likely to be guarded about their obsessions and compulsive behaviors, generally making the disorder easily recognizable to parents and teachers. In childhood, boys are more likely than girls to present with OCD.

Adults with OCD may enter counseling as a result of significant distress and disability caused by the disorder, occupational difficulties, impairments in social functioning and relationships, and comorbid diagnoses. Clients with OCD may present with substance use disorders, anxiety disorders, depression, Tourette's disorder, eating disorders, and attention-deficit/hyperactivity disorder.

The embarrassment surrounding OCD may make clients reluctant to disclose information about their symptoms, especially if they recognize that the obsessions and compulsions are irrational, or are related to socially undesirable content (e.g., disturbing sexual or aggressive obsessions). Clients will often be perfectionistic, have a rigid conscience, and may feel inappropriate guilt or remorse. As such, it is paramount that counselors focus on empowering the client and creating a sense of hope. Frequently reassuring clients that treatment can increase their quality of life will be immensely helpful in encouraging them to continue treatment. The need to quickly build trust with clients with OCD is important because clients may be reluctant to disclose the true nature and severity of their symptomology. Patience is required in working with this population, especially in encouraging clients to disclose material that they identify as unacceptable, embarrassing, and irrational. Counselors should be mindful of their body language and speech so as not to appear judgmental, particularly with clients who have intrusive thoughts with disturbing content. Counselors should also be careful not to mistakenly assume that a client's intrusive thoughts, such as fears of committing a violent act, are indicative of intent to commit the act.

Planning the direction of sessions will be helpful with OCD clients, as structure and routine can help to create a safe and comfortable treatment environment. A predictable environment will also help clients know what to expect in upcoming sessions, which may help to reduce anxiety and increase the likelihood of continuing in counseling.

OCD can significantly impair social functioning and the ability to maintain interpersonal relationships. Clients may limit their social interactions with others due to embarrassment and fear of ridicule from others. Relationships with family members can be strained by OCD as others may not understand the client's inability to resist irrational obsessions and compulsions, and thus become frustrated. Clients with OCD may demand that family members participate in rituals. Tensions can also arise if a family member or friend discloses information about the client's OCD, as it is often a source of embarrassment and is a deeply private subject. Stress within the family can be exacerbated in situations in which the client is a primary source of income and is unable to work due to the severity of OCD symptoms. Symptoms can severely inhibit a client's ability to arrive at work on time or at all, complete assigned tasks, and work with others. Because of the stigma surrounding the disorder, OCD symptoms can also prevent clients from seeking and maintaining intimate relationships. Intrusive thoughts and obsessions related to cleanliness, sex, and violent behavior can also interfere with intimacy, potentially causing relationship problems.

Counselors may want to encourage clients to involve family members and those in clients' support network to become involved in the treatment process. Direct psychoeducation from the counselor, or providing the client with informational handouts about OCD to share with their significant others, can help the client's support network understand the disorder and how they can assist the client. Members of the client's support network who are educated about the disorder may be more likely to provide support, reassurance, and encouragement to continue treatment.

Another consideration should be the environment in which counseling will take place. Clients with OCD may be easily distracted or triggered by stimuli in the counselor's office, and care should be taken to create an environment that reduces these possible distractions to help keep the clients focused. Distracting stimuli can include clutter, crooked picture frames, or any objects that the client may have a compulsion to rearrange.

Treatment Models and Interventions

The literature is abundant with randomized controlled studies addressing the treatment of OCD, and these will be discussed in the following sections. While efficacious interventions exist, as previously stated, clients with OCD may be particularly reluctant to begin treatment due to anxiety, feelings of embarrassment and guilt, and doubts about the helpfulness of the treatment. Psychoeducation, motivational interviewing, viewing a taped treatment session, and providing connections to people who have successfully completed the treatment have all been shown to encourage reluctant clients with OCD to enter and continue in treatment (Maltby & Tolin, 2005).

COGNITIVE BEHAVIORAL THERAPY (CBT)   Variations of CBT have long been considered the most efficacious treatment for OCD, and they have consistently been supported for use by randomized controlled studies. A recent meta-analysis of 16 randomized controlled studies using CBT to treat OCD revealed that clients completing CBT outperformed those assigned to control groups in posttreatment symptom reduction, and that subtypes of groups receiving cognitive therapy and exposure and response prevention (both are discussed in the following section) were relatively equal in efficacy (Olatunji, Davis, Powers, & Smits, 2013). CBT is also effective in treating OCD in children and adolescents (Williams et al., 2010). CBT utilizes techniques aimed at modifying cognitive (e.g., intrusive thoughts) and behavioral (e.g., compulsive behaviors) components to produce changes in the overall condition. In the following sections, examples of CBT approaches that are useful in treating OCD will be provided.

Exposure and Response Prevention (ERP)   ERP, a behavior therapy method, requires clients to directly confront the intrusive thoughts and images, situations, and objects that provoke psychological distress. This approach can elicit anxiety, and clients and counselors should be prepared for feelings of discomfort. Challenging thought patterns can help clients to recognize that their obsessions are unreasonable, and thus they become more open to resisting compulsive behaviors. Repeated exposure to anxiety-provoking stimuli assists clients in learning to cope with their feelings of discomfort and gain confidence in their abilities to resist compulsive behaviors.

When initiating ERP, counselors will first ask a client to disclose the stimuli that cause discomfort. Next, the client is asked to place the stimuli in a hierarchy based on the amount of distress associated with each. The least anxiety-provoking stimulus will be addressed first, as approaching a highly distressing stimulus may cause undue discomfort and discourage the client from returning to treatment. Several exposures to the anxiety-provoking stimulus will take place over the course of treatment, starting with exposures eliciting minimal discomfort and moving to those evoking higher levels of anxiety. Clients are then asked to refrain from engaging in compulsive behaviors. For example, a client with obsessions related to contamination may avoid touching doorknobs, and when doing so, may have a strong compulsion to wash his or her hands. The counselor can invite the client to first imagine touching a doorknob in a public place and refrain from hand washing. Future sessions may progress to viewing actual doorknobs, then eventually making contact with doorknobs, and refraining from hand washing. Clients who achieve greater levels of comfort with these tasks in session are then encouraged to practice resisting compulsive behaviors outside of sessions.

The literature has consistently recommended ERP as the gold-standard treatment for OCD; however, several challenges have limited ERP from more widespread use in the field. First, many counselors are not trained in ERP, and thus the modality of treatment is underutilized (Tolin, Diefenbach, & Gilliam, 2011). Next, this variation of CBT can be more time intensive, and thus more expensive than some alternative CBT approaches. Modifications can be made to ERP treatment to make counseling more cost effective in terms of both time and money. Group counseling settings are a viable alternative to individual counseling for clients with OCD (Jonnson, Hougaard, & Bennedsen, 2010), and can minimize treatment costs. Group counseling may also provide clients with support and encouragement to continue treatment; however, because clients with OCD may be reluctant to disclose due to feelings of embarrassment, counselors must take great care in determining the most appropriate treatment setting. Some research suggests that brief CBT treatment is as efficacious as full-term treatment (Bolton et al., 2011). Workbooks and activities can be completed independently to increase the development of coping skills and support the continued reduction of symptoms after termination (Bolton et al., 2011).

 Clinical Toolbox 6.1: In the Pearson etext, click here to view a video demonstration of exposure and response prevention techniques.

Cognitive Therapy   Cognitive therapy is typically used in conjunction with ERP in addressing OCD (Olatunji et al., 2013). This approach focuses primarily on the thoughts, attitudes, and feelings surrounding the client's obsessions. Cognitive therapy is aimed at helping clients modify dysfunctional beliefs about their obsessions. The goal is to help clients recognize their distortions in thinking, which would eventually diffuse the anxieties reinforcing the ritual thus leading to an extinction in the compulsive behavior. Clients are asked to identify the triggers of their obsessions and compulsions, recognize distortions in thinking, and challenge the validity of their thought patterns. For example, a client may think that if he or she does not complete a morning prayer ritual, a loved one will be killed. A counselor may help this client to challenge this thought, with the goal being for the client to eventually recognize that fears of a person coming to harm do not equate to the inevitability of this event occurring.

Mindfulness-Based Cognitive Therapy   Because many clients with OCD refuse treatment with ERP, alternative therapies, such as mindfulness-based cognitive therapy (MBCT; Segal, Williams, & Teasdale, 2013), have been suggested. While this is a relatively new treatment approach, the literature suggests that mindfulness may help clients with OCD to regain a sense of control and break the link between automatic thought patterns and subsequent compulsive behaviors (Wilkinson-Tough, Bocci, Thorne, & Herlihy, 2010). MBCT seeks to help the client to observe intrusive thought patterns without judgment.

Techniques of this approach involve clients being mindful of patterns of thoughts, feelings, and bodily sensations. Breathing exercises, meditation, and body scanning techniques are commonly utilized in MBCT. Research supports that MBCT helps clients with OCD to better regulate negative emotions and reduce symptoms (Hertenstein et al., 2012). This approach also encourages self-acceptance in clients and assists them in releasing feelings of guilt and embarrassment associated with their obsessions and compulsions.

Acceptance and Commitment Therapy (ACT)   ACT (Hayes, Luoma, Bond, Masuda, & Lillis, 2006) for OCD offers an alternative approach to traditional exposure-related therapies that are inherently anxiety-provoking. ACT allows clients to confront their obsessions and compulsions without increasing anxiety. Clients are encouraged to shift their focus to developing positive aspects of their lives, rather than on controlling their symptoms, and thus increase psychological flexibility. During counseling sessions, clients learn skills in acceptance, defusion, separating the self from the content of experiences, being aware of the present moment, examining values, and committed action. Counselors encourage clients to engage in behaviors and activities that they had withdrawn from due to their obsessions and compulsions, and while in these situations, to practice the skills learned during counseling sessions. Clients are taught to view their obsessions in a nonjudgmental manner and to commit to participating in activities that are important to them. In a randomized clinical trial, ACT was an efficacious treatment for OCD, and also reduced symptomology related to comorbid diagnoses (Twohig et al., 2010).

PSYCHOPHARMACOTHERAPY   Medication has been shown to be effective in treating OCD. Antidepressant medications, specifically selective serotonin reuptake inhibitors (SSRIs), are commonly used to treat this disorder. Selective serotonin reuptake inhibitors are typically prescribed in higher dosages in the treatment of OCD than in the treatment of depression (Preston, O'Neal, & Talaga, 2013). Currently, the FDA has approved the SSRIs citalopram (i.e., Celexa), fluoxetine (i.e., Prozac), fluvoxamine (i.e., Luvox), paroxetine (i.e., Paxil), and sertraline (i.e., Zoloft) for the treatment of OCD. Other SSRIs may be used "off label" to treat this condition based upon a physician's determination. SSRIs take a minimum of six weeks to produce a noticeable effect on symptoms and do not provide instant relief. SSRIs are especially helpful in treating clients with comorbid anxiety and depression. Because cessation of medication results in very high rates of relapse, continued treatment with a combination of medication and counseling is recommended (Preston et al., 2013).

anxiolytics

Before beginning any course of treatment including psychotropic medications, it is important to gather a thorough history of potential substance abuse. This is necessary as concurrent substance use can alter the metabolism of the psychotropic medication.

In general, medication is considered for the treatment of OCD when the symptoms range from moderate to severe, and in cases where the client is not responding to counseling interventions. Additionally, interventions including the use of medication should be considered when the client has a first-degree relative with OCD or a related condition, as this suggests a potential biological etiology of the disorder.

The tricyclic antidepressant clomipramine (i.e., Anafranil) is also sometimes used to treat OCD. Because the SSRIs have fewer side effects, they are more commonly prescribed to treat OCD than tricyclic antidepressants. The incidence of side effects are important to consider when treating clients with medication, as these can interfere with compliance. Furthermore, it is not uncommon for clients to try several different types of

CREATIVE TOOLBOX ACTIVITY 6.1   Being the Anchor in the Storm

Matthew J. Paylo, PhD, LPCC-S

Activity Overview

In this creative intervention, clients with body-focused repetitive behaviors (e.g., skin picking, nail biting, hair pulling) or compulsions (e.g., checking, hand washing, counting) learn to use an imagery technique focused on mindfulness-based skills to enhance their ability to tolerate stressful situations. Clients are asked to imagine that they are an anchor in the midst of a storm during times when they begin to sense an increased desire to engage in a body-focused repetitive behavior or compulsion. Clients are invited to be mindfully in the present moment and welcome the fear response, rather than fight it or run from it.

Treatment Goal(s) of Activity

The primary goals of this activity are to help clients (a) increase their awareness of times when they may engage in body-focused repetitive behaviors or compulsions; (b) implement these mindfulness-based interventions in real-life settings rather than acting on the urges or compulsions; and (c) tolerate the fear and anxiety in the present, until it passes.

Directions

1. The counselor and client process the client's body-focused repetitive behaviors and/or compulsive behaviors. This discussion enhances the client's awareness of the existence of antecedents of these behaviors. Additionally, the counselor and the client identify precursors to the urges and compulsions. This step is foundational to the rest of the activity. Invite the client to practice (e.g., in session first) acting as an anchor would in the midst of a storm.
2. Ask the client to stand. This change of positioning is vital to the implementation of this mindfulness-based intervention.
3. Ask the client to focus on body sensations in the present moment. This can be done by asking the client to close his or her eyes, and feel the breaths coming into his or her mouth and running down the windpipe and into the lungs. Next, the client is asked to envision he or she is pushing out all of the air from the lungs through the mouth.
4. Next, ask the client not only to focus awareness on his or her breathing, but to embrace the anxiety and fear that is welling up within.
5. Ask the client to begin to anchor him or herself with deep breaths. The counselor can also advise the client to grip the floor with his or her feet and to utilize this as another means of grounding himself or herself in the present moment.
6. The client is now instructed to welcome the fear and to envision that as it enters, it will eventually run through him or her and then exit through the feet. It will then dissipate into the ground.
7. The client is then invited to practice this mindfulness-based intervention in a real-life situation during the week between sessions.

Process Questions

1. How did you utilize the mindfulness-based intervention this week. What was that like for you?
2. Were you able to tolerate the urge or compulsion until it left you?
3. What did you notice about your thoughts, feelings, and behaviors after utilizing the intervention?
4. What was the most and/or least challenging aspect of this exercise for you?

medication before finding one that works for them in terms of symptom reduction and workable medication side effects.

Antianxiety medications can be used to immediately reduce anxiety levels and may be helpful for use during exposure and response prevention (ERP) therapy. Treatment with benzodiazepines presents a risk for abuse and dependence and may not be appropriate for long-term use to treat OCD, as it alters the symptoms but not the underlying pathology (Preston et al., 2013). Additionally, clients may build a tolerance for these medications, and the efficacy may be reduced.

Less frequently, typical and atypical antipsychotics may be prescribed to treat OCD. The literature has reported favorable responses in some with the use of antipsychotics, such as pimozide (i.e., Orap) and haloperidol (i.e., Haldol), when used in conjunction with SSRIs (Keuneman, Pokos, Weerasundera, & Castle, 2005). However, antipsychotic medications have numerous side effects, particularly when used long-term (e.g., tardive dyskinesia or "rabbit syndrome," which is characterized by involuntary, fine, rhythmic motions of the mouth along a vertical plane, without involvement of the tongue).

Prognosis

Research suggests that treatment with medication and psychotherapy effectively reduces OCD symptomology, and in many cases may lead to a full recovery. Comorbidity with substance abuse and other mental disorders may make treatment more difficult, and treatment gains may be more modest than in clients without these additional diagnoses (Hansen, Vogel, Stiles, & Götestam, 2007). While counseling may not completely alleviate all symptoms of OCD, symptoms can be significantly reduced and the quality of life enhanced. Clients may need to attend "maintenance" treatment sessions to prevent relapse and maintain treatment gains.

HOARDING DISORDER

Description of the Disorder and Typical Client Characteristics

In previous editions of the *DSM*, hoarding behaviors were informally addressed under obsessive-compulsive disorder (OCD) or obsessive-compulsive personality disorder. There is some relationship between OCD and hoarding behaviors (Sheppard et al., 2010), but hoarding is not simply a diagnostic feature of OCD. As such, HD is now listed as a separate diagnosis under Obsessive-Compulsive and Related Disorders in the *DSM-5* (APA, 2013).

Approximately 2 to 5% of the population experiences hoarding behaviors, which suggests that this is a relatively prevalent problem (Tolin, Meunier, Frost, & Steketee, 2010). Tolin et al. (2010) surveyed 751 adults with self-reported hoarding behaviors and found that most experienced symptoms before the age of 20; it was uncommon for hoarding behaviors to develop after the age of 40. Most often, people begin to develop hoarding behaviors between the ages of 11 and 15 (Tolin et al., 2010). Hoarding disorder appears to occur cross-culturally and have similar characteristics across cultures; however, limited information is available pertaining to cross-cultural hoarding behavior, and most of the research has been conducted with people in Western, more industrialized countries (APA, 2013). Some people living in poverty may hold onto items because of legitimate fears that they will not be able to acquire the item should they need it in the future; these types of poverty-related cultural considerations should be assessed and considered in diagnosing HD. In terms of gender, males and females have similar prevalence rates, but females tend to engage in more excessive acquisition (e.g., excessive buying) than males (APA, 2013).

People with HD find value in items that other people might not find valuable; as a result, they find it difficult to discard a variety of material possessions. Those with HD might fear misjudging an item's worth; accidentally discarding something valuable might cause negative emotional feelings (Timpano, Buckner, Richey, Murphy, & Schmidt, 2009). Or, they might hoard items that hold emotional or sentimental value. These strong feelings of attachment to material possessions make it difficult for clients to discard them.

Because people with HD have a strong urge to keep a lot of material possessions, the copious amounts of personal possessions in their homes can cause significant personal health risks (Timpano et al., 2009; Tolin et al., 2011). Hoarded items could range from newspapers and paper coffee cups, to statues, collectibles, and decorations, or any variety of objects. People with HD clutter their homes with these items, minimizing their ability to move unimpeded from room to room.

HD also poses a public health risk (Timpano & Schmidt, 2013). Homes that are overrun with hoarded items are more likely to catch fire, which puts the person with HD and those in surrounding buildings at risk. In addition, homes of people with HD may have pets that are not properly cared for (i.e., their waste is not effectively removed from the home), and this increases bacteria in the home and the neighborhood. Because pests (e.g., cockroaches, rats) cannot be properly controlled in the homes of those with HD, these pests are more likely to spread to neighboring buildings.

Most people with HD are aware that it is not healthy or helpful to keep so many possessions in their home, and they experience significant distress as the result of their lifestyle. They might become isolated from others, and they most likely will not freely allow other people (even family members or caregivers) into their homes. In addition to their social life, people with HD might also experience impairment in their occupational life. Their emotional attachment to objects might be evident at their workplace as well. People with HD are only able to part with their material possessions with help from others, such as family members, caregivers, mental health workers, or even local authorities who have to enforce public safety laws (Whitfield, Daniels, Flesaker, & Simmons, 2012).

Counselor Considerations

It is important for counselors to rule out alternative causes, other than HD, that might lead to hoarding behaviors. First, these behaviors must not be the result of a general medical condition, such as a brain injury (APA, 2013). Also, counselors must ensure that the client's symptoms are not better accounted for by a different diagnosis, such as OCD, major depressive disorder (in which the client might simply have limited energy to properly clean the home), or schizophrenia that might cause possession-related delusions (APA, 2013).

Some research suggests a possible relationship between HD and attention-deficit/hyperactivity disorder (ADHD), and counselors should also consider that ADHD may be comorbid (Frost, Steketee, & Tolin, 2011; Sheppard et al., 2010). Counselors will have greater success treating clients' HD if they alter their treatment plans to address comorbid ADHD symptoms as well (Tolin, 2011).

Although HD and depression are two independent disorders, there is a strong rate of comorbidity between these disorders (Frost et al., 2011). It is important for counselors to consider this correlation in two ways. First, counselors must remember that the effects of HD are socially and emotionally debilitating, and might result in depression. This could potentially further exacerbate the hoarding behaviors by reducing clients' energy and motivation to discard personal belongings. Second, depression might contribute to some of the clients' unhelpful or irrational beliefs about the value of their material possessions. The relationship between HD and depression is still unclear (i.e., does depression contribute to HD or is it a result of HD; Frost et al., 2011), but it is important for counselors to address depressive symptoms in the treatment plans of clients with HD.

Counselors must also be aware of additional factors that might make some people more vulnerable to HD. For example, some research suggests that those with HD have significantly higher levels of anxiety sensitivity than the general population, which means that clients with HD might actually hoard to avoid any potential of feeling anxious as the result of wrongly discarding something valuable (Timpano et al., 2009). However, this self-defeating cycle actually results in greater anxiety as the result of having an incredibly cluttered living space. Relatedly, those who hoard have been found to have significantly lower distress tolerance than the general population (Timpano et al., 2009). This limited ability to cope effectively with anxiety might increase clients' anxiety sensitivity, which further contributes to the hoarding cycle.

People with HD acquire objects and save them in order to avoid distressing feelings (Timpano et al., 2009; Wheaton et al., 2011), and they tend to have low levels of self-control (Timpano & Schmidt, 2013). When working with clients with HD, counselors should remember that clients genuinely feel distressed about the prospect of discarding items, and counselors should validate and support these fears. Counselors should identify ways that clients can overcome these difficult emotions and increase their distress tolerance and self-control.

Treatment Models and Interventions

Counselors should consider a biopsychosocial approach to assessing and treating HD (Tolin, 2011). Biologically, strong links among ADHD, depression, and HD suggest there is a strong genetic component to HD (Frost et al., 2011; Sheppard et al., 2010), and it may be responsive to psychotropic medications. Psychologically, HD may be associated with traumatic events in the client's history (Tolin, 2011). HD also affects the emotional well-being of the client (Frost et al., 2011). Counselors must also understand the social contributors to HD (e.g., avoidance of stressful experiences; Wheaton et al., 2011), and the social consequences of HD, including isolation and even eviction (Whitfield et al., 2012). As counselors begin to create an integrated, holistic understanding of the contributors and consequences of HD, they can better understand the intricate interplay of biological, psychological, and social factors. The following treatments can be used in treating HD using a biopsychosocial lens.

COGNITIVE BEHAVIORAL THERAPY (CBT)   CBT is the only treatment approach supported as an efficacious treatment for HD in children, adolescents, and adults (Gilliam & Tolin, 2010; Muroff et al., 2009; Steketee, Frost, Tolin, Rasmussen, & Brown, 2010; Tolin, 2011). CBT can be used in conjunction with psychopharmaceuticals and community support (see the following section).

When working from a CBT approach, interventions will address clients' information-processing difficulty, attachment to possessions, irrational or unhelpful beliefs, and associated behaviors (Gilliam & Tolin, 2010). Counselors start by exploring the biopsychosocial factors experienced by the client, and by validating his or her experience with HD. During this time, the counselor should work to build a strong therapeutic relationship with the client, and help the client establish safety within the therapeutic relationship.

As counselors listen to the client's story, they should work to identify irrational or unhelpful cognitions, such as "This magazine is just so interesting that I know it is going to be worth a lot of money someday." Additionally, counselors should use psychoeducation to explain contributing biological factors, low distress tolerance, and avoidance of unpleasant experiences or emotions that contribute to HD. These irrational thoughts can be explored by the counselor and client with the client's new knowledge of the etiology and functions his or her cognitions and behaviors serve.

Once trust has been established, the counselor can use the downward arrow technique to illustrate how an irrational statement leads to hoarding behaviors. For example, consider the statement "This magazine is just so interesting that I know it is going to be worth a lot of money someday" made by a male client. First, the statement is written down, and the counselor asks the client to explain what happens when this statement enters his mind. The client will probably say that he keeps the magazine. The counselor would take time to help the client identify his fears surrounding discarding the object (i.e., that the magazine will become valuable and he will regret discarding it), and that the hoarding behavior is actually a tool he uses to avoid negative feelings. The counselor would then take time to explore the client's distress tolerance techniques and help him build better coping skills.

Next, the counselor will ask the client to explain what happens once he keeps the magazine. He might explain that it (a) adds to the clutter in his house (which actually increases his anxiety), (b) he becomes even less likely to allow people into his home (which increases isolation), and (c) the magazine never actually becomes valuable (and any potential value would probably not be worth the negative consequences of hoarding). The counselor should take time throughout each step on the arrow to process the client's cognitions and fears, and ways in which the client can begin to identify similar irrational thoughts in his daily life. The counselor and client work together to build coping skills and more rational thoughts that the client can use to manage his hoarding symptoms.

The counselor might also use behavioral experiments in which negative thoughts or fears of the client are identified and disproved. For example, a client might state, "If I throw away that stack of books, I will regret it." The counselor might ask the client to identify one book that the client is willing to part with temporarily and ask the client to gauge (on a scale of 1 to 10) how much anxiety it will produce to part with it. Note that such experiments should start very small and gradually become more difficult. The client can then give the book to a friend or family member (as this is not as permanent as discarding it), and then gauge the level of actual distress. Any discrepancy in predicted verses actual distress can be addressed, and the counselor can help the client identify healthier ways of tolerating such distress. The client can eventually progress to permanently discarding the book and continue with even more helpful behavioral experiments.

Group CBT (G-CBT) is also effective in treating those with HD (Muroff et al., 2009). Because it is more cost affordable, G-CBT allows greater access to services. Additionally, G-CBT provides a much needed social outlet for those with HD, who often experience social isolation. Within G-CBT, cognitive and behavioral interventions, as mentioned above, should be used in an adapted form that is suitable for a group. The group leader should ensure that safety is built within the group and that each member is validated in his or her struggle with HD. The counselor should help group members identify irrational thoughts, ways to combat such thoughts with more healthy ones, and ways to increase each member's distress tolerance and willingness to experience uncomfortable feelings. Additionally, behavior experiments should be used to gradually expose group members to distressing situations and to dispel irrational beliefs through the practical application of new behaviors.

COMMUNITY SUPPORT   Those with HD experience a variety of consequences in addition to emotional discomfort and isolation. They may be evicted from their homes if it is found that the clutter poses a public safety hazard, either as the result of pests or fire hazards. Additionally, they often have comorbid health problems due to unsanitary living conditions (e.g., mice droppings, bedbugs, dust, debris).

Whitfield et al. (2012) implemented a community support program in which a variety of community agencies (e.g., social workers, home health care nurses, geriatric neuropsychologists and nurses, fire and safety investigators, safety officer, public health workers) worked together under the direction of a local seniors association. The collaboration between community organizations helped clients get the care that they needed and offered practical services, such as trash removal and professional organization of hoarded materials. As a result of such collaboration, participants in this program were able to stay in their own homes without facing eviction or such extreme safety hazards, and their isolation was reduced. Additionally, participants in the program reported feeling more empowered, and community members gained valuable insight into this often debilitating disorder (Whitfield et al., 2012).

Related to community support, it can be helpful to provide mental health support for family, friends, and caregivers of those who have HD (Tompkins, 2011), or to otherwise integrate family into treatment. Clients with HD often refuse treatment or have high rates of noncompliance. It is difficult for family members and caregivers to understand the client's disorder and to cope with the negative consequences of HD. As such, counselors can offer support and psychoeducation to family members and caregivers of those who have HD (Steketee et al., 2010).

PSYCHOPHARMACOTHERAPY   First, counselors should consider that those with HD may be prone to losing medications in a cluttered home, and this may present a challenge to medication compliance. Psychopharmaceuticals can be helpful in treating clients who have HD (Saxena, 2011). However, the research on the use of medication to treat HD is currently limited. Selective serotonin reuptake inhibitors (SSRIs) appear to be particularly helpful in treating this population (Saxena, 2011), and counselors should collaborate with psychiatrists in order to inform the physician of the client's psychological symptoms so that they can best identify the particular medication that will work best for individual client's symptoms.

Similar to the treatment of OCD, it is possible to augment HD treatment with SSRIs with the use of antipsychotic medication, such as in cases in which the antidepressant alone is not yielding significant results (Rothschild, 2010). As previously mentioned, the significant side effects associated with antipsychotic medications should be considered.

Prognosis

HD often begins to develop during childhood or adolescence. The earlier this population receives treatment, the better the prognosis (Storch et al., 2011). With treatment and other forms of collaborative support, people with HD can go on to live productive lives. The occurrence of co-occurring disorders can complicate the clinical picture, resulting in a poorer prognosis. In general, HD can be a challenging disorder to treat.

BODY DYSMORPHIC DISORDER

Description of the Disorder and Typical Client Characteristics

Body dysmorphic disorder (BDD) is characterized by an excessive and time-consuming preoccupation with a perceived flaw or defect in physical appearance that results in significant psychological distress and impairment. The perceived flaws are very minor, if at all noticeable to others. This disorder has undergone several changes in the transition from the *DSM-IV-TR* to the *DSM-5* (APA, 2013). Because of the intrusive and persistent thoughts and compulsive behaviors associated with BDD, it is now classified as an obsessive-compulsive and related disorder rather than a somatoform disorder.

People with this disorder often obsess over the size and shape of body parts. Any body area can be focused on, but the skin (e.g., wrinkles, color, blemishes), hair (e.g., too much or too little), breasts, genitals, stomach, and nose are among the most common. Concerns with body fat and size can also be encompassed by this diagnosis, but only when the symptoms are not better accounted for by an eating disorder. Muscle dysphoria is a type of BDD that occurs predominantly in males, and is indicative of a preoccupation with muscularity and leanness. This population typically has poor insight into the functions and dynamics of the disorder, and they do not usually recognize that their concern and preoccupations are inaccurate.

These perceived imperfections cause intense distress that results in compulsive mental acts or behaviors such as comparing one's self to others, picking skin, exercising or grooming excessively, checking or avoiding mirrors, asking for reassurance about appearance, repetitively touching the perceived imperfection, camouflaging the body part (e.g., with makeup, strategically placed clothing, wigs), using steroids, or seeking cosmetic procedures. Unfortunately, those who undergo cosmetic procedures are often dissatisfied with the outcome and may experience more distress than prior to the surgery. People with severe BDD may even perform cosmetic modifications on themselves.

The psychological distress associated with BDD can severely impair all areas of functioning. Beliefs that others are focusing on their flaws and the time-consuming nature of camouflaging methods may cause them to avoid social situations and miss school or work. The thought of going out in public can provoke significant anxiety. They are also typically very self-conscious and may even refuse to appear in photographs. Family members, friends, and significant others may have an especially difficult time understanding the client's preoccupation with the flaw which, if even present, is likely to be minor.

Counselor Considerations

Clients with BDD may enter counseling presenting with a number of co-occurring disorders including major depressive disorder, social anxiety disorder, obsessive-compulsive

[handwritten margin note: Relationships impacted, social isolation may occur]

disorder, and/or substance use disorders. Suicidal ideation and attempts may be present as a result of the severity of psychological distress associated with BDD. Clients with BDD may also have delusions of reference, in which they believe others are noticing and ridiculing their imperfections. Female clients with BDD are more likely to present with comorbid eating disturbances (APA, 2013)

A cultural conceptualization of the client's presenting concerns about his or her body is necessary, especially in the case of those of Japanese descent. *Shubo-kyofu,* a condition that exists in the Japanese population, is characterized by the fear of having a deformed body. The symptoms of *shubo-kyofu* resemble those of BDD and can result in social isolation. *Koro,* a condition that exists in Southeast Asia, also has symptoms consistent with BDD. Those with *koro* have an intense fear and preoccupation that their genitals will recede into the body and potentially lead to death (Phillips, 2004). Despite cultural variations, body dysmorphic disorder symptoms are quite reliable across cultures. Variations in presentation of BDD are most apparent when looking at differences in which body parts are the focus of the preoccupation. This is consistent with the notion that standards of attractiveness vary among cultures.

Clients with BDD may be hostile toward counselors, particularly if they have been referred to counseling by a physician refusing to perform a cosmetic procedure. They will be intensely self-conscious and distressed by their appearance; however, counselors must be very careful about commenting on the client's appearance. The perceived flaws or imperfections that clients with BDD focus on are typically very slight or completely unnoticeable to others. Counselors must be mindful when discounting the perceived flaw or complimenting clients' appearances, as this may frustrate clients. Clients may perceive dismissals or compliments as dishonest and it may feel like the counselor is minimizing the concerns. This client perception will prevent disclosure and hinder the formation of a therapeutic relationship. Those with BDD will likely be hypersensitive to criticism, and counselors must also be mindful of this.

Counselors should be supportive and encouraging, as clients with BDD may feel shameful, embarrassed, and unlovable because of their perceived imperfections. Embarrassment may be heightened if clients have insight into their condition and have even a slight understanding that their concerns may not be reasonable. Those with BDD may enter therapy because their relationships with their family members and significant others have been impaired. Preoccupations with appearance may cause clients to be perceived as vain, self-centered, and selfish by their loved ones. Clients may also experience strain in relationships related to financial difficulties. Clients may spend large amounts of money on cosmetic procedures, clothing, and beauty products to camouflage or "fix" their flaw. Counselors should also be aware of their own perceptions of these clients so as not to react verbally or nonverbally in ways that could be harmful to the therapeutic relationship.

Counselors may collaborate with physicians to treat clients with BDD. Clients who are at risk due to steroid use, extreme dieting, or self-performed cosmetic procedures should be referred to a physician.

Treatment Models and Interventions

In general, interventions for BDD should address social inhibition, impaired relationships, and diminished assertiveness associated with the disorder. One meta-analysis of BDD treatment approaches reported that behavior therapy, cognitive behavioral therapy, and pharmacological interventions effectively treated the disorder (Williams, Hadjistavropoulos,

& Sharpe, 2006). Psychotherapy interventions are generally found to be more effective at reducing BDD symptomology during treatment, and are associated with better follow-up outcomes and relapse prevention than medication use alone (Williams et al., 2006).

BEHAVIOR THERAPY (BT) BT for BDD typically includes exposure and response prevention (ERP) training (See the OCD treatment section; Prazeres, Nascimento, & Fontenelle, 2013; Williams et al., 2006). This training involves exposing clients to anxiety-provoking stimuli (e.g., the site of their perceived flaw) and preventing response behaviors (e.g., camouflaging or hiding the body part). The ERP training begins with exposure to stimuli that provoke a minimal amount of anxiety and progresses to include stimuli that induce high amounts of distress. The training continues until the client's anxiety responses are brought down to a manageable level. ERP has been reported as an efficacious treatment for BDD (Prazeres et al., 2013; Williams et al., 2006), but this technique is most commonly used in conjunction with cognitive therapy techniques in treatment.

COGNITIVE BEHAVIORAL THERAPY (CBT) Both group and individual CBT interventions have been found to effectively treat BDD (Prazeres et al., 2013). However, because of the shame and embarrassment that is associated with this disorder, care should be taken to ascertain whether a group setting is appropriate for a client. CBT techniques often include ERP training in conjunction with recognizing automatic thoughts, identifying cognitive distortions, and thought modification. Randomized controlled studies have supported CBT as an effective treatment for BDD and associated depressive symptoms (Veale et al., 1996).

INFERENCE-BASED THERAPY (IBT) Inference-based therapy is a cognitive-based approach that was originally developed for use with clients with OCD. IBT has been suggested as an alternative to CBT, and has been shown to be successful in reducing both BDD and co-occurring depressive symptoms (Taillon, O'Connor, Dupuis, & Lavoie, 2013). An IBT intervention for BDD combats clients' personal narratives about themselves; narratives that support their negative self-perceptions. The focus of IBT is upon addressing faulty inferences and overvalued, obsessional thoughts. Primary inferences are those a person makes based upon his or her own imagined possibilities, rather than through reality-based sources (e.g., five senses, common sense). Primary inferences would include thoughts about imperfections and flaws. The importance of these inferences is often overvalued by the client, and also leads to secondary inferences (e.g., I am flawed, and therefore unacceptable). IBT approaches address BDD by contrasting reality-based inferences versus imagination-based inferences, and encouraging a shift towards trusting information gained from the senses (i.e., reality) rather than the imagination.

PSYCHOPHARMACOTHERAPY At this time, there are no medications indicated specifically for the treatment of BDD. Antidepressant medications including tricyclics (e.g., clomipramine, desipramine) and selective serotonin reuptake inhibitors (e.g., fluvoxamine, fluoxetine, citalopram) have been used to treat BDD. In one meta-analytic study on the treatment of BDD, it was found that a combination of SSRIs and CBT was an effective treatment for the disorder (Ipser, Sander, & Stein, 2009). The use of antidepressant medication may help to alleviate the depressive symptomology that frequently co-occurs in clients with BDD.

Antipsychotic medication may be prescribed to augment SSRI treatment, particularly *and counseling* in the presence of delusions related to BDD (Phillips, 2004). Side effects, particularly those that may alter appearance (e.g., weight gain), are associated with the use of antidepressant and antipsychotic medications. These potential side effects should be considered when treating a client with BDD.

Prognosis

BDD typically emerges gradually with subclinical symptomology beginning around the ages of 12–13 and developing into the full diagnosis by ages 16–17. Early-onset BDD (before age 18) is associated with higher rates of comorbid diagnoses and suicide attempts (Bjornsson et al., 2013). Comorbidity and level of insight into diagnosis will affect each client's prognosis. Symptom severity decreases with treatment and can be maintained after treatment is discontinued. A greater quality of life can be achieved, and symptoms can be reduced to manageable levels (Taillon et al., 2013).

TRICHOTILLOMANIA (HAIR PULLING DISORDER)

Description of the Disorder and Typical Client Characteristics

Trichotillomania involves the repetitive removal of body hair with an accompanying sense of gratification, pleasure, or relief from anxiety. This condition typically results in noticeable hair loss, but depends on the frequency and duration of the behavior, as well as the area from which the hair is being removed. The scalp, eyebrows, and eyelashes are the areas from which hair is most commonly pulled (Woods, Wetterneck, & Flessner, 2006), but some clients may pull hair from their armpits, chest, face, and pubic areas. As clients with trichotillomania age, the number of sites where hair pulling occurs often increases (Flessner, Woods, Franklin, Keuthen, & Piacentini, 2009). Hair may be pulled out in clumps, but it is more common for clients with trichotillomania to pull single strands of hair at a time. Clients may pull hair out from the root, or twist hair until it breaks. In addition to pulling their own hair, people with trichotillomania may also feel the urge to pull hair from other people or objects (e.g., a pet or a doll). Hair-like fibers may also be pulled out of carpets and clothing to achieve the same sense of gratification or tension release. Combs, brushes, tweezers, and fingers are frequently used to remove hair (Walther, Ricketts, Conelea, & Woods, 2010). Often, those with trichotillomania enjoy examining the root of each strand of hair, and some may even place strands of hair in their mouth, pulling the strands between their teeth. Ecophagia, the consumption of hair, may also occur. Trichotillomania appears to manifest with similar characteristics across cultures (APA, 2013).

Several general medical conditions are associated with trichotillomania. Hair pulling may result in skin infections, tissue irritation and inflammation, and bleeding. Ecophagia *consumption of hair* is associated with esophageal erosion, bowel obstructions, production of trichobezoars (i.e., hairballs), nausea and vomiting, abdominal pain, and anemia. If undetected and untreated, bowel obstructions and trichobezoars can be fatal.

People with trichotillomania are often secretive about their behavior, and as such, researchers have had difficulties estimating the true prevalence of this condition. It is estimated that three million people in the United States, or 1–2% of the population, has trichotillomania (APA, 2013; Duke, Keeley, Geffken, & Storch, 2010). In children, this disorder affects boys and girls equally; however, as age increases, trichotillomania becomes more common in women (APA, 2013).

Trichotillomania symptoms can wax and wane over time, and symptom-free interludes may exist. Some clients may have binges in which they pull significant amounts of hair within a short period of time, or may have a consistent pattern of behavior. Great variation exists in the length of time that clients engage in hair-pulling episodes. Clients may engage in plucking hair for hours at a time. Stress exacerbates symptoms, and anxiety-provoking situations may increase the urge to pull (Duke et al., 2010).

Duke et al. (2010) proposed that trichotillomania can be categorized into three non–mutually exclusive types: early onset, automatic, and focused. Early-onset trichotillomania occurs before the age of eight, and often discontinues without intervention. This subtype is not typically associated with urges to pull or feelings of relief, gratitude, or pleasure. Clients in the automatic subtype engage in hair-pulling behaviors while they are immersed in other tasks (e.g., watching television, reading a book) or during downtime. The behavior takes place mostly out of the client's awareness, as opposed to the focused subtype, in which people experience urges and engage in hair pulling as a means of achieving feelings of satisfaction.

Trichotillomania is often compared to obsessive-compulsive disorder (OCD). The focused subtype is similar to OCD in that clients have urges to engage in the behavior, and the act relieves tension. However, the automatic subtype differs from OCD behavior, as hair pulling is engaged in during times of distraction, and no obsessive thoughts are present to precipitate the behavior.

Counselor Considerations

Clients with trichotillomania may be reluctant to disclose their behavior. Counselors should be prepared to exercise patience, as clients may become defensive or blatantly deny the behavior. Because clients may have limited social supports secondary to the significant impairment in social functioning that is associated with trichotillomania, encouragement and support will be especially important. The counselor may be the only person with whom the client is willing to share his or her condition, and feelings of judgment can discourage continued treatment. Those entering treatment are likely embarrassed about their behavior and their inability to control it, especially if it has resulted in noticeable changes to their physical appearance. Clients may be ridiculed for their hair loss, especially adolescents, as the teenage years are already a time of increased self-consciousness about appearance. Clients may feel abnormal and alone in their struggles with this condition, and reassurances and psychoeducation from the counselor may help to diminish these feelings.

Clients with trichotillomania may enter treatment presenting with co-occurring eating, depressive, and/or anxiety disorders (Duke et al., 2010; McDonald, 2012). The disorder is also sometimes associated with intellectual disabilities. The majority of people with this disorder also engage in other body-focused repetitive behaviors such as nail biting, skin picking, or lip chewing (APA, 2013).

Social functioning is often diminished in clients with noticeable hair loss, and they may begin to avoid social activities and situations because of lowered self-esteem and increased self-consciousness. Clients may also prefer to stay home or in an environment in which they can engage in hair pulling in private. Insecurity and body image dissatisfaction can also be associated with feelings of depression and anxiety, which can further impair clients' occupational or academic functioning.

Relationships with family members may be strained, as they may not understand why the client engages in the behavior, and they may also be embarrassed about the client's change in appearance. It may be helpful to include partners or family members in treatment.

Being mindful of nonverbal behavior will also be an important consideration for counselors, as clients with this condition may be highly self-conscious about their appearance. The physical appearance of a client may be drastically affected, and counselors should take care not to stare or convey negative nonverbal messages. Referral to a physician for examination to determine if the hair-pulling behavior is related to a general medical condition is recommended. Counselors should also be careful to ascertain whether the hair pulling is the result of a client's hallucinations or delusions, as this would warrant the exploration of a different diagnostic path.

Treatment Models and Interventions

Variations of behavior and cognitive behavioral therapies are the preferred treatment for trichotillomania. Among this group of therapies, the most commonly used treatment in addressing trichotillomania is habit reversal training, which is typically used in conjunction with other therapeutic interventions. The following sections will detail the types of treatments typically used to treat this disorder.

BEHAVIOR THERAPY   Habit reversal training (HRT) and stimulus control are the two behavior therapy interventions that are most commonly found to be efficacious in treating trichotillomania. HRT is considered the most efficacious intervention, and therefore it is a first-line treatment for treating trichotillomania (Duke et al., 2010; McDonald, 2012). HRT can be broken down into three components: awareness training/self-monitoring, competing response training, and social support. Clients are first encouraged to monitor their hair pulling and to become aware of the thoughts, feelings, and triggers of the behavior. Next, clients are taught to use a behavior that opposes hair pulling. For example, clients can clench their fists for 60–90 seconds when experiencing an urge to pull their hair. The last element, social support, asks clients to involve family members and friends in treatment. Members of the clients' social support network can encourage them to practice competing response training skills when they feel the urge to pull. Additional techniques from other therapeutic approaches are often incorporated into HRT to produce optimal results (McDonald, 2012).

Stimulus control (SC) is another behavior therapy intervention often used inconjunction with HRT (McDonald, 2012; Walther et al., 2010). SC requires clients to examine the stimuli that prompt their hair-pulling behaviors. For example, clients who are stimulated to pull hair after touching their skin or scalp may wear gloves or rubber fingertips to avoid the stimulating sensation. Those who stand in front of a mirror while engaging in hair pulling may cover the mirror. Situations in which the client experiences the urge to pull may also be avoided as a part of SC (e.g., refraining from sitting for long periods of time in front of the television if this is a trigger for the behavior).

CREATIVE TOOLBOX ACTIVITY 6.2   The Grab Bag

Matthew J. Paylo, PhD, LPCC-S

Activity Overview

In this creative intervention, clients with body-focused repetitive behaviors (e.g., skin picking, nail biting, hair pulling) enhance their utilization of problem-solving skills learned in treatment, while attempting to increase their ability to tolerate stressful situations. Clients are asked to create a list of competing activities that they can utilize when the urge to pick, bite, or pull becomes overwhelming. Clients then transfer those activities or ideas, which have been practiced in sessions, on individual pieces of paper. These pieces of papers are then put in a small bag that can be placed within a purse or client's pocket for use in a situation that may require the use of a competing activity.

Treatment Goal(s) of Activity

The primary goals of this activity are to help clients (a) identify times when they may engage in picking, biting, or pulling; (b) construct a list of competing activities; and (c) implement these competing activities in real-life settings rather than acting on the urge to pick, bite, or pull.

Directions

1. The counselor and client process the client's body-focused repetitive behaviors. This discussion increases the client's awareness of the dynamics and associated antecedents of these behaviors. Additionally, the counselor and the client need to identify precursors to these urges and sensations. This is foundational to the rest of the activity.
2. Provide the client with a piece of construction paper. Brainstorm with the client possible competing activities that could be utilized in times of intense urges. These identified activities need to be accessible to the client for use in a variety of circumstances. An additional question that can be asked when creating a list of possible competing activities is to ask the client if he or she has ever felt an urge, yet was able to do something else instead of engaging in the urge. These exceptions can help highlight competing activities that may be more beneficial to the client.
3. Ask the client to list each competing activity that may be an option.
4. Ask the client to practice each idea in session. If an idea is unable to be practiced in session, ask the client to walk you through his or her process step-by-step.
5. Next, ask the client to cut out each idea (on a small square of paper) and place those ideas in a small bag. The counselor can provide this bag. Essentially, this bag will need to be placed in an area that is always accessible to the client (e.g., purse, wallet, pocket).
6. Instruct the client to pull one competing activity/idea out of this bag each time he or she is presented with the urge to pick, bite, or pull. If after engaging in this competing activity, the client is still filled with the urge to pick, bite, or pull, then he or she is instructed to select another competing activity.

Process Questions

1. How did you utilize the bag this week? What was that like for you?
2. What did it feel like to be utilizing the competing activity/idea in that situation?
3. Talk about being able to distract yourself from the urge.
4. What did you notice about your thoughts, feelings, and behaviors after utilizing a competing activity?
5. Which competing activities appear to work better than others?
6. What was the most and/or least challenging aspect of this activity for you?

ACCEPTANCE AND COMMITMENT THERAPY (ACT)   A randomized controlled study reported that ACT (a type of cognitive behavioral therapy; Hayes et al., 2006) used in combination with habit reversal training effectively reduced trichotillomania symptoms, and treatment gains were maintained at a 3-month follow-up assessment (Woods et al., 2006). One example of an ACT intervention for use with trichotillomania is encouraging clients to begin participating in the activities that they once enjoyed, but withdrew from as a result of their hair pulling. Instead of rejecting and avoiding feelings, thoughts, and urges related to their hair pulling, clients are taught through ACT interventions to be aware and accepting instead. ACT also encourages clients to refrain from activities that bring temporary pleasure (e.g., hair pulling), but impair progression toward goals that are important to the client (e.g., spending time with others). As time spent engaging in positive activities increases, time spent pulling hair will decrease. As clients' avoidance decreases, they are able to move toward their valued goals with less obstruction. A nonjudgmental awareness may also reduce the negative emotions that clients attach to their trichotillomania. Approaches similar to ACT that stimulate awareness may be particularly useful with clients with automatic hair pulling behaviors, as it helps them to be more conscious of the behavior.

DIALECTICAL BEHAVIOR THERAPY (DBT)   DBT is a form of cognitive behavioral therapy that emphasizes learning and strengthening the skills needed to regulate emotions (Linehan, 2000). DBT interventions for trichotillomania emphasize learning emotion regulation and distress tolerance skills (Keuthen et al., 2010b). From a DBT perspective, hair pulling is viewed as a maladaptive emotion regulation strategy, and clients are thus taught to enhance adaptive emotion regulation strategies to reduce the severity of hair-pulling behaviors. Skills similar to those of HRT can be incorporated into DBT interventions that include helping the client to become more aware and mindful of behavior and associated thoughts, emotions, and sensations, and also training in stimulus control, competing responses, and habit prevention.

> **Clinical Toolbox 6.2:** In the Pearson etext, click here to read about a creative activity that can be used to help clients construct a timeline of their trichotillomania, and contextualize the relationship between trichotillomania and various life experiences.

PSYCHOPHARMACOTHERAPY   Randomized controlled studies have reported that behavior therapy approaches are superior to medication use alone in addressing trichotillomania (Duke et al., 2010). At this time, no medications are indicated specifically for the treatment of trichotillomania. The use of psychopharmacological interventions may be more appropriate for use in treating disorders that are present comorbidly with trichotillomania. Lithium, atypical antipsychotics (e.g., olanzapine), dopamine blockers (e.g., pimozide), opioid agonists (e.g., naltrexone), and tricyclic antidepressants (e.g., clomipramine) have been utilized in treatment yielding mixed results, but published support of pharmacological interventions utilizing randomized controlled studies does not exist at this time (McDonald, 2012).

As anxiety may worsen trichotillomania symptoms, it is reasonable to assume that treatment with antianxiety medications may reduce hair pulling. However, benzodiazepine medications are not recommended for long-term usage in general, as they are associated with high risks of dependency and abuse. Antidepressant medications indicated for the treatment of anxiety symptoms may provide a better option, as the risk of abuse is low. Additionally, medications that target glutamate receptors are being explored for the treatment of trichotillomania, as this neurotransmitter has been indicated as contributing to compulsive behaviors (Grant, Song, & Swedo, 2010). These medications include lamotrigine and riluzole. The amino acid N-acetyl-cysteine has also shown promise in reducing hair-pulling behaviors (Grant, Odlaug, & Kim, 2009).

Prognosis

Because the condition often fluctuates in severity over time, outcomes vary. Some clients may have consistent periods in which they engage in hair pulling, while others may have intermittent periods of time in which they are symptom free. In children with early-onset trichotillomania, prognosis is favorable, and full remission of the behavior is common (Duke et al., 2010). Psychotherapy interventions can improve trichotillomania symptomology, as well as associated depression, anxiety, and low self-esteem (Duke et al., 2010).

EXCORIATION (SKIN PICKING) DISORDER

Description of the Disorder and Typical Client Characteristics

Excoriation (skin picking) disorder is a disorder newly added to the *DSM-5* (APA, 2013). A relatively common disorder, excoriation is estimated to affect between 1.4 and 5.4% of the general population (Hayes, Storch, & Berlanga, 2009; Keuthen, Koran, Aboujaude, Large, & Serpe, 2010a). Excoriation disorder seems to be highly correlated with depressive, anxiety, and obsessive-compulsive symptoms (Hayes et al., 2009; Tucker, Woods, Flessner, Franklin, & Franklin, 2011), with an onset occurring either in early adolescence or in middle adulthood (i.e., 30s or 40s). The severity, prevalence, and course of this disorder has yet to be explored in children (McGuire et al., 2012).

Excoriation disorder involves excessively and impulsively scratching, rubbing, or picking normal skin, which creates skin lesions. The essential component of this disorder is the person's sense of powerlessness and the perception that he or she is unable to control these behaviors. These picking behaviors can cause significant, visible skin and tissue scarring, and potentially lead to infections and pigmentation changes. Although most people utilize their fingers or fingernails, some utilize their teeth as well as instruments (e.g., spoons, tweezers, nail files) to fulfill picking urges. While most locate specific sites on their bodies that are easily accessed (e.g., face, arms, neck), they may pick at multiple sites, and may perform rituals such as tactile stimulation (i.e., sliding fingers over skin) before and after they engage in picking behaviors (Snorrason, Belleau, & Woods, 2012).

Those with excoriation disorder often find it difficult to resist the urge to act, and to identify their patterns of behaviors, and they believe their behaviors are unchangeable. Picking behaviors are often divided into two types: automatic and focused (Christenson & Mackenzie, 1994). *Automatic* picking happens outside of one's level of awareness (e.g., picking that occurs while engaged in another activity such as watching television or reading a book). *Focused* picking is within one's awareness and usually occurs when one is feeling anxious and/or as an attempt to regulate strong feelings. Either one of these picking behaviors can impair daily functioning and cause significant embarrassment, distress, and an overwhelming sense that one lacks control and cannot stop the behavior (Odlaug, Chamberlain, & Grant, 2010). The compulsive and obsessive nature of this disorder, along with the similarities with trichotillomania (Snorrason et al., 2012) and body dysmorphic disorder (Tucker et al., 2011), are a primary reason for their reclassification within the *DSM-5* (APA, 2013) into the obsessive-compulsive and related disorders category. These disorders are compulsive in nature and people often present with an overwhelming urge to act, which is often followed by a brief sense of relief once the behavior has been engaged and completed; only to have the urge inevitably arise again. Limited research has been conducted to explore cultural differences in excoriation; however, it is believed to present similarly across cultures (Lester, 2012).

Counselor Considerations

Because of their embarrassment and a belief that their behavior cannot be controlled or changed, people with excoriation disorder do not typically seek treatment. They are often referred to treatment by family members, friends, and significant others who are worried about their perceived level of impairment and distress. On average, only about 50% of those with this disorder seek treatment, and those who seek treatment often report that providers are relatively uninformed and lack the training needed to help them (Tucker et al., 2011). Once in treatment, they are often guarded and apprehensive about treatment; therefore, counselors need to build a strong working alliance with these clients. One way to facilitate this is by helping clients explore how these behaviors are problematic, identifying patterns of repetitive behaviors, and instilling hope that change is indeed possible.

Because this disorder involves skin damage, referral to a medical provider is an important aspect of treatment. Skin lesions can trigger clients to pick. As such, medical interventions that minimize lesions may reduce picking (e.g., if a client has acne, medication may reduce skin lesions and reduce the client's skin picking).

Treatment Models and Interventions

Few randomized controlled trials exist for the treatment of excoriation disorder (Tucker et al., 2011). The treatments found to be useful in treating this disorder are similar to those used in treating trichotillomania. Several randomized controlled trials suggest that cognitive behavioral therapy (Schuck, Keijsers, & Rinck, 2011), habit reversal training (Teng, Woods, & Twohig, 2006), and psychopharmacotherapy (Grant & Odlaug, 2009) are the most effective treatments for those with excoriation disorder. These approaches are in their infancy stages in terms of validation, have yet to be replicated, and warrant further exploration (Tucker et al., 2011). Additionally, some preliminary case studies and pilot research has suggested acceptance and commitment therapy as an emerging approach in treating this disorder (Flessner, Busch, Heideman, & Woods, 2008; Twohig, Hayes, & Masuda, 2006).

COGNITIVE BEHAVIORAL THERAPY (CBT)   When used in the treatment of those with excoriation disorder, CBT addresses distorted and dysfunctional thoughts related to picking behaviors by identifying, challenging, and modifying these beliefs (Schuck et al., 2011). In applying a CBT approach, counselors must first gather information related to the nature of the behaviors (e.g., locations, symptoms) and provide a psychoeducational component to teach clients about the development and maintenance of these unwanted behaviors. Counselors can use Socratic questioning to highlight the fundamental beliefs and the automatic thoughts associated with these behaviors (e.g., Why do you believe this thought? Are there reasons to doubt this belief?). Some examples of the dysfunctional thoughts associated with excoriation disorder are: I can't resist this urge; I had a stressful day, therefore, I should be able to do this; I will be unable to relax until I do this, so I should just do it: and/or, I have to squeeze harder to remove this irregularity. The validity of irrational and maladaptive thoughts are tested and subsequently replaced with more functional thoughts. For example, clients may feel they need to pick their arms to relax after stressful situations. When the validity of this idea is tested, they may realize after questioning it that they may be able to relax more readily by taking a shower or even walking their dog around the block. A client can then adopt a more realistic thought (e.g., "I may become anxious, but that is okay. I can tolerate it. I don't have to pick to relieve stress, I can take a shower to relieve my stress, or I can walk this stress right off").

CBT can also include behavior-based interventions, which involve enhancing clients' awareness of skin-picking behaviors, and using behavioral alternatives. This could involve the use of gloves or bandages on one's hands during critical or stressful times. Another behavior intervention could be to delay clients' picking behaviors by encouraging them to engage in another activity in place of the picking behaviors (i.e., listening to music, calling a friend, cleaning). Homework is another essential component of this approach. For example, an assignment could include having a client chart his or her picking behaviors (e.g., frequency, precipitating events, thoughts, emotions), and then having the client implement a delaying technique, or an alternative behavior in place of those picking behaviors. Finally, a CBT approach highlights the need for clients to be prepared for relapse and assists clients in planning ahead for these future urges and situations.

HABIT REVERSAL TRAINING (HRT)   HRT is a behavioral treatment approach aimed at treating a wide variety of repetitive behavior disorders (e.g., skin picking, nail biting, trichotillomania). HRT focuses on enhancing clients' awareness of their behaviors, developing a competing response for their picking behaviors, creating a contingency management system (e.g., the use of reinforcement to increase their desired behaviors), and generalizing their new behaviors to alternative situations (Teng et al., 2006).

The first component of HRT involves defining the skin-picking behaviors and enhancing clients' awareness of the existence of the behaviors and associated antecedents. For example, a counselor may have clients look into a mirror to see how their behaviors "look" or are being displayed, or they may role-play these behaviors, asking clients to better identify their exact behaviors. As their awareness develops, clients are instructed to be more mindful of when the initial stages of these behaviors commence, or cease. Not only can clients then identify situations that exacerbate their urges, but they can also identify the early warning signs and precursors to their urges and sensations.

After their awareness has improved, a competing response to those behaviors must be developed. These responses should be something that can be carried out with little to no preparation in a host of situations. For example, having clients clench their fists for a whole minute can occupy their hands and make picking difficult until their urge dissipates or at least diminishes in intensity. These responses need to be developed collaboratively with clients so the responses occur more frequently.

Next, a system of reinforcements should be implemented. Systems such as a token economy or a contingency contract with the counselor are two ways to implement a contingency management plan that can be used in real-life situations. These reinforcements need to be meaningful, manageable, and timely. Once some mastery over these behaviors is accomplished in sessions, clients are then encouraged to implement these techniques in other real-life situations.

Clinical Toolbox 6.3: In the Pearson etext, click here to watch a video demonstration of habit reversal techniques.

ACCEPTANCE AND COMMITMENT THERAPY (ACT) ACT is a cognitive behavioral therapy that incorporates acceptance, mindfulness, and behavior-change strategies (Flessner et al., 2008). In the early stages of treatment, clients learn to distinguish the differences between urges (e.g., thoughts, sensations, feelings) and actual picking behaviors. The counselor aids clients in exploring their past attempts to control, diminish, and even decrease their urges to pick. These attempts highlight that most people are only able to extinguish these urges by acting on them; yet this solution only brings temporary relief because their urges ultimately return. Counselors can use this as an opportunity to utilize metaphors to help clients realize that their past attempts to deal with the problem are what is actually maintaining their problem behaviors (Hayes, Strosahl, & Wilson, 1999; Twohig et al., 2006). ACT draws on these metaphors and mindfulness exercises to promote greater self-acceptance and promote being in the present moment (i.e., being a mindful observer), rather than focusing on future-oriented thoughts or concerns. Clients are encouraged to notice their emotional responses, tolerate discomfort, and ultimately engage in more valued behaviors.

Creative hopelessness is an ACT technique that involves encouraging clients to assess what they have tried to change, considering whether it has truly worked, and creating space for something new or creative to happen. It is in this space of creative hopelessness that new strategies can be developed without the overemphasis on previous rules used to govern their behavior.

Clinical Toolbox 6.4: In the Pearson etext, click here to read an acceptance and commitment therapy (ACT) metaphor (i.e., Man in the Hole) that can be used to create a context for the ACT concept of creative hopelessness.

Treatment involves changing clients' thinking and the feelings associated with their urges. This can be done through addressing the different components of the "hexaflex" model, which proposes that six processes contribute to healthy, flexible living: (a) attention to the present moment; (b) acceptance; (c) defusion (i.e., the ability to "step back" and separate from thoughts and language); (d) self-as-context (i.e., the realization that you are not your thoughts, feelings, and memories; although they are a part of you, they are not the essence of who you are); (e) values; and (f) committed action. Finally, treatment ends with a review of treatment gains and a plan for relapse and maintenance.

PSYCHOPHARMACOTHERAPY Selective serotonin reuptake inhibitors (SSRIs), in particular fluoxetine (i.e., Prozac), have demonstrated efficacy in the treatment of body-focused repetitive behaviors such as obsessive-compulsive disorder, trichotillomania, and excoriation disorder (Grant & Odlaug, 2009). However, not all clients report clinically significant improvements from SSRIs; therefore, the results of these studies should be "interpreted cautiously" (Grant & Odlaug, 2009, p. 286).

It is possible to treat symptoms that trigger skin-picking behaviors, such as feelings of anxiety and depression, with medication. Antidepressant and antianxiety medications may be helpful in these cases. Temporary use of antianxiety medications may also be useful when clients are applying learned behavioral skills that may cause discomfort. However, it is important that clients prescribed benzodiazepine antianxiety medications be monitored for abuse and dependency.

If the skin-picking behaviors are related to "bumpiness" or blemishes, clients should be referred to a dermatologist to obtain medication to improve their complexion, thus possibly helping to reduce the picking behaviors. Sensations such as itchiness may be reduced by using topical antihistamine medications. Topical analgesics may also be considered to aid in decreasing the physical sensations that sometimes trigger skin picking. Only physical health care providers are competent to prescribe medications (even over-the-counter medications), thus medication recommendations should come only from the client's medical providers.

Prognosis

The prognosis for people with excoriation disorder is unclear at this time. Because of the paucity of research, significant differences in severity of symptoms, and the relative newness of the disorder, the literature is lacking in significant support for evidenced-based treatment. Many clients experience a recurrence of symptoms after treatment (Keuthen et al., 2010). Therefore, counselors must prepare clients for relapse, so that treatment gains can be maintained.

TREATMENT PLAN FOR JOHN

This chapter began with a discussion of John, a 40-year-old married art teacher who has excessive, intrusive obsessions and compulsive behaviors. John meets the criteria for obsessive-compulsive disorder. A counselor must consider the contextual factors, diagnosis, and the necessary levels of care before moving ahead with a strength-based treatment approach. The following I CAN START conceptual framework outlines treatment considerations, which may be helpful in working with John.

C = Contextual Assessment

John is a middle-aged man. He has stable employment and lives in a middle-class environment that is safe and comfortable; all of his basic needs are met. He is a Latino male, but reports he is not especially connected to his cultural group from a community perspective. He reports that he lives and works with mostly middle-class Caucasians and he doesn't place much emphasis on his cultural heritage. Developmentally, he is middle-aged and appears to have traversed all developmental stages in a typical fashion. At present he is navigating generativity versus stagnation, and appears to find meaning in multiple areas in his life. Additionally, he has strong religious convictions and regularly attends church services. His spirituality is important to his sense of self, and he volunteers regularly for his church's youth group.

A = Assessment and Diagnosis

Diagnosis = Obsessive-Compulsive Disorder 300.3 (F42)

N = Necessary Level of Care

Outpatient, individual counseling (once per week)

S = Strength-Based Lens

Self: John is an intelligent, insightful, and creative individual. He is gainfully employed at a local school as an art teacher and is respected among his peers at the school. Additionally, John is passionate about his art and his teaching. He is an excellent artist who has begun to sell his own artwork within his community.

Family: John is married with two daughters. Although there is some discord with his wife, she is loving and supportive. He has a solid relationship with his two daughters. His eldest daughter is creative and has begun to share her father's interest and passion in art.

Community: John is actively engaged in his local church and has long-standing relationships with other parishioners. He has become more involved with the art community in his local area (e.g., annual art festival participant; promoting arts in schools). He appears to have a supportive, positive friend base.

T = Treatment Approach

Behavioral Therapy with Exposure and Response Prevention (ERP) and Cognitive Therapy (CT)

Marital counseling once obsessions and compulsions are stabilized

A = Aim and Objectives of Treatment (3-month objectives)

John will maintain medication compliance → John will have 100% compliance in taking prescribed medications and will miss 0 psychiatry appointments. If issues arise with medications, he will contact his psychiatrist and counselor.

John will increase his ability to tolerate anxiety and discomfort → John will create a hierarchy of stimuli that causes anxiety and discomfort (e.g., steering wheel; sink; checking behaviors; washing hands). John will gradually resist compulsive behaviors in exposure situations at least 75% of the time. He will learn how to tolerate these thoughts and situations in the moment, realizing that they do not produce the horrible outcomes which dominate thoughts.

John will become aware of how his intrusive thoughts affect his behaviors and emotions, and he will use skills to change his thoughts and behavior → John will identify and learn 2 CT skills (e.g., thought stopping, restructuring, coping strategies) that will be used to help him examine how his thought patterns are impacting his behaviors and emotions; he will examine ways to challenge his intrusive thoughts and alter his behaviors and emotions 75% of the time.

John will continue to create artwork and use this task as a form of anxiety management → John will use creating and selling his artwork as a means to reduce his overall anxiety 3 times a week.

R = Research-Based Interventions (based on CBT)

Counselor will help John develop and apply the following skills:
• Challenging intrusive thoughts
• Tolerating anxiety (without utilizing compulsive behaviors)
• Engaging in healthy coping strategies

Counselor will effectively utilize cognitive restructuring techniques with John. This restructuring will be aimed at his intrusive thoughts and misconceptions about anxiety and his own overestimations of the threats and danger around him.

Counselor will assist John in learning that these intrusive thoughts and compulsive behaviors are tolerable and will not lead to his worst fears.

Counselor will help John identify alternative behaviors he can use to help him manage his symptoms.

T = Therapeutic Support Services

Referral to a psychiatrist for consultation regarding medication currently prescribed by his primary care physician for his OCD

Medical consultation for his dermatitis

Weekly individual counseling

Community-based support groups with other individuals with obsessive-compulsive disorder

References

American Academy of Child and Adolescent Psychiatry. (2011, December). Obsessive compulsive disorder in children and adolescents. *Facts for Families, 60.* Retrieved April 25, 2013, from: http://www.aacap.org/galleries/FactsForFamilies/60_obsessive_compulsive_disorder_in_children_and_adolescents.pdf

American Psychiatric Association (APA). (2013). *Diagnostic and statistical manual of mental disorders* (5th ed. [DSM-5]). Washington, DC: Author.

Bjornsson, A. S., Diddie, E. R., Grant, J. E., Menard, W., Stalker, E., & Phillips, K. A. (2013). Age at onset and clinical correlates in body dysmorphic disorder. *Comprehensive Psychiatry.* pii: S0010-440X(13)00079-5.

Bolton, D., Williams, T., Perrin, S., Atkinson, L., Gallop, C., Waite, P., . . . Salkovskis, P. (2011). Randomized controlled trial of full and brief cognitive-behaviour therapy and wait-list for paediatric obsessive-compulsive disorder. *Journal of Child Psychology and Psychiatry, 52,* 1269–1278.

Christenson, G. A., & Mackenzie, T. B. (1994). Trichotillomania. In M. Hersen & R. T. Ammerman (Eds.), *Handbook of prescriptive treatment for adults* (pp. 217–235). New York, NY: Plenum.

Duke, D. C., Keeley, M. L., Geffken, G. R., & Storch, E. A. (2010). Trichotillomania: A current review. *Clinical Psychology Review, 30,* 181–193.

Flessner, C. A., Busch, A. M., Heideman, P. W., & Woods, D. W. (2008). Acceptance-enhanced behavior therapy (AEBT) for trichotillomania and chronic skin picking: Exploring the effects of component sequencing. *Behavior Modification, 32,* 579–594.

Flessner, C. A., Woods, D. W., Franklin, M. E., Keuthen, N. J., & Piacentini, J. (2009). Cross-sectional study of women with trichotillomania: A preliminary examination of pulling styles, severity, phenomenology, and functional impact. *Child Psychiatry and Human Development, 40,* 153–167.

Frost, R. O., Steketee, G., & Tolin, D. F. (2011). Comorbidity in hoarding disorder. *Depression and Anxiety, 28,* 876–884.

Gilliam, C. M., & Tolin, D. F. (2010). Compulsive hoarding. *Bulletin of the Menninger Clinic, 74,* 93–121.

Grant, J. E., & Odlaug, B. L. (2009). Update on pathological skin picking. *Current Psychiatry Reports, 11,* 283–288.

Grant, J. E., Odlaud, B. L., & Kim, S. W. (2009). N-acetylcysteine, a glutamate modulator, in the treatment of trichotillomania: A double-blind, placebo-controlled study. *Archives of General Psychiatry, 66*(7), 756–763.

Grant, P., Song, J. Y., & Swedo, S. E. (2010). Review of the use of the glutamate antagonist riluzole in psychiatric disorders and a description of recent use in childhood obsessive-compulsive disorder. *Journal of Child and Adolescent Psychopharmacology, 20*(4), 309–315.

Hansen, B., Vogel, P., Stiles, T., & Götestam, K. G. (2007). Influence of co-morbid generalized anxiety disorder, panic disorder and personality disorders on the outcome of cognitive behavioural treatment of obsessive-compulsive disorder. *Cognitive Behaviour Therapy, 36*, 145–155.

Hayes, S. C., Luoma, J. B., Bond, F. W., Masuda, A., & Lillis, J. (2006). Acceptance and commitment therapy: Model, processes and outcomes. *Behaviour Research & Therapy, 44*, 1–25.

Hayes, S. L., Storch, E. A., & Berlanga, L. (2009). Skin picking behaviors: An examination of the prevalence and severity in a community sample. *Journal of Anxiety Disorders, 23*, 314–319.

Hayes, S. C. Strosahl, K. D., & Wilson, K. G. (1999). *Acceptance and Commitment Therapy: An experiential approach to behavior change*. New York, NY: Guilford.

Hertenstein, E., Rose, N., Voderholzer, U., Heidenreich, T., Nissen, C., Thiel, N., . . . Kulz, A. (2012). Mindfulness-based cognitive therapy in obsessive-compulsive disorder—A qualitative study on patients' experiences. *BMC Psychiatry, 12*, 185–194.

Ipser, J., Sander, C., & Stein, D. (2009). Pharmacotherapy and psychotherapy for body dysmorphic disorder. *Cochrane Database of Systematic Reviews (Online)*, (1), CD005332. Retrieved from: http://www.ncbi.nlm.nih.gov/pubmed/19160252

Jonnson, H., Hougaard, E., & Bennedsen, B. E. (2010). Randomized comparative study of group versus individual cognitive behavioural therapy for obsessive compulsive disorder. *Acta Psychiatrica Scandinavica, 123*, 387–397.

Keuneman, R. J., Pokos, V., Weerasundera, R., & Castle, D. J. (2005). Antipsychotic treatment in obsessive compulsive disorder: A literature review. *Australian and New Zealand Journal of Psychiatry, 39*, 336–343.

Keuthen, N. J., Koran, L. M., Aboujaude, E., Large, M. D., & Serpe, R. T. (2010a). The prevalence of pathologic skin picking in US adults. *Comprehensive Psychiatry, 51*, 183–186.

Keuthen, N. J., Rothbaum, B. O., Welch, S. S., Taylor, C., Falkenstein, M., Heekin, M., . . . Jenike, M. A. (2010b). Pilot trial of dialectical behavior therapy-enhanced habit reversal for trichotillomania. *Depression and Anxiety, 27*, 953–959.

Lester, R. J. (2012). *Self-mutilation and excoriation*.

In T. F. Cash (Ed.), *Encyclopedia of body image and human appearance* (pp. 724–729). San Diego, CA: Academic Press.

Linehan, M. (2000). The empirical basis of dialectical behavior therapy: Development of new treatments versus evaluation of existing treatments. *Clinical Psychology: Science and Practice*, 7, 113–119.

Maltby, N., & Tolin, D. F. (2005). A brief motivational intervention for treatment-refusing OCD patients. *Cognitive Behaviour Therapy, 34*, 176–184.

McDonald, K. E. (2012). Trichotillomania: Identification and treatment. *Journal of Counseling & Development, 90*, 421–426.

McGuire, J. F., Kugler, B. B., Park, J. M., Horng, B., Lewin, A. B., Murphy, T. K., . . . Storch, E. A. (2012). Evidence-based assessment of compulsive skin picking, chronic tic disorders and trichotillomania in children. *Child Psychiatry and Human Development, 43*, 855–883.

Muroff, J., Steketee, G., Rasmussen, J., Gibson, A., Bratiotis, C., & Sorrentino, C. (2009). Group cognitive and behavioral treatment for compulsive hoarding: A preliminary trial. *Depression and Anxiety, 26*, 634–640.

Odlaug, B. L., Chamberlain, S. R., & Grant, J. E. (2010). Motor inhibition and cognitive flexibility in pathologic skin picking. *Progress in Neuro-Psychopharmacology & Biological Psychiatry, 34*, 208–211.

Olatunji, B. O., Davis, M. L., Powers, M. B., & Smits, J. A. (2013). Cognitive-behavioral therapy for obsessive-compulsive disorder: A meta-analysis of treatment outcome and moderators. *Journal of Psychiatric Research, 47*, 33–41.

Phillips, K. A. (2004). Body dysmorphic disorder: Recognizing and treating imagined ugliness. *World Psychiatry, 3*(1), 12–17.

Prazeres, A. M., Nascimento, A. L., & Fontenelle, L. F. (2013). Cognitive-behavioral therapy for body dysmorphic disorder: A review of its efficacy. *Neuropsychiatric Disease and Treatment, 9*, 307–316.

Preston, J. D., O'Neal, J. H., & Talaga, M. C. (2013). *Handbook of clinical psychopharmacology for therapists* (7th ed.). Oakland, CA: New Harbinger.

Rothschild, A. J. (2010). *The evidence-based guide to antipsychotic medications*. Arlington, VA: American Psychiatric Publishing.

Saxena, S. (2011). Pharmacotherapy of compulsive hoarding. *Journal of Clinical Psychology: In Session, 67*, 477–484.

Schuck, K., Keijsers, G. P., & Rinck, M. (2011). The effects of brief cognitive behaviour therapy for pathological skin picking: A randomized comparison to wait-list control. *Behaviour Research and Therapy, 49,* 11–17.

Segal, Z. V., Williams, J. M. G., & Teasdale, J. D. (2013). *Mindfulness-based cognitive therapy for depression* (2nd ed.). New York, NY: Guilford.

Sheppard, B., Chavira, D., Azzam, A., Grados, M. A., Umana, P., Garrido, H., & Mathews, C. A. (2010). ADHD prevalence and association with hoarding behaviors in childhood-onset OCD. *Depression and Anxiety, 27,* 667–674.

Snorrason, I., Belleau, E. L., & Woods, D. W. (2012). How related are hair pulling disorder (trichotillomania) and skin picking disorder? A review of evidence for comorbidity, similarities and shared etiology. *Clinical Psychology Review, 32,* 618–629.

Steketee, G., Frost, R. O., Tolin, D. F., Rasmussen, J., & Brown, T. A. (2010). Waitlist-controlled trial of cognitive behavior therapy for hoarding disorder. *Depression and Anxiety, 27,* 476–484.

Storch, E. A., Rahman, O., Park, J. M., Reid, J., Murphy, T. K., & Lewin, A. B. (2011). Compulsive hoarding in children. *Journal of Clinical Psychology: In Session, 67,* 507–516.

Taillon, A., O'Connor, K., Dupuis, G., & Lavoie, M. (2013). Inference-based therapy for body dysmorphic disorder. *Clinical Psychology and Psychotherapy, 20,* 67–76.

Teng, E. J., Woods, D. W., & Twohig, M. P. (2006). Habit reversal as a treatment for chronic skin picking: A pilot investigation. *Behavior Modification, 30,* 411–422.

Timpano, K. R., Buckner, J. D., Richey, J. A. Murphy, D. L., & Schmidt, N. B. (2009). Exploration of anxiety sensitivity and distress tolerance as vulnerability factors for hoarding behaviors. *Depression and Anxiety, 26,* 343–353.

Timpano, K. R., & Schmidt, N. B. (2013). The relationship between self-control deficits and hoarding: A multimethod investigation across three samples. *Journal of Abnormal Psychology, 122,* 13–25.

Tolin, D. F. (2011). Understanding and treating hoarding: A biopsychosocial perspective. *Journal of Clinical Psychology: In Session, 67,* 517–526.

Tolin, D. F., Diefenbach, G. J., & Gilliam, C. M. (2011). Stepped care versus standard cognitive-behavioral therapy for obsessive-compulsive disorder: A preliminary study of efficacy and costs. *Depression and Anxiety, 28,* 314–323.

Tolin, D. F., Meunier, S. A., Frost, R. O., & Steketee, G. (2010). Course of compulsive hoarding and its relationship to life events. *Depression and Anxiety, 27,* 829–838.

Tompkins, M. A. (2011). Working with families of people who hoard: A harm reduction approach. *Journal of Clinical Psychology, 67,* 497–506.

Tucker, B. T., Woods, D. W., Flessner, C. A., Franklin, S. A., & Franklin, M. E. (2011). The skin picking impact project: Phenomenology, interference, and treatment utilization of pathological skin picking in a population-based sample. *Journal of Anxiety Disorders, 25,* 88–95.

Twohig, M. P., Hayes, S. C., & Masuda, A. (2006). A preliminary investigation of acceptance and commitment therapy as a treatment for chronic skin picking. *Behaviour Research and Therapy, 44,* 1513–1522.

Twohig, M. P., Hayes, S. C., Plumb, J. C., Pruitt, L. D., Collins, A. B., Hazlett-Stevens, H., . . . Woidneck, M. R. (2010). A randomized clinical trial of acceptance and commitment therapy versus progressive relaxation training for obsessive-compulsive disorder. *Journal of Consulting and Clinical Psychology, 78,* 705–716.

Veale, D., Gournay, K., Dryden, W., Boocock, A., Shah, F., Willson, R., . . . Walburn, J. (1996). Body dysmorphic disorder: A cognitive behavioural model and pilot randomised controlled trial. *Behaviour Research and Therapy, 34,* 717–729.

Walther, M. R., Ricketts, E. J., Conelea, C. A., & Woods, D. W. (2010). Recent advances in the understanding and treatment of trichotillomania. *Journal of Cognitive Psychotherapy, 24,* 46–64.

Wheaton, M. G., Abramowitz, J. S., Franklin, J. C., Berman, N. C., & Fabricant, L. E. (2011). Experiential avoidance and saving cognitions in the prediction of hoarding symptoms. *Cognitive Therapy Research, 35,* 511–516.

Whitfield, K. Y., Daniels, J. S., Flesaker, K., & Simmons, D. (2012). Older adults with hoarding behavior aging in place: Looking to a collaborative community-based planning approach for solutions. *Journal of Aging Research.* Retrieved from: http://www.hindawi.com/journals/jar/2012/205425/cta

Wilkinson-Tough, M., Bocci, L., Thorne, K., & Herlihy, J. (2010). Is mindfulness-based therapy an effective intervention for obsessive–intrusive thoughts: A case series. *Clinical Psychology and Psychotherapy, 17,* 250–268.

Williams, J., Hadjistavropoulos, T., & Sharpe, D. (2006). A meta-analysis of psychological and pharmacological treatments for body dysmorphic disorder. *Behaviour Research and Therapy, 44,* 99–111.

Williams, T. I., Salkovskis, P. M., Forrester, L., Turner, S., White, H., & Allsopp, M. A. (2010). A randomised controlled trial of cognitive behavioural treatment for obsessive compulsive disorder in children and adolescents. *European Child and Adolescent Psychiatry, 19,* 449–456.

Woods, D. W., Wetterneck, C. T., & Flessner, C. A. (2006). A controlled evaluation of acceptance and commitment therapy plus habit reversal for trichotillomania. *Behaviour Research and Therapy, 44,* 639–656.

Trauma- and Stressor-Related Disorders

Victoria E. Kress, Holly Hartwig Moorhead, and Chelsey A. Zoldan

CASE STUDY: IMANI

Imani is a 15-year-old African American female. She lives with her sister and her mother. She has been pulled from her mother's care on numerous occasions, but has had unsuccessful foster care placements and has always been returned to her mother. Children's Services believed her mother provided a level of care that was minimal, but "appropriate enough" to return her to her home.

Imani's mother is addicted to crack, and her ex-boyfriend forced her (the mother) to prostitute for drugs; the prostitution continued after he left, secondary to her escalating addiction. Imani's mother has also been abused and battered in numerous past relationships, and some of her ex-boyfriends have also abused Imani.

Imani's mother has a long history of mental illness. Imani's mother has psychotic breaks and once threatened to pour gasoline on herself and her children and set them on fire. She does manage to keep food in the apartment, and there are times when she is alert and attentive.

In the past, two of her mother's boyfriends sexually abused Imani. These are the experiences that most haunt her, and she expresses feelings of shame, "deserving" the abuse, and blaming herself because a part of her sometimes valued the attention; attention she was not receiving anywhere else.

Imani struggles with intrusive thoughts about her sexual abuse, as well as memories of her mother being battered. She frequently has nightmares about the abuse. Imani used to share a room with her sister, but her nightmares and occasional bed-wetting embarrassed her. She now sleeps on the couch in the family room.

Imani has taken on a parental role with her sister and wants to protect her from the abuses that she suffered and witnessed. When her mother is fighting with a boyfriend, or is experiencing a psychotic break, Imani will take her sister to the park or another area to get away from the chaos. She encourages her sister to do well in school and helps her with her homework. They sometimes visit the library, and Imani hopes that she and her sister may be able to attend the local community college one day. Imani wants to get counseling so that she can be a "good role model" for her sister. She hopes to be able to work and save up enough money to rent a small apartment for herself and her sister when she turns 18.

Although Imani has been able to work small jobs doing yard-work for neighbors and stocking shelves at a small neighborhood convenience store, reminders of her abuse get in the way. While working at the store she would see men who reminded her in some way of her abusers, and her intrusive memories of the abuse would start. Her heart would race, and she would sometimes have to hide in the bathroom. She constantly feels unsettled and fears something bad is about to happen.

She had saved up money from an entire summer of work and hid it under her bed, but her mother found the money and used it to buy drugs. The husband and wife who own the neighborhood convenience store, the Campbells, have been very supportive of Imani. After learning of Imani's mother having taken her earnings, the Campbells offered to help Imani set up a savings account at a local bank. They sometimes invite Imani and her sister to dinner or give them food to take home, knowing that they sometimes go long periods of time without food. The Campbells also invite the girls to come to church with them, and Imani looks forward to attending church each week. She has found strength in religion and enjoys the caring and sense of belonging she feels with the congregation members.

Imani has no transportation to receive counseling services. She is the kind of client who would typically slip between the cracks and not receive any services. However, she is so committed to "rising above" her experiences that she either walks rides a friend's bike, or takes the bus three miles to attend her counseling sessions. Whenever the Campbells are able to, they bring her to counseling. She is considering asking some other members of the church congregation to help her get to counseling.

Because of her addiction and mental health problems, her mother is unable to come in to meet with the counselor or to be supportive of Imani's counseling process. Someday Imani wants to have a family, but fears she will never be able to be intimate with a male because of her abuse. She feels damaged and ashamed of her body. She expresses identity struggles and says, "I know what to say, but I feel like I am faking it. I just don't know where to begin getting my life together."

Imani demonstrates insight into the complexities of her life circumstances. She expresses that she "wants to get out of it . . . move forward." She talks about how she is so sad and ashamed that it is sometimes hard to go to school. Since she isn't being monitored she doesn't have to go to school, but she tries to challenge herself to get there. At school Imani has a difficult time concentrating. She does have one close friend, whom she has known since early childhood, who has experienced traumas similar to Imani's. They have relied on each other for support for many years and have a deep bond because of their shared understanding. Imani hopes that by going to counseling she can set an example for her friend, so that she too will seek counseling in the future.

DESCRIPTION OF THE TRAUMA- AND STRESSOR-RELATED DISORDERS

This chapter addresses the treatment of trauma- and stressor-related disorders (as described in the *DSM-5*; American Psychiatric Association [APA], 2013), which include reactive attachment disorder, disinhibited social engagement disorder, posttraumatic stress disorder, acute stress disorder, and adjustment disorders. These disorders are characterized by exposure to a traumatic or stressful event that results in impairment warranting clinical attention. Diagnosis of these disorders requires that an identifiable traumatic event or stressor occurred that influenced the onset of the symptoms. Trauma- and stressor-related disorders share common symptomology with anxiety disorders (e.g., hyperarousal, insomnia, poor concentration), obsessive-compulsive and related disorders (e.g., persistent intrusive thoughts), and dissociative disorders (e.g., derealization, depersonalization). Distress after a traumatic or stressful experience varies across individuals and may present as fear, anxiety, aggression, anhedonia, and dysphoria. The disorders in this category vary in terms of their symptoms and severity.

COUNSELOR CONSIDERATIONS

While the disorders in this category are diverse, there are many broad considerations that can be addressed when approaching counseling with this population. First, counselors can work with the client to determine if the stressor can be reduced or removed and assess whether the client is currently experiencing ongoing traumatic events. Issues of safety must be a priority, and current victimization, continued exposure to traumatic events, and any accompanying homicidal or suicidal ideation must be addressed.

Child abuse is one of the most common causes of trauma in children; many of the clients counselors see are, or have been, victims of child abuse. Counselors have a mandatory duty to report suspected child abuse or neglect to the appropriate child welfare social service agency within their jurisdiction. It is important that counselors remember that they are not investigators, but rather mandated reporters of suspected abuse, and thus any reasonable suspicions of abuse should be presented (Kress, Adamson, Paylo, DeMarco, & Bradley, 2012). Counselors should also be vigilant about reporting any new instances of abuse or neglect that occur, even after an investigation has been closed.

Despite counselors' efforts to report and rectify children's abusive and neglectful living environments, some counselors may witness institutional discrimination against their clients. As such, they may need to advocate or otherwise address inadequate responses and witnessed injustices children experience (American Counseling Association [ACA], in press). Children's discrimination could be based on their race, gender, or socioeconomic status. Counselors have an ethical obligation to advocate for their clients while still maintaining the clients' right to privacy and privileged communication, and while not violating any therapeutic boundaries. Counselors should use their judgment and regularly consult to determine the appropriate course of action when faced with such barriers (Kress et al., 2012).

Beyond a counselor's duty to report suspected child maltreatment, counselors' top priority must be to facilitate their minor—and adult—clients' safety; safety must be obtained before any secondary needs of the client can be addressed. Removal from the unsafe environment can certainly achieve the goal of safety, but this is not always what happens even when child welfare agencies become involved. Also, in violent relationships, people often return a number of times before they leave. As such, counselors should always integrate a child or adult safety plan into their work with those at risk for violence (see Chapter 3). Also, attempts to enhance and promote clients' safety should be a part of the ongoing counseling process.

As is the case with many other diagnoses, referral to a physician for a physical examination is recommended when working with those who have experienced traumas. This is especially important when counselors suspect that clients may have physical injuries associated with the traumatic experience. For example, people experiencing ongoing intimate partner violence may have physical health issues that need to be addressed (e.g., brain damage) if they are to move forward and be able to do the work associated with counseling.

Because counselors must use their own clinical judgment to determine whether a reaction to a stressor is maladaptive, emotional and behavioral reactions should be examined within the scope of the client's cultural norms. Cultural factors may also impact the preference for a counselor of a specific gender, especially when issues of abuse and interpersonal victimization are involved. For example, a female client of a specified culture who has been sexually victimized may feel it is inappropriate to share her struggles with someone from outside of her culture. Issues of counselor gender should also be considered in cases in which the client was abused. For example, a female client with a history of childhood sexual abuse by a male perpetrator may not feel comfortable working with a male counselor. In these cases, counselors should be prepared to provide referrals.

Building trust with clients who have experienced a trauma or stressor can be difficult, and patience is crucial. Counselors should avoid pressuring clients to disclose information before they are ready, as this may negatively affect the therapeutic relationship and diminish the likelihood that the client will return to counseling. By displaying an optimistic attitude, counselors can instill hope and help clients feel empowered. It may be helpful to provide clients with reassurances that while memories of the stressor or trauma and negative thoughts will not diminish completely, they are capable of reaching a higher level of functioning and can learn more productive coping strategies. Using strategies to bolster clients' empowerment can aid them in restoring a sense of control over their lives. Identifying client strengths and resources can help clients to move toward a more optimistic future. Fostering social connection and support can be especially helpful in preventing social isolation and withdrawal, and in providing clients with a source of care and encouragement outside of counseling sessions.

Working with clients who have experienced trauma puts counselors at risk for developing vicarious trauma and burnout. Counselors should be careful to look for signs of vicarious trauma, especially if they have experienced trauma in the past. Self-care activities and seeking individual counseling, consultation, and supervision can help identify signs of burnout and vicarious trauma.

Clinical Toolbox 7.1: In the Pearson etext, click here to read more about what counselors need to know about managing and preventing vicarious trauma.

PROGNOSIS

The prognosis of trauma and stressor disorders varies greatly based on the specific diagnosis and each client's unique characteristics (e.g., resiliency, optimism, spirituality). The presence of comorbid diagnoses also impacts prognosis.

Adjustment disorders typically have a very favorable prognosis, with clients able to return to their former level of functioning in as early as a few months. Treatment improves prognosis, and early interventions are especially important in preventing additional stressors and impairment. Those who functioned at a high level before experiencing the trauma or stressor also have a more positive prognosis. While a myriad of biopsychosocial factors influence the severity and course of a diagnosis, the frequency and severity of trauma is the factor most associated with the extent of the individual's reaction (Friedman et al., 2011).

There is a firm foundation of evidence-based practices for use in treating PTSD and ASD. Cognitive behavioral and behavior therapy approaches have empirical support and can be quite efficacious in treating these disorders and in supporting positive long-term outcomes (Schnurr, 2008).

Less is known about attachment disorders, and their prognosis and effective treatment methods. Children with attachment disorders can have significant, long-term impacts if the disorder is not addressed. Early identification and intervention is key in changing the course of this disorder.

Trauma experiences also increase the likelihood a person will develop additional mental disorders. For example, clients who have been sexually abused are more likely to develop posttraumatic stress disorder, anxiety disorders, depression, eating disorders, sleep disorders, and to attempt suicide over their lifetimes (Chen et al., 2010). Clients who experienced maltreatment during childhood (i.e., those with attachment disorders or attachment disruptions) may be at a higher risk for future depression, suicide attempts, substance abuse, and behavior problems (Widom, Czaja, Bentley, & Johnson, 2009). While effects of the trauma, such as memories and intrusive thoughts, may not be extinguished completely, clients can achieve a better quality of life.

REACTIVE ATTACHMENT DISORDER AND DISINHIBITED SOCIAL ENGAGEMENT DISORDER

Description of the Disorders and Typical Client Characteristics

Disorders of attachment, or attachment disorders, are relatively rare diagnoses given to children who have experienced seriously negligent care by their primary caregivers, and who consequently do not form necessary, healthy emotional attachments with their caregivers and others. These disorders include reactive attachment disorder (RAD) and disinhibited social engagement disorder (APA, 2013). The *DSM-IV-TR* indicated children diagnosed with RAD could have one of two types of RAD: the inhibited type, or the more commonly observed disinhibited type. However, the *DSM-5* has distinguished the former "disinhibited type" of RAD as its own independent diagnosis, disinhibited social engagement disorder (DSED).

Children who have an attachment disorder consistently display, usually before the age of 5, distinct and inappropriate behaviors that are not explained by other developmental delays or disorders. It is difficult to precisely determine the exact prevalence of these disorders since few reliable empirical studies regarding attachment disorders exist, and because it is often difficult to definitively determine whether before the age of 5 the child exhibited inappropriate social behaviors that are part of the diagnostic criteria.

Attachment theory (e.g., Ainsworth, Blehar, Waters, & Wall, 1978; Bowlby, 1969), and current research highlight the need for all children to have basic emotional and physical needs met early in life by one or more dependable caregivers. When these needs are met, children can develop healthy attachments. These attachments are critical to how children learn to love and trust others; foundations that children need to establish healthy relationships throughout their lives. Infants and children may not be able to form these necessary attachments in environments where caregivers provide negligent care, characterized by repeated failure to appropriately respond to children's needs for comfort, stimulation, affection, and physical nurturance.

Negligent care associated with attachment disorders may also include inconsistency in who serves as a primary caregiver. Exposure to gross negligent care can prevent children from establishing stable and trustworthy attachments over time, which can develop into attachment disorders. However, it is important to note that neglect alone may not fully explain the etiology of attachment disorders. Some children who have been victims of profound neglect demonstrate resiliency in the face of such challenges and exhibit a keen susceptibility to heal, or they do not develop attachment disorders. Genetic or temperamental idiosyncrasies may be protective factors against developing attachment disorders and may determine variations in how children react to neglect.

Children with RAD persistently fail to initiate or respond in developmentally appropriate ways to social interactions. They may be excessively inhibited in social exchanges with others, or they may be hypervigilant around people. They may also give highly ambivalent and contradictory responses. Since they have not established secure attachments upon which to engage in and explore normal, healthy social interactions with others, they may demonstrate what seem to be incongruent patterns. For example, children with RAD may approach or initiate a social connection with caregivers, but then suddenly change and avoid or resist their caregivers' attempts to respond to them. In other circumstances, children with RAD may seem hypervigilant and intensely watch caregivers' responses.

As previously stated, disinhibited social engagement disorder (DSED), formerly considered to be a subtype of RAD, is now an independent diagnosis in the *DSM-5* (APA, 2013). Both DSED and RAD are believed to result from childhood maltreatment and neglect. Children diagnosed with DSED may have encountered caregivers who were unresponsive, but able to provide some form of affection. Because children must be developmentally capable of forming select attachments, a diagnosis of DSED can only be ascribed after the child reaches the developmental age of nine months. While RAD symptomology is primarily focused on attachment *insecurity*, DSED symptoms are predominantly characterized by the *inability* to form committed intimate social relationships. Children with DSED do not show a preference for social contact with caregivers and relatives over strangers. Of note, DSED has been observed more often in children who have been institutionalized, where they likely had limited opportunities to form secure attachments and social relationships.

In contrast to RAD, children with DSED may form attachments that are socially or otherwise inappropriate (APA, 2013). For example, children with DSED may not demonstrate appropriate connections with their own caregivers, yet be overfamiliar with strangers. Familiarity with strangers may include inappropriate physical contact, such as hugging and hand holding. These children may even react emotionally when being separated from strangers. Socially inappropriate behaviors exhibited by children with DSED can also include excessive comfort seeking from adults other than the primary caregivers, exaggerated helplessness while completing tasks, and behavior considered immature for their age. This indiscriminate behavior can lead to potentially awkward and dangerous situations. While children with DSED do not exhibit "stranger anxiety," they may generally appear anxious.

Once language skills have developed, overfamiliarity may present itself both physically and verbally in children with attachment disorders. Children may also have issues authentically expressing their emotions. School-aged children with attachment disorders will experience problems in relationships with their peers. They may experience bullying as a result of trouble relating to classmates, or they may act aggressively toward other children. These children may be very disruptive in classroom settings as evidenced by their throwing "temper tantrums," provoking reactions from peers, demanding a great deal of attention from teachers, and behaving inappropriately immature for their developmental age (e.g., making loud noises, crawling on the floor).

Many complications are associated with attachment disorders. For example, developmental delays (i.e., physical, cognitive, and emotional), learning disorders, mood disorders, anxiety disorders, feeding disorders, and academic problems are associated with attachment disorders. General medical conditions related to maltreatment may also be present. Attention-deficit/hyperactivity disorder is often diagnosed concurrently with DSED, and depressive symptoms commonly accompany a diagnosis of RAD. Issues of antisocial behavior, such as aggressiveness and perceived lack of empathy, may be present, but are not symptoms of attachment disorders. As they transition into adulthood, substance abuse issues may present in those with attachment disorders.

Counselor Considerations

Attachment disorders can be difficult to assess; assessment for attachment disorders must be done prudently and include a process to rule out the existence of other disorders, including potential psychiatric and developmental disorders that may also be explained by attachment disorder–related symptoms. Currently, there are no empirically supported, universally accepted screening assessments specifically for use in assessing attachment disorders. Thus, it may be helpful for counselors to use a multimodal assessment strategy to diagnose attachment disorders that includes collaborating with medical personnel, administering global assessment and attachment-specific measurements, performing direct observations, and obtaining clinical interviews with families and others involved in caregiving.

In the absence of universally accepted, empirically supported assessments specifically designed for evaluating attachment disorders, various screening measures, some used individually to assess for attachment disorders and others used as part of a comprehensive assessment plan to evaluate related aspects of attachment disorders, can be utilized to assess for attachment disorders or symptomatology associated with attachment disorders (Sheperis et al., 2003). Some of these assessments include the Behavior Assessment System for Children (BASC; Reynolds & Kamphaus, 1992); the Child and Adolescent Psychiatric Assessment–RAD module (CAPA-RAD; Angold & Costello, 2000); the Child Behavior Checklist (CBCL; Achenbach, 1991); the Eyberg Child Behavior Inventory (ECBI;

Eyberg, 1999); the Reactive Attachment Disorder Checklist (RAD-C; Hall, 2007); the Randolph Attachment Disorder Questionnaire (RADQ; Minnis, Pelosi, Knapp, & Dunn, 2001); and the Relationship Problem Questionnaire (RPQ; Minnis, Rabe-Hesketh, & Wolkind, 2002). See Sheperis et al. (2003) for a discussion of how some of these assessments may be used together to assess for RAD.

Interviewing primary caregivers is an important place to begin the observational assessment process in order to obtain (as accurately as possible) any history of neglect and anomalies within children's attachment behaviors. Next, children should be directly observed interacting with their primary caregivers and interacting with strangers, respectively, to assess for inhibited or uninhibited nonattachment behaviors. It is especially helpful during this process to intentionally structure opportunities to observe how children react to being separated from and reunited with both caregivers and strangers, respectively, in order to evaluate how children demonstrate attachment under stress.

Cultural issues should also be considered when assessing attachment issues. Symptoms such as limited eye-contact may be indicative of cultural norms, rather than pathology. Attachment disorders are believed to present similarly across cultures; however, it is advised that counselors exercise caution when diagnosing these disorders in clients of cultures in which attachment has not yet been studied (APA, 2013).

Treatment Models and Interventions

Currently, there are no uniformly accepted, identified effective treatments for children with attachment disorders, though there are several general protocols that counselors are encouraged to follow that have some evidence base. Because DSED was considered a subtype of RAD before the publication of the *DSM-5*, separate treatment approaches have not yet been developed or examined in the literature. Since an attachment disorder diagnosis involves the experience of severe neglect, children's safety should be evaluated and addressed before any other assessment is undertaken.

After assessing for safety, counselors may consider utilizing various attachment-based interventions to encourage the development of attachment between caregivers and children who already have some form of selective attachment. Essential elements of attachment disorder treatments include proper diagnosis, establishing secure and nurturing environments, applying empirically-based parent training, practically addressing family systems issues, and providing therapy that extends into the natural environments of children and families.

Attachment-based interventions that place a focus on relationship-based caregiver training that helps caregivers learn to appropriately and effectively react to an inappropriate lack of responsiveness from children may be a useful treatment option. One empirically supported approach that has been proposed as a family (or caregiver) approach to treating children with an attachment disorder and complex trauma experiences is dyadic developmental psychotherapy (DPP; Becker-Weidman & Hughes, 2008). DPP is a structured and systematic approach, grounded in attachment theory. Using DPP, counselors attempt to establish, as the foundation for the interventions used in this approach, strong therapeutic alliances between the counselor and child, between caregiver and child, and between counselor and caregiver. DDP is used to identify, regulate, and integrate parallel processes that exist between caregivers and children, counselors and caregivers, and counselors and children. This is done in ways that help caregivers become more secure resources for children, so children can build trust and develop greater security with them. In doing so, DPP addresses prominent areas of trauma associated with an attachment disorder, including impairment related to self-regulation, attachment, biological processes, regulating affect, defenses, behavior control, cognitive regulation, and self-concept.

There are several essential principles of DPP. First, counselors and caregivers must have their own attachment issues resolved before beginning work with children. Second, counselors and caregivers intentionally invite children to verbally and nonverbally share their intersubjective experiences (e.g., affect, awareness, attention). Moreover, children's disclosures of these experiences are overtly respected in counseling as an intentional intervention, especially since these experiences often are not recognized in abuse and neglect situations. Third, both counselors and caregivers display attitudes that promote healing, such as playfulness, acceptance, curiosity, and empathy. Fourth, conflicts and misunderstandings experienced by any party involved in DPP treatment are addressed directly with the attitudes previously mentioned. Throughout the implementation of DPP, counselor nonverbal attending behaviors (e.g., eye contact, facial expressions, voice modulation, gestures, and postures) are incorporated to help children feel safe, self-regulate emotion, and develop the ability to create new meanings of traumatic experiences.

The ultimate goal of DPP is to promote children's safety and freedom to explore in counseling. Helping children and caregivers recognize the influence of prior traumatic experiences on current functioning is another key part of this approach. Critical to reaching this goal is counselors' support and monitoring of caregivers as active participants in children's treatment.

In sum, attachment-based interventions, including DPP, are intended to help children with an attachment disorder learn to express their experiences and cope with the intense by-products of trauma with the essential support of their caregivers. However, not all attachment-based approaches are appropriate; a group of aversive treatment approaches is explicitly not recommended. These approaches include interventions that involve holding or binding, rebirthing, reparenting, rage reduction, withholding food or water, forced eating or drinking, or purposefully triggering anger. Proponents of these types of interventions have suggested that children who experience trauma early in life develop suppressed rage, which eventually manifests as antisocial behavior. Therefore, the aforementioned interventions are intended to encourage expression of this rage so that children stop resisting attachment and submit to their caregivers. However, these interventions do not have empirical support and are considered harmful because of (a) the potential for children to experience physical and psychological harm as a result of being subjected to these interventions; and, (b) the incompatibility between children being unable to extricate themselves from these types of activities and their need to receive caregiving that is especially sensitive, responsive, and emotionally responsive.

Currently, there are no medications specifically prescribed for use with attachment disorders. However, medications may be prescribed to treat significant co-occurring symptoms of attachment disorders, such as explosive anger, insomnia, depression, anxiety, or hyperactivity.

While medication is not specifically indicated for aggressive behavior, some medications may be used to treat certain symptoms of the disorder. Anticonvulsant medications may address poor impulse control and labile mood, antipsychotic medications can address disorganized behavior, lithium may be used for treating labile mood and impulsivity, and clonidine may be used to treat anxiety and agitations (Preston, O'Neal, & Talaga, 2013). Additionally, symptoms of aggression may respond to selective serotonin reuptake inhibitors (SSRIs; Preston et al., 2013).

Medication may also be helpful in treating comorbid ADHD in clients with attachment disorders. Stimulants, some antidepressants, and alpha-2 adrenergic agonists are often used to treat ADHD in children and adolescents. These medications include medications such as methylphenidate and dextroamphetamine (Preston et al., 2013). Antidepressant medications that work on dopamine and norepinephrine pathways, such as bupropion, can also be used to treat ADHD (Preston et al., 2013). Because SSRIs affect serotonin, these are not recommended for the treatment of ADHD, unless being used to address comorbid symptoms.

Because clients with attachment disorders are, by definition, children and adolescents, additional considerations are necessary when utilizing medication. In particular, the use of antidepressant medication should be monitored in children and adolescents, as an increased risk of suicide has been found in this age group (Preston et al., 2013). Substance abuse issues may present in these clients during their transition to adulthood, and counselors may want to monitor for potential abuse or dependency issues related to prescribed medications.

Prognosis

Attachment disorders are not commonly diagnosed. Many families who have a child with an attachment disorder do not recognize the occurrence of the disorder, or seek help. Moreover, there is little empirical data to suggest effective treatments for attachment disorders, and what is known about attachment disorders is largely based on case studies with limited generalizability. There is also a lack of research on attachment disorders in older children who have experienced severe neglect in their early years.

Children affected by attachment disorders can be significantly negatively affected in various areas of their physical, psychological, and emotional development. Without appropriate help, children with attachment disorders may experience myriad difficulties in the aforementioned areas, including a higher risk of developing depression, aggression and hostility, lying, stealing, bullying, a lack of empathy, learning difficulties, behavior problems, poor self-esteem, and difficulties forming healthy relationships.

Additionally, children with attachment disorders who do not receive necessary treatment may potentially develop conduct disorder and oppositional defiant disorder, and go on to meet the criteria for various other serious mental disorders (e.g., borderline personality disorder, antisocial personality disorder). Fortunately, it is possible for children with attachment disorders to learn to trust others and to live healthy lives. A key determinant in terms of prognosis is early identification and intervention.

Voices from the Trenches 7.1: In the Pearson etext, click here to watch a counselor discuss a profile of attachment disorders.

POSTTRAUMATIC STRESS DISORDER AND ACUTE STRESS DISORDER

Description of the Disorders and Typical Client Characteristics

Whether precipitated by civilian, military, or naturally occurring events, trauma has increasingly received greater attention from various sources, including mental health professionals, medical personnel, and governmental entities. It is normal for human beings to have strong, intense reactions to traumatic events for many reasons, including the inherent instinct to survive. However, both posttraumatic stress disorder (PTSD) and acute stress disorder (ASD) are serious, debilitating reactions to trauma that endure over time and significantly impair a person's ability to function in daily life (APA, 2013). These diagnoses both have, as their root cause, specific traumatic stressors.

For U.S. adults, the projected lifetime risk of developing PTSD is approximately 8% (APA, 2013). However, only about half of those who have PTSD ever receive treatment (Wang et al., 2005). Among children and adolescents, approximately 4% of 13- to 18-year-olds develop PTSD, with girls more frequently developing PTSD than boys (Merikangas et al., 2010).

Both ASD and PTSD involve exposure to trauma that presents a threat of severe injury or death. Consequently, people who experience these types of events may develop maladaptive reactions primarily in four areas: intrusion (e.g., experiencing intrusive thoughts or feelings); avoidance (e.g., intentionally avoiding events, people, emotions, cognitions that elicit memories of the trauma); negative changes in cognitions or mood (e.g., developing depression, anger, anxiety); and altered states of arousal or reactivity (e.g., extreme lethargy or hypervigilance).

Despite these general similarities, ASD and PTSD primarily differ with respect to when symptoms begin and how long symptoms persist (APA, 2013). ASD is characterized by the onset of symptoms within four weeks of the traumatic event, and the duration of symptoms is between two days and four weeks. Clients with persistent and recurrent feelings of being detached from their bodies, as if observing their own thoughts and actions, can be diagnosed with the specifier *depersonalization* (APA, 2013). Those who persistently experience feelings of unreality of their surroundings, as if in a dreamlike or distorted environment, can be diagnosed with the specifier *derealization* (APA, 2013). The dissociative experiences must not be associated with the use of a substance or general medical condition. PTSD can also have delayed expression, in which case the criteria for diagnosis are not met until at least six months after the occurrence of a traumatic event. According to the *DSM-5*, a PTSD diagnosis also may be further specified as PTSD with "delayed onset" if symptoms occur at least six months after the trauma occurs; PTSD "dissociative subtype" if symptoms include depersonalization and derealization; and PTSD "preschool type" for children six years of age or younger who meet the diagnostic criteria (APA, 2013). Some people experience PTSD as a chronic psychiatric disorder that persists over a lifetime.

Numerous types of traumatic events may precipitate the development of ASD and/or PTSD. Some examples of trauma-inducing events include war, torture, physical assault, sexual assault, child sexual abuse, natural or human disasters, terrorism, violence, motor vehicle accidents, refugee status, and military trauma.

While different people may experience the same type of traumatic event, their reactions to trauma are not homogeneous; they will react in diverse ways to various types of trauma. People may be exposed to different traumatic events throughout their lives, all of which may influence their reactions to traumatic events that occur later. The range of ASD and PTSD symptoms can include survivor guilt, shame, disinterest in activities that were once enjoyed, lack of sexual desire, difficulty in emotional expression, distrust of others, fear, anxiety, insomnia and other sleep disturbances, nightmares, flashbacks, anger, aggressive behavior, grief, somatic complaints, and chronic pain. Those who experience ASD or PTSD may develop other co-occurring problems which include maladaptive coping strategies, suicidal ideation, homicidal ideation, and substance abuse.

Cultural risk factors that increase the likelihood of developing PTSD and ASD include low socioeconomic status, history of childhood adversity, and minority racial or ethnic status (APA, 2013). Children living in impoverished environments are at a greater risk for experiencing multiple traumatic events due to a lack of resources, and because of the circumstances that correlate with poverty (e.g., mental illness and drug and alcohol abuse in those around them, community violence, fewer quality child care options and poor schools, fewer enrichment opportunities). Layered risk factors also compound the possibility of developing PTSD.

Cultural characteristics such as fatalistic (i.e., a belief that all events are predetermined by fate and are therefore unalterable) or self-blaming coping strategies are also associated with elevated risk of developing PTSD or ASD (APA, 2013). Presentation of PTSD and ASD may vary across cultures. Those in Cambodia may experience symptoms they describe as *khyal* attacks, which include shortness of breath, dizziness, and palpitations (APA, 2013). These attacks are brought on by upsetting cognitions and may present as a symptom of ASD or PTSD. Clients from Latin America may present with *ataque de nervios*, which consists of a broad range of somatic, anxiety, and depressive symptoms (APA, 2013).

ASD or PTSD typically relate to a distinct or a time-limited traumatic event (e.g., a motor vehicle accident, a one-time assault). Therefore, these diagnoses do not adequately describe unique reactions to chronic, prolonged, or repeated exposure to trauma (e.g., trauma associated with emotional or physical captivity or abuse perpetrated by other people). However, the concepts of *developmental trauma, complex trauma,* or *complex trauma disorder* have been proposed to more accurately categorize unique symptoms that victims of chronic trauma often experience in areas of emotion regulation, dissociation, negative self-perceptions, distortions of perpetrators, impaired social relationships, and establishing personal meaning. Sometimes these symptoms may be misdiagnosed as personality disorders instead of being more accurately identified as traumatic responses specific to complex trauma.

Clinical Toolbox 7.2: In the Pearson etext, click here to read more about complex trauma and strategies for treating people with complex trauma.

Many people who have experienced interpersonal abuses (e.g., violence in intimate relationships, sexual abuse) do not develop the symptoms of PTSD or complex trauma, but still seek and can benefit from counseling. While there are a number of reasons they may seek counseling, it is not uncommon for people to wish to process shame and embarrassment, issues associated with disclosing the situation to others (e.g., romantic partners), or ways the abuse may be impacting their relationships or other aspects of their lives.

Adult victims of childhood abuse seek treatment for a number of reasons, but most fail to recognize the effects past traumas or abuses may have had on their development and their problems in living. Similarly, the caregivers of children who have been traumatized often fail to identify current or past abuse or trauma as related to their child's struggles. Further complicating efforts to treat the trauma and support children is the fact that many abusive caregivers do not consider their behaviors to be aberrant.

Children who have experienced child abuse are especially vulnerable to developing PTSD (or complex trauma). Possible reactions to child abuse may include difficulty with making and sustaining attachments, depression, anxiety, academic struggles, disruptions to the child's emotional well-being (e.g., lowered self-esteem), and anger, which can be manifested in behavioral problems. In addition to the traditional PTSD symptoms previously discussed, child abuse victims may demonstrate the following reactions: loss of interest in activities (i.e., anhedonia), worries about dying at an early age, moodiness, showing sudden and extreme emotional reactions, somatic symptoms such as headaches and stomachaches, sleep problems, irritability or angry outbursts, difficulties concentrating, regression or acting younger than their age (e.g., thumb sucking and being clingy or whiny), showing increased alertness to the environment, and repeating behavior that reminds them of the trauma (e.g., through play or in art).

Developmental disruptions may also occur in children secondary to repeated maltreatment. These developmental or complex trauma reactions might include alterations in self-perception (e.g., a sense of chronic guilt, shame, helplessness), difficulties regulating emotions, alterations in relationships with others (e.g., being isolating, distrustful), and alterations in their sense of meaning (e.g., a sense of despair and hopelessness). These developmental reactions can have long-term, significant effects on a child's functioning, and it is important that these developmental reactions are addressed in counseling in addition to the traditional PTSD symptoms more typically targeted in treatment.

Despite the deleterious effects that child maltreatment can invite, it is important for counselors to understand that most children (and adults) do not develop ongoing trauma reactions secondary to abuse or exposure to traumatic events; they can, and do, adapt, move forward, and live productive lives. Secondary to their experiences, people can even experience posttraumatic growth and develop resources such as greater self-knowledge and self-appreciation, additional survival skills, increased empathy for others, and a broader understanding of the complexities of people and the world. It is important that counselors believe that all people with whom they work can heal and thrive.

Counselor Considerations

The first step when contemplating a diagnosis of ASD or PTSD is to conduct an accurate assessment. This is an essential precursor to rendering an appropriate diagnosis, especially since ASD or PTSD often occur alongside other physical or mental health conditions. Therefore, identifying what is and is not related to ASD or PTSD symptomatology is critical. However, before formal assessment begins, counselors must consider several issues. First, clients' safety (i.e., a client is not currently being victimized) and psychological stability (e.g., not experiencing active psychosis or suicidal or homicidal ideation) must be verified (Rubin & Springer, 2009). If clients are experiencing acute physical, situational, or psychological crises, they should receive appropriate medical or other psychological assistance to stabilize them before further assessment or treatment continues. Second, in this initial safety verification stage, as well as throughout assessment and treatment processes, it is important to attend to cultural factors that relate to how clients may demonstrate symptoms. Finally, sensitivity should be directed toward the potential for clients to experience psychological and/or physiological arousal while undergoing any part of the assessment (e.g., becoming too activated by sharing their experiences) and treatment phases and this should be considered in relation to prioritizing client safety.

There are myriad empirically supported screening assessments for PTSD and related issues like trauma exposure and ASD that may be selected as assessment tools. These assessments include multimethod measures created for use with different populations, within diverse cultures, and in various settings. Regardless of the specific assessments chosen, using structured interviews in the assessment process is recommended to thoroughly examine the existence and severity of all PTSD diagnostic criteria, explore trauma across the lifespan, evaluate symptomatology related to other psychiatric or comorbid disorders, and identify differential diagnoses (Foa & Yadin, 2011).

For additional PTSD assessment information, readers are invited to visit the National Center for PTSD and the International Society for Traumatic Stress Studies websites to review different PTSD assessment measures that may be administered to or used as self-report measures by adults and children.

When working with a child in the child welfare system who has PTSD (e.g., a child who has been identified as being a victim of maltreatment), there will be many different professionals charged with helping the child. It is important that counselors work with the child's team to ensure that the child receives the treatment he or she requires. Team members might include medical personnel who follow the child's growth and development, a child welfare system worker, and if the child has been removed from the home, the team may include temporary caregivers (e.g., foster parents). Whenever appropriate, other therapeutic support providers and services should be a part of the child's treatment team. An hour a week of counseling is not always enough to help a child who has PTSD, and a team approach to helping children can serve to further supplement and support the work done in individual counseling.

When working with traumatized children it is also important that counselors provide a consistent, safe space and a nurturing relationship within which the child may experiment with adapting to a safer world. Traumatized children also often do well when counselors work with them in group settings. Group counseling can be especially empowering with children who have been abused as it reduces their feelings of shame, and empowerment-oriented groups can help them co-create a strength-based identity.

Finally, when working with traumatized children, certain characteristics may insulate them from the long-term negative effects of maltreatment, and these factors should be considered when counseling this population. These factors include, but are not limited to, maintaining a healthy sense of spirituality, having at least one supportive relationship, possessing external attributions of blame (e.g., "the abuse was her fault, not mine"), having a positive self-regard, and holding to a positive outlook on life (Folger & Wright, 2013). Whenever possible, the aforementioned factors should be identified, developed, and amplified in clients via counseling and the client's treatment plan.

Treatment Models and Interventions

Since PTSD treatments are typically used to treat ASD, we will simply refer to PTSD treatments in this section. Treatment should be started as soon as possible following trauma exposure and, if possible, even before symptoms begin to emerge. When a traumatic event has just occurred, psychological first aid (PFA) may be initially provided to victims prior to initiating pharmacotherapy and psychotherapy (Nash & Watson, 2012).

 Clinical Toolbox 7.3: In the Pearson etext, click here to read more about the use of psychological first aid in helping people who are in disaster or crisis situations.

In years past, critical incident stress debriefing (CISD) had been used to address the immediate aftermath of traumatic events, especially by nonprofessional mental health responders, but it was not widely effective in treating distress following trauma, or in preventing the development of PTSD (Friedman, 2013). Therefore, the National Center for PTSD and the National Center for Child Traumatic Stress developed PFA as an evidence-informed early intervention to address trauma, especially by laypersons. More information can be learned about PFA by visiting their website. After attending to the initial needs of trauma victims and providing PFA, if necessary, counselors must determine which of the many different theoretical and therapeutic approaches should be used in treatment.

When feeling overwhelmed by trauma memories, clients with PTSD may become emotionally inflamed and may cope by becoming agitated, or by dissociating or numbing. Grounding techniques can be used to help clients regulate strong emotions or reconnect with their environment. Grounding techniques aim to help clients attain a balance between being conscious of reality and being able to tolerate it. Grounding techniques help to anchor clients to the present via shifting clients' attention outward to the external world, rather than inward toward the self. Grounding can be conceptualized as a form of distraction, healthy detachment, mindfulness, or an attempt to center or otherwise help clients feel safe. Physical grounding techniques involve the client focusing on the senses (e.g., touch, hearing; feeling your body in the chair, pushing your heels into the ground, holding a grounding object that pulls one into reality). Mental grounding involves focusing one's mind (e.g., counting things in the environment, cognitively organizing things into categories, reciting a positive self-talk statement) in an attempt to come into the present. Every counselor working with this population should have some basic knowledge of how to apply grounding skills.

There is a solid foundation of evidence-based practices for use in treating PTSD. Cognitive behavioral and behavior approaches are widely used and have empirical support in treating PTSD (Schnurr, 2008).

Alongside preparing to utilize effective pharmacotherapy and psychotherapy treatment options, the type of milieu, individual or group therapy contexts, in which to utilize psychotherapy approaches must be considered. Current research does not provide especially strong support for the use of group therapy. Yet group therapy proponents suggest that this modality uniquely allows clients to share traumatic experiences with others who have similar experiences, especially veterans, victims of sexual assault, and people affected by natural disasters. A combined individual and group cognitive processing therapy approach has been shown to be effective in treating PTSD (Schnurr, 2008).

Voices from the Trenches 7.2: In the Pearson etext, click here to read about lessons and insights that two counselors have accrued over the years secondary to providing trauma treatment.

Many different approaches have been proposed to treat PTSD, but not all have acceptable empirical support. In the following section, we review the evidence-based treatment approaches that are most commonly used to treat PTSD (Foa, Keane, Friedman, & Cohen, 2009). Most of these approaches are cognitive behavioral-based therapies that have been specifically tailored to address trauma reactions. In general, trauma-focused CBT approaches focus on restructuring cognitions associated with traumatic events by incorporating exposure and cognitive processing therapy (Friedman, 2008; Ponniah & Hollon, 2009).

PROLONGED EXPOSURE THERAPY (PET; EXPOSURE THERAPY) Building on the exposure therapy techniques historically used to treat anxiety disorders, PET, a cognitive behavioral approach, was specifically designed to treat PTSD (Foa & Yadin, 2011). The purpose of PET is to help clients recall trauma and associated fears, develop new information about the trauma and their responses, and learn new ways of reframing and coping with pathological fear associated with the trauma. Among people with acute stress disorder, exposure therapy has demonstrated decreased PTSD symptoms compared to other cognitive interventions. In fact, it is recommended that exposure therapy be used as an early intervention for people with ASD who have a high risk of developing subsequent PTSD (Bryant et al., 2008). Furthermore, individually provided exposure therapy has been well studied and empirically supported as a treatment for PTSD, and in fact, has been found to be the most effective of all CBT approaches (Foa et al., 2009; Foa & Yadin, 2011).

PET is typically offered within eight to 15 sessions, each session lasting between 60 and 90 minutes. Different formats may be used, such as meeting once or twice per week, using guided imagery, incorporating in vivo exposure, or utilizing recordings. The most effective method is combining imaginal exposure of the trauma memory with in vivo exposure to people, places, and situations associated with the trauma that do not pose a realistic risk of harm (Foa et al., 2009).

Regardless of variations in how this approach is conducted, the critical aspect of PET therapy is facilitating client exposure to the part of a specific traumatic event that elicits the greatest fear in order to gradually reduce fear and anxiety. Using visual imagery, virtual reality, or a combination of both, clients emotionally engage with the recollection. In doing so, they confront the feared event, identify and acknowledge their fears, and learn that expected disasters do not occur when they encounter the feared stimuli.

Revisiting trauma as part of therapy helps clients organize their memories of the traumatic event(s); reevaluate negative cognitions about their involvement with the trauma; develop new perceptions about themselves and others; differentiate between recalling the trauma and re-experiencing the trauma; develop skills to allow them to recall the trauma without experiencing undue anxiety; and understand that memories of the trauma will not harm them (Foa & Yadin, 2011).

COGNITIVE PROCESSING THERAPY (CPT)   The International Society for Traumatic Stress Studies indicates that CPT (Resick & Schnicke, 1992) is the next best supported PTSD treatment approach, following exposure therapy (Foa et al., 2009). CPT is an empirically supported cognitive behavioral treatment that has been used successfully with both civilian (especially victims of rape and sexual assault) and military personnel who have PTSD (Monson et al., 2006). It can be used as an alternative to pure exposure-based interventions since it incorporates both cognitive and exposure components. CPT is typically delivered within 12 sessions that can be held once or twice weekly, in individual or group formats.

 Clinical Toolbox 7.4: In the Pearson etext, click here to read about an activity that can be used to reduce trauma symptoms via the use of trauma narratives.

In the first treatment session, clients are provided psychoeducation about PTSD symptoms and given the opportunity to write about the traumatic event and their beliefs about why it occurred. A key part of the CPT approach is exposing clients to traumatic memories by having them write about the events and then read and reflect upon their thoughts, feelings, and beliefs associated with the traumatic events. This helps clients identify the range of emotions elicited by trauma exposure while simultaneously challenging maladaptive cognitions that may accompany emotional and behavioral responses.

In the second session, clients read their narratives aloud, focusing on problematic beliefs and cognitions in their account of the event. Counselors help clients begin to recognize how events, thoughts, and feelings are connected, and clients practice identifying these connections as homework between sessions.

During session three, self-monitoring homework is reviewed. Clients also are instructed to write a specific account of the worst traumatic event (i.e., the *worst* event, even if multiple traumas have occurred) that has occurred, and read the narrative each day before the next session.

During session four, clients rewrite the traumatic event, and are challenged in this re-writing to connect with more detail and to allow themselves to tolerate their strong emotions. They then read this narrative daily until the next session.

In session five, clients read aloud this rewritten account and the counselor facilitates the process of challenging cognitions, teaching clients how to question their assumptions and self-statements. Both in sessions four and five, clients are assisted in recalling the traumatic events about which they have written, developing more accurate contextual understandings of why the events occurred, and experiencing emotions they may have suppressed after the events occurred. In these two sessions, clients learn how to use worksheets daily to challenge themselves and then modify maladaptive thoughts and beliefs about traumatic experiences. During the final five sessions, clients examine irrational beliefs about themselves and others with respect to the following areas: safety, trust, power and control, esteem, and intimacy. Closure and reflection about treatment progress are part of the final session.

 Clinical Toolbox 7.5: In the Pearson etext, click here to read an example of how therapeutic stories can be used to help clients re-story their trauma experiences.

CREATIVE TOOLBOX ACTIVITY 7.1   Finding a Safe Place

Victoria E. Kress, PhD, LPCC-S, NCC

Activity Overview

Through the identification and visualization of a safe place, this activity helps clients develop an ability to connect with a sense of security and safety during times when they most need it.

Treatment Goal(s) of Activity

Clients who have experienced trauma often struggle to feel safe; the world often feels like a frightening, dangerous place. Clients can benefit from developing an ability to connect with a sense of safety and security, especially during the times when they feel unsafe. This activity addresses treatment goals related to developing and applying relaxation skills when feeling anxious or hyperaroused.

Directions

1. Identify places where you have felt safe and secure. If you cannot identify a place, identify an imaginary place. This safe place can be located anywhere you'd like it to be.
2. If it feels safe, close your eyes. Allow yourself to begin to see, in your imagination, the place that feels safe to you. If at any time anything in the safe place feels uncomfortable, replace it with something comforting.
3. Consider features of the environment: What do you see that is comforting? What else can you add to the space that you could visualize that would make it feel more safe? What is the temperature or climate in the space? What can you add to this space to make it feel more comforting? What comforting smells are in your space? What can you add to this space to make it smell more comforting? What comforting textures, or things that you can feel, are in your space? What textures can you add to this space to make it feel more comforting?
4. Open your eyes and draw a picture of your safe space. Add any additional elements that you identify that would make the safe place feel even more comforting.

Process Questions

1. Tell me about the significance and purpose of each feature in your safe place.
2. How can you connect with this safe place during times in your life when you feel unsafe? Do you need to add a visual element to the image to help lift you to your safe place (e.g., a helicopter or an escalator)?
3. Where can you post your picture so that you have it as a cue or a reminder of your safe place?
4. Is there an actual physical space in your life that you can create or establish as your safe place? If so, what objects might you add to make it feel safer?

STRESS INOCULATION TRAINING (SIT)   SIT (Meichenbaum, 1996), a cognitive behavioral approach, has some empirical support as a treatment for PTSD, and is often used in conjunction with other cognitive approaches. The SIT treatment approach has been found to be efficacious primarily with female victims of sexual assault (Foa et al., 2009).

Typically, SIT is delivered within eight to 15 sessions, though it can be adapted to meet the needs of individual clients and incorporated into individual or group approaches. Although SIT can be adapted into long-term therapy formats, it can also be utilized in acute settings within as little as a 20-minute session as well as in more traditional 60- to 90-minute sessions. There are three distinct phases of SIT: (a) conceptualization; (b) skills acquisition and rehearsal; and (c) application and follow-through. In the conceptualization phase, the counselor provides the client psychoeducation about stress and trauma, including physiological and psychological responses to trauma. Threats and fears are reframed as problems to be solved, and clients identify aspects of problems that can and cannot be solved. One of the goals of this treatment phase is to help clients focus on problems or emotions in the traumatic situation and develop short-term, intermediate, and long-term coping goals (Meichenbaum, 1996).

During the skills acquisition and rehearsal phase, clients develop and practice using flexible coping skills in session with the counselor, and then rehearse these coping skills to use in real-life situations specific to the unique stressors they encounter. Coping skills may include emotional self-regulation, self-soothing, self-acceptance, relaxation, cognitive restructuring, problem solving, communication skills training, and developing and using support systems. In the final application and follow-through phase, clients apply coping skills they have learned to stressors that increase in intensity. Key aspects of this phase of treatment include helping clients proactively work toward relapse prevention, accept ownership of their progress, and prepare to follow through using the coping skills in daily life.

CREATIVE TOOLBOX ACTIVITY 7.2   Cues for Safety and Relaxation

Victoria E. Kress, PhD, LPCC-S, NCC

Activity Overview

In this activity, clients learn to use an object or symbol to connect with feelings of relaxation and comfort. This activity can be used by clients when they are feeling fearful, anxious, or hyperaroused.

Treatment Goal(s) of Activity

Clients who have been traumatized often experience hyperarousal, and they typically struggle to decompress and relax. Clients can benefit from developing an ability to connect with a sense of relaxation. This activity addresses treatment goals related to developing and applying relaxation skills.

Directions

1. If it feels safe, close your eyes. Think about a time in your life when you have felt safe and comfortable.
2. Notice the details of that experience with special reference to sights, sounds, and sensations.
3. Take some time to enjoy and connect with this experience.
4. Consider making adjustments to the scene that would further enhance the comfort and security of the experience. Take as much time as you need to fully connect with the experience.
5. When the experience feels just right, lift a finger to let me know.
6. Lean into this experience a little more, and while doing this, pick an object that serves to remind you of this pleasant experience in the future, a sort of souvenir, a symbol. The symbol may be a sight, sound, or sensation that evokes the experience of safety that you are experiencing.
7. To orient the client to the present, invite him or her to refocus on the environment.
8. Suggests to the client that he or she can use the symbol itself to connect with feelings of safety and security during times when he or she feels scared, anxious, overwhelmed, or dissociative.
9. Invite the client to draw, paint, or write about the object—in the session—to deepen his or her memory of the experience.
10. Assess where or how the client can obtain a physical object that represents the identified symbol.
11. Discuss how these symbols can be used to help the client when he or she is feeling anxious, hyperaroused, or dissociative, and needs to connect in the present moment with a sense of safety and being safe in his or her reality.

Process Questions

1. Tell me about the symbol you selected. Why did you select that and what does it mean to you?
2. How can you use the symbol during times in your life when you feel anxious/hyperaroused/dissociative?
3. Where can you keep your symbolic object as a reminder to connect with this sense of security it evokes?

EYE MOVEMENT DESENSITIZATION REPROCESSING (EMDR)   EMDR has been proposed as another treatment for PTSD (Shapiro, 2002), and although promising results have been observed using EMDR to treat PTSD, criticisms persist that EMDR does not have enough rigorous scientific research to demonstrate its effectiveness compared to other treatments, such as CBT. Some argue that its effectiveness lies in the exposure therapy aspects of the approach, which overlap with the previously mentioned treatments (Schubert & Lee, 2009). Nevertheless, given the prevalence of EMDR as a treatment for PTSD, it is important for counselors to understand this approach and its value in treating PTSD.

In sum, the EMDR approach involves integrating exposure (i.e., evoking the memory of a traumatic event), cognition (i.e., recognizing negative thoughts), relaxation (i.e., intentional breathing exercises), and guided eye movements to help individuals learn to access, process, and resolve traumatic memories. There are eight phases of the EMDR approach that may be conducted separately in multiple sessions, or some phases (e.g., phases one through three) may be combined into a single session. Regardless of how the phases are incorporated into treatment, each stage must be completed and facilitated sequentially. Phase one involves obtaining client history, making a diagnosis, evaluating a client's readiness to engage in EMDR, and developing a treatment plan. In phase two, the counselor develops the essential therapeutic relationship and prepares the client for EMDR. During phase three, the counselor conducts an assessment, identifying the trauma target that will be processed using EMDR, and helps the client begin reprocessing the trauma. Desensitization occurs within phase four, wherein the client focuses on troubling emotions and sensations associated with the trauma, rates the intensity of the sensations, and makes specific eye movements with the facilitation of the counselor. In the fifth phase of treatment, the client begins to reprocess and reintegrate positive sensations associated with the traumatic event. In phase six, the client mentally revisits the traumatic event and conducts a body scan to assess whether residual tension or sensations remain. If no disturbances are identified during the body scan, the client moves to phase seven to bring closure to the experience and prepare for reprocessing that may emerge outside of the session. If disturbances remain during the body scan, the process can be repeated. Phase eight entails clients and counselors reevaluating previous EMDR sessions, identifying new areas needing treatment, and continuing to reprocess new targets.

Clinical Toolbox 7.6: In the Pearson etext, click here to view a brief video demonstration of EMDR.

TRAUMA-FOCUSED COGNITIVE BEHAVIORAL THERAPY (TF-CBT) An example of an evidence-based practice that can be used to treat traumatized children is TF-CBT (Cohen, Mannarino, Kliethermesb, & Murray, 2012). TF-CBT is a conjoint child and caregiver psychotherapy approach used with children and adolescents (and their families) who are experiencing significant emotional and behavioral difficulties secondary to traumatic life events. It is a model that integrates trauma-sensitive interventions with cognitive behavioral techniques, humanistic principles, and family involvement to decrease trauma symptomology. TF-CBT teaches children and caregivers new skills that can help them process thoughts and feelings related to traumatic life events; manage and resolve distressing feelings, thoughts, and behaviors that are related to the traumatic life events; and develop an enhanced sense of safety, personal growth, parenting skills, and improved family communication (Cohen et al., 2012). A free 10-hour certificate training program on TF-CBT can be completed through the TF-CBT website (Medical University of South Carolina, 2005). This training program can be completed by any helping professionals or by students currently enrolled in a graduate training program in a mental health discipline. This training is an excellent means of deepening one's understanding of trauma treatment concepts.

PSYCHOPHARMACOTHERAPY When comparing psychotherapy, particularly CBT approaches, with pharmacotherapy, psychotherapy demonstrates greater success in treating PTSD (Friedman, 2008). As part of a pharmacotherapy approach to treating symptoms of PTSD, selective serotonin reuptake inhibitors (SSRIs), a type of antidepressant medication, are most commonly prescribed. Specifically, the U.S. Food and Drug Administration has approved the SSRIs sertraline (e.g., Zoloft) and paroxetine (e.g., Paxil) to treat PTSD, since studies have demonstrated positive results when these medications have been used

(Friedman, 2008). Studies of other medications such as venlafaxine (e.g., Effexor) and nefazodone (e.g., Serzone) also have yielded positive results in treating PTSD (Friedman, 2008). Although commonly prescribed, SSRIs are not consistently effective in treating PTSD, especially chronic PTSD. However, intrusive experiences, emotional avoidance, hyperarousal, depression, and panic attacks may respond well to treatment with SSRIs (Preston et al., 2013).

Apart from SSRIs, atypical antipsychotic medications and antiadrenergic agents have been proposed to treat PTSD symptoms. Among people with PTSD who have not responded positively to SSRIs, atypical antipsychotic medications like risperidone (e.g., Risperdal) and olanzapine (e.g., Zyprexa) have been studied on a limited basis, and some favorable outcomes have been noted. Other medications like antiadrenergic agents also have been used to treat PTSD symptoms, specifically to block neurotransmitters released when a person is under stress. In some studies, prazosin (e.g., Vasoflex), an antiadrenergic agent, has demonstrated some efficacy in preventing the nightmares associated with PTSD (Friedman, 2008). Still, no single medication has been identified to adequately treat the complex symptoms of PTSD, although various medications can be used to treat different symptoms associated with PTSD (e.g., depression, anxiety, sleep disturbances).

Prognosis

Some symptoms associated with PTSD may be conceptualized as normal, acute responses (e.g., depression, anxiety, fear, avoidance) to being exposed to significant trauma. Responses to trauma can become pathological when they persist, impair daily functioning, or become maladaptive coping tools. Most people exposed to trauma do not develop PTSD, experiencing symptoms that only last for a short time. However, some trauma victims do develop PTSD and experience significant impairment. There are mixed projections for PTSD recovery, typically dependent on the severity of symptoms and the amount of time that the symptoms have been present. People who experience PTSD and have the best prognosis for recovery are those who had strong social support and healthy functioning before being exposed to the trauma, those who receive early treatment, and those who are symptomatic for less than six months. People who have less favorable prognoses for recovery from PTSD are those with delayed onset of symptoms and those who also experience a co-occurring disorder. While it may not be possible to eradicate memories of trauma, evidence-based PTSD treatments can help clients cope in healthier ways with trauma responses and memories, and they can live functional lives. Some clients may recover relatively quickly, within approximately six months, while others may experience relapses or endure PTSD as a chronic mental health condition.

Since strong social support is one factor associated with a more favorable prognosis, counselors may proactively encourage clients to intentionally establish and strengthen social supports as a preventive measure for coping with unexpected trauma.

Voices from the Trenches 7.3: In the Pearson etext, click here to read a case study of a woman with PTSD.

ADJUSTMENT DISORDERS

Description of the Disorder and Typical Client Characteristics

Adjustment disorders are characterized by maladaptive emotional or behavioral symptoms that are the result of an identifiable stressor. Symptoms must develop within three months of a stressor and dissipate within six months after the stressor or its consequences are removed. Adjustment disorder subtypes include: with depressed mood, with anxiety, with mixed anxiety and depressed mood, with disturbance of conduct, with mixed disturbance of emotions and conduct, and unspecified (APA, 2013). These disorders are hard to define, and clear diagnostic criteria are not available for each subtype. The adjustment disorder diagnosis is often made when clients have symptoms that are impacting their lives, but the symptoms are not at a level that meets the criteria for any other diagnosis. It is estimated that 5–20% of clients in outpatient settings have an adjustment disorder, but true prevalence rates are difficult to determine because no large-scale studies have assessed their prevalence in the general population (APA, 2013).

Clients with adjustment disorders may present in counseling with a variety of comorbid disorders. Adjustment disorders often present as conduct problems in childhood and adolescence, and as depression and anxiety in adulthood.

Clients from disadvantaged backgrounds may be more likely to enter counseling with these disorders as they are exposed to more life stressors. Those recently diagnosed with a debilitating or terminal medical condition (e.g., cancer, HIV), or those preparing to undergo a major medical procedure (e.g., cardiac surgery) may develop an adjustment disorder. Adjustment disorders are the most frequently diagnosed mental health disorder in settings where military personnel are deployed (Fielden, 2012). Both military clients and their family members may develop these disorders in response to life changes related to deployment. The elderly are particularly at risk for developing adjustment disorders (Casey, 2009) because of the many stressors associated with this lifespan stage, including illness, losses (e.g., spouse, friends, independence), and transitioning into assisted living environments.

Counselor Considerations

Adjustment disorders are characterized by maladaptive reactions to life stressors. The classification of a reaction as maladaptive is largely determined by counselors' clinical judgment, and as such, it is important that reactions are viewed within the client's cultural context. For example, a stressor such as poor academic performance may elicit a greater negative response from an individual who is from a culture that highly values academic success. Care should also be taken in determining whether a reaction is truly disproportionate to the stressor; an examination of the meaning the client ascribes to the event can help to this end.

Counselors should be especially mindful of clients' histories of substance use. Clients may use alcohol or drugs to cope with stress. As such, adjustment and transition times may invite the development or escalation of substance use problems. Counselors therefore have an important role to play in prevention and early intervention of substance use disorders.

Adjustment disorders have a favorable prognosis, with most clients returning to their former levels of functioning. Counselors should educate their clients about the nature of these disorders and demonstrate their confidence that the client's functioning will be restored. Clients who have never experienced extended periods of behavioral and emotional change may feel out of control and frightened. In cases in which the reaction is disproportionately greater than the stressor, the client may feel embarrassed and frustrated because of others' lack of understanding about this reaction. Encouragement and continual reminders about the ability to overcome adjustment disorders can support clients to use their coping skills and to begin to make improvements. When working with clients with adjustment disorders, counselors have an important role to play in preventing additional problems or disorders from developing.

To encourage the use of social supports as a coping strategy, counselors may want to include family members and friends in counseling. Support from others can encourage the client to continue treatment, reduce uncomfortable emotions, and prevent social withdrawal. Including others may be particularly helpful if the stressor is related to the family or relationships with significant others. Additionally, loved ones may be able to provide ideas for strategies that can reduce the client's emotional distress, and they can actively participate in helping the client to use adaptive coping strategies.

Counselors must be attuned to signs of suicidal ideation in clients presenting with adjustment disorders. Suicide risk is increased in those with adjustment disorders, and the progression from initial suicidal ideation to completed suicide is shorter and fluctuates more rapidly than in clients diagnosed with major depressive disorder (Carta, Balestrieri, Murru, & Hardoy, 2009). Additionally, suicide is more likely to be unplanned, occur shortly after the development of the stressor, involve substance use, and occur without prior behavioral or emotional indications in clients with adjustment disorders than in other mental disorders (Carta et al., 2009; Fielden, 2012).

Adolescents with adjustment disorders are especially at risk for suicide, and upon psychological autopsy, up to one-fifth of adolescents who completed suicide may have had an adjustment disorder (Pelkonen, Marttunen, Henriksson, & Lonnqvist, 2005).

Treatment Models and Interventions

The scarcity of literature on the treatment of adjustment disorders presents a challenge in treatment planning. There is little evidence for the superiority of one treatment approach over another; there are a lack of randomized controlled trials in the literature. Because of the lack of research on adjustment disorders and their treatment, it is suggested that counselors incorporate established treatment methods based on the subtype of the adjustment disorder. For example, some treatment techniques used to address major depressive disorder may be useful with clients diagnosed with adjustment disorder with depressed mood.

Several types of counseling and pharmaceutical interventions have been explored with promising results. While adjustment disorders are time-limited diagnoses, early interventions can be especially helpful in reducing the impairments in functioning that clients could face. Brief counseling is generally recommended since the disorder dissipates with time; however, longer treatment may be helpful in situations in which the stressor is chronic, or if the client has a pattern of maladaptive reactions to stressors.

Both individual and group counseling are appropriate for treating these disorders. Group counseling can facilitate the development of social support networks and can help normalize clients' struggles. For clients facing a common stressor (e.g., death of a spouse, diagnosis of a chronic medical condition), groups can provide an encouraging and supportive environment to share advice and enhance coping strategies (Strain & Diefenbacher, 2008). Group counseling can be used in conjunction with individual counseling for a more comprehensive treatment plan.

Psychotherapeutic interventions addressing adjustment disorders should (Strain & Diefenbacher, 2008): (a) identify client concerns and conflicts, (b) explore ways to reduce stressor(s), (c) strengthen coping skills, (d) assist the client in gaining perspective about his or her experience, and (e) facilitate the establishment of a support network to help manage stressors and self. It is important to help clients transfer their emotions into words or productive actions, rather than destructive means that could further impair their functioning (e.g., social withdrawal, substance use).

COGNITIVE BEHAVIORAL THERAPY (CBT)   CBT approaches for treating adjustment disorders focus on reducing or removing the stressor, facilitating adjustment to the stressor, and altering the response to the stressor (Fielden, 2012). A recent study examined the use of CBT to treat adjustment disorders (van der Heiden & Melchior, 2012). The approach utilized a combination of psychoeducation about adjustment disorders and stress reactions and CBT techniques. Treatment adhered to the following progressive framework: (a) self-monitoring symptoms of stress (e.g., record in a diary) to learn to identify triggers; (b) making lifestyle improvements (e.g., eating healthier foods, exercising) and participating in "RES" activities (i.e., *r*elaxing, *e*xercising, *s*ocializing); (c) engaging in RES activities when noticing triggers; and (d) engaging in thought modification (e.g., questioning evidence supporting cognitions, trying behavioral experiments). At follow-up, treatment effects were maintained, and participants reported feeling more capable of taking action. Modifications in coping strategies (i.e., the development of proactive coping skills) resulted in symptom reduction.

CBT interventions for adjustment disorders have decreased symptomology in members of the military (Nardi, Lichtenberg, & Kaplan, 1994), and in terminally ill cancer patients (Akechi et al., 2004). One RCT examined the use of a CBT approach similar to stress inoculation training (van der Klink, Blonk, Schene, & van Dijk, 2003). While the study did not yield differences in symptom reduction between the intervention and control groups, the duration of work leave was significantly shorter in the intervention group, reducing occupational impairment.

INTERPERSONAL PSYCHOTHERAPY (IPT)   IPT is a time-limited approach that helps clients regain control over their mood and functioning (Klerman, Weissman, Rounsaville, & Chevron, 1984). IPT approaches utilize psychoeducation, a here-and-now framework, formulation of the problems from an interpersonal perspective, exploration of options for changing dysfunctional patterns of behavior, identification of focused interpersonal problem areas, and the confidence counselors gain from the systematic approach and problem formulation provided by this treatment (Markowitz, Klerman, & Perry, 1992).

This approach was originally developed for the treatment of depression and may be especially well suited to treat clients who have an adjustment disorder diagnosis with depressive symptoms. A randomized clinical trial (not a controlled trial) reported that IPT was effective in reducing depressive symptoms in adolescents (Mufson et al., 2004). In another randomized clinical trial, IPT was compared to CBT, supportive psychotherapy, and supportive psychotherapy with medication, in addressing depressive symptoms in outpatients diagnosed with HIV (Markowitz et al., 1992). Participants receiving IPT treatment had greater improvements than those receiving CBT or supportive psychotherapy. For a more detailed discussion of IPT, please see Chapter 4.

SOLUTION-FOCUSED BRIEF THERAPY (SFBT) Because adjustment disorders are, by definition, time-limited diagnoses, brief therapy approaches such as SFBT (De Shazer, 1991) can be useful in helping clients to quickly identify and begin working toward goals. SFBT is future-focused and goal-oriented, and builds upon the strengths, abilities, and resiliencies that clients possess. This approach helps clients to focus their attention on solutions, rather than on the stressor that caused the disorder and its consequences. Clients formulate solutions through the identification of exceptions to their problems, and through the development of solutions. SFBT has a positive and optimistic emphasis that can empower clients to take an active role in their treatment, and its brief nature is consistent with research suggesting that most clients expect to attend about eight counseling sessions, and only seek counseling to alleviate a presenting problem.

BRIEF PSYCHODYNAMIC PSYCHOTHERAPY Because of the time-limited nature of adjustment disorders, brief psychodynamic psychotherapy may be considered as a treatment option (Maina, Forner, & Bogetto, 2005). However, clients who are more vulnerable to maladaptive reactions to stressors related to underlying personality pathology may benefit from more long-term psychodynamic treatment. Brief psychodynamic psychotherapy focuses on one central issue that is agreed upon by the counselor and the client. The counselor takes an active role in maintaining the focus on the primary presenting issue, so that goals can be worked toward in a timely manner. Brief approaches do not typically involve allowing the client to freely associate or digress to unrelated topics. Counselors utilize interpretation and transference techniques, with a typical overall goal of reducing symptoms.

In one randomized controlled trial, brief psychodynamic therapy was compared with supportive therapy and a control group in addressing depressive symptoms in those with adjustment disorder with depressed mood, dysthymia, and depressive disorder not otherwise specified (Maina et al., 2005). While both groups receiving psychotherapy improved over the control group, the group receiving brief psychodynamic therapy maintained treatment gains at a six month follow-up evaluation.

An ego-enhancing approach (i.e., an approach that helps to develop one's self-esteem or positive self-perceptions) has been studied for use in treating older adult clients who have adjustment disorders (Frankel, 2001). This psychodynamic approach assumes that the client has effective coping skills, but is overwhelmed by the stressor. Treatment enhances the client's ego functions by facilitating the acknowledgment of the stressor and promoting the use of coping strategies. Life review and active therapeutic stance techniques can help clients to gain a sense of mastery over the stressor (Strain & Diefenbacher, 2008).

PSYCHOPHARMACOTHERAPY Brief counseling is generally considered to be the treatment modality of choice for adjustment disorders; however, several studies have demonstrated that medication can be effective in reducing adjustment disorder symptomology. However, there are currently no medications marketed for the treatment of adjustment disorders, and these diagnoses typically dissipate without medication.

Medication can be used in conjunction with counseling, especially if the client's symptoms are not improving with counseling, and may be prescribed to treat associated symptoms such as anxiety, insomnia, panic attacks, inability to concentrate, hyperarousal, irritability, and restlessness. Anxiolytics (both benzodiazepines and nonbenzodiazepines), antidepressants, and sedatives may be used to treat symptoms, typically for short-term use and in low dosages (Preston et al., 2013). Because adjustment disorders can be associated with substance use, caution should be taken in prescribing medications that could be addictive (e.g., benzodiazepines).

Prognosis

Clients with adjustment disorders typically have a favorable prognosis and return to their former level of functioning. Adult clients are unlikely to develop future mental disorders secondary to having an adjustment disorder. The presence of behavioral and chronic symptoms is the strongest predictor of poor outcome (Carta et al., 2009). Early interventions can improve prognosis by preventing further impairment and stimulating recovery (Casey & Bailey, 2011).

TREATMENT PLAN FOR IMANI

This chapter began with a discussion of Imani, a 15-year-old female who has experienced an extensive abuse and trauma history, yet possesses a number of strengths. The following I CAN START conceptual framework outlines treatment considerations that may be helpful in working with Imani.

C = Contextual Assessment

Imani has connected with a church and finds peace and safety through this venue. She has gender considerations in terms of a family history of devaluation and abuse of women, and being sexually victimized as a child by males in authority roles in her life. She lives in a neglectful and sometimes abusive and unsafe family/home. She has developmental struggles around her identity. She lives in a culture of poverty with her mother, who is often neglectful and sometimes abusive; she lacks a father figure or any extended family she can call on for support. She has medicaid insurance, which allows her access to a variety of health care services.

A = Assessment and Diagnosis

Diagnosis = Posttraumatic Stress Disorder 309.81 (F43.10)

N = Necessary Level of Care

Outpatient, individual counseling (once per week), and a support group/group counseling for girls who have been sexually abused (once per week); referral for in-home family therapy (because of her mother's noncompliance with attending outpatient sessions) to address family roles and responsibilities and family system dynamics

S = Strength-Based Lens

Self: Imani is a survivor. Despite all of her life struggles, she has a will and a desire to succeed and to thrive. Her character strengths have endeared her to others and people are reaching out to support her. She is also intelligent and does well in school. She has a strong work ethic. She genuinely likes other people, despite all she has been through, and can connect with a sense of community through her new church. She is hopeful about her future and she actively seeks help from others.

Family: Imani cares about her sister and wants to be the best person she can be to help support her sister. While her mother is generally an unreliable caregiver and neglectful in many ways, she is resourceful enough to figure out ways she can feed the children and provide shelter.

Community: Imani has a developed a relationship with her employers, and they want to see her succeed and be well. They have connected her with their church, where she reports finding solace and peace. She attends high school and aspires to go to college. She has a best friend who is a source of support for her and, like her sister, motivates her to want to be the best person she can be.

T = Treatment Approach

Prolonged Exposure Therapy

A = Aim and Objectives of Treatment (3-month objectives)

Imani will learn foundational relaxation skills that she needs to help her relax and manage anxiety associated with facing her traumatic experiences in treatment → Imani will complete the Finding a Safe Place activity and the cues for safety and relaxation (see Creative Toolboxes 7.1 and 7.2) and learn basic breathing techniques, and she will use these skills 90% of the time when she is feeling anxious or unsafe.

Imani will decrease the occurrence of intrusive PTSD symptoms by participating in exposure therapy → Imani will participate in exposure therapy and will experience a decrease in flashbacks from 7 to 4 (on a 10-point scale) and experience a reduction in nightmares from once a week to once every other week.

Imani will decrease self-blame and shame related to her abuse experiences → Imani will identify the self-blaming thoughts she has related to her abuse and develop alternative cognitions. When she finds herself engaging in self-blame, she will use these alternative thoughts 80% of the time. She will attend weekly support groups where she will have an opportunity to see that she is not alone in her experiences.

Imani will develop a clearer sense of her capacities and her identity → Each day, Imani will write down three positive things about herself (i.e., her character, her wishes, her hopes and dreams) and/or her actions. She will use support people in her church as well as her friend, her sister, and the Campbells to help her identify her personal capacities.

R = Research-Based Interventions (Prolonged Exposure Therapy)

Counselor will help Imani: Develop skills needed to allow her to recall the trauma without experiencing undue anxiety

Organize and integrate her memories of the trauma/abuse

Reevaluate negative cognitions about her involvement with the trauma/abuse

Develop new perceptions about herself and others

T = Therapeutic Support Services

Referral to a psychiatrist for a consultation

Weekly individual counseling and a counseling support group

Involvement with the school counselor to help her (a) navigate the school and her schoolwork in the context of her symptoms; (b) work on ensuring she gets to school each day

Transportation services through the agency to help her with transportation to individual counseling and her support group

Referral for an assessment for in-home family therapy

References

Achenbach, T. M. (1991). *Manual for the Child Behavior Checklist/4-18 and 1991 Profile*. Burlington, VT: University of Vermont, Department of Psychiatry.

Akechi, T., Okuyama, T., Sugawara, Y., Nakano, T., Shima, Y., & Uchitomi, Y. (2004). Major depression, adjustment disorders, and posttraumatic stress disorder in terminally ill cancer patients: Associated and predictive factors. *Journal of Clinical Oncology, 22*, 1957–1965.

Ainsworth, M. D., Blehar, M. C., Waters, E., & Wall, S. (1978). *Patterns of attachment: A psychological study of the strange situation*. Hillsdale, NJ: Erlbaum.

American Counseling Association. (in press). *2014 ACA code of ethics*. Alexandria, VA: Author.

American Psychiatric Association (APA). (2013). *Diagnostic and statistical manual of mental disorders* (5th ed. [DSM-5]). Washington, DC: Author.

Angold, A., & Costello, E. J. (2000). The Child and Adolescent Psychiatric Assessment (CAPA). *Journal of the American Academy of Child and Adolescent Psychiatry, 39*, 39–48.

Becker-Weidman, A., & Hughes, D. (2008). Dyadic Developmental Psychotherapy: An evidence-based treatment for children with complex trauma and disorders of attachment. *Child and Family Social Work, 13*, 329–337.

Bowlby, J. (1969). *Attachment and loss* (Vol. 1). New York, NY: Basic Books.

Bryant, R. A., Mastrodomenico, J., Felmingham, K. L., Hopwood, S., Kenny, L., Kandris, E., . . . Creamer, M. (2008). Treatment of acute stress disorder: A randomized controlled trial. *Archives of General Psychiatry, 65*, 659–667.

Carta, M. G., Balestrieri, M., Murru, A., & Hardoy, M. C. (2009). Adjustment Disorder: Epidemiology, diagnosis and treatment. *Clinical Practice and Epidemiology in Mental Health, 5*, 15–29.

Casey, P. (2009). Adjustment disorder: Epidemiology, diagnosis and treatment. *CNS Drugs, 23*, 927–938.

Casey, P., & Bailey, S. (2011). Adjustment disorders: The state of the art. *World Psychiatry, 10*(1), 11–18.

Chen, L. P., Murad, M. H., Paras, M. L., Colbenson, K. M., L, Sattler, A. L., Goranson, E. N., . . . Zirakzadeh, A. (2010). Sexual abuse and lifetime diagnosis of psychiatric disorders: systematic review and meta-analysis. *Mayo Clinic Proceedings, 85*, 618–629.

Cohen, J. A., Mannarino, A. P., Kliethermesb, M., & Murray, L. A. (2012). Trauma-focused CBT for youth with complex trauma. *Child Abuse and Neglect, 36*, 528–541.

De Shazer, S. (1991). *Putting difference to work*. New York, NY: Norton.

Eyberg, S. M. (1999). *Eyberg Child Behavior Inventory*. Odessa, FL: Psychological Assessment Resources.

Fielden, J. S. (2012). Review: Management of adjustment disorder in the deployed setting. *Military Medicine, 177*, 1022–1027.

Foa, E. B., Keane, T. M., Friedman, M. J., & Cohen, J. A. (Eds.). (2009). *Effective Treatments for PTSD* (2nd ed.). New York, NY: Guilford.

Foa, E. B., & Yadin, E. (2011). Assessment and diagnosis of Posttraumatic Stress Disorder: An overview of measures. *Psychiatric Times, 28*, 1–8.

Folger, S. F., & Wright, M. (2013). Altering risk following child maltreatment: Family and friend support as protective factors. *Journal of Family Violence, 28*, 325–337.

Frankel, M. (2001). Ego enhancing treatment of adjustment disorders of later life. *Journal of Geriatric Psychiatry, 34*, 221–223.

Friedman, M. J. (2008). Treatments of PTSD: Understanding the evidence—Pharmacotherapy. *PTSD Research Quarterly, 19*(8), 1–11.

Friedman, M. J. (2013). *PTSD history and overview.* Retrieved from: http://www.ptsd.va.gov/professional/pages/ptsd-overview.asp

Friedman, M. J., Resick, P. A., Bryant, R. A., Strain, J., Horowitz, M., & Spiegel, D. (2011). Classification of trauma and stressor-related disorders in DSM-5. *Depression and Anxiety, 28,* 737–749.

Hall, C. (2007). *Reactive Attachment Disorder Checklist– RAD-C.* Department of Psychology, East Carolina University, Greenville, North Carolina.

Klerman, G. L., Weissman, M. M., Rounsaville, B. J., & Chevron, E. S. (1984). *Interpersonal psychotherapy of depression: A brief, focused, specific strategy.* New York, NY: Basic Books.

Kress, V. E., Adamson, N. A., Paylo, M., DeMarco, C., & Bradley, N. (2012). The use of safety plans with children and adolescents living in violent families. *The Family Journal, 20,* 249–255.

Maina, G., Forner, F., & Bogetto, F. (2005). Randomized controlled trial comparing brief dynamic and supportive therapy with waiting list condition in minor depressive disorders. *Psychotherapy and Psychosomatics, 74,* 43–50.

Markowitz, J. C., Klerman, G. L., & Perry, S. W. (1992). Interpersonal psychotherapy of depressed HIV-positive outpatients. *Hospital & Community Psychiatry, 43,* 885–890.

Medical University of South Carolina. (2005). *TF-CBT-Web: A web-based learning course for Trauma-Focused Cognitive-Behavioral Therapy.* Retrieved from: http://tfcbt.musc.edu/

Meichenbaum, D. (1996). Stress inoculation training for coping with stressors. *The Clinical Psychologist, 49,* 4–7.

Merikangas, K. R., He, J., Burstein, M., Swanson, S. A., Avenevoli, S., Cui, L., . . . Swendsen, J. (2010). Lifetime prevalence of mental disorders in U.S. adolescents: Results from the National Comorbidity Study-Adolescent Supplement (NCS-A). *Journal of the American Academy of Child Adolescent Psychiatry, 49,* 980–989.

Minnis, H., Pelosi, A. J., Knapp, M., & Dunn, J. (2001). Mental health and foster career training. *Archives of Disease in Childhood, 84,* 302–306.

Minnis, H., Rabe-Hesketh, S., & Wolkind, S. (2002). Development of a brief waiting room observation for behaviours typical of Reactive Attachment Disorder. *Child and Adolescent Mental Health, 15,* 73–79.

Monson, C. M., Schnurr, P. P., Resick, P. A., Friedman, M. J., Young-Xu, Y., & Stevens, S. P. (2006). Cognitive Processing Therapy for veterans with military-related Posttraumatic Stress Disorder. *Journal of Consulting and Clinical Psychology, 74,* 898–907.

Mufson, L., Dorta, K. P., Wickramaratne, P., Nomura, Y., Olfson, M., & Weissman, M. M. (2004). A randomized effectiveness trial of interpersonal psychotherapy for depressed adolescents. *Archives of General Psychiatry, 61,* 577–584.

Nardi, C., Lichtenberg, P., & Kaplan, Z. (1994). Adjustment disorder of conscripts as a military phobia. *Military Medicine, 159,* 612–616.

Nash, W. P., & Watson, P. J. (2012). Review of VA/DOD clinical practice guideline on management of acute stress and interventions to prevent posttraumatic stress disorder. *Journal of Rehabilitation Research & Development, 49,* 637–648.

Pelkonen, M., Marttunen, M., Henriksson, M., & Lonnqvist, J. (2005). Suicidality in adjustment disorder: Clinical characteristics of adolescent outpatients. *European Child & Adolescent Psychiatry, 14,* 174–180.

Ponniah, K., & Hollon, S. D. (2009). Empirically supported psychological treatments for adult Acute Stress Disorder and Posttraumatic Stress Disorder: A review. *Depression and Anxiety, 26,* 1086–1109.

Preston, J. D., O'Neal, J. H., & Talaga, M. C. (2013). *Handbook of clinical psychopharmacology for therapists* (7th ed.). Oakland, CA: New Harbinger.

Resick, P. A., & Schnicke, M. K. (1992). Cognitive processing therapy for sexual assault victims. *Journal of Consulting and Clinical Psychology, 60,* 748–756.

Reynolds, C. R., & Kamphaus, R. W. (1992). *Behavior Assessment System for Children (BASC).* Circle Pines, MN: AGS Publishing.

Rubin, A., & Springer, D. W. (Eds.). (2009). *Treatment of traumatized adults and children: Clinician's guide to evidenced-based practice.* Hoboken, NJ: Wiley.

Schnurr, P. P. (2008). Treatments of PTSD: Understanding the evidence—Psychotherapy. *PTSD Research Quarterly, 19(8),* 1–6.

Schubert, S., & Lee, C. W. (2009). Adult PTSD and its treatment with EMDR: A review of controversies, evidence, and theoretical knowledge. *Journal of EMDR Practice and Research, 3,* 117–132.

Shapiro, F. (2002). (Ed.). *EMDR as an integrative psychotherapy approach: Experts of diverse orientations explore the paradigm prism.* Washington, DC: American Psychological Association Books.

Sheperis, C. J., Doggett, R. A., Hoda, N. F., Blanchard, T., Renfro-Michel, E. L., Holdiness, S. H., . . . Schlagheck, R. (2003). The development of an assessment protocol for Reactive Attachment Disorder. *Journal of Mental Health Counseling, 25*, 291–310.

Strain, J. J., & Diefenbacher, A. (2008). The adjustment disorders: The conundrums of the diagnoses. *Comprehensive Psychiatry, 49*, 121–130.

van der Heiden, C., & Melchior, K. (2012). Cognitive-behavioral therapy for adjustment disorder: A preliminary study. *The Behavior Therapist, 35*, 57–60.

van der Klink, J. J., Blonk, R. W., Schene, A. H., & Van Dijk, F. J. (2003). Reducing long-term sickness absence by an activating intervention in adjustment disorders: A cluster randomised controlled design. *Occupational Environmental Medicine, 60*, 429–437.

Wang, P. S., Lane, M., Olfson, M., Pincus, H. A., Wells, K. B., & Kessler, R. C. (2005). Twelve-month use of mental health services in the United States. *Archives of General Psychiatry, 62,* 629–640.

Widom, C. S., Czaja, S. J., Bentley, T., & Johnson, M. S. (2009). A prospective investigation of physical health outcomes in abused and neglected children: New findings from a 30-year follow-up. *American Journal of Public Health, 102*, 1135–1144.

Substance-Related and Addictive Disorders

Rachel M. Hoffman O'Neill

CASE STUDY: DIANNA

Dianna is a 30-year-old biracial female who reports, "I'm sick and tired of living this life." She has struggled with addiction to substances since first experimenting with marijuana at age 13. Dianna states, "Back then, everyone smoked a little weed, it wasn't a big deal. But after a while, weed just wasn't enough for me, I needed a better high." She began drinking alcohol at about age 15. She states, "At first I'd just smoke some weed and drink some beer at parties. Then I found myself stealing alcohol from my parents and my friends' parents. By the time I was 16, I was drinking 4–5 nights a week, in my room, by myself." She gradually started experimenting with other substances, including cocaine, MDMA (i.e., ecstasy or "molly"), and prescription pills, including benzodiazepines (e.g., Xanax) and opioids (e.g., Oxycontin). Eventually she tried heroin because a friend told her "the high was like no other drug." Within two months of snorting heroin for the first time, she had progressed to using the drug intravenously and stopped using all other drugs. At present, Dianna uses heroin every day, "or else I'll be sick." She is afraid of overdosing or contracting HIV/AIDs or hepatitis C as a result of her intravenous use. Tearfully, she expresses, "This isn't what I thought my life would be."

Dianna is the oldest of five children. Her parents divorced when she was six years old, and she spent her childhood divided between two households. She felt that once her parents divorced, she and her siblings were neglected as her parents became wrapped up in their "new lives." Being biracial, she feels as though she has never "fit in." Secondary to "not fitting in," when she was 13, she started hanging around with the "wrong crowd," and spent time with a group of friends who were several years older than she was. She liked feeling as though she was accepted and cared about by this new group of friends. It was through this group of friends that Dianna was first introduced to marijuana and alcohol. Dianna explained that by this time, both parents had remarried, and, in her opinion, were "busy raising their new families." She comes from a "blue-collar steel town family" and no one in her family has ever attended college or received formal education. She graduated from high school, but has worked in the food service industry, mainly serving at "dive bars" and "strip joints."

Dianna has one child, a 6-year-old daughter who is currently in the custody of Dianna's mother. Dianna's goal is to be reunited with her child, although she acknowledges she has never had a meaningful relationship with her daughter because of her continued substance use. Dianna wishes to achieve sobriety "and be the best mom I can be." Financially, she struggles and is worried about her ability to meet her child's basic material needs.

Dianna's longest period of sustained sobriety was two months. During this time, she was involved with the local child welfare agency and was submitting random urine screens in order to maintain visitation privileges with her daughter. She describes her sobriety as a time of being "white knuckled"; she goes on to say, "I might not have been using, but that's all I thought about doing every day." She did not attend any community-based 12-step meetings nor did she receive treatment. Dianna reported that eventually the cravings got to be too much for her to resist and she returned to using heroin.

At present, Dianna is technically homeless. She had been living with a friend, but her friend uses heroin as well. Dianna believes that if she returns to the house, she'll be "shooting up within the hour." She wants to stop using, but fears withdrawal symptoms: "The last time I quit, I felt terrible. Like I had the flu, and was being beaten by a stick. I'm afraid I won't get through it this time."

DESCRIPTION OF THE SUBSTANCE USE AND ADDICTIVE DISORDERS

Addiction is a complex concept. Put simply, an addiction represents a *pathological relationship* between an individual and a substance, or a process. For purposes of clarification, it is important to distinguish between the terms *addiction* and *physiological dependence*. As previously mentioned, an addiction represents a maladaptive, problematic relationship with a substance that continues despite increasingly negative consequences; a person can have an addiction that does not involve physiological dependence (e.g., gambling). A physiological dependence, however, involves a physical reaction within the body in which the body begins to crave, or require, a substance in order to maintain a certain level of homeostatic functioning. The *DSM-5* (American Psychiatric Association [APA], 2013) does not use the term *addiction* in a diagnostic capacity, but rather uses the more neutral term *substance use disorder*. Substance use disorders (SUDs) can be characterized by a loss of control over consumption, obsessive thoughts about the substance, and continued use despite negative consequences (APA, 2013). The following example can help distinguish between these concepts: Consider a man gets in a car accident and has a back injury, and he is prescribed something like Oxycontin (i.e., an opioid) for pain. Over time, his body will develop a physiological dependence on that medicine. In other words, the opioid receptors will require that substance, and if the man misses a dose, he might experience some symptoms of opioid withdrawal (e.g., stomach upset, chills). It doesn't mean that he is *addicted* to the substance, only that his body has developed a physiological dependence on the medication. Depending on the dosage of the medication, these physical symptoms will subside within a few days. Some physicians will also prescribe other medications (e.g., Phenergan, an antihistamine used to treat nausea; Klonopin, a benzodiazepine used to treat anxiety and prevent seizures) to clients who are discontinuing opioid medication to help them manage some of the associated symptoms.

In an effort to be consistent with the *DSM-5*, the term *substance use disorders (SUDs)* will be used throughout this chapter. In past editions of the *DSM*, substance-related concerns have been categorized as occurring within four main categories: (a) substance abuse disorders, (b) substance dependence disorders, (c) substance-induced disorders, and (d) substance intoxication disorders. The *DSM-5* now divides substance-related disorders into two main categories: *substance use disorders* and *substance-induced disorders*. The *DSM* system no longer distinguishes between substance abuse and substance dependence.

In the *DSM-5*, substance use is conceptualized as occurring on a continuum from *mild,* to *moderate,* to *severe*. The *mild* specifier is used when an individual meets two or three of the diagnostic criteria. The *moderate* specifier suggests that an individual has four or five of the criteria, and the *severe* specifier is used in cases where the individual meets criteria for six or more symptoms. The *DSM-5* (APA, 2013) defined the essential feature of SUDs as a "cluster of cognitive, behavioral, and physiological symptoms indicating that the individual continues using the substance despite significant substance-related problems" (p. 483). People with SUDs have adopted a "pathological pattern of behaviors related to the use of the substance" (p. 483).

The diagnostic criterion for substance use disorders illustrates the chronic, progressive nature of the condition. People with SUDs may experience difficulty controlling their use of the substance, they may have had unsuccessful past attempts to cut down or abstain from use, and they may experience *cravings* (i.e., an intense desire for the substance; APA, 2013). There is no clear etiology for the development of substance disorders. Numerous models (i.e., moral, psychological, family, disease, biological, sociocultural, multicausal) have been proposed to help explain the potential origins of substance use disorders (Capuzzi & Stauffer, 2012). Chronic substance use is likely a result of a combination of genetic, social, environmental, and psychological factors (Kranzler & Li, 2008). Regardless of the etiology of substance use disorders, it is important to note that biological changes in brain circuitry occur with repeated use of substances, and these changes likely persist even if the person abstains from further use (APA, 2013).

The *DSM-5* (APA, 2013) postulates that some behavioral conditions do not involve ingestion of substances, yet share similarities to substance-related disorders. These behavioral-based conditions are often referred to as *process addictions*. Currently, only one process addiction disorder, gambling disorder, is included in the *DSM-5*. Gambling involves risking something of value in the hope of obtaining something of greater value (APA, 2013). Those with problem gambling habits generally engage in few social activities apart from gambling, and they often consider gambling the only pleasurable activity in which they participate (Petry, 2005).

Prevalence estimates suggest that about 1–2% of the U.S. population engage in pathological gambling (Petry, 2005). Gambling disorder often co-occurs with other mental health issues (e.g., depression, substance use). There is also an associated risk of suicide with estimates suggesting that upwards of half of those in treatment for gambling disorder demonstrate suicidal ideation, and about 17% of those actually attempt suicide (Petry & Kiluk, 2002).

Problem gambling can develop through three distinct pathways (Blaszczynski & Nower, 2002). In Pathway 1, those who have no clear biological or psychosocial vulnerabilities develop gambling problems as the result of behavioral reinforcement. For example, repeated visits to a casino in which the person wins even moderate amounts of money can reinforce his or her desire to engage in gambling behaviors. In Pathway 2, those with premorbid mental health issues (e.g., depression, anxiety), poor coping skills, and/or negative family experiences develop gambling problems as a means to modulate negative affective states. For example, someone might engage in gambling as a means to escape a negative family environment. In Pathway 3, people display the psychological and environmental vulnerabilities of those in Pathway 2, yet they also exhibit impulsivity, inattention, and antisocial personality features. In this pathway, negative emotions and environmental pressures are believed to exacerbate preexisting impulsivity and contribute to gambling and other impulsive behaviors.

COUNSELOR CONSIDERATIONS

There are numerous models that may partially explain the development of substance use disorders. Counselors who work with clients with substance use disorders need to have an understanding of the classic *disease concept* of addiction (Jellinek, 1960). This model conceptualizes SUDs as a progressive illness that, if left untreated, can result in significant life impairment or death. According to the disease concept of addiction, SUDs are a *brain disease*. As previously mentioned, even if a person abstains from substances he or she once used, the brain circuits may not return to pre-substance-use functioning. These brain changes might contribute to repeated episodes of relapse and intense substance cravings.

In addition to considering the disease model, counselors also need to be aware of issues related to dual diagnosis. The co-occurrence of a mental illness and a substance use disorder is common and should be considered the *expectation* rather than the *exception* when assessing patients with SUDs (Buckley, 2006). The relationship between substance use disorders and other mental health disorders is complex and may be rooted in attempts to self-medicate, genetic vulnerability, environment or lifestyle, and/or a common neural substrate (i.e., the set of brain structures that underlies a specific behavior or psychological state; Buckley, 2006). There are numerous complications associated with dual diagnosis, including poor medication compliance, physical comorbidities and poor health, poor self-care, increased suicide risk or aggression, increased risky sexual behavior, and possible incarceration (Bizzarri et al., 2009; Buckley, 2006). Effective treatment for dual diagnosis issues often involves an *integrated approach* to services, an approach that will be discussed later in this chapter.

Counselors who work with addiction issues need to have an understanding of the process of assessing *level of care,* or the minimum intensity level of treatment required to address the client's treatment needs. A level of care assessment takes into consideration all elements of the client's presentation to determine the appropriate treatment setting. On their website, the American Society of Addiction Medicine (ASAM) provides a helpful continuum of five levels of care, ranging from prevention to medical intervention, that can be used in guiding treatment decisions.

In Level 0.5: Early Intervention, clients have not yet demonstrated any substance use issues; however, they may be at risk for developing these issues based on factors such as family history, environment, or mental health–related concerns. The focus in Level 0.5 is on prevention, rather than on treatment. In Level I: Outpatient Services, clients generally meet on a weekly basis for one-on-one or group counseling sessions. Level II: Intensive Outpatient/Partial Hospitalization Services is characterized by services that occur during the day, before or after work/school, in the evenings, and on the weekends. Programs generally range from 9 to 12 hours per week, but might occur more or less frequently depending on unique client needs. In Level III: Residential/Inpatient Services, clients receive 24-hour-a-day services in a residential setting or a setting where he or she temporarily lives. They generally receive a mixture of individual, group, and supportive case management services. Level IV: Medically Managed Intensive Inpatient Services are used when the client requires a planned regimen of 24-hour medically directed evaluation, care, and treatment of mental and substance-related disorders in an acute care inpatient setting. Clients in a Level IV placement typically receive medical detoxification services (i.e., supervised, and in some cases, medication-assisted, withdrawal from substances).

It is also helpful for counselors to have an understanding of the physiological processes associated with substance abuse, their mechanisms of action, and their half-life (i.e., how long it takes for half of the substance to be eliminated from the bloodstream). Counselors also need to understand the concept of *biological testing,* or what is colloquially referred to as *drug testing,* as this is often an important indicator of client sobriety. Biological testing most often involves routine urinalyses of clients; however, blood tests, hair tests, and breathalyzer tests may also be used in some situations. Biological testing is an important indicator of client sobriety as it provides another source of data beyond simply using clients' self-reports, which are often suspect, especially early in treatment.

Clinical Toolbox 8.1: In the Pearson etext, click here to read about the use of biological testing for substance use; testing used to provide objective data about a client's continued sobriety.

Most biological drug detection tests will measure for commonly abused drugs (e.g., marijuana, cocaine, opioids, amphetamines); however, more specific drug detection tests are available to measure other types of abused drugs (e.g., synthetic cannabis [often referred to as K2 spice], 80-hour ethyl glucuronide [measures alcohol use within the past 3–4 days], benzodiazepines). As mentioned above, there are four main drug detection tests (i.e., hair, urine, blood, and breath); however, the urine drug screens are the most widely used test in substance use treatment. Urine screens are most often used when there are immediate concerns about a client's substance use. Drug detection times vary for each of the major classes of substances, with most substances having a detection window of hours, days, or in some cases, weeks.

Relapse is also a consideration for counselors who work with people who have SUDs. Relapse is defined as a return to substance use (or a process addiction) after a period of abstinence from use (Moss & Cook, 2012). The National Institute on Drug Abuse (NIDA, 2002) has suggested that the relapse rate is about 40–60% for those who have SUDs. It can be helpful to think about SUDs, and process addictions such as gambling, as *relapsing conditions* (Moss & Cook, 2012) that are analogous to a physical disease such as diabetes; a disease that involves constant maintenance and relapse (i.e., they often return to the disease after a period of full or partial recovery).

Another consideration for counselors who work with SUDs is the presence of co-occurring trauma symptoms. Abstinence from substances will not resolve comorbid trauma-related disorders, and for many patients, the trauma symptoms may worsen in the absence of substance use. Women with trauma histories tend to abuse the most severe substances and are vulnerable to relapse, as well as repeated victimization. Treatment programs do not typically offer integrated treatments for SUDs and trauma, which can result in poorer overall treatment outcomes.

 Clinical Toolbox 8.2: In the Pearson etext, click here to read about trauma-informed addictions treatment.

Research estimates have suggested a strong relationship between criminal activity and substance use. Almost two-thirds of prison inmates meet the diagnostic criteria for SUDs, and nearly a quarter of these individuals have co-occurring drug use and mental disorders (Center on Addiction and Substance Use at Columbia University, 2010). These associated legal charges represent a considerable burden to society. Nordstrom and Dackis (2011) presented several clinical considerations associated with the relationship between criminal behavior and SUDs. First, with respect to criminal activity, it is important to note that not all people with SUDs commit crimes. Second, criminally active drug users are made up of (a) a group that gets involved with crime before or at the same time they get involved with drugs (i.e., those who have shared psychological and social risk factors for deviant behavior in general), and (b) a group that gets involved with crime only after they become involved with drugs (i.e., those for whom the onset of addiction is a turning point and causes them to initiate a criminal career). Third, the combination of SUDs and criminal activity serves to maintain lifestyle patterns and peer affiliations which further reinforce substance use and criminal activity. Drug addiction does not turn nonviolent criminals into violent criminals, but active addiction increases the frequency of criminal activity (Nordstrom & Dackis, 2011).

Counselors who work with people who have substance use disorders should also consider legal and ethical issues that may pertain to their practice. Perhaps the most important ethics consideration is related to the protection of clients' confidentiality. Especially with substance use disorders, these issues are sensitive. Counselors who work with those who have substance use disorders are legally obligated to follow an additional confidential restrictions under the federal law (i.e., *Code of Federal Regulations [CFR] 42, Part 2. 42 CF;* Office of the Federal Register, 1994). These restrictions prohibit any unauthorized disclosure of the records of any client in a federally funded program that provides screening or treatment for drug or alcohol abuse. The intent of *42 CFR* is to encourage people to seek substance use treatment without fear of negative consequences (e.g., potentially losing their job or experiencing legal ramifications; Reiner, 2000). Counselors who work in substance use treatment facilities should become familiar with *42 CFR* prior to beginning their work with clients.

PROGNOSIS

Addiction issues can be complex to treat; however, many evidenced-based approaches have demonstrated success in working with those who have both substance and process addictions. People enter treatment for addictions via a number of different pathways, which include self-referral (i.e., the person decides to seek treatment on his or her own), court-referral (i.e., the person is in treatment to avoid some sort of associated legal consequences), or family-referral. In some cases, people may feel coerced into treatment and they may withdraw from the counseling process (Juhnke, 2002). This tends to be especially true of those who seek treatment to avoid legal or family consequences. The use of an empowerment-based treatment strategy, such as motivational interviewing, can be helpful in supporting client autonomy, and in encouraging clients to identify personal motivations for change, thus improving prognosis.

The prognosis for addictions can vary according to the nature of the addiction, age at first use, and other factors, such as family support. Treatment discontinuation is a common concern early in recovery from substances. Researchers (e.g., Day & Strang, 2011) estimate that approximately 50% of clients do not complete detoxification treatment, suggesting that many clients may not be able to tolerate the unpleasant effects associated with withdrawal from substances. Relapse is a common concern for those in early recovery (Douaihy, Daley, Marlatt, & Spotts, 2009). Relapse can be viewed as part of the natural course of the disorder, and relapse prevention should be built into all SUD treatment programs and treatment plans.

ALCOHOL-RELATED DISORDERS

Description of the Disorder and Typical Client Characteristics

In the *DSM-5*, the specific alcohol-related diagnoses include: alcohol use disorder, alcohol intoxication, alcohol withdrawal, other alcohol-induced disorders, and unspecified alcohol-related disorder (APA, 2013). Alcohol, a central nervous system depressant, is a legal substance in the United States. Although alcohol is legal and readily available, counselors should be aware of its addictive potential. Alcohol tends to be the most abused substance in the United States, with the 12-month prevalence of alcohol use disorder estimated to be 8% within the adult population (APA, 2013).

Alcohol use disorder tends to have an associated family component. It is not uncommon for alcohol abuse to begin in adolescence. Alcohol use disorder tends to run in families, with about 40–60% of the variance of risk explained by genetic influences (Schuckit, 2009). People who have a family member with an alcohol use disorder are three to four times more likely to also develop an alcohol use disorder.

An estimated 3.6% of the world population (15–64 years old) currently meets diagnostic criteria for an alcohol use disorder, with a lower prevalence found in the African region, a higher rate found in the American region (North, South, and Central America and the Caribbean), and the highest rates being found in the Eastern European region (APA, 2013). Males have a higher prevalence rate of alcohol-related disorders than females; however, females who drink heavily may be more vulnerable to some of the physical consequences associated with alcohol (e.g., liver disease; APA, 2013).

Most people can consume alcohol without developing any associated problems. However, others, through a complex set of genetic and environmental factors, may be at risk for developing an alcohol addiction. Alcohol use disorder is often associated with problems similar to those associated with other substances (e.g., cannabis; cocaine; heroin; amphetamines; sedatives, hypnotics, or anxiolytics).

Alcohol use disorder is defined by a cluster of behavioral and physical symptoms, which can include withdrawal, tolerance, and craving (APA, 2013). The critical ingredient in alcohol is ethanol, and most people report that ingesting alcohol results in feelings of relaxation and euphoria. Ethanol is readily absorbed into the bloodstream through the stomach, and intoxication effects are usually evident within 20 minutes of consuming an alcoholic beverage (Veach, Rogers, & Essic, 2012). Intoxication effects are moderated by factors such as food in the stomach, body weight, gender, and tolerance to alcohol (Veach et al., 2012). It is important for counselors to note that alcohol intoxication represents a potentially life-threatening presentation, as clients are at risk for alcohol poisoning, respiratory arrest, or aspiration of vomit.

Counselor Considerations

Counselors must be able to effectively assess the severity of a client's alcohol use, as clients who are physiologically dependent on the substance might require inpatient detoxification. Alcohol withdrawal can represent a significant clinical presentation, with 10% of those who develop alcohol withdrawal developing life-threatening symptoms (e.g., severe autonomic hyperactivity, tremors, alcohol withdrawal delirium; APA, 2013). Awareness of the physiological effects of alcohol is also important and must include an understanding of the effects of the substance during intoxication, withdrawal, and the long-term effects of continued use.

Withdrawal from alcohol is characterized by a pattern of symptoms that develop approximately 4–12 hours after the reduction of intake following prolonged, heavy alcohol ingestion (Schuckit, 2009). An episode of acute alcohol withdrawal usually lasts 4–5 days and typically occurs only after extended periods of heavy drinking (APA, 2013). Mild alcohol withdrawal is often colloquially referred to as a *hangover*. However, with chronic use, alcohol withdrawal can represent a significant and deadly condition.

Alcohol withdrawal symptoms can be grouped into three main categories: central nervous system excitation (e.g., restlessness, agitation, seizures), excessive function of the autonomic nervous system (e.g., nausea, vomiting, tachycardia, tremulousness, hypertension), and cognitive dysfunction (Blondell, 2005). Alcohol withdrawal is serious and in some cases, life-threatening. People who, upon cessation of alcohol use, are at risk for alcohol withdrawal should be monitored by a team of medical professionals to ensure a safe detoxification process. Medication-assisted treatments may also be used to help with the detoxification process.

Those who abuse alcohol generally spend a great deal of their time drinking, making sure they can get alcohol, and recovering from alcohol's effects, all of which can often occur at the expense of other activities and responsibilities. Chronic alcohol use is associated with difficulties in all major areas of a person's life, and can include violence and aggression, physical complications, relationship difficulties, and occupational impairment. All of these issues will need to be addressed in treatment.

Counselors must also be prepared to work with co-occurring mental health issues as there is a significant overlap between alcohol use and other mental health disorders. People with preexisting severe and persistent mental disorders (e.g., schizophrenia, bipolar disorder, major depressive disorder) are at a high risk specifically for alcohol use disorder (APA, 2013). It is important to note that the intoxication and withdrawal effects of alcohol can mimic many mental health disorders (e.g., depression, bipolar disorder, psychosis), thus, it is important to rule out intoxication or withdrawal effects before diagnosing a co-occurring mental health condition in a client with alcohol use disorder.

Counselors must manage *countertransference* reactions that can develop during the course of addictions treatment. Countertransference refers to the unconscious needs, feelings, and wishes that the counselor projects onto the client. Those with SUDs have the capacity to engender powerful countertransference reactions, especially in helpers who have been touched by another's—or their own—substance abuse. The client may present as oppositional, resistant, and manipulative; and, as a result, may evoke a strong emotional reaction within the counselor. It strains the most objective counselor not to experience emotional reactions to these processes, and countertransference reactions are not uncommon among those who work with SUDs.

What follows are four common countertransference reactions seen in professionals who work with SUDs (Imhof, Hirsch, & Terenzi, 1983): (a) acting in the role of a good parent rescuing a bad, impulsive child; (b) reacting with anger when the client challenges the counselor's knowledge or authority; (c) aligning with the client by identifying with antiauthority stories or by vicariously romanticizing the drug addict lifestyle; and (d) emotionally withdrawing, becoming indifferent, or feeling bored, angry, or burnt out. It can be helpful for the counselor to seek supervision to help manage these possible reactions.

The *disease concept,* which is endorsed by all mental health care–related professional organizations, including the World Health Organization (WHO), the American Medical Association (AMA), and the American Psychiatric Association (APA), has been used to explain the progressive, often debilitating nature of alcoholism. Jellinek (1960) described four phases of alcoholism, consistent with a disease model: the *prealcoholic phase*, the *prodromal phase*, the *crucial phase*, and the *chronic phase*. In the prealcoholic phase, the person's use of alcohol might be limited to social situations; however, he or she soon experiences psychological relief (i.e., negative reinforcement) in the drinking situation. Over time, the person begins to perceive alcohol use as a means to manage emotions, and he or she might experience an increase in tolerance (i.e., greater amounts of the substance are needed to achieve the desired results).

In the prodromal phase, the person begins to endorse alcohol use as a means of psychological escape from tensions, problems, and inhibitions. People at this stage may not experience any significant negative consequences as a result of their use; however, their alcohol consumption becomes habitual, and it may have resulted in some problematic situations (e.g., blackouts, hangovers).

In the crucial phase, people begin to exhibit difficulty maintaining control over their alcohol consumption. They may feel unable, or may be unwilling, to refrain from use. They tend to experience feelings of guilt and shame related to their use. Often, they may experience pressure from family, friends, or employers related to their ongoing use. They typically begin to experience negative consequences (e.g., DUIs, legal charges) associated with their ongoing substance use.

Those in the chronic phase tend to experience a complete lack of control over their drinking. They may be chronically intoxicated over a period of several days (sometimes referred to colloquially as a *bender*). They tend to experience difficulty maintaining a commitment to their obligations, such as family, friends, and employment. They may also begin to experience significant physical health concerns (e.g., tremors, liver problems) as a result of their continued use. Those who do not receive treatment are likely to experience long-term, often irreversible complications, including Karsakoff's syndrome, Wernicke's disease, cirrhosis of the liver, pancreatitis, or even death.

Counselors should be aware of cultural considerations, even considerations unique to specific aspects of a person's circumstances (e.g., regional uniqueness, aspects of their job that involve substance use), and how they may relate to clients' treatment. For example, a client who works in an environment where socializing around alcohol use is an aspect of his or her job (e.g., many traveling sales positions) will have unique relapse prevention considerations.

Treatment Models and Interventions

There are several evidence-based treatments for use with alcohol use disorders: cognitive behavioral therapy, 12-step facilitation, social skills training, and medication-assisted treatments. Each of these approaches has demonstrated success in helping clients sustain long-term recovery. Behavioral self-control training will also be addressed. While this treatment approach and its assumption that this population is able to engage in controlled drinking is controversial, it has some demonstrated utility with people who have mild to moderate alcohol use problems.

As previously mentioned, the client's severity of substance use symptoms is generally assessed using the ASAM levels of care placement. Depending on the client's symptom severity, a number of level care treatment options including medical detoxification, residential treatment, and intensive/outpatient services will be considered. Current methods of intervention also tend to incorporate an *integrated treatment* approach, which means that co-occurring substance abuse and mental health disorders are treated concurrently (Davis et al., 2006).

MEDICAL DETOXIFICATION People who have extensive histories of alcohol abuse may require medically supervised detoxification in order to ensure their safety during the withdrawal process (Di Nicola et al., 2010). Withdrawal from alcohol can be significantly uncomfortable and in some cases life-threatening, depending on the history and extent of the client's use. Medical detoxification of alcohol use usually takes place over the course of 3–7 days and involves a combination of medications designed to help alleviate some of the withdrawal symptoms associated with discontinuing alcohol use (e.g., nausea, vomiting, chills). Medical staff also closely monitor patients to ensure that all vital signs are within normal limits. Generally, clients will also receive a combination of individual and group counseling services during their detoxification period.

RESIDENTIAL TREATMENT Residential programs are generally used to stabilize those individuals with chronic substance use disorders. Programs usually begin after the point of detoxification and can range from 28 to 90 days in length, and usually incorporate some combination of individual, group, and family counseling (Wilkinson, Mistral, & Golding, 2008). The emphasis of residential programs is usually on removing the client from an environment that has been supporting his or her addiction. For example, a client who lives with his girlfriend who is also using substances is unlikely to be able to maintain his sobriety in an outpatient level of care.

Other types of residential options for treatment might include supportive housing programs, which generally offer opportunities for a client to reside in a supportive, sober community. Typically, supportive housing programs include some element of treatment (e.g., group counseling, individual counseling), as well as vocational and other case management services. Clients are often expected to pursue employment or educational opportunities, attend 12-step support meetings, and comply with all facility rules and guidelines during their stay in residential treatment.

OUTPATIENT-BASED TREATMENTS   Outpatient-based treatments include *intensive outpatient programs (IOP)* and *outpatient (OP)* services. In traditional IOP, clients receive three hours of group, three times per week for a total of nine hours of group per week. Clients may also receive one individual or family counseling session per week. The length of stay in IOP programs varies, although most programs last for a minimum of 24 weeks. Clients are often expected to engage in other therapeutic activities outside of the IOP schedule, which may include attending 12-step support meetings (e.g., AA/NA).

Other outpatient options may include weekly or biweekly group or individual counseling sessions. These programs are generally reserved for clients who have completed a higher level of care (e.g., residential, IOP) treatment. Occasionally, those who have relapsed on substances after a period of sustained sobriety might be placed in an outpatient program for a brief stabilization of the relapse.

CREATIVE TOOLBOX ACTIVITY 8.1   Goodbye Letter to Your Addiction

Rachel M. Hoffman O'Neill, PhD, PCC-S

Activity Overview

In an attempt to externalize from an addiction and take control over it, clients are invited to write a letter to their addiction and inform the addiction that they are no longer under its control.

Treatment Goal(s) of Activity

This activity can deepen a clients' motivation to change. It may also enhance clients' efficacy related to making behavioral changes. The goal of the activity is to utilize a narrative therapy technique to externalize the problem of addiction. Encouraging clients to consider what their life might be like without the addiction can help them visualize the possibilities associated with a sober lifestyle.

Directions

Invite the client to consider what role his or her addiction has played in his or her life. Ask the client to consider what he or she would like to say to the addiction, as he or she prepares to move on from it. Often, it can be helpful to frame this as if the client were *breaking up with the addiction*. After considering these issues, the client is directed to write a letter to the addiction, explaining why he or she is leaving the relationship, the negative effects the relationship has had on his or her life, and what he or she will gain by moving on from the addiction. To further externalize it, clients can also be invited to draw a picture of the addiction.

Process Questions

1. What was it like to consider the effect that addiction has had on your life?
2. What was the easiest thing about saying goodbye to the addiction?
3. What was the hardest part about saying goodbye?
4. If your addiction could respond, what do you think it would say? How might it try to convince you to stay?

MOTIVATIONAL INTERVIEWING (MI)   MI, sometimes referred to as motivational enhancement, is considered by many to be an effective approach when working with those who abuse substances. Motivational interviewing is an active, directive, client-centered counseling approach used to elicit behavior change by exploring and resolving client ambivalence (Miller & Rollnick, 2012). The foundations of MI include three main elements: (a) collaboration, (b) evocation, and (c) autonomy (Miller & Rollnick, 2012). The concept of *collaboration* highlights the importance of an egalitarian therapeutic relationship, which honors the experiences and perspectives of the client. *Evocation* refers to developing the client's inherent resources and intrinsic motivation for change. The final concept, *autonomy,* refers to a value of the client's right and capacity for self-direction and informed consent within the treatment process.

A goal of MI is to alter how the client sees, feels, and responds to problematic behaviors, with the counselor amplifying any discrepancy between the client's present behavior and goals that he or she verbalizes to be important (Britt, Blampied, & Hudson, 2004). Motivational interviewing creates a supportive, nonjudgmental, directive environment to facilitate the exploration of one's motivations, readiness, and confidence levels for change, as well as ambivalence about change (Miller & Rollnick, 2012). In addition to its utility with alcohol use disorders, MI is generally considered effective in working with those who have dual diagnosis issues (Barrowclough, Haddock, Fitzsimmons, & Johnson, 2006).

 Clinical Toolbox 8.3: In the Pearson etext, click here to view a video demonstration of motivational interviewing.

COGNITIVE BEHAVIORAL THERAPY (CBT)   CBT approaches are well researched and generally considered a best practice in the treatment of addictions. CBT approaches include behavioral self-control training, community reinforcement, contingency management, behavioral contracting, and social skills training (Osborn, 2012). CBT approaches focus on helping clients change their addiction-supportive thought processes, and develop their basic coping skills.

CBT is a structured, goal-oriented approach that focuses on addressing the immediate problems associated with alcohol use. CBT is generally flexible, and it can be adapted to a wide range of clients as well as a variety of settings (e.g., inpatient, outpatient) and formats (e.g., group, individual). CBT for substance use generally involves two main components: functional analysis and social skills training (Carroll, 1998). When using functional analysis, the counselor and client identify the client's thoughts, feelings, and circumstances before and after substance use. Early in treatment, the functional analysis plays a critical role in helping the counselor and client determine the high-risk situations that are likely to lead to substance use, and it can help provide insights into some of the reasons the person may be using substances (Carroll, 1998). Later in treatment, functional analyses of episodes of substance use may identify those situations or states in which the person still has difficulty coping.

The second component, social skills training, involves teaching clients to effectively use coping strategies. Social skills training strengthens and broadens the individual's range of coping styles with skills training focusing on both intrapersonal (e.g., coping with craving) and interpersonal (e.g., refusing substances) skills (Carroll, 1998). The aim of CBT is to help the client eliminate substance use, while simultaneously imparting skills that can benefit the client after treatment ends, thus preventing relapse and encouraging long-term health.

CBT may be especially beneficial in treating those with dual diagnosis issues. The utility of CBT for those with co-occurring substance use and mental health issues may be rooted in the recognition of escalating symptoms and other warning signs; coping with cravings; coming up with healthy alternative activities; normalizing substance use; developing plans for lapse or relapse; and cognitive restructuring to counteract unproductive beliefs about substance use (Barrowclough et al., 2006).

Clinical Toolbox 8.4: In the Pearson etext, click here to read about a creative activity that can be used to help clients identify current and past unresolved struggles that they need to address in order to maintain their sobriety.

BEHAVIORAL SELF-CONTROL TRAINING (BSCT) BSCT is a controversial behavior therapy approach that has been used in treating alcohol use disorders. BSCT (Marlatt, Latimer, Baer, & Quigley, 1993) involves teaching clients controlled drinking strategies so that they can consume alcohol in a moderation. This approach is more appropriate with clients who have only mild to moderate alcohol abuse. Walters (2000) identified the core components of BSCT as following six principal elements: blood alcohol concentration (BAC) discrimination training (i.e., teaching clients to estimate their BAC by attending to intoxication cues), rate control (i.e., teaching the client to expand the time frame between the drinks, prolong the duration of a drink, switch to a lower-proof beverage), functional analysis (i.e., identifying high-risk situations), self-monitoring, goal-setting, and contingency management. The principles of BSCT are based on the idea that substance-abusing clients can control their drinking, a belief that is contradictory to the basic premise of the disease concept and the Alcoholics Anonymous program.

Opponents of BSCT verbalize concern related to clients' continued usage of alcohol as clients with alcohol use disorders generally demonstrate past unsuccessful attempts to moderate their alcohol intake. Numerous studies have demonstrated BSCT's usefulness for motivated clients with mild to moderate problematic drinking behaviors, yet for those with more severe dependency and/or motivation issues (i.e., mandated or coerced), BSCT treatment is less successful (Thombs & Osborn, 2013). As such, the overall utility of BSCT with clients with alcohol use disorders is limited, and this treatment approach should be used with caution.

TWELVE-STEP FACILITATION Participation in 12-step fellowships such as Alcoholics Anonymous (AA) might be one of the best indicators of future recovery status (Humphreys et al., 2004; Moos & Moos, 2004). Participation in 12-step fellowships is considered to be a significant predictor of decreased stress in early recovery (Laudet & White, 2008), and reduced alcohol/drug use at 2-year (McKellar, Stewart, & Humphreys, 2003), 5-year (Ritsher, McKellar, Finney, Otilingam, & Moos, 2002) and 16-year follow-up (Moos & Moos, 2007).

Clinical Toolbox 8.5: In the Pearson etext, click here to read an activity that can be used early in a client's recovery to help him or her underscore ongoing personal responsibility related to recovery.

Although the 12-step fellowship is not considered *treatment*, counselors who use 12-step facilitation methods can help prepare and support clients for utilizing this support group. Twelve-Step Facilitation Therapy is a manual-guided treatment that was developed for use in the treatment of substance use disorders (Nowinski, Baker, & Carroll, 1992). The overall goal of Twelve-Step Facilitation Therapy is to promote abstinence by facilitating patients' active involvement and participation in the fellowship of 12-step recovery programs (e.g., NA, CA, AA). Active involvement in 12-step programs is regarded as the single most important factor responsible in maintaining sustained recovery from drug dependence, and therefore, it is the desired outcome of participation in this treatment.

 Clinical Toolbox 8.6: In the Pearson etext, click here to view a clinical demonstration of 12-step facilitation.

SOCIAL SKILLS TRAINING Social skills training (also discussed under CBT treatment), a CBT counseling approach used in mental health settings, involves teaching clients prosocial techniques for everyday living (Liberman, 2007). Social skills training uses goal setting to help the individual achieve specific, attainable, interpersonal goals. Goals are collaboratively developed by the counselor and client, and they focus on contemporary social situation that are meaningful to the client (Liberman, 2007). Modeling, role-playing social interactions, and positive feedback are all core components of social skills training. Social skills training is one element of a broader treatment program (Liberman, 2007).

Specific to alcohol use disorders, social skills training teaches clients how to develop alcohol refusal skills and how to effectively manage the social pressures that might lead to drinking behavior. For example, clients might be taught how to refuse alcohol for the customary New Year's Eve toast at midnight. Teaching clients drink refusal and social pressures skills training may result in significantly better clinical outcomes (Witkiewitz, Villarroel, Hartzler, & Donovan, 2011).

FAMILY THERAPY For those with substance use disorders, family involvement is likely to support overall treatment outcomes (Lewis, 2014). Family or friends who remain involved can be a knowledgeable and responsive resource, and can have a significant impact on clinical outcomes and recovery. Family therapy for addiction generally involves those most affected by the individual's substance use, typically people who may reside in the same household as the person with the addiction. Substance use usually disrupts relationships among family members, which can result in significant relational difficulties. Overall, the entire family can benefit from psychoeducation on the disease model of addiction, as well as an understanding of how family roles and dynamics can encourage or support alcohol abuse.

PSYCHOPHARMACOTHERAPY There are three main alcohol-related conditions that can be treated through the use of pharmacological approaches: (a) withdrawal, (b) abstinence, and (c) cravings. Benzodiazepines are generally used to treat alcohol withdrawal symptoms. Typically, benzodiazepines (e.g., lorazepam, diazepam) are effective in reducing the intensity of symptoms associated with withdrawal. It is important to note, however, that following acute withdrawal, symptoms of anxiety, insomnia, and autonomic dysfunction may persist for up to 3–6 months at lower levels of intensity (APA, 2013); thus, longer term medication management of these symptoms might be necessary.

Disulfiram (e.g., Antabuse) is perhaps one of the most well-known addiction medicines. Antabuse is considered an aversion treatment; if a client on Antabuse ingests alcohol, he or she will experience unpleasant side effects (e.g., nausea, vomiting). The rationale for the use of Antabuse is that, by blocking the pleasurable effects of alcohol and replacing them with negative experiences, clients will begin to develop an aversion to alcohol.

Acamprosate (e.g., Campral) has demonstrated efficacy in the treatment of alcohol-related cravings. Campral is designed for use in individuals who have some period of sustained sobriety; it is not likely to be helpful to a person who has not already quit drinking. Campral has demonstrated efficacy in maintaining abstinence from alcohol in clients who have undergone detoxification (Ross & Peselow, 2009).

Prognosis

Alcohol is a neurotoxin and repeated use can result in damage to numerous organ systems (Doweiko, 2011). Chronic alcohol use, if untreated, can result in significant legal, health, and family consequences. People who abuse alcohol are at greater risk for numerous health problems, including memory problems, liver damage, cancers, and alcohol-related brain damage. One of the most serious health complications is Wernicke-Korsakoff syndrome, which can result in vision changes, memory complications, and ataxia (i.e., a lack of voluntary coordination of muscle movements).

Those who abuse alcohol are likely to experience several setbacks, or relapses, on the way to sustained long-term sobriety. Estimated rates of relapse vary and may be difficult to accurately detect because of the reliance, to some extent, on client self-report. It can also be difficult to maintain contact with clients postdischarge from treatment, which can further complicate efforts to assess relapse at 3-, 6-, and 12-month intervals. Researchers (e.g., McKay, Franklin, Patapis, & Lynch, 2006; Walitzer & Dearing, 2006) estimated relapse rates in the range of 40 to 60% within the first several months posttreatment, and estimates of relapse are as high as 70 to 80% by the end of 1 year. However, Dawson, Goldstein, and Grant (2007) completed a 3-year follow-up of alcohol-dependent clients and found that only about 25% experienced a relapse and only about 5% experienced the recurrence of alcohol dependency.

A small percentage of those who are alcohol dependent may be able to return to some form of controlled drinking; however, long-term research has suggested that such people are likely to eventually return to problematic alcohol use, and total abstinence from alcohol use is the best treatment strategy (Vaillant, 2003). It is important for counselors to consider the potential protective factors that may help guard against relapse. Those with strong personal resources and fewer alcohol-related deficits have the greatest likelihood of sustained remission (Moos & Moos, 2007). Other protective factors in recovery may include the client's desire to avoid legal consequences and sustained employment (Best et al., 2010).

DRUG-RELATED DISORDERS

Description of the Disorders and Typical Client Characteristics

In this section, an overview of each of the remaining non-alcohol-based substance use disorders will be provided along with considerations related to counseling clients with each disorder. After a brief discussion of these disorders has been presented, a discussion of considerations and evidence-based treatments will follow. The prognosis section addresses each of the disorders presented in this section.

CAFFEINE-RELATED DISORDERS   Caffeine is the most widely used psychoactive substance in the world (Ogawa & Ueki, 2007). Nationwide, caffeine consumption averages approximately 210–238 mg/per person per day (Ogawa & Ueki, 2007). Large doses of caffeine can result in mild sensory disturbances, increased heart rate, agitation, restlessness, and increased bowel mobility (APA, 2013). Heavy, chronic caffeine use is associated with depression, anxiety, and illicit drug abuse and dependence (Kendler, Myers, & O'Gardner, 2006). There may be shared genetic or environmental factors between psychiatric disorders and caffeine use phenotypes (Bergin & Kendler, 2012). An observable withdrawal pattern, including headache, lethargy, and irritability, occurs when caffeine use is abruptly discontinued.

CANNABIS-RELATED DISORDERS   Estimates suggest that about 7% of the U.S. population report using marijuana (SAMHSA, 2011). People who use cannabis may use the substance throughout the day; thus an individual may spend many hours a day under the influence of the substance (APA, 2013). Cannabis intoxication usually begins with the person feeling a high, followed by feelings of euphoria, sedation, impaired judgment, and sensory deficits (APA, 2013). Tolerance to the effects of cannabis can develop rapidly, with the person needing more of the substance in order to achieve a high (Doweiko, 2011).

Many clients minimize the negative effects of repeated cannabis use. However, it is important to note that there are long-term problems associated with chronic cannabis use. The negative effects of cannabis use include decreased lung capacity, lowered testosterone levels, and decreased muscle capacity. The recent nationwide trend towards legalizing this substance may serve to reinforce the myth that cannabis, like alcohol, does not pose any significant associated health risks.

HALLUCINOGEN-RELATED DISORDERS   The *DSM-5* distinguishes between two types of hallucinogen-related disorders: phencyclidine disorders and other hallucinogen disorders. Phencyclidine includes PCP, ketamine, and other substances. In low doses, phencyclidine produces feelings of separation of mind and body; in high doses, stupor and coma can result (APA, 2013). Repeated hallucinogen use is of concern, given the likely consequences of neural damage, memory impairment, and possible symptoms of psychosis (Parrott, 2001).

Hallucinogen disorders involve the use of substances like MDMA (i.e., ecstasy, Molly), DMT, and LSD. The perceptual disturbances and impaired judgment associated with hallucinogen use can result in injury or potential fatal outcomes (APA, 2013). A person usually begins to experience the positive effects of the substance within 5–10 minutes, and the user may experience increased blood pressure, nausea, and muscle weakness (Doweiko, 2011). Hallucinogenic drugs are not generally believed to have physiologically addicting properties such as tolerance or withdrawal (Veach et al., 2012). Use of hallucinogenic substances appears to be on the rise; during the past decade, rates of MDMA use and associated morbidity and mortality have risen in the United States, and in other countries (Patel, Wright, Ratcliff, & Miller, 2004).

INHALANT-RELATED DISORDERS   Inhalants include a diverse category of substances that are inhaled, such as cleaning agents, pesticides, gasoline, glue, paint thinner, computer cleaner, and felt-tipped pens. Inhalants have the potential to be fatal on first use, with some substances producing *sudden sniffing death* (APA, 2013). At low doses, inhalants may cause the user to experience a sense of euphoria, a floating sensation, decreased inhibition, amnesia, and excitement (Doweiko, 2011). The long-term risks associated with inhalant use include a risk of tuberculosis, depression, anxiety, asthma, and bronchitis (APA, 2013).

Inhalant use is most likely to occur in adolescents, with nearly 16% of U.S. eighth-grade students reporting at least one episode of inhalant use (Garland & Howard, 2011). Many adolescents might mistakenly believe that inhalant use is not harmful; however, repeated use is associated with significant health concerns. Youth with higher levels of prior traumatic experiences and trait impulsivity, elevated levels of poly-substance use, more frequent use of inhalants, and self-medication use of inhalants, have an elevated risk of negative consequences (e.g., unprotected sexual activity, self-harm behaviors; Garland & Howard, 2011).

OPIOID-RELATED DISORDERS   Opioid related disorders are the fastest growing addiction in the U.S. In 2010, there were 140,000 persons age 12 or older who had used heroin for the first time, and 5.1 million people who had reportedly used prescription opioid pain relievers within the past 12 months (SAMHSA, 2011). The associated risk of fatal overdose is a concern for counselors who work with opioid-abusing clients. According to the National Center for Health Statistics, the number of fatal poisonings involving opioid analgesics more than tripled from 4,000 to 13,800 from 1999 through 2006 (Warner, Chen, & Makuc, 2009).

Opioids fall into three broad classes: (a) natural opiates, (b) semisynthetic opioids, and (c) synthetic opioids. Natural opiates, such as morphine and codeine, are obtained directly from opium. Semisynthetic opioids like heroin, are chemically altered derivates of naturally occurring opiates. Synthetic opioids for example methadone, are created in laboratories and are not at all derived from natural opiates.

Opioids can produce a rapid sensation of euphoria. Tolerance to opioids generally develops rapidly, and people might find themselves needing increased amounts of the substance in order to achieve the same sense of euphoria. The withdrawal pattern for opioids can often include nausea, vomiting, chills, and body aches. A common pathway to opioid abuse involves the misuse of prescription opioid substances (e.g., Oxycontin, Vicodin). Over time, some people may switch from prescription drugs to other opioids such as heroin.

Opioid abuse is associated with other related-risk factors (e.g., prostitution and criminal behavior; Öhlund & Grönbladh, 2009). Due to their intravenous substance use, those who inject heroin are also at an increased risk for contracting HIV/AIDS or hepatitis C. Estimates suggest as many as 90% of all intravenous drug users test positive for acute or chronic hepatitis C infection (Dinwiddie, Shicker, & Newman, 2003). Psychoeducation around needle sharing is an important component of effective treatment, and it may help decrease the risk of contracting HIV/AIDS or hepatitis C. For those who have HIV/AIDS and a substance use disorder, integrated treatment (i.e., concurrent treatment of the medical condition and the substance use) has been shown to improve HIV and other health outcomes (Batkis, Treisman, & Angelino, 2010).

benzodiazapines
carbamates
barbiturates

SEDATIVE/HYPNOTIC-RELATED DISORDERS Sedative disorders include the abuse of benzodiazepines, barbiturates, and barbiturate-like hypnotics. Sedatives are depressants and they tend to produce a calming effect. Significant levels of tolerance and withdrawal can develop with repeated use of these substances (APA, 2013). Those who have been abusing benzodiazepines for a significant amount of time might require a gradual *taper* in order to control the withdrawal process (Doweiko, 2011). Repeated use of these substances could result in potentially fatal outcomes, as the person may be at risk for sudden respiratory depression and hypotension (APA, 2013).

Women are more likely to be prescribed benzodiazepines compared to men. There are many concerns related to chronic benzodiazepine use, including impaired cognitive abilities, memory problems, mood swings, and potential overdose, especially if mixed with other depressants (e.g., alcohol). Those who abuse benzodiazepines tend to have relatively high rates of additional substance use disorders, and co-occurring psychiatric symptoms (Schuckit, Smith, Kramer, Danko, & Volpe, 2002).

STIMULANT-RELATED DISORDERS There are several types of substances that fall under the category of stimulant-related disorders: cocaine, amphetamine, amphetamine-like medications, and ephedrine (Doweiko, 2011). Stimulants usually produce feelings of well-being and euphoria. Some people may experience aggression, hallucinations, or paranoia. Withdrawal symptoms include hypersomnia, increased appetite, dysphonia, and enhanced cravings (APA, 2013).

Methamphetamine (colloquially referred to use "meth" or "crystal meth"), a common stimulant of abuse, can be taken orally, snorted, smoked, or injected. Tolerance to methamphetamine usually develops quickly, which can lead a person to begin taking large dosages of the substances. The effects of amphetamines and amphetamine-like drugs are similar to those of cocaine (APA, 2013). Compared to cocaine, amphetamines are longer acting, and thus, are used fewer times per day (Cruickshank & Dyer, 2009).

Cocaine users generally report a sense of increased self-esteem, euphoria, and well-being; however, with repeated use, an individual will begin to experience negative symptoms (e.g., depression, anxiety, paranoia). Cocaine can be used via intranasal means, intravenously, or smoked (i.e., crack cocaine). The route of administration may cause several problematic medical conditions. Intranasal users may experience sinusitis, nasal irritation, nosebleeds, or a perforated nasal septum (APA, 2013). Those who smoke crack cocaine are at increased risk for respiratory concerns, such as bronchitis. Intravenous users have an increased risk of HIV/AIDS and hepatitis C infections (APA, 2013).

TOBACCO-RELATED DISORDERS Tobacco is a stimulant and includes substances such as cigarettes, smokeless tobacco, and chewing tobacco. Smoking is the leading cause of preventable morbidity and mortality in the U.S., with smoking-related diseases claiming more than 440,000 lives annually. Epidemiological data suggest that more than 70% of all adult smokers would like to quit (Centers for Disease Control and Prevention, 2002). The majority of adolescents have experimented with tobacco use, with about 20% of those 18 years or older reporting that they smoke at least monthly. Prevention of smoking in adolescents appears to be the key to avoiding later adulthood use, as initiation of smoking after age 21 is rare (APA, 2013).

Cessation of tobacco is accompanied by a common withdrawal syndrome, which may include headaches, nausea, sleep issues, and irritability. Research suggests a strong relationship between tobacco use and other mental health disorders, including depression, anxiety, other drug use disorders, schizophrenia, and bipolar disorders (APA, 2013). The long-term effects of chronic tobacco use are problematic and include an increased risk of cardiovascular problems, cancers, and respiratory illnesses.

Counselor Considerations

Although it is common for clients to have a clear preference for a substance (often referred to as a *drug of choice*), in clinical practice, most clients abuse multiple substances (e.g., a client who prefers cocaine, but also uses alcohol, cannabis, and tobacco). Counselors must be prepared to work concurrently with each of the presenting substance use concerns.

Because of the impairment associated with substance abuse, clients may experience a host of negative consequences. Clients who abuse substances are at a higher risk for legal-related consequences. Possession of certain drugs may result in legal fines, and even first-time offenders can receive lengthy criminal sentences. This is true for almost all illegal drugs, as the Controlled Substances Act (1970) treats marijuana and other hallucinogens with the same severity as narcotics, such as heroin and methamphetamines.

Researchers have suggested a high rate of comorbidity between addiction-related issues and other mental-health related concerns, with reported rates of 50 to 80% of clients experiencing co-occurring disorders (Bride, MacMaster, & Webb-Robins, 2006). There is also a relationship between addiction and learning disabilities or behavior disorders, with reported rates of 40 to 60% (National Institute on Drug Abuse, 2000). Most treatment models emphasis an *integrated approach* to mental health and substance abuse treatment (Burnett, Porter, & Stallings, 2011). Counselors who work with clients with addiction and mental health disorders must be prepared to simultaneously address both concerns.

Effective counselors will also provide integrated case management services, which can also help address co-occurring psychosocial issues, such as homelessness, legal consequences, or physical health concerns. Similarly, counselors must be prepared to work closely with referral sources, as clients may be involved with probation officers, physicians, child welfare officers, and other collaborating providers.

Posttraumatic stress disorder (PTSD) is prevalent among adults in treatment for substance use disorders; however, many clients in treatment for substance abuse disorders are not evaluated for PTSD, nor offered PTSD-specific treatment. Substance abuse can exacerbate PTSD symptoms. Substances that increase or depress the body's arousal level tend to heighten hyperarousal and hypervigilance. Some research (e.g., Saladin, Brady, Dansky, & Kilpatrick, 1995) suggests that the type of substances used may reflect the pattern of PTSD symptoms experienced. Hyperarousal can lead to attempts to reduce anxiety and tension through self-medication or the use of stimulant drugs in order to maintain a state of high arousal. Hypervigilance may be sustained by the use of drugs that artificially increase the ability to maintain alert watchfulness. Psychoactive substances may be used to reduce distress associated with intrusive reexperiencing and to provide temporary avoidance of traumatic memories (i.e., self-medication). Other psychosocial issues, such as homelessness (Burnett et al., 2011) may be more common in those with co-occurring PTSD and substance use issues.

Voices from the Trenches 8.1: In the Pearson etext, click here to watch a counselor discuss treatment planning with clients who have experienced trauma and have addictions.

Physical health concerns are another consideration for counselors who work with those who abuse drugs. Traumatic brain injury (TBI) and spinal cord injury (SCI) are two other medical concerns that share a relationship with substance use, with prevalence rates of about 25% and 75% for SCI, and about 50% for TBIs (Benshoff & Janikowski, 2000). Substance users might be more likely to place themselves in high-risk situations, which could result in a greater likelihood of TBI- and SCI-related injuries.

There are noteworthy cultural considerations among the different classes of drugs. An understanding of these cultural issues can help counselors understand clients' risk of abuse, prevention, and cultural considerations that may relate to treatment.

Cannabis, the world's most commonly used illicit substance, is frequently among the first drugs of experimentation for all cultural groups in the U.S. (APA, 2013). Similarly, the prevalence of inhalant use disorder appears to be most common among 12- to 17-year-olds, with near equal prevalence among adolescent males and females. Ketamine appears to be abused more by Caucasian youth compared to youth from other cultures (APA, 2013). Opioid use disorder and stimulant use disorder occur with near equal prevalence among most racial/ethnic groups (APA, 2013). Although, historically, those from ethnic minority populations living in economically deprived areas have been overrepresented among those with opioid use disorder, opioid abuse has become much more common among the Caucasian, middle-class population, especially females and medical personnel (APA, 2013).

From the 1960s to the 1990s, the prevalence of tobacco use declined in the United States; however, this decline has been less evident in African American and Hispanic populations (APA, 2013). Tobacco use disorders tend to be more prevalent in developing countries than in developed nations (APA, 2013).

It is important to note that some substances may have historically been used as part of cultural or religious traditions. For example, hallucinogens have been used as part of established religious practices, such as the use of peyote in the Native American Church (APA, 2013). A thorough assessment of the client's cultural endorsement and cultural practices can help the counselor determine to what degree, if any, substance use is part of a cultural practice, and what this means in terms of the client's recovery from substance abuse.

Treatment Models and Interventions

There are a number of treatment options available for clients who abuse drugs. Generally, a combination of individual, group, and family counseling can be effective in helping the client navigate the process of recovery. Several common treatment options are discussed below.

Voices from the Trenches 8.2: In the Pearson etext, click here to watch a video of a counselor discussing the importance of being comfortable with counseling people who have addictions and complex case presentations.

COGNITIVE BEHAVIORAL THERAPY (CBT)   CBT is well established in the counseling literature as an evidence-based approach in the treatment of all substance-related disorders. CBT approaches have some variability in their focus and application, but they typically include social skills training, self-control training, community reinforcement, challenging irrational thoughts, contingency management, and stress-management training (Finney, Wilbourne, & Moos, 2007). The overarching focus of all of CBT approaches is to help clients match their abilities and skills (e.g., assertion, problem-solving, communication, interactions) with the demands of their environment. Many clients with SUDs have deficits in their abilities to navigate social interactions, express their thoughts and feelings, receive feedback and criticism from others, and they lack the skills they need to refuse a substance (Finney et al., 2007).

CBT approaches tend to be highly goal-oriented and structured. These approaches involve aiding clients in the cognitive restructuring of their irrational thoughts and beliefs, as well as increasing their skills (e.g., social, coping, self-control, stress toleration, emotional regulation). Treatment often involves challenging irrational thoughts and beliefs, skill development, role-playing, emotional regulation, and relapse prevention. The most effective treatments aim to increase clients' self-efficacy; therefore, utilizing multiple components of CBT approaches (e.g., coping skills, contingency management, self-control training) are essential in the effective treatment of substance related disorders (Litt, Kadden, Kabela-Cormier, & Petry, 2008).

FAMILY THERAPY   A family systems perspective can be helpful in understanding and modifying the dysfunctional patterns that might occur in a family with a substance abusing member. The treatment of an addictive disorder involves the identification and modification of whatever dysfunctional system allowed the addiction to develop (Bowen, 1985). Generally, family treatment involves identifying dominant family roles (e.g., chief enabler, scapegoat, lost child, hero), and helping families develop a new system of functioning. Families can benefit from involvement in a support group, such as Al-Anon.

There are two primary tasks of family therapy for substance use disorders (Chamberlain & Jew, 2003): (a) the family must create safety from internal and external sobriety triggers, and (b) each family member must explain the trauma of the addiction from his or her perspective. It is generally also effective to provide family members with psychoeducation about the disease of addiction, the person's drug of choice, and the possibility of relapse.

TWELVE-STEP FACILITATION   As mentioned in the alcohol-use disorder section, participation in 12-step fellowship is generally considered useful in early recovery. Similar to AA, Narcotics Anonymous (NA) is open to all people with drug addictions, regardless of the particular drug or combination of drugs used. When adapting AA's First Step, the word "addiction" is substituted for "alcohol," thus removing drug-specific language (Narcotics Anonymous World Services, 2012). The core concept of Twelve-Step Facilitation is to support a client's involvement and participation in the 12-step community.

[handwritten margin note: Emphasis on addiction as a disease]

MOTIVATIONAL INTERVIEWING (MI)   As previously mentioned, MI can be an effective treatment approach for those who use substances. MI works well with all types of SUDs because, and it is inherently empowering and engaging. It is founded on the idea that all clients have some motivation to change, and that this motivation can be enhanced through counseling. A more detailed discussion of this approach is provided in the alcohol treatment section.

CREATIVE TOOLBOX ACTIVITY 8.2   Use, Consequences, Significant Life Events, and Secrets

Meghan J. Fortner, PCC-S

Activity Overview

This creative intervention engages clients in a dialogue regarding their substance use history in a way that allows them to identify both the positive and negative consequences of their substance use, secrets they kept from themselves and others, as well as significant life events throughout their period of substance use. Clients are given a piece of paper and asked to draw a chart. In each column they document their age, associated substance use in that year, and then outline the consequences, secrets, and life events that occurred in that time frame.

Treatment Goal(s) of Activity

This activity aims to help increase clients' insight regarding the need to change their personal substance use, and it helps facilitate their change process. More specifically, the primary goals of this activity are to assist clients in: (a) creating a timeline for the progression of their substance use; (b) increasing personal insight regarding the connections between their substance use and the negative events/consequences in their lives; and (c) beginning change talk about decreasing/discontinuing substance use (begin movement from precontemplation to the contemplation stage of change, as conceptualized in motivational interviewing and the transtheoretical model's stages of change process).

Directions

1. The counselor should assess the client's current stage of change (as defined by the transtheoretical or stages of change model).
2. Provide the client with a blank sheet of paper (any size, but legal or larger is recommended).
3. Ask the client to draw six columns on the paper and title each column with the following: Age, Use, Positive Consequences, Negative Consequences, Secrets, and Significant Life Events.
4. Allow the client(s) to decorate their charts any way they would like before, during, or after they complete their charts.
5. Ask clients to start the first row under the titles of the columns, writing in their age and any substances used at that time under the first column.
6. For the columns following "Age," clients can fill in the related information under each column for that year of age across the chart. For example: under age in column one, the client writes "14—used tobacco, alcohol, and marijuana." Then they move on to "Negative Consequences" and fill that in for the age of 14 when they used those substances.
7. Some clients may struggle with the activity while others complete it without much trouble. You may assist the clients in completing the rest of their chart by using some open-ended questions regarding their use and probes for continued sharing.
8. After they have completed their chart, process the chart with the clients.

PSYCHOPHARMACOTHERAPY AND MEDICATION-ASSISTED TREATMENT Medications can be useful in treating the comorbid disorders that contribute to, or sustain, clients' substance use. They are also used as a means of medical intervention intended to help modify clients' substance use (i.e., medication-assisted treatment or MAT). In other words, in a highly controlled circumstance, clients use a different substance to change their patterns of use and break their addiction patterns (e.g., a client who takes methadone to aid in getting off heroin). Most MATs are designed to serve as an adjunct to other forms of treatment, including individual and group counseling (Kelch & Piazza, 2011).

MAT is generally considered the standard of practice in the treatment of chronic, severe opioid use disorders. Methadone, a full opioid agonist, is used as a replacement therapy with opioid-dependent clients. Methadone works by binding to the opioid receptor, which decreases an individual's withdrawal symptoms associated with heroin and prevents cravings associated with use. Methadone is administered under federal guidelines at a daily dosing methadone clinic. Methadone is administered orally and typically suppresses opioid withdrawal and drug craving for 24 to 36 hours in most people with opioid addictions (Center for Substance Abuse Treatment, 2005).

Other medication-assisted treatments for opioid dependence include naltrexone (e.g., Revia) and a combination of buprenorphine and naltrexone (i.e., Suboxone). Buprenorphine is a partial opioid agonist (i.e., it does not fully bind to the opioid receptor). Similar to methadone, buprenorphine is used in the treatment of opioid dependence. Federal guidelines govern the prescription of Suboxone, as well as methadone, when prescribed for addiction treatment. Thus, Suboxone can be prescribed on an outpatient basis and does not require daily dosing. Naltrexone is an opiate antagonist; it blocks and reverses the physical effects of opioids (i.e., one cannot get "high" on an opioid while on naltrexone). When given to patients who have or are being treated using psychosocial treatments for opioid addiction, it not only decreases craving for these types of drugs, it also prevents patients who use opioids while taking naltrexone from experiencing the euphoria associated with their use.

When administered appropriately, methadone and buprenorphine/naltrexone are associated with several side effects. The most common adverse effects reported by patients are constipation, sweating, insomnia, early awakening, and decreased sexual interest and/or performance. Similarly, clients on naltrexone may experience gastrointestinal side effects. Other side effects of naltrexone include anxiety, insomnia, headaches, joint or muscle pain, and fatigue.

Although less commonly used, medications for the treatment of cocaine use might serve to support treatment outcomes. Bupropion (i.e., Wellbutrin) and anti-Parkinson's agents (i.e., dopamine agonists) have shown some success in supporting abstinence from cocaine use. Both bupropion and anti-Parkinson's agents are generally well tolerated with minimal side effects. Side effects of bupropion are usually mild and include agitation, weight loss, dry mouth constipation, and headaches. Side effects of anti-Parkinson's agents can range from mild to severe and may include irregular heartbeat, hypotension, nausea, vomiting, and headache. Disulfiram (i.e., Antabuse) has also been noted to decrease cocaine cravings in alcoholics with concurrent addiction to cocaine, although there is currently no FDA-approved medication for treating stimulant addictions. Side effects of disulfiram may include eye pain, mood changes, and stomach pains.

Medication-assisted treatment of tobacco use disorders has been well documented, and it includes such approaches as nicotine gum, nasal spray, patch, and sublingual tablets. These approaches are generally referred to as *nicotine replacement therapy*, and they work by lessening the withdrawal symptoms associated with abrupt nicotine cessation. Additionally, bupropion (i.e., Wellbutrin, an antidepressant) has also increased the smoking abstinence rate of individuals, and gains were maintained in a 12-month follow-up (O'Brien & McKay, 2007). All forms of nicotine replacement have side effects, but the types of side effects may vary depending on the type of therapy used. Common side effects with nicotine gum can include stomach upset, hiccups, or jaw pain from excessive gum chewing. Common side effects of nicotine nasal spray include a cough and sore throat. Side effects of the nicotine patches include skin rash and sleep difficulties.

Clients with SUDs are especially vulnerable to developing new addictions to medicines with such potential (e.g., benzodiazepines used to manage co-occurring anxiety, psychostimulants used to treat co-occurring attention-deficit/hyperactivity disorder, and clients' use of these medications should be monitored closely. Concerns of abuse should be processed with clients and their physicians. Finally, experts in the field of addictions contend that for medications to be successful in the treatment of substance use disorders, they must be combined with evidence-based psychosocial treatments (O'Brien & McKay, 2007).

Prognosis

As mentioned earlier, numerous factors impact a client's treatment prognosis. Additionally, due to the chronic nature of these disorders and the high relapse rates, effective treatments are usually longer in duration, and require sustained effort from clients (Finney et al., 2007). Many contextual, variables contribute to a better prognosis in treatment such as family support (e.g., family involvement, support, intact relationships), individual factors (e.g., motivation, less severe mental disorders, no legal involvement), and the early detection of a substance use disorder paired with the appropriate evidence-based treatments.

Those with SUDs are also sensitive to life crises, especially interpersonal conflicts and losses, and these experiences make this population vulnerable to relapse (Najavits, 2009). As such, the development of coping and life skills that help them manage these situations (see the CBT and Social Skills Training treatment sections for examples) may be helpful in preventing relapses. When working with this population, relapse prevention will need to be integrated into treatment to ensure clients can navigate stressful and frustrating life experiences; experiences which can invite relapses.

GAMBLING DISORDER

Description of the Disorder and Typical Client Characteristics

The *DSM-5* (APA, 2013) identifies one non-substance-based addictive disorder: pathological gambling. Internet gaming disorder is listed under the "Conditions for Further Study" section of the *DSM-5*, and may be formally included in future editions of the *DSM*.

Pathological gambling includes a problematic pattern with the act of risking something with hopes of gaining something of greater value (APA, 2013). Addiction is conceptualized by an inability to consistently abstain from a problematic behavior (Smith, 2012). Thus, an individual with pathological gambling disorder has demonstrated the inability to abstain from gambling behavior, despite experiencing significant consequences (e.g., loss of job) as a result of the behavior (APA, 2013). Pathological gambling also tends to co-occur with other *DSM* disorders, including substance use disorders, depressive/bipolar disorders, ADHD, and personality disorders (Petry & Steinberg, 2005).

While pathological gambling cuts across age, gender, and socioeconomic status, the form of gambling that people engage in can be related to certain demographic variables. For example, in a study of 347 problematic gamblers, Petry (2003) found that *horse/dog-race gamblers* were generally older, male, and less educated; they also began gambling regularly at a young age, and spent relatively greater amounts of money gambling compared to others who gamble. Comparatively, those who gambled on *sporting events* tended to be younger males with intermediary gambling problems, and relatively high rates of current substance use in the absence of other psychiatric problems. Chronic *card players* spent low to moderate amounts of time and money gambling, and this type of gambling behavior is generally associated with fewer alcohol problems, and less psychiatric distress compared to the other groups. *Slot machine gamblers* were older, more likely to be female, and they generally began gambling later in life. This population also had high rates of bankruptcy and numerous psychiatric difficulties. Finally, *scratch/lottery gamblers* spent the least amount of money gambling, yet they gambled the most frequently and had relatively severe alcohol and psychiatric symptoms.

Problem gamblers may engage in few social activities other than gambling and thus, after treatment, they may experience considerable unstructured time and inadequate social skills (Jackson, Francis, Byrne, & Christensen, 2013). Teaching clients leisure skills and providing clients with an opportunity for positive peer supports outside of gambling is likely to result in overall better outcomes (Jackson et al., 2013). Perhaps even more concerning is that only about 1 in 10 gamblers with gambling dependence will ever seek treatment (Cunningham, 2005). Thus, it is likely that most pathological gamblers may not seek services for their gambling behaviors.

Counselor Considerations

Counselors must consider the potential for gambling problems to exist in their clients. Despite its increasing prevalence, gambling disorders remain largely untreated (Ashley & Boehlke, 2012). A thorough assessment of any gambling-related concerns should be routinely integrated into initial diagnostic assessments, especially in alcohol and drug treatment settings. Counselors must also be prepared to deal with co-occurring disorders and psychosocial stressors. As previously stated, among pathological gamblers, there are increased rates of depressive/bipolar disorders, attention deficit disorders, substance abuse, impulse-control disorders, and cluster B personality disorders (APA, 2013).

Perhaps one of the most significant concerns associated with chronic gambling is the potential for financial troubles. People with gambling disorders may spend significant amounts of money on their gambling, which often results in their inability to maintain financial obligations. There is a certain amount of shame that can accompany a gambling disorder, and people with this condition are often secretive, even with family members, about their gambling behavior. The costs associated with gambling disorder are significant and can include bankruptcies, job loss, and involvement in criminal activities in an attempt to pay off debts. Pathological gambling can strain family relationships and may result in numerous deleterious effects to family members, and this should be considered in treatment planning.

There are some cultural differences in gambling, with some cultures endorsing specific preferences for gambling activities (e.g., pai gow, cockfights, blackjack, horse racing; APA, 2013). There are also gender differences, with males developing gambling disorders at a higher rate than females (APA, 2013). There are gender preferences with regard to gambling behaviors, with cards, sports, and horse race gambling being more prevalent among males, and slot machine and bingo gambling more common among females (APA, 2013). Counselors should ensure they monitor their stereotypes of what types of gambling are and are not problematic; a broad conceptualization of pathological gambling is important if counselors are to accurately detect and treat this disorder.

Treatment Models and Interventions

Research into the effectiveness of treatments for gambling disorders is in its infancy and as such, treatment guidance is relatively limited (Petry, Weinstock, Ledgerwood, & Morasco, 2008). However, many of the approaches previously discussed in relation to treating substance abuse may also demonstrate effectiveness in the treatment of gambling disorder. Motivational interviewing and 12-step approaches commonly used to treat substance use disorders have been used successfully to treat gambling disorder (Ashley & Boehlke, 2012). Similarly, cognitive behavioral strategies used in the treatment of addictions have also showed promise in the treatment of gambling-related disorders (Cowlishaw et al., 2012). Gamblers Anonymous (GA), based on the 12-step approach to addictions treatment, is a self-help group for compulsive gamblers, which might be helpful in sustaining long-term recovery from problematic gambling.

In addition to the treatments mentioned above, behavioral interventions are also useful when treating this population. Self-exclusion and money-management strategies can help facilitate abstinence and/or gambling behavior modification (Ashley & Boehlke, 2012). For example, someone may give his or her ATM card to a trusted family member/friend to avoid the temptation that might be associated with making a quick trip to a casino. Self-help approaches have demonstrated efficacy in supporting recovery in those who self-identify as problematic gamblers (LaBrie et al., 2012).

In vivo exposure with response prevention (ERP), a behavioral approach to gambling treatment, appears to be successful in treating problem gambling (Hodgins & Peden, 2008). In ERP sessions, clients are typically exposed to potentially triggering places or stimuli (e.g., being in a casino with money), and they are directed to use coping skills to refrain from engaging in the desired behavior (i.e., gambling) during the exposure. ERP treatment generally begins gradually. For example, a client may be asked to drive by a casino on his way to the counseling session. It is only after the client has demonstrated the ability to utilize coping skills that he or she would be placed in a more potentially triggering situation (e.g., walking into a casino). It may be helpful for clients to involve a friend or family member in an exposure activity to ensure that the client has additional support during the experience.

Recent research (e.g., Brewer & Potenza, 2008) has suggested that medication might be helpful in the treatment of process (i.e., behavioral) addictions such as gambling disorder. Naltrexone and nalmefene have demonstrated efficacy in supporting abstinence for those with chronic gambling conditions (Grant, Kim, Hollander, & Potenza, 2008). The use of medication to support the treatment of gambling disorder is still in its infancy.

Prognosis

Similar to substance addictions, pathological gambling is characterized as a chronic relapse disorder (Grant, Williams, & Kim, 2006), with relapse rates as high as 90% in the first year following treatment (Shaffer et al., 2004). Although a causal relationship has not been established, some research (e.g., Hodgins, Mansley, & Thygesen, 2006) has suggested an increased risk of suicide among those with pathological gambling problems. Specifically, the hopelessness and lack of viable financial options associated with problematic gambling may encourage the client to consider suicide a viable solution.

TREATMENT PLAN FOR DIANNA

This chapter began with a discussion of Dianna, a 30-year-old female with a history of opioid use. In addition to opioid use, Dianna is also experiencing a myriad of other concerns, which must be addressed in order to fully assist her in maintaining sobriety. The following I CAN START conceptual framework provides a strength-based model for effectively working with Dianna.

C = Contextual Assessment

Diana is biracial and reports identity confusion and a sense of never fitting in. These issues and their implications should be considered as she moves forward in her treatment. Her parents divorced at age 6, and she is the oldest of 5 children. She is from a "blue-collar" family and has not had access to the education or training needed to help her find a job that will support her child. Dianna's substance use began early, at age 13, and it progressed rapidly, therefore she has not been able to traverse or move through many of the normal developmental stages that adolescents and adults learn to navigate (e.g., identity, intimacy). She is a single parent with economic struggles and no support from her child's father, and the stress associated with these issues needs to be addressed as a part of her relapse prevention plan.

A = Assessment and Diagnosis

Diagnosis = Opioid Use Disorder—Severe 304.00 (F11.20)

Refer client for a physical examination to rule out any medical conditions; refer client to addictionologist to plan for medication-assisted treatment (i.e., methadone or Suboxone); utilization of the Addiction Severity Index (ASI; McLellan, Luborsky, O'Brien, & Woody, 1980) to assess for ongoing addiction symptoms.

N = Necessary Level of Care

Inpatient residential treatment for a proposed duration of 60 days. Daily individual and group counseling sessions, and a once-a-week family session with her mother. Engagement in 12-step support groups (e.g., NA) during treatment and after the completion of residential treatment, as well as access to a step-down intensive outpatient program (IOP).

S = Strengths

The client is resilient and motivated and desires sobriety. She is committed to being a more stable mother to her 6 year-old daughter. She has a past history of 2 months of sustained sobriety. She has been able to maintain stable employment despite her ongoing drug dependence, and she has an excellent work ethic. She has not been involved in the criminal justice system, and is self-referred to treatment.

T = Treatment Approach

Medication-assisted treatment to help address withdrawal symptoms and stabilize cravings. Motivational interviewing to explore client's ambivalence toward changing her substance use behavior. 12-step facilitation to encourage the client's involvement in the 12-step community.

A = Aim and Objectives of Treatment (60-day objectives)

Dianna will abstain from using any mood-altering and illicit substances → Dianna will produce 1 negative urine specimen per week.

Dianna will engage in a program of medication-assisted recovery → Dianna will take all medications as prescribed. Dianna will meet with the addictionologist on a once-weekly basis, and immediately report any withdrawal symptoms, cravings, or associated, concerns regarding her medication to a treatment professional.

Dianna will utilize 12-step support to maintain sobriety → Dianna will attend (3) 12-step support groups per week; Dianna will complete Step 1 (of the 12 steps).

Dianna will actively engage in psychosocial addiction treatment → Dianna will participate in all programs in the therapeutic environment, and will attend and actively participate in all daily individual and group counseling sessions that are part of her inpatient residential treatment.

R = Research-Based Interventions (Based on Medication-Assisted Treatment, Motivational Interviewing, and 12-Step Facilitation)

Counselor will help Dianna develop and apply the following skills:
- Self-management of medication-assisted treatment
- Understanding of the disease concept of addiction by providing psychoeducation related to this topic
- Understanding of the concept of *powerlessness* (i.e., Step 1 of the 12 steps) and how it relates to her addiction
- Completion of a decisional balance sheet (i.e., a motivational interviewing technique that addresses the pros and cons of different choices and helps someone

decide what to do in a certain circumstance, with a focus on addressing ambivalence) related to Dianna's continued substance use

*T = **Therapeutic Support Services** (Case Management, Community Supports, Medication Referral)*

Medication-assisted treatment

Case management to help with receiving housing services, food stamps, and any other financial resources needed to support her and her daughter should they be reunified

Referral for medical evaluation to rule out any physical health considerations

Exploration of logistics of reunification plan with her daughter with Children's Services

References

American Psychiatric Association (APA). (2013). *Diagnostic and statistical manual of mental disorders* (5th ed. [DSM-5]). Washington, DC: Author.

Ashley, L. L., & Boehlke, K. K. (2012). Pathological gambling: A general overview. *Journal of Psychoactive Drugs, 44,* 27–37.

Barrowclough, C., Haddock, G., Fitzsimmons, M., & Johnson, R. (2006). Treatment development for psychosis and co-occurring substance misuse: A descriptive review. *Journal of Mental Health, 15,* 619–632.

Batkis, M. F., Treisman, G. J., & Angelino, A. F. (2010). Integrated opioid use disorder and HIV treatment: Rationale, clinical guidelines for addiction treatment, and review of interactions of antiretroviral agents and opioid agonist therapies. *AIDS Patient Care and STDs, 24,* 15–22.

Benshoff, J. J., & Janikowski, T. P. (2000). *The rehabilitation model of substance abuse counseling.* Belmont, CA: Wadsworth/Thomson.

Bergin, J. E., & Kendler, K. S. (2012). Common psychiatric disorders and caffeine use, tolerance, and withdrawal: An examination of shared genetic and environmental effects. *Twin Research and Human Genetics, 15,* 473–482.

Best, D., Groshkova, T., Loaring, J., Ghufran, S., Day, E., & Taylor, A. (2010). Comparing the addiction careers of heroin and alcohol users and their self-reported reasons for achieving abstinence. *Journal of Groups in Addiction & Recovery, 5,* 289–305.

Bizzarri, J. V., Rucci, P., Sbrana, A., Miniati, M., Raimondi, F., Ravani, L., . . . Cassano, G. B. (2009). Substance use in severe mental illness: Self-medication and vulnerability factors. *Psychiatry Research, 165,* 88–95.

Blaszczynski, A., & Nower, L. (2002). A pathways model of problem and pathological gambling. *Addiction, 97,* 487–499.

Blondell, R. D. (2005). Ambulatory detoxification of patients with alcohol dependence. *American Family Physician, 71,* 495–502.

Bowen, M. (1985). *Family therapy in clinical practice.* Northvale, NJ: Jason Aronson.

Brewer, J. A., & Potenza, M. N. (2008). The neurobiology and genetics of impulse control disorders: Relationships to drug addictions. *Biochemical Pharmacology, 75,* 63–75.

Bride, B. E, MacMaster, S. A., & Webb-Robins, L. (2006). Is integrated treatment of co-occurring disorders more effective than nonintegrated treatment? *Best Practices in Mental Health, 2,* 43–57.

Britt, E., Blampied, N. M., & Hudson, S. M. (2004). Motivational interviewing: A review. *Australian Psychologist, 38,* 193–201.

Buckley, P. F. (2006). Prevalence and consequences of the dual diagnosis of substance abuse and severe mental illness. *Journal of Clinical Psychiatry, 6,* 5–9.

Burnett, R., Porter, E., & Stallings, K. (2011). Treatment options for individuals with dual diagnosis. *Journal of Human Behavior in the Social Environment, 21,* 849–857.

Capuzzi, D., & Stauffer, M. D. (2012). History and etiological models of addiction. In D. Capuzzi & M. D. Stauffer (Eds.) *Foundations of addictions counseling* (2nd ed.). Upper Saddle River, NJ: Pearson.

Carroll, K. (1998). *NIDA therapy manuals for drug addiction: A cognitive behavioral approach: Treating cocaine addiction*. National Institute on Drug Abuse, NIH Publication Number 98-4308.

Center on Addiction and Substance Abuse at Columbia University (CASA). (2010). *Behind Bars II: Substance Abuse and America's Prison Population*. Retrieved from http://www.casacolumbia.org/addiction-research/reports/substance-abuse-prison-system-2008

Centers for Disease Control and Prevention. (2002). Annual smoking attributable mortality, years of potential life lost, and economic costs—United States, 1995–1999. *Morbidity and Mortality Weekly Report, 51,* 300–303.

Center for Substance Abuse Treatment. (2005). *Medication-assisted treatment for opioid addiction in opioid treatment programs*. Rockville, MD: Author. Available from: http://www.ncbi.nlm.nih.gov/books/NBK64158/

Chamberlain, L., & Jew, C. L. (2003). Family assessment of drug and alcohol problems. In K. Jordan (Ed.), *Handbook of couple and family assessment* (pp. 221–239). Hauppauge, NY: Nova Science Publishers.

Cowlishaw, S., Merkouris, S., Dowling, N., Anderson, C., Jackson, A., & Thomas, S. (2012). Psychological therapies for pathological and problem gambling. *The Cochrane Database of Systematic Reviews, 11.* CD008937. doi: 10.1002/14651858. CD008937.pub2

Cruickshank, C. C, & Dyer, K. R. (2009). A review of the clinical pharmacology of methamphetamine. *Addiction, 104,* 1085–1099.

Cunningham, J. A. (2005). Little use of treatment among problem gamblers. *Psychiatric Services, 56,* 1024–1025.

Davis, K. E., Devitt, T., Rollins, A., O'Neill, S., Pavick, D., & Harding, B. (2006). Integrated residential treatment for persons with severe and persistent mental illness: Lessons in recovery. *Journal of Psychoactive Drugs, 38,* 263–272.

Dawson, D. A., Goldstein, R. B., & Grant, B. F. (2007). Rates and correlates of relapse among individuals in remission from DSM-IV alcohol dependence: A 3-year follow-up. *Alcoholism: Clinical and Experimental Research, 31,* 2036–2045.

Day, E., & Strang, J. (2011). Outpatient versus inpatient opioid detoxification: A randomized controlled trial. *Journal of Substance Abuse Treatment, 40,* 56–66.

Di Nicola, M. M., Martinotti, G. G., Tedeschi, D. D., Frustaci, A., Mazza, M., Sarchiapone, M., . . . Janiri, L. (2010). Pregabalin in outpatient detoxification of subjects with mild-to-moderate alcohol withdrawal syndrome. *Human Psychopharmacology: Clinical and Experimental, 25,* 268–275.

Dinwiddie, S. H., Shicker L., & Newman T. (2003). Prevalence of Hepatitis C among psychiatric patients in the public sector. *American Journal of Psychiatry, 160,* 172–174.

Douaihy, A., Daley, D. C., Marlatt, G. A, & Spotts, C. R. (2009). Relapse prevention: Clinical models and intervention strategies. In R. Ries, D. Fiellin, S. Miller, & R. Saitz (Eds.), *Principles of addiction medicine* (4th ed.). Chevy Chase, MD: ASAM.

Doweiko, H. E. (2011). *Concepts of chemical dependency* (8th ed.). Pacific Grove, CA: Brooks/Cole.

Finney, J. W., Wilbourne, P. L., & Moos, R. H. (2007). Psychosocial treatments for substance use disorders. In P. E. Nathan & J. M. Gorman (Eds.), *A guide to treatments that work* (pp. 179–202). New York, NY: Oxford.

Garland, E. L., & Howard, M. O. (2011). Adverse consequences of acute inhalant intoxication. *Experimental and Clinical Psychopharmacology, 19,* 134–144.

Grant, J., Kim, S., Hollander, E., & Potenza, M. (2008). Predicting response to opiate antagonists and placebo in the treatment of pathological gambling. *Psychopharmacology, 200,* 521–527.

Grant, J. E., Williams, K. A., & Kim, S. W. (2006). Update on pathological gambling. *Current Psychiatry Report, 8,* 53–58.

Hodgins, D. C., Mansley, C., & Thygesen, K. (2006). Risk factors for suicide ideation and attempts among pathological gambling. *Journal of Counseling and Consulting Psychology, 72,* 72–80.

Hodgins, D. C., & Peden, N. (2008). Cognitive-behavioral treatment for impulse control disorders. *Revista Brasileira de Psiquiatria, 30,* (Suppl. 1), S31–S40.

Humphreys, K., Wing, S., McCarty, D., Chappel, J., Gallant, L., Haberle, B., . . . Weiss, R. (2004). Self-help organizations for alcohol and drug problems: Toward evidence-based practice and policy. *Journal of Substance Abuse Treatment, 26,* 151–158.

Imhof, J., Hirsch, R., & Terenzi, R. E. (1983). Countertransferential and attitudinal considerations in the treatment of drug abuse and addiction. *International Journal of Addictions, 18*, 491–510.

Jackson, A. C., Francis, K. L., Byrne, G., & Christensen, D. R. (2013). Leisure substitution and problem gambling: Report of a proof of concept group intervention. *International Journal of Mental Health Addiction, 11*, 64–74.

Jellinek, E. M. (1960). *The disease concept of alcoholism.* New Haven, CT: Hillhouse.

Juhnke, G. A. (2002). *Substance abuse: Assessment and diagnosis.* New York, NY: Routledge.

Kelch, B. P., & Piazza, N. J. (2011). Medication-assisted treatment: Overcoming individual resistance among members in groups whose membership consists of both users and nonusers of MAT: A clinical review. *Journal of Groups in Addiction and Recovery, 6,* 307–318.

Kendler, K. S., Myers, J., & O'Gardner, C. (2006). Caffeine intake, toxicity and dependence and lifetime risk for psychiatric and substance use disorders: An epidemiologic and co-twin control analysis. *Psychological Medicine, 36,* 1717–1725.

Kranzler, H. R., & Li, T-K. (2008). What is addiction? *Alcohol Research and Health, 31,* 93–95.

LaBrie, R. A., Peller, A. J., LaPlante, D. A., Bernhard, B., Harper, A., Schrier, T., . . . Shaffer, H. J. (2012). A brief self-help toolkit intervention for gambling problems: A randomized multisite trial. *American Journal of Orthopsychiatry, 82,* 278–289.

Laudet, A. B., & White, W. L. (2008). Recovery capital as a prospective predictor of sustained recovery, life satisfaction, and stress among former poly-substance abusers. *Substance Use and Misuse, 43,* 27–54.

Lewis, T. F. (2014). *Substance abuse and addiction treatment: Practical application of counseling theory.* Columbus, OH: Pearson.

Liberman, R. P. (2007). Dissemination and adoption of social skills training: Social validation of an evidenced-based treatment for the mentally disabled. *Journal of Mental Health, 16,* 595–623.

Litt, M. D., Kadden, R. M., Kabela-Cormier, E., & Petry, N. M. (2008). Coping skills training and contingency management treatments for marijuana dependence: Exploring mechanism of behavior change. *Addiction, 103,* 638–648.

Marlatt, G. A., Latimer, M. E., Baer, J. S., & Quigley, L. A. (1993). Harm reduction for alcohol problems: Moving beyond the controlled drinking controversy. *Behavior Therapy, 24,* 461–504.

McKay, J. R., Franklin, T. R, Patapis, N., & Lynch, K. G. (2006). Conceptual, methodological and analytical issues in the study of relapse. *Clinical Psychology Review, 26,* 109–127.

McKellar, J., Stewart, E., & Humphreys, K. (2003). Alcoholics Anonymous involvement and positive alcohol-related outcomes: Cause, consequence, or just a correlate? A prospective 2-year study of 2,319 alcohol-dependent men. *Journal of Consulting and Clinical Psychology, 71,* 302–308.

McLellan, A. T., Luborsky, L., O'Brien, C. P., & Woody, G. E. (1980). An improved diagnostic instrument for substance abuse patients: The Addiction Severity Index. *Journal of Nervous & Mental Diseases, 168,* 26–33.

Miller, W. R., & Rollnick, S. (2012). *Motivational interviewing: Preparing people for change* (3rd ed.). New York, NY: Guilford.

Moos, R. H., & Moos, B. S. (2004). Long-term influence of duration and frequency in participation in Alcoholics Anonymous on individuals with alcohol use disorders. *Journal of Consulting and Clinical Psychology, 72,* 81–90.

Moos, R. H., & Moos, B. S. (2007). Protective resources and long-term recovery from alcohol-use disorders. *Drug and Alcohol Dependence, 86,* 46–54.

Moss, R., & Cook, C. C. H. (2012). Maintenance and relapse prevention. In D. Capuzzi & M. D. Stauffer (Eds.), *Foundations of addictions counseling* (2nd ed.). Upper Saddle River, NJ: Pearson.

Najavits, L. M. (2009). Seeking safety: An implementation guide. In D. W. Springer & A. Rubin (Eds.), *Substance abuse treatment for youth and adults: Clinician's guide to evidence-based practice* (pp. 311–347). Hoboken, NJ: Wiley.

Narcotics Anonymous World Services. (2012). *Information about NA.* http://www.na.org/admin/include/spaw2/uploads/pdf/PR/Information_about_NA.pdf

National Institute on Drug Abuse. (2000). *Substance abuse and learning disabilities: Peas in a pod or apples and oranges?* New York, NY: National Center on Addictions and Substance Abuse, Columbia University.

National Institute on Drug Abuse (NIDA). (2002). *Comparing methamphetamine and cocaine. NIDA Notes, 13.* Retrieved April 26, 2013 from: http://archives.drugabuse.gov/NIDA_Notes/NNVol13N1/Comparing.html

Nordstrom, B. R., & Dackis, C. A. (2011). Drugs and crime. *Journal of Psychiatry and Law, 39,* 663–687.

Nowinski, J., Baker, S., & Carroll, K. M. (1992). *Twelve step facilitation therapy manual: A clinical research guide for therapists treating individuals with alcohol abuse and dependence*. NIAAA Project MATCH Monograph Series, Volume 1, DHHS Publication No. (ADM) 92-1893. Rockville, MD: National Institute on Alcohol Abuse and Alcoholism.

O'Brien, C. P., & McKay, J. (2007). Psychopharmacological treatments for substance use disorders. In P. E. Nathan & J. M. Gorman (Eds.), *A guide to treatments that work* (pp. 145–177). New York, NY: Oxford.

Office of the Federal Register. (1994). *Code of Federal Regulations [CFR] 42. Part 2*. Washington, DC: U.S. Government Printing Office.

Ogawa, N., & Ueki, H. (2007). Clinical importance of caffeine dependence and abuse. *Psychiatry and Clinical Neurosciences, 61,* 263–268.

Öhlund, L. S., & Grönbladh, L. (2009). Patterns of deviant career in the history of female methadone clients: An exploratory study. *International Journal of Social Welfare, 18,* 95–101.

Osborn, C. J. (2012). Psychotherapeutic approaches. In D. Capuzzi & M. D. Stauffer (Eds.), *Foundations of addictions counseling* (2nd ed.). Upper Saddle River, NJ: Pearson.

Parrott, A. C. (2001).Human psychopharmacology of ecstasy (MDMA): A review of 15 years of empirical research. *Human Psychopharmacology, 16,* 557–577.

Patel, M. M., Wright, D. W., Ratcliff, J. J., & Miller, M. A. (2004). Shedding new light on the "safe" club drug: Methylenedioxymethamphetamine (ecstasy)-related fatalities. *Academy of Emergency Medicine, 11,* 208–210.

Petry, N. M. (2003). A comparison of treatment-seeking pathological gamblers based on preferred gambling activity. *Addiction, 98,* 645–655.

Petry, N. M. (2005). *Pathological gambling: Etiology, comorbidity, and treatment*. Washington, DC: American Psychological Association.

Petry, N. M., & Kiluk, B. D. (2002). Suicidal ideation and suicide attempts in treatment-seeking pathological gamblers. *Journal of Nervous Mental Disorders, 190,* 462–469.

Petry, N. M., & Steinberg, K. L. (2005). Childhood maltreatment in male and female treatment-seeking pathological gamblers. *Psychology of Addictive Behaviors, 19,* 226–229.

Petry, N. M., Weinstock, J., Ledgerwood, D. M., & Morasco, B. (2008). A randomized trial of brief interventions for problem and pathological gamblers. *Journal of Consulting and Clinical Psychology, 76,* 318–328.

Reiner, S. M. (2000). Ethical and legal issues in substance abuse counseling. In P. Stevens & R. L. Smith (Eds.), *Substance abuse counseling: Theory and practice* (pp. 390–414). Upper Saddle River, NJ: Merrill.

Ritsher, J. B., McKellar, J. D., Finney, J. W., Otilingam, P. G., & Moos, R. H. (2002). Psychiatric comorbidity, continuing care and mutual help as predictors of five-year remission from substance use disorders. *Journal of Studies on Alcohol, 63,* 709–715.

Ross, S., & Peselow, E. (2009). Pharmacotherapy of addictive disorders. *Clinical Neuropharmacology, 32,* 277–289.

Saladin, M. E., Brady, K. T., Dansky, B. S., & Kilpatrick, D. G. (1995). Understanding comorbidity between PTSD and substance use disorders: Two preliminary investigations. *Addictive Behaviors, 20,* 643–655.

Schuckit, M. A. (2009). An overview of genetic influences in alcoholism. *Journal of Substance Abuse Treatment, 36,* 5–14.

Schuckit, M. A., Smith, T. L., Kramer, J., Danko, G., & Volpe, F. R. (2002). The prevalence and clinical course of sedative-hypnotic abuse and dependence in a large cohort. *The American Journal of Drug and Alcohol Abuse, 28,* 73–90.

Shaffer, H. J., LaPlante, D. A., LaBrie, R. A., Kidman, R. C., Donato, A. N., & Stanton, M. V. (2004). Toward a syndrome model of addiction: Multiple expressions, common etiology. *Harvard Review of Psychiatry, 12,* 367–74.

Smith, D. E. (2012). Editor's Note: The process addictions and the new ASAM definition of addiction. *Journal of Psychoactive Drugs, 44,* 1–4.

Substance Abuse and Mental Health Services Administration (SAMHSA). (2011). *Results from the 2010 National Survey on Drug Use and Health: Summary of National Findings*, NSDUH Series H-41, HHS Publication No. (SMA) 11-4658. Rockville, MD: Substance Abuse and Mental Health Services Administration.

Thombs, D. L., & Osborn, C. J. (2013). *Introduction to addictive behaviors* (4th ed.). New York, NY: Guilford.

Vaillant, G. E. (2003). A 60-year follow-up of alcoholic men. *Addiction, 98,* 1043–1051.

Veach, L. J., Rogers, J. L., & Essic, E. J. (2012). Substance addictions. In D. Capuzzi & M. D. Stauffer (Eds.), *Foundations of addictions counseling* (2nd ed.). Upper Saddle River, NJ: Pearson.

Walitzer, K. S., & Dearing, R. L. (2006) Gender differences in alcohol and substance use relapse. *Clinical Psychology Review, 26,* 128–148.

Walters, G. D. (2000). Behavioral self-control training for problem drinkers: A meta-analysis of randomized control studies. *Behavior Therapy, 31,* 135–149.

Warner, M., Chen, L. H., & Makuc, D. M. (2009). Increase in fatal poisonings involving opioid analgesics in the United States, 1999–2006. *National Center for Health Statistics Data Brief, 22,* 1–8.

Wilkinson, S. S., Mistral, W. W., & Golding, J. J. (2008). What is most and least useful in residential rehabilitation? A qualitative study of service users and professionals. *Journal of Substance Use, 13,* 404–414.

Witkiewitz, K., Villarroel, N., Hartzler, B., & Donovan, D. M. (2011). Drinking outcomes following drink refusal skills training: Differential effects for African American and non-Hispanic White clients. *Psychology of Addictive Behaviors, 25,* 162–167.

Personality Disorders

Victoria E. Kress, Matthew J. Paylo, and Chelsea A. Zoldan

CASE STUDY: JANE

Jane is a withdrawn, 35-year-old Caucasian female from the Midwest who attended one year of community college while in her 20s. When asked about her religious and spiritual beliefs and practices, she says, "If there were a God, he wouldn't have let my life turn out this way." Jane expresses some interest in Buddhism; she would like to learn more about this religion, and "develop her spirituality."

She has lived with her mother her entire life and has struggled to maintain stable friendships. Jane's relationships have been tumultuous and often end with people pushing her away as they increasingly perceive her as being "needy" and "depressing." She describes a pattern of relationships that begin with an intense feeling of connection, yet end with her feeling victimized and rejected. She often lashes out in anger as these relationships begin to unravel, and even slashed the tires of one friend after that relationship ended. She has identity struggles, and it is difficult for her to describe herself, her interests, beliefs, values, and hopes for her future. She tends to take on the interests of the people with whom she is associating with as her own. In talking with her, she is negativistic in her thinking; she often sees the world in black-and-white terms.

As a child, Jane experienced an extensive sexual abuse history by both her older brother and her father's best friend. Jane does not believe that her mother was aware of the sexual abuse she experienced, and to this day, Jane has maintained these "family secrets." Jane was repeatedly and violently sexually abused from the age of approximately 4 to about 14, when her brother left the home. Adding to her shame and confusion is the fact that her older brother now works as a high-ranking military general and is what she calls the "family hero." In her family, Jane received the message that women were less valued than men. She witnessed her mother being physically and emotionally abused by her father until his death when Jane was 18. Jane has internalized the family belief that her brother is special, makes excuses for his abuse of her, and expresses no anger toward him. Jane indicates that she is leery of most men, and she generally only seeks relationships with women. She has never had any sexual or romantic contact with men or women, and the thought of doing so makes her feel exceptionally anxious.

Since she was about 20 years old, Jane has engaged in severe self-injury. She has had upwards of 15 stitches during various incidents in which she has self-injured. She also sometimes bangs her head against the wall, and she will self-burn using bathroom cleaning chemicals. Jane self-injures about three times per week. Jane's self-injury is typically precipitated by either conflicts with her mother or people with whom she works; feelings of loneliness and emptiness that sometimes overwhelm her, especially when she has unstructured down time or by flashbacks and intrusive memories of her past sexual abuse.

Every few months, Jane experiences what she calls "dark times" when she is overwhelmed by feelings of sadness and hopelessness, during which she spends her weekends in bed. She denies having made any suicide attempts since her teen years, however she regularly wishes she were dead and fantasizes about suicide.

Jane also has a history of bulimia that ensued from the age of 13 until she was about 23 years of age. As her bulimia dissipated, the rate at which she self-injured increased. She refers to herself as "the original self-injurer" and takes pride in her knowledge of the topic. Jane has read a great deal about self-injury and has even shared her story with a local newspaper that published a special story on the topic.

Jane also has asthma, and she is able to induce asthma attacks, which result in her making frequent trips to the emergency room at her local hospital. She has been to the emergency room at least twice a week for the past year, and only feels "safe" and "loved" when receiving medical treatment at the hospital. Jane is especially fond of a female medical intern with whom she perceives she has made a special connection with over the past few months.

Jane has spent the past two years in counseling. She refers to her counselor as her "surrogate mother." Jane used the Internet to find her counselor's home address, and she used to drive by the counselor's house when she felt agitated and needed to self-soothe. Jane also secured her counselor's phone number and would frequently call her at home, resulting in the counselor setting firm boundaries with Jane around out-of-session contact. Jane was initially angry when her counselor set these boundaries, and she left treatment. Eventually Jane settled and returned to treatment.

Four years ago, Jane was fired from her previous job because she self-injured at work with a box cutter after an altercation with a colleague. Despite Jane's interpersonal struggles, she has maintained employment at a factory for the past four years. She reports that some of her colleagues are hostile toward her and she has occasional conflicts, but for the most part her job is stable. She perceives that working in an all-male environment is adaptive for her, as she isolates herself from her colleagues and rarely has a need to interact with them.

Jane is intelligent and creative, enjoys photography and nature, and has a passion for taking wildlife photos; but recently, she has not been engaged in this activity. She is also intermittently involved in a wildlife photography club in her community. She is interested in possibly returning to school to earn a graphic arts degree, but her mother has been discouraging this, stating that she "does not see the point in it." While she describes her relationship with her mother as "cold," Jane's mother, in some ways, serves as a source of support. Jane also has occasional contact with a friend from high school whom she admires and respects. Jane is able to seek help and support, and she is quite knowledgeable about many of the issues with which she struggles. She presently takes Paxil as prescribed by her primary care physician.

DESCRIPTION OF THE PERSONALITY DISORDERS

Personality refers to people's traits, coping styles, and ways of interacting with others and the world around them. Personality begins to emerge in childhood and typically solidifies by late adolescence and early adulthood. Most people have fairly adaptable personalities; they are able to bend to the demands of society and social expectations. Those who have personality disorders are inflexible in their interactions with the world, and they demonstrate rigid, problematic, and deeply ingrained patterns of relating to the world and in how they perceive themselves. For example, people with avoidant personality disorder will continue to avoid relationships with new people who enter their world even though they feel lonely and yearn to make meaningful connections.

According to the *DSM-5* (American Psychiatric Association [APA], 2013), to qualify as having a personality disorder, one's behavior must be *pervasive*, *inflexible*, and *stable* over a *long duration*. In addition, it must cause *significant distress* or *impairment in functioning*, and be demonstrated in at least two of the following areas: cognition, affectivity, interpersonal functioning, or impulse control. The characteristic traits and patterns that this population demonstrates are replayed in all new situations they encounter, and they do not adapt their behavior in response to experiences. People with personality disorders are known to incite much distress in the lives of the people around them, and they do not typically see their personality and behaviors as problematic. Their behavior is ego-syntonic, which means that to them, their behaviors, values, and feelings are acceptable to the needs and goals of their ego; they are consistent with their ideal self-image. Often, they do not seek treatment unless mandated to do so, at the insistence of another, or because they seek assistance for discomfort associated with comorbid issues.

There is wide variability in the severity and form of personality disorders. In milder cases, people are able to function at fairly high levels, and they may appear to be fairly adaptive or even successful to an outsider. Others with more severe personality disorders experience significant impacts in their functioning, and may face incarceration, recurrent hospitalizations, and even commit suicide or homicide.

Personality disorders are, by definition, stable and enduring personality patterns, and because personality is established early in one's life, so are personality disorders. There are 10 personality disorders included in the *DSM-5*: borderline personality disorder, antisocial personality disorder, histrionic personality disorder, obsessive-compulsive personality disorder, avoidant personality disorder, dependent personality disorder, schizotypal personality disorder, schizoid personality disorder, paranoid personality disorder, personality change due to another medical condition, and other specified personality disorder and unspecified personality disorder. It is believed that approximately 9% of the United States population meets the criteria for one of the personality disorders (APA, 2013). Gender distribution of the personality disorders varies depending on the disorder. Refer to Table 9.1 for an overview of the personality disorders.

Interestingly, a comprehensive meta-analysis (Verheul & Widiger, 2004) indicated that unspecified personality disorder is the most common personality disorder diagnosed

TABLE 9.1   OVERVIEW OF KEY PERSONALITY DISORDERS

Antisocial	Avoidant	Borderline	Dependent	Histrionic
Blatant disregard and violation of the rights of others	*Inhibited; feelings of inferiority*	*Unstable relationships; poor self-image; lack of emotion regulation*	*Enmeshment; desires/ requires external guidance and support from others.*	*Attention-seeking; self-dramatization*
Prevalence	**Prevalence**	**Prevalence**	**Prevalence**	**Prevalence**
0.2–3%	2%	2–6%	0.5%	2%
Characteristics	**Characteristics**	**Characteristics**	**Characteristics**	**Characteristics**
• Egocentric mindset • Goals based on personal gratification • Absence of internal standards to conform to lawful and ethical behaviors • Lack of concern for others' needs, feelings, concerns • Lack of remorse when hurting others • Use of coercion, intimidation, and dominance to control others	• Excessive feelings of shame and inadequacy • Low self-esteem • Perceives self as inept • Sensitivity to rejection and criticism by others • Reluctant to get involved with others unless certain of being liked • Lack of initiation and avoidance of close attachments (friends or sexual relationships)	• Poorly developed, unstable self-image • Compromised ability to recognize others' feelings • Feelings of emptiness; excessive self-criticism • Instability in relationship due to mistrust, neediness, or threats of abandonment • Marked impulsivity • Interpersonal hypersensitivity • History of self-harm	• A need to be taken care of • Lacks initiative • Feelings of helplessness • Inability to separate in relationship; clingy behaviors • Preoccupied with fears of abandonment • Desires for others to assume responsibility • Difficulty in making decisions	• A need to be the center of attention • Rapidly changing moods and emotions • Attention-seeking (provocative) behaviors • Tendency to be irritable; angry outbursts if attention is not given • Suggestible • Excessively emotional • Uses physical appearance to draw attention

Narcissistic	Obsessive-compulsive	Paranoid	Schizoid	Schizotypal
Requires excessive admiration; overvaluation of others opinions and reactions	*Inflexible; perfectionistic; values order and rules*	*Suspicious; a general mistrust of others*	*Inability and lack of desire to form social relationships*	*Interpersonal deficits; odd, eccentric behaviors; perceptual disturbances*
Prevalence	**Prevalence**	**Prevalence**	**Prevalence**	**Prevalence**
0–6%	2–8%	2–4%	3–5%	4–5%

(Continued)

TABLE 9.1 (Continued)

Characteristics	Characteristics	Characteristics	Characteristics	Characteristics
• Grandiose (exaggerated sense of self) • Goals based on approval from others • Inability to recognize others' feelings and needs • Superficial relationships • Admiration seeking • Arrogant; a sense of entitlement • Self-promoting behaviors	• Sense of self derived from productivity • Rigid and unreasonably high standards • Difficulty understanding others' ideas, feelings, and behaviors • Rigid perfectionism • Persistency with tasks (even with repeated failures)	• Preoccupation with doubts of others' intentions • Bears grudges • Always on guard; perceives others are seeking to harm or hurt • Questions the motives of others • Reacts angrily to others • Reads into the meaning (or the hidden agenda) of behaviors	• Detached, flat affect • Lacks close relationships • No desire for sexual or platonic relationships • Indifferent to praise or criticism • Selects activities that involve solitude • Deficient in social skills	• Odd, unusual thoughts and behaviors • Suspicious or paranoid ideation • Confused boundaries (between self and others) • Difficulty understanding impact of behaviors on others • Impairments in making close connections • Emotionally restricted • Avoidance of social contact and social activities

in clinical practice. Although officially used only for disorders of personality functioning that "do not meet the full criteria for any of the personality disorders' diagnostic class" (APA, 2013, p. 684), this diagnosis is often used in a variety of ways in real-world practice. Some clinicans use the diagnosis to suggest a personality disorder that involves features of more than one personality disorder, but does not meet the full criteria for any specific one. Some may use it to suggest a person meets the criteria for a personality disorder that has been removed with evolving editions of the *DSM* (e.g., passive-aggressive personality disorder). Others may use it to convey that a person has a personality disorder, but cannot yet identify which specific one is present (Verheul et al., 2003).

At this time, it is widely accepted that personality disorders are rooted in both biological and psychosocial factors, While social and environmental circumstances impact a disorder's development, genetic factors such as temperament also play an important role in the development of these disorders.

COUNSELOR CONSIDERATIONS

As is the case when counseling all clients, a strong therapeutic relationship is essential. However, because of their guardedness, trust issues, and emotional sensitivity, a strong relationship is especially important when counseling those who have personality disorders. This population may be especially vulnerable to any type of confrontation, and the risk of therapeutic alliance ruptures and premature therapy termination is high.

Counselors who work with this population should seek regular consultation and supervision, and be especially mindful of monitoring their personal reactions to clients. To help manage their reactions when counseling this population, counselors might consider clients' resistance and therapy-disrupting behaviors as stemming from their protective defense mechanisms, or attempts to guard their egos.

Compared to other categories of disorders, there is a paucity of research on treating personality disorders. Most of the literature has focused on the treatment of borderline personality disorder. Very little empirical research has addressed the treatment of the other personality disorders. Research suggests that the Cluster C personality disorders (i.e., dependent, avoidant, and obsessive-compulsive) may be more responsive to treatment than the Cluster B (i.e., antisocial, borderline, narcissistic, and histrionic; Butcher, Mineka, & Hooley, 2010), or the Cluster B (paranoid, schizoid, and schizotypal) disorders.

To understand the treatment literature related to personality disorders, it is important to understand the limitations associated with diagnosing personality disorders. Of all the *DSM* categories, personality disorders have the weakest diagnostic reliability and are more often misdiagnosed than any other category in the *DSM* classification system. Even using highly structured interview assessments, short-term test-retest reliabilities of .54 for specific personality disorders and .56 for any personality disorder are reported (Chmielewski & Watson, 2008). When considering longer term assessment of reliability, test-retest reliabilities of .51 have been found for any personality disorder and .34 for specific personality disorders, and significant diagnostic changes have been found over as little as six months (Shea et al., 2002). These findings suggest that personality disorders are *not* reliably diagnosed, even under the best of conditions.

One factor that complicates the research related to the treatment of personality disorders is the high comorbidity among personality disorders. For example, in one study of 900 psychiatric outpatients, it was found that 45% qualified for at least one personality disorder diagnosis, and of those, 60% qualified for more than one with 25% qualifying for two or more (Zimmerman, Rothchild, & Chelminski, 2005). Again, with such a high comorbidity among personality disorder diagnoses, it is difficult to make determinations about the effectiveness of a treatment on a given disorder.

The difficulties with reliability are rooted, in part, in the structure of the personality disorders. For example, in considering the possible symptom variations required to meet the criteria to receive a borderline personality disorder diagnosis (using the *DSM-IV* criteria), there are 256 different symptom profile possibilities (Johansen, Karterud, Pedersen, Gude, & Falkum, 2004). In other words, people can meet the criteria for the same personality disorder, yet have few, if any, features in common with others diagnosed with the same disorder. For example, one client may present with odd beliefs, thinking, and speech, or magical thinking, ideas of reference, unusual perceptual experiences, and paranoid ideation. Another client may have few friends, be suspicious, experience excessive social anxiety, have an odd appearance and constricted affect. Yet, both of these clients will meet the diagnostic criteria for schizotypal personality disorder.

The difficulties with diagnostic reliability confound the treatment literature on personality disorders; if there is uncertainty about the diagnoses of a population, it is difficult to then assess for treatment effectiveness. As Butcher et al. (2010) stated: "this virtually ensures that few obtained research results will be replicated by other researchers even though the groups studied by the different researchers have the same diagnostic label" (p. 343).

It should also be considered that people who have personality disorders and who seek treatment for issues other than their personality disorder (e.g., depression or anxiety) do not tend to fare as well in treatment as those who seek treatment and do not have a personality disorder (Critis-Christoph & Barber, 2007). This population's dysfunctional personality characteristics can impede the therapeutic relationship, and clients are less likely to engage in the activities they need to in order to make behavioral changes.

Those with personality disorders often struggle to function across a variety of domains and have a propensity to decompensate, or to have their symptoms worsen, under stress (Sperry, 2003). Clients may need access to a variety of levels of care where they can receive access to medication management, individual and group therapy, and case management services. In terms of levels of care, they may require access to crisis stabilization services, such as hospital care, for times when they are actively suicidal or homicidal, and/or partial hospitalization as a step down from a hospital setting or as a means of preventing a hospitalization. For clients who have severe personality disorders, access to residential treatment centers where they can receive services in a structured, monitored, therapeutic environment is essential.

Some people with personality disorders may struggle to function across a number of life domains and may benefit from access to a variety of supportive services. Career and vocational counseling, shelter and housing needs, and access to various social services may be required.

Historically, psychodynamic theories have contributed a great deal to an understanding of personality disorders and their etiology and treatment. In more recent years, behavioral, cognitive behavioral, and integrated treatments have received attention (e.g., Beck, Freeman, & Davis, 2004; Young, Klosko, & Weishaar, 2003). Because of the wide variability of symptoms associated with each of the personality disorders, a summary of the treatment literature will not be provided in this section; instead treatment will be addressed in each of the specific personality disorder sections.

PROGNOSIS

It is commonly suggested that personality disorders are fairly intractable. By definition, personality disorders involve enduring, inflexible, and pervasive patterns of behavior, and as such, are difficult to change. Personalities evolve over time, and once established, they are difficult to alter. All people can struggle to make even simple behavior changes; changing the foundations of personality though can be a monumental task.

However, while it is difficult to change personality dynamics and personality disorders are the disorder category widely considered to be most resistant to change, clients can make meaningful progress. As is true with all clients, those who have a reason or motivation to change are most likely to be successful in treatment. When working with this population, success can be achieved if attainable treatment goals are established. For example, while changing one's personality is a difficult task, changing specific behaviors that the client is motivated to change will likely result in a more satisfying outcome; it is important to have realistic treatment outcomes.

While personality disorders are often viewed as intractable, the prognosis for these disorders may be better than was once thought. Some research on client functioning over time suggests significant individual variations in terms of the long-term prognosis of those who have personality disorders (e.g., Kvarstein & Karterud, 2011). What is more likely is that associated comorbid disorders (e.g., substance use) and various contextual life factors (e.g., a lack of positive supports or financial resources) also play a role in determining the prognosis of those with personality disorders.

The presence of comorbid disorders can negatively impact the prognosis of a personality disorder, and it is important that counselors develop a thorough understanding of all of the disorders the client may have, and integrate these considerations into their case conceptualization and treatment plan. For example, it is important to assess for a past abuse and trauma history and associated PTSD, as neglecting traumatic stress disorders may result in unsuccessful treatment. If a client is having flashbacks and avoidance symptoms that are related to unacknowledged trauma, he or she may struggle to apply skills addressed in his or her treatment plan.

Substance use is another issue that can complicate the prognosis of personality disorders. Those with personality disorders have higher rates of substance use disorders than the general population (Straussner & Nemenzik, 2007). Some literature addresses the treatment of these co-occurring disorders, but is limited to those with borderline personality disorder and antisocial personality disorder. Studies suggest that the presence of both a personality disorder and substance use disorders may increase symptom severity and worsen prognoses (Straussner & Nemenzik, 2007). However, there is evidence to suggest that appropriate concurrent treatment of both disorders can be successful and needs to be provided. As such, co-occurring substance use should always be assessed and treated, or the counselor will likely struggle to have success in treating the personality disorder.

BORDERLINE PERSONALITY DISORDER

Description of the Disorder and Typical Client Characteristics

Borderline personality disorder (BPD) is one of the most common personality disorders seen in clinical practice (APA, 2013). Its prevalence, combined with many treatment challenges related to working with this population, may be why more attention and research have been given to BPD than any of the other personality disorders. Negative moods, which often move from feelings of anger to depression in short periods of time, disinhibition as evidenced by risk-taking and engaging in impulsive behaviors, unstable relationships with others, and a poor and fluctuating self-image are some of the characteristics of people who have BPD. In an attempt to regulate their negative feelings and self-soothe, those with BPD may impulsively engage in maladaptive behaviors such as self-injuring, substance abuse, shoplifting, or various disordered eating behaviors (especially binging and purging).

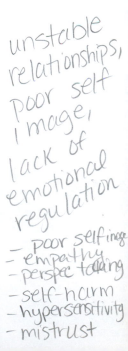

(handwritten margin notes: unstable relationships, poor self image, lack of emotional regulation — poor self image — empathy — perspec taking — self-harm — hypersensitivity — mistrust)

Clinical Toolbox 9.1: In the Pearson etext, click here to read about a creative counseling activity that can be used to help clients who self-injure better manage their behaviors.

CREATIVE TOOLBOX ACTIVITY 9.1   Protective Shields

Victoria E. Kress, PhD, LPCC-S, NCC

Activity Overview

This activity uses guided imagery to help clients imagine a protective shield that can be used as a means of preventing self-injury.

Treatment Goal(s) of Activity

The protective shields activity is intended to teach clients a relaxation skill that can be used when they feel an impulse to self-injure. This activity helps clients develop their emotion regulation skills and provides an alternative coping skill to self-injury.

Directions

1. Introduce the exercise to the client as an activity that can be used for relaxation and to self-soothe when experiencing urges to self-injure.
2. Invite the client to close his or her eyes, or keep them open, depending on which feels more comfortable.
3. Instruct the client to bring his or her attention to the part/s of the body where they self-injure.
4. Ask the client to take a few moments to establish a connection with the area of the body, noticing the color, weight, texture, movements, shape, and form of the particular area of the body.
5. Ask the client to notice the body part and continue to be aware of the function, mobility, and ability to support and work together with the rest of the body.
6. Invite the client to consider how this body part connects him or her to the surrounding world.
7. Instruct the client to take a few moments to relax and continue to deepen his or her sense of a connection to his or her body.
8. Direct the client to imagine a protective shield over the part/s of the body where he or she has urges to self-injure.
9. Ask the client about the texture, color (intensity, multiple colors), and shape of the shield. Also, ask the client to consider when he or she thinks he or she will need to connect with the shield. Invite the client to reorient to his or her surroundings.
10. After the client has a clear picture of the protective shield in mind, invite the client to use the materials to draw the shield. Be sure to have the materials ready for use to allow the client to begin working immediately.

Process Questions

1. What was this activity like for you?
2. How did you visualize the part of the body that you typically self-injure?
3. What did it feel like for you to build this shield?
4. How can you use this activity to help prevent self-injury in the future?

Chaotic relationships are a hallmark of those who have this disorder, and their relationships are typically intense and stormy. "Splitting," or the overvaluation and then devaluation of others, is a common occurrence. This devaluation of others is often triggered by a fear of rejection or abandonment and an inability to integrate and balance contrasting feelings within the self and/or about others. Early in relationships, those with BPD may idealize people and see them as all "good," kind, and nurturing, but because of their interpersonal hypersensitivity and fear of rejection, they move to seeing people as all "bad," cruel, and rejecting.

Women are more often diagnosed with this disorder, with an estimated gender ratio of 3 to 1. However, the disorder may be missed in men who have the disorder, and they are more likely to receive diagnoses of antisocial or narcissistic personality disorders. Men should be just as carefully assessed for BPD as women, as more recent epidemiological studies of community, non-help-seeking samples suggest a more equal gender ratio than the documented prevalence research suggests (e.g., Lynam & Widiger, 2007). Symptoms similar to BPD are seen across cultures and can be misidentified in individuals experiencing issues such as identity crises, substance abuse, sexual orientation conflicts, and pressure to determine a career path (APA, 2013).

Counselor Considerations

As with any counseling relationship, it is important that the therapeutic alliance be built on a trusting, nonjudgmental relationship. Repeated rejection, abuse, and self-destructive behaviors have left most people with this disorder feeling stigmatized and shamed. It is especially important that counselors monitor their own reactions to clients' experiences and sustain a compassionate approach to treatment.

It is typical that at some point in treatment, clients with BPD will idealize their counselors and see them as people who will rescue them. However, as counselors cannot live up to these unrealistic expectations, clients often rapidly shift to vilifying their counselors. In a counseling relationship, this devaluation of the counselor is usually incited by clients feeling frustrated or angry about a limit established by the counselor. When these behaviors threaten the client's ability to continue in treatment, counselors can either process this transference dynamic with the client, or consider changing the treatment approach.

Because of the nature of the symptoms associated with this disorder, many clients with BPD are treated in residential, partial hospitalization, or acute care settings such as hospitals. In these settings, they are treated by a team of professionals. It is especially important that when working as part of a treatment team, team members avoid being pulled into clients' splitting dynamics. Regular team communication and team member awareness of such dynamics are helpful ways to avoid unproductive dynamics.

With this population it is especially important that counselors are firm, consistent, and reliable in their treatment approach. When counseling people who have BPD, it is important that counselors take an active approach to managing sessions and setting limits around the treatment process. It can be helpful to approach each session with a hierarchy of preidentified tasks. The most important tasks might be addressing suicidal and self-destructive behaviors, with an eye to evaluating risk factors and helping to facilitate safety. Since clients with BPD may engage in multiple self-destructive behaviors, counselors may find themselves spending a great deal of time setting limits around clients' destructive behaviors. Counselors are challenged to address these behaviors, yet ensure that they do not become embroiled in a countertransference situation in which they police the behavior to the point that treatment becomes unproductive.

While it is important to establish a detailed treatment plan with all clients, it is especially important to do so with this population. A clear treatment plan will help establish the necessary therapeutic boundaries. Depending on the theoretical approach of the counselor and the limitations of the setting (i.e., agency policies, private practice, hospital setting, rural communities), counselors will have different expectations of clients' behavior. Counselors should be certain to specify the frequency with which sessions will be held, a plan for managing between-session crises, session tardiness, missed sessions, between-session assignment completion, active participation in sessions, clarification of the clients' and counselors' roles, and clarification of counselors' between-session availability.

Counselors must also communicate to clients the consequences of boundary violations. Collaboratively involving clients in discussions about boundaries and why they are important can be a useful way to reinforce counselor expectations. Clients with BPD will frequently violate boundaries (e.g., request between-session contacts), and as such, it is important that counselors are consistent in reinforcing and sustaining these boundaries. For example, if a client asks for the counselor's home phone number, a counselor might say: "If you were to contact me in between our sessions, you would be missing out on an opportunity to develop your support networks and to use the skills you have learned to manage your distress." Or, if a client inquires about a counselor's personal life, a counselor might say: "Time spent addressing personal questions about me detracts from our ability to help you achieve your goals, which is the focus of our treatment," or "Tell me about what you imagine about that piece of my life in the absence of not knowing." Clients with BPD often violate boundaries in an attempt to assess whether the treatment situation is a safe and consistent enough environment in which to make themselves vulnerable. Thick clinical boundaries may ultimately reinforce a perception that the counseling environment is one that is in fact predictable, and as such, safe.

People who have BPD commonly experience suicidal ideation, with approximately 8 to 10% of this population committing suicide, and 60–70% attempting suicide (Oldham, 2006). As such, safety issues should be given priority not only in the initial assessment, but throughout clients' treatment. The results of these evaluations, combined with a review of clients' functioning and circumstances, will determine the level of care that clients need at any given time. Depending on clients' evolving circumstances, the severity of their struggles, and their comorbid disorders, this population may experience rapid shifts in their required level of care. People with BPD are one of the largest populations found in inpatient acute care settings, residential treatment, and partial hospitalization programs (Sperry, 2006).

There are a wide variety of disorders that are comorbid with BPD, and assessment for these disorders should be completed early in treatment. Depressive and bipolar disorders, eating disorders, PTSD, anxiety disorders, obsessive-compulsive and related disorders, panic disorders, and ADHD are just some of the disorders that often co-occur with BPD. Consideration of co-occurring disorders should be addressed as a part of a comprehensive treatment plan. Depressive disorders are most commonly comorbid with BPD, and depressive symptoms can be particularly difficult to ferret out from the BPD, as there is some overlap in symptoms. Depressive features that may be subsumed under borderline personality disorder are emptiness, self-condemnation, abandonment fears, hopelessness, self-destructiveness, and repeated suicidal gestures.

Substance use disorders are also common in those who have BPD. Substance abuse has important implications for treatment, since patients with BPD who abuse substances tend to have poorer outcomes and are at a higher risk for suicide and for death or injury secondary to accidents. A thorough substance abuse evaluation should be conducted when working with this population, and aggressive treatment of substance abuse disorders will be required before or during the treatment of BPD.

While not all people who have BPD have childhood trauma histories, most people with BPD have endured a variety of childhood abuse (e.g., sexual, physical, emotional, neglect; Arntz, van Genderen, & Drost, 2009). By appreciating the connections between early childhood abuses and clients' present-day behaviors, counselors' empathy toward those with BPD may be deepened. The characteristic BPD symptoms of affective instability, a negative self-image, relationship instability, and abandonment fears can all be tied back to early childhood experiences. Most people believe that it is better to wait until a later phase of treatment, when a strong alliance has been established and destructive symptoms have been stabilized, before directly tackling these trauma issues. In addition, before addressing trauma issues in those with BPD, it may be helpful to consider the clients' present functioning including current life stressors and transitions, and their level of agitation as related to the traumatic events. In the later phase of treatment, it is helpful for clients to engage in the PTSD treatments discussed in Chapter 7. It is important to help clients realize that they were not responsible for their past abuse and neglect, but they can control their reactions and behavior in the present. Too much of a focus on past traumas at the expense of connecting these events to present behaviors and functioning may be detrimental to clients. As clients integrate their traumatic experiences, cognitively restructure their experiences and memories, grieve their losses, and develop a healthy identity, they are better able to separate their past experiences and reactions from their present-day relationships, and ultimately develop more adaptive and stable ways of interacting with others.

Treatment Models and Interventions

All effective treatments for use with this population include some common features. One common feature is the validation of clients' experiences and the establishment of a foundational therapeutic alliance. Monitoring and addressing self-injurious and suicidal behaviors will also be an important aspect of all the therapies used to treat this population. It is recommended that all counselors establish a hierarchy that delineates priorities related to treatment, with safety considerations being at the top of that hierarchy. Because of the variety of comorbid issues, strengths, and weaknesses characteristic of this population, it is also important that counselors take a flexible approach to treatment planning; recognizing that clients' needs may rapidly evolve and shift. Additionally, because of the nature of the disorder, longer-term, intensive treatment is usually indicated. Depending on the approach used, the treatment for BPD is quite lengthy (APA, 2013), with a combination of weekly individual and group therapy sessions for 1–2 years being most useful.

If clients with BPD are participating in counseling groups, it is generally recommended that they also receive individual counseling so that they have an ability to process and apply group material. There is a limited body of research on the use of couples and family therapy, but it is not recommended as a primary source of treatment. Since clients with BPD often have complex familial relationships, counselors should be cautious when integrating family members into treatment.

Voices from the Trenches 9.1: In the Pearson etext, click here to watch a video in which tips for treating borderline personality disorder are presented.

DIALECTICAL BEHAVIOR THERAPY (DBT) DBT is a cognitive behavioral therapy approach specifically developed to treat BPD that has been found to reduce anxiety, anger, and self-harming behaviors in this population (Linehan, 1993; Linehan et al., 2006). It is widely used to treat BPD and has received a considerable amount of research over the past 20 years. Randomized controlled trials suggest that DBT is effective in reducing the symptoms of BPD, especially the associated self-injurious and suicidal symptoms (Linehan et al., 2006; Verheul et al., 2003). Those participating in DBT also tend to stay in treatment longer than those in control groups and require fewer hospitalizations. A number of controlled studies have been published that support these findings (see Lynch, Trost, Salsman, & Linehan, 2007 for a review of this literature).

At the heart of DBT is the idea that people with BPD struggle to tolerate strong negative emotional states, and as such, the goal of this approach is to help people learn to tolerate negative emotions in adaptive ways, without engaging in self-destructive or maladaptive behaviors. Linehan's treatment approach is based on a hierarchy of goals: (a) decreasing suicidal and other self-injurious behaviors; (b) decreasing therapy-interfering behaviors (e.g., lying to the counselor, missing sessions); (c) decreasing quality of life interfering behaviors (e.g., substance abuse, eating disorder behaviors); and (d) increasing behavioral skills that can be used to regulate negative emotions, increase distress tolerance, and enhance interpersonal skills.

Voices from the Trenches 9.2: In the Pearson etext, click here to watch a video which contains suggestions for integrating distress tolerance skills into treatment.

DBT is support-oriented in that it helps clients to identify their unique strengths and builds on them so that the person can feel empowered to make changes. As mentioned, DBT is a type of CBT therapy, and as such, it aims to help clients identify and change the thoughts, beliefs, and assumptions that make their lives harder (e.g., changing "I have to be perfect at everything I do in order for people to care about me" to "I don't need to be perfect at everything for people to care about me"). DBT is also collaborative in that it requires constant attention to the therapeutic relationship; a collaborative therapeutic relationship is seen as essential if clients are to trust the counselor and engage in the work of treatment. DBT is active in that it requires clients to complete homework assignments, role-play, practice new ways of interacting with others in individual sessions and groups, and practice using a variety of skills such as self-soothing and distress tolerance when upset.

The skills taught in DBT are conveyed through weekly lectures, reviewed in weekly homework groups, and referred to in nearly every group and individual counseling session.

Dialectical behavior therapy integrates both individual and group counseling, with clients being asked to commit to at least 6–12 months of treatment. Each week, clients participate in individual counseling, which usually lasts for about an hour, as well as one 2–2.5 hour skill-building group. Individual counseling focuses more on the client's individual needs and how the client is applying information learned through skill groups. As a part of individual therapy, clients are asked to complete weekly diary cards on which they document therapy interfering behaviors, in other words, behaviors that derail them from reaching their goals (i.e., lying to the counselor, not completing diary cards, "yes but-ing" everything the counselor says). In individual counseling clients follow a treatment hierarchy of issues: (a) issues of suicide and self-injury are addressed; (b) behaviors that are not directly harmful to one's self or others, but interfere with the client's success are addressed; and finally, (c) the counselor and client work on applying the DBT skills. The skills group component of DBT focuses more on learning and applying various skills such as distress tolerance, emotion regulation, and interpersonal skills. Both the individual and group components are seen as necessary to clients' success.

There are four modules or skills that are taught as a part of DBT, with all of these skill sets involving a variety of activities and acronyms intended to aid in their comprehension. First, the idea of mindfulness is essential to DBT and its implementation. *Mindfulness* involves the capacity to pay attention—in a nonjudgmental way—to the present moment, and to experience one's senses fully, but with perspective and a sense of acceptance. A variety of meditative skills are used to teach this concept. *Distress tolerance* involves developing one's skills and ability to self-soothe strong emotions. The goal of distress tolerance is to become capable of calmly connecting with negative situations and their impacts, rather than becoming overwhelmed by them, or hiding from them. In enhancing distress tolerance skills, clients are better able to tolerate strong emotions and make deliberate decisions about how to respond to situations. Radical acceptance is an aspect of distress tolerance. Radical acceptance is the process of accepting experiences, beliefs, and perceptions without offering judgments or believing that things should be different from what they are.

Clinical Toolbox 9.2: In the Pearson etext, click here to read about a creative counseling intervention that uses the DBT skill of radical acceptance to help clients tolerate distressing experiences.

Emotion regulation skills are a third set of skills emphasized in DBT. The emotion regulation skills include the identification of ways clients can effectively regulate and manage strong emotions as they occur. *Interpersonal effectiveness* skills are the final set of skills emphasized in DBT. These skills include effective strategies for communicating what one needs, saying no, and managing interpersonal conflict.

One popular DBT technique that can be used in reducing clients' self-harming behavior is a chain analysis (Linehan, 1993). A chain analysis is a detailed evaluation of a chain of behaviors that led up to an event in which one self-injured. (Linehan, 1993). Chain analysis involves a detailed recall of problem behaviors, events that promoted the self-harm, and the consequences of the behavior. When using a chain analysis, the identified behavior, the antecedent events that increase the reoccurrence of the behavior, and the consequences of the behavior are closely examined.

The development of a detailed chain analysis may reduce clients' shame and enhance their problem-solving abilities, thus helping them to feel more in control of their behaviors and emotions.

 Clinical Toolbox 9.3: In the Pearson etext, click here to read about an intervention, behavior chain analysis, that can be used to reduce and stabilize self-harming behaviors.

DBT takes into account and integrates a number of treatment considerations unique to working with clients with BPD. For example, as a part of a DBT program, there is a treatment team that regularly meets to process and assess clients' progress in treatment and to ensure that all team members are collaborating effectively. Another helpful aspect of DBT is phone coaching, which is a structured approach to managing client contact between sessions (Ben-Porath, 2004). In phone coaching, clients are instructed to call their counselor prior to any suicidal or self-injurious behaviors. The goal of phone coaching is to assist clients in generalizing their learned skills to their natural environment while simultaneously *not* reinforcing crisis-oriented behavior. Phone coaching skills—as well as any of the DBT skills—can easily be integrated into a variety of therapeutic approaches.

 Clinical Toolbox 9.4: In the Pearson etext, click here to read a case application of DBT phone coaching techniques.

SCHEMA THERAPY (ST)   ST has some evidence to suggest its effectiveness in treating BPD (Young et al., 2003). Several randomized controlled trials suggest ST is effective at decreasing personality dysfunction, increasing quality of life, decreasing suicidality, and decreasing treatment dropout rates (Giesen-Bloo et al., 2006; Farrell, Shaw, & Webber, 2009), and is more cost effective than transference-focused psychotherapy (a modified ego-psychology approach) and object relations theory treatment approaches (Clarkin, Yeomans, & Kernberg, 1999). By nature, ST is integrative. While this integrative approach may be attractive to counselors trained in different models, it makes ST a difficult treatment to evaluate, as there are not standardized treatment applications.

ST is commonly referred to as a modified cognitive behavioral treatment. However, ST is an integrative psychotherapy (Kellogg & Young, 2006), which incorporates psychodynamic theory tenets along with CBT principles. As is consistent with the psychodynamic object relations and attachment theories, ST emphasizes the internalization of early relationships into cognitive-affective representations, and suggests that BPD dynamics involve the dominance of maladaptive representations, of these relationships, or maladaptive schemas. In other words, the reactive emotional states that people with BPD experience can be seen as regressions to states they experienced as children.

Maladaptive schemas develop early in life and in response to family environments. People who develop BPD experience their families as demeaning, unstable, unsafe, neglectful, or punitive. Over time and with repeated exposure, these experiences develop into schemas that become core aspects of one's personality structure. The modes involved with BPD are (a) the abandoned and abused child; (b) the angry and impulsive child;

(c) the detached protector; (d) the punitive parent; and (e) the healthy adult (Kellogg & Young, 2006). Those with BPD will respond to their relationships in accordance with these schemas, often rapidly flipping between different modes. For example, when facing the withdrawal of affection from a partner, a client with BPD may enter the abandoned child mode, and then move into the angry and impulsive child mode and act out, and then move into the punitive parent mode in which the client blames himself or herself for being "bad" and causing the withdrawal of affection.

ST attempts to modify these schemas through the use of interventions from various treatment models, including not only CBT, but emotion-focused therapies (Kellogg & Young, 2006). As with DBT, the empathic therapeutic relationship is considered to be foundational to ST (Kellogg & Young, 2006). This approach suggests clients participate in two individual counseling sessions per week over an average of three years (Arntz et al., 2009). The techniques involved in this approach include various emotion-focused and gestalt techniques, altering behavioral patterns, and cognitive restructuring (Arntz et al., 2009; Kellogg & Young, 2006). Experiential and gestalt techniques consist of imagery work related to early dysfunctional relationships as well as dialogues between the different schema modes. Cognitive behavioral interventions include the use of homework exercises, challenging beliefs, and the modification of maladaptive behaviors. Table 9.2 provides examples of the core beliefs and assumptions that can be challenged when working from a CBT perspective with clients who have BPD.

PSYCHODYNAMIC Most theories of the etiology of BPD are rooted in psychodynamic principles, and as such, this approach has been widely used to treat those with BPD. While many criticize the psychodynamic approaches for being time and resource intensive and lacking in empirical support, there is evidence to suggest they may be useful in treating this population (Bateman & Fonogy, 2001; Leichsenring & Rabung, 2008).

From a psychodynamic perspective, there are different schools of thought about the origins of BPD, but all of these approaches view BPD as a developmental disorder involving a disturbance of self that evolves in relation to experiences with others in their childhood environments. Psychoanalysts hold that people carry these childhood images and representations as objects within their subconscious and that these object representations are then carried or projected into adult relationships. An application of this idea is the adult who experienced abuse in childhood and then expects people in authority positions to engage in abusive behaviors, and as such, responds aggressively to all authority figures.

All psychodynamic treatments emphasize a restorative therapeutic relationship that invites client regression and transference into the therapeutic relationship, and then uses it as a means of enhancing client insight and creating corrective experiences. As such, psychodynamic approaches use present experiences to identify and change reactions that are believed to be rooted in the past.

Mahler's separation individuation theory is an example of a psychodynamic object relations theory, and it provides insights into the development of BPD and its treatment (Mahler, Pine, & Bergman, 1973). Mahler's theory focuses on how people develop a sense of themselves as separate and unique from others. Mahler believed that disruptions in the fundamental process of separation-individuation during the first three years of life could result in disturbances in the ability to maintain a reliable sense of individual identity later in life. Children whose needs are not met do not develop the healthy sense of security needed to appropriately separate and individuate from their caretakers. As such, they struggle to develop a healthy sense of themselves as unique, autonomous individuals.

In terms of evidence-based applications of psychodynamic theory to working with those who have BPD, there is evidence to suggest that mentalization-based therapy (MBT) may be effective in treating BPD (Bateman & Fonagy, 2008b, 2009). The enduring efficacy of MBT was demonstrated in an 8-year follow-up of MBT (versus a treatment as usual group; Bateman & Fonagy, 2008b), and enduring treatment effects were also found in an 18-month follow-up study in which subjects were randomly assigned to a MBT treatment (Bateman & Fonagy, 2009).

MBT is based on attachment theory, another popular psychodynamic theory, and holds that those with BPD suffer from disorganized attachments and have failed to develop a mentalization capacity within the context of a healthy attachment relationship. Mentalization is the process by which people understand their mental state as well as that of others. It is best viewed as a form of imaginative mental activity, which allows people to perceive and interpret others' behavior in terms of intentional mental states (e.g., desires, needs, feelings, beliefs, goals, purposes, and reasons). In enhancing mentalization, clients are able to develop a more stable sense of themselves and others, and their relationships are thus enhanced. The enhancement of mentalization is placed at the forefront of this approach; while insight is important, applying mentalization in the present is what is deemed most important. Relatedly, the past is important as it relates to clients' current mental state. MBT is a manualized treatment, and it typically involves two sessions a week with sessions alternating between group and individual counseling.

During MBT sessions, counselors aim to activate clients' attachment systems through the exploration of current and past attachment relationships, and by encouraging and regulating clients' attachment bonds with the counselor. In the group counseling setting,

CREATIVE TOOLBOX ACTIVITY 9.2   Wall of Defenses

Suzanne N. Olesko, LPC, RN

Activity Overview

In this activity, clients are invited to use a set of children's blocks to concretely design a "wall of defenses." The wall of defenses is made up of issues that are contributing to a client's difficulty in reaching his or her life goals (e.g., relationship problems).

Treatment Goal(s) of Activity

The goal of this activity is for clients to identify defenses that are creating stuck points in their lives and then assign each of these issues to a block, noting the size, shape, and color of the block in order to represent the different "sizes" of the roles these issues are playing in their lives. Additionally, clients are then asked to work in the session to deconstruct their wall one block at a time; processing their identified issue using whatever evidence-based treatment may be appropriate for that treatment and client at that time (e.g., a client who identifies fear as an issue may work with a cognitive behavioral approach in session to challenge irrational thoughts that contribute to the fear).

Directions

1. Clients are asked to construct a list of defenses that make up their need for a "wall of defenses" to protect them from the outside world (e.g., trust, abandonment, fear).
2. Clients are introduced to a set of blocks of varying shapes and sizes and asked to label various blocks, which are selected based on their representation of the defense (i.e., based on shape and color).

   Note: Clients may alter shapes or combine blocks to make the block better fit how their identified issue looks.

3. Clients are then asked to construct their wall of defenses using their labeled blocks with the issues that the client believes are the most engrained or will be the most difficult to process at the base of the wall.
4. The counselor and client then begin to deconstruct the wall built by the client utilizing evidence-based approaches that apply to the identified issue.

   Note: The process of deconstructing the wall will likely take many sessions, and the client should be asked at the beginning of each counseling session to reconstruct the wall as the construction may change as issues are processed. The client or counselor can take a picture of the wall and use it as an ongoing tool in counseling.

Process Questions

Pre-Activity

1. What makes up your need for a wall of defenses?
2. In what ways do you think the wall is helpful to you?
3. In what ways do you think the wall holds you back or interferes with your life?

Deconstruction of Wall

1. Assess with the client his or her reasoning for the label assigned to each block.
2. What significance does the color of the block have?
3. What color or shape for the block would make it a less significant part of the wall?
4. What changes need to occur for the shape or color of the block to change?

counselors attempt to create attachment bonds between members of the group, with these bonds then being used as a part of the counseling process.

STEPPS GROUP THERAPY   Group therapy is often viewed as a cost-effective way of providing treatment to clients with BPD. Because of the high frequency with which those with BPD are placed in acute care or residential settings, and because partial hospitalization and/or group therapy is a common part of the step-down process in moving from a greater to a lesser restrictive setting, effective group therapy treatment models are a useful modality of intervention with this population. Systems training for emotional predictability and problem solving (STEPPS; Blum et al., 2008) is a group treatment model that has demonstrated success in randomized controlled trials (Blum et al., 2008). This treatment was found to reduce impulsivity, relieve depression, improve overall functioning, and decease emergency room visits during treatment and follow-up (Blum et al., 2008). This approach integrates CBT and a systems model into a 20-week, manualized, outpatient group treatment format.

PSYCHOPHARMACOTHERAPY Psychopharmacological intervention is not generally used to treat BPD per se, but medications can be helpful in targeting specific symptoms of BPD. Antidepressant medications, such as the SSRIs, are often used in treating mood shifts, anger, and anxiety, as well as impulsive symptoms such as self-injury and angry outbursts (Koenigsberg, Woo-Ming, & Siever, 2007).

This population may abuse or misuse medications (e.g., overdose), and it is sometimes recommended that medications with an abuse potential (e.g., benzodiazepines) be avoided, and medications with a low toxicity be used and prescribed in a way that limits abuse potential. SSRIs generally have a low toxicity when taken in overdose, thus minimizing the potential for completed suicides if taken in high quantities (Preston, O'Neal, & Talaga, 2013). Trazodone, bupropion, and venlafaxine are other antidepressant medications with low toxicity (Preston et al., 2013).

Medications can be helpful in addressing comorbid diagnoses. Low-dose antipsychotic medications are sometimes used to treat suicidality, impulsive aggression, rejection sensitivity, and any psychotic symptoms that may be evident (Koenigsberg et al., 2007). Mood-stabilizing medications may be useful in reducing irritability, suicidality, and impulsive and aggressive behaviors (Koenigsberg et al., 2007). Anticonvulsant medications may also be useful in treating the angry-impulsive symptomology and labile mood (Preston et al., 2013). Benzodiazepines may be associated with emotional dyscontrol and increased suicidality, thus they are not generally used to treat BPD and its accompanying symptoms (Preston et al., 2013).

Prognosis

Because of the high comorbidty of other disorders with BPD, and because of the pervasive nature of the disorder, improvements can come slowly. Some research suggests that BPD has a poorer prognosis than other personality disorders (e.g., Zanarini, Frankenburg, Hennen, Reich, & Silk, 2005); while other research suggests that in fact, BPD has a more favorable prognosis than some other personality disorders (i.e., avoidant personality disorder or paranoid personality disorder), and that positive changes in functioning can occur over time and may remit with age (APA, 2013; Kvarstein & Karterud, 2011).

The occurrence of severe self-injury, repeated suicide attempts, and other impulsive, high-risk behaviors invites the risk of deliberate or accidental death, and these behaviors must be monitored to ensure client safety. Structured, comprehensive treatments that integrate medication management and provide access to required levels of care as needed may be most effective in creating enduring change within this population. Symptoms tend to gradually reduce with age, and this shift may be due to those with this disorder gaining greater stability in their relationships, identity, and vocations, and because of biological shifts or having learned more adaptive coping skills in response to natural consequences.

ANTISOCIAL PERSONALITY DISORDER (DYSSOCIAL PERSONALITY DISORDER)

Description of the Disorder and Typical Client Characteristics

People with antisocial personality disorder (ASPD) or dyssocial personality disorder are identified by persistent disregard for and violation of the rights of others (APA, 2013). The diagnosis of ASPD is given to those who have continued these antisocial patterns into adulthood and have previously met the criteria for the childhood diagnosis of conduct disorder with an onset before the age of 15 (see Chapter 12 for a detailed discussion of conduct disorder).

This population has a pervasive pattern of reacting impulsively and aggressively toward others and thwarting socially expected laws, rules, and norms. These patterns of behaviors are not situationally bound, meaning in response to life circumstances, but are consistent ways of interacting with the world. They typically experience no remorse for their actions and rationalize exploiting or hurting other by directly blaming victims (e.g., "it was their fault" or "they should have known better"). They may not be able to govern many normal aspects of adulthood such as sustained employment and relationships, but depending on their intelligence and other characteristics, they may be able to find careers in which their traits allow them to function fairly well. Their egocentric, self-centered mindset, compounded by their impulsive, reckless, and irresponsible decision-making behavior, often contributes to difficulties in maintaining stable life circumstances. Difficulties negotiating life roles (e.g., employee, spouse, parent) are common, and it may be difficult to maintain relationships because of their persistent rule breaking, exploitative nature, deceitfulness, and blatant disregard for the feelings or welfare of others.

People with ASPD are often impulsive in their decision making and desire instant gratification. They are often drawn to exciting, reckless activities that have a high stimulation factor. Because of their persuasive nature, they are often able to sway or convince others to do or engage in reckless activities. They often value impressing others, and despite their swiftness in providing verbal judgment, they typically have difficulties managing others' rejection and judgment.

They have significant difficulties maintaining close personal relationships that are egalitarian in nature. Usually tumultuous in nature, their relationships are laced with power differentials that favor the person with the disorder. This inequality often leads to multiple romantic partner changes. Additionally, this population struggles to take the perspective of others. They tend to think in a linear fashion, anticipating others' reactions only after they have first acted upon their own wishes or desires. These interpersonal difficulties directly affect a person's ability to sustain gainful employment. The submissive nature of working for another person or agency is often too much for a person with ASPD to tolerate, and this may lead to persistent job changes.

Criminality and involvement in the criminal justice system are common, yet not all have committed criminal acts per se. Some turn their self-absorbed drive into vocational success. For example, a drive for material goods and/or power may be translated into more socially acceptable arenas (e.g., politics, business).

ASPD is rooted in both genetic and environment factors. In one meta-analytic review of behavioral genetic etiological studies, it was concluded that 56% of the variance in ASPD can be attributed to genetic predispositions, with 11% being due to shared experiences such as family socialization processes (e.g., internalized culture and developed identity), and 31% being attributed to unique individual influences and experiences such as head injuries and infections (Ferguson, 2010).

Although genetic predispositions play a vital role in the development of ASPD, environmental contributions are also important (Gelhorn, Sakai, Price, & Crowley, 2007). Prevalence rates are higher among those who have experienced adverse socioeconomic or sociocultural factors such as poverty and immigration (APA, 2013). In the families of people who have ASPD, discipline is often inconsistent and erratic, and sometimes involves harsh parenting. Conversely, many people with this disorder experience an absence of parental supervision in late childhood and adolescence. This lack of supervision can create a void of guidance and invite opportunities for conduct problems, which are a major risk factor for the development of ASPD in adulthood. They may also struggle to understand that inappropriate behaviors may be temporally pleasurable, but are often associated with significant long-term consequences. Again, an inconsistent home environment and a lack of supervision and guidance may contribute to difficulties in connecting consequences to actions. Secondary to erratic, unsupportive home environments and defensive communication patterns within the family, they may learn to focus only on themselves and their own needs, thus breeding an egocentric mindset (Hiatt & Dishion, 2008). Clients presenting with ASPD are much more likely to be male, but this diagnosis should not be ruled out in females as they too can have ASPD (APA, 2013).

Counselor Considerations

This population does not typically seek treatment to relieve antisocial symptoms; they are more likely to seek treatment to relieve secondary symptoms (e.g., anxiety, depression), or they may be forced into treatment by an external force such as the legal system or a persistent loved one. Since those with ASPD are not generally internally motivated to change aspects of their personality, counselors can benefit from utilizing external motivations to facilitate the change process, and the motivational interviewing and enhancement techniques often used in treating substance use disorders (see Chapter 8) may be useful in increasing their motivation to change.

Counselors should establish a supportive yet structured approach to treatment, which seeks to avoid judgment and punitive positions and provides firm, clear limits around the counselors' and clients' roles and responsibilities (Sadock & Sadock, 2007). The approach used with this population should aim to assist clients in considering the long-term consequences and risks associated with antisocial behaviors. Counselors should avoid an approach that attempts to develop or enhance a sense of remorse or guilt over past actions (as these are rarely helpful), and instead focus on the substantial benefits of prosocial behaviors. Some counselors may experience feelings of animosity and distaste for clients who have a history of exploitive acts (Gunderson & Gabbard, 2000); therefore, appropriate consultation and supervision needs to be in place when working with this population.

When evaluating clients with ASPD, counselors need to fully assess the following areas: antisocial behaviors; personality function including the client's strengths and limitations; any possible comorbid mental disorders (e.g., depression, anxiety, drug and alcohol misuse/abuse/dependence, posttraumatic stress disorders, and other personality disorders); and treatment needs including psychological treatment, or vocational considerations and domestic violence/abuse issues.

Treatment Models and Interventions

The literature offers minimal guidance on evidence-based treatments and interventions for use in treating clients who have ASPD (Duggan, 2009). No randomized controlled trials are currently reported in the literature (Critis-Christoph & Barber, 2007; Duggan, 2009). Because this population is often able to see the advantages of antisocial behaviors, but not the costs of them, many people throughout history have suggested that ASPD is untreatable (Sadock & Sadock, 2007). As previously stated, clients' immediate motivation to change is usually external (e.g., by a court order or another individual), and often only lasts as long as these external pressures are present. Prevention and early intervention with ASPD is needed, and programs geared toward using evidence-based models of intervention with conduct-disordered youth are important. Chapter 12 provides a review of approaches that are useful in treating conduct disordered youth, and thus preventing the development of adult ASPD. This section reviews treatments that provide the most promise for treating those who have ASPD.

While psychotherapies have been routinely associated with success in treating those with ASPD, schema therapy (Young et al., 2003), mentalization-based therapy (Bateman & Fonagy, 2008a), and cognitive behavioral therapy (Rodrigo, Rajapakse, & Jayananda, 2010) show promise.

SCHEMA THERAPY (ST)   ST is an innovative approach that integrates cognitive therapy, behavior therapy, object relations therapy, and gestalt therapy into a unified approach to treatment (Young et al., 2003). This approach is often associated with treating people with borderline personality disorder (see the discussion of this approach in the BPD section for additional information about this therapy), but it also shows promise in treating clients with ASPD. According to ST, early in life people with ASPD develop maladaptive schemas, which are played out in their current relationships. These themes are self-defeating and repeat throughout people's lives. Maladaptive schemas from childhood can be thought of as forming when a child's needs (e.g., safety, acceptance, respect, nurturance, approval) are unmet.

The enhancement of coping styles is another important aspect of ST. From the ST perspective, coping skills can be conceptualized as an individual's behavioral response to their internalized schema. While their responses attempt to compensate for the schema, they often inadvertently reinforce it through their behavior and actions; thus, they create a self-fulfilling prophecy. People who have personality disorders often have maladaptive coping strategies that are overcompensating, surrendering, or avoidant in nature. For example, a person with an abandonment schema may behave out of self-preservation, and therefore limit intimacy in the relationship in a protective stance against past hurts. This withdrawal from others will then only serve to limit intimacy, and ultimately expedite the demise of their relationships.

Schema modes, another aspect of ST, are the daily emotional states made up of a person's schemas and can be thought of as a "temporary way of being" (Young et al., 2003, p. 37). Young et al. (2003) outlined a schema mode specifically for people with ASPD called "bully-and-attack mode." This overacting and even hurting of someone else due to the mistrust, abuse, and feelings of defectiveness experienced in youth characterize this schema mode.

The aim of ST is to help clients heal maladaptive schemas and stop engaging in maladaptive coping styles. This is accomplished by aiding clients in getting their needs met (within and outside the therapeutic relationship), resisting previously controlling schemas and modes, and constructing healthier (more adaptive) schemas and modes.

Interventions that are utilized in this approach consist of imagery rescripting (e.g., revising a difficult childhood memory with an attachment figure and clarifying the connect between memories and triggers), flashcards (e.g., written statements addressing a foreseen difficult situation for review between sessions), chair work (e.g., gestalt chair work between schema [or parts of self] or between figures to resolve unfinished business), and diaries (e.g., structured writing exploring thoughts, feelings, behaviors, schemas, and healthy perspective taking).

MENTALIZATION-BASED THERAPY (MBT)   MBT like schema therapy, is often used when treating people with borderline personality disorder. Mentalization-based therapy also holds promise for treating people with ASPD (Bateman & Fonagy, 2008a). It is a psychodynamic approach that aims to increase people's capacity for mentalization (i.e., ability to recognize one's thoughts, feelings, and desires as they are connected with behaviors and interactions), which theoretically increases their ability to regulate affect and have more meaningful relationships with others.

Those with ASPD often have a long history of misinterpreting others' motives. This misinterpretation in turn creates rigid relationships with very elementary ways of relating and functioning with others. This inflexibility leaves some emotionally vulnerable, for if another person challenges them, they experience this as humiliation. This threat of humiliation is then preemptively met with violence, aggression, and the desire to control others. This lapse in one's ability to mentalize mental states can often be their gateway to violence. Increasing their ability to maintain personal integrity of their own mental states when threatened becomes the focus of treatment. The central goals of MBT are to aid clients in increasing their control over these reactive behaviors, enhancing their ability to regulate affect, developing more meaningful relationships, and increasing their ability to reach their life goals. This approach is intensive in that it integrates individual sessions and group counseling sessions.

COGNITIVE BEHAVIORAL THERAPY (CBT)   CBT offers promise as an effective treatment for those with ASPD (Rodrigo et al., 2010). Some though have argued that counselors should use caution when utilizing CBT because it provides these clients with the needed skills to become better manipulators (Butcher et al., 2010). In a meta-analysis (e.g., using nonrandomized controlled trials), CBT was the most successful intervention for treating antisocial behaviors (Salekin, 2002).

The fundamental goal of CBT is to alter people's thinking, which will in turn impact and alter their behavior (Beck et al., 2004). The structured and directive nature of this approach is well suited for people with ASPD. While some approaches to treating ASPD directly address moral development (i.e., building moral structures externally through perspective taking), CBT attempts to address moral development indirectly by improving a client's cognitive functioning (Beck et al., 2004). Therefore the aim of treatment is to aid clients in moving from more concrete thinking (e.g., impulsive) to more abstract thinking (e.g., alternative options based on situations). These shifts in cognitive functioning can be accomplished through the use of problem-focused work, linking thoughts to maladaptive behaviors, building coping skills, and making constructive choices (Beck et al., 2004).

Taking a structured, problem-focused approach when counseling this population keeps them focused on treatment, and not on treatment distractions (e.g., minimization of problems, attempting to control sessions). Beck et al. (2004) outlined six self-serving beliefs of those with ASPD: justification (e.g., "My desires justify my actions"); thinking is believing (e.g., "My thoughts are fact"); personal infallibility (e.g., "I don't make bad decisions"); feeling makes facts (e.g., "If it is wrong, why does it feel good"); impotence of others (e.g., "Others are irrelevant"); and low-impact consequences (e.g., "Consequences won't happen or won't affect me"). These self-serving beliefs influence automatic thoughts and reactions. Being unaware of these influences, people with ASPD are often confused by others' reactions to them.

The enhancement of coping skills is another intervention that can be utilized when treating people with ASPD. From a CBT perspective, this population may lack the skills needed to interact successful, and thus by developing these skills, meaningful changes can occur. Skills training with these clients involves teaching them perspective taking, communication, emotion regulation, assertiveness, consequential thinking, frustration tolerance, and impulse control (Beck et al., 2004).

Theoretically, the development of these skills can expand their problem-solving skills and ultimately increase appropriate social interactions. For example, by teaching people how to be more consequential in their thinking, they are able to evaluate behaviors before acting. They are then able to select a decision with the best possible outcome. This transition from instant to delayed gratification can enable people with ASPD to avoid the undesirable or painful consequences of impulsive choices.

Making constructive choices is another intervention that can be utilized in CBT treatment. This can be done in a collaborative way using a cost versus benefit ratio as related to decision-making. When developing a ratio, the counselor and the client construct a systematic review of all of the risks and benefits for every alternative to a situation. Table 9.2 provides examples of the core beliefs and assumptions that can be challenged when working from a CBT perspective with this population.

TABLE 9.2   Cognitive Treatment Aims for Those with Personality Disorders

Personality Disorder	Beliefs	Assumptions	Behaviors	Possible Treatment Aims
Antisocial	I am vulnerable Others are exploitive and hurtful	If I act first, then I will not get hurt; If I take what I want, then I will be superior (in charge/in control)	Exploit and take advantage of others	Social sensitivity; reciprocity; develop empathic behaviors
Avoidant	I am defective/broken Others will judge me harshly and see that I am lacking	If people know the real me, they will reject me; If I act like someone else, maybe others will accept me	Avoid others and close relationships; avoid intimacy	Self-assertion; sociability; self-confidence
Borderline	I am unlovable/needy/weak/helpless Others will reject and leave me	If people know the "real me" they will reject me; People will take advantage of me if I let them; People will only pay attention to me if I act in extreme ways	Guarded; feelings get out of control; overidentify with others; strong desire to have someone around at all times; self-sabotaging relationships	Safety; decrease impulsivity/self-injury; emotional regulation; an awareness of their interpersonal impacts, strengths, and deficits
Dependent	I am helpless Others need to take care of me	If I depend on myself, I will fail; If I depend on others, I'll survive	Rely on other people	Self-reliance; self-sufficiency; reciprocal relationships

(Continued)

TABLE 9.2 (Continued)

Personality Disorder	Beliefs	Assumptions	Behaviors	Possible Treatment Aims
Histrionic	I am worthless/nothing Others will not value me	If I am not entertaining and engaging, others will not be attracted to me; If I am not dramatic, I will not get others' attention	Attention-seeking behaviors (by entertaining; by being overly dramatic)	Self-discipline; self-control
Narcissistic	I am inferior Others will not value me "as I am"	If people do not acknowledge me in a special way, then I am inferior	Demanding special treatment and considerations; treating others as if they are inferior; acting as if they are superior	Empathy; reciprocal relationships
Obsessive-Compulsive	I need control Others are irresponsible	If I am not in control, things will fall apart; I need to structure my environment with rules and expectations (rigidly), and then everything will be fine	Control others rigidly	Spontaneity; unconstrained behaviors
Paranoid	I am exposed/vulnerable Others are out to get me	If I trust others, they will harm me; If I am on guard, I can protect myself	Be suspicious of everyone	Trust; reciprocal relationships
Schizoid	I am a loner/different/not normal Others are cruel and out to get me	If I try to befriend others, they will pick up that I am different and ridicule me; If I engage people, they will hurt me	Avoid all contact with others	Intimacy; closeness; affectionate relationships
Schizotypal	I am different/abnormal/worthless Others are cruel and dangerous	If I befriend others, they will reject me; If I have unusual experiences, they must be important; If I let people see me upset, then they will hurt me	Adopt eccentric speech and dress to garner attention; simultaneously avoiding social situations	Self-confidence; reciprocal relationships; awareness of social interactions

PSYCHOPHARMACOTHERAPY A systematic review of controlled studies provided no convincing evidence to suggest the utilization of medications as an intervention in the treatment of ASPD per se (Duggan, 2009). However, medications can be used to treat the secondary symptoms of anxiety, depression, impulsivity, and irritability often found in this population.

Some data suggest that the use of medications in the treatment of impulsive aggression is helpful, but the generalizability of these medications to addressing the whole spectrum of ASPD symptoms is unclear (Markovitz, 2001; Sadock & Sadock, 2007). Anticonvulsant medication (e.g., divalproex, carbamazepine, lithium) may be useful in addressing the symptoms of labile mood and impulsivity (Preston et al., 2013). Selective serotonin reuptake inhibitors (SSRIs) have implications in treating sudden "attacks" of anger, and the blood pressure medication clonidine may reduce levels of agitation and anxiety (Preston et al., 2013).

Prognosis

The treatment prognosis for those with ASPD is not favorable. This may be because they often lack motivation to alter their behaviors, their behaviors have become entrenched, and/or because they are more susceptible to an increased risk of co-occurring disorders such as substance use and depressive disorders. The course or height of symptomology tends to develop around late adolescence and is often persistent throughout adulthood. Treatments tend to be long, structured, and aimed at increasing a client's self-awareness, self-control, social skills, and delayed gratification. While the prognosis for each client varies, some symptoms may diminish with age, leading to the expression of more somatic issues as they age (APA, 2013; Sadock & Sadock, 2007).

NARCISSISTIC PERSONALITY DISORDER

Description of the Disorder and Typical Client Characteristics

As defined by the *DSM-5*, to qualify as having narcissistic personality disorder (NPD) one must have at least five of the following symptoms: a grandiose sense of self-importance; a need for excessive admiration; a sense of entitlement; a belief that one is special and unique; interpersonally exploitive behaviors; a lack of empathy for others; enviousness of others and a perceptions that others are envious of him or her; arrogant behaviors; and finally, a preoccupation with fantasies of success, power, brilliance, beauty, or ideal love (APA,2013). While on the surface, people with NPD appear to be self-aggrandizing and have an inflated sense of self-importance, these characteristics are believed to actually mask a fragile ego.

Those with NPD often seek relationships with people whom they can idealize, and thus see as idealized extensions of themselves; but these relationships are shallow and lack genuine intimacy. A preoccupation with fantasies of superiority, power, beauty, intelligence, or ideal love is common. Their inner lives lack substance, and as such, they engage in pursuits that cover what self-psychology theorist Kohut (1984) referred to as their narcissist wounds. They are especially sensitive to criticism from others, and perceived transgressions can fuel their drive to achieve in ways that garner them the accolades they seek. Those with NPD often engage in self-comparison and experience heightened negative emotions in situations where they feel threatened by another. In work settings, those with NPD easily delegate tasks to others, and people working on a task with a person with NPD may experience frustration at having to complete a disproportionate amount of work. People with NPD do not generally believe that rules and restrictions apply to them, and they will generally cheat or violate rules when they believe there is a limited risk of being caught.

Issues and comorbid disorders such as depression, marital discord, legal issues, and substance abuse may bring clients with NPD into treatment, but they are unlikely to associate their narcissism with their life problems. Clients with NPD often enter counseling by way of significant others or family members who seek help to cope with their problematic behaviors (e.g., infidelity, callous behavior). Clients with NPD may be difficult to work with in counseling as they prefer to view themselves as perfect and have little motivation to change. Furthermore, due to their self-deceptive tendencies, they are unlikely to recognize that their behavior patterns are incongruent and problematic, and many with this disorder mistakenly perceive themselves as possessing noble and admirable qualities. An example of this is the politician who builds an identity around having a strong, altruistic character and sees himself as a pillar of the community, all the while exploiting others for his benefit, lying to the people he "cares" about to get whatever it is he wants, and hurting others to preserve this faux image of "character." Outside of their interpersonal relationships, those with NPD may have the skills and abilities to be high functioning, and their confidence can lead others to believe they are more competent and important than they are.

During initial sessions, clients with NPD will typically spend most of their time attempting to establish a basis for their self-importance. Rather than blatantly boast about their perceived superiorities, they may casually drop this information into conversation to appear nonchalant, especially if they are intelligent and seasoned, and have learned what skills they need to use to get what they want. In group therapy settings, they will frequently give unsolicited advice to other members and attempt to take over as a leader.

For those with NPD, healthy, adaptive social interactions and relationships are significantly hindered because of their concerns with themselves and with keeping up the appearances that are important to them. Those with NPD will take advantage of others to further their own interests, and relationships with others will be superficial. While those with NPD will often idealize their chosen significant other at the onset of a romantic relationship, they will often devalue their partner as time goes on. They may see their children as extensions of themselves, and when their children achieve in ways they see as desirable, they are quick to boast about these successes; yet when their children do not live up to their exacting standards, they place the responsibility on them and are angry and disappointed with them. Tendencies to exaggerate their own accomplishments and minimize those of others can also add strain to relationships with co-workers and significant others. Clients with NPD will be resistant to accepting responsibility for personally and socially destructive behavior, as this would require an admission of fallibility. In situations where an apology or explanation is warranted, a person with NPD will usually blame others or another external factor.

Those with NPD tend to be envious of others and are continually trying to achieve more of whatever it is that feeds their ego. Similarly, they tend to project onto others that they are envious of them and want what they have across a variety of contexts (e.g., wealth, physical appearance, relationships, status positions).

Counselor Considerations

Counselors must be aware that those with NPD can be very manipulative, and they are experts at deceiving themselves, and often others as well. Of clients diagnosed with NPD, 50–75% are male (APA, 2013). Talking about accomplishments can be used as a way to direct counselors' attention away from topics that are perceived as shortcomings. Clients with NPD are guarded, hypervigilant, and easily provoked when they perceive the fidelity of their fragile ego is at stake; they are quick to engage the counselor or others in arguments when feeling threatened. Those with NPD may often interrupt the counselor, as they feel that what they have to say is of greater importance.

To heal what Kohut called their narcissist wounds (1977, 1984), it is necessary to identify these wounds, recognize the role they play in a person's functioning, and actively work on changing these behaviors and reactions. Because people with NPD are so guarded and unamenable to considering their fallibilities or weaknesses, counseling with this population can be challenging. This population rarely seeks counseling unless mandated, and when they do, it is often for relief from co-occurring mental disorders. Counselor feedback and a genuine desire to help may be viewed by clients as domineering or critical behavior. Employing an attentive, validating, respectful, task-focused, and consistent interaction style is advantageous when working with this population. Ronningstam (2012) recommended that counselors working with clients who have NPD do the following to build a strong therapeutic alliance: (a) identify the client's presenting problems and motivation to seek treatment, (b) encourage the client's coherent narrative of internal experiences, (c) build mutually agreed upon perspectives and understanding between client and counselor, (d) focus on the client's divergent, opposite, and incompatible perspectives of self and others, and (e) attend to the client's criticism and transference reactions of anger, disappointment, and retaliation.

Masterson (1981) emphasized that because of the emotional fragility of this population, an extrasupportive therapeutic alliance is required to help heal their developmental arrests. Additionally, a strong *here-and-now* focus in which empathy is conveyed and mirrored (Kohut, 1984) is also helpful. When counseling this population, the therapeutic alliance can be volatile because of their need to continually test others for safety, which in their eyes means being seen in a positive light (Masterson, 1981). Counselors may inadvertently activate clients with NPD, and in these situations, it is important to manage these alliance ruptures or breakdowns. Clients with NPD may shamefully withdraw or become hostile when presented with information that threatens their egos. Masterson (1981) describes counselors' management of these ruptures as similar to the swaddling of a baby who is upset, or like managing a toddler's tantrum. In enveloping, containing, and managing these breakdowns, counselors gain the trust of their clients. If counselors fail to pass these tests, clients' narcissistic injuries will likely result in them dropping out of treatment. Counselors should be comfortable with confrontation should the client act in a deprecatory manner toward the counselor, and be assertive in maintaining personal treatment guidelines should the client challenge them. Monitoring emotions and being self-aware can help counselors to avoid falling into a mutual pattern of engaging in power struggles or ego-defensiveness with a client who has NPD.

Treatment Models and Interventions

No randomized controlled studies on treating NPD could be found in the literature. This section reviews the treatments that have been most frequently discussed in the literature for use with NPD.

PSYCHODYNAMIC As previously mentioned, an understanding of NPD and how to treat it has been most informed by psychodynamic approaches. From a psychodynamic approach, the most effective treatment will be longer-term, insight-oriented, and focused on the relationship between the counselor and client (Kohut, 1984; Kernberg, 2000). With regard to treating narcissism from a psychodynamic approach, two overlapping approaches dominate the literature: the self-psychology approach (Kohut, 1977, 1984), and the object relations approach (Kernberg, 2000). These theories are dynamic and complex, and a thorough review of them is beyond the scope of this text. Readers are invited to read the cited classic references to garner a greater understanding of these theories and their applications. Following is a greatly simplified overview of the two leading psychodynamic theories that relate to treating pathological narcissism, self-psychology and object relations theory.

Heinz Kohut's self-psychology (1984) is considered foundational to an understanding of narcissism. Kohut suggested that narcissism is a component of everyone's psychology. We are all born as narcissists, but over time, our infantile narcissism matures into a healthy adult narcissism. Kohut suggested that our sense of self develops early in life and in response to our interactions with early caregivers. Children fail to develop healthy self-esteem when parents do not respond with approval to their children's displays of competency. Kohut believed that when parents respond to children with warmth, respect, and empathy, children develop healthy self-esteem.

According to Kohut, children whose self-esteem is neglected do not develop an ability to accept or tolerate their own shortcomings, and thus they develop narcissistic wounds. Repeated wounds can then develop into pathological narcissism, thus resulting in repeated attempts to bolster one's sense of self through unending quests for love, approval, and success. These efforts to fill one's self up in this way can be viewed as external attempts to shield oneself from vulnerability and ensure that narcissistic wounds are not exposed.

An important term relating to Kohut's theory is mirroring. Mirroring involves a self–object transference of mirroring and idealization. To clarify, Kohut believed that all children have a normal need to idealize and emotionally identify with the idealized competence of figures whom they admire (i.e., caregivers). They also need to have their self-worth reflected back by these trusted, idealized figures. Kohut suggested that pathological narcissism results from a normal, maturationally determined need to be mirrored by and to idealize the parental figures during early stages of development (i.e., the pre-oedipal phase of development). If the child's need for mirroring is not adequately responded to, the child searches in all relationships for what was experienced as missing.

Conceptually, Kohut's model of narcissism can be understood as involving a type of arrested development. It is the counselor's task, according to Kohut, to meet the client where he or she became arrested. The counselor does this by providing an environment in which the client has the experience of having his or her narcissistic needs responded to in such a way as to allow the client to develop a more cohesive self-system.

Kohut (1984) saw client resistance and defensiveness as a predictable, healthy part of the treatment process and stated: "My personal preference is to speak about the defensiveness of patients and to think of their defensive attitudes as adaptive and psychologically valuable and not of their resistances" (p. 114).

Kernberg's object relations theory of narcissism (1976, 2000) is based on Mahler's theory of the separation-individuation process in infancy and early childhood (which was discussed in relation to borderline personality disorder earlier in this chapter). To summarily review, Mahler's model addressed the ways a developing child gains a stable self-concept by successfully mastering different separation individuation stages in infancy and early childhood. Kernberg believed that those with pathological narcissism are unable to successfully master the rapprochement subphase (age 14 to 24 months) of Mahler's model and become fixated. The practicing subphase (age 10 to 14 months) precedes the rapprochement subphase and is the developmental stage during which the child learns to walk. This ability to freely move about gives the child a new perspective of the world and provides the child with a sense of grandiosity and omnipotence (which closely resemble the experience of those with NPD). During the subsequent stage, the rapprochement subphase (age 14 to 24 months), the child discovers that he or she is not omnipotent, and that there are limits and consequences related to what he or she can do. Kernberg suggested that if the child is severely frustrated at this stage, he or she can adapt by returning to the practicing subphase, which affords him or her the psychological security associated with a sense of grandiosity and omnipotence.

In Kernberg's object relations theory, objects (e.g., other people) are viewed as an extension of the self. Often the person chooses to merge with objects that represent aspects of the self that the person feels are inferior. For example, if a person feels unintelligent he or she will seek to merge with someone who is perceived to be intelligent. If someone feels powerless, he or she will merge with someone perceived to be powerful. Slightly less pathological, some acknowledge the separateness of the object; however, they view the object as similar to themselves in the sense that they share a similar quality or makeup. In other words, the person perceives the object is "just like me." The least of the pathological ways of relating to objects is when the object is seen as both separate and different, but the person is unable to appreciate the object as a unique and separate person. The object thus becomes perceived as useful only to the extent of its ability to aggrandize the person's false identity.

While Kernberg and Kohut's theories have much in common, they are, in many ways, unique. Kernberg's (2000) theory of narcissism diverged from Kohut's work in several ways. First, they differed in their emphasis on normality. Kernberg believed that narcissism does not result from arrests in the normal maturation of infantile narcissism, but instead narcissism represents a fixation in a developmental period of early childhood. More specifically, someone with pathological narcissism becomes fixated at a developmental stage in which the person cannot differentiate between the self and others.

Kernberg (2000) also suggested that the job of the counselor is to actively interpret the client's narcissistic defenses while at the same time highlighting the client's negative transferences. Kernberg believed the objective of treatment was to eradicate or diminish the client's grandiose sense of self by directly confronting defenses.

Kernberg placed a strong emphasis on people's aggression and aggressive impulses as contributing to pathological narcissism. He suggested that aggressive impulses contributed to the person developing narcissistic defenses. Kernberg, more than Kohut, also emphasized analyzing narcissistic resistances. He believed that it was only by confronting and interpreting these resistances, particularly the transference resistances, that one could expose and work through his or her defenses.

In contrast, Kohut advocated for an empathic approach to working with this population, one in which the counselor encourages the client's grandiosity and promotes the development of idealization as a part of the transference process. Kohut cautioned against tearing down clients' defenses.

In practice, most psychodynamic practitioners fuse elements of both Kernberg's and Kohut's psychodynamic approaches to treating narcissism. An approach that emphasizes flexibility and an empathic understanding of the clients' needs that honors their need for narcissistic defenses combined with a thorough exploration of those defenses is generally preferred.

COGNITIVE BEHAVIORAL THERAPY (CBT)   CBT approaches view narcissistic tendencies as compensatory reactions stemming from core beliefs of unimportance or inferiority. When using CBT, counselors will help clients recognize their maladaptive thinking styles, replace them with healthy alternatives, and change their resulting behavior. Beck et al. (2004) suggested that the following NPD/CBT treatment objectives: (a) exploring the meaning of success as related to the desire for goal attainment and mastery; (b) increasing interpersonal skills (e.g., self-awareness of boundaries and the perspectives of others); and (c) constructing alternatives to maladaptive beliefs about self-worth and emotions. Role-playing and exercises in which clients are given an opportunity to test their core beliefs about themselves and others can be particularly helpful. Table 9.2 provides examples of the core beliefs and assumptions that can be challenged when working from a CBT perspective with this population.

SCHEMA-FOCUSED THERAPY (ST)   ST (Young et al., 2003) was discussed in some detail with regard to antisocial personality disorder and borderline personality disorder treatment, and as such, a thorough review of its tenets will not be provided in this section. Again, when using ST, treatment focuses on adjusting maladaptive narcissistic schemas that clients formed during childhood and young adulthood when their needs were not met. The counselor educates the client about schemas and helps the client to recognize the schemas that contribute to his or her behavior in maladaptive ways. Clients are asked to identify and confront their cognitive distortions (e.g., need for perfection) and maladaptive coping strategies that they developed as a result of their schema development (i.e., narcissistic patterns of thinking and behavior). The counseling relationship serves as a healing environment in which missed steps of childhood development can be completed.

METACOGNITIVE INTERPERSONAL THERAPY (MIT)   The goal of an MIT approach to treating NPD is to decrease clients' unconscious fears of vulnerability and build their confidence so that they will be less sensitive to feedback from others (DiMaggio & Attina, 2012). Through an MIT approach, anger and hostility in social interaction will be reduced, and clients can learn to value their efforts, even if they do not meet their high expectations (DiMaggio & Attina, 2012). MIT requires the client to discuss autobiographical information in great detail, while the counselor uses this information to collaboratively work with the client to identify emotional states and triggers in the narratives. The counselor then works to help clients recognize the connections between their emotional triggers and their resulting reactions. A primary focus on helping the client gain insight into his or her dysfunctional patterns of thinking and behaving is required before change can take place. Assisting clients in setting realistic standards, becoming more aware of their own and others' emotions, increasing empathy, and incorporating healthier patterns of thinking and behaving into their lives can be used as vehicles for positive change (DiMaggio & Attina, 2012).

PSYCHOPHARMACOTHERAPY   As with the other personality disorders, there is no medication that has been established as useful in treating the symptoms of NPD. However, medications may be useful in addressing comorbid disorders. SSRIs may decrease vulnerability to criticism, anger, and impulsivity in this population. Anxiety and depression that present with NPD can be treated with medication and may diminish the severity of some NPD symptoms.

Prognosis

People with NPD are challenging to treat and may require years of treatment before any enduring change is noted (Sperry, 2003). As with all disorders, higher levels of functioning predict better treatment outcomes. It is important to note that counseling will not "cure" clients of narcissistic tendencies, but rather, it helps them to deal with their NPD in ways that will enhance their quality of life. Prognosis varies and depends on factors such as the client's motivation to change, his or her level of insight into problems, comorbid diagnoses, and the severity of the disorder.

OBSESSIVE-COMPULSIVE PERSONALITY DISORDER

Description of the Disorder and Typical Client Characteristics

Obsessive-compulsive personality disorder (OCPD) is characterized by an excessive and inappropriate concern with maintaining order and control, and it is diagnosed twice as often in males as in females (APA, 2013). This population is typically preoccupied with schedules, lists, rules, and organization, and they use these as a vehicle for maintaining a sense of control. While many of these tendencies may be adaptive and increase work efficiency, people with this disorder take them to an extreme, and they are often counterproductive. Because of a pervasive need for control and fear of making mistakes, they often become immersed in minor details and are unable to complete tasks in a timely manner. They may also focus on work to the extent that they struggle to integrate leisure activities into their lives.

Decision-making can be problematic for people with OCPD because they fear making the wrong choice. A preference is shown for situations in which there is a clear "right" answer. They are unlikely to be generous in sharing time or money for any activity that they do not feel is rewarding, and they are often viewed by others as very frugal. While they may excel at work, deficits exist in social functioning and interpersonal relationships.

They often enter counseling secondary to threats of losing a job or a significant relationship, stress-related medical problems, anxiety, and/or depression. They typically do not recognize the connections between their problems and their behavior. In sessions, they may take a perfectionistic approach towards the counseling process, and have difficulty staying focused on the concepts behind treatment interventions.

Relationships with significant others and family members will likely be strained because of the client's tendencies to be critical, demanding, and controlling. Rigid adherence to ethical, moral, and religious beliefs and expecting others to accept them can be a source of conflict for those interacting with people with OCPD. They are often intolerant of their own perceived flaws, as well as those of others, which can be problematic in social functioning. Little true emotion is displayed as it is viewed as a source of vulnerability, and affect is generally limited and pervaded by hostility. Concepts of intimate relationships may be skewed from the norm, and they may appear emotionally detached. Loyalty and trust are expected from significant others, but emotional vulnerability is avoided. Problems in the home may also be exacerbated by a need to hoard money and items of no apparent value. They may be reluctant to discard items, though they are broken or no longer serve a discernable purpose. Frugality and unwillingness to part with money for any cause that does not directly reward the client can also create difficulties in interpersonal relationships.

While many clients with OCPD excel at work secondary to their habitual diligence, their interactions with coworkers and employers may be troubled. Others may view them as perfectionistic, serious, stubborn, rigid, and inflexible, especially in relation to values, ethics, and morals. They often experience difficulties delegating tasks, supervising, or collaborating with others, because they may view others as incompetent or unable to work to their personal standards (McGlashan et al., 2005). They may take issue with superiors and authority figures whom they view as incompetent, or as not providing deserved recognition for their work. Their competitive nature, difficulty being aware of and communicating feelings, and general view of others as incompetent, make collaboration difficult for those with OCPD. Perfectionistic tendencies can also negatively impact the completion of their own work and cause clients to miss time deadlines. Although clients with OCPD may have substantial accomplishments, they may not be satisfied or acknowledge their accolades. In times of crisis and discomfort, clients will display an even stricter adherence to their obsessive-compulsive behaviors.

Clients presenting with OCPD may have experienced a rigid upbringing in which parents were overprotective, unavailable, or controlling. As children, their parents may have expected total obedience and called attention to mistakes through punishment. Cultural and religious backgrounds that emphasize strict adherence to set morals and values (e.g., out of fear of punishment by God, to protect the honor of the family) may also play a role in the development of OCPD personality traits.

OCPD is distinguishable from obsessive-compulsive disorder (OCD), but it can be diagnosed comorbidly. While symptomology may be similar, clear-cut differences exist between these disorders. Those with OCPD typically view their tendencies as adaptive, while OCD sufferers identify their symptoms as problematic and burdensome. OCD causes difficulty in functioning in all aspects of daily life, while OCPD causes deficits primarily in social functioning. Obsessions and compulsive behavior do not vary with time in OCPD, and are typically consistently present throughout the lifespan.

Counselor Considerations

Counselors must be aware that clients who have OCPD are often uncomfortable entering counseling because of a perceived lack of control in the situation, discomfort with discussing emotions, and limited insight into personal problems. Because they generally feel that others are incompetent, the formation of a therapeutic relationship is challenging and may take a considerable amount of time. They may have difficulty in engaging the counselor and can appear mechanical in conversation.

Formation of a therapeutic alliance in the early stages of counseling is fundamental, as it has been shown to be predictive of a reduction in pathological personality symptoms in clients with OCPD (Strauss, Hayes, & Johnson, 2006). Placing little value on interpersonal relationships and mistrust of others can impede the establishment of rapport. Patience is required in working with this population, as they may spend a great deal of time questioning and challenging the counselor. Counselors should also be sure to avoid engaging in a power struggle with this population.

Clients may react with hostility toward the counselor, most notably when changes or encouraging assumption of responsibility have been suggested. Counselors should monitor their verbal and nonverbal behavior, as clients with OCPD may be selectively attuned to behavior that can be interpreted as criticism or rejection in anticipation of negative social interaction. This population may challenge the competency of their counselors and assert that they do not require counseling. Counselors should also be mindful of clients' attempts to avoid discussing emotional information and be willing to redirect the conversation. Clients with OCPD may attempt to take control of the session by changing the subject or disputing the counselor. It is also common for clients with OCPD to avoid discussing uncomfortable emotions by sharing elaborate anecdotes with little actual detail. People with OCPD often have grievances against others and are quick to place blame for their problems on them.

This population is likely to terminate treatment prematurely. Treatment goals should be realistic and take into account the discomfort and anxiety they experience in situations of change, uncertainty, and emotional vulnerability. Counselors should be comfortable involving the client in the formulation of appropriately attainable goals, as this will give clients a sense of control and security. Counselors should also be alert for signs that a client is being superficially compliant in lieu of actual change.

Treatment Models and Interventions

No randomized controlled studies of treatments for OCPD have been documented in the literature. In this section, the treatments that have been most frequently discussed in the literature for use with this population, cognitive behavioral therapy (CBT) and dialectical behavior therapy (DBT), will be reviewed. In addition to CBT and DBT, psychodynamic therapy (Simon, 2009) and metacognitive interpersonal therapy (Dimaggio, Semerari, Carcione, Nicolò, & Procacci, 2007 have been used to treat OCPD.

Regardless of the treatment approach, a recent meta-analysis revealed that OCPD tends to be more apt to change than any other Cluster C personality disorder (Simon, 2009). Additionally, those with a Cluster C diagnosis appear to benefit more from therapeutic intervention than clients with a Cluster A or Cluster B personality disorder diagnosis (Simon, 2009). Interventions across therapeutic orientations may focus on one or more of the following universal goals in working with clients with OCPD: (a) decreasing obsessive thought patterns, (b) reducing participation in compulsive behavior, (c) gaining awareness into one's own emotions and those of others, (d) decreasing fear of emotional vulnerability, (e) increasing range of emotional expression, (f) reducing need to control others and situations, and (g) developing more appropriate expectations of self and others.

Medication is generally not recommended for the treatment of OCPD (de Reus & Emmelkamp, 2012). However, comorbid diagnoses, such as anxiety and depression, may benefit from treatment using medication.

COGNITIVE BEHAVIORAL THERAPY (CBT) CBT is the most researched treatment modality for use with those who have OCPD. The active, structured, problem-focused, and concrete approach that CBT employs may be more suitable for this population than insight-oriented approaches, which place a premium on self-analysis and the expression of emotion; characteristics that are antithetical to those who have OCPD (Beck et al., 2004; Millon, Grossman, Millon, Meaghern, & Ramnath, 2004). Challenging dichotomous and automatic thinking may be particularly useful with this population, as these thinking patterns are characteristic of the diagnosis. Role-reversal exercises between the counselor and client can assist in recognizing and disputing automatic thoughts. Development of coping-statements to manage automatic thoughts may also be helpful.

Cost-benefit analysis can be used to assist clients in gaining insight into how their behaviors are affecting their lives and others. Taking a problem-solving approach that highlights prioritizing problems, setting an agenda, and approaching one issue at a time can provide clients with a linear, logical, and thus comfortable, approach to addressing their problems. Counselors must be careful in selecting exercises and in using appropriate timing so as not to cause the client increased distress. Asking a client to engage in an experiment to change compulsive behavior early in the treatment process may result in significant anxiety and premature termination. Table 9.2 provides examples of the core beliefs and assumptions that can be challenged when working from a CBT perspective with this population.

DIALECTICAL BEHAVIOR THERAPY (DBT) DBT, commonly used for the treatment of borderline personality disorder, has also been suggested for use with clients with OCPD. In applying DBT, counseling sessions are used to teach the client skills that increase flexibility to new experiences, decrease rigid thinking, and reduce compulsive behavior so as to increase the client's overall quality of life. Lynch and Cheavens (2008) suggested a sequential model of therapy that: (a) decreases behavioral avoidance; (b) decreases negative emotions toward others (e.g., hostility, bitterness, distrust); (c) decreases emotional suppression; (d) decreases rigid thinking patterns; and (e) decreases compulsive behavior (e.g., bias toward confirmatory information, checking for mistakes). Homework may be assigned to practice skills acquired in sessions and can include participating in leisure activities, being mindful of own/others' judgments, and practicing prosocial behavior (Lynch & Cheavens, 2008).

Prognosis

The prognosis for those with OCPD varies, and without appropriate interventions, symptoms will likely remain relatively stable over time. Although their adherence to details, rules, order, and neatness tend to isolate them from others, their rigidity to these ideals, as well as their inability to deal with the unexpected, prevent most from experiencing dramatic changes even with treatment. The risks and challenges associated with making behavioral changes may invoke too much anxiety and preclude any attempts to make significant changes. They may only seek or stay in counseling to address comorbid issues, and not personality functioning.

AVOIDANT PERSONALITY DISORDER

Description of the Disorder and Typical Client Characteristics

People who have avoidant personality disorder (AVPD) tend to be timid, socially hypersensitive, and inhibited in new situations because of their feelings of inadequacy (APA, 2013). While they can present as being withdrawn, they typically desire close relationships. Because of their intense feelings of inferiority and fear of rejection, they warrant unconditional acceptance before ever entering into a relationship. Since this is not normally afforded to people in emerging relationships, they often have very few close relationships. In turn, they tend to be self-effacing and may go out of their way to please others.

Hypersensitivity to rejection and emotional frailty are the hallmarks of those with AVPD. The possibility of rejection leads them to be socially withdrawn; they tend to be averse to taking social risks and are plagued by fears of humiliation (e.g., being evaluated due to not behaving in a socially acceptable way). Without treatment, they often remain withdrawn, socially detached, and distrustful of others.

Traits of social anxiety, self-consciousness, shyness, and inhibition are highly inheritable. Some argue, though, that genetic predispositions alone are insufficient to cause AVPD, and in fact, environmental conditions and experiences are necessary to transfer these traits into a long-standing pattern of avoidant behaviors (Eggum et al., 2009). Some suggest that avoidant behaviors are the manifestation of persistent thoughts of inferiority and irrational cognitions, which perpetuate an inverted stance when interacting with others (Beck et al., 2004). Deficits in interpersonal functioning have an accumulative effect on this population's sense of insecurity and shyness secondary to their continual experience of perceived embarrassment and judgment.

Family of origin issues may provide some insight into the development of this disorder. Some suggest that families of those with AVPD may have been controlling and overly critical, frequently requiring their child to present in a positive light (Sperry, 2003). As a result, the child was not able to fully develop social skills (e.g., an ability to respond to conflict), and thus developed a limited social competence. As such, the child became socially withdrawn, shy, timid, and had poor peer relationships. This internalized experience, whether coupled with parental rejection or not, led the child to internalize intense fears of rejection and harsh self-criticism; and to develop a strong mistrust of others, which then led to behavioral, emotional, and cognitive avoidance of interactions with others.

Counselor Considerations

Because of their self-consciousness and fear of possible embarrassment, those with AVPD rarely seek treatment. When they do seek treatment, they often do so to address anxiety symptoms usually related to stifling social anxiety disorder (First & Tasman, 2004), or depressive symptoms. Once in treatment, this population is unlikely to fully disclose the spectrum of their symptoms, and they usually present with depressive or anxiety issues.

Counselors should recognize that people with AVPD have pervasive pathology involving interpersonal insecurity and low self-esteem, which is different from the typical shyness observed within the general population. It is paramount that a counselor conveys availability, empathy, acceptance, and support, and builds on the clients' strengths.

Counselors working with this population may become frustrated because of the slow change process. Sustaining this population in treatment is often difficult because of the nature of their disorder; they may avoid attending sessions by cancelling, coming late, or not coming prepared for sessions. Counselors can utilize these avoidance opportunities to be supportive while also enhancing their awareness of the feelings, attitudes, and behaviors that are related to the avoidance. Additionally, counselors need to consistently evaluate their own levels of countertransference as it may relate to this disorder. For example, some counselors may feel overprotective of clients with this disorder, or they may establish unrealistic treatment goals (Sperry, 2003).

Counselors must assess the potential role of cultural factors in influencing a client's avoidant behavior. Differences in cultural norms and problems related to acculturation may lead to behaviors that are interpreted as avoidant or reserved (APA, 2013).

Because of their fears of rejection and humiliation, this population often has issues with employment, and they may require career counseling or access to vocational services. Their interpersonal fears may drive them to assume job positions that are significantly below their competency level because they believe they will be evaluated less harshly (Sperry, 2003). Additionally, these lower level positions may require little social interactions and may be void of possible advancement, thus precluding any possibility of rejection. Usually, if a person with this disorder is forced into social situations in the workplace, he or she may remain shy and timid around others, being hypervigilant about rejection and requiring constant reassurance.

Treatment Models and Interventions

Only two randomized controlled studies have been conducted on the treatment of AVPD (Alden, 1989; Emmelkamp et al., 2006). Both studies suggested that a behavior therapy or a cognitive behavioral therapy approach were beneficial. In the following sections, behavior therapy, cognitive behavioral therapy, schema therapy, and psychopharmacotherapy will be discussed in relation to treating people with AVPD.

BEHAVIOR THERAPY (BT) BT is one of the more researched treatment approaches used with clients who have AVPD (Critis-Christoph & Barber, 2007). Whether utilizing it as a stand-alone treatment or integrating it into another treatment modality, BT and the interventions associated with it should be an essential component in providing treatment to this population. The following interventions (i.e., gradual exposure, social skills training, and guided imagery) are associated with BT and the treatment of AVPD (Alden, 1989; Renneberg, Goldstein, Phillips, & Chambless, 1990).

Gradual Exposure or Systematic Desensitization The utilization of gradual exposure or systematic desensitization is an effective intervention with people who have AVPD (Alden, 1989; Renneberg et al., 1990). This behavioral intervention has historically been effective in treating social phobias and may be helpful in addressing the social anxiety component of AVPD. Systematic desensitization, which is based on classical conditioning tenets, attempts to substitute a relaxation response for an anxiety or fear response. To provide the greatest impact, this behavioral intervention needs to be tailored to the person's specific fears or anxieties. A counselor can aid this process by having clients with AVPD construct a gradual hierarchy of fears (e.g., starting with the least feared situations and moving to the most feared situations). Concurrently, clients are trained in relaxation techniques that can be used to lessen their anxiety as they approach the fears. These relaxation techniques can involve deep breathing, progressive muscle relaxation, or even visualization. Utilization of relaxation techniques takes practice; therefore, in-session skill building is recommended. This in-session skill building is called behavioral rehearsal. Behavioral rehearsal involves practicing new behaviors in the safety of sessions through the use of demonstrations and role-play; this is essential to the transfer of skills into real-world scenarios. Additionally, relaxation skills are critical, because once mastered, the client can eventually either visually imagine the stressful social situations (i.e., in vitro) or gradually experience the anxiety-producing social situation (i.e., in vivo). While additional research is warranted, this treatment intervention suggests some promise in treating AVPD.

Interpersonal Social Skills Training   Interpersonal social skills training is an important component of effective treatment for those who have AVPD (Alden, 1989; Renneberg et al., 1990). This population typically needs behavioral skills training in nonverbal communication, engaging in conversations, being assertive, discussing sexuality, and dealing with issues of conflict management. These skills can be modeled and practiced in sessions and then replicated outside of sessions.

The "acting as if" intervention is an example of one intervention that can be helpful in transitioning from within-session practice to outside-of-session implementation. Using this intervention, clients are invited to act "as if" they have the skill they seek. For example, if clients have difficulty talking to someone new because they lack confidence, they might act "as if" they do have confidence. Clients are often surprised by how well they are able to connect with these ideal behaviors. The "acting as if" intervention provides clients with an opportunity to examine the desired behavior in a given situation.

Guided Imagery   Guided imagery is a behavior therapy intervention involving the intentional, directed use of imagery techniques. Often, guided imagery is used to induce a relaxed state and to visualize an improved life circumstance and a more mindful experience of a situation. In utilizing all of a client's senses, a counselor can verbally walk through a situation using positive thoughts and regulating negative emotional experiences. Guided imagery can be used with those with AVPD as a means of helping them to visualize improved social situations, thus allowing them to connect with a better way of managing stressful interpersonal situations. Guided imagery helps to develop a client's ability to connect with positive and optimistic images of their present and their future. Guided imagery, then, is a helpful intervention in increasing one's comfort with and ability to tolerate and manage social situations.

COGNITIVE BEHAVIORAL THERAPY (CBT)   Considering the underlying assumptions of persons with AVPD (e.g., fear of rejection, self-criticism, irrational assumptions about relationships, misevaluation of others' reactions, discounting positive data), and the fact that they often utilize behavioral, emotional, and cognitive avoidance to deal with dysphoria, CBT is an approach that may help this population. Through CBT a counselor can test clients' automatic thoughts, challenging and aiding in the replacement of these thoughts so as to help counter self-criticism, negative prediction, maladaptive assumptions, and misevaluation of others' reactions. Beck et al. (2004) suggested four stages of treatment that can be useful when working from a CBT perspective with this population: (a) establishing a trusting relationship with clients and discussing their fears of rejection; (b) increasing clients' abilities to perceive their patterns of self-defeating, self-destructive thoughts and behaviors; (c) utilizing the therapeutic relationship to aid clients in evaluating beliefs and increasing skills through role-plays that then can be implemented in the real world; and (d) integrating affect management to increase clients' abilities to tolerate dysphoria and anxiety. These recommendations are helpful in laying the foundation for counselors working from a CBT approach.

The counselor's central aim in treating those with AVPD from a CBT perspective is to increase their emotional tolerance and reduce avoidance. By evoking emotions in sessions and then not allowing them to distract or avoid discussing them, a counselor can highlight clients' avoidance patterns and target their dysfunctional automatic thoughts. Because people with AVPD often avoid these negative emotions and thoughts, any interventions that educate them and expose them to these experiences can help them to tolerate and become more comfortable being with their negative feelings. One way to aid clients in building assertiveness is to ask clients to fill out a counselor feedback form at the end of each session. This form can rate a counselor's ability to listen, communicate expectations, and any relevant components of the process or content of sessions. If the counselor assumes a nondefensive stance in reviewing the feedback (during the start of the next session), the client can see how assertiveness can alter relationships and be reinforced to eventually provide feedback verbally in sessions.

An additional consideration in the treatment of persons with AVPD is relapse prevention. Due to the nature of avoidant symptomology, clients can easily slip into old patterns of interacting. Often, through treatment, progress is made in behavioral arenas (e.g., developing new relationships, expressing opinions, being assertive when appropriate, taking on new tasks at home and work) and cognitive arenas (e.g., becoming aware of automatic thoughts, underlying assumptions, responding to negative cognitions). One intervention that may be helpful in ensuring changes are retained is the use of flashcards. Clients can utilize flashcards with an old belief (e.g., "If people really knew me, they would leave me") on one side with the evidence against that belief (e.g., "Ava, my neighbor, knows me and is still my close friend") under it. Then on the other side of the flashcard, a client can put the new, more functional belief (e.g., "People do like me and do not leave me"). After treatment, these flashcards can remind clients of their progress, while also providing a means to prevent slips toward old patterns. Table 9.2 provides examples of the core beliefs and assumptions that can be challenged when working from a CBT perspective with this population.

 Clinical Toolbox 9.5: In the Pearson etext, click here to read an example of an activity that can be used to help clients challenge avoidant thought processes.

SCHEMA THERAPY (ST) In a qualitative study, Coon (2004) reported successful treatment of ASPD utilizing ST. Clinical gains were observed at termination and at follow-up. ST

(Young et al., 2003) is discussed (in detail) in the BPD and ASPD sections of this chapter. As previously stated, maladaptive schemas from childhood can be thought of as occurring when a child's needs (e.g., safety, acceptance, respect, nurturance, approval) are unmet. If unmet, these needs can transform into personality disorders or patterns of interacting with the world in adulthood. People who have personality disorders often have maladaptive coping strategies that are overcompensating, surrendering, or avoidant in nature.

According to ST, avoidance strategies are believed to stem from unmet needs such as approval, self-expression, acceptance, and attention. The aim of treatment is to make a client aware of these strategies, connect present behaviors with childhood events, and replace them with more adaptive strategies. Imagery can be utilized to help clients reflect on a significant childhood event and engage others associated with those events in an attempt to see how unmet needs and maladaptive schemas developed. When using schema therapy, throughout treatment, counselors will challenge clients to find evidence to refute their maladaptive schemas. An example of this may be a person holding to the schema that "I'm unlikable and defective." The person is supported and challenged to confront this assumption by finding examples of when people have liked him or her. Additionally, a counselor can facilitate a hypothetical debate between the emerging healthy-side of the adult with the maladaptive schema-side (e.g., chair work intervention). Letter writing to caregivers, role-plays, imagery, flashcards, and structured diaries are other interventions often associated with ST.

PSYCHOPHARMACOTHERAPY Medications are not generally used to treat AVPD per se. This population may feel uncomfortable with the idea of taking psychotropic medications. In situations where clients' feelings of anxiousness and social anxiety are markedly disruptive to their current functioning, medication may be helpful in alleviating symptoms. Medication may aid in overcoming the initial overwhelming feelings of fear and anxiety associated with treatment and help clients engage in treatment.

People with AVPD may respond well to anxiolytic medications and antidepressants (e.g., monoamine oxidase inhibitors [MAOIs] and selective serotonin reuptake inhibitors; Koenigsberg et al., 2007; Markovitz, 2001). Studies have demonstrated that MAOIs can successfully reduce rejection sensitivity and other symptoms related to a fear of social interaction (Preston et al., 2013). Imipramine, a tricyclic antidepressant, may be useful in treating high levels of separation anxiety and panic attacks (Sadock & Sadock, 2007). The use of benzodiazepines may be useful during behavioral experiments to reduce anxiety, but will not alter the cause of anxiety and presents a risk of dependence and abuse with long-term treatment (Preston et al., 2013). While medication may alleviate some symptoms associated with AVPD, psychosocial therapies are recommended to address underlying pathology and stimulate long-term change (Preston et al., 2013).

Prognosis

The prognosis for those with AVPD varies and can depend on the severity of the disorder as well as comorbid issues. Like all of the personality disorders, change can be slow due to the pervasive nature of the disorder. The tendency to avoid, which is central to this disorder, can make AVPD more difficult to treat than some other personality disorders (Kvarstein & Karterud, 2011). Clients with AVPD may prematurely terminate counseling and may avoid fully engaging in the treatment process.

While behavioral change can occur, most people with AVPD wrestle with feelings of inferiority and self-doubt (Sadock & Sadock, 2007). Within protected environments, this population is able to function marginally. However, if social support systems fail, they risk an increase in the possibility of social avoidance, anxiety, and depression (Sadock & Sadock, 2007).

DEPENDENT PERSONALITY DISORDER

Description of the Disorder and Typical Client Characteristics

Those with dependent personality disorder (DPD) are identified by their long-standing and excessive need to be taken care of, which leads to their intense fear of separation; and thus subservient, clinging behaviors (APA, 2013). Beck et al. (2004) stated that those with DPD often hold onto two assumptions that feed their disorder: (a) they are inadequate and helpless in a dangerous, frightening world; and (b) they need to find someone who can help them navigate this world, someone who will protect and care for them. People with this disorder find it difficult to make life decisions independently, often needing significant reassurance before making any decisions. They tend to depend on others and will avoid disagreements because of their fears of rejection. They are considered "people pleasers" and are hypersensitive to others' rejection, disapproval, and criticism.

The fear of abandonment is crippling for people with DPD, resulting in overreliance, submissiveness, and clinging behaviors in relationships. People with DPD tend to experience significant distress and worry excessively when separated from a close, dependent relationship. If a close relationship should happen to be terminated, they will, although emotionally overwhelmed, attempt to replace that individual with another whom they deem competent to care for them. In turn, this new individual will then adopt a dominant, decision-making role in their life.

Those with DPD typically have low self-esteem, low self-confidence, and are self-critical. They assume they have nothing of value to offer others, and therefore they place themselves in submissive roles (e.g., a one-down position), believing this is the only way they will be accepted by another. They often think in dichotomous, rigid, absolute terms (e.g., "I am too inadequate to handle my life, I need someone else" or "If I was independent, I would be all alone"), and they have a tendency to catastrophize (e.g., "If I am independent, I will be completely alone, I can't survive like that, I will fall apart"; Beck et al., 2004; Millon et al., 2004).

Childhood environmental factors may impact the development of DPD (Eskedal & Demetri, 2006). Authoritarian and overprotective parenting styles appear to create dependency in children (Bornstein, 1996). As children, this population often displayed fearful, sad, and withdrawing temperaments. They have been excessively submissive, and they may have had chronic physical complaints and separation anxiety issues during childhood (APA, 2013). Within the home, personal autonomy may have been significantly discouraged, and expectations to behave perfectly may have been placed on the child (Millon et al., 2004). These families may have been overly controlling, overly protective, and discouraging of all forms of self-expression. As children, they may have been filled with self-doubt, withdrawn, avoided competitive activities, and experienced frustrating social interactions (Sperry, 2003).

Those with DPD tend to have few significant relationships, and they may even be dissatisfied with their current, dependent relationships, but stay because of their fears of abandonment (or their fears of being alone). They will often endure abusive, unfaithful relationships to maintain their sense of attachment. Overall, people with DPD may experience little happiness and have an underlying pessimistic attitude towards life.

Occupationally, they may function in competent ways if they are within rigidly structured environments where feedback and approval is continual. They struggle significantly when asked to be creative, think independently, or take the initiative on an assignment or a project. People with DPD often feel helplessness when others externally require them to be independent. They may often appear indecisive, incompetent, and consumed by anxiety. Because of their lack of self-confidence, they often experience intense anxiety even in anticipation of new responsibilities.

Counselor Considerations

Those with DPD often seek treatment after the loss of an attachment figure (e.g., divorce, death), or secondary to the request of another (e.g., partner, family member, friend). Secondary symptoms (e.g., anxiety, depression, substance-related issues) are often the initial focus of treatment with themes of dependency emerging throughout treatment. They tend to be relatively passive in the beginning of treatment, often having little interest in becoming more assertive or taking more responsibility for their own decisions. They will often abdicate power and the direction of counseling to the counselor, considering the counselor to be the expert on the direction and process of treatment.

In counseling, people with DPD will typically work hard in an attempt to please the counselor. This drive to please can be redirected to create a sense of rapport and understanding. With a therapeutic alliance in place, the counselor can then encourage clients to begin enhancing their own independence. Assuming a supportive yet structured approach is helpful when working with this population. People with DPD can easily become overly dependent on counselors for direction, advice, and personal support. Additionally, counselors need to be aware that clients may develop dependence or even romantic feelings for the counselor; therefore, clear boundaries need to be established and maintained throughout treatment.

The overall goals of treatment with people with DPD are centered on the promotion of greater self-reliance, self-expression, and independence. This must first be established within the safety of the counseling sessions, and then transferred to relationships and settings outside of treatment. As treatment concludes, termination is another issue for a counselor to consider. Often, those with DPD have experienced rejection and abandonment in significant relationships. Termination becomes an opportunity for the client to have a deliberate, corrective, positive disengagement of a relationship.

Work with this population can present unique clinical challenges. Five challenges may arise when working with people with DPD (Perry, 2005): (a) requesting advice from the counselor; (b) placing the counselor in the dominant decision-making role; (c) not making changes outside of treatment to maintain the emotional attachment with the counselor; (d) the presentation of stories of mistreatment, which can personally affect the counselor (e.g., the counselor may attempt to control the client's patterns); and (e) avoiding dealing with separation issues within counseling sessions. These challenges can present significant issues in the treatment of people with DPD and should be considered before and during treatment.

Diagnostic issues related to the overlap between DPD and AVPD have been addressed throughout the clinical literature (Fossati et al., 2006). Based on the symptom clusters of the two disorders, 43% of those with AVPD could be diagnosed with DPD; conversely, 59% of people diagnosed with DPD could be diagnosed with AVPD (Fossati et al., 2006). This calls into question whether the criteria for these two personality disorders can even be clearly distinguished. Additionally, depression and DPD have very similar criteria that overlap, including hopelessness, helplessness, lack of initiative, and difficulty making decisions (Beck et al., 2004); these issues need to be considered when diagnosing DPD.

When assessing a person with DPD, counselors need to fully evaluate the following areas: interpersonal relationships, decision-making processes, self-reliance, personality function including clients' strengths and limitations, domestic violence/abuse issues, and any common comorbid mental disorders (e.g., depression, phobias, obsessive-compulsive disorders, substance use, or other personality disorders).

Additionally, cultural factors must be thoroughly assessed in both applying this diagnosis and in developing a treatment plan. Perceptions of the concepts of dependence and independence are highly culturally relative. For example, some cultures value politeness, passivity, and differential treatment of others, and these characteristics may present as traits of this disorder (APA, 2013). A diagnosis of DPD should be rendered when the dependent behaviors are in excess of cultural norms. Even in the cases where the person meets the DPD criteria, his or her culture should be considered in developing the treatment plan.

Treatment Models and Interventions

Little is known about DPD in terms of treatment, and it is one of the least researched personality disorders (Fossati et al., 2006). While there are a variety of treatment approaches for use in working with people with DPD, no randomized controlled trials have been documented in the literature (Critis-Christoph & Barber, 2007). Most of the treatment literature involves case studies, uncontrolled studies, and some clinical trials that contain a mixture of all of the personality disorders (Perry, 2005). Two approaches that seem promising in working with DPD are psychodynamic (short- and long-term) and cognitive behavioral therapy (Simon, 2009).

PSYCHODYNAMIC APPROACHES Psychodynamic approaches may be effective in treating clients with DPD (Eskedal & Demetri, 2006; Perry, 2005). This approach allows clients to revisit and more fully resolve past relationship struggles through the identification of transference that occurs in the therapeutic relationship. The client gains insight through this process and develops emotionally by working through issues of separation and loss. Working from a psychodynamic perspective, clients who are dependent may develop a dependence on their counselors, and this can then be used to develop a cohesive and supportive therapeutic relationship. Through this relationship, the counselor can attempt to uncover the underlying conflicts that are perpetuating the maladaptive behaviors (i.e., dependency), and help clients gain insight by exploring these behaviors.

COGNITIVE BEHAVIORAL THERAPY (CBT) CBT approaches (e.g., Beck et al., 2004) view dependency tendencies as compensatory reactions stemming from core beliefs of helplessness. These clients often perceive the world as being cruel and dangerous, and they believe they need someone to care for them and navigate life for them. The aim of CBT treatment then is to help clients with DPD recognize their maladaptive thinking styles, replace them with healthy alternatives, and change their resulting behaviors. Beck et al. (2004) recommended utilizing guided discovery and Socratic questioning with these clients as a way for the counselor to avoid being in the authoritarian role. This can aid clients in reaching their own solution rather than abdicating power and implementing the direct suggestions of their counselor. Counselors may want their clients to reduce their dependency on others and establish more independence, but they should monitor their own desires and not become overly pushy with clients; client empowerment is most important, and attempts to control clients may leave the counselor in an authoritarian role. The counselor should utilize a collaboratively negotiated list of problems the client seeks to address. In being collaborative, clients are empowered to become more independent. This hierarchy of goals will then become the focus of treatment.

As a counselor works within the clients' hierarchy of goals, the opportunity to explore their dichotomous view of independence will likely arise. Exploring this dichotomy may be helpful for clients. Their thinking usually ranges from one extreme of being totally dependent and helpless, to the other extreme of being totally isolated and alone. Beck et al. (2004) suggested drawing this dichotomy on a continuum (e.g., total independence to total independence). Allowing the client to see the steps between these two ideals can make the client feel less frightened about smaller steps that can be made along the way. Additionally, the counselor can aid the client in challenging the cognitive distortions that maintain this dichotomy in thinking.

The utilization of role-playing, social skills training, gradual exposure, in vivo experiences, and exercises in which clients are given an opportunity to test their core beliefs about themselves and others is also helpful (Simon, 2009). One such activity is utilizing the Dysfunctional Thought Record (e.g., situation, emotions, automatic thoughts, and rational response). This activity can be used to increase clients' awareness of the thoughts and emotions associated with a given situation, and it provides a mechanism to record their responses to these situations. The Dysfunctional Thought Record is ideal for monitoring and then challenging automatic thoughts and is an essential intervention utilized in CBT. Table 9.2 provides examples of the core beliefs and assumptions that can be challenged when working from a CBT perspective with this population.

PSYCHOPHARMACOTHERAPY   There are currently no known medications effective in treating the symptoms of DPD (Koenigsberg et al., 2007). The use of medication in treatment is often considered when associated disorders such as depression and anxiety are present. Clients with high levels of separation anxiety and panic attacks may benefit from imipramine (i.e., Tofranil; Sadock & Sadock, 2007).

Studies have reported that MAOIs have successfully treated the DPD symptoms of fear of rejection, separation anxiety, and social anxiety (Preston et al., 2013). Benzodiazepines may also be used to address symptoms of anxiety, but long-term use is not recommended because of their potential for addiction (Preston et al., 2013). While not indicated specifically for this use, antidepressant medications, specifically SSRIs, can reduce separation anxiety (Preston et al., 2013).

Prognosis

Overcoming their intense and ingrained patterns of dependency and submissiveness can be difficult, but with the aid of treatment, those with DPD have a more favorable prognosis than those with some of the other personality disorders (Eskedal & Demetri, 2006).

They tend to be more self-aware of their pathology, desire to change, and are more willing to undergo treatment than others with personality disorders (Eskedal & Demetri, 2006). Because of their ability to form relationships, trust others, and make commitments to change, people with DPD may significantly benefit from counseling.

SCHIZOTYPAL PERSONALITY DISORDER

Description of the Disorder and Typical Client Characteristics

Schizotypal personality disorder (STPD), a schizophrenia spectrum disorder, is characterized by a pervasive pattern of eccentricities of behavior, cognitive or perceptual distortions, and interpersonal deficits (APA, 2013). The symptomology of STPD includes positive symptoms (e.g., cognitive and perceptual distortions) and negative symptoms (e.g., social aversion and withdrawal) that are similar to those found in schizophrenia.

Secondary to symptoms of magical thinking, ideas of reference, and peculiar thoughts, people with STPD are often perceived as being odd. They often experience cognitive or perceptual distortions without the psychosis (i.e., hallucination, delusions, disorganized thoughts, disorganized behaviors, and negative symptoms). Compared to those with schizophrenia, people with STPD have better interpersonal skills, greater awareness of their social environment, a higher level of functioning, and do not typically suffer from hallucinations.

People with STPD have interpersonal struggles, as well as hygiene struggles, (e.g., they may appear unkempt and disheveled). Their unique communication style may lead them to appear confused. Additionally, when discussing a specific topic, they often have the tendency to either overelaborate a point or appear vague. Sometimes they will intermingle material from their past and present experiences without adequate explanation.

They typically have few close relationships and find it difficult to maintain employment. This is usually due to the deficits in sustained social relationships and difficulties in communicating in typical ways in social interactions. Additionally, sustained focus and attention to detail may be challenging for this population. They may complete some tasks, but often become sidetracked due to their own cognitive peculiarities of thought. They may find multisequential tasks difficult to complete.

People with STPD also experience subclinical psychotic symptoms such as mild delusions (e.g., others want to harm them; others are talking about them), and feelings of suspiciousness. With these difficulties and the deficits of social relating and interacting with others, people tend to perceive those with STPD as odd and unapproachable. Others' social withdrawal serves to reinforce this population's feelings of suspiciousness, thus leading to further social isolation.

Both genetic and environmental factors seem to play a role in the development of this disorder. With regard to genetics, this population is more likely to have a close family member or relative who has been diagnosed with schizophrenia (First & Tasman, 2004). Environmental stressors such as depravity, maltreatment, neglect, childhood trauma, and isolation in childhood appear to increase the risk of developing this disorder. For these people, their schooling tended to be difficult because of social impairment secondary to eccentric ideas or interests. They were often bullied and teased by their peers, thus reinforcing social isolation. This population is often drawn to subgroups that support aberrant beliefs and reinforce ideas consistent with their magical thinking. They tend not to marry and regularly live alone, or with their family of origin.

Counselor Considerations

This population rarely seeks treatment for their difficulties. Therefore, counselors are challenged to engage them and must build trust, create a safe environment, and develop a strong connection with this population. Because of the communication and speech deficits associated with this group, counselors need to stay focused on creating a structured environment and a solid therapeutic alliance. This population is not typically manipulative, and once trust has been established they will often talk freely about their lived experiences and inner world (Sperry, 2003).

Odd, eccentric behaviors are more malleable as a result of treatment, but other symptoms such as cognitive or perceptual distortions tend to be more resistant to change. Counselors need to be prepared to manage their own discomfort with clients' strange, odd, and eccentric reactions, ideas, and behaviors. Counselors need to be as nonjudgmental as possible in the face of their unique presentation.

Clients must be evaluated for STPD within their cultural context. Some beliefs and behaviors that are linked to culture may be misinterpreted as eccentric or odd. In particular, religious beliefs and rituals, such as voodoo, the evil eye, and shamanism, could appear as symptomatic of STPD to an uninformed counselor (APA, 2013).

Early in counseling, too much personal exploration should be avoided due to clients' propensity to potentially decompensate. Reality testing (i.e., the relationship between the objective "real world" and someone's subjective view of the world) is a critical component in treating this population. Clients need significant assistance in distinguishing internal distortions from external events and reality.

Social and occupational impairments often continue into adulthood. This population is often drawn to subgroups that support aberrant beliefs and reinforce ideas consistent with their magical thinking. They tend to not marry and regularly live alone, or with their family of origin.

When under a great deal of stress and anxiety, those with STPD may decompensate (i.e., have worsening symptoms), and display more identifiable psychotic symptoms. These episodes are often brief in duration and dissipate quickly. Maybe more than some of the other personality disorders, counselors need to be mindful of connecting this population with the resources and community services they require to be successful.

Counselors need to assess for common disorders that co-occur with STPD. These disorders include other personality disorders (i.e., borderline, avoidant, and paranoid) and disorders such as major depressive disorder, brief psychotic disorder, and anxiety disorders.

Treatment Models and Interventions

There is little research on treating clients who have STPD (Hayward, 2007), and at present, there are no randomized controlled trials currently reported in the literature (Critis-Christoph & Barber, 2007). When it comes to treating this population, little is known about what psychosocial treatments are effective (Critis-Christoph & Barber, 2007). Psychoeducation, cognitive behavioral therapy, case management, and psychopharmacotherapy have the most clinical potential and promise for working with people with STPD.

PSYCHOEDUCATION   The aim of psychoeducation is for clients to better understand and manage the nuances of their mental disorder. Essentially, psychoeducation is the transfer of knowledge of symptomology, known causes, treatments, and prognosis of a mental disorder. It can aid the client, family members, or other loved ones directly involved. Additionally, psychoeducation can provide knowledge of other modalities of treatment (e.g., psychotropic medications), and a fuller understanding of psychosocial therapies and their aims. Additionally, through the use of psychoeducation, counselors can address clients' personal hygiene, their daily living skills, and their isolating behaviors, in an attempt to aid in the establishment of greater independence and awareness.

COGNITIVE BEHAVIORAL THERAPY (CBT)   CBT (Beck et al., 2004) may be helpful in treating those who have STPD. Once a supportive relationship has been developed, a counselor is well positioned to address some of the maladaptive thoughts normally associated with this diagnosis, including suspicious or paranoid thoughts, ideas of reference, superstitions and magical thoughts, and illusions (Beck et al., 2004). By addressing these thoughts, along with the distorted emotional reasoning associated with them, a counselor can begin to aid a client in managing them.

Another CBT strategy that appears to have clinical significance with this population is the promotion of self-awareness through the utilization of reality testing. For example, a counselor may ask for the evidence for and/or against a distortion in relation to the specific situation being discussed (e.g., people are looking at me and want to humiliate me). Additionally, utilizing behavior therapy techniques such as skill training, exposure therapy, and imagery can significantly improve a client with STPD's interpersonal social skills and overall awareness. Table 9.2 provides examples of the core beliefs and assumptions that can be challenged when working from a CBT perspective with this population.

CASE MANAGEMENT   Case management, or the coordination of services provided by various agencies and social programs, is often an important part of treatment planning with this population. People with STPD often have difficulties navigating community mental health services as well as managing other psychosocial concerns (e.g., housing, employment, paperwork, and obtaining medication). Case management may involve the assessment of needs, planning of services and meetings, implementation of community mental health resources, and a consistent review of clients' adaptive functioning and progress in relation to the provided services. Additionally, those with STPD may benefit from increased access to a crisis support system, and a case manager or a counselor can help facilitate this access.

PSYCHOPHARMACOTHERAPY   A combination of psychotropic medication and psychosocial therapies is the most effective approach in addressing the needs of people who have STPD. Atypical antipsychotics (e.g., risperidone, olanzapine) may be beneficial in treating some of the mild psychotic symptoms experienced by those with STPD (Koenigsberg et al., 2007). In trials, low-dose antipsychotics reduced cognitive disturbance, ideas of reference, anxiety, depression, social dysfunction, and negative self-image (Koenigsberg et al., 2007). Compared to typical antipsychotics, atypical antipsychotics are associated with a lower incidence of both immediate, and long-term side effects (Preston et al., 2013); as such, atypical antipsychotics are generally better tolerated.

Additionally, pharmacotherapy can be utilized to treat secondary symptoms of anxiety (i.e., anxiolytics) and depression (e.g., antidepressants). The use of the antidepressant bupropion (i.e., Wellbutrin) must be carefully monitored, as STPD clients may experience transient psychosis, which can be exacerbated by this medication in prepsychotic clients (Preston et al., 2013).

Prognosis

The prognosis for those with STPD varies. Situational experiences, as well as case studies have outlined that treatment with this population is a slow and lengthy process (Beck et al., 2004; First & Tasman, 2004). Those with STPD, even with medications and psychosocial therapy, often have eccentric behaviors, distortions, and impairments in social interactions. Throughout their lifetime, they often wrestle with cognitive impairment, social isolation, and milder psychotic symptoms. Their symptomology is fairly stable and does not remit with age (First & Tasman, 2004). Therefore, goals for treatment should address overall adaptive functioning, and aid clients in continued mental health treatment, case management, psychoeducation, and medication management.

SCHIZOID PERSONALITY DISORDER

Description of the Disorder and Typical Client Characteristics

Those with schizoid personality disorder (SPD) are identified by their long-standing patterns of social detachment and their limited range of emotions within social interactions (APA, 2013). Characterized by a lack of desire for interpersonal relationships, this population does not tend to seek treatment because they do not view their behaviors as problematic. Additionally, they often display negative symptoms (i.e., lack of affect, limited emotional expression, social withdrawal, apathy, and anhedonia) in the absence of any other psychotic symptoms (i.e., hallucinations, delusions, disorganized behaviors, disorganized thoughts).

They tend to avoid close relationships, even with family members, because they do not desire these types of interactions. The avoidance of social relationships in people with SPD and avoidant personality disorder (AVPD) are fundamentally different in that people with SPD do not desire or miss social relationships, whereas people with AVPD experience pain and fear around relationships, yet desire to engage with others. Those with SPD derive little satisfaction from contact with others; therefore, they choose to spend the majority of their time alone or with only minimal controlled interpersonal contact.

They tend to be autonomous and self-sufficient (Esterberg, Goulding, & Walker, 2010), and they choose vocations and activities that can be performed in solitude and are typically below their level of ability (Beck et al., 2004). People with this disorder do not appear to take pleasure in vocational or recreational activities, and they generally report indifference toward them. Some with SPD may totally avoid employment and live with family members, although most tend to live reclusively. Most engage in all life tasks relatively independently, and view others more as business transactions rather than as social beings. They often function fairly well as long as social expectations are not placed upon them.

This group finds it difficult to establish emotional attachments with others. They often establish emotional attachments to inanimate objects, or even animals, rather than with other human beings (Esterberg et al., 2010). This may be due to their lack of desire for social interaction, or it may be due to their difficulties in displaying, experiencing, and reciprocating emotions. Their void of emotions appears odd to others, diminishing others' ability to fully connect with them emotionally. For example, they may find it challenging to express their frustration or anger, and they may respond passively to significant life events (e.g., death of a parent, marriage of a sibling, eviction notice). This often leads others to perceive them as being isolated, withdrawn, and bored with social interactions (Esterberg et al., 2010).

People with SPD do not normally have close friends. Because of their poor social skills, they are perceived as lacking empathy and introspection. They do not often develop or maintain sexual or even platonic relationships, appearing indifferent to both. They tend to believe that relationships will ultimately be frustrating and disappointing. This rationale leads them to perceive themselves as being different from others, odd, eccentric, and even worthless in some cases.

They also tend to keep others at a relatively safe distance because they are uncomfortable and fearful of intimacy and living interdependently (Parpottas, 2012). Finding their emotions difficult to regulate and demonstrate to another, they convey to others that they are distant and unattached emotionally (Parpottas, 2012). In turn, others avoid them and they avoid other people.

People with SPD typically have significant impairments in their ability to communicate with others. They are perceived as being vague or even concrete in the way they communicate, in that they display more rudimentary cognitions, inappropriate speech tones, and reduced eye contact (Beck et al., 2004). This impoverished speech and non-verbal communication (e.g., gesturing, eye contact) significantly hampers their ability to communicate. This population is often perceived as being aloof. They present as flat and void of emotions, appearing to others as lethargic and lacking motivation and drive. This marked restriction of affect is especially evident in relation to normally stimulating external events (e.g., promotion at work, death of family member). They often have vivid and complex inner worlds and tend to fantasize, but do not lose contact with reality.

Environmental stressors such as rejection, bullying, and abuse may exacerbate the disorder (Beck et al., 2004). They learn to cope by avoiding these negative experiences and adopting a more isolated, private way of living. People with this disorder may have been raised in homes where there were few, if any, warm, emotional interactions, by caregivers who were themselves aloof and withdrawn (Sperry, 2003). Because of this environment, they did not learn or experience appropriate social interactions and skills.

Historically, SPD has been associated with delusional disorder, schizophrenia, major depressive disorder, or other personality disorders (Esterberg et al., 2010). While this disorder, like other cluster A personality disorders (i.e., paranoid, schizotypal), can be a precursor for a psychotic disorder, it is more often associated with other coexisting personality disorders (e.g., avoidant, schizotypal, antisocial).

Counselor Considerations

Obviously, therapeutic trust is one of the most essential characteristics needed in treating people with SPD. With little experience in expressing feelings, engaging in relationships, and trusting others, they are often mistrusting and fearful of the intentions of others. Counselors need to consider ways to enhance trust, reduce scrutiny, and increase their level of comfort with the counseling process. If a counselor is able to create a more corrective emotional experience by enhancing optimism and decreasing a desire to withdraw, the counselor may preemptively reduce early termination.

Those with SPD typically only seek counseling because of the encouragement and prodding of family members, or an employer. While not typically internally motivated to change, the external motivations for seeking counseling should be utilized and fully explored. By being active, positive, and encouraging a sense of trust, the counselor can begin to slowly move the external motivation for treatment to an internally focused pursuit of what the client may want out of treatment. Concurrently, those with SPD are often ambivalent about social interactions, and they may begin to see the utility of social relationships when another person openly accepts them as they are. The therapeutic change process is likely to be slow due to the significant anxiety triggered by the forced social interactions, and a counselor needs to place reasonable expectations on the process and treatment.

When assessing those with SPD, counselors need to fully evaluate the following areas: interpersonal functioning, eccentric behaviors, social aversion and withdrawal, personality function including clients' strengths and limitations, and any common comorbid mental disorders (i.e., delusional disorder, schizophrenia, major depressive disorder, or other personality disorders [i.e., paranoid, schizotypal, avoidant]).

Counselors should also determine whether cultural and situational factors may better account for the client's behavior. Defensive behaviors and styles of interaction may be the norm in some cultures and should not be viewed as a sign of SPD. Additionally, those who move from rural to metropolitan areas, or those who have recently emigrated from another country, may display restricted affect, participate in solitary activities, and avoid social interaction while adjusting to new surroundings (APA, 2013). Cultural and life adjustment factors should be considered and integrated into clients' treatment plans.

Treatment Models and Interventions

The literature provides minimal guidance on the best treatments for use with this population (Hayward, 2007), with no randomized controlled trials currently being reported in the literature (Critis-Christoph & Barber, 2007). Behavior therapy and cognitive behavioral therapy seem to have the most clinical potential and promise for working with this population. The literature provides no suggestions or guidance on the use of medications in treating SPD.

BEHAVIOR THERAPY   Behavioral change techniques can be utilized to improve a client's social skills, assertiveness, and overall communication skills. Clients with SPD do not typically respond well to reinforcement, therefore counselors need to monitor certain aspects of behavioral treatment that a client may deem as intrusive and controlling. Taking an educational approach to increasing social skills, assertiveness, and overall communication skills may be appropriate when working with this population. The use of role-plays and exercises in which the clients are given an opportunity to practice social skills learned in session may be helpful (First & Tasman, 2004).

COGNITIVE BEHAVIORAL THERAPY (CBT)   CBT approaches (e.g., Beck et al., 2004) view schizoid tendencies as compensatory reactions stemming from core beliefs of feeling odd, worthless, and isolated. People with SPD often perceive the world as being cruel and hostile. CBT attempts to help clients with SPD recognize their maladaptive thinking styles, replace them with healthy alternatives, and change their resulting behaviors. Beck et al. (2004) provided two recommendations for counselors working with clients with SPD:

(a) collaboratively negotiate a problem list, and (b) monitor reactions to the client. When developing a problem list or a hierarchy of goals, the counselor needs to actively listen to what the client is motivated to work on in treatment. This may be significantly different from what the counselor speculates or perceives should be the initial focus. For example, a client with SPD may state he or she wants to address the following concerns the issue of not having enough money, not having anything to do during the days, feeling worried, and not accomplishing anything. This becomes the hierarchy of goals for treatment, and thus the focus. The counselor may want to reduce the client's isolation and help him or her establish a sense of intimacy with others, but the counselor should not push a personal agenda at the expense of the client's stated goals. If a client is pushed too quickly to discard isolating behaviors, he or she may experience intense anxiety, and ultimately abandon treatment altogether (Beck et al., 2004).

The utilization of role-playing, in vivo experiences, gradual exposure, and exercises in which clients are given an opportunity to test their core beliefs about themselves and others are useful. Additionally, guided discovery can be utilized to identify a client's interests and increase a client's involvement in those perceived pleasurable activities.

Prognosis

SPD symptoms are difficult to change and as such, significant behavior changes are not typically seen in treatment. Case studies have described treatment with those who have SPD as a being a slow and lengthy process (Beck et al., 2004; First & Tasman, 2004). Many with SPD do not seek treatment or prematurely terminate counseling. While many are often able to function in everyday living, they do not typically have many meaningful relationships. They are often comfortable with their lifestyle patterns, and lack a motivation to change. Therefore, they have a high probability of either maintaining or returning to their isolating behaviors, regardless of treatment interventions.

HISTRIONIC PERSONALITY DISORDER

Description of the Disorder and Typical Client Characteristics

Those who have histrionic personality disorder (HPD) desire to be at the center of attention and are excessively emotional (APA, 2013). They crave and seek attention, often appearing colorful and sometimes sexually proactive and seductive. They are often perceived by others to be vain, self-centered, disingenuous, and insincere, yet they have an extraverted, dramatic style that many, initially anyway, find charming. They are prone to excitability and require a great deal of stimulation, and their lives can be quite theatrical, with them being on the center stage.

Excessive emotionality is a hallmark of HPD, and they often experience rapidly shifting emotions and use emotional outbursts to get what they desire. Their emotional reactivity leads them to be easily swayed and influenced, and they tend to base their strongly held—yet fleeting—convictions on minimal evidence. They not only seek attention, but also approval from others, and they are uncomfortable when they are *not* the center of attention. They are also easily influenced by others and are quick to become interested—and then disinterested—in fads. They also tend to be self-centered and self-absorbed.

While they may be quick to enter into relationships with new people and verbally express strong emotion, these relationships are shallow and superficial, and lack depth and true intimacy. Others are generally not able to keep up with their demands for attention and as such, relationships are fragile and quickly unravel. They also quickly become bored and disinterested in their relationships, and they seek the thrill of new relationships. While they may manipulate others to get their way, they are simultaneously often dependent on and deeply attached to others; in other words, their ego is very fragile.

Their adventure seeking, need for change, challenge, and stimulation, and tendency to quickly grow bored can translate to many transitions within their relationships, career, and leisure pursuits. They tend to be highly energetic and can be successful in these pursuits if they are well matched with people or environments that fit with their needs. In their relationships, they may become bored when they receive the very relationship they seek, and then move on to a new relationship, forever seeking an idealized mate. This population tends to be quite vain and frequently uses their appearance, sexuality, and a flirty, energetic style to seek the attention they crave. Aging may be difficult for those with HPD, because as they age, they may be less able to rely on appearances or their sexuality to garner attention.

It has been hypothesized that HPD develops secondary to early childhood experiences. Sperry (2003) suggested that the families of these individual are frequently chaotic and dramatic, with family members often having personality disorders or addictions. In these environments, they only received nurturing when they were ill, or for external factors such as their appearance, specific talents, and/or achievements. As such, they came to expect that the only way they could receive attention and love was through external, dramatic presentations.

Counselor Considerations

Clients with HPD may initially be actively engaged in the counseling process. They do not typically seek counseling to address their own personality issues and their consequences (Millon et al., 2004). Rather, they seek counseling because of comorbid disorders or secondary to feelings of hurt or rejection (e.g., not getting something they desired, the termination of a relationship). Impaired functioning at work and in relationships with others may also bring clients with HPD into counseling. As clients, they are initially very engaged and motivated, aiming to please their counselor and receive his or her approval. As counseling moves forward, they may become disinterested or even annoyed with their counselor should he or she not provide them with the positive attention they seek.

Cultural, age, and gender differences in factors such as emotional expression, interaction styles, seductiveness, and sociability should be explored, as these may account for the client's behavior (APA, 2013). Many of the symptoms of HPD are culturally dependent, and counselors should be aware of their own biases and attitudes related to emotional expressiveness and the other HPD symptoms. To warrant a diagnosis of HPD, the client's behavior must cause significant distress or impairment in functioning. Clients' cultural standards should always be taken into account when developing a treatment plan.

Care should be taken not to appear critical of this population, as they will be quick to flee counseling should they feel they are being judged. If those with HPD can feel safe in counseling, they may stay engaged and active as the opportunity to receive attention from their counselor, and to talk about themselves, is attractive to them. Counselors need to be especially careful to structure sessions and create a therapeutic climate in which the sessions do not become overly focused on clients' sharing or storytelling at the expense of their exploring more meaningful therapeutic material. Counselors should be cautious of taking clients' accounts at face value, as there is a tendency of those with HPD to over-exaggerate. Taking a questioning, but nonjudgmental approach with clients may help them to recognize their own distortions in reasoning. Examining and clarifying emotions in each session can also help clients to gain more awareness into their behavior.

Many challenges exist in retaining clients with HPD in counseling, and in maintaining a healthy therapeutic relationship. Because of their need for change and stimulation, they may be hesitant to engage in an ongoing counseling relationship. Regularly challenging clients in a nonthreatening way can facilitate interest in continuing treatment.

Counselors should also be aware of client behaviors that may be detrimental to the therapeutic relationship and process, and explore their personal feelings surrounding them. It is not uncommon for clients with HPD to find the counselor attractive, and act in a provocative manner during sessions. Other distorted views of the therapeutic relationship may exist and may cause the client to form an unhealthy dependency upon the counselor. Dependency may also be encouraged by the client's constant need for reassurance. To avoid or confront these issues, counselors should set firm boundaries with these clients and explore these issues as they arise. Having unclear boundaries and allowing a client to continue to have a distorted perception of the therapeutic relationship will hinder the therapeutic process and prohibit client empowerment.

Counselors should also explore their feelings related to working with a client who exhibits the behaviors characteristic of HPD. The intense, dramatic behavior seen in this population may prompt emotional reactions in counselors. An awareness of potential nonverbal and verbal emotional reactions to clients with HPD is necessary. Monitoring for countertransference is also crucial, as clients with HPD are more impressionable, and clients may take on a counselor's attitudes and values, even if they do not agree with them.

It is important to note that mention of suicide should not be minimized because of the tendency of those with HPD to behave dramatically or overexaggerate. Suicidal behavior is common within this population and warrants consistent, on-going assessment throughout treatment. Counselors may monitor suicidal ideation through making inquiries during each session. Other types of self-destructive behavior such as nonsuicidal self-injury may also be present with HPD and should also be continually monitored.

 Clinical Toolbox 9.6: In the Pearson eText, click here to review questions that can be used to assess nonsuicidal self-injurious behavior.

The development of a safety plan may be helpful in preventing self-destructive behavior and can offer clients a concrete, healthy course of action to follow when experiencing a desire to self-harm.

Treatment Models and Interventions

As is common with most other personality disorder diagnoses, the majority of the treatment literature is based on narrative case studies of individual clients. No controlled studies on treating HPD could be found in the literature (Critis-Christoph & Barber, 2007). In this section, the treatments that have been most frequently discussed in the literature for use with HPD will be reviewed.

Both group and individual treatment may be helpful with this population. Groups can provide a unique opportunity for this population to receive feedback on their interpersonal style, and to learn and practice new and more adaptive ways of interacting with others. Care should be taken to ensure a client is able to manage the stimulation of a group without being disruptive or monopolizing.

FUNCTIONAL ANALYTIC PSYCHOTHERAPY (FAP) FAP (Kohlenberg & Tsai, 1991) has been suggested as an efficacious, psychodynamic approach for treating HPD (Callaghan, Summers, & Weidman, 2003). The role of the counselor is to bring awareness to the problematic behaviors that appear in counseling, and to encourage clients to practice more adaptive behaviors that promote and enhance their functioning. As such, the counselor can use these in-session interactions as a vehicle for promoting client change. This approach is based on the assumption that changes made during sessions can be generalized to behavior outside of counseling sessions (Callaghan et al., 2003). Interpretation and exploration into past issues is not a focus, but rather, attention is given to present behaviors.

Initial sessions are used to gather information about the client's treatment goals, and to identify problematic behaviors relevant to treatment. Goals are then periodically reviewed during sessions. Using this approach, one of the most important factors identified as facilitating client improvement was the ability of the therapist to recognize and call attention to problematic behaviors as they occur in sessions (Callaghan et al., 2003). For example, in the case of HPD, a client who behaves flirtatiously and seductively during a session will be assumed to do so outside of counseling sessions. The counselor will bring attention to this behavior, track its progression, and help the client explore more appropriate ways of interacting.

COGNITIVE ANALYTIC THERAPY (CAT) CAT (Ryle, 1990) is another psychodynamic approach that has some demonstrated success in treating HPD (Kellett, 2007). CAT is a time-limited approach that involves three phases of therapy: reformulation, recognition, and revision. During the reformulation phase, the counselor assesses a client's problems and explores the problems' origins in the client's past history. The counselor then writes a letter to the client expressing his or her understanding of the problems, their origins, and their effects on the client's life. The client reads the letter and works collaboratively with the counselor to address the issues.

During the recognition phase, the counselor asks the client to begin to become aware of his or her problematic behaviors through journaling or recording behaviors on a worksheet. These exercises are used in sessions to help clients conceptualize their problems through creating a diagrammatic representation, referred to as a sequential diagrammatic reformation. Patterns of feelings, contextual factors, and resulting behaviors will emerge. For example, a diagram may display how a client feels ignored and insecure, desires more attention, and acts out to fulfill this need.

The third phase of CAT, revision, focuses on breaking away from the identified cyclical patterns through the identification of "exits." In reference to the aforementioned example, an "exit" from that pattern may be to increase tolerance for not having constant attention. At the conclusion of counseling, the client and counselor will write each other "goodbye" letters reviewing changes made during the course of counseling, identifying potential challenges ahead, and discussing the feelings that may arise at termination.

COGNITIVE BEHAVIORAL THERAPY (CBT) CBT theorists hold that those with HPD have erroneous beliefs and are focused around the idea that they need attention from others to validate their self-worth. For example, they may believe that "Unless people desire me, I am nothing," or "If I cannot entertain people, they will abandon me" (Beck et al., 2004). Table 9.2 provides examples of the core beliefs and assumptions that can be challenged when working from a CBT perspective with this population. Counselors working from a CBT approach can help clients recognize cognitive distortions and automatic thought patterns, and ways to challenge their validity.

In applying the behavioral aspect of CBT, assertiveness training may be used to help those with HPD to develop healthier interpersonal relationships. Behavioral techniques such as modeling and rehearsal can be helpful in teaching clients with this disorder to behave in more appropriate ways in social or work situations. A cost-benefit analysis can also be helpful in demonstrating how identified behaviors are detrimental to their functioning. The development of basic problem-solving skills may also help reduce impulsive behavior.

 Clinical Toolbox 9.7: In the Pearson etext, click here to read about a creative activity that can be used to help clients understand and develop appropriate interpersonal boundaries.

PSYCHOPHARMACOTHERAPY There is no medication used specifically to treat HPD. However, medications may be helpful in treating comorbid disorders that commonly occur with HPD (e.g., major depressive disorder). This population is prone to suicidal gestures and as with the treatment of BPD, careful attention should be given when prescribing medication that can potentially increase suicide risk, or may be lethal when ingested in high amounts. Because of their potential to become addicted to medications, any addictive medications should be monitored for abuse. Benzodiazepines for the treatment of comorbid anxiety present a high risk of abuse, dependence, and lethality in the case of overdose; trazodone, bupropion, and venlafaxine are antidepressant medications that present a lower risk of harm through overdose, and may be more appropriate for use with those who have HPD and comorbid anxiety or depression (Preston et al., 2013).

Prognosis

The prognosis of those with HPD varies and symptoms tend to be modulated by time and age. This may be due to a reduction of the energy required to maintain the symptoms associated with this disorder. It may also be that with time, this population learns more adaptive ways of coping or settles into a more stable identity that is less grounded in receiving attention from others. Clients who do engage in treatment can improve their functioning in work and interpersonal relationships. Unfortunately, many with HPD are unable to modify their patterns of behaviors and terminate treatment early.

PARANOID PERSONALITY DISORDER

Description of the Disorder and Typical Client Characteristics

Those with paranoid personality disorder (PPD) have a projected, pervasive distrust of others (APA, 2013). They are constantly suspicious, defended, hypervigilant, and scanning the horizon for signs of people attempting to harm them and their interests. They fear others will exploit them, cause them to feel helpless, or criticize them and as such, they struggle to make and maintain relationships because they are preoccupied with the idea that others will be malicious, disloyal, or otherwise hurt them. They tend to blame others for their problems, as they believe them to be hostile. They typically hold grudges, often ruminate about perceived injustices, and are generally reactive and angry in their interactions with others. These personal characteristics lead to numerous interpersonal conflicts and difficulties, with others often describing them as hostile, bitter, rigid, controlling, angry, snarky, sarcastic, argumentative, irritable, and lacking a sense of humor. They tend to be very guarded and share little about themselves or their experiences with others. They pursue their many perceived injustices with a moralistic, self-righteous tenacity.

They often misperceive themselves as the focus of others' interests. They also frequently believe that others are being hostile or are trying to sabotage them, even if this is not the case. For example, if the mail carrier accidentally places their mail in the neighbor's mailbox, they may believe that the mail carrier is doing so intentionally to annoy them. They tend to be very sensitive to issues associated with authority, class, power, and rank, and they are jealous of people who have things they do not. They tend to be protective of their independence and they desire power and status. Because of their hypervigilance, this population appears very tense, and this tension typically escalates when they are under stress or face their greatest fears: humiliation or failure (Sperry, 2003).

Their rigidity and need for control can create stress for them as well as the people who live and work around them. If they can find a job, career, and family circumstance that that is functional to their need for obedience and organization, they can strike a relatively adaptive homeostasis. However, because of their mistrust, they are often jealous and suspicious of others (e.g., their romantic partners' faithfulness), and this stability is often tenuous, especially when under stress. The nature of this disorder leads this population to isolate themselves from others, or at least to not be forthcoming about their perceived injuries. This isolation feeds the disorder, as they do not receive reality checks that might provide more adaptive perspectives about others' intentions. They typically desire to have relationships with others, but their guarded, suspicious approach makes this difficult.

Counselor Considerations

Those with PPD do not typically seek counseling because they are prone to externalizing, lack insight into how they contribute to their situation, and thus blame others for their problems. As such, they see no need to look to themselves as a source of change. They may take pride in their sterile rigidity and controlled expressions, viewing themselves as psychologically strong, and as such, they are likely to view expressions of emotions as a sign of weakness. Attempts to explore emotions should be approached with caution.

Counselors must consider the client's cultural background before diagnosing this disorder. Individuals of minority groups, immigrants, and refugees are among the populations of people who may display guarded and defensive behaviors that could be interpreted as paranoid (APA, 2013). Additionally, language barriers may contribute to the inability to confide in others, and may appear as reluctance or mistrust. A differentiation between acculturation and paranoid personality disorder symptoms is necessary to produce an accurate diagnosis, and these cultural factors should also be considered in developing a treatment plan.

Because of their fear of exploitation, this population does not typically trust others, and as such, open disclosures to counselors are not typically forthcoming. They struggle with intimacy in all relationships secondary to this distrust. Providing them with control over the frequency of sessions, encouraging them to be active in developing counseling goals and tasks, and allowing them to determine the session focus may help ease their defenses and prevent premature termination. Beck et al. (2004) also suggested that meeting less frequently, earlier in the therapeutic relationship, may help clients approach counseling and its requisite disclosures at a safe and comfortable pace.

Counselors also need to be mindful of their personal reactions when working with this population. These clients' anger and hostility should not be personalized. Conversely, counselors should avoid being overly effusive; displays of emotion may be viewed by this population as fake or manipulative. As they are prone to see insults where none exist and quick to take offense when none was intended, counselors must take care to convey a strong sense of empathy, while also appearing confident and strong.

It is important that counselors differentiate between PPD and several other disorders, which may appear similar to PPD. The paranoia experienced by those with PPD is not typically of a psychotic nature, they have a clear connection with reality, and their functioning is not as impacted by their disorder as it is for those who have paranoia associated with schizophrenia. Those who have schizophrenia experience many more symptoms such as disorganized thinking, losses of contact with reality, and hallucinations and delusions. PPD may also resemble delusional disorder with a persecutory subtype. The main difference between these two disorders is that those with PPD rarely experience delusions, and if they do, they are fleeting. Also, those with PPD have a lifelong history of being constantly hypervigilant, watchful, and suspicious of others.

Those with PPD also tend to have comorbid personality disorder diagnoses, most commonly narcissistic, avoidant, or obsessive-compulsive personality disorders. They also frequently have co-occurring anxiety and depressive disorders (Millon et al., 2004).

Treatment Models and Interventions

No controlled studies on treating PPD could be found in the literature. In addition, very little has been written on the treatment of this disorder. Individual treatment is preferred over group treatment; the nature of their disorder will heighten their defenses when in group situations that involve confrontation and emotional exposure. This section reviews the treatments that have been discussed in the literature for use with PPD.

BEHAVIOR THERAPY (BT) Because insight and emotion-oriented approaches may feel threatening to this population, the active, structured approach taken in BT may be a good therapeutic fit (First & Tasman, 2004). When using BT, clients may feel a greater sense of control over the sessions, and the teaching approach utilized in BT may be more engaging to clients than some other approaches.

In terms of BT techniques, the use of appropriate assertiveness skills may help these clients engage in appropriate, not aggressive, communication patterns with others. Additionally, stress management may help reduce the chronic tension this population is prone to experiencing. Finally, the development of basic problem-solving skills such as the use of a cost benefit analysis may help them learn how to make adaptive decisions. The development of these skills may help them modify the suspicious and guarded approach they take towards others and will ideally help them understand that their interpersonal style may invite the very behaviors they fear.

COGNITIVE BEHAVIORAL THERAPY (CBT)   Like behavior therapy, CBT is an active, focused approach, which provides clients with a sense of control over the therapeutic process. CBT theorists hold that those with PPD harbor many problematic beliefs that fuel their disorder. They tend to magnify negative experiences (i.e., overfocus on negative events that do occur), overgeneralize (i.e., take one event and apply it to multiple other situations), and engage in black-and-white/all-or-nothing thinking. Through CBT, clients can begin to explore alternative explanations of their situations (Beck et al., 2004). For example, this population often believes, "If I trust others, they will harm me." Through CBT, they can explore alternative ways of thinking about the world, ideally coming to a place of thinking instead, "If I trust others, they will likely not harm me." Table 9.2 provides examples of the core beliefs and assumptions that can be challenged when working from a CBT perspective with this population.

PSYCHOPHARMACOTHERAPY   Medication is generally not recommended for the treatment of PPD. Because of their distrust of others, this population will be reluctant to take psychotropic medications. Even suggesting they seek a psychiatric consultation may offend them, and may lead to client dropout or noncompliance; it is important that counselors approach this subject delicately. Medication may be useful in treating the anxiety or depressive symptoms that are frequently comorbid in this population. Antipsychotic medications may also be useful in treating the paranoid ideation associated with the disorder; however, research is limited with regard to using medication with this population.

Prognosis

Little is known about the course and prognosis of PPD, but one recent 5-year longitudinal study suggested that those with PPD and avoidant personality disorder had fewer positive changes in functioning over time than those who had other personality disorders (Kvarstein & Karterud, 2011). As previously mentioned, it is best to focus on realistic, concrete, and attainable goals as opposed to personality changes. This approach will allow the counselor and the client to experience a sense of satisfaction with the treatment process. Willingness to seek treatment and the ability to form some level of trust with a counselor will likely produce more favorable outcomes. Though managing PPD will be a lifelong process for those with the diagnosis, counseling can reduce symptoms to a manageable level and help clients make improvements in overall functioning.

TREATMENT PLAN FOR JANE

This chapter began with a discussion of Jane, a 35-year-old female who meets the criteria for borderline personality disorder, major depressive disorder, and posttraumatic stress disorder. A counselor must consider multiple factors before moving ahead with a strength-based treatment approach. The following I CAN START conceptual framework outlines treatment considerations that may be helpful in working with Jane.

C = Contextual Assessment

No religious involvement, but she is interested in exploring Buddhism; a limited connection with her culture or her values and beliefs as related to her culture; gender struggles—female working in an all-male environment, devaluation and abuse of women within her family, sexually victimized as a child by males in authority roles in her life; developmental struggles around the autonomy, initiative, industry, identity, and intimacy stages; no one in her family has gone to college, and she has a limited understanding of how to be successful in college.

A = Assessment and Diagnosis

Diagnosis = Borderline Personality Disorder 301.83 (F60.3); Major Depressive Disorder (recurrent, moderate) 296.32 (F33.1); Posttraumatic Stress Disorder 309.81 (F43.10).

Beck Depression Inventory (at initial session and then as needed for follow-up)

Assessment of her self-injury (on a weekly basis)

Assessment of suicidality (on a weekly basis)

N = Necessary Level of Care

Outpatient, individual (once per week) and group therapy (once per week); acute/hospital care should be readily accessible should her self-injury and suicidal intent escalate; possible family therapy with her mother at some point in the future when her self-injurious behaviors have become more stable, and she has developed basic emotion regulation skills.

S = Strength-Based Lens

Self: Jane is a creative, intelligent woman. She has a hobby about which she is passionate and can express a motivation to return to school and better her career circumstances. She is good at researching issues with which she struggles, and she seeks help. In isolating herself from intimate relationships with males, Jane has been able to keep herself physically and emotionally safe from further abuse. Jane is a survivor as she has endured a great deal, yet still finds a will to move forward.

Family: Jane cares about her mother, and she is invested in having a relationship with her mother. Her mother is a possible social support resource.

Community: She has a friendship she has maintained since high school. She is engaged in a photography club.

T = Treatment Approach

Dialectical Behavior Therapy

A = Aim and Objective of Treatments (6-month objectives)

Jane will use her coping skills to not self-injure → Jane will have 0 suicide attempts and reduce her incidents of self-injury to no more than 1 episode per week, and she will engage in appropriate wound care. She will utilize at least 2 DBT skills (i.e., mindful meditation, distress tolerance, emotional regulation, and interpersonal effectiveness) 100% of the time when she has urges to self-harm.

Jane will be active and committed to her treatment → Jane will attend all individual and group counseling sessions; she will adhere to all the rules related to between-session contact with her counselor; she will be open, forthcoming, and honest with her counselor; she will complete *all* homework assignments (e.g., diary cards).

Jane will learn and utilize mindful meditation skills and use these to help her tolerate her negative thoughts → Jane will apply at least 1 mindful meditation activity (e.g., observe non-judgmentally, living in the moment, experience emotions) 2 times per day when she finds she is having destructive or judgmental thoughts.

Jane will implement learned skills to better tolerate stressful situations → During times of distress, Jane will identify and utilize at least 1 distress tolerance skill (e.g., distraction, self-soothing, pros and cons, accepting reality) 90% of the time to increase her ability to tolerate distress. If the initial skill used is unsuccessful, Jane will try a different distress tolerance skill.

Jane will use learned skills to better regulate strong negative emotions → Jane will identify and utilize at least 1 emotion regulation skills (e.g., reducing vulnerabilities, building positive experiences, using mastery) 90% of the time to increase her ability to regulate strong negative emotions. If the initial skill used is unsuccessful, Jane will try a different emotion regulation skill.

Jane will learn and develop more effective ways to interact with others → Jane will learn and engage in at least 5 learned interpersonal skills (e.g., asking for what you need, saying no, coping, and managing interpersonal conflict) a week.

Jane will connect with her social supports and interests as a means of increasing her self-esteem and positive life experiences → Jane will take pictures at least 1 time per week. She will reconnect with her friends from the photography club and attend at least 1 photography club meeting per month.

Jane will develop a clearer sense of her spiritual identity → Jane will select and read a book on Buddhism, consider how a Buddhist philosophy applies to her and her life, and how it relates to the mindfulness skills she is learning. She will reflect weekly on this connection by journaling about her emerging spiritual identity.

R = Research-Based Interventions (based on Dialectical Behavior Therapy)

Counselor will effectively structure the boundaries of the therapeutic process so as to help Jane be successful.

Counselor will help Jane develop and apply the following skills:

- Emotion regulation skills
- Interpersonal effectiveness skills
- Distress tolerance skills
- Mindfulness skills

T = Therapeutic Support Services

Medication management by her psychiatrist

Weekly DBT group therapy and individual therapy sessions

Access to a secure setting should her symptoms escalate

Physician will monitor health concerns including her asthma and any new self-inflicted wounds

References

Alden, L. (1989). Short-term structured treatment for avoidant personality disorder. *Journal of Consulting and Clinical Psychology, 57,* 756–764.

American Psychiatric Association (APA). (2013). *Diagnostic and statistical manual of mental disorders* (5th ed. [DSM-5]). Washington, DC: Author.

Arntz, A., van Genderen, H., & Drost, J. (2009). *Schema therapy for borderline personality disorder.* Malden, MA: Wiley.

Bateman, A., & Fonagy, P. (2001). Treatment of borderline personality disorder with psychoanalytically oriented partial hospitalization: An 18-month follow-up. *The American Journal of Psychiatry, 158,* 36–42.

Bateman, A., & Fonagy, P. (2008a). Comorbid antisocial and borderline personality disorders: Mentalization-based treatment. *Journal of Clinical Psychology, 64,* 181–194.

Bateman, A., & Fonagy, P. (2008b). 8-year follow-up of patients treated for borderline personality disorder: Mentalization-based treatment versus treatment as usual. *The American Journal of Psychiatry, 165,* 631–638.

Bateman, A., & Fonagy, P. (2009). Randomized controlled trial of outpatient mentalization-based treatment versus structured clinical management for borderline personality disorder. *The American Journal of Psychiatry, 166,* 1355–1364.

Beck, A. T., Freeman, A., & Davis, D. D. (2004). *Cognitive therapy of personality disorders* (2nd ed.). New York, NY: Guilford.

Ben-Porath, D. D. (2004) Intercession telephone contact with individuals diagnosed with borderline personality disorder: Lessons from dialectical behavior therapy. *Cognitive and Behavioral Practice, 11,* 222–230.

Blum, N., St. John, D. Pfohl, B., Stuart, S., McCormick, B., Allen. J., . . . Black, D. W. (2008). Systems training for emotional predictability and problem solving (STEPPS) for outpatients with borderline personality disorder: A randomized controlled trial and 1-year follow-up. *The American Journal of Psychiatry, 165,* 468–478.

Bornstein, R. F. (1996). Dependency. In C. G. Costello (Ed.), *Personality characteristics of the personality disordered* (pp. 120–145). New York, NY: Wiley.

Butcher, J. N., Mineka, S., & Hooley, J. M. (2010). *Abnormal psychology* (14th ed.). New York, NY: Allyn & Bacon.

Callaghan, G. M., Summers, C. J., & Weidman, M. (2003). The treatment of histrionic and narcissistic personality disorder behaviours: A single-subject demonstration of clinical improvement using functional-analytic psychotherapy. *Journal of Contemporary Psychotherapy, 33,* 321–339.

Chmielewski, M., & Watson, D. (2008). The heterogeneous structure of schizotypal personality disorder: Item-level factors of the schizotypal personality questionnaire and their associations with obsessive-compulsive disorder symptoms, dissociative tendencies, and normal personality. *Journal of Abnormal Psychology, 117,* 364–376.

Clarkin, J. F., Yeomans, F., & Kernberg, O. F. (1999). *Psychotherapy of borderline personality.* New York, NY: Wiley.

Coon, D. W. (2004). Cognitive-behavioral interventions with avoidant personality: A single case study. *Journal of Cognitive Psychotherapy: An International Quarterly, 8,* 243–253.

Critis-Christoph, P., & Barber, J. P. (2007). Psychological treatments for personality disorders. In P. E. Nathan & J. M. Gorman (Ed.), *A guide to treatments that work* (pp. 641–658). New York, NY: Oxford Press.

de Reus, R. M., & Emmelkamp, P. G. (2012). Obsessive-compulsive personality disorder: A review of current empirical findings. *Personality and Mental Health, 6*(1), 1–21.

DiMaggio, D., & Attina, D. (2012). Metacognitive interpersonal therapy for narcissistic personality disorder and associated perfectionism. *Journal of Clinical Psychology: In Session, 68,* 922–934.

Dimaggio, G., Semerari, A., Carcione, A., Nicolò, G., & Procacci, M. (2007). *Psychotherapy of personality disorders: Metacognition, states of mind and interpersonal cycles.* London: Routledge.

Duggan, C. (2009). A treatment guideline for people with antisocial personality disorder: Overcoming °attitudinal barriers and evidential limitations. *Criminal Behaviour and Mental Health, 19,* 219–223.

Eggum, N., Eisenberg, N., Spinrad, T. L., Valiente, C., Edwards, A., Kupfer, A. S., . . . Reiser, M. (2009). Predictors of withdrawal: Possible precursors of avoidant personality disorder. *Developmental and Psychopathology, 21,* 815–838.

Emmelkamp, P. M., Benner, A., Kuipers, A., Feiertag, G. A., Koster, H. C., & Apledoorn, J. (2006). Comparison of brief dynamic and cognitive-behavioural therapies in avoidant personality disorder. *The British Journal of Psychiatry, 189,* 60–64.

Eskedal, G. A., & Demetri, J. M. (2006). Etiology and treatment of cluster C personality disorders. *Journal of Mental Health Counseling, 28,* 1–17.

Esterberg, M. L., Goulding, S. M., & Walker, E. F. (2010). Cluster A personality disorders: Schizotypal, schizoid and paranoid personality disorders in childhood and adolescence. *Journal of Psychopathology and Behavioral Assessment, 32,* 515–528.

Farrell, J. M., Shaw, I. A., & Webber, M. A. (2009). A schema-focused approach to group psychotherapy for outpatients with borderline personality disorder: A randomized controlled trial. *Journal of Behaviour Therapy and Experimental Psychiatry, 40,* 317–328.

Ferguson, C. (2010). Genetic contributions to antisocial personality and behavior: A meta-analytic review from an evolutionary perspective. *Journal of Social Psychology, 150,* 160–180.

First, M. B., & Tasman, A. (2004). *DSM-IV-TR mental disorders: Diagnosis, etiology, & treatment.* Hoboken, NJ: Wiley.

Fossati, A., Beauchaine, T. P., Grazioli, F., Borroni, S., Carretta, I., DeVecchi, C., . . . Maffei, C. (2006). Confirmatory factor analyses of DSM-IV cluster C personality disorder criteria. *Journal of Personality Disorders, 20,* 186–203.

Gelhorn, H. L., Sakai, J. T., Price, R. M., & Crowley, T. J. (2007). DSM-IV conduct disorder criteria as predictors of antisocial personality disorder. *Comprehensive Psychiatry, 48,* 529–538.

Giesen-Bloo, J., van Dyck, R., Spinhoven, P., van Tilburg, W., Dirksen, C., van Asselt, T., . . . Arntz, A. (2006). Outpatient psychotherapy for borderline personality disorder. *Archives of General Medicine, 63,* 649–658.

Gunderson, J. G., & Gabbard, G. O. (2000). *Psychotherapy for Personality Disorders.* Washington, DC: American Psychiatric Press.

Hayward, B. (2007). Cluster A personality disorders: Considering the "odd-eccentric" in psychiatric nursing. *International Journal of Mental Health Nursing, 16,* 15–21.

Hiatt, K. D., & Dishion, T. J. (2008). Antisocial personality development. In T. P. Beauchanie & S. P. Hinshaw (Eds.), *Child and adolescent psychopathology* (pp. 370–404). Hoboken, NJ: Wiley.

Johansen, M., Karterud, S., Pedersen, G., Gude, T., & Falkum, E. (2004). An investigation of the prototype validity of the borderline DSM-IV construct. *Acta Psychiatrica Scandinavica, 109,* 289–298.

Kellett, S. (2007). A time series evaluation of the treatment of histrionic personality disorder with cognitive analytic therapy. *Psychology and Psychotherapy: Theory, Research and Practice, 80,* 389–405.

Kellogg, S. H., & Young, J. E. (2006). Schema therapy for borderline personality disorder. *Journal of Clinical Psychology, 62,* 445–458.

Kernberg, O. F. (1976). *Object-relations theory and clinical psychoanalysis.* New York, NY: Jason Aronson.

Kernberg, O. F. (2000). *Borderline conditions and pathological narcissism.* New York, NY: Jason Aronson.

Koenigsberg, H. W., Woo-Ming, A. M., & Siever, L. J. (2007). Psychopharmacological treatment of personality disorders. In P. E. Nathan & J. M. Gorman (Eds.), *A guide to treatments that work* (pp. 659–680) New York, NY: Oxford University Press.

Kohlenberg, R. J., & Tsai, M. (1991). *Functional analytic psychotherapy: Creating intense and curative therapeutic relationships.* New York, NY: Plenum.

Kohut, H. (1977). *The restoration of the self.* New York, NY: International Universities Press.

Kohut, H. (1984). *How does analysis cure?* Chicago, IL: University of Chicago Press.

Kvarstein, E. H., & Karterud, S. (2011). Large variations of global functioning over five years in treated patients with personality traits and disorders. *Journal of Personality Disorders, 26,* 141–161.

Leichsenring, F., & Rabung, S. (2008). Effectiveness of long-term psychodynamic psychotherapy: A meta-analysis. *Journal of the American Medical Association, 300,* 1551–1565.

Linehan, M. M. (1993). *Cognitive behavioral treatment of borderline personality disorder.* New York, NY: Guilford.

Linehan, M. M., Comtois, K. A., Murray, A. M., Brown, M. Z., Gallop, R. J., Heard, H. L., . . . Lindenboim, N. (2006). Two-year randomized controlled trial and follow-up of dialectical behavior therapy vs. therapy by experts for suicidal behaviors and borderline personality disorder. *Archives of General Psychiatry, 63,* 757–766.

Lynam, D. R., & Widiger, T. A. (2007). Using a general model of personality to identify the basic elements of psychopathy. *Journal of Personality Disorders, 21,* 160–178.

Lynch, T. R., & Cheavens, J. S. (2008). Dialectical behavior therapy for comorbid personality disorders. *Journal of Clinical Psychology, 64,* 154–167.

Lynch, T. R., Trost, W. T., Salsman, N., & Linehan, M. M. (2007). Dialectical behavior therapy for borderline personality disorder. *Annual Review of Clinical Psychology, 3,* 181–205.

Mahler, S., Pine, F., & Bergman, A. (1973). *The psychological birth of the human infant.* New York, NY: Basic Books.

Markovitz, P. (2001). Pharmacotherapy. In W. J. Lively (Ed.), *Handbook of personality disorders* (pp. 475–493); New York, NY: Guilford Press.

Masterson, J. F. (1981). *The narcissistic and borderline disorders*. London, England: Brunner-Routledge.

McGlashan, T. H., Grilo, C. M., Sanislow, C. A., Ralevski, E., Morey, L. C., Gunderson, J. G., . . . Pagano, M. E. (2005). Two-year prevalence and stability of individual criteria for schizotypal, borderline, avoidant, and obsessive-compulsive personality disorders: Toward a hybrid model of axis II disorders. *The American Journal of Psychiatry, 162,* 883–889.

Millon, T., Grossman, S., Millon, C., Meagherm S., & Ramnath, R. (2004). *Personality disorders in modern life* (2nd ed.). Hoboken, NJ: Wiley.

Oldham. J. M. (2006). Borderline personality disorder and suicidality. *American Journal of Psychiatry, 163,* 20–26.

Parpottas, P. (2012). A critique on the use of standard psychopathologicial classification in understanding human distress: The example of "schizoid personality disorder." *Counselling Psychology Review, 27,* 44–52.

Perry, J. C. (2005). Dependent personality disorder. In G. O. Gaggard, J. S. Beck, & J. Holmes (Eds.), *Oxford Textbook of Psychotherapy* (pp. 321–328). New York, NY: Oxford University Press.

Preston, J. D., O'Neal, J. H., & Talaga, M. C. (2013). *Handbook of clinical psychopharmacology for therapists* (7th ed.). Oakland, CA: New Harbinger.

Renneberg, B., Goldstein, A. J., Phillips, D., & Chambless, D. L. (1990). Intensive behavioral group treatment of avoidant personality disorder. *Behavior Therapy, 21,* 363–377.

Rodrigo, C., Rajapakse, S., & Jayananda, G. (2010). The "antisocial" person: An insight into biology, classification and current evidence on treatment. *Annals of General Psychiatry, 9,* 1–12.

Ronningstam, E. (2012). Alliance building and narcissistic personality disorder. *Journal of Clinical Psychology: In Session, 68,* 943–953.

Ryle, A. (1990). *Cognitive Analytic Therapy: Active participation in change*. Chichester, England: John Wiley & Sons.

Sadock, B. J., & Sadock, V. A. (2007). *Kaplan and Sadock's synopsis of psychiatry: Behavioral sciences/ clinical psychiatry* (10th ed.). Philadelphia, PA: Lippincott Williams & Wilkins.

Salekin, R. T. (2002). Psychopathy and therapeutic pessimism. Clinical lore or clinical reality? *Clinical Psychology Review, 22,* 79–112.

Shea, M. T., Stout, R., Gunderson, J., Morey, L. C., Grilo, C. M., McGlashan T., . . . Keller MB (2002). Short-term diagnostic stability of schizotypal, borderline, avoidant, and obsessive-compulsive personality disorders. *American Journal of Psychiatry, 159,* 2036–2041.

Simon, W. (2009). Follow-up psychotherapy outcome of patient with dependent, avoidant and obsessive-compulsive personality disorder: A meta-analytic review. *International Journal of Psychiatry in Clinical Practice, 13,* 153–165.

Sperry, L. (2003). *Handbook of diagnosis and treatment of DSM-IV-TR personality disorders* (2nd ed.). Philadelphia, PA: Brunner-Routledge.

Sperry, L. (2006). *Cognitive behavior therapy of DSM-IV-TR personality disorders* (2nd ed.). New York, NY: Routledge.

Strauss, J. L., Hayes, A. M., & Johnson, S. L. (2006). Early alliance, alliance raptures, and symptoms change in a nonrandomized trial of cognitive therapy for avoidant and obsessive-compulsive personality disorders. *Journal of Counseling and Clinical Psychology, 74,* 337–345.

Straussner, S. L. A., & Nemenzik, J. M. (2007). Co-occurring substance use and personality disorders. Current thinking on etiology, diagnosis, and treatment. *Journal of Social Work Practice in the Addictions, 7,* 5–23.

Verheul, R., Van Den Bosch, L. M. C., Koeter, M. W. J., De Ridder, M. A. J., Stijnen, T., & Van Den Brink, W. (2003). Dialectical behaviour therapy for women with borderline personality disorder: 12-month, randomised clinical trial in the Netherlands. *The British Journal of Psychiatry, 182,* 135–140.

Verheul, R., & Widiger, T. A. (2004). A meta-analysis of the prevalence and usage of the personality disorder not otherwise specified (PDNOS) diagnosis. *Journal of Personality Disorders, 18,* 309–319.

Young, J. E., Klosko, J. S., & Weishaar, M. E. (2003). *Schema therapy: A practitioner's guide*. New York, NY: Guilford.

Zanarini, M. C., Frankenburg, F. R., Hennen, J., Reich, D. B., & Silk, K. R. (2005). Psychosocial functioning of borderline patients and axis II comparison subjects followed prospectively for six years. *Journal of Personality Disorders, 19,* 19–29.

Zimmerman, M., Rothchild, L., & Chelminski, I. (2005). The prevalence of DSM-IV personality disorders in psychiatric outpatients. *American Journal of Psychiatry, 162,* 1911–1918.

CHAPTER

10

Schizophrenia Spectrum and Other Psychotic Disorders

Casey A. Barrio Minton and Elizabeth A. Prosek

CASE STUDY: MITCHELL

Mitchell is a 28-year-old African American male who lives in the southern region of the United States. He entered the workforce after graduating from high school, and he lives at home with his parents; however, he frequently comments about his desire to live independently. Mitchell's mother has never worked outside of the home. His father is a pastor at the local neighborhood church, where the family frequently volunteers. Mitchell does not have siblings, but he references cousins with whom he played throughout his childhood.

His employment record is inconsistent. Mitchell describes difficulty maintaining employment, especially when "the devil" is in his head. When he speaks of the devil, his voice is quiet, he limits eye contact, and he seems to withdraw. He provides an example of when the devil "got into [his] head" and he could not leave the house. It becomes evident that Mitchell stops going to work and isolates himself when he hears the devil, and this has resulted in his losing jobs. His longest term of employment was about one month.

When prompted, Mitchell openly discusses his relationship with the devil. He highlights how the devil says "mean things" about him, which make him feel "sad," and at times agitated. He reports his desire to have a girlfriend and go on dates, but the devil tells him he is not good enough to date. When Mitchell feels lonely, he isolates himself in

321

his bedroom where he will eat all of his meals, watch TV, or read comic books. He also reports that he enjoys drawing, mostly graphic art. Mitchell unfolds a piece of paper from his pocket; it is a picture of a superhero. He explains that the hero, Angeldefender, defeats evil in the world and is adored by all. He smiles, and reports that Angeldefender has many girlfriends who love him very much. Mitchell continues to display excitement as he describes the hero's material possessions, which include expensive sports cars. He leans in and quietly reports that Angeldefender needs to keep his real identity secret, or else the devil will come to Earth.

Mitchell's parents describe his childhood with limited detail. They report he was always a "good boy." There is evidence that he was frequently teased at school, and he needed extra supports in the classroom. Mitchell reports that he does not like to talk or even think about school, because it reminds him of how the other kids teased him.

His parents express concern about Mitchell's inability to maintain a job and live independently. They worry that he will not be able to live safely away from them. They describe several significant incidents over the last two years that required police intervention. During one incident, Mitchell demanded money and threatened a bank teller with a steak knife. When the police arrived for his arrest, Mitchell reported he needed the money to pay off the "evil guards of hell." The judge ordered Mitchell into inpatient hospitalization in lieu of a prison sentence. After his hospital release, he was linked to a psychiatrist in the community and began taking medications.

During the second incident, he assaulted his mother, "shaking her down" for money, again to pay debts to evil characters. Although his mother did not call the police, a neighbor did, and Mitchell was again admitted to inpatient hospitalization for psychiatric stabilization.

Mitchell is an artistic and sensitive young man. His hobbies include graphic novel drawing and writing letters. He frequently purchases car magazines and comic books, and keeps a large collection in his bedroom. He reports a strong desire to gain employment, live independently, and maintain relationships, including a romantic relationship. He has not received counseling in the past, but he meets with a psychiatrist once a month for medication management. Upon his last release from inpatient hospitalization, he was assigned a case manager who linked him to counseling services.

DESCRIPTION OF THE SCHIZOPHRENIA SPECTRUM AND OTHER PSYCHOTIC DISORDERS

According to the *DSM-5* (American Psychiatric Association [APA], 2013), psychotic disorders "are defined by abnormalities in one or more of the following five domains: delusions, hallucinations, disorganized thinking (speech), grossly disorganized or abnormal motor behavior (including catatonia), and negative symptoms" (p. 87). In this chapter, we address schizophrenia, and delusional, brief psychotic, schizophreniform, and schizoaffective disorders (see Chapter 9 for information on schizotypal personality disorder, a disorder on the spectrum).

The myriad of technical terms used to describe and define the psychotic disorders can be overwhelming. Table 10.1 provides an overview of the symptoms most frequently associated with the psychotic disorders and includes brief examples of each.

The examples in Table 10.1 highlight the range of experiences those with psychotic disorders may navigate. The simple presence of psychotic symptoms does not necessarily

TABLE 10.1   Symptoms Associated with Schizophrenia Spectrum and Psychotic Disorders

Term	Definition	Examples
Delusions	Strongly fixed beliefs that are not grounded in reality and are inflexible even when presented with contrary evidence. Delusions tend to be *persecutory, referential, somatic, religious, grandiose,* or *bizarre* in nature.	• Despite numerous clear medical tests, Danica believes that her husband and children are slowly poisoning her. • Luca is convinced that a newscaster is sending him special messages and instructions during the evening news.
Bizarre Delusions	Fixed beliefs that are not seen as plausible or understandable within one's culture. Bizarre delusions tend to involve beliefs that one's mind (e.g., thought withdrawal or thought insertion), or body (e.g., delusions of control) is being controlled by outside forces.	• An unidentified woman presents to a local emergency room requesting that her teeth be replaced with pennies so outside forces can no longer read her mind. • Isaac is afraid to go to sleep because the FBI is planning a brain transplant to more fully control him.
Hallucinations	Lifelike experiences in which a person senses (sees, hears, feels, tastes, or smells) something despite a complete lack of external stimulus for the experience. *Auditory,* followed by *visual* hallucinations, are most common, but hallucinations can also involve the senses of touch (*tactile*), smell (*olfactory*), and taste (*gustatory*). Often, tactile hallucinations are related to substance intoxication or withdrawal, and olfactory and gustatory hallucinations are related to medical concerns.	• Ava hears people calling her name and voices whispering around her; occasionally, the voices become loud enough that she can understand what they are saying. • Frederick is arrested after using a shotgun to shoot several holes through the side of his home. Upon interview, he states that he was defending his home from the "purple bugs and little green army men" who he saw outside.
Disorganized Speech or Thought	Disorganized thinking manifests in one's speech. This may include switching of topics (*derailment* or *loose associations*), unrelated answers to questions (*tangentiality*), sentence structures that are so disorganized one cannot understand them (*incoherence* or *word salad*), and made-up words (neologisms).	• Hayden speaks rapidly and with purpose; however, you are unable to follow his flow of thought. It appears as if the sentences are not related to each other, and he frequently changes topics even within sentences.
Grossly Disorganized or Abnormal Motor Behavior	When one is not able to react to the environment, the behavior may be labeled as *catatonic*. Examples of catatonic behavior include resistance to instructions (*negativism*), rigid or bizarre posture, lack of verbal responses (*mutism*), and lack of motor responses (*stupor*). Abnormal motor behavior may also include echoing speech and sounds, staring, or making repeated movements.	• Family members bring Grace to a local hospital where she blankly stares straight ahead and does not respond to any attempts at conversation. • Max sits rigidly in the waiting area; approximately every 10 seconds, he jerks his head up and to the left.

(Continued)

TABLE 10.1 *(Continued)*

Term	Definition	Examples
Negative symptoms	Whereas other symptoms involve the addition of behaviors or experiences not otherwise expected, negative symptoms refer to experiences that are missing or not present. The *DSM-5* includes five examples of negative symptoms: *diminished emotional expression* (reduction in amount of nonverbal emotions expressed), *avolition* (decrease in purposeful activity), *alogia* (decrease in speech), *anhedonia* (inability to experience pleasure), and *asociality* (lack of interest in social interactions).	• Jerry stays in bed all day and refuses to take care of daily living activities such as bathing, eating, and cleaning his living space. • Hope observes her family from a distance. She usually does not speak; when she does, she rarely uses more than 2–3 words. • Marcus rarely smiles, laughs, or shows interest in anything. When he speaks, he does so in a quiet monotone.

mean one will be diagnosed with schizophrenia or another psychotic disorder. Medical concerns including neurological conditions, cancers, dementia, delirium, autoimmune disorders, and metabolic conditions can cause symptoms of psychosis or even psychotic disorders. Even something as simple as a urinary tract infection in an older adult can result in psychosis. In these cases, the *DSM-5* has a special category of psychotic disorders called *Psychotic Disorder Due to Another Medical Condition.*

Use of, or withdrawal from, prescription or recreational drugs can also result in psychotic symptoms. Of course, the use of hallucinogens can cause hallucinations; however, so can cannabis (marijuana), inhalants, sedatives, stimulants, and even prescription steroids (APA, 2013). Alcohol withdrawal can cause various types of agitation and hallucinations, as can withdrawal from sedatives, hypnotics, and anxiolytics. These experiences may be diagnosed within the *substance-related and addictive disorders* section of the *DSM-5*, or they may be severe enough to fit within a *DSM-5* diagnostic category called *substance/medication-induced psychotic disorders* (APA, 2013). Finally, psychotic symptoms may be a symptom of a major depressive or manic episode, or the reexperiencing and flashbacks associated with posttraumatic stress disorder.

Although psychotic experiences are not rare, schizophrenia spectrum and other psychotic disorders are relatively rare. The disorders discussed in this chapter are diverse, and the people diagnosed with these disorders may appear and function differently depending on the specific constellation of symptoms, the ways in which individuals experience symptoms, and the duration of the symptoms. In some cases, individuals may remain quite functional despite their symptoms, and they may only need to manage symptoms for a short period of time. In other cases, the psychotic disorder can be disabling, all-consuming, and lead to a lifetime of impaired functioning. One's experience also depends on the specific nature of symptoms, underlying causes of symptoms, age of onset, quality of care received early in the illness, and family and social support.

Table 10.2 provides an overview of the major types and characteristics of primary psychotic disorders included in the *DSM-5*.

TABLE 10.2 Overview of Key Psychotic Disorders

Delusional Disorder	Brief Psychotic Disorder	Schizophreniform Disorder	Schizophrenia	Schizoaffective Disorder
Presence of delusions in the absence of other psychotic symptoms	*Sudden onset of psychotic symptoms lasting at least one day but not more than one month*	*Psychotic symptoms lasting at least one month but not more than six months*	*Psychotic symptoms and impairment of occupational and social functioning lasting at least six months*	*Psychotic symptoms characteristic of schizophrenia and major mood episodes*
Prevalence	**Prevalence**	**Prevalence**	**Prevalence**	**Prevalence**
0.2%	9% of cases of first-onset psychosis	Up to five times lower than schizophrenia	0.3–0.7%	0.3%
Characteristics	**Characteristics**	**Characteristics**	**Characteristics**	**Characteristics**
• Presence of delusions for at least 1 month • Functioning is not markedly impaired • No evidence of additional psychotic symptoms, overlap with manic or major depressive episodes, or overlap of substance use or other medical conditions	• Presence of delusions, hallucinations, disorganized speech, or grossly disorganized or catatonic behavior • Duration of 1 day to 1 month with full return to functioning • May be associated with marked stressor or postpartum onset	• Presence of delusions, hallucinations, disorganized speech, grossly disorganized or catatonic behavior, and/or negative symptoms • Duration of 1 month to 6 months • May be associated with or without good prognostic features	• Presence of delusions, hallucinations, disorganized speech, grossly disorganized or catatonic behavior, and/or negative symptoms for at least 1 month • Impairment in major life areas • Duration of combined symptoms for at least 6 months	• Presence of delusions, hallucinations, disorganized speech, grossly disorganized or catatonic behavior, and/or negative symptoms for at least 1 month and in the absence of mood episodes • Major depressive or manic episode concurrent with psychotic symptoms and present for the majority of the time

COUNSELOR CONSIDERATIONS

Although the therapeutic relationship is essential to all good counseling, it can be particularly difficult to establish a therapeutic relationship with individuals who are experiencing psychotic symptoms. Most counseling literature focuses on developing relationships with clients after they have stabilized on medication, perceive reality more accurately, and can communicate more readily (Walsh, 2011). However, it is still important to develop relationships with individuals who are experiencing active psychotic symptoms. It can be challenging to develop relationships with clients when they are out of contact with reality, have difficulty concentrating and focusing, feel stigma or denial, are agitated or terrorized from their symptoms, have difficulty trusting the counselor due to paranoia or other delusions, or are not interested in social relationships as a result of their negative symptoms.

The costs of mental health stigmas are high, and counselors should be alert to the likelihood that they have internalized stigmas, stereotypes, and fear regarding people who have psychotic disorders. Beliefs and biases that this population is untreatable, violent, and hopeless can get in the way of developing a strong therapeutic relationship with clients who may already experience a great deal of isolation and rejection. Counselors must always remember that experiences and emotions related to psychosis are very real for the client; compassion and understanding are essential, even—and especially—when symptoms and behaviors may appear bizarre and incomprehensible.

In addition to the well-known interpersonal benefits of a strong therapeutic relationship, it is also associated with both attitudes toward, and adherence to, antipsychotic medications, even after adjusting for clients' symptom severity and unique provider effects (McCabe et al., 2012). In addition to supporting medication adherence, the therapeutic alliance is also linked to higher levels of functioning, fewer symptoms, and less required medication among clients who have psychotic disorders (Rubin & Trawver, 2011).

Walsh (2011) outlined five recommendations for mental health providers who need to establish therapeutic communication with clients experiencing psychosis. These included:

1. Remembering that the counseling relationship may be the "sustaining link between the client and the external world, and provides the client with an environment of safety" (p. 4)
2. Expanding the client's perspective by exploring thoughts or feelings regarding areas of concern and then anchoring statements rather than arguing about their perceived reality
3. Processing distress by taking care that the structure of the conversation does not lead to the client feeling activated and overwhelmed
4. Facilitating new understanding of situations by slowly and gently confronting or providing alternative explanations of experiences
5. Introducing possibilities for action and activity in their social world

Counselors who transcend stigma and develop meaningful relationships with this population will maximize the power of the therapeutic relationship.

Most treatments for clients who have chronic psychotic disorders include a team approach in which a client is served by a variety of professionals including psychiatrists, case managers, and mental health professionals. Counselors who work with this population must possess interdisciplinary skills and an interest in working as a part of a team environment, be comfortable in uncomfortable or unpredictable situations, and demonstrate creativity and flexibility. This is particularly important because counselors may see clients on a short-term basis in crisis stabilization settings, *or* they may be called upon to develop long-term relationships in settings focused on managing severe and persistent mental illnesses such as schizophrenia. This may include providing in-home or case-management services in addition to more traditional counseling services. Creativity and flexibility are important because individuals who are experiencing psychosis may not be able, or willing, to share elements of their history; elements that are important in understanding their needs. Thus, counselors need to be able to build alliances with the client while collaborating with family members and significant others who can provide important information regarding the history of the illness, treatment, and impacts on functioning. Because some clients who have psychotic disorders will require involuntary or court-supervised treatment at the height of their illness, counselors should also be prepared to balance ethical principles of autonomy, beneficence (i.e., counselor actions that benefit clients), and nonmaleficence (i.e., not harming clients), and engage with the legal system as needed to ensure appropriate care and protection.

Accurate assessment is especially important when counseling clients with psychotic disorders. At a minimum, an accurate assessment of clients' symptoms will determine appropriate levels of care, treatment plan considerations, and medication needs. The *DSM-5* (APA, 2013) includes a Clinician-Rated Dimensions of Psychosis Symptom Severity assessment tool, which provides scales for the dimensional assessment of the primary symptoms of psychosis. The primary symptoms assessed include hallucinations, delusions, disorganized speech, negative symptoms, and abnormal psychomotor behavior. The assessment also includes the evaluation of symptoms related to cognitive impairment and mood (e.g., depression and mania). The assessment is an 8-item measure that is completed by the counselor. The counselor rates the severity of the indicated symptoms over the past 7 days on a scale from 0 (not present) to 4 (present and severe).

Cultural competence is particularly important because schizophrenia spectrum disorders are among the disorders that occur cross-culturally (Eriksen & Kress, 2005). Schizophrenia, in particular, is one of the few mental health disorders believed to occur worldwide, with individuals across cultures experiencing similar levels of prevalence and course. Cultural sensitivity is especially important because communication style, expression of distress, content of delusions, and nature of hallucinations vary among cultures. For example, individuals in one culture may hold religious ideas believed to be delusional by those from another culture. In some cultures, it is considered normal to hear voices as part of religious experiences, or to be visited by ghosts of recently deceased loved ones. Similarly, an uninformed counselor may unwittingly interpret a client's differences in verbal and nonverbal communication as signs of disorganized speech or behavior.

In all, counselors need to remain culturally alert so they do not interpret culturally normal events and experiences as pathological—or miss signs of distress different from their cultural expectations. As will be discussed in the following sections, one's experience with schizophrenia, including symptoms experienced, degree of impairment in functioning, and necessary treatment, is highly individual. Cultural competence may help a counselor to avoid the overdiagnosis of psychotic symptoms that tends to happen with clients from diverse backgrounds, and best understand how to support individuals and their families within their cultural context.

There is a significant body of literature related to treating schizophrenia spectrum disorders; however, that research tends to be grounded in psychiatry, psychiatric nursing, and social work. Treatment approaches tend to focus on two primary areas: medication management and psychosocial support. In most cases, medication management is essential for helping to reduce or eliminate positive symptoms such as hallucinations, delusions, disorganized thinking, and disorganized behavior. Although negative symptoms are not as likely to respond to treatment, some medications may help manage negative symptoms. Psychopharmacotherapy is often the focus during times of crisis, when clients' most severe symptoms are at their peak. During these crisis times, clients may need hospitalization in order to remain safe and secure.

Once a client has been stabilized on medication, treatment usually shifts to medication compliance, psychosocial support, and lifestyle management in an outpatient setting. Together, these elements help clients manage symptoms, function optimally, and participate in the least restrictive level of care. This level of care will vary by individual, but may include case management and counseling services while an individual lives independently, lives with loved ones, or takes part in supportive living programs. Regardless of their living arrangement, clients who experience severe and persistent mental illnesses are likely to participate in a variety of long-term services such as supported employment and social services designed to maximize independence and community living.

 Clinical Toolbox 10.1: In the Pearson etext, click here to review a plan that can be used to help prevent and manage psychotic symptom relapses.

In the literature, little attention is paid to the role of professional counselors per se in working with clients who have psychotic disorders. However, counselors frequently provide services to this population, and they play an essential role in helping clients uncover strengths, develop resiliency, and institute adaptive behaviors known to be associated with positive outcomes. Counselors can also help clients develop communication skills for working with their treatment team, and respond to subtle changes in environments that may trigger relapse, and/or lead some individuals to decompensate. Counselors can also provide support to loved ones who help provide care and support to individuals with these disorders. It is very important for counselors to understand symptoms, illness course, and typical treatment processes, so that these can be conveyed to clients and their support people.

PROGNOSIS

The prognosis of the disorders discussed in this chapter varies dramatically depending on the specific nature of the disorder, quality of early intervention services provided, family history, available social support, and the client's pre-illness level of functioning. For some, managing schizophrenia spectrum disorders may be a lifelong challenge. Others, however, may experience a psychotic episode, participate in appropriate treatment, and go on to live healthy and fulfilling lives.

SCHIZOPHRENIA

Description of the Disorder and Typical Client Characteristics

Schizophrenia is the most commonly known and understood of all the psychotic disorders. According to the *DSM-5* (APA, 2013), schizophrenia is characterized by several key features. First, an individual must experience at least a month during which two of the following psychotic symptoms are present: delusions, hallucinations, disorganized speech, grossly disorganized or catatonic behavior, or negative symptoms (see Table 10.1 for definitions and examples). At least one of the symptoms must include delusions, hallucinations, or disorganized speech. In addition, these symptoms must be accompanied by a decrease in ability to function in major life areas such as relationships, work, and school.

Together, the client must experience at least a six-month disturbance in functioning, even if some of the symptoms are present in attenuated or reduced form. Although previous editions of the *DSM* system included five diagnostic subtypes of schizophrenia (i.e., paranoid, disorganized, undifferentiated, residual, and catatonic), the *DSM-5* discontinued using subtypes because mental health providers had difficulty using the subtypes in a reliable manner, and because subtype identification did not necessarily inform treatment. However, these subtype references are still commonly found in the literature and in the settings where this population is treated.

According to the National Institute of Mental Health (National Institute of Mental Health [NIMH], 2009), schizophrenia affects about 1% of men and women in communities around the world. Symptoms usually begin to appear during late adolescence and early adulthood, with males developing symptoms at somewhat earlier ages than females. The onset of schizophrenia is rare in children and in adults over the age of 40. Early emergence of symptoms is associated with longer and more severe illness impacts (Gearing & Mian, 2009; Pagsberg, 2013). As will be discussed in the prognosis section, not everyone who develops schizophrenia will struggle with the disorder for the rest of his or her life. However, a majority of individuals with schizophrenia experience lifelong distress and disability.

Causes of schizophrenia are unknown. However, researchers describe schizophrenia as a brain disorder and believe there to be strong genetic and physiological contributors to the disorder (APA, 2013; Gaebel, 2011; NIMH, 2009). Having a parent, brother, or sister with schizophrenia increases one's risk of developing schizophrenia from 1% to 10%; having an identical twin with schizophrenia increases one's risk to 40–65%. Emerging neuroscience research suggests that people with schizophrenia have different brain structures, brain functions, and activity of neurotransmitters called dopamine and glutamate. In particular, reduced brain volume, changes in frontal and temporal cortexes, and a variety of neurological signs are all associated with schizophrenia and may be implicated in its etiology (APA, 2013).

Counselor Considerations

Counselors are most likely to provide services to clients with schizophrenia in two distinct settings: (a) inpatient crisis stabilization hospitals, where individuals may present with more noticeable or dramatic positive symptoms such as delusions, hallucinations, disorganized thought, disorganized behaviors, and responses to symptoms that threaten their immediate safety and ability to function, and (b) community mental health centers, where individuals may participate in long-term medication management and psychosocial services to promote independent living and prevent deterioration that may require hospitalization. Regardless of setting, counselors work with multidisciplinary teams to support functioning, remain hopeful regarding the possibility of positive outcomes, and work with the reality that schizophrenia often presents a life-long challenge in need of care. Each member of the team will bring unique strengths, perspectives, and resources that can assist the client.

Professional counselors bring a strength-based, collaborative, and developmental perspective to treatment; a perspective which highlights the development of collaborative treatment goals aimed at managing long-term symptoms. Counselors can also aid in building on strengths and supports that can be used in treatment. Research suggests that the more coping strategies this population has, the better they function (Phillips, Francey, Edwards, & McMurray, 2009). These findings suggest the value of counselors helping clients develop a variety of flexible coping strategies that can be used—over their lifespan—to aid in symptom management.

Neurocognitive deficits are a core feature of schizophrenia (Horan, Harvy, Kern, & Green, 2011), thus problems in cognitive processing persist and may be stable throughout adulthood, even when people with schizophrenia are not experiencing an active psychotic episode. Horan et al. (2011) identified four key areas that should be addressed in counseling: real-world functioning in work, independent living, and social domains; well-being and satisfaction with life; ability to engage successfully in treatment; and functional capacity in social situations. It is important that counselors assess for strengths and needs in these areas, and consider ways to attend to life needs while building on the resources associated with positive outcomes.

Counselors may also play an important role in assessing symptoms and other life experiences of clients with schizophrenia. This population often experiences a number of coexisting mental health concerns such as substance abuse, lack of insight, anxiety, problems in cognitive functioning, hostility, and behavioral disturbances (Potuzak, Ravichandran, Lewandowski, Ongür, & Cohen, 2012). People with schizophrenia have often had significant exposure to traumatic events, and many experience co-occurring depressive and anxiety disorders (Rubin & Trawver, 2011). Approximately 50% of those diagnosed with schizophrenia also experience a substance use disorder (Rubin & Trawver, 2011). The most commonly used substances included alcohol, tobacco, amphetamine, and cannabis (marijuana); some individuals use substances to cope with symptoms (e.g., help their voices go away, alleviate anxiety), but the use of some substances (e.g., cannabis) can actually induce or worsen psychotic symptoms (Raby, 2009).

Unfortunately, people with schizophrenia have much lower life expectancies compared to the general population. This is due to increased suicide risk (approximately 10% of this population completes suicide), increased risk of medical complications, and decreased engagement in health-promoting activities (APA, 2013; Rubin & Trawver, 2011). Researchers are uncertain whether these experiences are endemic to schizophrenia or represent unique mental health concerns that occur secondary to having the disorder. Counselors who work with this population should carefully assess and remain alert to the likelihood of confounding physical health concerns.

Whether the client is an adolescent or adult, family engagement and support are critical in the treatment of schizophrenia (Gearing, 2008; Rössler, 2011). Counselors should be mindful of ways in which they facilitate communication among members of the client's treatment team including, and especially, family members. As will be discussed in the following sections, counselors often play key roles in educating clients and their family members about schizophrenia and coping strategies, and they provide many of the direct services discussed in the treatment models and interventions section.

Treatment Models and Interventions

The literature on treatment and management of schizophrenia is largely based in psychiatry (i.e., the use of medications as a form of interventions) and social work (i.e., traditionally, placing an emphasis on connecting clients to community resources). Rössler (2011) identified three main pillars of treatment for schizophrenia: medications to relieve symptoms and prevent relapse, psychosocial interventions to help clients and families cope with the illness and prevent relapse, and vocational rehabilitation to reintegrate into the community and regain occupational functioning. It is essential that treatment for schizophrenia go beyond active symptom management (such as dealing with hallucinations and delusions), and move to promoting higher levels of functioning in everyday life tasks such as school, work, and social relations (Horan et al., 2011).

The American Psychiatric Association (APA, 2004) recommended that treatment goals and focus be tailored to the specific phase of illness. The following are recommendations from APA's (2004) *Practice Guideline for the Treatment of Patients with Schizophrenia*. Clients who are experiencing a crisis associated with the *acute phase* of the illness will need treatment approaches focused on minimizing harm while reducing key symptoms such as hallucinations, delusions, and disorganized behavior. Treatment in this phase includes attention to thorough assessment, medication, and psychosocial interventions focused on ensuring the most stable and safe environments possible. This phase will also involve the education and support of family members.

During the *stabilization phase* (in the months following the acute phase), treatment goals are focused on reducing stress, providing support, and promoting recovery. This includes the continuation of medication, the continuance of structured and directive psychosocial interventions, and a heavy focus on education.

During the *stable phase*, counselors focus on relapse prevention via psychosocial interventions. Key psychosocial treatments include psychoeducation, skills training, cognitive behavioral therapy, behavioral modification, family intervention, supported employment, and assertive community treatment (Kopelowicz, Liberman, & Zarate, 2007).

PSYCHOPHARMACOTHERAPY Most people with schizophrenia need to take medications to manage their symptoms and function effectively. Psychopharmacotherapy is essential during active phases of the illness and is important in preventing relapse. The APA practice guidelines outline three phases of psychopharmacological treatment for schizophrenia. During the acute phase, usually lasting 4–8 weeks, physicians focus on managing hallucinations, delusions, and agitation. During the stabilization phase, symptoms may be controlled, but clients are at high risk of relapse if medications are interrupted or new stressors are introduced; generally, this phase includes about six months of maintenance on medications. During the maintenance phase, the focus turns to preventing relapse and enhancing functioning through medication. For clients who have experienced multiple episodes of psychosis, this may mean indefinitely continuing antipsychotic medications. Because noncompliance with medication is the most common cause of symptom relapse, the focus in this stage turns to medication, education, and the management of side effects.

Medication management is both an art and a science. In some cases, it may take a client and physician many years and attempts to find the combination of medications that promotes optimal functioning and includes tolerable side effects. This trial and error process may be frustrating to physicians, clients, and family members alike. Although counselors will not be prescribing medication, they play a critical role in supporting medication compliance. If appropriately trained, counselors may provide psychoeducation to clients and families regarding medication, help clients find creative ways to fit medication into their daily lives, and help clients develop the skills they need to talk with their physician regarding side effects and medication concerns.

Counselors should be familiar with the common medications and side effects of medications used to treat schizophrenia. These medications focus almost exclusively on the treatment of positive symptoms (e.g., hallucinations, delusions), although some newer medications may assist with reduction of negative symptoms and associated cognitive impairments. Generally speaking, psychiatrists will rely on two major types of medications in the treatment of schizophrenia: typical and atypical antipsychotics (NIMH, 2012; Schizophrenia Medications, 2013). Depending on the client's specific symptoms, psychiatrists may also supplement antipsychotic medications with antidepressants, antianxiety drugs, lithium, antiepileptic drugs, and estrogen replacement for women (Schizophrenia Medications, 2013).

Typical antipsychotics include longstanding drugs such as chlorpromazine (e.g., Thorazine) and haloperidol (e.g., Haldol). These drugs are considered effective for treating positive symptoms such as hallucinations and delusions, and some may be administered via monthly injections to enhance medication compliance. Unfortunately, side effects may be extreme and include a range of cognitive, emotional, and physical symptoms. Of particular concern with typical antipsychotics are risk of symptoms that may lead to irreversible Parkinson-like symptoms, risk of sudden drop in blood pressure, and fatal side effects related to cardiac arrest and neuroleptic malignant syndrome (NIMH, 2012; Schizophrenia Medications, 2013).

Atypical antipsychotics include newer drugs such as clozapine (e.g., Clozaril), risperidone (e.g., Risperdal), olanzapine (e.g., Zyprexa), quetiapine (e.g., Seroquel), ziprasidone (e.g., Geodon), aripiprazole (e.g., Abilify), and paliperiodone (e.g., Invega). These drugs are considered effective at treating positive symptoms, may reduce negative symptoms, and may also reduce cognitive impairment, depression, hostility, and suicide risk (NIMH, 2012). They tend to have fewer severe side effects than typical antipsychotics; however, they may still cause a number of uncomfortable and potentially dangerous cognitive and physical effects. Atypical antipsychotics are associated with significant weight gain and metabolic changes leading to diabetes and high cholesterol. They may also cause extrapyramidal side effects (i.e., movement disorder). although not to the same extent as typical antipsychotics. Clozapine is also associated with problems with white blood cell counts (NIMH, 2012; Schizophrenia Medications, 2013).

Typical (e.g., haloperidol) and atypical (e.g., risperidone, aripiprazole) antipsychotics are also available in long-acting injectable form. These medications are delivered on a regular basis ranging from once weekly to once monthly. Benefits of injectable antipsychotic medications include increased compliance, especially for individuals who may struggle to remember to take medication, take medication incorrectly, or be tempted to discontinue due to unpleasant side effects or influences of delusions. On the other hand, injection format is not available for all medications, may be unpleasant for those who have a fear of needles, and may present a threat to autonomy.

PSYCHOSOCIAL INTERVENTIONS Psychosocial interventions are focused on helping clients and their families cope with the illness and its far-reaching effects including stigma, discrimination, worry about being a burden, and access to quality care (Rössler, 2011). Psychosocial treatments include certain types of psychotherapy, psychoeducation, and social and vocational training. They are helpful in providing support, education, and guidance to people with mental illnesses and their families. Psychoeducation is especially important when working with this population. A meta-analysis of randomized controlled trials on the use of psychoeducation demonstrated that these interventions had a medium-sized effect on relapse and rehospitalization for approximately 1 year; interventions that involved family members produced stronger and more lasting results (Lincoln, Wilhelm, & Nestoriuc, 2007).

Often held in group formats, psychoeducation tends to be experienced positively by clients with schizophrenia (Chadzynska & Charzynska, 2011). Benefits of psychoeducation include gaining knowledge, enhancing mood, developing adaptive relationships with others, learning strategies for coping with symptoms, general education about their illness, and understanding triggers and signs of escalating symptoms.

The Substance Abuse and Mental Health Services Administration's (SAMHSA) *Family Psychoeducation Evidence-Based Practices Kit* (2010) is an excellent free resource focused on evidence-based practices for conducting psychoeducation. In addition, the UCLA Clinical Research Center for Schizophrenia and Psychiatric Rehabilitation offers a series of evidence-based skills-training modules focused on the key needs of clients with schizophrenia. These modules include a focus on medication management, symptom management, recreation, basic conversations, community reentry, job seeking, and workplace fundamentals.

Another type of psychosocial intervention for use in treating schizophrenia is cognitive behavioral therapy for psychosis (CBTp; e.g., Beck, Rector, Stolar, & Grant, 2009; Kingdon & Turkington, 2002). Meta-analyses have found a small moderate, but positive, impact of CBTp in treating schizophrenia (Jolley & Garety, 2011). The focus on CBTp is on helping clients to develop insight, or understanding, regarding schizophrenia and the actions they can take to increase their chances for improvement (Jolley & Garety, 2011). Counselors use CBTp to help clients learn how to test the reality of their thoughts and experiences while also managing overall symptoms (NIMH, 2009). At least 16 sessions of CBTp should be used to target persistent symptoms, reduce number and length of hospital stays, and improve mood and functioning (Jolley & Garety, 2011).

Clinical Toolbox 10.2: In the Pearson etext, click here to read about distraction and interaction techniques that can be used by clients to help them manage auditory hallucinations.

CREATIVE TOOLBOX ACTIVITY 10.1   Listening with Fuller Understanding

Robert C. Schwartz, PhD, PCC-S

Activity Overview

In this activity, clients who have auditory or visual hallucinations are invited to listen, with a fuller understanding, to their hallucinations. This activity helps clients to gain a more concrete and in-depth understanding of the meaning behind their hallucinations. Clients are provided two blank sheets of paper and asked to draw two separate images depicting the most relevant aspects of their hallucinations. The first image depicts, as closely as possible, what is heard or seen. The second image depicts the most important message that the first image represents to them (i.e., a phenomenological interpretation of the hallucination).

Treatment Goal(s) of Activity

This activity aims to help clients who have hallucinations (a) more clearly and fully tune into and document their hallucinatory experiences (to lessen fear and psychological avoidance of the experiences); and (b) identify what meaning their hallucinatory experiences have (to enhance self-reflection, and to gain a greater sense of control over the experiences).

Directions

1. Ascertain client readiness to engage in this intervention, and secure client agreement to engage in drawing images (which may seem awkward or embarrassing at first). This intervention may be inappropriate for clients who are in a state of heightened anxiety/distress due to florid psychotic symptomatology. This intervention may also be inappropriate for clients who, due to severe neurocognitive deficits associated with severe forms of psychosis (e.g., schizophrenia disorganized or catatonic type), are unable to understand the content or purpose of the intervention.

2. Discuss the purpose of the activity with the client and attempt to empower the client toward a willingness to experiment with learning how to better manage the distressing hallucinations.

3. Present the client with two blank pieces of paper and writing utensils (colored pencils and an eraser are recommended so clients can revise images as needed).

4. On the first piece of paper, ask the client to choose one recent visual *or* auditory hallucination. Ask the client to draw an image of what has been seen or said as fully as possible. After the image has been completed, clarify the image with the client, summarizing its aspects (both to reinforce counselor understanding and the client fully grasping the image content).

5. On the second piece of paper, ask the client to draw an image of what the first image means to him or her. For example, if the first (hallucinatory) image depicts a house with someone running away from the structure into the street because the client is being told to leave as he is in danger, the second (meaning) image may show bright red and yellow colors in the form of a sun with jagged sharp edges depicting a sense of fear or panic. After the image has been completed, clarify the image with the client, focusing on the emotional content and personal messages drawn (both to reinforce counselor understanding and the client fully processing the image's meaning).

6. Follow the client's lead while he or she is engaged in the creative process. Show empathy and support as the client attempts to document what is in his or her mind.

7. After the client has completed his or her drawings, process them.

Process Questions

1. What does this image represent to you (depiction #1)?
2. What stands out most for you as you look at this image (depiction #1)?
3. What does this picture tell you about the first image (depiction #2)?
4. What feelings come up for you as you look at this picture (depiction #2)?
5. What does this picture tell you about yourself as you reflect on this experience (depiction #2)?

REHABILITATION RESOURCES Finally, treatment for schizophrenia would not be complete without attention being paid to the need for coordination of services and care when promoting long-term management (Rössler, 2011). Rehabilitation resources typically include a type of case management program that connects individuals to mental health, housing, or rehabilitation agencies or services. In some cases, counselors may be called on to provide rehabilitation resources and services directly. In other cases, counselors may collaborate with case managers and social workers who are tasked with ensuring that clients have the services they need in order to live in the community as independently as possible. Clients with schizophrenia may participate in Assertive Community Treatment (ACT) and other focused programs which include access to housing resources and supports and supported employment/vocational opportunities (APA, 2004; Rössler, 2011).

ACT is an intensive, multidisciplinary team approach that allows those with severe and persistent mental illnesses access to services needed to maintain independent living. Services are tailored to the individual and are often provided in-home by a consistent team of professionals. Key features of ACT include psychiatric medication management, individual counseling, mobile crisis intervention, hospitalization, substance abuse treatment, skills training, supported employment, supported education, family skills training, family collaboration, and legal and advocacy services (National Alliance on Mental Illness, 2013). SAMHSA also offers a free *Assertive Community Treatment Evidence-Based Practice Kit* (2008) for those who would like to learn more about this treatment modality.

Supported employment is a service available to those with disabilities. Supported employment involves special training and support to secure and maintain employment activities. SAMHSA (2010) offers a free *Supported Employment Evidence-Based Practice Kit* that can help counselors design optimal programs. Supportive housing programs are designed to foster independent living within the community to the extent possible. This care may include financial assistance as well as help with daily tasks and household demands.

Prognosis

While no less than one-third of all people with schizophrenia have relatively benign outcomes, for the majority, the illness has a profound, lifelong impact on personal growth and development. The initial symptoms of the disorder are not strongly predictive of the pattern of course, but the mode of onset (acute or insidious), the duration of illness prior to diagnosis and treatment, the presence or absence of substance use, as well as background variables such as premorbid adjustment, educational and occupational achievement, and availability of a supportive social network, allow a reasonable accuracy of prediction in the short to medium term (2–5 years; Gaebel, 2011).

In all, for more than one-half of those individuals diagnosed with schizophrenia, the disorder will prove to be a lifelong disability (Gaebel, 2011). Those with more positive prognoses are those who have a later age of onset and higher social development and functioning at the disorder's initial onset (Rubin & Trawver, 2011).

SCHIZOPHRENIFORM DISORDER

Description of the Disorder and Typical Client Characteristics

With the exception of duration and long-term impact, symptom criteria for schizophreniform disorder are identical to those for schizophrenia. These symptoms include two or more of the following over a one-month period: delusions, hallucinations, disorganized speech, grossly disorganized or catatonic behavior, and negative symptoms (APA, 2013). At least one of the symptoms must be delusions, hallucinations, or disorganized speech.

Unlike schizophrenia, the symptoms in schizophreniform disorder last at least 1 month, but not more than 6 months. In essence, schizophreniform disorder is considered a gateway, or precursor diagnosis, to schizophrenia. Characteristics of individuals who have schizophreniform disorder are similar to those who have schizophrenia; however, the incidence of schizophreniform disorder is only about 20% that of schizophrenia (APA, 2013).

Psychotic Break = gateway to Schizophrenia [handwritten margin note]

Counselor Considerations

Because this disorder is on the schizophrenia spectrum, the counselor considerations for working with clients who have schizophreniform disorder are nearly identical to those mentioned in the previous section. Attention to medication considerations, immediate safety, psychoeducation, and family support is critical. By definition, clients who have schizophreniform disorder are experiencing new or first-episode psychosis. This means that clients and their families may need special attention and support as they learn about the disorder and its implications, and navigate mental health systems for the first time. Counselors must balance a realistic appraisal of the situation with an optimistic realization that "the course of these disorders is not fixed, with deterioration in social and occupational functioning being the norm and a poor prognosis inevitable, but rather, as fluid and malleable" (McGorry & Goldstone, 2011, p. 142).

Treatment Models and Interventions

Treatment models and interventions for schizophreniform disorder are nearly identical to those used in the initial and stabilization phases of schizophrenia. However, there is an emerging body of literature regarding treatment considerations for those with first-episode psychosis. For example, Valencia, Juarez, and Ortega (2012) proposed an integrated treatment approach specific to clients with first-episode psychosis, and conducted a randomized controlled trial to investigate its effectiveness. Consistent with recommendations for treating schizophrenia, the integrated treatment included medication, psychosocial approaches, and psychoeducation. Nearly all (95%) of those in the integrated group reported remission of symptoms compared to just 59% of those in the medication-only group. Similarly, 57% of individuals in the integrated approach experienced functional remission (returning to normal psychosocial functioning) compared to just 4% of those who received medication only. Careful attention to early support and intervention may have a considerable impact on quality of life and even the course of the illness.

Prognosis

Approximately one-third of those who are diagnosed with schizophreniform disorder recover completely; the other two-thirds of individuals go on to meet criteria for schizophrenia or schizoaffective disorder (APA, 2013). Researchers have identified several prognostic features for schizophreniform disorder. Rapid onset of positive symptoms, confusion or distress in relation to the symptoms, optimal occupational and social functioning prior to episode onset, and absence of negative symptoms such as flat or blunted affect, are all associated with good prognostic features (APA, 2013). On the other hand, clients who have a slow deterioration in functioning and presence of negative symptoms are more likely to go on to develop schizophrenia.

BRIEF PSYCHOTIC DISORDER

Description of the Disorder and Typical Client Characteristics

Brief psychotic disorder is described as the presence of psychotic symptoms similar to those seen in schizophrenia (e.g., delusions, hallucinations, bizarre behavior; APA, 2013). However, as the name implies, the client experiences the symptoms for a short amount of time, not less than 1 day, and not more than 1 month. In general, brief psychotic disorder is triggered by a traumatic or stressful event. If the symptoms continue beyond 30 days, the diagnosis of brief psychotic disorder serves as a precursor to schizophreniform disorder.

The *DSM-5* outlines three subtypes of brief psychotic disorder for counselors to consider. The first is brief psychotic disorder with a marked stressor(s). In this type, there is an identifiable stressor, trigger, or combination of events that lead to the development of symptoms. The second subtype is brief psychotic disorder without a marked stressor(s). In this case, the onset of the psychotic episode cannot be linked to a particular stressful situation or event. Although the etiology of the psychosis is unknown, the symptoms alleviate within the 30-day limitation. The third subtype is brief psychotic disorder with postpartum onset. In this type, the psychotic episode occurs after childbirth, usually within 4 weeks.

Counselor Considerations

Because brief psychotic disorder symptoms remit fairly quickly, it is a rare disorder for counselors to come across. The sudden and severe onset of brief psychotic disorder may leave clients feeling disoriented and confused. As clients work toward stabilization, counselors need to attend to clients' struggles to understand their experiences. Because psychotic symptoms are unexpected and new to clients with this disorder, counselors must be attentive to clients' overall health and well-being (e.g., nutrition and hygiene). During times of psychosis, clients may be at a higher risk for self-harm, including suicide, thus clients' safety should also be a priority.

The nature of a brief psychotic disorder requires counselors to be mindful of the timeline of symptoms, especially when establishing a marked stressor or series of traumatic events. It may behoove counselors to utilize additional sources of information when collecting information on the presenting symptoms (e.g., family members or friends of the client). This may be especially important in a crisis situation when the client is actively experiencing a psychotic episode, and cannot accurately provide such information.

The diagnosis of brief psychotic disorder mandates that the symptoms *not* be due to other psychotic disorders such as schizophrenia, schizoaffective disorder, or delusional disorder. Therefore, when assessing a client's mental health history, it is important to identify whether the presenting psychosis is the first psychotic episode experienced. Counselors must also consider if the psychotic symptoms are related to a manic episode, and thus possibly associated with a bipolar disorder. Differential diagnosis of substance use or a medical condition is imperative for an accurate assessment of the etiology of the psychotic symptoms. As such, counselors should recommend all clients with new-onset psychosis be medically screened and evaluated to ensure symptoms are not related to a medical condition or substance issue. The *DSM-5* suggests a potential link between personality disorders and the development of a brief psychotic episode. An accurate understanding of the client's mental health history is imperative to establishing a holistic treatment plan.

Treatment Models and Interventions

The treatments for brief psychotic disorder vary and depend on the severity and onset of the symptoms. However, generally, the previously mentioned treatment protocols used to treat the acute phase of schizophrenia are used to treat brief psychotic disorder. The least restrictive treatment modality that maintains the client's safety is ideal. If psychotic symptoms are

[handwritten margin notes: Psychosocial: ↑ coping skills — Better respond in the future; ↑ awareness to triggers; address catalyst]

severe, the client may be hospitalized for stabilization and to minimize the risk of harm to self or others. Atypical antipsychotics may be used to alleviate the psychotic symptoms. Common atypical antipsychotics used in the treatment of clients experiencing brief psychotic disorder include olanzapine (e.g., Zyprexa) and intramuscular ziprasidone (e.g., Geodon).

Once the psychosis has diminished, individual counseling is appropriate. Counseling interventions may include exploration of the triggering traumatic event (if one is present), and enhancing coping skills in order to prevent severe responses to stressful situations in the future. Group counseling for stress management or conflict resolution may also be appropriate, depending on the situation surrounding the psychotic episode.

Prognosis

The prognosis for those diagnosed with a brief psychotic disorder that resolves within 30 days is very good. It is common for clients to experience the symptoms of psychosis for only a few days before stabilization is reached. The long-term outcomes for clients with this disorder are more reflective of the treatment for the trauma or stressor, if one exists, that served as the catalyst for the disorder's onset.

DELUSIONAL DISORDER

Description of the Disorder and Typical Client Characteristics

Delusional disorder involves the presence of nonbizarre cognitive distortions. The cognitive nature of this disorder makes it challenging to diagnose. Clients with delusional disorder do not usually present with the traditional psychotic symptoms, or bizarre behavior discussed in relation to the other disorders addressed this chapter. Instead, the delusions are potentially plausible stories that counselors may not interpret as unusual. These believable delusions must be present for at least one month before counselors can consider the diagnosis of delusional disorder.

Delusional disorder is categorized by the underlying theme of the delusion and diagnosed by a corresponding subtype (APA, 2013). The *erotomanic type* encompasses beliefs related to romantic relationships. Clients with this disorder believe that someone else (often a famous person or a superior) is in love them. It is not uncommon for the object of their affection to be a stranger. The *grandiose type* represents beliefs related to exceptional talent or groundbreaking innovation. The *jealous type* involves the belief that one's partner is being unfaithful. The *persecutory type* involves the belief that others want to do the client harm, even though there is no evidence to support that the client is being persecuted. The client's perception that others want to harm him or her may lead to legal system involvement should a client decide to retaliate. The *somatic type* describes beliefs associated with bodily functions or sensations. Counselors may diagnose *mixed type* when clients do not meet the full criteria for any one subtype, but instead demonstrate symptoms from more than one delusional category. *Unspecified type* is assigned if the belief cannot be categorized into any of the defined subtypes.

Counselor Considerations

Generally, there is a relatively limited impact on the psychosocial functioning of a client experiencing a delusional disorder (APA, 2013), which leads to difficulties in diagnosing the disorder. Counselors may be attuned to subtle clues that suggest a potential for these nonbizarre delusions within the client's story. For example, counselors may be alerted by the client's disproportionate sensitivity, irritability, or hostility when a belief is questioned. Counselors working with clients with delusional disorder may observe the belief to be time consuming. Clients may describe related stories to the foundational delusion at length, or find ways to focus most of the counseling sessions on the theme of the delusion. For the most part, the delusion appears nondisruptive; however, if unusual or disruptive behavior does occur, it tends to be in direct relation to the delusion itself. For example, it is not uncommon for those diagnosed with delusional disorder *erotomanic* type to stalk the objects of their affection. Or clients experiencing persecutory symptoms may begin to isolate themselves for protection from those they believe to be threatening them.

Although overall intellectual or occupational functioning may not be negatively affected by the delusion, a client may experience distress in social or personal relationships. Counselors must be attuned to the impact of delusions on those relationships closest to clients. For example, with the *jealous* type, more aggressive symptoms or anger may develop as accusations are made, which will significantly impact the personal relationship. Many counselors may never encounter a client with a delusional disorder, as the estimated prevalence rate is only 0.03% (APA, 2013).

Treatment Models and Interventions

Clients diagnosed with delusional disorder may demonstrate limited insight, which can present a therapeutic challenge for counselors. There is also variability in the course of the disorder based on type. For example, the *persecutory* type (the most common subtype) may be chronic in nature, whereas other types may demonstrate periods of full remission. Counselors may need to track the evolution of the delusion over time. The focus of treatment may be to increase insight and combat the faulty assumptions of the delusion. Counselors should also pay attention to any resulting emotional distress related to the delusion. For example, a counselor may assist with anger management for those diagnosed with the *jealous* type or help to alleviate depressive symptoms for those diagnosed with the *erotomanic* type. Clients experiencing the *somatic* type symptoms may became anxious that medical tests are not revealing a disease, or medical treatments are not alleviating perceived symptoms. Counselors can work with clients to develop new coping strategies to alleviate anxiety. The literature includes two types of treatment for clients with delusional disorder: acceptance and commitment therapy and psychopharmacotherapy.

ACCEPTANCE AND COMMITMENT THERAPY (ACT) When applied to treating clients with delusional disorder, ACT focuses on helping clients to accept their disruptive thoughts and behaviors (Bach & Hayes, 2002). By acknowledging the situation and increasing their mindfulness surrounding difficult situations, clients are able to reduce associated harmful thoughts and feelings. In a randomized controlled trial, researchers demonstrated reductions in hospitalizations for clients diagnosed with various psychotic disorders, including delusional disorder, after receiving ACT treatment (Bach & Hayes, 2002). In follow-up reviews, the clients who participated in ACT were better able to identify delusional thoughts. Although more research is needed on using ACT, the foundational tenets appear to support increased insight for clients with this disorder.

CREATIVE TOOLBOX ACTIVITY 10.2   Mindful Relaxation

Robert C. Schwartz, PhD, PCC-S

Activity Overview

This activity invites clients with psychotic symptoms to gain mindful awareness of their distress in order to reduce psychological avoidance and unconscious reactivity experienced secondary to psychosocial stressors. Clients are asked to learn mindfulness-based techniques that may lead to acceptance of painful experiences, and ultimately a more thoughtful and deliberate response to these situations.

Treatment Goal(s) of Activity

The primary goals of this activity are to provide a technique to help clients (a) gain an increased self-awareness of their own mental activity; (b) manage emotional stress resulting from psychotic symptomatology (e.g., reduced ability to manage daily living skills), or social tension (e.g., stigma or isolation); and (c) accept, rather than avoid, their internal experiences in order to develop a fuller and richer sense of self.

Directions

1. Ascertain client readiness to engage in this intervention, ensuring that the client is able to engage in calming/mindfulness-based exercises. This intervention may be inappropriate for clients who are in a state of heightened anxiety/distress due to florid psychotic symptomatology.
2. Discuss the purpose of mindful relaxation with the client. Educate the client on mindfulness, and how it enhance calmness and help the client feel better (i.e., less stress).
3. Ask the client to sit with both feet flat on the ground (a comfortable chair or firm couch is often more helpful).
4. Ask the client to take three deep breaths in through the nose (to the count of 3) and out through the mouth (to the count of 5). It is recommended that the counselor engage in the same actions to both model the position, and to desensitize the client to the intervention. Repeat this intervention 2–3 times after a short break in between.
5. Ask the client to feel bodily changes—tension release, coolness in his or her head, calmness in his or her body. Ask the client to report the main bodily changes experienced.
6. Then, ask the client to close his or her eyes and take three deep breaths in through the nose (to the count of 3) and out through the mouth (to the count of 5). Repeat this intervention 2–3 times after a short break in between.
7. Ask the client to feel changes in his or her body. Ask the client to report the main bodily changes he or she noticed.
8. Then, suggest that the client picture a person or thing that usually invites negative feelings (e.g., a critical friend, a stressful encounter that day). Ask the client to report what the image is, and also bodily changes noticed as the image is pictured (e.g., more bodily tension, headache). Suggest that the client not attempt to push away or avoid the image, but rather just see it and accept it as a temporary picture in his or her mind. Note: It is not necessary to process what the image means to the client.
9. With eyes closed and the same image pictured, ask the client to reengage in the breathing exercises (#6 above).

10. Again, ask the client to feel changes in his or her body after the mindfulness exercise. Ask the client to report the main bodily changes observed.
11. Ask the client to open his or her eyes and process the evolution of the experiences, focusing on how both mental activity, and our response to this activity can be better under our control with patience, acceptance, and practice.

Process Questions

1. How did it feel to breathe deeply and slowly?
2. What were the main changes noticed in your body when a stressful picture was called up?
3. Did your body/mind change, even with the stressful picture, when you simply noticed it?
4. Did you find that calming your mind, even with the stressful image pictured, helped to change your body/reaction?
5. During which other times today could you have used this technique, and how would you have done that?

PSYCHOPHARMACOTHERAPY   There is mixed research on the use of antipsychotic medications in the treatment of delusional disorder. Historically, it was thought that antipsychotic medications were not effective; however, newer research suggests that antipsychotic medication can be helpful (Pillmann, Wustmann, & Marneros, 2012), at least for those diagnosed with *somatic* and *persecutory* types. Pillmann et al. (2012) estimated positive responses to antipsychotic medication treatments at a rate of 50%. Further research is needed to ascertain more substantial support for the use of antipsychotic medication in treating delusional disorder.

Prognosis

In general, clients diagnosed with delusional disorder demonstrate higher levels of functioning when compared to those with perceptual psychotic symptoms (e.g., schizophrenia; APA, 2013). However, because clients lack awareness that there is a problem, and they rarely seek treatment, it is challenging to predict the prognosis of this disorder.

SCHIZOAFFECTIVE DISORDER

Description of the Disorder and Typical Client Characteristics

Schizoaffective disorder involves the presence of both psychotic and mood symptoms. Clients present with the psychotic symptoms described in this chapter (i.e., delusions, hallucinations, and/or bizarre behavior), yet they experience these psychotic symptoms concurrently with a predominant depressive episode and/or a manic episode (APA, 2013).

The mood episode will determine the subtype of schizoaffective disorder. In diagnostic practice, counselors will specify *bipolar type* when a manic episode is part of the presentation, and *depressive type* if the mood disturbance is accounted for by a major depressive episode in the absence of a history of manic episodes. The key to distinguishing schizoaffective disorder from schizophrenia is the prominent presence of mood symptoms. It is suggested in the *DSM-5* (APA, 2013) that counselors consider a diagnosis of schizophrenia if psychotic symptoms become prominent in proportion to mood symptoms.

Counselor Considerations

There is a great deal of debate in the literature on how to view schizoaffective disorder in relation to schizophrenia and depressive/bipolar disorders. There are some experts who insist schizoaffective is not a valid disorder, but rather two distinct diagnoses: schizophrenia and a depressive or bipolar disorder. Others view schizoaffective disorder as being on a continuum in which schizoaffective falls somewhere in between schizophrenia and depressive/bipolar disorders (Kantrowitz & Citrome, 2011). To receive this diagnosis, the *DSM-5* requires the person have a 2-week period in which hallucinations and/or delusions are present, but there is an absence of the (or markedly fewer) mood symptoms (APA, 2013). This criterion is especially important, as it differentiates schizoaffective disorder from mood disorders with psychotic features. Some researchers argue, though, that there is no scientific evidence to support a 2-week absence of mood symptoms as suggested in the *DSM-5* (Lake & Hurwitz, 2008), and the *ICD-10* does not include this criterion in its disorder requirements. Controversy over the reliability and validity of schizoaffective disorder has lead many researchers to conclude that there is frequent misdiagnosis—or overdiagnosis—of schizoaffective disorder (Casecade, Kalali, & Buckley, 2009; Heckers, 2012; Lake & Hurwitz, 2008). Thus, it is imperative that counselors consider the timing of symptoms carefully when assessing for schizoaffective disorder. Careful attention to timing of symptoms will help counselors differentiate between schizoaffective disorder (which includes considerable overlap between psychotic experiences and mood episodes), and bipolar or major depressive disorders with psychotic features (which include primarily mood concerns with some psychotic experiences).

Clients diagnosed with schizoaffective disorder generally demonstrate better cognitive functioning than clients diagnosed with schizophrenia (Kantrowitz & Citrome, 2011). Many helping professionals consider schizoaffective disorder to be a less impairing disorder as compared to schizophrenia.

Treatment Models and Interventions

Treatment for schizoaffective disorder includes a combination of psychotic and mood symptom intervention strategies. Clients who are experiencing debilitating psychosis and/or mood symptoms may need inpatient hospitalization to ensure safety. Once clients are stabilized, outpatient treatment is similar to treatment interventions for schizophrenia. In terms of research, clients diagnosed with schizoaffective disorder are often combined in sample populations with those diagnosed with schizophrenia. Thus, using similar treatment strategies to treat both populations is common practice. Please reference the previous treatment sections in this chapter as well as those in Chapter 4 for a comprehensive review of the treatment approaches which may be useful in treating schizoaffective disorder.

In addition to the previously discussed treatments (i.e., for schizophrenia/ schizophreniform and depressive/bipolar disorders), psychosocial interventions for schizoaffective disorder may include psychoeducation and social skills training.

Psychopharmacotherapy tends to include a combination of antipsychotics and mood stabilizers. As with schizophrenia, a multidisciplinary approach is most common when helping clients with schizoaffective disorder; therefore, it is imperative that counselors communicate with other professionals (e.g., psychiatrists, case managers) involved in the client's treatment.

Successful employment predicts better long-term outcomes for clients diagnosed with schizophrenia and schizoaffective disorders (Wallace, 2003). Thus, supported employment or vocational rehabilitation counseling may serve as important pieces of a holistic treatment plan for this population.

PSYCHOEDUCATION Counselors can facilitate clients' knowledge of schizoaffective disorder through psychoeducation interventions. Through psychoeducation, clients are empowered to understand their disorder and may be more open to treatment interventions. *medication side effects*

Family involvement and education is also helpful in treatment. Family members who understand the symptoms of psychotic disorders can better support clients in adhering to their treatment plan (Torrey, 2006). Family members may also find that involvement with the National Alliance on Mental Illness (NAMI) assists with helping them advocate for their family members (see their website for more information).

Voices from the Trenches 10.1: In the Pearson etext, click here to watch a counselor discuss the importance of understanding and empathizing with how psychotic symptoms can impact a client's daily functioning.

SOCIAL SKILLS TRAINING Social skills training is an evidence-based intervention that can be used with clients diagnosed with schizoaffective disorder, or any of the schizophrenia spectrum disorders (Bellack, Mueser, Gingerich, & Agresta, 2004). Through social skills training, clients learn—or relearn—socially acceptable behaviors intended to increase positive relationships and experiences in the community. Social skills training with this population can improve communication skills and enhance compliance with medication management (Bellack et al., 2004; Patterson et al., 2003). It can also contribute to improvements for clients in navigating community (e.g., transportation), and household (e.g., financial organization) matters (Patterson et al., 2003).

PSYCHOPHARMACOTHERAPY As with other psychotic disorders, many clients are prescribed antipsychotics to provide relief from symptoms. In a sample of individuals diagnosed with schizoaffective disorder, 93% were prescribed an antipsychotic as one piece of their treatment plan (Casecade et al., 2009). However, it is fairly common to work with clients who are prescribed a combination of drugs to alleviate the symptoms of schizoaffective disorder, both psychotic and mood related. In a sample of clients diagnosed with schizoaffective disorder, 20% were prescribed an antipsychotic and a mood stabilizer; 19% an antipsychotic and an antidepressant; and 18% an antipsychotic, a mood stabilizer, and an antidepressant (Casecade et al., 2009). The most common atypical antipsychotics prescribed for the treatment of schizoaffective disorder are ziprasidone, olanzapine, and risperidone (Jager, Becker, Weinmann, & Frasch, 2010).

Typical antipsychotics such as fluphenazine and haloperidol are also commonly prescribed (Jager et al., 2010). Mood stabilizers with evidence-based research to support effectiveness with schizoaffective disorder included lithium and carbamazepine (Jager et al., 2010).

Counselors working with clients diagnosed with schizoaffective disorder need to be educated on the prescription drug regimens of clients and the potential side effects. Common side effects (e.g., weight gain, increased risk for diabetes and cardiac problems, and sedation) may be distressing to clients. Counselors may need to help clients cope with such adverse side effects.

Prognosis

Compared to schizophrenia, schizoaffective disorder has a better long-term prognosis. Adherence to a holistic treatment plan will support better outcomes for clients diagnosed with schizoaffective disorder. Counselors can support the multidisciplinary approach by effectively communicating among all pertinent parties including clients, families, psychiatrists, and case managers.

TREATMENT PLAN FOR MITCHELL

This chapter began with a discussion of Mitchell, a 28-year-old male who presented with auditory hallucinations (i.e., the devil talks to him) and delusions (i.e., the existence of a superhero). Mitchell had been in inpatient psychiatric treatment, and is presently working with a psychiatrist and a case manager. A counselor needs to consider Mitchell holistically before creating a strength-based treatment approach. The I CAN START conceptual framework can help the counselor work with Mitchell's treatment team to formulate a plan to meet his unique needs.

C = Contextual Assessment

Mitchell has strong familial supports, including a mother who has been able to stay at home to care for him, and a church family with whom he has been involved his entire life. Mitchell is African American, and the diagnosis of schizophrenia is made with an awareness of the documented disproportionate rates of psychotic disorders among people of color. On a personal level, Mitchell presents with a preoccupation with financial worries and limited successful employment history. He is motivated to experience interpersonal relationships, and he is artistic and creatively expressive.

A = Assessment and Diagnosis

Diagnosis = Schizophrenia, continuous, 295.90 (F20.9). Mitchell's counselor will assess his symptoms of psychosis and overall impairment utilizing the Clinician-Rated Dimensions of Psychosis Symptom Severity scale (APA, 2013), and the World Health Organization Disability Assessment Schedule 2.0 (WHODAS 2.0) provided in the *DSM-5* (APA, 2013). Mitchell will undergo a general medication evaluation by a physician, and continue to meet with his psychiatrist for medication management.

N = Necessary Level of Care

Outpatient (i.e., individual counseling once per week; regular case management services, monthly visits with his psychiatrist); available acute/inpatient hospitalization when psychosis escalates, and/or if there is risk of harm to self or others.

S = Strength-Based Lens

Self: Mitchell is an artistic and creative man. He identifies hobbies he enjoys and that help him to express his emotions (e.g., drawing and letter writing). He reports a strong desire to build relationships with others and maintain employment.

Family: Mitchell and his parents demonstrate a strong family bond. His parents want to be supportive, but are not always sure how that support might look. Currently his parents provide financial support and ensure all Mitchell's basic needs (e.g., housing, food, transportation) are met. His family is willing and able to participate in his treatment.

Community: Mitchell is active in his church where he has a social support network. Again, he actively wants to develop friendships and a partnership.

T = Treatment Approach

Mitchell's treatment approach will follow the previously addressed APA (2004) practice guidelines for treating people with schizophrenia. His treatment will include medication management and psychosocial services with a focus on social skills training incorporated into behavioral-based counseling. Therapeutic support services will include attention to vocational rehabilitative resources that will support Mitchell's ability to function as independently as possible.

A = Aim and Objectives of Treatment

Mitchell will engage in all therapeutic and rehabilitative services necessary to achieve stabilization and maintain recovery → Mitchell will attend monthly medication management sessions with his psychiatrist; he will take all medications as prescribed. Mitchell will attend bimonthly sessions with the case manager in which he reviews current functioning, participates in the treatment planning process, and discusses any obstacles or concerns regarding adhering to the treatment plan.

Mitchell will develop his skills in managing his hallucinations and delusions → Mitchell will attend all individual counseling sessions; he will communicate with the counselor how often the devil is speaking to him and discuss alternatives to the devil's requests of him. Mitchell will bring his graphic drawings to session to help assess the presence of the Angeldefender and devil-related delusions. He will learn two new skills that he can use to help him in managing his symptoms. He will use these skills 80% of the time he experiences hallucinations/delusions.

Mitchell will increase social relationships → Mitchell will reduce isolation by engaging in social activities with his peers. Mitchell will join a young adult group at his church, actively attending social events at least once per week. He will also attend a weekly schizophrenia support group offered through the local community mental health agency. In session, he will identify new friendships in his developing social network and describe interactions with his peers. Social skills training will support Mitchell's successful communication with peers.

Mitchell will secure and maintain employment → Mitchell will complete all shifts on his job with the assistance of his vocational rehabilitation counselor (job coach). Mitchell will call his job coach and employer if he needs to take a sick day at least 4 hours before his shift begins. He will work cooperatively with his job coach to maintain appropriate dress, hygiene, and boundaries at work. In session, Mitchell will articulate job responsibilities and areas of challenge. He and the counselor will discuss options for coping with challenges at work.

R = Research-Based Interventions *(based on Social Skills Training)*

Counselor will provide consistent support to Mitchell, promoting his strengths as he learns and relearns appropriate interactions with others and the community. Counselor will help Mitchell develop and apply the following skills:
• New coping strategies to respond to his hallucinations and delusions
• Using his artwork and letter writing interests as means to express emotions
• Interpersonal skills to promote social relationships and successful employment

T = Therapeutic Support Services

Medication management by his psychiatrist

Weekly individual counseling

Case manager to assist with stabilization in the community

Vocational rehabilitation counselor to monitor employment placement

Weekly schizophrenia support groups

References

American Psychiatric Association (APA). (2004). *Practice guideline for the treatment of patients with schizophrenia* (2nd ed.). Arlington, VA: Author. Retrieved from: http://psychiatryonline.org/content.aspx?bookid=28&sectionid=1665359

American Psychiatric Association (APA). (2013). *Diagnostic and statistical manual of mental disorders* (5th ed.). Washington DC: Author.

Bach, P., & Hayes, S. C. (2002). The use of Acceptance and Commitment Therapy to prevent the rehospitalization of psychotic patients: A randomized controlled trial. *Journal of Consulting and Clinical Psychology, 70,* 1129–1139.

Beck, A. T., Rector, N. A., Stolar, N., & Grant, P. (2009). *Schizophrenia: Cognitive theory, research, and therapy.* New York, NY: Guilford.

Bellack, A. S., Mueser, K. T., Gingerich, S., & Agresta, J. (2004). *Social skills training for schizophrenia* (2nd ed.). New York, NY: Guilford.

Casecade, E., Kalali, A. H., & Buckley, P. (2009). Treatment of schizoaffective disorder. *Psychiatry (Edgmont), 6,* 15–17.

Chadzynska, M., & Charzynska, K. (2011). The participation of patients with schizophrenia in psychoeducation—the analyses from the patient's perspective. *Archives of Psychiatry and Psychotherapy, 2,* 67–72.

Eriksen, K., & Kress, V. E. (2005). *Beyond the DSM story: Ethical quandaries, challenges, and best practices.* Thousand Oaks, CA: Sage.

Gaebel, W. (2011). *Schizophrenia: Current science and clinical practice.* Hoboken, NJ: Wiley-Blackwell.

Gearing, R. E. (2008). Evidence-based family psychoeducational interventions for children and adolescents with psychotic disorders. *Journal of Canadian Academy of Child and Adolescent Psychiatry, 17,* 2–11.

Gearing, R. E., & Mian, I. (2009). The role of gender in early and very early onset of psychotic disorders. *Clinical Schizophrenia & Related Psychoses, 2,* 298–306.

Heckers, S. (2012). Diagnostic criteria for schizoaffective disorder. *Expert Reviews Neurotherapeutics, 12*(1), 1–3.

Horan, W. P., Harvy, P., Kern, R. S., & Green, M. F. (2011). Neurocognition, social cognition and functional outcome in schizophrenia. In W. Gaebel (Ed.), *Schizophrenia: Current science and clinical practice* (pp. 68–107). Hoboken, NJ: Wiley-Blackwell.

Jager, M., Becker, T., Weinmann, S., & Frasch, K. (2010). Treatment of schizoaffective disorder: A challenge for evidence-based psychiatry. *Acta Psychiatry Scandinavia, 121,* 22–32.

Jolley, S., & Garety, P. (2011). Cognitive-behavioural interventions. In W. Gaebel (Ed.), *Schizophrenia: Current science and clinical practice* (pp. 185–215). Hoboken, NJ: Wiley-Blackwell.

Kantrowitz, J. T., & Citrome, L. (2011). Schizoaffective disorder: A review of current research themes and pharmacological management. *CNS Drugs, 25,* 317–331.

Kingdon, D. G., & Turkington, D. (2002). *Cognitive-behavioral therapy of schizophrenia.* New York, NY: Guilford.

Kopelowicz, A., Liberman, R. P., & Zarate, R. (2007). Psychosocial treatments for schizophrenia. In P. E. Nathan & J. M. Gorman (Ed.), *A guide to treatments that work* (pp. 243–269). New York, NY: Oxford Press.

Lake, C. R., & Hurwitz, N. (2008). Schizoaffective disorder—its rise and fall: Perspectives for DSM-V. *Clinical Schizophrenia & Related Psychoses, 2*(1), 91–97.

Lincoln, T. M., Wilhelm, K., & Nestoriuc, W. (2007). Effectiveness of psychoeducation for relapse, symptoms, knowledge, adherence and functioning in psychotic disorders: A meta-analysis. *Schizophrenia Research, 96,* 232–245.

McCabe, R., Bullenkamp, J., Hansson, L., Lauber, C., Martinez-Leal, R., Rössler, W., . . . Priebe, S. (2012). The therapeutic relationship and adherence to antipsychotic medication in schizoprehnia. *PLoS ONE, 7,* 1–5. doi:10.1371/journal.pone.0036080

McGorry, P. D., & Goldstone, S. (2011). Early recognition and prevention of schizophrenia. In W. Gaebel (Ed.), *Schizophrenia: Current science and clinical practice* (pp. 142–160). Hoboken, NJ: Wiley-Blackwell.

National Alliance on Mental Illness. (2013). *PACT: Program of assertive community treatment.* Retrieved from http://www.nami.org

National Institute of Mental Health (NIMH). (2009). *Schizophrenia* (NIH Publication No. 09-3517). Retrieved from: http://www.nimh.nih.gov/health/publications/schizophrenia/

National Institute of Mental Health (NIMH). (2012). *Mental health medications* (NIH Publication No. 12-3929). Retrieved from: http://www.nimh.nih.gov/health/publications/mental-health-medications/nimh-mental-health-medications.pdf

Pagsberg, A. K. (2013). Schizophrenia spectrum and other psychotic disorders. *European Child & Adolescent Psychiatry, 22,* S3–S9. doi: 10.1007/s00787-012-0354-x

Patterson, T. L., McKibbin, C., Taylor, M., Goldman, S., Davila-Fraga, W., Bucardo, J., & Jeste, D. V. (2003). Functional Adaption Skills Training (FAST): A pilot psychosocial intervention study in middle-aged and older patients with chronic psychotic disorders. *American Journal of Geriatric Psychiatry, 11,* 17–23.

Phillips, L. J. Francey, S. M., Edwards, J., & McMurray, N. (2009). Strategies used by psychotic individuals to cope with life stress and symptoms of illness: A systematic review. *Anxiety, Stress, & Coping, 22,* 371–410.

Pillmann, F., Wustmann, T., & Marneros, A. (2012). Acute and transient psychotic disorders versus persistent delusional disorders: A comparative longitudinal study. *Psychiatry and Clinical Neurosciences, 66,* 44–52.

Potuzak, M., Ravichandran, C., Lewandowski, K. E., Ongür, D., & Cohen, B. M. (2012). Categorical vs. dimensional classifications of psychotic disorders. *Comprehensive Psychiatry, 53,* 1118–1129.

Raby, W. N. (2009). Comorbid cannabis misuse in psychotic disorders: Treatment strategies. *Primary Psychiatry, 16,* 29–34.

Rössler, W. (2011). Management, rehabilitation, stigma. In W. Gaebel (Ed.), *Schizophrenia: Current science and clinical practice* (pp. 217–246). Hoboken, NJ: Wiley-Blackwell.

Rubin, A., & Trawver, K. (2011). Overview and clinical implications of schizophrenia. In A. S. Rubin, D. W. Springer, & K. Trawver (Eds.), *Psychosocial treatment of schizophrenia: Clinician's guide to evidence-based practice (pp. 1–22).* Hoboken, NJ: Wiley-Blackwell.

Schizophrenia Medications. (2013, March). Retrieved from: http://health.nytimes.com/health/guides/disease/schizophrenia/medications.html

Substance Abuse and Mental Health Services Administration (SAMHSA). (2008). *Getting started with evidence-based practices: Assertive community treatment* (SAMHSA Publication SMA08-4345). Washington, DC: Author.

Substance Abuse and Mental Health Services Administration (SAMHSA). (2010). *Getting started with evidence-based practices: Family education* (SAMHSA Publication SMA09-4423). Washington, DC: Author.

Substance Abuse and Mental Health Services Administration (SAMHSA). (2010). *Getting started with evidence-based practices: Supported employment* (SAMHSA Publication SMA08-4365). Washington, DC: Author.

Torrey, E. F. (2006). *Surviving schizophrenia: A manual for families, patients, and providers* (5th ed.). New York, NY: HarperCollins.

Valencia, M., Juarez, F., & Ortega, H. (2012). Integrated treatment to achieve functional recovery in first-episode psychosis. *Schizophrenia Research and Treatment, 2012.* doi: 10.1155/2012/962371

Wallace, C. J. (2003). *Final report to the National Institutes of Mental Health on Project 1RO2MH57029: A clinical pilot of the workplace fundamentals module.* Los Angeles, CA: University of California at Los Angeles.

Walsh, J. (2011). Therapeutic communication with psychotic clients. *Clinical Social Work Journal, 39,* 1–8.

Feeding and Eating Disorders

Denise D. Ben-Porath, Kelly Bhatnagar, and Michelle Gimenez Hinkle

CASE STUDY: ALICIA

Alicia is a 32-year-old Caucasian female from the Midwest region of the United States. She graduated with a degree in law from Cornell University, and works as an attorney at a midsize law firm. Alicia finds her work rewarding, but says that at times it can be overwhelming to always have to "be on her game." She is married to a cardiologist who works long hours and is often on call. Alicia identifies as Catholic and feels a strong connection to her religion.

Alicia has been married for four years to her husband John. Alicia describes the first two years of their marriage as "fine." She stated, "We both wanted the same things out of life. We would take great vacations, spend time with my family, and spend money on the house." However, she describes her marriage as becoming increasingly tense and strained over the past two years. She says, "John is constantly focused on having a baby, and it is all he talks about." While they have been attempting to conceive, they have not been successful. Alicia states that she is ambivalent about having a baby. She also reports that she feels increasing pressure from John to have a baby, and while she wants to start a family sometime in the future, she is not sure that now is the right time.

She describes her relationship with her parents as "good." Her father, a successful attorney, has always placed high expectations on Alicia. He insisted that she attend an Ivy League law school. Although Alicia has work acquaintances with whom she occasionally goes out to dinner, she describes her mother as her primary and sole confidant. Alicia often confides in her mother regarding her marital dissatisfaction and stressors.

As a teenager, Alicia participated in competitive dance and was accepted as a member of an elite dance company when she was 14. Her mother, a former dancer, was considerably invested in Alicia's success as a dancer, often insisting that she practice dance an additional hour after her mandatory three hour company practice in order to get "that competitive edge."

Since the age of 17, Alicia has engaged in binge eating, purging, and excessive exercise. She can recall a defining moment when her dance instructor told her that she would not advance in her company unless she lost 10 pounds. It was at that point that she began to restrict her caloric content, generally eating an 800-calorie-a-day diet. She rarely eats certain food groups (e.g., meat or grains), and her daily food intake consists mainly of greens and vegetables. This restriction would then set her up for a binge, during which she would go to her "secret cache" of Twinkies and Pringles. Other times she would find herself upset about her dance performance and come home and binge to soothe herself. To compensate for the calories ingested, she would often vomit and/or commit to do intense aerobic activity the next day. Her symptoms went unnoticed for years until her mother observed that her knuckles were calloused and bleeding from the self-induced vomiting. Upon discovering Alicia's secret, her mother helped her secure outpatient counseling.

Alicia has had periods of her life when she has not engaged in eating-disordered behaviors. She reports having gone up to a year at a time with no such struggles. At present, Alicia is engaging in 4–7 episodes of binging and purging each week. Her purging episodes involve both vomiting and excessive exercise (upwards of 2–3 hours at a time). She is actively trying to reduce her binge-purge behaviors. There have been times in her recent history when she would purge twice a day. She has noticed that as the stress with her husband has escalated, so has her binging and purging. She also reports that as her binge-purge behaviors escalate, she finds herself isolating herself from other people and limiting her involvement in the activities that boost her self-esteem (i.e., creating art).

Alicia is intelligent, artistic, and athletic. She enjoys the arts, especially visual and performing arts. She has dabbled in ceramic making and pottery and has sold a few of her pieces at local art shows. She also enjoys going to the ballet and has season tickets; however, she reports that it can be difficult to attend dance shows as she is prone to "obsessing" about the ballerinas' small frames.

DESCRIPTION OF THE EATING DISORDERS

Eating disorders (EDs) are serious, potentially life-threatening disorders, characterized by abnormal eating behaviors. In this section, anorexia nervosa, bulimia nervosa, and binge eating disorder will be discussed. People who have bulimia and anorexia nervosa have maladaptive beliefs surrounding weight, and bodily shape and appearance (American Psychiatric Association [APA], 2013). Although disordered eating behaviors vary by disorder, both anorexia nervosa and bulimia nervosa share an overevaluation of shape and weight (Fairburn, Cooper, & Shafran, 2003), which leads people with these disorders to base their sense of self-worth largely on their shape and/or weight, and their perceived ability to control them. Overevaluation of shape and weight may be expressed in a variety of ways, including intense concern about weight, frequent weighing, repetitive checking of body parts, avoidance of body information (e.g., refusal to look in mirrors), and extreme body dissatisfaction. Not surprisingly, these expressions of overevaluation can have a profound impact on social functioning and interpersonal relationships (Fairburn et al., 2009).

Overevaluation of shape and weight can have a significant impact on eating behaviors (Fairburn et al., 2009). It may result in extreme attempts to limit food intake and other maladaptive weight management behaviors such as self-induced vomiting, excessive exercise, and laxative or diuretic abuse. These dangerous behaviors can be life-threatening and have dire medical consequences. For example, excessive dietary restriction causes decreased bone density, dry and thin skin, abdominal bloating, delayed gastric emptying, cardiac abnormalities, renal complications, and endocrine and metabolic irregularities (Pomeroy, Mitchell, Roerig, & Crow, 2002). Recurrent compensatory behaviors such as self-induced vomiting and laxative abuse cause cardiac hypotension, permanent erosion of dental enamel, esophageal tears, and a depletion of the body's sodium and potassium (Pomeroy et al., 2002). The combined medical and psychological consequences of eating disorders lead to substantially high mortality rates when compared to other mental health conditions (Klump, Bulik, Kaye, Treasure, & Tyson, 2009). As such, immediate and aggressive treatment is warranted upon identification of eating disorder symptomatology.

Binge eating disorder is a disorder new to the DSM system (it was added in the *DSM-5*). Binge-eating disorder involves recurrent episodes of binge eating in the absence of compensatory behaviors. The binge eating episodes must occur at least one time per week for three months. As is the case with anorexia and bulimia nervosa, people with this disorder are also at risk for serious health issues. Because it is a newly classified disorder, less is known about it, and its treatment, in comparison to anorexia and bulimia nervosa.

COUNSELOR CONSIDERATIONS

When presenting for treatment, many individuals with eating disorders wish to figure out the "root" of the illness. It is important for counselors to keep in mind that the precise etiology of eating disorders is not entirely understood. There is substantial evidence that the development of an eating disorder can be attributed to an interaction between genetics and environment, but the complex nature of this interaction is still being studied. In 2009, the Academy for Eating Disorders (AED) published a position paper arguing for the recognition of eating disorders as biologically based, serious mental illnesses (Klump et al., 2009). The AED contended that eating disorders require the same level of treatment consideration as other conditions classified as serious mental illnesses (e.g., schizophrenia, bipolar disorder, depression, and obsessive-compulsive disorder). Eating disorders negatively influence brain functioning (Kerem & Katzman, 2003; Muhlau et al., 2007), metabolism (Katzman, 2005), and neurochemistry (Kaye, Strober, & Jimerson, 2009), thus impairing cognitive functioning (Roberts, Tchanturia, Stahl, Southgate, & Treasure, 2007; Southgate, Tchanturia, & Treasure, 2008), decision making (Cavedini et al., 2004), and emotional stability, and severely limiting the life activities of sufferers (de la Rie, Noordenbos, Donker, & Van Furth, 2007; Keel, Mitchell, Miller, Davis, & Crow, 2000).

The level of impairment associated with eating disorders requires that the counselor's attention immediately be drawn to variables thought to be maintaining the illness rather than variables thought to have caused the illness. Sessions initially focusing too heavily on the "root" of the illness may be doing so at the expense of resolving disordered eating behaviors that have the potential to lead to death. Additionally, clients and counselors may find insight-oriented counseling difficult, frustrating, and unproductive while the client is in a malnourished state (as is the case when working with clients who have anorexia nervosa), and these discussions may be better suited to a time when physical and psychological health has been fully restored.

PROGNOSIS

In general, while eating disorders are serious disorders with life-threating implications, there is an emerging treatment literature suggesting that with the application of evidence-based treatments and a comprehensive, team-based approach, eating disorders have a positive prognosis. In 2004, the National Institute for Health and Care Excellence (NICE) published guidelines for core interventions in the treatment and management of eating disorders. The guidelines currently list family-based treatment (FBT; also known as the Maudsley Approach; Lock & Le Grange, 2012) as the treatment of choice for adolescent anorexia nervosa, and FBT and cognitive behavior therapy (CBT) with family involvement as the treatment of choice for adolescent bulimia nervosa. NICE does not specify a treatment of choice for adult anorexia nervosa, but strongly recommends that treatment take place in a "setting that can provide the skilled implementation of refeeding with careful physical monitoring . . . in combination with psychosocial interventions" (NICE, 2004). CBT is currently recommended by NICE for adults suffering from bulimia nervosa, binge eating disorder, or an eating disorder not otherwise specified. Other approaches, such as dialectical behavior therapy (DBT; Linehan, 1993), also show promise.

ANOREXIA NERVOSA

Description of the Disorder and Typical Client Characteristics

Anorexia nervosa (AN) is a serious and potentially life-threatening mental disorder characterized by dietary restriction that leads to a significantly low body weight. Significantly low body weight is defined as a weight that is less than minimally normal relative to one's age, sex, developmental trajectory, and/or physical health. For children and adolescents, this includes maintaining a weight that is less than that minimally expected based on historic growth patterns. There are two subtypes of AN: *restricting type* and *binge-eating/purging type*. *Restricting type* AN describes presentations in which weight loss is attained primarily through dieting and sometimes exercise. Individuals with restricting type do not regularly engage in binge-eating or purging/compensatory behaviors such as self-induced vomiting, excessive exercise, or misuse of laxatives, diuretics, or enemas. Conversely, those with *binge-eating/purging type* of AN do regularly engage in binge-eating and/or compensatory purging behaviors, which may further complicate the diagnostic picture. Other characteristics of AN include maladaptive beliefs surrounding weight, shape, and appearance and often a persistent disregard for the seriousness of low body weight. Individuals suffering from AN generally demonstrate an intense fear of gaining weight or becoming fat, even though they are at a significantly low body weight (APA, 2013).

Approximately 0.5–1% of the population suffers from AN, and it is estimated to be 10 times more common in women than in men (Hoek & van Hoeken, 2003). It is important to note, however, that estimates of AN in men are likely misrepresented due to the historic cultural stigma of AN being a "woman's disease." This stigma leads to health care professionals being less likely to assess, and thus identify, AN in men. Coupled with the fact that men are less likely than women to seek treatment, it is very possible that incidence rates in men could be much higher than originally suggested. For women over the age of 20, incidence rates have remained constant, but there has been a significant increase in prevalence for females age 15–19 years (Hoek & van Hoeken, 2003).

The onset of AN typically occurs during adolescence, with the mean age being approximately 17 years. The causes of AN are still unknown; however, most counselors and researchers agree that many factors may contribute to the onset of AN. It is clear that AN has a strong biological basis, and it is likely an interaction between genes and environment that contributes to the development of the illness. Risk factors for developing AN include a family history of AN, teasing by peers, low self-esteem, poor body image, and belonging to a family that is heavily preoccupied with dieting.

Counselor Considerations

Treatment of AN is complex and requires attention be paid to the broad medical, nutritional, and psychological aspects of the disease. It is important for counselors working with clients with AN to be closely connected with a multidisciplinary treatment team that ideally includes a physician, dietitian, and psychiatrist, all of whom hold expertise in the treatment of eating disorders.

A thorough medical evaluation by a physician is a key step in the initial assessment, and in the ongoing treatment of AN. The medical evaluation includes a complete physical and laboratory tests (e.g., blood tests, electrocardiogram, blood urea nitrogen, creatinine, thyroid study, and urine specific gravity) to test for the physical effects of AN on the body. Chronic malnutrition can lead to major medical complications including dehydration, orthostasis (drastic changes in heart rate and blood pressure when moving from lying down to standing up, which manifests as dizziness), bradycardia (low heart rate) and heart arrhythmias (irregular heartbeats), hypothermia (low body temperature), cold intolerance, skin changes, and lanugo (sudden growth of fine hair all over the body). Clients with AN who engage in self-induced vomiting may experience hypokalemia (low potassium levels), esophageal tears, and tooth erosion (Academy of Eating Disorders, 2011).

Collaboration with a specialized dietitian can help counselors working with this population better understand their nutritional needs. Meal plans are frequently used for clients with AN and can assist in monitoring caloric intake to make sure clients are eating adequately to reverse malnutrition. Counselors should work with a dietitian to ensure sound nutritional recommendations are made to parents, especially as they work to refeed their malnourished child and help avoid nutrition-related complications such as refeeding syndrome (i.e., a metabolic disorder that occurs as a result of reinstitution of nutrition to those who have been severely malnourished).

Clinical Toolbox 11.1: In the Pearson etext, click here to read about a therapeutic meal support intervention.

Partnership with a psychiatrist specializing in eating disorders can help counselors manage psychiatric comorbidities that may complicate treatment. Counselors working with this population should be aware of common regularly co-occurring psychiatric disorders. Depression, anxiety, and especially obsessive-compulsive disorder, is found in relatively high rates among adults and adolescents with AN (Keel, Klump, Miller, McGue, & Iacono, 2005).

Treating clients who have EDs, particularly those who have AN, involves important ethical considerations. Because treatment with these individuals is often rife with life-threatening medical complications, counselors must be certain that they are adequately trained to treat these individuals and to assess when a higher level of care is warranted. Not making referrals as required can potentially involve death when working with this high-risk population. Because clients who are malnourished are unable to think logically, it is often necessary to involve their family (if they are appropriate resources) in treatment, so that clients' treatment needs can be encouraged and supported.

AN is found across cultures although it is more common in industrialized, higher income countries such as many European countries, the United States, Japan, Australia, and New Zealand (APA, 2013). With respect to cultural considerations, AN is, comparatively, more predominant in Caucasian females than in African Americans, Asians, and Latinos living in the United States (APA, 2013). However, some suspect that AN is on the rise in diverse communities, but these individuals may be more reluctant to seek help. In fact, these populations are less likely to seek mental health services, which may result in perceived lower rates of occurrence (APA, 2013). Because these populations are under-represented at treatment centers and in research studies on eating disorders, it is not clear if they are insulated from anorexia or if social and cultural factors impose barriers to treatment. Counselors should be sensitive to the experience diverse populations may have in disclosing and managing anorexia.

Counselors should also be aware that there can be differences cross-culturally in terms of the presentation of weight concerns. For example, people from certain Asian communities may not experience the intense fear of gaining weight that others do. Also, the Latino population may have less of a fear of weight gain (APA, 2013). Differing symptom profiles for AN need to be taken into account when assessing and treating patients from different cultures. Counselors must also be aware of their stereotypes about who develops anorexia and ensure they do not let these negatively impact their clients' treatment.

Treatment Models and Interventions

A significant body of research has emerged suggesting evidence-based approaches to treating AN. In recent years, family-based treatment has been demonstrated to have a high success rate in treating adolescents with AN. CBT approaches also have some demonstrated success. As previously mentioned, early intervention and a comprehensive team approach to treating AN are necessary.

FAMILY-BASED TREATMENT (FBT) In adolescents, AN severely affects physical, emotional, and social development, and it is important that treatment address each of these components. Family-based treatment (FBT), or the Maudsley Approach (Lock et al., 2010; Lock & Le Grange, 2012) is an outpatient treatment model developed at the Maudsley Hospital in London. FBT is intended to take approximately one year, and it was originally designed to treat adolescents age 18 or younger who live at home with their families.

The overall philosophy of FBT is that the adolescent is embedded in the family and that parental involvement in treatment is crucially important for treatment success. The adolescent is viewed as unable to make sound decisions about eating and related behaviors because of distortions associated with AN. Therefore, it is the parents' responsibility to take control of their child's eating and activity behaviors until the child is able to do so for himself or herself. FBT is also highly focused on adolescent development and aims to guide parents in assisting their adolescent with navigating normal developmental tasks (Lock et al., 2012).

FBT typically proceeds through three clearly defined phases. Phase I: Weight Restoration usually lasts 3–5 months, with therapy sessions scheduled at weekly intervals. Therapy in Phase I is almost entirely focused on the eating disorder. Parents are encouraged to work out for themselves how best to help their child gain weight and return to normalized eating, while the counselor provides ongoing support for these efforts. Problem-solving is a key therapeutic tool used to assist parents in making appropriate decisions for their child's food intake. The family meal, which occurs during session two, is an opportunity to assess and provide feedback surrounding mealtime family dynamics, and to empower parents to take charge of the illness by successfully coaching the adolescent to take "just one more bite" than he or she was originally prepared to eat.

When steady weight gain is evident and parents believe they have a manageable grasp on the illness, Phase II: Transitioning Control of Eating Back to the Adolescent, begins. During Phase II, sessions are held every 2–3 weeks over the course of approximately three months. Eating disorder symptoms remain central in discussions, and the counselor works with the family to slowly transition developmentally appropriate control over eating and activity back to the adolescent (under close parental supervision). As Phase II progresses, other familial issues that had to be postponed to focus on weight restoration may now be introduced. The issues are only processed, however, in relation to the effect that they have on the family's ability to continue refeeding, and/or maintain a healthy weight for the adolescent.

Phase III: Adolescent Issues and Termination is initiated when the client achieves a stable weight (e.g., minimum of approximately 90% of expected body weight), and eating disordered behaviors are no longer occurring. Sessions are held monthly or every other month over the course of approximately three months. The primary goal of Phase III is to help the adolescent establish a healthy relationship with parents so that the distorted eating does not make up the basis of the familial interactions. This entails working toward achieving personal autonomy, establishing appropriate familial boundaries, practicing effective problem-solving, and preparing for upcoming transitions in stages of life.

FBT is currently considered the gold standard, first-line treatment for adolescents with AN (NICE, 2004). There is substantial evidence supporting family-based treatment as an effective immediate and long-term treatment option for adolescent AN (Lock, Agras, Bryson, & Kraemer, 2005; Lock et al., 2012). Overall, the data indicate that FBT, used with young clients with AN who have a relatively short duration of illness, is promising and that the beneficial effects of the treatment appear to be sustained in 2- to 5-year follow-up studies (Eisler, Simic, Russell, & Dare, 2007; Lock et al., 2005).

COGNITIVE BEHAVIOR THERAPY (CBT)   CBT focuses on the cognitive, affective, and behavioral dimensions of the disorder that initiate and maintain the disorder. Fairburn's (1981) approach is a classic CBT treatment for use with this population. It is divided into three stages, with each stage progressively treating the eating disorder. Stage 1 is primarily behavioral in nature. In this stage, clients are asked to keep a diary of ED behaviors (e.g., bingeing, inappropriate compensatory behaviors), and to engage in self-monitoring of food intake. Additionally, clients are prescribed a balanced meal plan, which includes eating a variety of foods from many different food groups. In session, clients review their food diary with their counselor, and the counselor and the client work together to identify triggers for ED behaviors, and to problem solve how to change or avoid them. Lastly, Stage 1 treatment also consists of psychoeducation about nutrition. Because many clients with an eating disorder have misinformation or distorted information about nutrition, psychoeducation designed to teach clients about balanced nutrition is important.

When working from this CBT perspective with this population, Stage 2 of therapy is designed to teach the client how to problem solve life's difficulties without resorting to ED behaviors. The problem-solving strategies include: (a) identifying the problem; (b) describing the problem as accurately and objectively as possible; (c) brainstorming solutions to the problem; (d) generating consequences to each solution; (e) choosing the best response; and (f) following through with the action.

The last stage, Stage 3, assists clients in identifying cognitions and behaviors that may lead to relapse. For example, dichotomous or black-and-white thinking (e.g., "No one will think I am special unless I am thin") may set a client up for a relapse. In this instance, the counselor may ask the client to develop an alternative cognition that reputes his or her current belief. For example, the counselor may ask the client to observe individuals he or she knows whom others value and respect who are not thin. Recognizing these cognitive distortions and challenging them is an important goal in preventing relapse in CBT treatment.

Several studies have demonstrated the effectiveness of CBT in treating those who have AN. For example, CBT has been demonstrated to be superior to nutritional counseling with, respect to relapse prevention, in those with AN (Pike, Walsh, Vitousek, Wilson, & Bauer, 2003). Furthermore, in a nonrandomized clinical trial, individuals diagnosed with AN who were treated with CBT had significantly longer periods without relapse as compared to those individuals who were provided a standard treatment (Carter et al., 2009).

ENHANCED COGNITIVE BEHAVIOR THERAPY FOR EATING DISORDERS (CBT-E) CBT-E is an adaption of CBT, and was specifically designed for use in treating all eating disorders, pulling on a transdiagnostic framework to address core pathology across all eating disorders (Fairburn et al., 2003; Fairburn, 2008). CBT-E was designed for use with adults; however, adaptations have been used with adolescents.

CBT-E sets out to construct a clinical formulation of the processes hypothesized to be maintaining the eating disorder. This clinical formulation is used to identify and prioritize features of the illness that need to be targeted in treatment. Thus, an individualized formulation (or treatment plan) is developed in the very beginning and revised throughout treatment.

The standard course of treatment for CBT-E is 20 treatment sessions over 20 weeks. It is an individual therapy model that uses specific strategies and procedures to address the targeted symptoms.

CBT-E is conducted in four stages. Stage 1 (weeks 1–4) goals include orienting and engaging the client to treatment, developing the personalized formulation, providing psychoeducation on eating disorders and weight change, and establishing a pattern of "regular eating" and "in-session weighing." Stage 2 (weeks 5–6) is considered a transitional stage in which the client and counselor review treatment progress, identify emerging barriers to change, and modify the personalized formulation. Stage 3 (weeks 7–14) is considered the crux of treatment, and the goal is to address the main mechanisms (mostly cognitive) thought to be maintaining the eating disorder. Stage 4 (weeks 15–20) is the final stage of treatment, and focuses on relapse prevention planning for the long-term. A review session held 20 weeks posttreatment is also offered to ensure changes are being maintained over time.

CREATIVE TOOLBOX ACTIVITY 11.1   House of Cards

Denise D. Ben-Porath, PhD

Activity Overview

Clients with eating disorders are often judgmental, not only of their bodies, but of many aspects of their lives. Several studies suggest that this population "compares up" when examining their own abilities and strengths, with the result being perpetual feelings of inadequacy. Because their inner dialogue is often a constant narrative of self-deprecating thoughts, clients often fail to notice these thoughts and the impact they can have on their mood and self-esteem. Thus, an important therapeutic task is to assist clients in recognizing and targeting judgmental thinking.

Treatment Goal(s) of Activity

This intervention focuses on redirecting clients' thinking and its impact on mood and behavior, and fits well within any cognitive or cognitive behavioral therapy framework. The primary goals of this activity are to help eating disordered clients: (a) identify judgmental thinking; (b) identify how judgmental thinking impacts their mood and behavior; (c) begin to "catch" judgmental thoughts, and redirect their focus away from negative thinking.

Directions

1. Give each client six playing cards.
2. Simply state: "I would like you to use these cards to make a house. You will have five minutes to complete this task." (If clients ask if they need to use all six cards, reply, "It is your choice.")
3. Record the time with a watch or clock.
4. After 5 minutes, follow up with the process questions.

Process Questions

1. Tell me what thoughts you had about this exercise.
2. What judgmental thoughts about your performance did you notice?
3. Did you notice yourself judging your house and comparing it to others? What impact did this have on your mood, performance, and so on?
4. How often do you notice judgmental thoughts about yourself in the course of a day? What impact does this have on your mood and functioning?
5. How can you apply what you learned here to the thoughts you have that relate to the eating disorder?

Research trials are currently underway testing the immediate and long-term effects of CBT-E. Results have been promising and indicate a decrease in global severity of eating disorder symptoms at the end of a 20-week treatment, and at a 60-week follow-up assessment (Fairburn et al., 2009).

PSYCHOPHARMACOTHERAPY   Antidepressant medications, both selective serotonin reuptake inhibitors (SSRIs) and tricyclics (TCAs), and antipsychotic medications have been suggested for use with clients with AN. Randomized controlled trials have typically reported an absence of efficacious pharmacological interventions for AN (Mitchell, Roerig, & Steffen, 2013). Despite this, psychotropic medication is widely prescribed for those diagnosed with AN (Fazeli et al., 2012). For example, in a survey of those with AN, one study found that approximately 53% of those surveyed reported being prescribed psychotropic medications (Fazeli et al., 2012).

Given the high comorbidity of depression and anxiety in individuals with AN, SSRIs have been widely prescribed to treat this population. However, randomized controlled trials have failed to demonstrate a beneficial effect in those diagnosed with AN when using these agents (Mischoulon et al., 2011). Additionally, potential side effects associated with SSRIs include bone loss with an increased risk of fracture (Ziere et al., 2008). Given that malnourishment places many patients with AN at risk for developing osteopenia or osteoporosis, the risks associated with prescribing SSRIs are even more significant in this population.

While the use of antidepressant medication in those with AN has remained relatively stable over the past decade, the use of atypical antipsychotic agents has doubled in this time (Fazeli, 2012). Because body image disturbance in those with AN can be so severe and profound, many researchers have conceptualized this distortion as bordering on delusional thinking. Subsequently, many researchers have begun to explore the use of antipsychotic medications in treating those diagnosed with AN. Furthermore, antipsychotic medications are known to stimulate hunger and promote weight gain, an additional benefit for those needing weight restoration.

The most promising antipsychotic agent to date is olanzapine (e.g., Zyprexa), which is an atypical antipsychotic agent (Attia et al., 2011). In five randomized controlled trials, olanzapine demonstrated superior outcomes in weight gain and decreased obsessions in those with AN as compared to a placebo (Brewerton, 2012). However, olanzapine is not without adverse side effects. Chief among these is an increased risk of diabetes and diabetes ketoacidosis (Lebow, Sim, Erwin, & Murad, 2012). Given the increased frequency of individuals with an eating disorder who are also diagnosed with the insulin-dependent form of diabetes mellitus, caution should be exercised when prescribing antipsychotics for those with AN. While most of the psychotropic medications discussed have the beneficial side effect of promoting weight gain in those with AN, clients are often noncompliant in taking their medications because of their intense fear of weight gain.

Prognosis

Many studies have looked at the short-term, immediate, and long-term posttreatment outcomes for those with AN. Most of these studies were conducted with adults, although it is reasonable to assume that many suffered from AN as a teenager as well. In general, the research suggests that approximately 50% have good outcomes, 25% have moderate outcomes, and about 25% do poorly after treatment. Most studies use successful weight and nutritional rehabilitation as the primary measures of outcome.

What makes AN so dangerous, however, is that it has the highest mortality rate of any psychiatric illness listed in the *DSM*, including depression and substance use disorders. The crude mortality rate is approximately 5% per decade for this population (APA, 2013). AN can become a chronic illness for many of its sufferers, and multiple hospitalizations and prolonged treatment can become a reality for many with this disorder. It is important that intervention occur as early as possible in order to prevent chronicity. There is strong evidence to suggest adolescents who are not ill for a long duration (less than three years) can make a full psychological and weight recovery if treatment is immediate and intensive (Lock et al., 2010).

BULIMIA NERVOSA

Description of the Disorder and Typical Client Characteristics

Bulimia nervosa (BN) is characterized by recurrent episodes of binge eating coupled with compensatory behaviors that are used to prevent weight gain. A binge is defined as the rapid consumption of an objectively large amount of food in a short time period (within two hours) accompanied by a feeling of loss of control (APA, 2013). Those diagnosed with BN also engage in inappropriate compensatory behaviors to prevent weight gain. These behaviors may include self-induced vomiting, misuse of laxatives, diuretics, enemas, insulin, excessive exercise, and/or fasting. A common misperception is that people must engage in purging behaviors in order to receive a BN diagnosis. However, nonpurging methods (e.g., fasting and exercise) can also be used to compensate for the binge episodes. Individuals may receive the diagnosis of BN if they have been engaging in binge behaviors and some form of inappropriate compensatory behaviors (e.g., purge or nonpurge) approximately once a week for the past three months (APA, 2013). To receive the diagnosis, the *DSM-5* also requires that the person's self-evaluation is significantly influenced by his or her body shape and weight.

Women are more often diagnosed with this disorder, with an estimated gender ratio of 10 to 1. Therefore, the diagnosis of BN may be missed in men because it is less commonplace and because societal perceptions lean toward viewing bulimia as a "female disorder." Despite this, an estimated 10–15% of people with bulimia are male. Higher rates of bulimia are sometimes found in male athletes, suggesting that sports, particularly those where weight control and muscle mass are linked to athletic success (e.g., wrestling, long-distance running, gymnastics, equestrians, body building), may place some men at an increased risk for BN. Thus, men should be carefully assessed for BN, particularly those who participate in at-risk sports.

Counselor Considerations

It is important that counselors who work with those with BN understand the medical consequences and complications that can result from the disease. Because excessive purging behaviors (e.g., diuretics, laxatives, vomiting, ipecac use) can result in an electrolyte imbalance that places the individual at risk for death (secondary to heart failure), it is important that counselors who work with this population coordinate clients' care with a physician. A routine physical, including a blood panel that assesses the levels of potassium (K+), magnesium (Mg+), and calcium (Ca+) in the blood, should be performed to rule out electrolyte disturbances. Esophageal tears are a rare, but serious, medical complication associated with self-induced vomiting. Esophageal tears most commonly occur when the individual is using objects or instruments to produce a gag reflex. While not life threatening, self-induced vomiting can also result in erosion of the tooth enamel, leaving the person vulnerable to dental disease. Swelling of the salivary (parotid) glands can also occur secondary to self-induced vomiting (Academy of Eating Disorders, 2011).

A second important consideration in treating individuals with bulimia is determining the proper level of care. Several studies indicate that the first four sessions are a good indicator of longer term treatment success (Bogh, Rokkedal, & Valbak, 2005; Fairburn, Agras, Walsh, Wilson, & Stice, 2004). Thus, if clients with BN cannot greatly reduce their incidents of purging in an unstructured setting, or if medical complications are not resolving, the counselor should consider a more structured setting such as day treatment or residential hospitalization. On their website, the American Psychiatric Association provides clinician guidelines for levels of care; this information can be used to guide counselors level of care decision making (American Psychiatric Association, 2006).

Lastly, several studies indicate that those with bulimia nervosa, particularly those who exhibit the purging subtype, are more prone to impulsive behaviors. BN has also been associated with cluster B personality disorders, impulsivity, affective instability, and disinhibition (Godt, 2008; Keel, Wolfe, Liddle, De Young, & Jimerson, 2007). Thus, counselors should assess for other possible comorbid impulsive behaviors in individuals with bulimia including gambling, substance abuse, reckless driving, unprotected sexual encounters, multiple sexual partners, and other impulsive, risky behaviors.

With respect to cultural issues, there appears to be less variability of BN in culture-specific prevalence rates than with anorexia. In the United States, those who present for treatment with BN are primarily Caucasian, but the disorder occurs in other ethnic groups with prevalence rates comparable to those of Caucasian samples (APA, 2013).

Treatment Models and Interventions

The treatment literature suggests effective treatments for use in addressing BN. Dialectical behavior therapy and family-based treatment (for use with adolescents) have both been found to be effective in treating BN.

Cognitive behavioral therapy (CBT) and interpersonal psychotherapy (IPT) have also both been evidenced as effective in the short- and long-term. In a randomized controlled trial, CBT was found to be superior to IPT in the treatment of BN. However, after a 12-month follow-up, no significant differences were found between the two treatments (Agras, Walsh, Fairburn, Wilson, & Kraemer, 2000). These results suggest that CBT may make quicker therapeutic strides in treatment, but no differences may be present in long-term follow-up.

COGNITIVE BEHAVIOR THERAPY (CBT)   CBT (e.g., Fairburn, 1981) and CBT-E (Fairburn, 2008) have been applied to the treatment of bulimia nervosa with success. For a more detailed description of these treatment approaches, please see the anorexia nervosa treatment section. To date, CBT has the strongest empirical support for the treatment of BN, with studies suggesting that approximately 50% of clients diagnosed with BN recover with CBT treatment (Hay, 2013). A prospective treatment study found that individuals suffering from BN who were treated with CBT did markedly better on treatment outcomes, and had a better prognosis, than those treated with just behavior therapy (Fairburn et al., 1995).

INTERPERSONAL PSYCHOTHERAPY (IPT)   A primary goal in IPT is to help the client address current interpersonal issues that are perpetuating ED symptoms. The *Initial Phase* of treatment consists of five sessions. In these sessions, the counselor obtains information regarding the course and history of the client's eating disorder. An ED diagnosis is given and the client is formally assigned to the "sick role." Consistent with the medical model, clients assigned to the "sick role" are informed that they are ill, that they are given permission to be ill, and thereby granted permission to work toward recovery.

Additionally, in the initial phase of treatment, a thorough examination of the client's social functioning, intimate relationships, and relationship patterns is conducted. How these relationships and expectations impact ED behaviors is explored with the client. Results from this examination lead to an "interpersonal formulation" whereby the counselor, in collaboration with the client, identifies a primary or core problem area for the client that is most associated with ED symptoms. Treatment goals are then established based on this primary problem area.

The *Intermediate Phase* is dedicated to addressing the primary problem area. This phase typically consists of 8–10 sessions. In this phase, treatment focuses on four key areas of the individual's life: (a) interpersonal deficits, or feelings of social isolation or involvement in empty, unfulfilling relationships; (b) interpersonal role disputes, or conflicts with significant others that originate from discrepancies in expectations; (c) role transitions, or difficulties transitioning to changes in status; and (d) grief, issues surrounding loss or bereavement. Counselors may choose to focus on more than one of these areas as needed if relevant to a client's ED symptoms. Goals in treatment are developed based on the identified area of concern. Thus, clients who are experiencing interpersonal deficits will work toward finding more meaningful, fulfilling relationships. Clients who are struggling with interpersonal role disputes will work toward conflict resolution with other individuals in their lives. Clients struggling with role transitions will focus on honoring both the positive and negative aspects of a changing role (e.g., wife to mother) and seek support for their transition. Lastly, those clients struggling with grief will work toward finding meaning in new relationships while allowing time to mourn.

The *Termination Phase* lasts approximately four to five sessions, and involves a focus on client empowerment. During this phase, the counselor summarizes the client's progress in treatment. The client is encouraged to reflect on his or her successes and accomplishments in treatment. Relapse prevention is addressed as clients are asked to identify early warning signs and triggers that could prompt a relapse. Lastly, counselors should be prepared to process with clients feelings of grief regarding the ending of the relationship.

DIALECTICAL BEHAVIOR THERAPY (DBT)   The previously mentioned approaches such as CBT and IPT do not fully address issues associated with affect regulation, which often contribute to the development and maintenance of BN. Although DBT was originally developed to treat emotion dysregulation in those with borderline personality disorder (Linehan, 1993), it has subsequently been applied to those with bulimia and other eating disorders.

What is commonly called the "University of Washington" DBT model involves treating clients with BN (or binge eating disorder) who have a comorbid diagnosis of borderline personality disorder (Chen, Matthews, Allen, Kuo, & Linehan, 2008; for a more thorough description of standard DBT, please see Chapter 9 and the borderline personality disorder treatment section). As in standard DBT, Target 1 behaviors include any life-threatening behaviors (e.g., suicide attempts, suicide threats or gestures, nonsuicidal self-injurious behaviors); Target 2 behaviors are therapy-interfering behaviors (e.g., not attending session, not following through on homework); and Target 3 behaviors are quality of life–interfering behaviors. Thus, in this model, eating disorder behaviors are considered Target 3 behaviors and constitute behaviors that interfere with one's quality of life.

As in standard DBT, all clients are assigned a DBT counselor who assists him or her in replacing maladaptive behaviors with more skillful and adaptive behaviors. Toward this end, behavior chain analyses and diary cards are used to address and track dysfunctional behaviors, including bingeing and purging and suicidal/nonsuicidal self-injurious behaviors.

Clients learn from skills trainers, in a didactic format, DBT skills designed to increase mindfulness, interpersonal effectiveness, emotion regulation, and distress tolerance. Attention is paid to making the focus of the skills relevant to eating disordered behavior (e.g., doing a pros and cons exercise related to purging behavior).

In this model, clients attend weekly individual DBT therapy and weekly group skills training for six months. This approach also includes the use of team consultation and DBT telephone consultation. In a small pilot study, eight women diagnosed with BN (or BED) and borderline personality disorder received six months of comprehensive dialectical behavior therapy. Reductions were observed in ED symptoms and suicidal behaviors, and these changes were maintained at a 6-month follow-up (Chen et al., 2008).

Safer, Telch, and Chen (2009) also developed a DBT model (sometimes referred to as the "Stanford University" model) that can be used to treat clients with bulimia (and BED) from a DBT perspective. In this model, clients attend 20 weekly individual sessions of DBT where elements of group skills training and individual DBT are combined in a 1-hour weekly therapy appointment. In these 20 sessions, clients are taught mindfulness, distress tolerance, and emotion regulation skills. Diary cards are used to track bingeing, purging, and "mindless eating." Mindless eating refers to being unmindful of eating and the process of eating (e.g., eating in front of the television or while on the phone). The Stanford model teaches clients to slow their eating down, to attend to the taste, smell, and experience of eating, and to do so mindfully.

 Clinical Toolbox 11.2: In the Pearson etext, click here to watch a video demonstration on how to review food diary cards with clients.

As in standard DBT, the treatment hierarchy prioritizes life-threatening behaviors, followed by therapy-interfering behaviors and then quality-of-life interfering behaviors. Additionally, relapse prevention is discussed as is dialectical abstinence. Dialectical abstinence involves helping clients commit to total and complete abstinence of bingeing and purging. However, if a relapse should occur, the pendulum moves toward acceptance and forgiveness, followed by a swift return and recommitment to total and complete abstinence of all ED behaviors. In a randomized controlled trial, 28% of clients with BN who were treated with DBT were abstinent from binge eating/purging behaviors as compared with participants in the wait-list control condition (Safer, Telch, & Agras, 2001).

Wisniewski and Kelly (2003) have also applied DBT to treating those with eating disorders. However, unlike the other two programs described above, their model includes the treatment of those with anorexia nervosa, bulimia nervosa, binge-eating disorder, and other specified feeding or eating disorder who meet criteria for a higher level of care, such as intensive outpatient and partial hospitalization. Additionally, this model infuses DBT with empirically supported CBT treatments for those with an ED. In this model, clients meet with an individual DBT counselor weekly and attend various CBT and DBT groups during treatment hours.

Given the symptom severity of this population, modifications to the DBT target hierarchy can be applied when working with those who have eating disorders. Target 1 behaviors (e.g., imminently life-threatening behaviors) can be not only defined as suicidal behaviors, but also as medical complications, secondary to an eating disorder that can result in imminent death (e.g., electrolyte disturbances). An adapted model of telephone consultation has also been developed to target eating disorder urges as well as suicidal thoughts (Wisniewski &

Ben-Porath, 2005). Similar to standard DBT, weekly team consultations occur to discuss cases within the DBT framework. Food diary cards are used to track skill use and dysfunctional ED behaviors and suicidal/nonsuicidal self-injurious behaviors. However, unlike the Stanford model and the University of Washington model, daily food intake and cues associated with hunger and satiety are recorded. Several studies suggest that this hybrid model of CBT/DBT for individuals who require a higher level of care is effective in reducing ED symptoms and enhances clients' ability to regulate affect (Ben-Porath, Wisniewski, & Warren, 2009; Federici, Wisniewski, & Ben-Porath, 2012).

Voices from the Trenches 11.1: In the Pearson etext, click here to watch a discussion of the role that emotion regulation can play in eating disorder treatment.

CREATIVE TOOLBOX ACTIVITY 11.2   Self-Soothing Kit

Denise D. Ben-Porath, PhD

Activity Overview

Clients with eating disorders often have difficulty regulating their emotions. Linehan (1993) has described self-soothing as a helpful intervention to reduce distress and assist clients in re-regulating strong emotions. An important therapeutic goal is to teach clients how to self-soothe and regulate intense painful emotions.

Treatment Goal(s) of Activity

This intervention provides clients with a tool they can use to self-sooth and regulate their emotions, thus avoiding eating disordered behaviors.

Directions

1. One week before the activity (which can be used in individual or groups sessions), orient the group to the exercise. State: "Next week we will be making a self-soothing kit. This will be a kit that you can use when you are feeling intense emotions and need to re-regulate those emotions." Next state, "Your only homework for the following week is to bring in a recording of your favorite soothing song. This is a song that relaxes and calms you. It may be that the lyrics are meaningful to you, or it may just be that the tune is comforting. The most important part of your assignment is that the song you choose is comforting. Bring this with you to our next group session."
2. Next session, have your clients sit at a long table. Give each client a shoebox and construction paper. Have them cover the shoebox lid and the box in construction paper.
3. Next provide them with several magazines. Have them look for inspirational quotes or messages in ads or titles. Examples may include: "You are amazing!";"Take time to smell the roses"; or "Respect yourself." Have them clip out these inspirational sayings and paste them to the outside of their box. While they are working on this activity, you can explain that the outside of the box with its inspirational quotes will be a way for them to visually self-soothe.

4. When they are finished, hand each person a stress ball. Explain that squeezing the stress ball is a tactile way they can self-soothe.
5. Next give each client a small candle. Explain that various scents are known to relax, and calm people. Have them smell the candle and then place it in their box. Explain that the candle will be a way for them to self-soothe using their sense of smell.
6. Now ask them to play the soothing song selected during the week. Explain that music can be a way for them to self-soothe using their auditory senses. Ask them to commit to using their self-soothing kit before the next session.

Process Questions

1. Did you use your self-soothing kit this week?
2. What sense did you find worked best for you when you needed to self-soothe?
3. Did you notice yourself feeling more calm and relaxed after using your self-soothing kit? If so, how long did it take before it started working?
4. What other items might be helpful to include in your self-soothing kit?
5. What else can you add to your kit to help you self-sooth?

FAMILY-BASED TREATMENT MODEL (FBT) FBT, the current gold standard approach for treating adolescent AN, has also been adapted to treat youth with BN (FBT-BN; Le Grange & Lock, 2007). Manualized FBT-BN includes 20 sessions that occur over the course of six months. Three individual sessions between the adolescent and the counselor are also recommended during the course of FBT-BN.

Similar to FBT-AN (i.e., for use in treating anorexia nervosa), FBT-BN has three well-defined phases. In *Phase I*, parents assist their adolescent in reestablishing healthy patterns of eating. In *Phase II*, parents oversee the adolescent's return to independence regarding eating behaviors. FBT-BN concludes with *Phase III*, in which the primary task is to discuss issues related to adolescent development in the context of the eating disorder.

When compared to FBT-AN, FBT-BN is considered more collaborative in Phase I, and the adolescent is more directly involved in plans for a return to normalized eating. FBT-BN emphasizes regulating food intake, breaking the binge-purge cycle, and addressing the secretive nature of these behaviors, as key to successful treatment. Also, it is suggested that counselors using FBT-BN exercise greater flexibility and creativity in their approach and style because of the heterogeneous presentation of BN adolescents (as compared to those with anorexia nervosa; Le Grange & Lock, 2007).

In terms of research support for FBT-BN, there has been one case study (Le Grange, Lock, & Dymek, 2003) and two large controlled trials that have investigated the efficacy of this approach (Le Grange & Schmidt, 2005). The results from all of the studies suggest strong support for the use of FBT-BN with this population. There is additional data to suggest that children with the anorexia nervosa binge-purge/subtype respond well to parental attempts at decreasing bulimic symptoms as described in the FBT-BN manual (Eisler et al., 2000).

Voices from the Trenches 11.2: In the Pearson etext, click here to watch an eating disorder expert discuss how parent empowerment can be integrated into eating disorder treatment.

PSYCHOPHARMACOTHERAPY   The primary pharmacological agents utilized in treating BN are antidepressants. A relatively modest number of clinically controlled trials have been conducted examining the efficacy of antidepressants in treating BN. The few studies that have been conducted have investigated tricyclics and SSRIs, and the findings have been mixed.

One exception worth noting is the use of the SSRI fluoxetine (e.g., Prozac) for treating BN; fluoxetine is the only FDA-approved medication for the treatment of this disorder. Not surprisingly, it is also the most widely researched with approximately 12 clinical trials having been conducted examining its efficacy. While treatment success has been difficult to define because there is not a consistent definition of what "recovered" means in the eating disorder literature, the data does suggest that the use of Prozac demonstrates a reduction in binge and purge episodes. In the longest maintenance trial to date, it was found that individuals diagnosed with BN reported a significant reduction in purging as compared to those who were administered a placebo (Romano, Halmi, Sarkar, Koke, & Lee, 2002).

In both research and clinical settings, adherence to medication treatment can be problematic, especially because of the side effects of medications. Adverse side effects are numerous and include nausea, dizziness, sedation, fatigue, insomnia, dry mouth, constipation, heart palpitations, sexual dysfunction, elevated pulse rate, declining systolic and diastolic blood pressures, and orthostatic hypotension. Not surprisingly, these side effects have contributed to high dropout rates in clinical trials, and could prevent clients from continuing the use of medication.

While other SSRIs and their effectiveness in treating BN have been studied, the results have been inconclusive. However, the use of antidepressant medications may be useful in treating comorbid diagnoses and additional affective symptoms (Mitchell et al., 2013). One notable exception is bupropion (i.e., Wellbutrin). Because Wellbutrin increases the risk of seizures in clients with BN, the medication is contraindicated for those suffering from an ED. Other studies have found that anticonvulsants, particularly the antiepileptic drug topiramate (e.g., Topamax), to be efficacious in the short-term treatment of BN as it reduces binge frequency (Arbaizar, Gomez-Acebo, & Llorca, 2008).

Voices from the Trenches 11.3: In the Pearson etext, click here to watch a physician discuss the physiological issues that need to be considered when treating people who have eating disorders.

Prognosis

Recovery rates for BN vary considerably depending on the study cited, with rates of remission ranging from 31–74%. Variability in these estimates is thought to be due to the differing lengths of posttreatment follow-up, and the varied definition of recovery used across treatment studies. A rapid reduction in symptoms during the first four weeks of treatment has been linked to a positive course for those diagnosed with bulimia (Bogh et al., 2005; Fairburn et al., 2004). While several researchers have attempted to identify prognostic factors in the treatment of bulimia, the results have been largely inconsistent and difficult to replicate. In a recent review of the literature, Steinhausen and Weber (2009) examined studies over the past 25 years that investigated prognostic factors in those with bulimia. Inconclusive or nonsignificant findings were found for various variables, including age of onset, severity of the illness, comorbid diagnoses (e.g., substance use disorders, borderline personality disorder), and personality characteristics (e.g., introversion, perfectionism, emotional lability, neuroticism). However, a handful of studies do seem to suggest that a history of familial obesity, multi-impulsive behaviors (e.g., self-injury, substance abuse, promiscuity), disturbed family relationships, and psychosocial distress have a negative impact on treatment outcome. Furthermore, a continued overemphasis on weight and body shape and continuous dieting posttreatment were also indicative of poor treatment outcome. Finally, several studies indicate that individuals diagnosed with bulimia who purge (e.g., self-induced vomiting), tend to present with higher levels of general psychopathology, greater impulsivity, and more severe ED symptoms (Nunez-Navarro et al., 2011), thus having a poorer prognosis.

BINGE-EATING DISORDER

Description of the Disorder and Typical Client Characteristics

Binge-eating disorder (BED) is characterized by recurrent episodes of binge eating in the absence of compensatory behaviors. A binge is defined by a rapid consumption of an objectively large amount of food in a short time period (within two hours). In a binge episode, the amount of food is considerably larger than what most people would eat in this time span and typically consists of high-caloric and/or dense foods with minimal nutritional value (e.g., ice cream, bread). Additionally, to receive this diagnosis, one must experience feeling a loss of control while binge eating. While most people occasionally overeat, a binge episode differs from overeating in that the food is consumed quickly, there is a self-perception of a loss of control over one's behavior, and the binge is often done in secret (APA, 2013). To qualify for the *DSM-5* diagnosis of BED, the binge eating must occur, on average, at least once a week for three months, and the symptom severity should be indicated (i.e., mild, moderate, severe, or extreme; APA, 2013).

Personality characteristics associated with those who binge are less well understood in comparison to those associated with anorexia nervosa and bulimia nervosa. A recent study found that approximately 25% of an outpatient sample being treated for BED presented with comorbid cluster C characteristics, particularly avoidant personality disorder and obsessive-compulsive personality disorder (Becker, Masheb, White, & Grilo, 2010). Similar to anorexia nervosa and bulimia nervosa, BED is more prevalent in women than men with a 3:2 ratio, respectively. While the age of onset is variable, many individuals diagnosed with BED report lifelong problems with overeating.

Counselor Considerations

Counselors working with clients who have BED should be keenly attuned to issues of shame. Because BED is characterized by frequent binge eating without compensatory behavior, individuals who carry this diagnosis also tend to have body mass index scores in the obese or morbidly obese range. In a recent literature review, studies found that those diagnosed with BED reported higher levels of body image concerns than individuals who are obese, but did not binge (Ahrberg, Trojca, Nasrawi, & Vocks, 2011).

Additionally, because binge eating is often done in secret, feelings of shame and guilt are often linked with the behavior of bingeing, making individuals with binge eating disorder reluctant to initially disclose their behaviors to a counselor for fear of being judged or shamed. Indeed, one study found that shame was a primary barrier to receiving treatment in those diagnosed with binge eating disorder (Hepworth & Paxton, 2007). Given these intense issues with shame and guilt, counselors need to approach these clients in a highly empathic, nonjudgmental manner.

Like AN and BN, the prevalence of BED is most pronounced in industrialized countries. With respect to diverse cultural groups, rates are comparable among Latinos, Asians, African Americans, and Caucasians (APA, 2013). Furthermore, while BED is more common in women than men, it is considerably more common in men than are the other EDs, such as AN and BN.

Treatment Models and Interventions

In part because BED is a disorder new to the DSM system, there are fewer treatment studies than there are for anorexia and bulimia nervosa. Research suggests that CBT, interpersonal psychotherapy, and DBT are treatment approaches that may be useful in treating BED. Enhanced cognitive behavior therapy for eating disorders (CBT-E; Fairburn, 2008) has been applied to the treatment of BED with success. For a more detailed description of CBT-E, please see the anorexia nervosa treatment section.

COGNITIVE BEHAVIOR THERAPY: SELF HELP (CBT-SH)   CBT-SH (Fairburn, 2013) is widely used in the treatment of binge eating disorder. Fairburn (2013) developed a 6-step self-help plan that pulls on numerous CBT techniques to help treat BED. This approach can be used by counselors with their clients who have BED, or it can be used by clients to self-treat their own BED symptoms.

In *Step 1,* clients are required to monitor their weekly food intake. In doing so, clients gain insight into the time of day that may be triggering, the types of foods that they are likely to binge on, and what locations make them particularly susceptible to a binge. Clients are also expected to weigh themselves once weekly, although significant weight loss is not always associated with a reduction in bingeing. *Step 2* involves establishing a pattern of regular eating. This can include up to six small meals a day. It is important not to let more than 3–4 hours elapse between meals. In *Step 2*, clients are encouraged to eat at the prescribed times according to their meal plan, and not according to feelings of hunger or urges to eat/binge. *Step 3* involves teaching clients alternatives to bingeing. Clients are encouraged to construct a list of alternative activities to use until the urge to binge passes. Examples include taking a hot shower, going for a walk, listening to music, or calling a friend. *Step 4* involves "taking stock" of what triggers a binge episode. Most binges are triggered by stressful or unpleasant environmental events; thus, *Step 4* involves identifying what the problem/situation is that triggers a binge and employing problem-solving techniques.

As in CBT for bulimia, problem solving involves the same six steps: (a) identifying the problem, (b) describing the problem as accurately and objectively as possible, (c) brainstorming solutions to the problem, (d) generating consequences to each solution, (e) choosing the best response, and (f) following through with the action. *Step 5* pertains primarily to people who binge in response to restrictive dieting, such as limiting their overall caloric intake, avoiding certain foods, and/or attempting to go for long periods of time without eating.

While *Step 4* is particularly helpful for those who binge in response to environmental stressors, *Step 5* is useful for those who "yo-yo" between restrictive dieting and bingeing. The protocol in *Step 5* is to gradually have the client introduce "forbidden foods," increase caloric intake, or decrease time between meals. By establishing a regular eating pattern and not depriving oneself of foods or food groups, binges are likely to decrease.

The last step, *Step 6,* involves preventing relapse. In this step, clients are educated about realistic expectations, are taught to differentiate between a "lapse" and a relapse, and taught how to identify stressors associated with, or likely to trigger, a relapse. In an evaluation of this self-help program, participants diagnosed with BED were randomly assigned to either a self-help condition, or a wait-list control condition for 12 weeks (Carter & Fairburn, 1998). After six months, approximately half of the individuals in the self-help group ceased to binge eat, whereas little to no change was observed in the wait-list condition.

INTERPERSONAL PSYCHOTHERAPY (IPT)   IPT has also been applied to the treatment of BED. For a more detailed description of this treatment, please see the bulimia nervosa treatment section. Similar to findings with IPT for bulimia nervosa, research has suggested that those diagnosed with BED who receive IP treatment report a considerable reduction in binge episodes. In a randomized controlled trial, participants were assigned to one of the following three conditions: IPT, CBT, or a behavioral weight loss treatment (Wilson, Wilfley, Agras, & Bryson, 2010). At the end of 12 months, there were no differences among the three groups on eating disorder pathology. However, at a 2-year follow-up, binge eating behaviors were significantly reduced in the IPT and CBT groups. Furthermore, a high frequency of binge eating at the onset of treatment was associated with poor outcomes in CBT and the behavioral weight loss treatment condition, but not the IPT condition, suggesting that IPT may be particularly useful for those who binge (Wilson et al., 2010).

DIALECTICAL BEHAVIOR THERAPY   The Stanford DBT model (described previously in the bulimia nervosa treatment section) used to treat bulimia can also be used to treat BED. One modification is that the 20-session format is conducted in a group setting for those with BED. Findings suggest that DBT is also an effective treatment for those diagnosed with BED, with as many as 89% of the women diagnosed with BED who received the 20-session group format being abstinent from binge eating at the end of treatment (Telch, Agras, & Linehan, 2001). Also, in another study, those who participated in DBT had a lower treatment dropout rate, and greater abstinence in binge eating as compared to an active comparison group therapy treatment (Safer, Robinson, & Booil, 2010).

Voices from the Trenches 11.4: In the Pearson etext, click here to watch an eating disorder expert review important considerations when treating people who have eating disorders.

PSYCHOPHARMACOTHERAPY   There is no one drug that is used to specifically treat BED. However, some medications are proven to be efficacious in reducing binging urges and episodes. The antiepileptic drug topiramate (e.g., Topamax) has been efficacious in reducing binge eating and stimulating weight loss (Arbaizar et al., 2008). Another antiepileptic medication, zonisamide (e.g., Zonegran), has been reported to reduce the frequency of binge eating (Mitchell et al., 2013). While anticonvulsants have some demonstrated success with this population, serious potential side effects exist with these drugs. These include an increase in suicidal thoughts and birth defects in pregnant women. Thus, counselors should monitor for suicidality in clients taking these drugs.

A review of pharmacological interventions for BED suggested that SSRIs are useful in reducing binge eating behaviors, but not in completely eradicating them (Mitchell et al., 2013). Vocks et al.'s (2010) review of BED treatments suggested that SSRIs had moderate effects on binge eating and depressive symptoms, but yielded virtually no improvements in eating and body-related cognitions. Because of these results, it is recommended that psychosocial treatments be used in conjunction with any medication treatment to ensure long-term behavior changes.

Prognosis

Generally, BED is considered to be more treatment responsive that anorexia and bulimia nervosa. Given that BED is a relatively new diagnosis, few studies have been conducted on the long-term course of the disorder. What is clear is that the mortality rate for binge eating disorder is considerably lower than it is for bulimia and anorexia nervosa, given that restriction and purging are not a part of the diagnostic picture.

DESCRIPTION OF THE FEEDING DISORDERS

In the *DSM-IV-TR*, feeding disorders were classified as *disorders usually first diagnosed in infancy, childhood, or adolescence*. In the *DSM-5*, this category of disorders was eliminated in an attempt to underscore how these disorders can continue to manifest at different stages of life, and how they may be a on a developmental continuum across the lifespan. As such, the disorders in this category were placed into other categories believed to be more descriptive of the symptomatology of the disorders. Feeding disorders were added to the eating disorder category of the *DSM-5*, and the category was retitled feeding and eating disorders. Despite the combination of feeding and eating disorders into one category, these disorders are unique.

Feeding disorders, including pica, rumination disorder, and avoidant/restrictive disorder, are associated with persistent symptoms that alter food intake or absorption and result in impaired health and functioning (APA, 2013). These disorders can occur throughout the lifespan and across populations; however, they are most prevalent in children and in those who have a developmental or intellectual disorder. When clients have a feeding disorder, they are subject to a multitude of medical and social complications as a result of the disorder. With intervention and support from counselors, clients can work to eliminate or manage symptoms, and any connected mental health and social impediments. The prevalence of feeding disorders is unclear (APA, 2013), and these are disorders that counselors encounter less frequently than many of the other disorders discussed in this text.

COUNSELOR CONSIDERATIONS

As with any counseling relationship, counselors should maintain an understanding and empathic therapeutic relationship when working with individuals who have been diagnosed with a feeding disorder. Counselors should be aware of the social implications that coexist with the particular disorder and be understanding of how the disorder directly impacts the individual. As many of the clients may be children, adolescents, or have a co-occurring developmental or intellectual disorder, the counselor should readily collaborate with parents and caregivers and be able to provide psychoeducation to those closest to clients. Counselors should also consider working with parents of children with a feeding disorder to diminish their stress and anxiety related to their children's symptoms (Fischer & Silverman, 2007). Little information is known about cultural demographics as they pertain to the prevalence of these disorders. As with any diagnosis, though, counselors should do their best to assess how cultural and societal norms influence the manifestation and maintenance or symptoms, as well as caregivers' response to the symptoms.

Because of the medical side effects and complications associated with these disorders, counselors should be able to deal with potentially life-threatening and emergency situations, and form collaborative relationships with medical professionals and other helping professionals who are involved with the client. A collaborative partnership with medical professionals helps to maintain a continuum of care for the client, and provides a medical resource to clients and counselors. To date, no medications have been suggested for use in treating the feeding disorders. Behavior therapy interventions have the most documented success in treating these disorders.

PROGNOSIS

The prognosis for feeding disorders varies and may be dependent on comorbidity factors such as developmental or intellectual disorders. When present in a typically developing child or adolescent, a feeding disorder may cease on its own or in response to treatment. When a client with a comorbid disorder struggles with a feeding disorder, prognosis may be dependent on the consistency of care across caregivers and family members. Nevertheless, for all populations of people with a feeding disorder, early diagnosis and treatment may be important in successfully eradicating the related symptoms, particularly to avoid life-threatening medical complications.

PICA

Description of the Disorder and Typical Client Characteristics

Pica is described as the "eating of nonnutritive, nonfood substances" for at least one month without being supported by developmental, cultural, or societal norms (APA, 2013, p. 329). Individuals with pica have repeated and compulsive cravings to ingest nonfood items such as clay, dirt, rocks, sand, chalk, hair, soap, paint chips, feces, urine, metal, ice, paper, fabric, or plastic. Depending on the substance that was consumed, they may be at risk for nutritional deficiencies, toxicity, infections, gastrointestinal complications, and even death. The diagnosis of pica can occur throughout the lifespan, although it is generally reported among children older than two years, and/or individuals with an intellectual disability, developmental disability, or other mental disorder. Pregnant women can also display symptoms of pica. Some have theorized that craving nonnutritive substances during pregnancy occurs because of nutritional deficiencies (Carter, Wheeler, & Mayton, 2004). Others have noted cultural and medicinal purposes for pica during pregnancy (Corbett, Ryan, & Weinrich, 2003). Many adults who display pica symptoms live in residential settings because of comorbid diagnoses; they require close supervision to keep pica symptoms under control, and prevent pica-related medical consequences. The severity of a co-occuring intellectual disability and the prevalence of pica may be positively correlated (APA, 2013).

Counselor Considerations

As the prevalence of pica is high among children and individuals with co-occurring disabilities or disorders, counselors should be aware that they will most likely be working closely with family members or caregivers of the primary client. Additionally, due to the medical risks of pica, regular communication with medical professionals and primary physicians will be important. Pica can cause serious medical emergencies (e.g., intestinal obstruction), and even death (APA, 2013). As such, it is important that counselors help clients and their caregivers create the safest environment possible.

Eating nonnutritive substances, particularly dirt or clay, can be acceptable in some cultures (Henry & Kwong, 2003). As a result, it is beneficial for counselors to consider pica symptoms in cultural and societal contexts. According to the diagnostic criteria (APA, 2013), in order to be considered as pica, symptoms must not be supported by cultural or societal norms. Counselors should obtain relevant information unique to the client in order to determine if symptoms can be better explained through the context of culture.

Because of the high prevalence of adults with pica living in residential facilities, clients may benefit from counselors creating a tight continuum of care with other residential staff. As pica is not well understood, counselors might consider conducting staff training and professional development sessions regarding pica symptoms, the dangers of the disorder, and prevention strategies, particularly with paraprofessional staff who work with facility clients on a daily basis (Williams & McAdam, 2012). Counselors should remain mindful that treatment for pica should be consistent and regular as pica symptoms for clients in residential settings will reappear after breaks in, or termination of, counseling (Williams, Kirkpatrick-Sanchez, Enzinna, Dunn, & Borden-Karasack, 2009). Open communication with staff regarding treatment can improve monitoring and supervision, which may result in decreased symptoms (APA, 2013).

Treatment Models and Interventions

Most research on pica treatment has been completed in residential settings with participants who are developmentally or intellectually disabled. To date, no randomized controlled trials have been conducted on the treatment of pica. Because of the serious medical risks associated with pica, including those that are life-threatening, the goal of treatment should be to eliminate all pica behaviors rather than just reducing them (Williams & McAdam, 2012).

Common treatment strategies for pica include behavioral techniques and the application of environmental controls. Multiple simultaneous behavioral interventions are most effective in decreasing pica (Hagopian, Gonzalez, Rivet, Triggs, & Clark, 2011).

BEHAVIORAL MANAGEMENT Behavioral treatment interventions, including the use of replacement behaviors, reinforcement, response interruption, redirection, and restrictive procedures, are frequently used when treating clients with pica (Williams et al., 2009). An example of a behavioral management technique is when providers or caregivers bait clients with items, and then impose reinforcements and restrictions, as appropriate, in an attempt to shape their behavior (Williams et al., 2009). For example, positive reinforcement may be given when clients turn in the inappropriate nonfood items, or when they choose edible items to put into their mouths.

Restrictive procedures, or responses that would reduce or restrict pica behaviors from occurring (e.g., reprimands, restraints, oral hygiene training), are examples of behavioral management procedures that can be used in response to pica behaviors, in order to eliminate the symptoms and keep clients safe (Hagopian et al., 2011). Reinforcement tactics are a technique that can be used to encourage positive behaviors: when the client places the simulated pica items in receptacles to encourage this behavior, the client receives a reinforcement. Blocking pica behaviors (e.g., putting things in the mouth), and redirecting attention elsewhere (e.g., toward neutral objects) in an effort to avoid pica may also be helpful.

Another behavioral treatment approach is to create a situation in which clients are exposed to noncontingent stimuli, or neutral objects that are specifically appealing to the client (e.g., a book, game, toy), alongside simulated pica look-a-like items that are safe. The counselor then ignores the client when he or she is engaged in pica behaviors with the simulated pica items, but engages with the client when he or she is engaged with the neutral objects, thus reinforcing positive behaviors (Hagopian et al., 2011).

Response blocking may also be helpful in treating pica (McCord, Grosser, Iwata, & Powers, 2005). Response blocking involves sweeping a person's hand away from his or her mouth in order to prevent the likelihood of ingesting a nonedible item. Pica exchange, in which a client gives a nonedible item to a caregiver or residential staff member for direct exchange of a highly desirable edible item, has also been used successfully in reducing pica behaviors (Carter, 2009).

ENVIRONMENTAL STRUCTURING Controlling the environment around an individual with pica is an important aspect of a treatment plan. Environmental structuring helps to facilitate safety by decreasing the availability of nonfood and dangerous items (Williams et al., 2009; Williams & McAdam, 2012), and can be used in collaboration with behavioral interventions. Caregivers can monitor the physical environment to remove all nonedible items that are commonly ingested. In residential settings, it is recommended that staff create check-in systems for necessary, but frequently consumed items, such as rubber gloves, and implement regular inspections of residential areas to ensure consistent supervision and safety for inpatient residents (Williams et al., 2009). Additionally, in the case of severe or life-threatening pica, some researchers have suggested the use of visual screens, which involve the client wearing an actual screen over his or her eyes. The screen is used to block the client's view of the dangerous item, and thus prevent its ingestion (Williams & McAdam, 2012).

Prognosis

The prognosis for individuals with pica varies and can be dependent on comorbid factors (e.g., intellectual disability, comorbid mental disorders). Children may outgrow the pica behaviors with consistent monitoring and behavioral interventions. For individuals who have comorbid factors, such as a developmental or intellectual disorder, consistent monitoring and long-term treatment is recommended (Williams et al., 2009).

RUMINATION DISORDER

Description of the Disorder and Typical Client Characteristics

Rumination disorder is characterized as repeated regurgitation of swallowed, or partially digested food, without an underlying medical condition (APA, 2013). Rumination disorder can be diagnosed across the lifespan. Infants diagnosed with rumination disorder typically have an onset age of 3–12 months. They may present as difficult to soothe, and exhibit low weight and even malnutrition leading to harmful aftereffects, and even death (APA, 2013). Some researchers have identified that neglectful circumstances or poor parent–child relations can be attributed to rumination disorder in infants and children. Rumination disorder can also be diagnosed in adolescence or adulthood, but it may manifest in a slightly different way than in infancy and childhood. While infants and children rechew and reswallow the regurgitated food, adolescents and adults consciously choose whether or not to reswallow or expel the regurgitated substance (Bryant-Waugh, Markham, Kreipe, & Walsh, 2010). Although this disorder can occur across the population, it is more commonly reported with people who have a developmental or intellectual disorder, and may be associated with self-soothing or self-stimulating behaviors (APA, 2013).

Counselor Considerations

Knowledge of the clinical features, as well as a thorough assessment for the disorder is important for counselors, as rumination disorder is often misdiagnosed (Chial, Camilleri, Williams, Litzinger, & Perrault, 2003). Medical professionals may diagnose rumination disorder, and subsequently refer the client to a counselor. Likewise, counselors may refer a client to his or her physician to have a physical examination to confirm or deny the existence of the disorder. Nevertheless, counselors should collaborate and consult closely with medical professionals because of the risk of medical complications of the disorder (e.g., weight loss and malnutrition). Due to the medical nature of the disorder, counselors should be aware of the role they play when working with clients and be careful not to step out of their appropriate scope of practice by offering advice on medical issues. Conversely, counselors should take note of the medical nature of this presenting problem, and refer clients to their physician when they have medically oriented questions or concerns. As individuals with cognitive and developmental disabilities frequently present with rumination behaviors, collaboration between caregivers, other mental health staff, and residential staff (if applicable) through psychoeducation and ensuring a continuum of care should be considered.

When working with infants or children with rumination disorder, it is likely that counselors will be working with parents or caregivers through family counseling. Infants and children with this disorder may have experienced negative relationships with caregivers, stressful home environments, or have attachment issues (e.g., reactive attachment disorder; Kronenberger & Meyer, 2001), therefore, working to improve family relationships can be beneficial in treatment for rumination disorder. When working with families, counselors should consider systemic approaches to counseling and parent education (Dalton & Czyzewski, 2009).

For adolescents and adults, there are social impacts related to rumination disorder, such as school and work absences, hospitalizations, extensive medical interventions (Chial et al., 2003), and avoidance of social occasions involving food (APA, 2013). Effective counseling for rumination disorder may involve evaluating the social impact of the disorder, as well as any co-occurring stress or anxiety. Working to create an empathic and trusting therapeutic alliance is important when working with a client who has been diagnosed with rumination disorder. Additionally, it is important that counselors have a genuine concern and understanding of the relational and social impacts that the client may be experiencing as a result of the disorder.

Treatment Models and Interventions

Models of treatment for rumination disorder vary; however, no randomized controlled trials of treatments could be found in the literature. In terms of psychosocial treatments, the literature has most often noted the use of behavioral interventions to treat rumination disorder. Some researchers have noted the usefulness of using multiple behavioral strategies simultaneously (Chial et al., 2003), primarily to increase the awareness of the behavior and then to decrease the symptoms (Dalton & Czyzewski, 2009). Additionally, family counseling has also been a recommended strategy for treatment.

DIAPHRAGMATIC BREATHING AND DISTRACTION   Diaphragmatic breathing is a behavioral intervention that can be taught to increase relaxation and distract clients from the desire to regurgitate, while simultaneously increasing their awareness of distractors (e.g., cognitions or physical activities; Dalton & Czyzewski, 2009). When using this type of breathing, clients are instructed to take deep belly breaths in which their abdomen expands, and is followed by an expulsion of all the air. This breathing is then linked to times in which clients feel the urge to spit up digested food; instead of regurgitating, they relax their muscles, and resist the reflex to purge. Clients who practice this relaxation skill can link other forms of distractions with the diaphragmatic breathing such as repeating a mantra, engaging in mindfulness activities, or redirecting the behavior during the breaths.

SELF-MONITORING/MONITORING   Charting, or asking parents and caregivers to chart regurgitating behaviors is another behavioral intervention that may be helpful in enhancing awareness of symptoms, tracking times when symptoms are more or less pronounced, and encouraging the use of coping strategies (e.g., swallowing, diaphragmatic breathing; Dalton & Czyzewski, 2009; Lyons, Rue, Luiselli, & DiGennaro, 2007). Clients and family members are asked to monitor regurgitation behavior and reinforce progress with tangible rewards. In case reports, self-monitoring and monitoring were found to be useful in the reduction of regurgitation behaviors for up to two years posttreatment (Dalton & Czyzewski, 2009).

AVERSIVE TECHNIQUES AND POSITIVE REINFORCEMENT   Aversive techniques, a behavior therapy intervention, involves the practice of linking unwanted or unpleasant stimuli with regurgitation to prevent it from reoccurring. Mild aversions such as swallowing the regurgitated material (Dalton & Czyzweski, 2009), using mouthwash, receiving a brief reprimand from a caregiver, or planned ignoring have been recommended (Lyons et al., 2007). Positive reinforcements such as a tangible reward, social praise and support, or time with a desired activity have been used to promote diminished symptoms (Dalton & Czyzweski, 2009; Lyons et al., 2007).

SATIATION Because rumination disorder is reinforced by the satisfaction of having something in their mouths, stomachs, or the act of swallowing, behavioral techniques such as food satiation and oral stimulation may be useful interventions (Fredericks, Carr, & Williams, 1998; Lang et al., 2011). Food satiation involves allowing the person to continue to consume food, to eat starchy foods, or to eat more slowly in at attempt to replicate the desired physical sensations (Lang et al., 2011). Other strategies such as gum-chewing (Rhine & Tarbox, 2009), or chewing a plastic ring (Lyons et al., 2007) focus on oral stimulation and have been successful at reducing symptoms.

FAMILY COUNSELING Because of to the possibility that rumination disorder may be related to poor parent–child relations, techniques that enhance family relationships and communication have been recommended (Dalton & Czyzewski, 2009). Working with parents and guardians on developing parenting skills and improving relationships with their children can be helpful in strengthening familial bonds. Promoting caregivers' empathy and understanding of their children's emotions, and supportive and nurturing responses, may also be beneficial in reducing rumination. Additionally, family counseling to help reduce stress in the home, and teach stress management skills that the whole family can use, may also be helpful.

Prognosis

According to the *DSM-5* (APA, 2013), rumination disorder can occur in isolated episodes, or be a continuous behavior until successfully treated. The disorder will sometimes cease on its own, or with treatment. Early recognition of the disorder may improve the likelihood of intervention, and prevent the adverse co-occurring social deficiencies clients might experience in conjunction with the disorder. (Chial et al., 2003). In cases in which rumination disorder is not successfully treated, serious complications or death may occur (APA, 2013).

AVOIDANT/RESTRICTIVE FOOD INTAKE DISORDER

Description of the Disorder and Typical Client Characteristics

Avoidant/restrictive food intake disorder (ARFID) is a diagnosis new to the *DSM* system, first added in the *DSM-5* (APA, 2013). It is characterized by a disturbance in feeding that results in weight loss, nutritional deficiency, dependence on nutritional supplements or alternative forms of food intake, and/or interference with social functioning. Disturbances in eating may manifest as avoiding certain foods based on their sensory characteristics of texture or smell, anxiety over certain foods, or a lack of interest in eating (APA, 2013; Bryant-Waugh et al., 2010). The avoidance or restriction of food intake for clients with this disorder is not accounted for by availability of food, cultural practices, anxiety over body weight and image, developmental aspects, or medical conditions (APA, 2013). Children with this disorder might refuse food, reject certain foods based on their texture, or "pack" or pocket food to avoid eating (Addison et al., 2012). ARFID symptoms occur most commonly in children and may be associated with anxiety, obsessive-compulsive disorder, or neurodevelopmental disorders. Other factors may include anxiety and disturbances in family and environmental settings, and/or a medical history of gastrointestinal complications.

Counselor Considerations

Parents and caregivers of children with symptoms related to ARFID will often initially present concerns to physicians. As with all of the feeding disorders, counselors should maintain collaborative relationships with medical professionals when working with a child who has ARFID. Counselors might also consider consulting with an occupational therapist who may work with clients who avoid food based on sensory integration issues.

Parents of children with feeding disorders, particularly those whose children refuse to eat or are disinterested in food, have reported high levels of stress during mealtime and negative interactions with their children (Didehbani, Kelly, Austin, & Wiechmann, 2011; Fischer & Silverman, 2007). As such, counselors should include parents in counseling as much as possible to improve child–parent interactions, and to help them create a more relaxed and enjoyable environment during mealtimes. Additionally, as with any disorder, counselors should consider ARFID symptoms in the context of culture. It is beneficial for counselors to assess the restrictive food intake to identify if there are explanations for the behavior such as a lack of availability of food for socioeconomic reasons, or for religious motivations, such as fasting (Kenney & Walsh, 2013).

Treatment Models and Interventions

Behavior therapy treatment models, and interventions that involve exposure to foods, have been most often researched and recommended for use with ARFID, particularly for the most severe cases (Sharp, Jaquess, Morton, & Herzinger, 2010). Currently, no randomized controlled trials have been conducted on effective treatments for this disorder. If the disorder is severe enough that tube feeding is required, medical interventions and monitoring may also be included in treatment. In terms of psychosocial treatments, the literature has focused on behavioral and familial intervention strategies, with the goal of increasing food intake, increasing tolerability of various food textures, and decreasing problem behaviors and stress during mealtimes.

CONTINGENCY MANAGEMENT Contingency management is a behavioral technique which involves evaluating antecedents and consequences in order to target problem behaviors (Fischer & Silverman, 2007). While working with parents, counselors can create a plan that reinforces optimal eating behaviors such as oral feeding, trying different-textured foods and drinks, taking sips and bites, and prolonging time in front of food. Other behaviors, such as undesirable attention from parents, should be removed via negative reinforcement. Escape extinction used with reinforcement has also been effective, particularly with severe cases of food avoidance and restriction. This intervention involves removing any form of escape from eating. Examples include placing a spoon in the child's mouth, using physical guidance to swallow food, or presenting food over and over until the child eats (LaRue et al., 2011; Sharp et al., 2010).

SHAPING Shaping is another behavior therapy technique that can be used to treat ARFID. One goal of treatment for those who have ARFID is to attain behaviors that are close in approximation to age-appropriate, and desired eating behaviors (Sharp et al., 2010). Through shaping, counselors and parents can track successful attempts that come close to the desired behavior of eating and reinforce them by slowly introducing new eating habits (Fischer & Silverman, 2007). This can be particularly useful when trying new textures, or when applying new eating skills and behaviors during mealtimes (Fisher & Silverman, 2007). For example, if a child will only eat French fries, parents can gradually move from frying the potatoes to frying zucchini and carrot sticks. Then they can exchange the fried foods for roasted potatoes and vegetable sticks. Finally, parents can introduce baked vegetables and potatoes to provide the child with a new texture, thus expanding the child's food choices. Another similar behavioral intervention that has been successful at increasing food intake, and decreasing "packing" food in the mouth while refusing to swallow, is to introduce a "chaser" of an accepted texture or consistency immediately following typically rejected foods (Vaz, Piazza, Stewart, Volkert, & Groff, 2012).

PARENT TRAINING AND FAMILY COUNSELING Working closely with parents and providing psychoeducation and training can also be helpful when working with families of children with ARFID (Fischer & Silverman, 2007). Counselors can provide parents with literature and information about the disorder, help parents practice ways to model healthy eating habits, and coach them through healthy interactions with their children about food, as well as their use of positive and negative reinforcements related to food intake. Counselors should also consider talking to parents about feeding structures at home and implement routines that encourage prolonged time at the meal table without distractions (Fischer & Silverman, 2007). Additionally, family counseling related to improving communication, and more healthy interactions surrounding food, can be beneficial to both children and parents.

Prognosis

Similar to the other feeding disorders, the prognosis for ARFID can vary based on the etiology and the characteristics of the clients with the disorder (e.g., typically developing children, children with autism spectrum disorder). Treatment consisting of behavioral and family interventions is recommended, and can provide positive outcomes (Sharp et al., 2010). Multidisciplinary collaboration with medical professionals, occupational therapists, and nutritionists might also be beneficial for creating a continuum of care and providing effective treatment (Sharp et al., 2010).

TREATMENT PLAN FOR ALICIA

This chapter began with a discussion of Alicia, a 32-year-old female who engages in binge-purging behaviors. Alicia meets the diagnostic criteria for bulimia nervosa. A counselor must consider a variety of factors before moving ahead with a strength-based treatment approach. The following I CAN START conceptual framework outlines treatment considerations that may be helpful in working with Alicia.

C = Contextual Assessment

Developmentally, Alicia is struggling as her husband wants to have children and she does not. Alicia is negotiating societal gender role expectations of women (e.g., "I should want to have a baby at my age") with her unique ideas of the life she wants, along with her husband's expectations. The stress of these struggles could be exacerbating the eating disorder symptoms, and these issues should be integrated into her treatment plan, and addressed as her behavior stabilizes. Alicia lives comfortably and has access to a variety of resources. She reports that her religion is important, and this can be used as a source of strength for her as she moves through her treatment process.

A = Assessment and Diagnosis

Diagnosis = Bulimia Nervosa—Moderate 307.51 (F50.2)
Eating Disorder Examination-Interview (conducted at initial assessment)

Eating Disorder Examination-Questionnaire (EDE-Q; Fairburn & Beglin, 1994) at initial session and then every 4 weeks to assess symptom severity

Physical examination by a physician to determine if there are any longstanding medical complications secondary to restriction and purging behaviors

N = Necessary Level of Care

Outpatient, individual (once per week) and group therapy (once per week); a higher level of care should be considered if symptoms do not improve.

S = Strength-Based Lens

Self: Alicia is an intelligent, motivated, tenacious person. She is also creative and has multiple interests and aspects of her life that bring her satisfaction (e.g., art, her career). She has been able to establish a solid career that more than meets all of her basic needs and allows her to have the financial resources she needs to entertain her leisure pursuits and interests.

Family: Alicia's husband and her mother are both a source of support. They are both committed to her treatment and will do whatever they can to support her. Her parents have also expressed that they will do whatever is necessary to ensure Alicia receives the best treatment.

Community: Alicia lives in a safe, stable community and has access to excellent health care resources. Her community also provides opportunities for her to display her art and indulge her interests (e.g., dance). She also has access to a wellness center where she finds some peace and solace in meditation and yoga.

T = Treatment Approach

Cognitive Behavior Therapy-Enhanced and Dialectical Behavior Therapy

A = Aim and Objectives of Treatment (3-month objectives)

Alicia will use her coping skills to prevent purging (i.e., vomiting) and excessive exercise → Alicia will have 0 episodes of vomiting after she eats, and will use—or attempt to use—her learned skills 100% of the time. Alicia will exercise 3–4 times a week for no more than 1 hour at a time.

Alicia will actively commit to and engage in the treatment process and complete all homework assignments → Alicia will attend all individual and group counseling sessions; she will complete food diary logs between sessions and bring these to sessions; she will complete all homework assignments.

Alicia will identify and challenge cognitive distortions related to food, body weight, shape, and/or size → Alicia will learn and use thought—challenging techniques to modify her dysfunctional thoughts 80% of the time.

Alicia will use coping skills to self-soothe and avoid bingeing → Alicia will learn and identify distress tolerance skills and use them at least 80% of the times when she feels dysregulated, or is having an urge to binge.

Alicia will continue to stay connected with activities that bring her personal satisfaction and do not place an emphasis on her weight or body image, and she will use these as a distraction skill when wanting to binge/purge → Alicia will work on her art when she has an urge to binge/purge, aiming to submit a piece of artwork to an art show within 6 months.

R = Research-Based Interventions *(based on Cognitive Behavior Therapy-Enhanced and Dialectical Behavior Therapy)*

Counselor will help Alicia develop and apply the following DBT and CBT skills:
- Self-soothing skills
- Distraction skills
- Identify and challenge cognitive distortions related to food, body weight, shape, and/or size

T = Therapeutic Support Services

Medication management by psychiatrist

On-going medical evaluation by a primary care physician with expertise in eating disorders

Weekly CBT/DBT group therapy and individual therapy

Access to a higher level of care should she need it

References

Academy of Eating Disorders. (2011). *Eating Disorders: Critical points for early recognition and medical risk management in the care of individuals with eating disorders* (2nd ed). Report published by the Academy of Eating Disorders, www.aedweb.org/Medical_Care_Standards

Addison, L. R., Piazza, C. C., Patel, M. R., Bachmeyer, M. H., Rivas, K. M., Milnes, S. M., . . . Oddo, J. (2012). A comparison of sensory integrative and behavioral therapies as treatment for pediatric feeding disorders. *Journal of Applied Behavior Analysis, 45,* 455–471.

Agras, W. S., Walsh, T., Fairburn, C. G., Wilson, G. T., & Kraemer, H. C. (2000). A multicenter comparison of cognitive-behavioral therapy and interpersonal psychotherapy for bulimia nervosa. *Archives of General Psychiatry, 57,* 459–466.

Ahrberg, M., Trojca, D., Nasrawi, N., & Vocks, S. (2011). Body image disturbance in binge eating disorder: A review. *European Eating Disorders Review, 19,* 375–381.

American Psychiatric Association (APA). (2006). Treatment recommendations for patients with eating disorders. *American Journal of Psychiatry, 163* (7 suppl), 1–54. See http://www.edtreatmenthelp.org/references/8_published_practice_guidelines.html

American Psychiatric Association (APA). (2013). *Diagnostic and statistical manual of mental disorders* (5th ed. [DSM-5]). Washington, DC: Author.

Arbaizar, B., Gomez-Acebo, I., & Llorca, J. (2008). Efficacy of topiramate in bulimia nervosa and binge-eating disorder: A systematic review. *General Hospital Psychiatry, 30,* 471–475.

Attia, E., Kaplan, A. S., Walsh, B. T., Gershkovich, M., Yilmaz, Z., Musante, D.,…Wang, Y. (2011). Olanzapine versus placebo for out-patients with anorexia nervosa. *Psychological Medicine, 41,* 2177–2182.

Becker, D. F., Masheb, R. M., White, M. A., & Grilo,

C. M. (2010). Psychiatric, behavioral, and attitudinal correlates of avoidant and obsessive-compulsive personality pathology in patients with binge-eating disorder. *Comprehensive Psychiatry, 51*, 531–537.

Ben-Porath, D. D., Wisniewski, L., & Warren, M. (2009). Differential treatment response for eating disordered patients with and without a comorbid borderline personality diagnosis using a Dialectical Behavior Therapy (DBT)-Informed approach. *Eating Disorders, 17*, 225–241.

Bogh, E. H., Rokkedal, K., & Valbak, K. (2005). A 4-year follow-up on bulimia nervosa. *European Eating Disorders Review, 13*, 48–53.

Brewerton, T. D. (2012). Antipsychotic agents in the treatment of anorexia nervosa: Neuropsychopharmacologic rationale and evidence from controlled trials. *Current Psychiatry Reports, 14*, 398–405.

Bryant-Waugh, R., Markham, L., Kreipe, R. B., & Walsh, B. T. (2010). Feeding and eating disorders in childhood. *International Journal of Eating Disorders, 43*, 98–111.

Carter, S. L. (2009). Treatment of pica using a pica exchange procedure with increasing response effort. *Education and Training in Developmental Disabilities, 44*, 143–147.

Carter, J. C., & Fairburn, C. G. (1998). Cognitive-behavioral self-help for binge eating disorder: A controlled effectiveness study. *Journal of Consulting and Clinical Psychology, 66*, 616–623.

Carter, J. C., McFarlane, T. L., Bewell, C., Olmsted, M. P., Woodside, D. B., Kaplan, A. S., . . . Crosby, R. D. (2009). Maintenance treatment for anorexia nervosa: A comparison of cognitive behavior therapy and treatment as usual. *International Journal of Eating Disorders, 42*, 202–207.

Carter, S. L., Wheeler, J. J., & Mayton, M. R. (2004). Pica: A review of recent assessment and treatment procedures. *Education and Training in Developmental Disabilities, 39*, 346–358.

Cavedini, P., Bassi, T., Ubbiali, A., Casolari, A., Giordani, S., & Zorzi, C. (2004). Neuropsychological investigation of decision-making in anorexia nervosa. *Psychiatry Residency, 127*, 259–266.

Chen, E. Y., Matthews, L., Allen, C., Kuo, J. R., & Linehan, M. M. (2008). Dialectical behavior therapy for clients with binge-eating disorder or bulimia nervosa and borderline personality disorder. *International Journal of Eating Disorders, 41*, 505–512.

Chial, H. J., Camilleri, M., Williams, D. E., Litzinger, K., & Perrault, J. (2003). Rumination syndrome in children and adolescents: Diagnosis, treatment, and prognosis. *Pediatrics, 111*, 158–162.

Corbett, R. W., Ryan, C., & Weinrich, S. P. (2003). Pica in pregnancy: Does it affect pregnancy outcomes? *American Journal of Maternal Child Nursing, 28*, 183–189.

Dalton, W. T., & Czyzewski, D. I. (2009). Behavioral treatment of habitual rumination: Case reports. *Digestive Diseases and Sciences, 54*, 1804–1807.

de la Rie, S., Noordenbos, G., Donker, M., & Van Furth, E. F. (2007). The patient's view on quality of life and eating disorders. *International Journal of Eating Disorders, 40*, 13–20.

Didehbani, N., Kelly, K., Austin, L., & Wiechmann, A. (2011). Role of parental stress on pediatric feeding disorders. *Children's Health Care, 40*, 85–100.

Eisler, I., Dare, C., Hodes, M., Russell, G., Dodge, E., & Le Grange, D. (2000). Family therapy for adolescent anorexia nervosa: The results of a controlled comparison of two family interventions. *Journal of Child Psychology and Psychiatry, 41*, 727–736.

Eisler, I., Simic, M., Russell, G., & Dare, C. (2007). A randomised controlled treatment trial of two forms of family therapy in adolescent anorexia nervosa: A five-year follow-up. *Journal of Child Psychology and Psychiatry, 48*, 552–560.

Fairburn, C. G. (1981). A cognitive behavioural approach to the management of bulimia. *Psychological Medicine, 11*, 707–711.

Fairburn, C. G. (2008). *Cognitive behavior therapy and eating disorders*. New York, NY: Guilford.

Fairburn, C. G. (2013). *Overcoming binge eating: The proven program to learn why you binge and how you can stop* (2nd ed.). New York, NY: Guilford.

Fairburn, C. G., Agras, W. S., Walsh, B. T., Wilson, G. T., & Stice, E. (2004). Prediction of outcome in bulimia nervosa by early change in treatment. *American Journal of Psychiatry, 161*, 2322–2324.

Fairburn, C. G., & Beglin, S. J. (1994). Assessment of eating disorders: Interview or self-report questionnaire. *International Journal of Eating Disorders, 16*, 363–370.

Fairburn, C. G., Cooper, Z., Doll, H. A., O'Connor, M. E., Bohn, K., Hawker, D. M., . . . Palmer, R. L. (2009). Transdiagnostic cognitive-behavioral therapy for patients with eating disorders: A two-site trial with 60-week follow-up. *The American Journal of Psychiatry, 166*, 311–319.

Fairburn, C. G., Cooper, Z., & Shafran, R. (2003). Cognitive behaviour therapy for eating disorders: A 'transdiagnostic' theory and treatment. *Behaviour Research and Therapy*, *41*, 509–528.

Fairburn, C. G., Norman, P. A., Welch, S. L., O'Connor, M. E., Doll, H. A., & Peveler, R. C. (1995). A prospective study of outcome in bulimia nervosa and the long-term effects of three psychological treatments. *Archives of General Psychiatry*, *52*, 304–312.

Fazeli, P. K., Calder, G. L., Miller, K. K., Misra, M., Lawson, E. A., Meenaghan, E., . . . Klibanski, A. (2012). Psychotropic medication use in anorexia nervosa between 1997 and 2009. *International Journal of Eating Disorders*, *45*, 970–976.

Federici, A., Wisniewski, L., & Ben-Porath, D. D. (2012). Description of an intensive dialectical behavior therapy program for multidiagnostic clients with eating disorders. *Journal of Counseling & Development*, *90*, 330–338.

Godt, K. (2008). Personality disorders in 545 patients with eating disorders. *European Eating Disorders Review*, *16*, 94–99.

Fischer, E., & Silverman, A. (2007). Behavioral conceptualization, assessment, and treatment of pediatric feeding disorders. *Seminars in Speech and Language*, *28*, 223–231.

Fredericks, D. W., Carr, J. E., & Williams, W. L. (1998). Overview of the treatment of rumination disorder for adults in a residential setting. *Journal of Behavioral Therapy and Experimental Psychiatry*, *29*, 31–40.

Hagopian, L. P., Gonzalez, M., Rivet, T. T., Triggs, M., & Clark, S. B. (2011). Response interruption and differential reinforcement of alternative behavior for the treatment of pica. *Behavioral Interventions*, *26*, 309–325.

Hay, P. (2013). A systematic review of evidence for psychological treatments in eating disorders: 2005–2012. *International Journal of Eating Disorders*, *46*, 462–469.

Henry, J., & Kwong, A. M. (2003). Why is geophagy treated like dirt? *Deviant Behavior*, *24*, 353–371.

Hepworth, N., & Paxton, S. J. (2007). Pathways to help-seeking in bulimia nervosa and binge eating problems: A concept mapping approach. *International Journal of Eating Disorders*, *40*, 493–504.

Hoek, H., & van Hoeken, D. (2003). Review of the prevalence and incidence of eating disorders. *International Journal of Eating Disorders*, *34*, 383–396.

Katzman, D. K. (2005). Medical complications in adolescents with anorexia nervosa: A review of the literature. *International Journal of Eating Disorders*, *37* (Suppl.), 552–559.

Kaye, W. H., Strober, M., & Jimerson, D. C. (2009). *The neurobiology of eating disorders*. New York, NY: Oxford.

Keel, P. L., Klump, K. L., Miller, K. B., McGue, M., & Iacono, W. G. (2005). Shared transmission of eating disorders and anxiety disorders. *International Journal of Eating Disorders*, *38*, 99–105.

Keel, P., Mitchell, J. E., Miller, K. B., Davis, T. L., & Crow, S. J. (2000). Social adjustment over 10 years following diagnosis with bulimia nervosa. *International Journal of Eating Disorders*, *27*, 21–28.

Keel, P. K., Wolfe, B. E., Liddle, R. A., De Young, K. P., & Jimerson, D. C. (2007). Clinical features and physiological response to a test meal in purging disorder and bulimia nervosa. *Archives of General Psychiatry*, *64*, 1058–1066.

Kenney, L., & Walsh, B. T. (2013). Avoidant/restrictive food intake disorder (ARFID): Defining ARFID. *Eating Disorder Review*, *24*(3). Retrieved from: http://www.eatingdisordersreview.com/nl/nl_edr_24_3_1.html

Kerem, N. C., & Katzman, D. K. (2003). Brain structure and function in adolescents with anorexia nervosa. *Adolescent Medicine*, *14*, 109–118.

Klump, K. L., Bulik, C. M., Kaye, W. H., Treasure, J., & Tyson, E. (2009). Academy for eating disorders position paper: Eating disorders are serious mental illnesses. *International Journal of Eating Disorders*, *42*, 97–103.

Kronenberger, W. G., & Meyer, R. G. (2001). *The child clinician's handbook* (2nd ed.). Boston, MA: Allyn & Bacon.

Lang, R., Mulloy, A., Giesbers, S., Pfeiffer, B., Delaune, E., Didden, R., . . . O'Reilly, M. (2011). Behavioral interventions for rumination and operant vomiting in individuals with intellectual disabilities: A systematic review. *Research in Developmental Disabilities*, *32*, 2193–2205.

LaRue, R. H., Stewart, V., Piazza, C. C., Volkert, V. M., Patel, M. T., & Zeleny, J. (2011). Escape as reinforcement and escape extinction in the treatment of feeding problems. *Journal of Applied Behavior Analysis*, *44*, 719–735.

Lebow, J., Sim, L. A., Erwin, P. J., & Murad, M. H. (2012). The effect of atypical antipsychotic medications in individuals with anorexia nervosa: A systematic review and meta-analysis. *International Journal of Eating Disorders*, *46*, 332–339.

Le Grange, D., & Lock, J. (2007). *Treating bulimia in adolescents: A family-based approach*. New York, NY: Guilford.

Le Grange, D., Lock, J., & Dymek, M. (2003). Family-based therapy for adolescents with bulimia nervosa. *American Journal of Psychotherapy, 57*, 237–251.

Le Grange, D., & Schmidt, U. (2005). The treatment of adolescents with bulimia nervosa. *Journal of Mental Health, 14*, 587–597.

Linehan, M. M. (1993). *Cognitive-behavioral treatment of borderline personality disorder*. New York, NY: Guilford.

Lock, J., Agras, W., Bryson, S., & Kraemer, H. (2005). A comparison of short- and long-term family therapy for adolescent anorexia nervosa. *Journal of the American Academy of Child & Adolescent Psychiatry, 44*, 632–639.

Lock, J., Brandt, H., Woodside, B., Agras, S., Halmi, W., Johnson, C., . . . Wilfley, D. (2012). Challenges in conducting a multi-site randomized clinical trial comparing treatments for adolescent anorexia nervosa. *International Journal of Eating Disorders, 45*, 202–213.

Lock, J., & Le Grange, D. (2012). *Treatment manual for anorexia nervosa: A family-based approach* (2nd ed.). New York, NY: Guilford.

Lock, J., Le Grange, D. Agras, W., Moye, A., Bryson, S., & Jo, B. (2010). Randomized clinical trial comparing family-based treatment with adolescent-focused individual therapy for adolescents with anorexia nervosa. *Archives of General Psychiatry, 67*, 1025–1032.

Lyons, W. A., Rue, H. C., Luiselli, J. K., & DiGennaro, F. D. (2007). Brief functional analysis and supplemental feeding for postmeal rumination in children with developmental disabilities. *Journal of Applied Behavior Analysis, 40*, 743–747.

McCord, B. E., Grosser, J. W., Iwata, B. A., & Powers, L. A. (2005). An analysis of response-blocking parameters in the prevention of pica. *Journal of Applied Behavior Analysis, 38*, 391–394.

Mischoulon, D., Eddy, K. T., Keshaviah, A., Dinescu, D., Ross, S. L., Kass, E., . . . Herzog, D. B. (2011). Depression and eating disorders: Treatment and course. *Journal of Affective Disorders, 130*, 470–477.

Mitchell, J. E., Roerig, J., & Steffen, K. (2013). Biological therapies for eating disorders. *International Journal of Eating Disorders, 46*, 470–477.

Muhlau, M., Gaser, C., Ilg, R., Conrad, B., Leibl, C., & Cebulla, M. H. (2007). Gray matter decreases of the anterior cingulate cortex in anorexia nervosa. *American Journal of Psychiatry, 164*, 1850–1857.

National Institute for Health and Care Excellence (NICE). (2004). *Core interventions in the treatment and management of anorexia nervosa, bulimia nervosa, and binge eating disorder* (National Clinical Practice Guideline CG9). Retrieved from: www.nice.org.uk/nicemedia/pdf/CG9FullGuideline.pdf

Nunez-Navarro, A., Jimenez-Murcia, S., Alvarez-Moya, E., Villarejo, C., Sanchez Díaz, I., Augmantell, C., . . . Fernández-Aranda, F. (2011). Differentiating purging and nonpurging bulimia nervosa and binge eating disorder. *International Journal of Eating Disorders, 44*, 488–496.

Pike, K. M., Walsh, B. T., Vitousek, K., Wilson, G. T., & Bauer, J. (2003). Cognitive Behavior Therapy in the posthospitalization treatment of anorexia nervosa. *American Journal of Psychiatry, 160*, 2046–2049.

Pomeroy, C., Mitchell, J. E., Roerig, J., & Crow, S. (2002). *Medical complications of psychiatric illness*. Washington, DC: American Psychiatric Press.

Rhine, D., & Tarbox, J. (2009). Chewing gum as a treatment for rumination in a child with autism. *Journal of Applied Behavior Analysis, 42*, 381–385.

Roberts, M. E., Tchanturia, K., Stahl, D., Southgate, L., & Treasure, J. (2007). A systematic review and meta-analysis of set-shifting ability in eating disorders. *Psychological Medicine, 37*, 1075–1084.

Romano, S. J., Halmi, K. A., Sarkar, N. P., Koke, S. C., & Lee, J. S. (2002). A placebo controlled study of fluoxetine in continued treatment of bulimia nervosa after successful acute fluoxetine treatment. *American Journal of Psychiatry, 159*, 96–102.

Safer, D. L., Robinson, A. H., & Booil, J. (2010). Outcome from a randomized controlled trial of group therapy for binge eating disorder: Comparing dialectical behavior therapy adapted for binge eating to an active comparison group therapy. *Behavior Therapy, 41*, 106–120.

Safer, D. L., Telch, C. F., & Agras, W. S. (2001). Dialectical behavior therapy adapted for bulimia: A case report. *International Journal of Eating Disorders, 30*, 101–106.

Safer, D. L., Telch, C. F., & Chen, E. Y. (2009). *Dialectical behavior therapy for binge eating and bulimia*. NY, New York: Guilford.

Sharp, W. G., Jaquess, D. L., Morton, J. F., & Herzinger, C. V. (2010). Pediatric feeding disorders: A quantitative synthesis of treatment outcomes. *Clinical Child and Family Psychology Review, 13*, 348–365.

Southgate, L., Tchanturia, K., & Treasure, J. (2008). Information processing bias in anorexia nervosa. *Psychiatry Residency, 160*, 221–227.

Steinhausen, H. C., & Weber, S. (2009). The outcome of bulimia nervosa: Findings from one-quarter century of research. *American Journal of Psychiatry*, *166*, 1331–1341.

Telch, C. F., Agras, W. S., & Linehan, M. M. (2001). Dialectical behavior therapy for binge eating disorder. *Journal of Consulting and Clinical Psychology*, *69*, 1061–1065.

Vaz, P. C. M., Piazza, C. C., Stewart, V., Volkert, V. M., & Groff, R. A. (2012). Using a chaser to decrease packing in children with feeding disorders. *Journal of Applied Behavior Analysis*, *45*, 97–105.

Vocks, S., Tuschen-Caffier, B., Pietrowsky, R., Rustenbach, S. J., Kersting, A., & Herpertz, S. (2010). Meta-analysis of the effectiveness of psychological and pharmacological treatments for binge eating disorder. *International Journal of Eating Disorders*, *43*, 205–217.

Williams, D. E., Kirkpatrick-Sanchez, S., Enzinna, D., Dunn, J., & Borden-Karasack, D. (2009). The clinical management and prevention of pica: A retrospective follow-up of 41 individuals with intellectual disabilities and pica. *Journal of Applied Research in Intellectual Disabilities*, *22*, 210–215.

Williams, D. E., & McAdam, D. (2012). Assessment, behavioral treatment, and preventions of pica: Clinical guidelines and recommendations for practitioners. *Research in Developmental Disabilities*, *33*, 2050–2057.

Wilson, G. T., Wilfley, D. E., Agras, W. S., & Bryson, S. W. (2010). Psychological treatments of binge eating disorder. *Archives of General Psychiatry*, *67*, 94–101.

Wisniewski, L., & Ben-Porath, D. D. (2005). Telephone skill-coaching with eating-disordered clients: Clinical guidelines using a DBT framework. *European Eating Disorders Review*, *13*, 344–350.

Wisniewski, L., & Kelly, E. (2003). The application of dialectical behavior therapy to the treatment of eating disorders. *Cognitive and Behavioral Practice*, 10, 131–138.

Ziere G., Dieleman, J. P., van der Cammen, T. J., Hofman, A., Pols, H. A., & Stricker, B. H. (2008). Selective serotonin reuptake inhibiting antidepressants are associated with an increased risk of nonvertebral fractures. *Journal of Clinical Psychopharmacology*, *28*, 411–417.

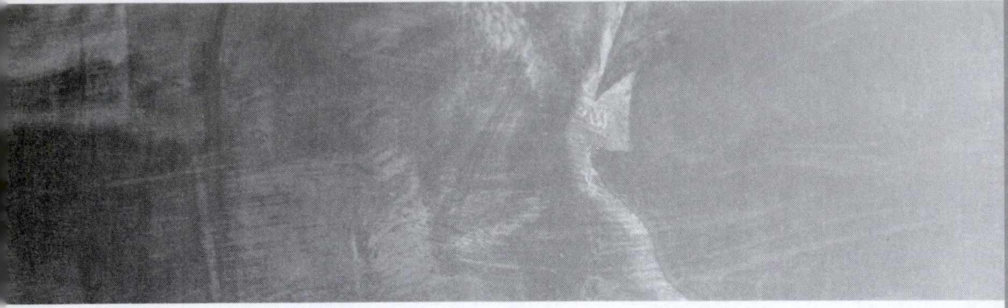

CHAPTER

12

MST - ↑ prosocial ↓ deviance
Family - understanding family system
PMT - parent change approach consistency structure

CBT
IT
Prob Solving
School
meds

Disruptive, Impulse-Control, and Conduct Disorders, and Elimination Disorders

Nicole A. Adamson, Emily C. Campbell, and Victoria E. Kress

CASE STUDY: ANDREW

Andrew is a hostile and inattentive 15-year-old Caucasian male from an urban city in the Northeast region of the United States. Andrew failed the seventh grade and currently is in the ninth grade. He attends an urban high school that is within walking distance from the apartment where he lives with his parents and four siblings. Andrew has very few friends. The friends he has are identified by his peers and school staff as "scary" and "troublemakers." Andrew and his friends are notorious for getting into physical altercations, possessing drugs, skipping school, and being suspended for their disruptive, disrespectful, and illegal behaviors.

The oldest of five children, Andrew comes from a low socioeconomic status home, where his father works two jobs (construction during the day, and as a security guard at the county jail at night), and his mother works the night shift at a local gas station five nights a week. As the oldest child, Andrew is in charge of helping to take care of his siblings, and he resents this role. Andrew's father drinks heavily and becomes aggressive when he drinks. Andrew and his mother tend to take the brunt of the abuse. Andrew's mother does the cooking and cleaning around the apartment, but isolates herself from the children on the weekends, providing very little support, structure, and discipline. The children frequently see her crying. Andrew's father drinks all weekend long, and only interacts with his wife and the children when he needs something (e.g., another beer), and he does this by yelling his demands. Everyone in the house is afraid of Andrew's father. Andrew and his father often arguments that escalate and become violent.

As early as the age of five Andrew was displaying anger, disobedience, stubbornness, tantrums, lying, stealing and aggressive behaviors towards his siblings and is parents. These behaviors continued to escalate as Andrew grew older. Andrew acted increasingly aggressive with family members and classmates, was verbally disrespectful of his parents and other adults, began disobeying the laws, and became a hazard to himself and to others.

Andrew has been involved in multiple incidences of hurting and killing animals. When he was six, Andrew's mother witnessed Andrew catch a frog and then kill it. She found it odd that he didn't show any emotion when he realized that the frog was not able to hop away, but she disregarded the incident. Andrew's mother reported that this behavior continued as Andrew grew older and that he escalated to injuring and killing larger animals. At the age of nine, Andrew found a stray kitten wandering around outside their apartment. He seemed to like the kitten and asked if the family could keep it. Andrew's mother agreed. Two days later, Andrew put the kitten in the microwave and killed it. His mother became very concerned as Andrew showed no remorse for his actions.

In late elementary and early middle school, Andrew's grades dropped, he became more aggressive, and he received many school suspensions for cheating, stealing, fighting, and sniffing substances. At the age of 11 he assaulted a girl at his school. His subsequent court involvement led to his first admission to a residential treatment facility. At the age of 12, Andrew was again involuntarily admitted to a local psychiatric hospital for seven days secondary to having threatened another student.

Over the past three years, with Andrew's escalating behaviors, Andrew's mother has withdrawn and become less involved in his life. Andrew has been admitted to hospitals for psychiatric care three other times over the course of the past three years. While his mother was involved in Andrew's inpatient therapy, his father was not. Andrew's parents have been inconsistent in following through with outpatient family therapy recommendations. Andrew always returns to his problematic behaviors soon after being released from the hospitals. He is currently not taking his prescribed medication. Several days ago, Andrew was involved in another physical altercation with a school peer during which Andrew threatened to kill the other student. Andrew was immediately expelled for the remainder of the school year. Andrew was then taken into legal custody, and transfered to a secure (i.e., "locked") residential intensive treatment center, for psychiatric assessment.

DESCRIPTION OF THE DISRUPTIVE, IMPULSE-CONTROL, AND CONDUCT DISORDERS

Disruptive, impulse-control, and conduct disorders include a number of diverse, disruptive behaviors (e.g., oppositional and aggressive outbursts, stealing) and disorders. In the *DSM-5*, the disruptive, impulse-control, and conduct disorders include oppositional defiant disorder (ODD), conduct disorder (CD), antisocial personality disorder (see Chapter 9 for a detailed discussion of this disorder and its treatment), intermittent explosive disorder (IED), pyromania, and kleptomania (American Psychiatric Association [APA], 2013).

IED, kleptomania, and pyromania are disorders which all involve difficulties in controlling impulses and behavior. In people with IED, these impulse control struggles manifest as a failure to control aggressive impulses, with resulting verbal aggression (e.g., temper tantrums, verbal altercations), or impulsive physical aggression (e.g., physically lashing out at others or property). With pyromania, people set fire to objects, and with kleptomania, people engage in impulsive stealing.

ODD and CD, colloquially referred to as disruptive behavior disorders, are the two most common child and adolescent disorders seen in counselor practice (Sadock & Sadock, 2007). Persistent disruptive behavior is a product of multiple interacting elements and includes biological, environmental, and psychological influences. Because of the multidimensionality of disruptive behaviors, it is difficult to identify the exact cause or primary contributing factors that support the development of disruptive behaviors.

According to the *DSM-5* (APA, 2013), diagnosable disruptive behavior disorders (i.e., ODD and CD) are characterized by behaviors that are persistent and contribute to severe impairment in social, academic, or occupational performance. In addition, diagnosis requires that these behaviors are pervasive, spanning interactions with peers, family, friends, and authority figures, and are consistent across different domains including home, school, and work systems. Disruptive behaviors are often rooted in anger and indicate an inability to effectively regulate emotion and implement effective coping mechanisms when in activating situations. The degree of noticeable dysfunction is contingent on unique individual characteristics.

Disruptive behavior disorders are considered to represent a continuum of behaviors, ranging from the early childhood onset of ODD to antisocial personality disorder in adulthood. Thus, the earlier the onset and the more pervasive and severe ODD is throughout childhood, the greater the chance these symptoms can manifest and develop into symptoms of CD. Similarly, more pervasive and severe CD throughout adolescence and young adulthood increases the likelihood of these symptoms progressing into symptoms of antisocial personality disorder as an adult. It is important that counselors competently differentiate among these disruptive behavior disorders and provide appropriate interventions.

Less is known about IED, kleptomania, and pyromania, than ODD and CD. People with these disorders rarely seek out treatment for issues related to these disorders, and as such, the literature provides minimal guidance on treatment considerations.

COUNSELOR CONSIDERATIONS

Developing a healthy therapeutic relationship is the first priority when working with any client. Many individuals with disruptive, impulse-control, and conduct disorders (especially CD and ODD) do not feel safe with others. Individuals with these disorders typically come to counseling with a preexisting message that the world is against them, and the counselor will not be any different from others who have hurt or disappointed them. A primary component of creating a working alliance with this population is developing a safe environment that fosters trust between the counselor and client. Once safety and trust are developed, the client's defenses and his or her need to defy authority figures typically decrease. The counselor–client relationship can serve as a corrective experience in which clients gain a sense of self-worth, self-efficacy, and self-mastery, learning new and more effective ways to control their disruptive behaviors.

Clients with disruptive behavior disorders can be challenging to work with in counseling. Work with this population will require that counselors possess a great deal of patience. This population is typically resistant to the counseling process and may act out verbally or behaviorally in session. It is important to not be intimidated and to create concrete and defined treatment boundaries. Counselors must be consciously aware of their own feelings regarding control, anger, aggression, defiance, and misbehavior. Counselors may have unresolved issues from their own adolescence that are triggered by this population. It is important to be cognitively aware of one's own trigger points to ensure that countertransference is managed.

One lens that is helpful for understanding poor emotion regulation and distancing-type behaviors is attachment theory (Ainsworth & Bowlby, 1991). In order to work effectively toward decreasing these negative behaviors, counselors must consider the poor emotion regulation systems these clients possess. Emotion regulation is determined through infant and primary caregiver interactions (Ainsworth & Bowlby, 1991), and from early childhood experiences. Youth with disruptive behaviors tend to demonstrate insecure attachment styles (Guttmann-Steinmetz & Crowell, 2006) including withdrawing from emotion, being fearful of intimacy, and being afraid of not being "enough" to the people who matter the most. These deeply ingrained emotions and psychological reactions are then manifested as disruptive behaviors. Play therapy and expressive arts techniques can be of use in helping children to express emotions.

Family dynamics must also be considered when working with children and adolescents with these disorders. Not only is it important to consider how the family system has contributed to the persisting negative, hostile, and deviant behaviors, but it is crucial to consider how to engage the family in the treatment process. Thus, a significant aspect of treating this population is developing a strong working alliance with the parents as well as the child (Gopalan et al., 2010). One of the most significant barriers to getting this population the mental health services they need is the clients' and their caregivers' lack of understanding of the complexity of the issues that need to be addressed, caregivers' lack of involvement in the counseling process, and caregivers' misbeliefs about the origins of the child's issues (Gopalan et al., 2010).

One of the primary factors that contributes to, or supports disruptive behaviors is the family system. Because children, especially oppositional children, are less likely to be aware of, or know how to talk about, emotional distress, it is important to consider that poor emotion regulation may be at the root of these disruptive behaviors. It is essential that families and/or caregivers be involved in treatment with children and adolescents who have disruptive behavior disorders.

PROGNOSIS

With regards to IED, kleptomania and pyromania, there is a lack of research, and little is known about the course of these disorders or their long-term prognosis. More research is needed on prognostic, therapeutic factors, and treatments that can best support these populations.

The prognosis for those with ODD/CD is highly contingent on other systems of influence. Because disruptive behaviors are so multidimensional in nature, it is difficult to effectively treat ODD/CD with individual counseling alone. In order to create lasting change, it is necessary to pull family and school systems into treatment. The best predictor of success is ongoing support from parents and their openness to parental training. In many cases, the caretakers of the youth will cease counseling prematurely, which leads to poor outcomes (i.e., no behavioral changes). Factors that predict a child's behavior change include those associated with parent–child interactions (i.e., abuse, neglect, conflict, inconsistency in punishment), and parents' mental health issues (e.g., substance use; Sadock & Sadock, 2007). Various stressors and difficulties getting the child to treatment appointments can also invite negative treatment outcomes. Caregivers' openness to being a part of the treatment plan, and their participation in parenting skills training are positive predictors of treatment outcome (Sadock & Sadock, 2007).

OPPOSITIONAL DEFIANT DISORDER AND CONDUCT DISORDER

Description of the Disorders and Typical Client Characteristics

Depression check Comorbid (handwritten annotation)

Oppositional defiant disorder (ODD) and conduct disorder (CD) share many similarities, with CD embodying ODD symptoms, but with greater scope and severity. As such, the treatments and counseling considerations for these two disorders are similar. Because of these similarities, in this section, ODD and CD will be presented together.

According to the *DSM-5* (APA, 2013), ODD is described as a persistent pattern of defiant and disobedient behaviors marked by hostile and negative demeanor that is specifically targeted at authority figures. ODD is characterized by anger, resentment, hostile emotions, vindictive and blaming behaviors, resistance to authority, low frustration tolerance, and gaining pleasure from resisting and annoying others. In comparison to children of a similar age and developmental stage in life, children diagnosed with ODD exhibit increased frequency and more severe levels of negative, disrespectful, and defiant behaviors marked by disobedience, power struggles, unwillingness to compromise or cooperate, argumentativeness, resisting authority, and angry outbursts (Sadock & Sadock, 2007). Specifically, younger children diagnosed with ODD are emotionally highly reactive to environmental stimuli, difficult to soothe once distressed, have a low tolerance for frustration, and act out through tantrums, kicking, and screaming. As these children get older, these emotions can be internalized into low self-esteem and low self-worth. As a result, these children may start acting aggressively and maliciously toward others, initiate verbal and physical altercations, curse, and experiment with drugs and alcohol.

2-3 grade (handwritten annotation)

ODD has an average prevalence estimate of 3% (APA, 2013). The prime age of diagnosis is eight and it is most prevalent between the ages of eight and 11. ODD is more prevalent in males than females (Sadock & Sadock, 2007). A person must display the ODD-related behaviors consistently for at least six months to receive the diagnosis (APA, 2013).

ODD is related to poor school performance, school suspension and expulsion, and higher dropout rates. Learning disabilities are also common in children who are diagnosed with ODD. ODD is significantly related to environmental factors, especially family dynamics. Depending on the family system, the family may be unaware of the severity of the disruptive behaviors and the degree to which it is hindering the child's success. If that is the case, the family may be a significant contributing factor to the origin of the disorder, and may continue to unconsciously reinforce and escalate the negative behaviors. Risk factors for ODD may include a number of interacting factors such as living in poverty, single-parent families, experiencing physical abuse, harsh and inconsistent punishments, neglect, multiple changing caretakers, and witnessing family violence.

CD has a 1-year median population prevalence of 4% (APA, 2013). According to the *DSM-5* (APA, 2013), CD is an enduring and repetitive pattern of defiance marked by deceitful, hostile, and destructive behaviors that violate self and others. CD is characterized by a lack of empathy and angry and hostile emotions that drive malicious behaviors toward others. Common CD behaviors include acting out aggressively, causing physical harm to other people or animals, destroying property, deceitfulness, theft, and not adhering to, and often intentionally going against, rules (APA, 2013). Children diagnosed with CD are more likely to intentionally start physical altercations, inflict harm by using objects (e.g., knife, bat) on people and animals, perpetrate a sexual assault, violate others' rights, and gain pleasure from seeing humans or animals suffer. Those diagnosed with CD are more likely to steal or deliberately destroy someone else's property, lie and manipulate others to get out of responsibilities, and struggle to adhere to small system (i.e., rules within the home) or large system (i.e., legal system laws) rules.

Children with CD have very poor interpersonal relationships and extreme difficulties engaging in intimate relationships, tend to have multiple sexual partners and start engaging in sexual activities at an early age, and intentionally dominate younger and more helpless individuals. Behaviorally, CD characteristics are divided into two categories, overt and covert behaviors. Overt behaviors are stereotypically found more often in males with CD and are demonstrated through observable behaviors that directly impact others, like initiating physical altercations, theft, assault, destroying property, setting fires, and killing animals. Covert behaviors are less confrontational and are found more often in females with CD. Some examples include, but are not limited to, lying, cheating, threatening others, verbal arguments, truancy, power struggles, and shoplifting.

Many children seen for mental health services are diagnosed with CD (APA, 2013), and these rates are exceptionally high in hospital and residential treatment settings. The *DSM-5* suggests a specifier of childhood onset of CD, which indicates the child exhibited these behaviors prior to the age of 10, and an adolescent specifier suggests the child began to exhibit these behaviors post age 10. The severity of the CD can also be specified (i.e., mild, moderate, severe), as can the specifier *with limited prosocial emotions* (i.e., a lack of remorse or guilt, callous and lacking empathy, unconcerned about performance, and/or shallow or deficient affect). CD is more prevalent in males than females with ratios that range from 4 to 1, to 12 to 1 (Sadock & Sadock, 2007).

Counselor Considerations

Family dynamics typically play an important role in the development and/or maintenance of ODD/CD. As such, counselors should always consider the role that family dynamics and family functioning play in these disorders.

All children wish to feel special and want people to notice and care about them. Some children act up as a way to have their emotional needs met. Because parents (or other adults) typically punish children for unwanted behaviors, children with ODD/CD often receive ample attention (although it is negative) for their destructive behaviors. For example, a child who hits his sibling will be reprimanded, possibly snatched up by a parent, and maybe placed in a time out. While in the time out, the parent generally monitors the child, and this can be a time-intensive process. Although the child is technically being punished, he is receiving a significant amount of the parent's time and energy, which can actually be reinforcing. Although the punishment is somewhat reinforcing, it provokes feelings of anger and inadequacy in the child, creates relational ruptures in the parental relationship, and reinforces the idea, for both the parent and the child, that the child is a problem. The mild reinforcement the child receives for being disruptive supports the child's future use of unhelpful behaviors during times of distress. As such, while punishment seems to be a viable solution in managing behavioral problems, it can reinforce negative and unhelpful behaviors.

The counselor must also attend to the way in which a child with ODD/CD affects the other children in the household. The client's siblings might feel as though the parents pay more attention to the client due to the misbehavior, and other siblings might tend to act out, or siblings might choose to avoid the negative behaviors displayed by the client in order to gain positive attention. If this occurs, it might lead to even more negative feelings in the client, and further invoke a sense of inadequacy and anger. It is important for counselors to attend to all of the family dynamics to identify strategies for helping the client and siblings get the positive attention they need to facilitate appropriate and helpful behaviors.

Similar to any other counseling relationship, it is important to create a strong working alliance with this population. Trust and safety are key elements in the counseling relationship and may be especially important. The construction of a working alliance allows the client to feel a sense of autonomy, mastery, and control within the therapeutic process, and helps to deescalate defensive and protective behaviors. Engaging the client in activities that he or she enjoys is a good way to facilitate the development of the relationship (e.g., talking while playing a card game).

At first, in an effort to maintain some sense of control, these clients will likely push the limits in counseling sessions. From the first session, the counselor must consider developing and implementing concrete and firm boundaries, and provide explicit consequences for violating these. The client must be given reasonable rules and responsibilities to adhere to, balanced with the freedom to make choices that give sessions direction. Clearly communicating expectations for these clients is a positive way of showing care and trust. The goal is to deescalate the emotional distress and disruptive behaviors, thus creating a secure and safe space, while empowering the client to make better decisions.

Counselors must also take care to assess for a physical, emotional, or sexual abuse history. Any abuse or trauma issues must also be addressed in a client's treatment plan.

Connecting with the child's experience and having empathy for the child will facilitate counselors' patience with this often challenging population. At the same time, it is important that counselors connect with the child's caregivers. Without this connection, caregivers may not be willing to be a part of the treatment process.

Counselors working with this population are challenged to apply evidence-based interventions in a developmentally appropriate, engaging fashion. Treatment interventions must be meaningful to clients. If they are not meaningful, clients will not take them seriously, and will not follow through on using learned skills. The use of creative media (e.g., art, music) can be engaging to clients and may help them better digest the concepts presented in treatment.

Cultural considerations should inform counselors' assessments and interactions with ODD/CD. According to the *DSM-5*, symptoms of ODD appear relatively similar across diverse populations. However, CD symptoms may present differently across diverse populations and with regard to race/ethnicity, socioeconomic status, and gender (APA, 2013). For example, CD can be overdiagnosed in high-crime areas because environmental circumstances are frequently overlooked as significant contributors to criminal behaviors. Similarly, gender is another significant contributor to how CD symptoms manifest. For example, males tend to demonstrate disruptive behaviors toward someone else (e.g., fighting, vandalism, stealing), while females are more likely to demonstrate symptoms that involve, to a greater degree, passive-aggressive behaviors such as lying, running away, or substance use (APA, 2013).

In addition, counselors are ethically responsible for informing minor clients about the limitations to confidentiality, specifically related to the client's age (i.e., parents have a right to information about the client and his or her treatment). With this population, counselors should also be very explicit that the counselor will need to report imminent harm to self and/or others to guardians/legal authorities, and take measures to enhance the safety of the client and those who may be at risk.

It is also imperative that counselors assess for comorbid difficulties when working with children with ODD/CD. This population is likely to experiment with drugs or alcohol (Sadock & Sadock, 2007). Substance use may provide temporary relief from clients' family stress, their own negative feelings, or their difficulties in social situations. However, drugs and alcohol ultimately complicate and exacerbate client symptoms, and this should be addressed in conjunction with—and typically before—any ODD/CD treatments are applied.

Treatment Models and Interventions

The symptoms of ODD/CD are informed and affected by the client's cognitive, psychological, and social influences (Powell et al., 2011). As such, counselors should take care to address the client's entire system, including intrapersonal, school, family, and social contexts.

Research suggests that multisystemic therapy is one of the most comprehensive and effective treatments for use with this population. As previously mentioned, treatments which involve the family are also important. Individual therapies that place an emphasis on the development of skills are also effective, and these include cognitive behavioral therapy, behavior therapy, and problem-solving skills training. Finally, school-based programs, or specialized school settings for children with behavior disorders may be required for children with severe behavior problems.

MULTISYSTEMIC THERAPY (MST)   MST (Henggeler & Schaeffer, 2010) is an intensive, ecological, family- and home-based approach used to address conduct behaviors in youth, and it is considered an evidence-based approach to treating children and adolescents with conduct issues (Henggeler & Schaeffer, 2010; Stambaugh et al., 2007). MST focuses on multiple interconnected systems (i.e., the self, family, neighborhood, school, peers, culture, and community), and includes multiple levels of intervention and care. MST is operationalized through nine core treatment principles: finding the fit (how the problem makes sense in the context of the system); focusing on positive strengths in all systems; increasing family members' responsibility; being present-focused, well-defined, and action-oriented targeting sequences of behaviors; being developmentally appropriate; applying continuous effort; consistently evaluating from multiple perspectives; and generalizing skills to multiple settings (Henggeler & Schaeffer, 2010). Client empowerment and creating and sustaining positive behaviors is the central aim of MST.

In MST, psychosocial treatment is utilized to enhance prosocial behaviors and diminish deviant behaviors (Masi et al., 2011). Treatment is focused on enhancing emotional self-awareness, and developing the skills needed to deescalate and manage anger. Role plays are used to help clients explore and discover more effective ways of responding to undesired situations, problem solving, and negotiating interpersonal conflicts. This type of treatment also involves daily individual counseling, along with multiple opportunities for family therapy (Masi et al., 2011).

FAMILY THERAPY   Family therapy (e.g., functional family therapy; Alexander & Parsons, 1982) is important if children with these disorders are to experience enduring change (Gopalan et al., 2010). Family therapy creates an opportunity for the counselor to gain a more holistic understanding of what is occurring within the family system, including observations of the interactions between parents and children, and can be efficacious in decreasing ODD/CD symptoms (Hendriks, van der Schee, & Blanken, 2012). Through family therapy, counselors can help parents develop the skills they can use to cope with their own negative reactions (e.g., anger) to the child's behavior. As parents learn new skills and how to deescalate situations, more space is created for parents to respond to the child with patience and care. These system changes can invite new and more adaptive family interactions. A recent meta-analysis of 47 randomized controlled studies of family therapy approaches addressing disruptive behavior disorders reported that regardless of treatment modality (e.g., individual family therapy, multifamily group therapy), family-based interventions produced significant changes in symptomology associated with these disorders and increased family functioning (Sydow, Retzlaff, Beher, Haun, & Schweitzer, 2013).

The goal of family therapy is to substantially decrease, if not eliminate, negative cycles of interaction between parents and children, including inconsistent and harsh punishments, and to increase the positive interactions that parents have with their children (Sadock & Sadock, 2007). As previously mentioned, the cycle of negative client behaviors is usually deeply embedded within family system dynamics, and it is important to help parents understand the ways in which punishment can actually reinforce negative client behaviors. Because hostile parenting styles have been associated with poor treatment outcomes with this population, addressing this factor in family therapy is beneficial (Scott et al., 2010). This therapy focuses primarily on identifying interactions and behaviors within the family that maintain the symptoms, and then moving to making adjustments to the entire family system that will reduce the problematic behaviors (Johnson & Waller, 2006). It is typically difficult for parents to initially begin focusing on positive client behavior while the client's negative behaviors still continue. However, as clients gain reinforcement and attention for desirable behaviors, their unhelpful behaviors will begin to diminish. Siblings can also play a role in the maintenance of problems, and as such, whenever possible, they should be included in family therapy.

Family therapy can be time intensive, and it is important that all family members be adequately invested in the therapeutic process. Counselors should map out family dynamics and cycles and help all family members gain insight and understanding into one another's experiences.

It can be helpful to conduct family therapy in the client's home (i.e., home-based family therapy; Gopalan et al., 2010) as this may further increase the applicability of counseling interventions to the family's real-world setting. Offering families services in the home is also helpful to those who have a difficult time transporting their child to individual counseling and/or family therapy. The provision of home-based services will depend on the policies and programs at the counselor's place of employment. Family therapy that takes place out of the home has its own merits though in that the clinical setting is a neutral place where family cycles and dynamics can be challenged.

Strength-based family interventions are geared toward focusing on what the family and client are doing well (Gopalan et al., 2010). Strength-based approaches focus on enhancing the strengths the family has and building onto those areas that seem to be working well for the family. This could include, but is not limited to, cultural strengths, support systems, decision making, and current level of competencies. The hope is that focusing on the strengths helps parents to feel validated, valued for their role in the family, and open to gaining more knowledge on how to better structure and manage the family. Empirically supported parent-training programs offer parents and caregivers the opportunity to explore and improve their interaction styles with their children and build new problem-solving skills. Many of these programs also include training for the children, which involves the enhancement of problem-solving skills and emotional regulation abilities.

Clinical Toolbox 12.1: In the Pearson etext, click here to read about an activity that can be used with families with children with disruptive behavior disorders to help them better identify their family strengths.

PARENT MANAGEMENT TRAINING (PMT) A number of applications of PMT models have been developed and several of these will be briefly discussed in this section. PMT is one of the most established ODD/CD treatment approaches. Its focus on training parents in the use of new skills makes it an important part of any treatment plan with this population. In fact, research suggests that parents' use of PMT can decrease the youth's aggressive and oppositional behaviors, and increase desired social behaviors (Webster-Stratton, 2011). PMT differs from traditional family therapy in its emphasis on teaching parents skills that they can use to help alter their child's behavior. PMT is an active, directive approach that is based largely on cognitive behavioral and behavior therapy principles. All PMT approaches teach parents to use consistent discipline strategies, the use of rewards to reinforce the child's positive behaviors, and the importance of monitoring the child's behavior.

Clinical Toolbox 12.2: In the Pearson etext, click here to view a brief demonstration of parent management training in practice.

The Oregon model of group-based parent management training (PMTO) was supported as one effective PMT intervention in one randomized trial (Kjøblie, Hukkelberg, & Ogden, 2013). This program works to identify and promote more effective methods by which parents can meet their child's needs. Parents are taught to avoid using aggressive or aversive behaviors to manipulate their child's environment. Parents are taught how to use various prosocial, positive interactions with their child. These new methods of parenting include the parent providing copious amounts of encouragement for desirable behaviors, the use of positive involvement with the child, consistent monitoring of the child's behaviors, appropriate discipline techniques (such as time outs), and the use of problem-solving skills (Kjøblie et al., 2013).

Others, such as Kazdin (2008), have developed PMT models for use in working with this population and their families. Using Kazdin's approach, parents are trained to manage their child's behavioral problems inside and outside of the home. Kazdin's (2008) model is based on social learning and behavior theory principles with an emphasis on applied behavior analysis and antecedents, behaviors, consequences, and repeated practice.

General parent management training has been demonstrated to be successful in treating CD (Costin & Chambers, 2007). General parent management training's primary focus is on working with parents to educate them on better ways of interacting with their child to positively change the child's oppositional behaviors (Costin & Chambers, 2007). This approach focuses more on the parent than the child, with the understanding that if parents change how they approach their child (i.e., rewarding, rules, boundaries, consequences, communication), then the child will adapt as well.

The Incredible Years is a parenting intervention geared towards parents who have younger children. The Incredible Years training protocol includes the use of videos, role plays, rehearsals, and homework assignments to actively reshape parents' interactions with their children (Webster-Stratton, 2011). This intervention was found to be effective when used just with parents, but it is recommended that in order to achieve optimal effectiveness, the child also be involved in treatment (Webster-Stratton, 2011). This program teaches parents to use positive disciplinary strategies, deal with stress more effectively, implement more helpful parenting skills, and strengthen children's social skills. When used with children, puppets and interactive games are used to help them gain insight into their behaviors and interpersonal relationships. The Incredible Years may be an effective way to restructure the familial and interpersonal interactions of parents and their children.

 Clinical Toolbox 12.3: In the Pearson etext, click here to read about an activity that can be used to facilitate communication between youth and their families.

INDIVIDUAL THERAPY Individual counseling is an important aspect of the treatment process when counseling ODD/CD youth. Especially with children who have mild symptoms, individual counseling may be an appropriate initial modality of treatment. Because of their entrenched negative behavioral patterns, most children with ODD/CD do not have many opportunities to receive individual attention that is positive, reinforcing, and corrective. Thus, individual counseling provides an opportunity for the client to have one-on-one time to work through emotional distress and learn new coping skills and adaptive responses to triggering stimuli (Sadock & Sadock, 2007).

By definition, this population is oppositional and may be resistant to change. One specific approach that can break down this resistance and enhance clients' motivation to want to change is motivational interviewing (MI; Miller & Rollnick, 2012). MI is a client-centered, collaborative, goal-directed therapeutic intervention used by the counselor to help encourage clients to want to make positive changes (see Chapter 8 for a more detailed discussion of MI). Through the use of open-ended questions, counselors facilitate a nonconfrontational, questioning conversation in which the client is encouraged to decide what changes are desired, and how he or she is going to make these positive changes. This approach helps clients actively work to discover the positives and negatives of their decisions by highlighting the gap between what they want in life and how their current behavior is not moving them towards their desired goals (Gopalan et al., 2010).

In individual counseling, the treatment focus will be on teaching the client to use new skills. These skills are typically rooted in behavior and cognitive behavior therapy (CBT) treatment principles. Problem-solving skills training is one CBT approach that has received a great deal of attention in the literature. In addition, William Glasser's choice therapy (i.e., reality therapy), provides an active, directive approach that may work well with this population, although no controlled research could be found to support its use with those who have ODD/CD.

Behavior Therapy (BT)   BT interventions are one of the most commonly applied approaches in treating ODD/CD (Sadock & Sadock, 2007). In general, the focus of treatment from a BT perspective is on teaching children adaptive coping skills. Because it is difficult to separate out thoughts from behavior, behavioral skills are nearly always intertwined with the cognitive behavioral skills. From a BT perspective, this population can benefit from learning new skills and applying them to real-world situations. Skills that are frequently taught include problem-solving skills, relaxation skills, anger management skills, and decision-making skills. Parent management training approaches are grounded in BT principles.

Cognitive Behavioral Therapy (CBT)   CBT is another theoretical approach commonly used with youth who have ODD/CD. There are a variety of specific CBT approaches that can be used with this population (Powell et al., 2011). These CBT approaches all focus on developing skills that can be applied to multiple realms of the client's life, including family, school, and personal/social. Working from a CBT perspective, the counselor will first help clients enhance their emotional awareness. Next, the counselor will help clients connect their thoughts with their emotions, and then connect their emotions and thoughts with their behaviors. As counselors teach clients how to shift their cognitions, the resulting emotions and behaviors will shift as well. In order to facilitate this process, CBT interventions also employ basic behavioral interventions such as problem-solving, decision-making, and social-skills training.

Anger management is a common CBT intervention used with this population. When applying anger management, clients learn to identify what typically triggers their anger, the bodily reactions they experience which cue them that they are angry, the automatic thoughts they have, and their typical aggressive reactions. To help client's change this pattern, counselors teach them about various cognitive distortions or thinking errors which support their anger and hostility (e.g., "I should always get what I want from others"), and how these can be challenged. Clients then practice (first with the counselor, but then moving to the real world) using these skills. A strong emphasis is placed on the thinking errors that support angry and aggressive responses. As a part of anger management training, clients also learn to use behavioral skills to manage their anger responses.

These skills may include the use of deep breathing or other relaxation skills (e.g., progressive muscle relaxation), counting backwards, or the use of distraction techniques (e.g., categorizing, in one's head, objects in a room; using imagery to imagine a safe place).

Clinical Toolbox 12.4: In the Pearson etext, click here to read a script that can be used with younger children to teach them how to use progressive muscle relaxation.

Problem-Solving Skills Training (PSST)   Clients with ODD and CD use unproductive means to get their needs met. PSST (e.g., Kazdin, 2010), a CBT approach, can be used to help clients learn the problem-solving skills they need to more effectively get their needs met. In PSST, clients are provided with concrete, step-by-step methods for solving interpersonal dilemmas. Although the steps may seem simple to high-functioning adults, clients may not have these skills; it is important to review each step in order to help clients identify new insights and learn the steps that they might be missing. For example, when dealing with a conflict with another person, clients must first cognitively recognize that there is an interpersonal problem, as opposed to just having an uncomfortable feeling and reacting in a negative way. In addition to concretely breaking down interpersonal social skills, PSST incorporates games and activities that help clients apply what they have learned to practical, real-life scenarios.

In PSST, clients are systematically reinforced for engaging in desirable behaviors. This reinforcement results in the likelihood that the positive behaviors will eventually reoccur. PSST involves 12–20 weekly individual sessions. Clients are initially reinforced with tokens or tangible items, but social reinforcers are primarily used to motivate clients to use prosocial behaviors (Substance Abuse and Mental Health Services Administration [SAMHSA], 2012).

It is also important that parents are able to help their children use PSST in the home environment. The counselor must take care to teach PSST to the parent and must not assume that these are skills that the parent has mastered. As previously mentioned, disruptive behavior disorders are highly systemic, and it is important to help parents identify how to use PSST. Once they fully understand PSST, parents can use it to help clients make more desirable choices outside of the therapeutic setting. Parents' use the PSST skills can serve as good modeling for the child.

CREATIVE TOOLBOX ACTIVITY 12.1   The Color of Anger Game

Nicholette Leanza, MEd, PCC-S

Activity Overview

Therapeutic techniques that invigorate the senses may stimulate clients' interest in counseling and improve their overall engagement in the treatment process. Using clients' sweet tooth as a motivator, this activity encourages clients to examine their difficulties with anger and how to effectively manage this complex emotion. Sensory techniques can help clients connect with concepts such as anger in that they tap into clients' direct experiences, which enables them to retain the learned skills more effectively. In this activity, clients learn to associate their anger experiences with different colored food items.

Treatment Goal(s) of Activity

The primary goals of this activity are to help clients (a) identify their anger triggers; (b) recognize the physical signs, or cues, of their anger; (c) consider the consequences of their aggressive behavior; and (d) develop constructive ways of expressing and managing their anger.

Directions

1. If used with a child, receive consent from the guardians to use candy or fruit snacks as part of the counseling process, and document this consent.
2. Present the client with a small portion (10–15 pieces), or one fun-size pack, of candy or fruit snacks. In this example, plain M&M's candy will be used.
3. Ask the client to sort the candy by color.
4. Provide the client with a list of questions that correspond to each candy color. This can be presented on a sheet of paper, or on an index card. Make sure the client receives at least one piece of candy of each color.

   Red: Talk about an experience that made you angry (i.e., anger triggers).

   Orange: Describe how your body feels when you are angry (i.e., anger cues).

   Yellow: Talk about a good choice you made when you were angry, one that helped the situation.

   Green: Describe what you often think when you are angry.

   Blue: What is one thing you can do to cool off when you're angry?

   Brown: Talk about a not-so-good choice you made when you were angry; one that made the situation worse.

5. Have the client select a piece of candy and answer the corresponding question. The counselor may need to provide examples or ask additional questions to assist the client in clarifying the questions or his or her answers.
6. After the client answers each question, he or she may eat the piece of candy.
7. After the activity, the counselor should guide the client into a deeper discussion about his or her anger, and process his or her feelings and reactions to the activity. The counselor can also point out how each color might represent a certain aspect of anger. For example:

   Red = the client's anger

   Orange = the client's bodily sensations

   Yellow = the client's good choices in dealing with anger

   Brown = the client's poor choices in dealing with anger

   Green = the client's thoughts pertaining to anger

   Blue = the client's coping strategies to manage anger

Process Questions

1. What was the most challenging part of this activity for you?
2. How is anger handled in your family?

3. How do your thoughts contribute to the escalation of your anger?
4. How can you change your thoughts to deescalate your anger?
5. How can you motivate yourself to change the way you deal with anger?
6. What are some consequences of angry outbursts or aggression toward others?
7. How are you affected by other people's anger?
8. How do you know when you are angry?
9. What are the positive aspects of anger?
10. How can you help others with their anger?

SCHOOL-BASED INTERVENTIONS School interventions are also important in supporting youth with ODD/CD. This population may require an Individualized Education Plan or a 504 plan that specifies special accommodations the child needs to support his or her learning in the context of the disorder. In situations where the child has severe behavior problems, the child may require placement in a school that specializes in educating—and maybe even treating—this population.

There are a number of programs that have been applied in schools for use with this population. Positive Attitudes toward Learning in Schools (PALS; Gopalan et al., 2010) is just one example of a program that is centered on improving student behaviors in the classroom through conjoining classroom-based interventions (e.g., reward systems, behavior contingencies, posting rules and consequences), and family-directed interventions (e.g., groups facilitated by parents). Depending on the state or county, different school and community programs will be available to help support the educational needs of children with disruptive behaviors. Counselors may need to be involved in supporting children and families in navigating the school environment. Many times, this means becoming the proactive liaison between the family and the school system, and helping families and schools develop behavioral strategies that can be used to help the child be successful in the school.

PSYCHOPHARMACOTHERAPY It is not uncommon for children with ODD/CD to be prescribed medications to manage their symptoms. Prescription treatments can be helpful in stabilizing the psychological and genetic components of the disorder. Some clients may need medications to help them improve their functioning to the point that they can benefit from psychosocial treatments. However, it is important that medication be used in conjunction with the aforementioned psychosocial interventions.

OCC/CD often co-occur with other disorders such as anxiety and depressive disorders, and medications are often used to treat these comorbid disorders. Mood stabilizers (e.g., Depakote) are sometimes prescribed for clients who have difficulty regulating their emotions and impulsiveness (Masi et al., 2007). Mood stabilizers help stabilize clients' moods so that they can better control their behavior.

Often, physiological symptoms associated with disruptive behavior disorders are the result of attention-deficit/hyperactivity disorder (ADHD), which is often diagnosed comorbidly (Wehmeier et al., 2011). Approximately 50% of clients with ODD also have ADHD (Turgay, 2009). Stimulants may allow clients with disruptive behavior disorders and ADHD to filter stimuli entering their perception, to ignore distracters, and to focus their attention on the desired activity.

Because clients with disruptive behavior disorders tend to not take their medications consistently, stimulants that are longer-acting are preferred over those that are short-acting (Turgay, 2009). Long-acting stimulants include Adderall XR, Concerta, and Ritalin LA. Short-acting stimulants include methylphenidate and dextroamphetamine (Turgay, 2009). Longer-acting stimulants are also preferred by clients' parents and teachers, as there is less need to enforce medication compliance, and the client benefits from the medication for longer periods of time.

There is a potential for clients to abuse stimulant drugs. Taking the drug in a greater dosage than what is recommended could result in a "high" feeling. Additionally, some clients may sell their medications or share them with friends. Overall, the use of medication with clients who have ODD/CD should be carefully monitored for abuse and/or dependence.

Prognosis

When families are more involved, children with ODD/CD tend to have better treatment outcomes (Sadock & Sadock, 2007). The more involved the parents are, the quicker and more effective the treatment is for children.

Outcomes are primarily dependent on the duration, frequency, and manifestation of the symptoms (Sadock & Sadock, 2007). Children who develop symptoms during early childhood and have a higher frequency and manifestation of symptoms are more likely to develop comorbid disorders as they age. In particular, depressive/bipolar disorders and substance use tend to be correlated with more severe, long-term issues. Children and adolescents who demonstrate mild or less invasive behaviors, and do not have comorbid disorders, have the best future prognosis. The duration of treatment will depend on the degree of severity of ODD/CD, and longer-term treatment is generally found to be the most effective (Steiner & Remsing, 2006).

INTERMITTENT EXPLOSIVE DISORDER

Description of the Disorder and Typical Client Characteristics

People with intermittent explosive disorder (IED) fail to control aggressive impulses, as manifested by being verbally aggressive (e.g., temper tantrums, verbal altercations) or physically aggressive (e.g., toward property, animals, or others). For an individual to receive the diagnosis, the *DSM-5* requires that at least three of the behavioral outbursts include damage or destruction to property, and/or a physical assault involving physical injury to animals or others (within a 12-month period; APA, 2013). If these violent outbursts are not better accounted for by another diagnosis that involves aggressive outbursts (e.g., conduct disorder), an IED diagnosis may be appropriate.

Those with IED often report an intense desire to act violently before an outburst, and this desire may be accompanied by physical symptoms such as racing thoughts or tingling in their bodies. After the outburst, they often report feeling fatigued and depressed and they often have trouble remembering the details of the aggressive incident (APA, 2013). Outbursts typically last for less than 30 minutes, and generally occur in response to a minor provocation involving an intimate friend or partner.

Males are more likely to have IED than females, and it typically appears in clients between childhood (the diagnosis cannot be given to children under age 6; APA, 2013) and early adulthood. It is common that an individual with IED has a first-degree relative (e.g., mother or brother) with the same disorder (Harvard Health Publications, 2011).

Also, it is more likely that the child of someone with IED will have a depressive/bipolar disorder, or substance use disorder (Ahmed, Green, McClosky, & Berman, 2010). The 1-year prevalence data suggest a prevalence of 2.7%, with the diagnosis being more prevalent in younger people (i.e., younger than ages 35–40; APA, 2013).

Counselor Considerations

Counselors should take care to explore any potential precipitating events or motivating factors that might suggest the aggressive acts are intentional or purposeful. So as to avoid legal or interpersonal repercussions, some may claim that they did not intentionally assault or harm a person or property.

Counselors should refer individuals who might have IED to a physician to ensure that the symptoms are not the result of a general medical condition (e.g., a brain injury). Relatedly, IED should not be diagnosed in a client whose outbursts are associated with a neurocognitive disorder. Substance use or withdrawal might be a factor in a client's aggressive outbursts, and this would also overrule a diagnosis of IED.

There are a number of other diagnoses that must be ruled out before ascribing an IED diagnosis. Oppositional defiant disorder and conduct disorder share many similar characteristics, and counselors should take care to identify whether these diagnoses better account for the explosive behaviors. ADHD involves impulsive behaviors, and this diagnosis should also be ruled out. People with schizophrenia or bipolar disorder (in a hypomanic/manic stage) might display symptoms that seem to align with IED, but are better explained by these disorders. Neurocognitive disorders (e.g., delirium), and personality change due to another medical condition should also be ruled out as they might explain aggressive outbursts. Clients with disruptive mood dysregulation disorder, by definition, have aggressive outbursts. Even people who have major depressive disorder might have aggressive outbursts secondary to the irritability associated with depression. Finally, antisocial and borderline personality disorders should be ruled out as these disorders might better explain aggressive outbursts. As such, IED should only be diagnosed when a counselor has gathered a thorough history of the client, and cannot find a more comprehensive diagnosis that fits his or her symptoms.

Culturally, IED is more prevalent in the United States than in some other countries, but it is not clear if this is because it is not explored or inquired about, or if it is because of a truly higher prevalence (APA, 2013). Similarly, IED is observed more frequently in males than females in some, but not all studies (APA, 2013). Also, IED is related to incidences of early life (up to age 20) physical and emotional trauma, and as such, any co-occurring trauma issues will need to be integrated into a client's treatment plan.

Especially with a stigmatizing disorder like IED, the consequences of others finding out about the disorder can be serious. Because of this, counselors must inform clients of the limitations of receiving such a diagnosis and of potential confidentiality issues. For example, should a client be involved in a custody battle, his or her records could be subpoenaed. The counselor should also be clear with clients about his or her mandate to report potential safety issues associated with harm to others, especially children who may be living in the home.

Treatment Models and Interventions

There is a paucity of research on treating IED. Cognitive behavioral therapy can be used to assess and change the client's thoughts, feelings, and behaviors. Additionally, psychopharmacological interventions can help stabilize the biological factors that contribute to the disorder.

COGNITIVE BEHAVIORAL THERAPY (CBT)   As applied to IED treatment, CBT holds that clients have at least some control over their aggressive episodes. When used with this population, CBT involves enhancing practical tools clients can use to identify the precursors of their outbursts and potentially calm themselves before committing violent acts (Harvard Health Publications, 2011). The first component of CBT is to help clients identify and restructure unhelpful or irrational thoughts. These thoughts might include "There is nothing I can do to control this." The counselor works with the client to identify these automatic thoughts and negate them, which allows more healthy thoughts to emerge.

Another component of CBT that may be helpful to those with IED is coping skills training. Clients are taught to recognize their anger cues (i.e., racing thoughts or tingling in their bodies) so that they can utilize an identified coping skill to try to calm these symptoms, and potentially avoid an aggressive outburst. Such coping skills might include exercising, listening to music, or utilizing a relaxation technique. Clients are also taught to identify thoughts that are soothing, such as focusing on a particularly pleasant thought or a positive mantra, such as, "I am in control."

Relaxation training is the final component of CBT that can be helpful for clients with IED. Clients are empowered to learn how to relax at will, and eventually, they translate this skill to situations where they are at risk for an outburst. Guided imagery, progressive muscle relaxation, and deep breathing are just several of the techniques that can be used to help facilitate relaxation. Just one example of a relaxation skill would be inviting clients to imagine that they have an elevator going from their belly button to their chin. The elevator goes up as they count to five and down as they count to six. There are many additional ways that clients can learn to relax their bodies through the use of mental visualization. The combination of restructuring irrational thoughts, utilizing coping skills, and implementing relaxation techniques may allow clients to feel more empowered and take control of this disorder.

CREATIVE TOOLBOX ACTIVITY 12.2   Coping Anger Through Imagination: Superheroes and Villains

Matthew V. Glowiak, MS, NCC, LPC

Activity Overview

Growing up, many people were at one time or another enthralled by superhero mythology; from Batman to Superman, to the Wolverine and Incredible Hulk, their adventures leave many people yearning for superpowers of their own. There is a therapeutic element in these stories that can be useful to some clients. By taking clients' love of, and familiarity with, superheroes and villains, and infusing it into a role-play situation where they discuss what powers they would have and how they could use these powers to overcome their struggles, counselors may potentially reach clients in ways not otherwise possible. This activity can be useful for clients who wish to better manage their emotions and change their behaviors, especially those over which they feel they have no control (e.g., angry outbursts).

Treatment Goal(s) of Activity

The primary goals of this activity are to help clients (a) learn to connect with and express their feelings and experiences in a manner that is safe to themselves and others, and (b) explore feelings and experiences they may keep hidden, or are unaware of.

Directions

1. For this type of role-play to be effective, it is important to first be aware of whether or not the client has an interest in superheroes and villains. Attempting this activity with a disinterested client will likely prove to be ineffective. Variations using other characters (e.g., anime characters) may also be effective.
2. Ask the client to describe a favorite superhero or villain.
3. Ask the client to share why that particular superhero or villain is his or her favorite, and what powers the figure possesses. Suggest the idea that everyone has his or her own blend of powers, which are represented by his or her individual strengths.
4. Discuss the activity with the client and gauge his or her willingness to engage in the activity. If the client is interested, ask the client to participate in the role-play as the selected superhero or villain.
5. While the client participates as the selected superhero or villain, encourage him or her to do so within the limits that most closely resonate with his or her personality, beliefs, values, wants, needs, and desires. Invite the client to consider the following: the persona that the mythical figure shows to the world; the persona the figure keeps hidden (what others are unaware of); and the superpower the figure possesses.
6. Follow the client's lead while engaged in the creative role-play process. Clients are typically slow to warm up with this activity, but they begin to connect with it as it moves forward.
7. Once the role-play is complete, process the experience with the client.

Process Questions

1. As this particular figure, how would your life be different?
2. What qualities of this figure do you wish you could possess?
3. How could a power like this be useful to you in managing the behavior you want or need to change (e.g., anger)?
4. If you had the said power, how would you be different—what thoughts, feelings, and behaviors would be different?
5. How would the figure deal with your behaviors you are trying to change?
6. What differences and/or similarities do you have to this figure?
7. What can you learn from this figure about your own behavior, or what changes can you make to how you respond to situations?
8. Removing any qualities that are unrealistic for real-life human beings to possess, what strengths do you have that you can use to take control of the behaviors with which you are struggling?

PSYCHOPHARMACOTHERAPY Medication options have had limited success in treating IED. However, some medications may be useful in treating its symptoms. While there are no specific medications designated as effective for the treatment of IED, clients are frequently prescribed medications to address the associated symptoms of the disorder. For example, if a client has issues with global anger and irritability, he or she may be treated with antidepressant medications (e.g., selective serotonin reuptake inhibitors). If a client has an associated labile mood, he or she may be treated with anticonvulsant medications (e.g., carbamazepine) and mood stabilizers (e.g., lithium; Preston, O'Neal, & Talaga, 2013).

Prognosis

Fewer than 20% of people with IED have received mental health services specifically for IED; those who have received counseling receive it for a co-occurring diagnosis, or another presenting concern (Harvard Health Publications, 2011). As such, the research on the treatment and prognosis of IED is somewhat limited at this time. Some individuals may experience IED chronically, and others might recover or experience it in episodes (APA, 2013). Overall, clients who receive a diagnosis and treatment for the disorder can become more aware of the etiology and possible ways to control some—or all—of the symptoms over their lifetime.

PYROMANIA

Description of the Disorder and Typical Client Characteristics

People with pyromania intentionally set fire to objects (e.g., buildings or vehicles) for personal satisfaction. They are not setting fires for secondary gain (e.g., to collect an insurance claim or to make a political statement). Individuals with pyromania set things on fire because they find pleasure in the fire itself, or in the aftermath of such a fire (e.g., a leveled house or destroyed car). People with pyromania typically have an intense curiosity or passion for fire, and they relieve a sense of tension, or overwhelming emotions, by setting fires (APA, 2013).

Behavioral because it is soothing

build up of wanting the fire

The onset of pyromania is typically in childhood or early adolescence (Fritzon, Lewis, & Doley, 2011b), and the population prevalence of this disorder is unknown (APA, 2013), suggesting it is a rare disorder. Although it has been reported in females, those diagnosed with pyromania are most often male (APA, 2013; Fritzon, Dolan, Doley, & McEwan, 2011a). Although adolescents are often aroused by fire and engage in antisocial behavior, pyromania is characterized by problematic behavior that potentially causes significant damage to valuable objects and is punishable by legal consequences.

Counselor Considerations

Counselors should take care to gather extensive information regarding the history and extent to which a client has started fires. Pyromania is not simply characterized by repeatedly setting fires; the motivation must be that of personal satisfaction and emotional relief. If clients have set fires out of curiosity, by accident, or as a cry for help, they most likely do not meet the criteria for this disorder.

Individuals with conduct disorder or antisocial personality disorder might set fires as part of their overarching symptoms, and the presence of these disorders should be ruled out. Individuals experiencing a manic episode or a schizophrenic delusion might impulsively set a fire, and again, care should be taken to rule out these diagnoses.

Counselors must also assess for any mental or physical difficulties that might impact a client's judgment. For example, a person with a neurocognitive disorder might accidentally set a fire. Finally, if drugs or alcohol impaired the individual's judgment, this would rule out pyromania. However, a strong link between alcohol use and pyromania has been found, and counselors must carefully assess for the extent to which the client was mentally aware and intentional about fire-setting behaviors.

Counselors must also consider safety issues. Counselors should assess the client's level of functioning and determine whether a secure setting is required to facilitate the client's and others' safety. If at any point the client appears to be at risk of harming himself or herself or others, the counselor has an ethical and legal obligation to seek other resources and supports to aid in ensuring safety. As such, the limits of confidentiality should be explained to clients at the onset of treatment. Counselors should also thoroughly check for comorbid disorders (i.e., substance use disorders, bipolar disorders, other disruptive behavior disorders, impulse-control disorders), as this can enhance the likelihood of impulsiveness and associated harm.

Treatment Models and Interventions

Little is known about effective treatments for pyromania; no randomized controlled treatment studies could be found in the literature. There are also currently no medications supported as useful in treating clients with pyromania. As people with this disorder are often socially isolated, family involvement may be helpful in supporting clients' sense of feeling heard, valued, and understood. What follows are treatment approaches that may be helpful in treating this disorder.

DIALECTICAL BEHAVIOR THERAPY (DBT)   DBT is a potentially useful treatment for treating pyromania. This approach has been successful in treating individuals who have borderline personality disorder, those who have a difficult time regulating strong emotions, and those who feel personal distress and dissatisfaction that is turned inward. It is theorized that fire setting is the result of similar negative feelings, which clients have a hard time regulating, and as such, DBT might be effective in treating this disorder (Fritzon et al., 2011b). The DBT skills that allow for increased awareness, emotional regulation, and social support might effectively rehabilitate individuals with pyromania.

COGNITIVE BEHAVIORAL THERAPY (CBT)   CBT has been used successfully with other behavior-based disorders, and it may be helpful when treating individuals who have pyromania (Fritzon et al., 2011a). The first step in applying CBT is to help clients identify their emotions associated with various fire-setting events; it is important to validate and normalize the emotions (not the behaviors) that the client associated with these events. Clients also learn to identify what triggers their fire-setting urges, and to recognize the physiological cues they experience when wanting to fire set. Next, clients are taught to link their thoughts with their feelings and accompanying physiological responses. Through feeling and thought recognition and identification, clients develop their awareness of the dynamics that are supporting and encouraging their fire setting behaviors. Next, clients are taught how to change their thinking patterns and behavioral responses to cease fire-starting behaviors. They may be taught how to use various behavioral skills (e.g., relaxation training, diaphragmatic breathing) to manage their feelings and avoid fire-starting behaviors.

Prognosis

Little is known about this disorder, its course, effective treatment, or its prognosis. Although several psychosocial treatment options are supported as potentially effective for clients with pyromania, the longitudinal effects of mental health treatment are currently unknown. Some clients may experience short periods of symptoms, and others might deal with the disorder throughout their lifetime. Secondary to experiencing a supportive counseling environment, clients with this disorder may feel safe enough to explore the dynamics which have encouraged and sustained their behavior, and make safe alternative behavioral choices.

KLEPTOMANIA

Description of the Disorder and Typical Client Characteristics

People with kleptomania steal and take things that are not theirs. They might steal from stores or individuals, and they are motivated to steal things for the satisfaction they experience while committing the act. Those with kleptomania do not have a need for the objects they steal, and they do not steal in order to seek vengeance from the people who rightfully own the objects. They typically experience tension before they commit an act of stealing, and then experience a sense of relief and satisfaction while stealing (APA, 2013); this relief serves to reinforce the behavior.

They typically fear being caught stealing, and they feel remorseful about their actions after they have committed the crime. They know that their stealing is inappropriate or unnecessary, but they have difficulty controlling their behavior (in part because it is self-reinforcing). First-degree relatives of individuals with kleptomania (i.e., siblings, parents, or children) are more likely to have obsessive-compulsive disorder than those who do not have a similar relative (APA, 2013). Overall, kleptomania is very rare and is found in less than 1% of the population (0.3–0.6%; APA, 2013; Grant, Odlaug, & Kim, 2010b). However, kleptomania occurs in about 4–24% of those arrested for shoplifting (APA, 2013). Culturally, little is known about kleptomania. Overall, approximately two-thirds of individuals diagnosed with kleptomania are female (APA, 2013).

Counselor Considerations

When working with those who have kleptomania, counselors should assess if clients were in an otherwise sound mental state when committing the acts of theft. That is, they cannot have active dementia and they must not have been experiencing schizophrenic delusions or a manic episode. Additionally, counselors must rule out differential diagnoses that might more completely explain the client behaviors, such as antisocial personality disorder or conduct disorder.

Stealing is a relatively common phenomenon in the United States and counselors must differentiate shoplifting, or theft that is motivated by some sort of gain, from the emotional relief experienced by people with kleptomania. For example, a person who steals something simply because he or she does not wish to purchase it and does not experience the tension and culminating relief would not meet the criteria for kleptomania. Additionally, counselors must try to ensure that clients are not portraying the symptoms of kleptomania in order to avoid prosecution for an act of theft or shoplifting. It will be helpful for counselors to obtain a thorough family history to determine if there are any genetic links or risk factors within the family.

Clients with this disorder may become involved with the legal system, and counselors should be aware of the ethical and legal implications of working with this population. Counselors should inform clients of the occasions when their records might be subpoenaed (e.g., criminal proceedings) and the implications of the limits of confidentiality. Counselors should fully inform clients of such limits to confidentiality, and counselors should not treat informed consent as a one time event; informed consent discussions should be considered an on-going aspect of counseling.

Treatment Models and Interventions

There are currently no medications supported for use in the treatment of kleptomania. However, medications are useful in treating the issues that often co-occur with this disorder.

Interestingly, recent treatment literature has compared kleptomania to substance abuse. Both disorders operate from the presence of urges to commit an act and relief as the act (either stealing or using drugs) is committed. As such, interventions that have been supported for substance abuse treatment are also indicated for the treatment of kleptomania (See Chapter 8; Grant, Kim, & Odlaug, 2010a; Grant et al., 2010b).

Basic behavior therapies are supported as helpful interventions for kleptomania and other impulse-control disorders (Grant et al., 2010b). When using this approach, counselors first focus on identifying the typical behaviors that lead up to a stealing event. The intention is for clients to begin to connect specific life events or moods with a desire to steal. Clients are then encouraged to identify alternative coping skills that they can use to relieve negative emotions (such as tension and anxiety), and they begin to practice using those behaviors in place of stealing. Such behavioral skills might include socializing or exercising. Next, clients rehearse these behaviors intentionally while continuing to track their emotions in relation to their stealing impulses, and the relief associated with specific coping skills.

Cognitive behavioral therapy adds a cognitive layer to basic behavioral interventions in that clients recognize and learn to change the cognitive processes that are supporting the behavior (Grant et al., 2010b). Clients also begin to link their desire to steal with past reinforcements they have received (secondary to stealing), and they begin to identify high-risk stealing situations, or situations that place them at a higher risk for wanting to steal. In recognizing these high-risk situations, clients can identify coping skills that might be most useful for them in avoiding or managing these situations. Thus, a cognitive component added to behavioral interventions allows clients to fully understand their thinking patterns, triggers, and high-risk situations (Grant et al., 2010b).

Clinical Toolbox 12.5: In the Pearson etext, click here to read about a guided imagery activity that can be used by clients to control unwanted impulses.

Prognosis

The prognosis for kleptomania is uncertain at this time due to limited treatment or longitudinal research on the disorder. Kleptomania may continue for years with the possibility of periods of spontaneous remission (APA, 2013).

DESCRIPTION OF THE ELIMINATION DISORDERS

Elimination disorders are diagnosed when an individual experiences difficulty with elimination of bodily waste. Elimination disorders are typically found in children and young adolescents, but can potentially be diagnosed in people of all ages. However, according to the *DSM-5*, encopresis cannot be diagnosed in an individual before the age of 4, and enuresis cannot be diagnosed before the age of 5 (APA, 2013). Before these ages, children do not have a firm grasp on waste management, and it would not be appropriate to label elimination difficulties with a mental health diagnosis.

Although toilet training is a difficult task for some, it is expected that the concept should be understood by the age of 4 or 5 (depending on the type of waste). As such, even if children have had difficulty with toilet training, they should not be displaying the signs of enuresis or encopresis at the age of 4/5 or older. Toilet training is typically conducted by an adult caregiver and there is potential for toilet training to be somewhat inconsistent. For example, a caregiver might be persistent about the child using the toilet, but then allow the child to use a diaper the next day because of a busy work schedule. This can be very confusing for a child. However, after the age of 4 or 5, caregiver inconsistency is still not a warranted reason for the symptoms of enuresis or encopresis.

The only time a child older than 4 or 5 might display the symptoms of an elimination disorder, but not warrant a diagnosis, is in the case of a developmental delay. If the chronological age of children is 4/5 or older, but their cognitive abilities are below that of an average 4/5-year-old, their difficulties with eliminating waste might not be related to a mental health diagnosis. A developmentally delayed client might need more time to understand the concept of eliminating waste in the toilet.

It is important to note that elimination disorders are diagnosed in accordance with chronological age regarding cognitive development, as opposed to physical development. If a child is experiencing other physical reasons for the elimination problems, these should be thoroughly explored before a mental health diagnosis is issued. For example, children with seizure disorders might lose control of their bladders during the course of a seizure. Although the child's difficulty using the toilet might initially seem to be the result of a cognitive difficulty, it is imperative to explore all physical explanations first.

The presence of enuresis or encopresis can be difficult for children. Most children are able to eliminate their waste in a toilet. Children with enuresis or encopresis might eliminate waste on their clothing or other obvious places, which makes their difficulty apparent to others. The extent to which children with elimination disorders are stigmatized by peers can exacerbate the mental health difficulties associated with their diagnosis. Coping with elimination disorders can be especially challenging for parents. Adult caregivers are often charged with the responsibility of cleaning the child's waste from their clothes, bed linens, or other household surfaces. This requires time and energy and it can fatigue caregivers. Some children with elimination disorders might need to wear diapers to bed, or even throughout the entire day. This can be financially and emotionally taxing for parents and they might share negative reactions with the child. This can further exacerbate the child's symptoms and the elimination difficulties. Therefore, it is important for counselors to explore ways to address the specific symptoms of the elimination disorder, the residual mental health effects that might accompany such a diagnosis, and to work with caregivers.

COUNSELOR CONSIDERATIONS

As mentioned, counselors must first ensure that a client with elimination difficulties meets the cognitive criteria for a mental health diagnosis. The counselor should take steps to assess the child's cognitive abilities via reports from his or her school, or even a cognitive evaluation. Cognitive evaluations can be completed by counselors if they have the proper training (e.g., meet the educational requirement determined by the instrument publisher, and understand how the client aligns with the population on which the instrument was normed), and if this is permitted by their state's counselor practice act (i.e., counselor licensure laws). If the counselor is unable to assess the client's cognitive ability, a referral can be made to another professional who meets the required training and expertise.

Counselors must explore the possibility of any medical causes for the improper elimination of solid or liquid waste. Counselors are not medical professionals, and should refer any client who might be diagnosed with an elimination disorder to a medical professional for a physical examination. It may be helpful to the family and the medical professional to gather comprehensive information about the symptoms so that caregivers can give this information to the medical professional.

Next, counselors should take care to respect the severity of diagnosing a child with a mental health disorder. It will be important for counselors to adequately explain the diagnosis and treatment options. A mental health diagnosis can be stigmatizing for children, and elimination disorders can be particularly embarrassing because waste elimination is typically a private act. Conversely, parents and children might be relieved to have a name and a formal explanation for the difficulty they have been experiencing; a formal diagnosis indicates that others have experienced similar problems and provides hope that it can be treated.

PROGNOSIS

Although elimination disorders are difficult on clients and their families, treatment for each disorder is relatively hopeful (APA, 2013). A variety of interventions for both diagnoses have been explored, and some key techniques have been found to be most effective in achieving complete symptom relief. For encopresis and enuresis, behavioral techniques and interventions are highly supported after medical causes for symptoms have been negated. Additional interventions are supported in accordance to the client's specific symptoms and needs.

With regards to enuresis, only 1% of cases are not effectively treated in children or adolescents (APA, 2013). Although several treatments might be tried before an effective one is found for each case, counselors have been successful in helping individuals identify ways in which they can control their urination. Additionally, many cases of enuresis spontaneously resolve without intentional interventions.

The chances of encopresis lasting throughout a client's lifetime are very rare. However, it can last for years after the original diagnosis (APA, 2013). With that said, the majority of cases that persist long-term are only problematic intermittently. It is likely that a child with encopresis can experience periods of time without any disturbances, and the symptoms will typically clear by late adolescence or adulthood. If a variety of treatments are implemented with the support of caregivers, encopresis can be completely ceased for about three-fourths of children, and for almost all adults (APA, 2013; Gontard, 2013).

For both disorders, it is important to involve the families of the client and to begin treatment as early as possible. Enuresis and encopresis have a strong behavioral component (Gontard, 2013). This suggests that clients who have these diagnoses are able to control the symptoms in some way. Early intervention allows clients to maintain a sense of control over their bodies; the longer the symptoms persist, the longer the clients will believe that they are powerless over their difficulties. Also, behavioral patterns can form quickly; habits that exist for shorter periods of time become less engrained in the child's behavioral routine. Family can serve as a strong source of motivation and encouragement for the client as they work together to find more helpful ways to deal with waste elimination.

ENURESIS

can be an indicator of sexual abuse

Description of the Disorder and Typical Client Characteristics

Enuresis is characterized by inappropriate elimination of urine into bedding or clothing. According to the *DSM-5* (APA, 2013), symptoms of the disorder include urination in bed or clothing at least twice per week for three consecutive months, or to the extent that it is causing significant client distress. As previously mentioned, clients diagnosed with enuresis must be at least five years of age, and it must not be due to a general medical condition.

In the *DSM-5*, there are three specifiers for enuresis used to indicate that the symptoms only occur at certain types of day (APA, 2013). *Nocturnal only* means that the client only experiences difficulty urinating in a proper facility during the nighttime. *Diurnal only* indicates that the client experiences the symptoms of enuresis only during the daytime. *Nocturnal and diurnal* involves a combination of the two subtypes.

Enuresis is one of the most common disorders diagnosed in young people (Shapira & Dahlen, 2010). It can affect up to 19% of children age 5–12 years (Hodgkinson, Josephs, & Hegney, 2010). However, it only affects approximately 1% of people age 15 years or older (APA, 2013). Nocturnal enuresis is more common in males, and diurnal incontinence is more common in females (APA, 2013). Environmental considerations are a potential risk factor for children who develop enuresis, as this disorder is more common in children who live in child care systems, institutions, and organizations such as orphanages (APA, 2013).

There are many potential causes of enuresis, including psychological factors, genetics, and biology. Many children who have been the victims of emotional or physical abuse experience enuresis (APA, 2013), but not all children with this disorder have an abuse history. Counselors should, however, take care to rule out the possibility of abuse when working with any child who has enuresis.

Genetic and biological factors are the primary contributors to the disorder (Shapira & Dahlen, 2010). About two-thirds of children with enuresis have a biological relative who experienced similar symptoms (APA, 2013). Potential biological contributors to the disorder are a lack of sleep arousal, low levels of antidiuretic hormones, reduced bladder capacity, or delayed maturation (Shapira & Dahlen, 2010). The connection between children's brains and their physical ability to regulate their waste management typically forms by the age of five, but some people simply tend to develop slower, even if they have otherwise average cognitive abilities. In addition to any other general medical conditions that might cause enuresis, these factors should be screened by a medical professional, and addressed by counselors via psychoeducation only.

Psychological factors that could contribute to enuresis include unstable parenting or other stressful life events (Shapira & Dahlen, 2010). However, the biological or genetic contributors are more salient in terms of the etiology of this disorder, and many children who have enuresis are otherwise happy and well-adjusted children. As such, it is important to have a working understanding of the biological and genetic contributors to the disorder, the ways in which these can be assessed by a medical professional, and the ways that counselors can develop and implement proven interventions in order to reduce or eliminate the symptoms.

Counselor Considerations

Counselors should take care to remember that psychological factors can, but do not always, contribute to enuresis. As such, it is important for counselors to thoroughly assess the client's psychosocial experiences, and the attachment between the child and caregiver(s). These potential stressors should be addressed in addition to the supported enuresis interventions. The biological and genetic contributors should be assessed by a medical professional and explained by the counselor, but treatment should focus on implementing psychosocial interventions.

Counselors should also take note that enuresis can be emotionally damaging for young people. Although emotional difficulties do not often cause enuresis, they might develop as a result of the disorder. As such, counselors should take care to address the stigma and shame that might emerge in clients, and celebrate even the smallest improvements as clients take control of their disorder.

Counselors have the responsibility of determining whether the enuresis is rooted in an environmental issue or a medical issue (APA, 2013). This will likely mean referring the client to a physician first, before continuing with treatment of the enuresis. If medical causes are ruled out, counselors must consider the safety of the child's home environment (e.g., parenting, nutrition, violence), and take appropriate action depending on the client's unique circumstances. Once all of these considerations are addressed, counselors can move on to exploring psychosocial treatments.

Treatment Models and Interventions

The most highly supported interventions for clients with enuresis apply behavior therapy principles to help clients retrain their bodies. In addition to counseling interventions that directly focus on the wetting behaviors, clients can sometimes benefit from counseling interventions that focus on any emotional needs that have emerged as a result of the enuresis.

ENURESIS ALARM The primary psychosocial treatment for nocturnal enuresis is the use of an enuresis alarm (Hodgkinson et al., 2010; Shapira & Dahlen, 2010). Because nocturnal bedwetting occurs while the child is sleeping, it is almost always involuntary and unintentional. The use of an enuresis alarm at night can also help children learn to control any daytime wetting symptoms.

This treatment protocol involves the use of any one of a variety of bedwetting alarms that can be independently purchased at online retailers. The search term for online purchases would be *enuresis alarm,* and they range in cost from $50 to $100. Depending on the specific brand, the components will vary. However, two main features are a sensor that indicates the moisture level of the child's undergarments, and an alarm that sounds (and/or vibrates) when moisture levels increase. The sensor can be wireless and typically clips onto the outside of the client's undergarments.

Although nocturnal bedwetting is involuntary, clients can learn to control the symptoms. When increased moisture levels are detected, the alarm goes off. This system uses two behavioral principles in order to decrease (and eventually eliminate) nocturnal enuresis. First, classical conditioning links the body's sensation of having to urinate with the act of waking up. At first, the association is mediated by the noise of the alarm. Thus, the association links sensation of urination, to a loud noise (or vibration), to waking up. Eventually, the client's body begins to link the urination sensation with the act of waking up. Next, the alarm promotes behavioral rehearsal of getting up and going to the bathroom in the midst of sleeping. Coupled with the client's ability to wake upon feeling the need to urinate, the client begins to independently use the restroom during the night instead of urinating in the bedding. It is especially effective to link the use of an enuresis alarm with other operant behavioral interventions (as discussed in the next section).

OPERANT BEHAVIORAL INTERVENTIONS When treating nocturnal enuresis, operant behavioral interventions pair nicely with the classical conditioning provided by an enuresis alarm. These techniques are also useful in treating children who experience diurnal enuresis (or symptoms throughout the waking hours). Operant behavioral interventions reward clients for desired behaviors, and they have been found to have a small, but significant, effect on treating enuresis (Hodgkinson et al., 2010).

Operant behavioral interventions come in two forms: reinforcement and punishment. Reinforcement increases the likelihood of desired behaviors, and punishment decreases the likelihood of unhelpful behaviors. However, reinforcement is generally more effective than punishment in motivating children. That is, children are more easily motivated to alter behaviors in order to obtain something desirable, rather than altering behaviors to avoid punishment. As such, counselors should focus on rewarding behaviors that are inconsistent with the unwanted behaviors. That is, counselors should help caregivers find ways to reward the client's use of the proper facilities, which is incompatible with wetting the bed.

Reinforcement schedules are an important component in using operant conditioning. At first, a one-to-one ratio should be used. That is, every time clients complete a desired behavior, they receive a reward. At first, successive approximations might need to be reinforced in order to shape the desired behaviors—that is, behaviors that are closer to the target behavior (e.g., running to the toilet as a client is urinating in clothing) should be reinforced. Eventually, the target behavior will be reached as their effort and practices continue to increase. Once the client achieves the desired behavior on a consistent basis, verbal praise should remain high, but tangible reinforcers can be systematically reduced.

Clinical Toolbox 12.6: In the Pearson etext, click here to read a case application of a behavioral intervention, an enuresis alarm, in the treatment of enuresis.

PSYCHOPHARMACOTHERAPY Medications may be used in conjunction with behavioral interventions to support the client's improvement. One possible reason for difficulty in controlling urination is that hormones are not at the levels required to control elimination. Medications such as desmopressin (e.g., DDAVP), a synthetic hormone, are sometimes used to simulate the hormone in the body that encourages water retention. This medication increases the client's ability to physically contain urine for longer periods of time.

It has been hypothesized that clients with enuresis have trouble identifying when they need to use the restroom. Tricyclic antidepressants (e.g., Tofranil) have been used to stimulate the body's responsiveness to recognizing and controlling the urge to eliminate waste (Shapira & Dahlen, 2010). These antidepressants increase clients' awareness and ability to use the restroom properly.

Although medication may be helpful when working with enuresis, there is a significant risk of relapse after clients cease taking the medication (Hodgkinson et al., 2010). If mental health and behavioral interventions are not used in conjunction with the medications, clients do not learn how to maintain their progress without the medications. The aforementioned counseling interventions should be used in lieu of or in conjunction with medicinal interventions, if at all possible.

Prognosis

The prognosis for enuresis is very good. In fact, only 1% of people over the age of 15 have this disorder, and it spontaneously clears in many cases. There are many biological indicators, such as a small bladder, decreased hormone levels, and slower neural maturation, that resolve independently over time. Additionally, behavioral interventions give clients a sense of control over their symptoms and ways to intervene, which allows them to quickly experience relief with a reasonable amount of effort.

ENCOPRESIS

Can be an indicator of sexual abuse

Description of the Disorder and Typical Client Characteristics

refer to medical professional

Encopresis is defined as involuntary or intentional passage of fecal matter into inappropriate places, such as clothing or onto floors (APA, 2013). This behavior occurs at least once per month for at least three months, and the client must be age four or older. Additionally, the behavior must not be due to a general medical condition. One exception to this is constipation, which can be considered a medical condition, but does not negate diagnosis of the disorder.

There are two subtypes of encopresis. *With constipation and overflow incontinence* indicates that the client does have regular constipation (or excessive stool that has not been eliminated by the body). This is the most common subtype and is generally involuntary. *Without constipation and overflow incontinence* indicates that constipation is not a consideration when assessing the client. This later subtype indicates more voluntary behavior and could possibly be related to the presence of oppositional defiant or conduct disorder (APA, 2013). Encopresis can be primary which indicates that the client has never reached a point of consistently defecating in a proper facility, or secondary which indicates that the client has intermittently displayed desirable defecating behaviors amongst the symptoms of encopresis.

Approximately 1% of 5-year-olds have encopresis and it is more common in boys (APA, 2013). Involuntary encopresis is generally the result of constipation. This constipation might be due to a general medical condition, dehydration, or anxiety related to defecation. Voluntary encopresis (without constipation) has a strong psychological component and is often found in children who have been abused or neglected.

Counselor Considerations

When treating encopresis, it is very important for the counselor to fully understand the client's symptoms and their etiology. Counselors will need to refer the client to a physician so that physical health–related issues can be assessed. Encopresis can result from physiological factors, such as dehydration, lack of exercise, or high-fat diets. Some of these factors lead to constipation, which makes defecation painful, or impossible, and limits the client's ability to control his or her bowels. Many children with encopresis have enuresis symptoms, and associated urinary reflux which may lead to chronic urinary tract infections. These infections typically remit with the treatment of the constipation and encopresis.

The counselor should also assess for cognitive delays, negative experiences with potty training, abuse or neglect, anxiousness, or possible difficulties with attention (which could impair children from focusing on proper defecation). Counselors should thoroughly review interventions that have been attempted with the client in the past.

Children with obsessive-compulsive disorder or learning delays might also experience encopresis. In these cases, the focus of treatment should be on the broader disorders in addition to the treatment of the encopretic symptoms.

Psychological problems that may contribute to voluntary encopresis include oppositional defiant disorder or conduct disorder. These disorders must be treated in conjunction with the encopresis. Also, counselors must take care to assess for abuse or neglect that might be contributing to encopresis. This could range from neglectful parenting to sexual abuse.

Treatment Models and Interventions

Early intervention is very important when working with encopresis (Coehlo, 2011). Withholding stool can cause physical damage to the client's body. At first, the withholding behaviors cause an overflow and loose stool escapes from the anus. This can lead to a stretched colon and damaged nerves. Eventually, clients lose the ability to determine when they need to defecate (due to both the nerve damage and the habit of withholding bowel movements). There are no psychotropic medications that are used to treat encopresis.

TOILET EDUCATION AND TRAINING   At some point, all children must learn to use the toilet to expel waste and it is important that clients with encopresis have been effectively taught. Proper toilet training is an important aspect of treatment for clients who are experiencing encopresis as the result of physiological difficulties, cognitive difficulties, or anxiety surrounding the process of defecating. It is important to ensure that clients can verbalize the steps of defecating in a toilet (e.g., notice the urge to defecate, go to the bathroom, sit on the toilet, defecate, wipe, flush, and wash hands), and their readiness to do so. It is also important to determine that clients are physically able to complete the steps associated with using a toilet to defecate, such as pulling pants up and down, wiping properly, and flushing the toilet upon completion.

It is important for parents to model toilet training behaviors to children, and to clearly teach children how to implement their behaviors independently (Coehlo, 2011). Additionally, punishment for undesirable defecation is not helpful. This further contributes to clients' anxiety around defecating. As such, parents should focus on praising positive behaviors associated with appropriate defecation.

Counselors and caregivers should work together to ensure that the client has a developmentally appropriate understanding of toilet training. This can be done through talk therapy, bibliotherapy (i.e., reading and processing stories), or other creative media interventions (e.g., DVDs or television shows that address the topic of toilet use). When choosing a story about proper toilet behaviors, take care to ensure that the main character is similar to the client in age and gender. Read the story with the client and take plenty of time to process ways in which the client is similar to the character and ways in which they differ.

NUTRITIONAL CHANGES/MEDICATIONS It is not generally appropriate for counselors to make dietary recommendations (unless they have specialized medical training and this is within the scope of practice of the license under which they practice). However, counselors should encourage clients to work with a medical professional to discuss nutritional changes or the use of laxatives or stool softeners, all of which may help treat encopresis.

When treating encopresis, fiber is the most important addition that should be made to a client's diet (Coehlo, 2011). Counselors can be helpful in working with clients and families to develop behavioral schedules that facilitate fiber consumption recommended by a medical professional. The fiber should improve the texture of the client's stool (e.g., higher water content and improved texture), which should make it easier to pass.

Clients might also try reducing their fat and sugar intake (which contributes to constipation and water retention) and decreasing their consumption of other foods that increase constipation (e.g., bananas). Again, counselors should refer clients to medical professionals for specific directions regarding a change in diet, but counselors can focus on lifting the barriers that might prevent clients from making such changes.

If clients are suffering from constipation, which leads to loss of bowel control, a laxative might help them increase their ability to properly control and expel waste. Over time, the use of a laxative can be tapered as clients gain greater efficacy around defecation.

Another over-the-counter medication that is often used to treat encopresis is stool softeners. Stool softeners allow a client to have a more predictable, less painful bowel movement. Stool softeners are helpful for clients who have painful or hard bowel movements, which often result from their diet (e.g., not enough water, too much cheese), food allergies, or may even be a side effect of different medications. Some clients who have painful or otherwise difficult bowel movements may appear to have encopresis, when in actuality they have a more straightforward physiological difficulty. Over-the-counter stool softeners such as MiraLax, Senokot, or mineral oil might be prescribed for clients to rule out physiological causes of the encopretic symptoms.

BEHAVIOR MANAGEMENT   Many caregivers use punishment as a way to control their child's behavior, but punishment is not an effective way to handle encopresis (Coehlo, 2011). However, children can be involved in cleaning up any improper defecation as this may help them become more personally invested in ceasing the behaviors. However, this should never be done in a punitive manner. Parents should simply explain that every person is responsible for his or her own actions. The child's cooperation can be rewarded with praise after successfully cleaning any messes.

Families must be supportive throughout the course of treatment, which will require a certain amount of energy on their part. Caregivers should first begin with helping the child develop a routine around the use of the bathroom. While consistently integrating any dietary changes recommended by a medical professional, parents should create a consistent routine for the child to eat and use the restroom.

Caregivers should implement a reinforcement schedule to solidify the child's healthy routine. As was mentioned with regard to enuresis, there are two types of reinforcers: positive and negative. Positive reinforcers give children something they want, such as extra time with friends, toys, prizes, or parental praise. The most effective (and free) reinforcer is verbal praise (e.g., "Nice work!"). It is important to be wary of using food or candy as a reinforcer because clients could begin linking accomplishments with eating, which can promote unhealthy eating habits or obesity, which may further complicate the disorder. Negative reinforcers remove something the child does not want, such as a chore or extra household responsibilities. If the client uses the facilities successfully, maybe he or she will not be required to complete a chore that day.

Both positive or negative reinforcement occurs after the child has successfully completed a desired behavior. This distinguishes operant conditioning from bribery in the sense that bribery uses a reward first in order to make an individual complete a desired behavior. This is ineffective because the client does not learn to do the desired behavior spontaneously on his or her own. Thus, all reinforcers should be given after the client independently completes a desired behavior, such as using the restroom instead of soiling his or her clothing.

Reinforcement schedules are an important component to using operant conditioning. At first, a one-to-one ratio should be used. That is, every time clients complete a desired behavior, they receive a reward. At first, successive approximations might need to be reinforced in order to shape the desired behaviors. That is, behaviors that are closer to the target behavior (e.g., running to the toilet as a client is defecating in clothing) should be reinforced. Eventually, the target behavior will be reached as increase their effort and practice.

Prognosis

The prognosis for encopresis is not as straightforward as it is for enuresis. Treatment can require up to a year of dedicated, consistent interventions from parents, medical professionals, and mental health professionals. Encopresis in certain populations (e.g., those who have intellectual disabilities) could require extensive, ongoing intervention and may involve a reoccurrence of symptoms. Interventions must be holistic and address cognitive, behavioral, and nutritional changes. With commitment, support, and validation, children experiencing the symptoms of encopresis can experience physical and emotional relief over time.

TREATMENT PLAN FOR ANDREW

This chapter began with a discussion of Andrew, a 15-year-old male who has severely disruptive behaviors. Andrew meets the criteria for conduct disorder. Andrew has multiple needs and a complex situation. A counselor must consider multiple factors before moving ahead with a strength-based treatment approach. The following I CAN START conceptual framework outlines treatment considerations that may be helpful in working with Andrew.

C = Contextual Assessment

Andrew is a 15-year-old Caucasian male. He has experienced physical and emotional abuse from his father since he was a young child and uses anger and aggression to cope with his family difficulties. Andrew's parents are both uninvolved with his life and the family lives in an urban, low socioeconomic status area. His father abuses alcohol and his mother struggles with depression, but both maintain some form of employment.

A = Assessment and Diagnosis

Diagnosis = Conduct Disorder (Childhood Onset, with limited prosocial emotions, severe) 312.81 (F91.1). The Conners Teacher Rating Scale-Revised (CTRS-R; Conners, Sitarenios, Parker, & Epstein, 1998) will be used to assess for ADHD (Shapira & Dahlen, 2010), and the Achenbach Child Behavior Checklist (CBCL; Achenbach & Edelbrock, 2009) will be used to assess Andrew's behavior. To assess Andrew's level of hostility and defiance, the Buss and Perry Aggression Questionnaire (B-P AQ; Buss & Perry, 1992), or Conners-Wells' Adolescent Self-Report Scale (CASS; Conners et al., 1997) will be used. Formal suicide and homicide assessments will also occur on an ongoing basis. A posttraumatic stress disorder assessment may also be used to rule out the possibility of trauma secondary to on-going abuse in the home.

N = Necessary Level of Care

Temporary psychiatric/stabilization care in a secure (i.e., "locked" facility) followed by an extended residential treatment placement is required. Upon discharge from residential treatment and release into the community, intensive outpatient treatment will be needed for Andrew and his family across settings (e.g., school and home).

S = Strength-Based Lens

Self: Andrew is an intelligent and determined adolescent who works hard to accomplish his goals. He has coped with family dysfunction independently. He is motivated to belong, and he protects himself from others.

Family: Andrew has four siblings in whom he confides and who understand his circumstances. Andrew's parents are still married, and both of his parents are employed. Until recently, Andrew's mother was somewhat involved in his life.

Community: Andrew and his family live in an urban area, and there are many therapeutic resources and activities within walking distance.

T = Treatment Approach

Andrew's treatment needs are complex. In the short term (i.e., over the next several days), Andrew needs to be psychiatrically stabilized and needs crisis intervention; placement in a secure setting where he cannot harm himself or others is necessary. Upon psychiatric stabilization, he needs to be placed in a residential treatment setting where he can (a) be further assessed and evaluated before being returned to the community, and (b) learn the skills he needs to better manage his behaviors and control his impulses. In residential treatment he will benefit from Behavior Therapy (BT) and Cognitive Behavioral Therapy (CBT) approaches. These approaches will help him develop various skills he needs to manage his aggressive impulses (e.g., anger management, social skills, problem-solving skills). Andrew's parents should receive Parent Management Training (PMT) before he returns home, and family therapy will be needed as he transitions back into the home. If available, Multisystemic Therapy (MST; intensive, wrap-around services) should be used to ease his transition back into the community, and to wrap Andrew and his family in supportive services. Placement in a specialized school for youth with behavior issues will be required secondary to his school expulsion. Intensive individual (e.g., BT/CBT) therapy will also be needed as Andrew transitions back into the community.

A = Aim and Objectives of Treatment (1 month treatment objective, which will begin upon admittance to a residential treatment facility)

Andrew will learn and use anger management skills to regulate his strong negative feelings (i.e., anger, frustration) so as to aid in his return to the community → Andrew will use his resourcefulness, intelligence, and BT/CBT skills learned in treatment to identify 3 anger triggers, 3 anger-inducing thoughts, 3 resulting emotions, 3 cues that he is becoming angry, and 3 ways he can adaptively manage his anger. He will use these identified behavioral alternatives to manage his anger 100% of the time while in residential treatment, resulting in 0 episodes of physical aggression.

Andrew will be medication compliant → Andrew will comply with taking all medications as prescribed by his psychiatrist.

Andrew and his family will begin to improve their family functioning → Andrew and his family will participate in family therapy twice each week for 90 minutes.

Andrew's parents will develop their parenting skills → Andrew's parents will enter a Parent Management Training program.

R = Research-Based Interventions (based on Behavior Therapy and Cognitive Behavioral Therapy)

BT and CBT are essential in the treatment of conduct disorder. Counselors will work to (a) develop a therapeutic relationship; (b) create concrete expectations; (c) utilize hands-on therapeutic activities (e.g., behavioral contract, emotion regulation workbooks); (d) help Andrew recognize his emotional triggers (e.g., people telling him what he should do) and emotional cues (e.g., fists start to clench when angry); (e) help Andrew develop and use his new coping skills; (f) set realistic and obtainable goals; and (g) assign skills he can practice.

T = Therapeutic Support Services

- Psychiatric/medication management
- Short-term psychiatric stabilization
- Intensive individual inpatient residential treatment (length of stay to be determined based on Andrew's progress)
- Outpatient therapy on release from residential treatment
- An alternative school that has the resources needed to support children with severe behavior problems
- Andrew's parents will participate in Parent Management Training (PMT)
- Multisystemic Therapy (MST) upon release from residential treatment will be optimally beneficial

References

Achenbach, M. T., & Edelbrock, C. (2009). *Manual for the Child Behaviour Checklist and revised Child Behaviour Profile*. Burlington, VT: University of Vermont.

Ahmed, A. O., Green, B. A., McCloskey, M. S., & Berman, M. E. (2010). Latent structure of intermittent explosive disorder in an epidemiological sample. *Journal of Psychiatric Research, 44*, 663–672.

Ainsworth, M., & Bowlby, J. (1991). An ethological approach to personality development. *American Psychologist, 46*, 333–341.

Alexander, J. F., & Parsons, V. B. (1982). *Functional family therapy: Principles and procedures*. Carmel, CA: Brooks-Cole.

American Psychiatric Association (APA). (2013). *Diagnostic and statistical manual of mental disorders* (5th ed. [*DSM-5*]). Washington, DC: Author.

Buss, A. H., & Perry, M. (1992). The aggression questionnaire. *Journal of Personality and Social Psychology, 63*, 452–459.

Coehlo, D. P. (2011). Encopresis: A medical and family approach. *Pediatric Nursing, 37*, 107–112.

Conners, C. K., Sitarenios, G., Parker, J. D., & Epstein, J. N. (1998). The revised Conners Parent Rating Scale (CPRS-R): Factor structure, reliability, and criterion validity. *Journal of Abnormal Child Psychology, 26*, 257–268.

Conners, C. K., Wells, K. C., Parker, J. D., Sitarenios, G., Diamond, J. M., & Powell, J. W. (1997). A new self-report scale for assessment of adolescent psychopathology: Factor structure, reliability, validity, and diagnostic sensitivity. *Journal of Abnormal Child Psychology, 25*, 487–497.

Costin, J., & Chambers, S. (2007). Parent management training as a treatment for children with oppositional defiant disorder referred to mental health clinic. *Clinic Child Psychology and Psychiatry, 12*, 511–524.

Fritzon, K., Dolan, M., Doley, R., & McEwan, T. E. (2011a). Juvenile fire-setting: A review of treatment programs. *Psychiatry, Psychology & Law, 18*, 395–408.

Fritzon, K., Lewis, H., & Doley, R. (2011b). Looking at the characteristics of adult arsonists from a narrative perspective. *Psychiatry, Psychology and Law, 18*, 424–438.

Gontard, A. (2013). The impact of DSM-5 and guidelines for assessment and treatment of elimination disorders. *European Child and Adolescent Psychiatry, 22*, 61–67.

Gopalan, G., Goldstein, L., Klingenstein, K., Sicher, C., Blake, C., & McKay, M. (2010). Engaging families into child mental health treatment: Updates and special considerations. *Journal of the Canadian Academy of Child and Adolescent Psychiatry, 19*, 182–196.

Grant, J. E., Kim, S., & Odlaug, B. L. (2010a). A double-blind, placebo-controlled study of the opiate antagonist, naltrexone, in the treatment of kleptomania. *Biological Psychiatry, 65*, 600–606.

Grant, J. E., Odlaug, B. L., & Kim, S. (2010b). Kleptomania: Clinical characteristics and relationship to substance use disorders. *American Journal of Drug and Alcohol Abuse, 36*, 291–295.

Guttmann-Steinmetz, S., & Crowell, J. (2006). Attachment and externalizing disorders: A developmental psychopathology perspective. *Journal of American Academy Child and Adolescent Psychiatry, 45,* 440–451.

Harvard Health Publications. (2011). Treating intermittent explosive disorder: Emerging data show medication and cognitive behavioral therapy may help some patients. *Harvard Mental Health Letter, 27*(10), 6.

Hendriks, V., van der Schee, E., & Blanken, P. (2012). Matching adolescents with a cannabis use disorder to multidimensional family therapy or cognitive behavioral therapy: Treatment effect moderators in a randomized controlled trial. *Drug & Alcohol Dependence, 125*(1/2), 119–126.

Henggeler, S. W., & Schaeffer, C. (2010). Treating serious antisocial behavior with multisystemic therapy. In J. R. Weisz and A. E. Kazdin (Eds.), *Evidence-based psychotherapies for children and adolescents* (2nd ed.; pp. 259–276). New York, NY: Guilford.

Hodgkinson, B., Josephs, K., & Hegney, D. (2010). Best practice in the management of primary nocturnal enuresis in children: A systematic review. *JBI Library of Systematic Reviews 8*(5), 173–254.

Johnson, M. E., & Waller, R. J. (2006). A review of effective interventions for youth with aggressive behaviors who meet diagnostic criteria for conduct disorder or oppositional defiant disorder. *Journal of Family Psychotherapy, 17,* 67–80.

Kazdin, A. E. (2008). Parent management training: Treatment for oppositional, aggressive, and antisocial behavior in children and adolescents. New York, NY: Oxford University Press.

Kazdin, A. E. (2010). Problem-solving management training for oppositional defiant disorder and conduct disorder. In J. R. Weisz and A. E. Kazdin (Eds.), *Evidence-based psychotherapies for children and adolescents* (2nd ed.; pp. 211–226). New York, NY: Guilford.

Kjøbli, J., Hukkelberg, S., & Ogden, T. (2013). A randomized trial of group parent training: Reducing child conduct problems in real-world settings. *Behaviour Research & Therapy, 51,* 113–121.

Masi, G., Manfredi, A., Milone, A., Muratori, P., Polidori, L., Ruglinoni, L., . . . Muratori, F. (2011). Predictors of nonresponse to psychosocial treatment in children and adolescents with disruptive behavior disorders. *Journal of Child and Adolescent Psychopharmacology, 21,* 51–55.

Masi, G., Perugi, G., Millepiedi, S., Toni, C., Mucci, M., Pfanner, C., . . . Akiskal, H. S. (2007). Bipolar co-morbidity in pediatric obsessive-compulsive disorder: Clinical and treatment implications. *Journal of Child and Adolescent Psychopharmacology, 17,* 475–486.

Miller, W. R., & Rollnick, S. (2012). *Motivational interviewing: Preparing people for change* (3rd ed.). New York, NY: Guilford.

Powell, M. P., Boxmeyer, C. L., Baden, R., Stromeyer, S., Minney, J. A., Mushtaq, A., . . . Lochman, J. E. (2011). Assessing and treating aggression and conduct problems in schools: Implications from the Coping Power program. *Psychology in the Schools, 48,* 215–222.

Preston, J. D., O'Neal, J. H., & Talaga, M. C. (2013). *Handbook of clinical psychopharmacology for therapists* (7th ed.). Oakland, CA: New Harbinger.

Sadock, B. J., & Sadock, V. A. (2007). *Kaplan and Sadock's synopsis of psychiatry: Behavioral sciences/clinical psychiatry* (10th ed.). Philadelphia, PA: Lippincott Williams & Wilkins.

Scott, S., Sylva, K., Doolan, M., Price, J., Jacobs, B., Crook, C., . . . Landau, S. (2010). Randomised controlled trial of parent groups for child antisocial behaviour targeting multiple risk factors: The SPOKES project. *Journal of Child Psychology and Psychiatry, 51,* 48–57.

Shapira, B. E., & Dahlen, P. (2010). Therapeutic treatment protocol for enuresis using an enuresis alarm. *Journal of Counseling & Development, 88,* 246–252.

Stambaugh, L., Mustillo, S., Burns, B., Stephens, R., Baxter, B., Edwards, D., . . . DeKraai, M. (2007). Outcomes from wraparound and multisystemic therapy in a center for mental health services system-of-care demonstration site. *Journal of Emotional and Behavioral Disorders, 15,* 143–155.

Steiner, H., & Remsing, L. (2006). *Practice parameters for the assessment and treatment of children and adolescents with oppositional defiant disorder: Work group report.* Washington, DC: American Academy of Child and Adolescent Psychiatry.

Substance Abuse and Mental Health Services Administration (SAMHSA). (2012, October 1). *Problem-Solving Skills Training (PSST) and Parent Management Training (PMT) for conduct disorder.* Retrieved October 13, 2013, from: http://www.nrepp.samhsa.gov/viewlegacy.aspx?id=75

Sydow, K., Retzlaff, R., Beher, S., Haun, M. W., & Schweitzer, J. (2013). The efficacy of Systemic

Therapy for childhood and adolescent externalizing disorders: A systematic review of 47 RCT. *Family Process, 52*(4), 576–618.

Turgay, A. (2009). Psychopharmacological treatment of Oppositional Defiant Disorder. *CNS Drugs, 23*, 1–17.

Warner-Metzger, C. M., & Riepe, S. M. (2013). *TDMH-SAS best practice guidelines: Disruptive behavior disorders in children and adolescents.* Retrieved from: http://www.tn.gov/mental/policy/best_pract/Pages%20from%20CY_BPGs_132-161.pdf

Webster-Stratton, C. (2011). *The incredible years: Parent, teachers, and children's training series.* Seattle, WA: Incredible Years.

Wehmeier, P., Schacht, A., Dittmann, R., Helsberg, K., Schneider-Fresenius, C., Lehmann, M., . . . Ravens-Sieberer, U. (2011). Effect of atomoxetine on quality of life and family burden: Results from a randomized, placebo-controlled, double-blind study in children and adolescents with ADHD and comorbid oppositional defiant or conduct disorder. *Quality of Life Research, 20*, 691–702.

Neurodevelopmental and Neurocognitive Disorders

In conjunction with speech + occupational therapist in school setting

MEREDITH A. RAUSCH, NATALIE F. WILLIAMS, AND VICTORIA E. KRESS

CASE STUDY: MELINDA

Melinda is a 27-year-old Caucasian female who works full-time, and is enrolled in graduate school in the evenings. She began graduate school six months ago. Melinda's friends describe her as "scatterbrained," and at times, she seems to have difficulties managing her responsibilities at work, home, and school. Melinda readily agrees that she tends to be "scatterbrained," but attributes this tendency to juggling multiple responsibilities. She often finds she double-books or overschedules herself secondary to her multiple interests and excitement related to different activities. She figures, "Who wouldn't forget a few things if they were as busy as I am?"

Melinda's one-bedroom apartment is messy, and every time she attempts to clean, she becomes distracted with a new recipe she found or an exciting workout routine she wants to try. Melinda does not have any pets or houseplants because she knows she would forget to water them or take them for walks, just as she did when she was younger. In the past six months, since starting graduate school, she has become increasingly anxious and seems to be forgetting important things like class assignments and paying her bills. She is forever thinking about trying a new organizational system or buying books she never reads on how to get organized and declutter one's life. In class, Melinda's mind wanders during lectures and she often makes minor, detail-related errors on exams. While Melinda struggles to stay on task during class, there are times when she is hyperfocused and able to complete complicated projects at work, finishing reports in one day that her coworkers usually finish in one week. When Melinda is in "go" mode, as she calls it, she is able to work for several hours at a time without taking a break. Melinda relishes her ability to focus and feel productive during these times. She feels as if, for the most part, she is very high functioning. However, she finds that during the times when she is in "go" mode, she does not answer her phone or check emails; her mind is totally focused on the task in front of her. This ability to work diligently on certain tasks has been beneficial for Melinda. She was able to graduate with a B average as an undergraduate, and she successfully completed her first semester in graduate school. However, there are times when Melinda will forget to mail a payment for a bill or complete a homework assignment that was due.

She feels a great deal of anxiety, as she frequently misplaces things such as her car keys and smartphone, and even her credit card. She has noticed that as she takes on more life responsibilities, she is even more prone to losing things, causing her to feel even more anxiety.

Melinda is single. Her last boyfriend ended their relationship because he felt she failed to listen or to pay attention to him during conversations or on dates. She would also forget to return texts until days after receiving a message from him. He would become frustrated with her because she could not sit still and watch television with him. Melinda argued that she did not understand why one would sit for hours in front of the television when they could be doing something more creative, active, engaging, or interesting.

Melinda has struggled with these behaviors as long as she can remember, certainly as early as first grade, but she assumed she was just forgetful or disorganized. She tried using planners, writing out a daily schedule, and setting alarms and reminders on her phone, but none of these things seemed to work for longer than one or two days. Over the years, she has compensated by working very hard to complete certain tasks, although she could never seem to get started until the night before a major deadline. Talking with other students, she finds that many of them struggle with procrastination, so she assumes this is a normal part of graduate school.

Melinda realized she needed to seek help when she returned home after class one night to find her apartment dark because she failed, for the second time this year, to pay her electric bill. After reflecting on her situation, she began to wonder if perhaps there were deeper issues at play, so she decided to see a counselor at her college.

DESCRIPTION OF THE NEURODEVELOPMENTAL DISORDERS

Neurodevelopmental disorders involve disruptions in the developmental process of the brain, resulting in impairments in cognitive functioning. These impairments can impact social and emotional behavior, leading individuals to seek the services of mental health professionals. The *DSM-5* neurodevelopmental disorders discussed in this chapter include intellectual disability autism spectrum disorder (ASD), attention-deficit/hyperactivity disorder (ADHD), communication disorders, specific learning disorder, developmental coordination disorder, stereotypic movement disorder, and tic disorders (American Psychiatric Association [APA], 2013). The aforementioned disorders span a wide array of experiences and symptoms. Many neurodevelopmental disorders are congenital, meaning the disorder is present at birth; however, corresponding symptoms may not be fully present, or observable, until the individual reaches a certain age or enters certain environments, such as formal educational settings, or experiences certain developmental transitions (e.g., having children).

Clients with neurodevelopmental disorders often enter treatment as children, referred for services by parents or guardians, teachers or school administrators, or pediatricians or other medical professionals. Before providing services to children and adults with neurodevelopmental disorders, counselors should reference state laws and agency policies regarding guardianship and capacity to consent to treatment. Some adults who have an intellectual disability are not their own guardians and cannot consent to treatment. Care should also be taken to ensure that, if appropriate, those with an intellectual disability understand all aspects of informed consent.

With younger children, symptoms are often manifested as observable behaviors. Parents of children with neurodevelopmental disorders should participate in treatment as this will enhance treatment success. Parents can join in during sessions and help clients generalize skills to other environments. Adults with neurodevelopmental disorders may be self-referred, referred by another professional, or mandated into mental health treatment.

COUNSELOR CONSIDERATIONS

Treatment for neurodevelopmental disorders depends on the presenting symptoms, but may include medication, specific psychosocial therapies, or a combination of both. Regardless of their reasons for seeking treatment, all clients with neurodevelopmental disorders present with individual strengths that will serve as assets in the treatment process. These strengths vary from person to person and depend on considerations such as age, diagnosis, gender, previous treatment history, and co-occurring disabilities, but may include diligence, persistence, a positive attitude, and high levels of energy and enthusiasm. While certain personal characteristics could present as problematic, these characteristics could also be reframed as assets and can be channeled for more appropriate use during the treatment process and beyond.

Counselors working with client populations with neurodevelopmental disorders often operate from behavior therapy orientations and use brief solution-focused therapy, modified cognitive behavioral therapy techniques, and other types of behavior therapy interventions. Effective counseling treatment for clients with neurodevelopmental disorders may include increased levels of repetition (i.e., reviewing concepts multiple times); a consideration of clients' unique developmental levels, skills, and abilities a consistent session structure, which may include the use of timers or written schedules to stay on task; displaying emotions using exaggerated facial expressions or gestures; and finally, including family members or caregivers in sessions, depending on the specific needs of the client. Visual tools such as dry erase boards, pictures, and handouts with words and images are also helpful additions to counseling sessions for adults and children with neurodevelopmental disorders.

PROGNOSIS

Neurodevelopmental disorders are developmental disorders that do not go away, but can be impacted through effective intervention. Neurodevelopmental disorders are often diagnosed in childhood (e.g., as with an intellectual disability), but sometimes they are not identified until well into adulthood (e.g., as with ADHD). Autism spectrum disorder is often diagnosed during the toddler years, and ADHD and specific learning disorders are more frequently diagnosed around the time a child enters a school setting, or during the school-age years.

Over time, without intervention, the negative symptoms of a disorder could intensify, decreasing the likelihood of success in educational or employment settings, and impacting the person's overall quality of life. However, with early intervention services, often from birth to age three, children with neurodevelopmental disorders have the opportunity for a healthier start, and may experience a decreased need for long-term treatment later in life. As children with neurodevelopmental disorders grow older, many are able to access special education services through the public school systems. Counselors who work in schools are often available to assist students with socioemotional needs as they arise. Later in life, many adults with neurodevelopmental disorders continue to participate in ongoing treatment, depending on their specific needs. With consistent participation in mental health treatment and the use of other supportive services as needed, many individuals with neurodevelopmental disorders go on to live full, productive lives, depending on the severity of symptoms. However, most individuals with neurodevelopmental disorders require some level of services or support throughout their lifetime.

INTELLECTUAL DISABILITY

Description of the Disorder and Typical Client Characteristics

In the *DSM-5* (APA, 2013), intellectual disability (also known as intellectual developmental disorder) is a diagnosis formerly referred to as mental retardation. Approximately 1% of the U.S. population has an intellectual disability (APA, 2013). To qualify for this diagnosis, the *DSM-5* requires the following three criteria be met: deficits in intellectual functioning (i.e., reasoning, problem solving, planning, learning from experience; which is confirmed by clinical assessment as well as standardized intelligence testing); deficits in adaptive functioning (i.e., communication skills, independent living); and, an onset of these intellectual and adaptive deficits that occurs during the person's developmental period. The *DSM-5* suggests four levels of intellectual disability severity: mild, moderate, severe, and profound. With the *DSM-5*, the APA moved away from an emphasis on IQ scores in determining severity, and instead focused more on adaptive functioning as a determinant of severity. However, it is still suggested that impairment in intellectual functioning refers to an intellectual quotient (IQ) at or below 70, as assessed using an individually administered standardized IQ test such as the Weschler Intelligence Scales for Children, Fourth Edition (WISC-IV; Weschler, 2004), or the Stanford-Binet Intelligence Scales, Fifth Edition (SB5; Roid, 2003).

Although an IQ at or below 70 is one characteristic of an intellectual disability, clients vary in their strengths and abilities based on their adaptive behavioral skills. Impairments in adaptive behavior refer to clinically significant limitations in conceptual, practical, or social skills. Examples of conceptual skills include reading, comprehension, and mathematical reasoning skills; practical skills include everyday living tasks such as preparing meals and maintaining employment; and social skills include the ability to maintain relationships and stay safe from victimization.

An intellectual disability can be caused by problems which occur before birth, as with a chromosomal disorder; complications during delivery, such as a loss of oxygen to the brain; or problems which occur during childhood, such as exposure to environmental toxins. The most common causes of an intellectual disability are Down syndrome, fragile X syndrome, and fetal alcohol spectrum disorder.

While all intellectual disabilities are developmental disabilities, only some developmental disabilities result in intellectual impairments. In the United States approximately 1 in every

6 children ages three to 17 has a developmental disability. Developmental disorders may be physical in nature, as with epilepsy, and may or may not coexist with cognitive limitations, as with cerebral palsy or autism spectrum disorder.

Counselor Considerations

Children and adults with an intellectual disability present with a range of needs that may require mental health treatment. In order to adhere to legal and ethical standards, counselors should request information regarding a client's guardianship status. This information will allow a counselor to determine whether an individual can consent to treatment, or if parental or guardian consent is required. Some clients with an intellectual disability seek mental health services for issues unrelated to the disability, such as depression, grief, or relationship problems, and many also have co-occurring mental health disorders that require treatment, such as ADHD, bipolar disorder, or PTSD. However, some clients with an intellectual disability have mental health needs that are related to the disorder, such as social skills training, decreasing inappropriate behavior, or anger management. Depending on the specific diagnosis, children and adults with an intellectual disability may engage in inappropriate or impulsive behaviors, have difficulties expressing feelings appropriately, or suffer from social isolation. Children and adults with an intellectual disability are also more vulnerable to abuse and victimization than other populations, and this abuse can also create a need for mental health treatment.

Counselors who treat co-occurring mental health disorders within this population often use more active and directive approaches, giving clear suggestions and guidance throughout the treatment process. Due to limited cognitive processing skills, more open-ended techniques, such as indirect questioning, may cause confusion or be misinterpreted by this population. Counselors can increase the likelihood of success by breaking the traditional 50-minute session into manageable segments of about 15 minutes each. The first 15 minutes could involve reviewing content from the previous session; the second 15–20 minutes could include the incorporation of new information; and the last 15 minutes might be spent reviewing the topic and discussing homework, small goals, or tasks to be completed before the next session. An enthusiastic, energetic approach—especially with young children—can also be helpful.

A less obvious consideration when working with this population is the level of preparedness a counselor has in treating individuals who have an intellectual disability. In more recent years, this population has been seeking services in "mainstream" settings as opposed to disability-specific agencies. Some counselors have limited training in treating disabilities, specifically intellectual disability, and they may question their abilities to adequately treat these disorders. Continuing education, training, and supervision can increase counselor competence in working with this population.

There is a long history of stigmatization associated with intellectual disability, both in the United States and globally. Adults with an intellectual disability and other types of cognitive impairments have often been treated either as perpetual children or as dangers to society. When working with this population, counselors should be aware of their own biases as well as the biases others have toward this population (APA, 2013). Intellectual quotient (IQ) test results should be interpreted within the context of an individual's language, family, and culture, with consideration given to the adaptive, practical, and social skills necessary to thrive in that environment.

Treatment Models and Interventions

Treatment for individuals with an intellectual disability depends on the specific needs of the client and the severity of the disability. While the approaches used to treat someone with a mild disability versus a severe disability are quite different, the use of case management is an essential component of an effective treatment plan with this population. Case management requires counselors to collaborate with other professionals and entities, provide advocacy for appropriate resources and services, and facilitate appropriate educational or career-related opportunities. Case management is especially important with young adults who are typically wrestling with job-related issues and housing concerns.

Behavioral models that incorporate social skills training, feelings identification and expression, and managing interpersonal relationships are crucial, especially for children and adolescents with intellectual and developmental disorders. The most common therapeutic approaches with this population include applied behavior analysis (ABA), behavior therapy, and cognitive behavioral therapy (CBT) approaches.

Clinical Toolbox 13.1: In the Pearson etext, click here to watch a demonstration of a behavior therapy technique used to reduce self-injury and aggressiveness with a man who has a severe intellectual disability, fetal alcohol syndrome, and autism.

Skinner's behavioral Principal of operant conditioning to elicit behavior change

While the effectiveness of ABA has been established by over 60 years of empirical research (see the autism spectrum disorder treatment section in this chapter for more detailed information on ABA), there is some evidence to support the effectiveness of other approaches, including CBT (Sturmey, 2012). Insight- and process-oriented talk therapies (e.g., person centered) are generally regarded as ineffective with this population, although as with all counseling, a strong therapeutic relationship is essential. Both individual and group counseling are appropriate methods of treatment delivery with this population.

Effective interventions include the use of active and concrete tools to illustrate concepts, such as role-play in group treatment, and the use of visual schedules to outline the plan for an individual session. Young children with intellectual disability may benefit from exaggerated facial expressions and gestures, which serve as models for age-appropriate behavior and feelings expression. Adolescents and adults with intellectual disabilities may benefit from repetition of important concepts and the use of behavior contracts, which serve as concrete reminders of commitments and goals. Token economies (i.e., a reward system using tokens or symbols), verbal praise, and small rewards (e.g., small toys or stickers) are types of positive reinforcement counselors use to promote prosocial behaviors with this population.

Voices from the Trenches 13.1: In the Pearson etext, click here to watch a video discussion of considerations that are important when working with people who have an intellectual disability.

CREATIVE TOOLBOX 13.1   Buddy Gets Mad

Natalie F. Williams, PhD, PC

Activity Overview

Using a concoction that bubbles up as a metaphor for anger, clients with an intellectual disability (or any other disorders that involve anger) are taught to recognize and appropriately express their feelings of anger.

Treatment Goal(s) of Activity

CBT can be an effective form of treatment for decreasing aggressive behavior in those with intellectual disabilities and complex communication disorders. This activity is designed for use with young children with ID and other disorders that may result in impairments in feelings expression and identification. The goal of this activity is to provide children with intellectual disabilities with developmentally-appropriate ways to identify, express, and cope with feelings of anger in a safe, healthy manner.

Directions

1. Gather the following materials: Feelings Flashcards (e.g., Todd Parr © 2010; or you can make your own using magazine pictures of faces pasted onto index cards or card stock paper), baking soda, distilled white vinegar, two spoons, a tray or shallow bucket, a hand puppet with an angry face (this can easily be made by the counselor), one small cup (about 4 oz in size) and one large cup (about 8 oz or larger), and food coloring.
2. Show the client the "angry" face flashcard and the puppet, and share a short story about a friend named Buddy. Talk about specific triggers that make Buddy mad and use examples that are relevant to the client. In your story, include examples of inappropriate behavior when angry, using the image on the flashcard or examples from the client's tantrums, as reported by the client or the parent. Use expressive language and gestures to indicate feelings of anger. Stop the story midway and continue to the next step.
3. Prompt the child to put four big scoops of baking soda in the small cup. Place the small cup in the middle of the tray or shallow bucket.
4. Next, pour about 5–6 oz of vinegar in the larger cup. Direct the child to add three drops of food coloring and stir.
5. Continue the story and end with, "Buddy got so mad that he exploded!" At this point direct the child to pour the liquid mixture on top of the baking soda. As the mixture fizzles up, act out "angry" behaviors—stomp your feet, raise your voice, and continue to describe Buddy's inappropriate expressions of anger.
6. After the mixture stops fizzing, ask the client to describe how it smells, what it looked like, and so on. Talk about how all of those angry feelings "bubbled up" inside Buddy and then he "exploded!"

Process Questions

1. What happened to make Buddy so mad?
2. What did Buddy do when he was mad?
3. Do you ever explode like Buddy?
4. What do you do when you are mad?

> 5. Do you feel good or do you feel yucky when you get really, really mad?
> 6. What could Buddy do next time he gets mad?
> 7. How can we help Buddy calm down?
> 8. Who/what helps you feel better when you are mad?

Those with an intellectual disability who also have co-occurring psychiatric disorders, such as depression and anxiety, are often prescribed medication to address these comorbid disorders and symptoms. Additionally, medications may be utilized to control certain undesirable behavioral components including agitation, self-injurious behaviors, aggression, and hyperactivity. While risperidone and other antipsychotic medications have been the most utilized medications in the treatment of behavior problems in individuals with intellectual disabilities (Deb & Unwin, 2007), stimulants have occasionally been used to increase concentration levels and restrict hyperactivity. The use of antipsychotics comes with side effects, which include weight gain, sedation or drowsiness, sexual dysfunction, and hyperlipidemia (i.e., high cholesterol; Ücok & Gaebel, 2008).

Prognosis

While intellectual disability is a lifelong, intractable disorder, early intervention is the best way to ensure positive outcomes and the effective management of problematic symptoms and behaviors. With consistent participation in treatment, individuals with an intellectual disability who have co-occurring mental health concerns can experience reduction in symptoms and an improvement in overall well-being.

AUTISM SPECTRUM DISORDER

Description of the Disorder and Typical Client Characteristics

S,R,SI

Approximately 1 in 88 children in the United States have autism spectrum disorder (ASD) (Centers for Disease Control and Prevention [CDC], 2012b), or 1% of the U.S. population (APA, 2013). ASD is four times more prevalent in boys than girls and is usually diagnosed during the toddler years, before age three (APA, 2013).

In the *DSM-IV-TR,* the following disorders were listed separately: autistic disorder, Asperger's disorder, childhood disintegrative disorder, and pervasive developmental disorder (not otherwise specified). In the *DSM-5,* these disorders were collapsed and are all referred to as autism spectrum disorder (ASD). Rather than listing specific diagnoses, ASD is the formal diagnosis with a specifier to indicate the severity of symptoms (i.e., Level 1, Level 2, or Level 3). In order to meet the criteria for diagnosis, symptoms must be present in early childhood and must cause clinically significant impairments in everyday life.

 Clinical Toolbox 13.2: In the Pearson etext, click here to view a summary of diagnostic changes that occurred as related to the autism spectrum diagnoses from the *DSM-IV-TR* to the *DSM-5.*

According to the *DSM-5,* ASD includes a range of impairments in two broad categories: (a) significant social communication and interaction impairments, not resulting from developmental delays; and (b) behavior, interests, or activities that are restrictive and repetitive. Along with these two symptom categories, some individuals with ASD—but not all—may also experience limitations in cognitive or adaptive skills. Some, but not all, people with ASD may engage in stereotyped behaviors. An example of a stereotypical behavior is self-stimulatory behavior, or "stimming" activities, such as hand-flapping or rocking back and forth. Examples of repetitive behaviors may include echolalia (i.e., repeating what is heard) or "scripting" (i.e., quoting lines from books or movies).

Children with ASD may also have sensory processing issues and experience physical and emotional dysregulation. These difficulties with emotion regulation are the root of many acting-out behaviors and tantrums. Related to this, many adults and children with ASD have difficulty with interpersonal relationships and with identifying and expressing feelings.

While some individuals with ASD have enhanced abilities in certain areas, they may also have delays in other areas when compared to their same-age peers without ASD. For example, a 3-year-old child with ASD may have memorized all of the states in the United States and their capitals, but he may be unable to play with peers. These sharp differences in skills and abilities are referred to as "splinter" skills.

As currently conceptualized in the *DSM-5*, ASD covers a broad range of symptoms and behaviors. Those with ASD may each present quite differently. For example, one man with ASD might be a college professor with an IQ of 140, who has had on-going interpersonal struggles, but because of other strengths and resources, has been able to function at a high level. At the other extreme is a man with ASD who has a severe intellectual disability (caused by fetal alcohol syndrome), and has severe behavior problems (i.e., self-injury, physical outbursts) which have resulted in his living his entire life in a secure group home setting. Counselors should consider that there are a number of co-occurring disorders and struggles, as well as unique client strengths, that influence the presentation, course, and treatment of a client with ASD.

Early signs of ASD include failure to meet certain developmental milestones, limited language development, and limited eye contact and social interaction with others. The specific causes for ASD are still under investigation; however, some scholars have explored the impact of environmental toxins and the interplay between genetic vulnerability and environmental risk factors. In the past, there was a suspected link between the MMR (measles, mumps, and rubella) vaccine and other vaccines that contain thiomersal, also referred to as thimerosal, and ASD but these studies have been largely discredited (CDC, 2012a).

Counselor Considerations

Because clients with ASD may have difficulties with receptive communication (i.e., understanding written or verbal messages) and interpretation of social nuances, such as metaphors and idioms, counselors should use concrete language and techniques when counseling this population. Because of their limited social skills, clients with ASD may struggle with age-appropriate identification and expression of emotions, and engage in inappropriate behavior. Patience is required, especially when serving children with ASD who may present with hyperactive or aggressive behaviors. Counselors can model appropriate behavior, tone of voice, and eye contact, and be prepared to offer additional prompting, reminders, and suggestions related to social skills as needed for children and adults with ASD. Children and adults with ASD typically prefer a regular routine and have difficulty coping with change; counselors should aim to avoid surprises during sessions and remain consistent regarding use of space, timing, and the structuring of sessions.

Counselors should also understand the role of family and caregivers and be open to collaborating with other providers in schools or community settings to enhance clients' opportunities for success. ASD can have a devastating impact on families; parents and caregivers of children with ASD may experience high levels of stress and anxiety, or even depression, as a result of their child's symptoms. The increased financial strain of expensive treatments and therapies for children with disabilities, specifically ASD, can be a contributing factor to the high parental divorce rates. Difficulty obtaining and maintaining childcare is also a major concern due to the limited number of trained providers who are able to manage the symptoms of the disorder. Siblings without disabilities are also impacted by their brothers or sisters with ASD and can benefit from counseling. Siblings may be a resource for clients and may even be integrated into a client's comprehensive treatment plan.

Because ASD is a developmental disorder, some third-party payers perceive that treatment can only minimally change its course. Therefore, third-party payers may not provide reimbursement for mental health services with an ASD diagnosis alone. However, third-party payers will often reimburse for the treatment of co-occurring mental health disorders such as anxiety, depression, or ADHD.

Counselors providing services to children and adults with ASD should be sensitive to cultural differences in communication and social interactions, and integrate these considerations into treatment plans. Although social niceties and idioms vary among languages and cultures, a diagnosis of ASD indicates a noticeable, marked, or severe deficit in social communication skills (APA, 2013).

Treatment Models and Interventions *Specialized*

Effective treatment of ASD must include a comprehensive assessment that is focused on determining a client's unique social and emotional needs. Ongoing psychoeducation can be beneficial to help the client and family understand the disorder and cope with symptoms. Tracking progress over time is useful for assessing the impact of treatment, specifically when targeting changes in behavior. Clients and/or caregivers can be taught to monitor symptoms at home and at school and provide updates to the counselor at counseling sessions. Almost all treatments for ASD include a focus on helping clients develop social skills and an ability to regulate their behavior.

Clinical Toolbox 13.3: In the Pearson etext, click here to read about a creative activity that can be used to help teach children with autism spectrum disorder to identify thoughts and feelings.

Several promising treatment approaches will be discussed in more detail in the following sections.

Clinical Toolbox 13.4: In the Pearson etext, click here to review a creative activity that can be used to help clients with autism spectrum disorder develop their social skills.

APPLIED BEHAVIOR ANALYSIS (ABA) The most widely researched and evidence-based form of treatment therapy for children and adults with ASD is ABA (e.g., Boutot & Hume, 2012; Matson et al., 2012). ABA is often delivered one-on-one in a school, home, or clinical setting. ABA can also be delivered in social skills group settings that sometimes incorporate siblings or peers without ASD to serve as models for appropriate behavior and social communication. ABA uses Skinner's behavioral principles of operant conditioning to elicit positive behavior change. ABA can be used to teach age-appropriate communication skills, social skills, adaptive behavior skills, and academic content to adults and children with ASD, while simultaneously decreasing negative behaviors such as tantrums and outbursts. ABA treatment is increasingly covered by a number of government and private insurance agencies.

The Early Start Denver Model (ESDM; Rogers & Dawson, 2009) is a form of ABA early intervention for toddlers with ASD, ages 1 to 4 years, that is useful in treating ASD. ESDM incorporates the following components: parental involvement, ABA techniques delivered in natural settings, age-appropriate sequencing of developmental skills, emphasis on positive interactions, and language and communication development (Rogers & Dawson, 2009).

Pivotal response treatment (PRT; Koegel & Koegel, 2006) is another well-researched ABA therapy for clients with ASD. PRT builds on ABA principles and incorporates child-centered play. PRT emphasizes natural reinforcement in the environment and focuses on "pivotal" or critical areas in a child's development. PRT is highly individualized and centers on communication, social skills, and play.

Early intensive behavioral intervention (EIBI; Lovaas, 1987) is a modified form of ABA therapy, which is used with children at the age of four years or younger, and usually continues for 2–3 years. EIBI is delivered one-on-one from 20 to 40 hours per week and focuses on teaching adaptive behavior, social, and communication skills. Caregivers play an important role in EIBI, and their involvement is crucial to the child's success beyond treatment settings. Although some studies show EIBI to be beneficial for children with ASD, additional research including randomized controlled trials is needed to evaluate the effectiveness of the EIBI approach (Reichow, Barton, Boyd, & Hume, 2012).

 Clinical Toolbox 13.5: In the Pearson etext, click here to watch a video demonstration of applied behavior analysis.

FLOORTIME THERAPY   Using floortime therapy (Greenspan & Wieder, 2009), parents and caregivers join in with their child in play, and gradually move to incorporating a focus on developing the child's communication and interpersonal skills. For example, if a toddler throws a ball in the air, her father can engage with her by throwing the ball back and forth, and add appropriate verbal comments, like "ball." The goal of floortime therapy is to promote social and emotional development, particularly for children with developmental delays. Two randomized controlled studies found floortime therapy to be an effective intervention for young children with ASD (Casenhiser, Shanker, & Stieben, 2013; Pajareya & Nopmaneejumruslers, 2011).

THE TEACCH METHOD   The Training and Education of Autistic and Related Communication Handicapped Children (TEACCH; Mesibov, Shea, & Schopler, 2004) model is often delivered in special education classrooms with children with ASD, but has also been used with adults with ASD in residential and community-based facilities. The TEACCH method emphasizes the use of visual tools, such as charts and schedules, to support learning and comprehension. The TEACCH method is assessment-driven and incorporates play and recreation, parent education, individual counseling, and supported employment, and it can be used with clients of all ages with ASD. One nonrandomized program evaluation of the TEACCH method (Panerai, Ferrante, & Zingale, 2002) found statistically significant differences between experimental and control groups on the following skills for a group of children with autism and other disorders: gross motor skills, cognitive performance, play and leisure, imitation, hand-eye coordination, perception, developmental age, and personal living skills. For adolescents and adults with ASD and severe disabilities, the TEACCH method was useful in increasing communication, independence, and prosocial behavior (Van Bourgondien, Reichle, & Schopler, 2003).

PSYCHOPHARMACOTHERAPY   Although there are currently no medications used to treat ASD per se, psychiatrists often prescribe medications to target specific symptoms such as hyperactivity or anxiety. Additionally, antipsychotic medications (e.g., risperidone and aripiprazole) have also been prescribed to manage the more severe behavioral problems sometimes associated with the disorder, such as severe temper tantrums, self-injurious behaviors, or increased aggression (CDC, 2013). As stated previously, the use of antipsychotics invites serious side effects that need to be considered including sedation or drowsiness, sexual dysfunction, weight gain, and hyperlipidemia (i.e., high cholesterol; Ücok & Gaebel, 2008).

Prognosis

Because ASD is a neurodevelopmental disorder, most children with ASD continue to struggle with symptoms as they age, especially if they are not actively involved in treatment. Outcome studies on behavior-based therapies and ASD have demonstrated these therapies are effective in decreasing the presence of negative symptoms and increasing adaptive behavior over the long-term (e.g., Eldevik et al., 2009; Virués-Ortega, 2010). However, dramatic changes in client symptomology are not typical. The most effective way to decrease symptoms is to identify and begin treating the disorder as early as possible (CDC, 2012b).

ATTENTION-DEFICIT/HYPERACTIVITY DISORDER

Description of the Disorder and Typical Client Characteristics

Attention-deficit/hyperactivity disorder (ADHD) is a neurological processing disorder, which is typically first identified and diagnosed in school-age children. Adults may also be diagnosed with ADHD, although clinically significant symptoms must be present before age seven to meet the *DSM-5* ADHD diagnostic criteria. Approximately 5% of school-age children and about 2.5% of adults have ADHD (APA, 2013). Recent research using chromosomal data supports the genetic inheritance of ADHD in families, leading scientists to look to heredity as the most important contributing etiological factor in the development of ADHD (Hebebrand et al., 2006; Mick & Faraone, 2008).

ADHD is an often-misunderstood disorder. The disorder's name implies attention deficiencies, but in reality, the disorder involves attention irregularities. While people with ADHD may struggle to attend to some tasks for a period of time, they also possess a unique ability to hyperfocus, or focus exceptionally attentively to tasks that interest them. Clients with ADHD may exhibit hyperactive behavior or be largely inattentive, or present

[handwritten margin note: Brain can't filter out excessive "noise" smaller brain that contributes to difficulties in executive functioning]

a combination of both. These impairments must be clinically significant and pervasive in multiple environments to meet the criteria for diagnosis. Children with ADHD often have trouble focusing in school and may have poor grades, and experience consequences secondary to negative behavior (often related to impulse control or inattentiveness), including referrals and suspensions. Students with ADHD may have problems with organization, fail to complete assignments, and struggle with the necessary self-regulation to stay on task during an 8-hour school day. Adults with ADHD may also experience similar symptoms, with the addition of strained interpersonal relationships and difficulties at work, or more severe outcomes, such as self-medication with alcohol and/or other drugs.

In children, ADHD symptoms present differently by gender, with girls with ADHD being twice as likely to report inattentiveness and greater co-occurring anxiety, and being less likely to use alcohol and/or other drugs than boys with ADHD (Biederman et al., 2002). Boys with ADHD are also more likely to have co-occurring behavioral, depressive, and learning disorders than girls with ADHD, although these struggles are still relatively common in all children who have ADHD (Biederman et al., 2002). As those with ADHD age, there are no significant differences between men and women in terms of severity of symptoms; however, men are more likely to engage in "acting out" or hyperactive behaviors as compared to women.

Counselor Considerations

Highly structured sessions with direct, concrete dialogue will help focus children and adults with ADHD. Counselors can provide firm, yet supportive redirection to ensure time is devoted to relevant tasks and clients stay focused on working towards their goals. Clients with ADHD may struggle with self-esteem issues and often report feeling "different" from others as a result of difficulties in work, school, or home environments. Counselors can work to build clients' self-esteem by offering praise for completion of tasks and consistent participation in treatment, and by pointing out their strengths and the ways that their ADHD symptoms can serve, at times, as a resource. For example, if a college-age client with ADHD has a tendency to hyperfocus when writing term papers, the counselor can work with the client to identify times when this behavior has been helpful in meeting important deadlines. Counselors and clients can also work together to figure out how to harness abilities and channel them in productive ways. Counselors can also help clients normalize symptoms by providing psychoeducation on ADHD, and assuring clients that their behavior is a result of a neurological condition, and that the disorder is not their fault or a strike against their character. Counselors who provide services to children with ADHD should also collaborate with other professionals, including psychiatrists, parents and caregivers, and teachers, to obtain updates on clients' progress outside of session. Involving these stakeholders can increase the likelihood of generalizing new skills to other contexts. For children and adults with ADHD, collaboration with other household members, including partners and children, may also be helpful in strengthening support symptoms; household members can benefit from better understanding ADHD and how to cope with it, and they can be solicited in supporting the clients' treatment goals.

 Clinical Toolbox 13.6: In the Pearson etext, click here to read about a creative activity that can be used to help children with ADHD control their impulsive behaviors.

Cultural factors may play a role in the identification or diagnosis of ADHD. In the United States, females, and African and Hispanic Americans have lower rates of ADHD diagnoses compared with Caucasian Americans (APA, 2013). Some research suggests that it may be missed and as such, underdiagnosed, in these populations (Bailey & Owens, 2005). Variations in what behaviors are seen as problematic within the culture may contribute to these differences in identification, and counselors should be aware of these uniquenesses in terms of identifying ADHD and when developing treatment plans.

In terms of gender, both female children and adults are less likely to be diagnosed with ADHD. The ratio of male-to-female ADHD diagnosis is 2 to 1 for children and 1.6 to 1 for adults, and females are more likely to present with inattentive features, when compared with males (APA, 2013). These differences in symptom manifestation should be considered when developing a treatment plan (e.g., placing more of an emphasis on inattentiveness as opposed to hyperactivity symptoms).

Treatment Models and Interventions

Treatment plans for children with ADHD should incorporate counselors, school personnel, medical professionals (e.g., psychiatrists), and caregivers. A combination of CBT and medication management has had positive outcomes in reducing symptoms of the disorder (Emilsson et al., 2011). An emerging body of literature also suggests neurofeedback may be an emerging effective form of treatment for clients with ADHD.

COGNITIVE BEHAVIORAL THERAPY (CBT)   Because ADHD is typically a chronic disorder, clients need to develop the skills necessary to effectively navigate its accompanying symptoms. CBT focuses on helping clients develop both the cognitive and behavioral skills needed to effectively manage their symptoms in the long term. CBT focuses on addressing clients' thoughts and the way their thoughts contribute to enduring beliefs about themselves, and thus influence the way they feel and act. Interventions using CBT techniques and skills also address the impact of the disorder on clients' social and emotional well-being. CBT skills can also be useful in enhancing one's ability to focus (Virta et al., 2010).

As applied to treating ADHD, CBT focuses on enhancing attention span, memory, impulse control, problem-solving skills, emotion regulation (e.g., anger management, self-soothing), social skills, and organizational skills. When working from a CBT focus, counselors place an emphasis on helping clients develop skills that they can apply in various life contexts to counteract their ADHD symptoms. For example, clients might learn self-regulation or self-mediation skills that they can use to help them regulate impulsive emotional reactions; reactions that may create problems in their interpersonal relationships. Research has suggested that CBT can decrease the major symptoms of adults with ADHD in both the short and long term (Emilsson et al., 2011).

In terms of skill development, CBT has a strong focus on helping clients with ADHD learn practical strategies and instructions to solve three of their most common struggles: organization, time management, and planning. For clients with ADHD, simple behavioral changes can go a long way to improving their day-to-day life circumstances and symptom management. For example, learning to use one's smartphone to receive reminders and to use time alarms can help prevent distractions and aid in time management. Clients might also learn self-talk strategies such as "If it isn't in my electronic calendar, I won't do it," to help them stay focused.

For clients with ADHD, the challenges they face often contribute to a negative view of themselves and their capabilities. As such, CBT has a heavy focus on helping clients alter their unproductive thoughts. Clients may be quick to avoid engaging in situations where they have had past failures because of this negative self-talk (e.g., "I failed at this in the past, so why try now?"); negative self-talk can be self-sabotaging. For example, many clients with ADHD may feel overwhelmed when faced with certain tasks that require a sustained focus or attention to detail. They may develop a characteristic way of thinking in these situations (e.g., "I cannot complete this task"). This negative thinking can magnify symptoms and complicate problem-solving abilities. This thinking can also lead to clients avoiding new learning situations and opportunities because of fears of failure. Changing one's thoughts can help clients enter into circumstances or activities with a way of thinking that promotes their success.

NEUROFEEDBACK   Neurofeedback or electroencephalography (EEG) feedback is a non-invasive procedure in which electrodes are placed on a client's scalp to monitor electrical signals in the brain. The electrodes are connected to a computer that provides immediate feedback from clients' brain waves. When a client is attentive and focused, as measured by theta and beta wave patterns, pleasant images appear on a computer screen. As clients monitor their brain activity using neurofeedback in sessions, they learn skills to increase attention and focus under certain conditions.

Recent research studies suggest neurofeedback has implications for the treatment of ADHD. Neurofeedback serves as a way to analyze brain activity levels in real time to help clients learn to increase attention, focus, working memory, and other executive functioning skills. In a review of all randomized controlled trials, neurofeedback has been suggested as "probably efficacious" in the treatment of ADHD (Lofthouse, Arnold, Hersch, Hurt, & DeBeus, 2011, p. 1).

PSYCHOPHARMACOTHERAPY   Various forms of prescription medication, primarily stimulants, have proven effective in reducing the symptoms associated with ADHD in both children and adults. ADHD is typically a chronic neurological disorder, and while prescription medications may be useful in managing symptoms, they do not cure or completely eliminate the disorder. Stimulants are effective in reducing symptoms for approximately one-half to three-fourths of all adults and children with ADHD. Stimulants increase the production of dopamine and noradrenaline in the brain, activating the parts of the brain that control inhibition, and enhancing focus. (Kooij, 2013).

Common stimulants prescribed for ADHD include Adderall, Ritalin and Focalin, available in short and extended-release, and the 12-hour Daytrana patch (Kooij, 2013). Short-release stimulants are less often preferred for children and adults with ADHD because up to six to eight doses could be needed daily. The likelihood of medication compliance is greater with long-release stimulants.

Common side effects of stimulants include loss of appetite, weight loss, headaches, and increased heart rate (Kooij, 2013). Other, less frequent side effects include dry mouth, difficulty sleeping, and an increase or reduction in blood pressure (Kooij, 2013).

Counselors can spend time processing a client's reactions to potential side effects of prescribed medication and collaborate with health care providers to ensure the best possible outcomes for the client. Prescriptions can be adjusted to increase medication compliance and prevent premature termination of medications because of discomfort with the medication's side effects.

While stimulants are the most common medications used to treat ADHD, antidepressants (i.e., bupropion [Wellbutrin], venlafaxine, atomoxetine) are also prescribed, but with less evidence of efficacy (Paykina, Greenhill, & Gorman, 2007). Stimulant medications are addictive, and this risk should be taken seriously, especially with this population that is already vulnerable to addictions. However, if taken as prescribed, the risk of addiction to most ADHD medication can be managed. Repeated reports of misplaced medication, failure to follow up after receiving prescriptions, and little improvement in symptoms over time could be signs of abuse of these medications (Kooij, 2013).

Prognosis

A common misconception is that people with ADHD outgrow their symptoms. While some do outgrow some symptoms with age, and certain symptoms may diminish (e.g., hyperactivity), some symptoms (e.g., inattentiveness) may worsen with age (Kooij, 2013), and most people continue to have symptoms throughout their lives. However, with consistent treatment, often including medication, counseling, and collaboration with other stakeholders, clients with ADHD are likely to learn strategies to successfully manage symptoms and live productive lives. In fact, many people with ADHD are able to turn certain aspects of the disorder into strengths (e.g., the ability to hyperfocus can lead to notable accomplishments in certain areas). Clients, along with their parents and caregivers, can request reasonable accommodations in work or school settings in order to increase the potential for long-term positive outcomes.

COMMUNICATION DISORDERS

Description of the Disorders and Typical Client Characteristics

In the *DSM-5*, the communication disorders category includes the following disorders: language disorder, speech sound disorder, childhood-onset fluency disorder (stuttering), social (pragmatic) communication disorder, and other specified and unspecified communication disorders. Language disorder involves a person having language skills that are below age expectations in one or more areas (i.e., spoken, written). Speech-sound disorder is a failure to produce language in an age-appropriate manner (e.g., leaving out consonants or substituting one sound for another). Childhood onset fluency disorder (formerly stuttering) is an interruption in the normal flow of speech patterns (e.g., repetition of words or sounds, pauses during speech) that is atypical based on age and development. Social communication disorder involves problems with verbal and nonverbal communication that are not the result of mental disabilities or grammar problems, but that significantly impact the development of interpersonal relationships.

Language delays are more prevalent in younger children, with rates of about 10–15% of all children under age three having some type of communication disorder; however, as children reach school age, the rates fall to between 3–7%. Some adults experience communication disorders as a result of accident, injury, or medical conditions. Clients with communication disorders may stutter, have difficulty enunciating certain sounds, distort sounds, or omit sounds where they should occur. Some clients may also engage in head jerking or eye blinking when attempting to generate words or sounds. These irregularities in communication can cause feelings of embarrassment in social situations. Clients with communication disorders may also have co-occurring medical conditions, such as cerebral palsy, which impact the motor and/or cognitive skills necessary for effective communication.

Counselor Considerations

Those with communication disorders may experience psychological distress as a result of the disorder. Typically, the counselor's role is to work to enhance clients' self-esteem, to help clients manage and/or cope with the symptoms, and to address any social and emotional issues that may occur secondary to the disorder's symptoms. Counselors will need to refer clients with these disorders to speech and language pathologists for treatment of the disorder. When addressing mental health concerns with this population, collaboration with speech and language pathologists will be helpful.

Counselors should always remain aware of the differences between receptive and expressive communication skills—some clients may actually understand (i.e., receptive communication) more information than they may be able to convey (i.e., expressive communication). Creative treatment approaches that include art or writing can provide an opportunity for clients with communication disorders to share their stories, cope with the associated problems, and overcome any personal barriers that may impede their success in life; the use of these alternative mediums may feel more comfortable to clients who struggle to communicate verbally.

Treatment Models and Interventions

Early intervention and prevention during the first three years of life is crucial for clients with communication disorders. Counselors, specifically those with early childhood expertise, can help parents identify important developmental milestones, and identify areas where children may be lacking in the development of language skills. Counselors can refer clients to appropriate professionals to treat the communication disorder, and offer services such as psychoeducation, self-esteem–building activities, and social skills training to help clients cope with the presenting symptoms related to the disorder. Because speech and language therapy are the primary treatments for communication disorders, there is limited research on the effectiveness of psychosocial interventions in treating these disorders. The treatments that follow are those which *may* be helpful in supporting this population.

SPEECH AND LANGUAGE THERAPY   Speech and language therapy is the primary form of treatment for communication disorders. Speech and language pathologists deliver services to clients with communication disorders in schools, private practice, and clinical settings such as hospitals or research facilities. They consider the developmental components associated with communication and target interventions to meet the client's individual needs. Thorough assessment is needed to identify gaps in developmental communication, and speech and language pathologists often work with teachers, parents, and family members to ensure skills are generalized from clinical settings to natural environments.

NARRATIVE THERAPY (NT)   No research could be found to support its use with communication disorders, but NT is one approach that may be helpful in empowering clients with communication disorders (Leahy, O'Dwyer, & Ryan 2012). In applying NT to work with this population, the counseling process might begin with clients sharing their experiences related to the impact of the disorder on their lives. Clients are then encouraged to explore their personal strengths and the challenges associated with the problem. In later sessions, clients are encouraged to identify specific times when they were able to overcome the problem. These positive experiences are then used to write a new narrative in which the client eventually creates a unique identity, separating himself or herself from the problem and building on the personal strengths that have been identified throughout treatment.

ACCEPTANCE AND COMMITMENT THERAPY (ACT) ACT is an intervention that has been used with some success with adults who stutter. In one study, both a clinician and a speech therapist facilitated ACT groups with participants. At the completion of eight ACT group sessions, all participants had statistically significant improvements in all of their psychosocial treatment goals, and had maintained those gains at a 3-month follow-up (Beilby, Byrnes, & Yaruss, 2012). The treatment goals addressed by the speech therapist included decreasing stuttering, enhancing fluency, and improving overall communication skills. Some of the psychosocial goals addressed by the clinician included increasing self-awareness and mindfulness skills, making commitments to change and identifying barriers to change, and identifying personal strengths.

COGNITIVE BEHAVIORAL THERAPY (CBT) CBT is another treatment intervention that has been used with some success with adults who stutter. The relationship between anxiety and stuttering has been well documented, and approximately 50% of all adults who stutter also have social anxiety disorder (Menzies, Onslow, & O'Brian, 2009). A randomized control trial by Menzies et al. (2008) found 12 weeks of CBT targeting anxiety, followed by intensive speech therapy, was effective in decreasing social anxiety disorder for adults who stutter; however, there was no observed difference in stuttering between the experimental and control groups. CBT for social anxiety and stuttering often includes (a) exposure, in which clients practice speaking skills in anxiety-provoking situations; (b) behavioral experiments, in which clients engage in activities such as voluntary stuttering to test their negative beliefs about how others will respond; (c) cognitive restructuring to challenge negative beliefs; and (d) attention training and mindfulness activities to stop the flow of negative thoughts (Menzies et al., 2012). Speech and language therapists and counselors can use CBT techniques to help clients with co-occurring communication and anxiety disorders restructure negative thoughts and feelings and confront negative behaviors such as social avoidance in both individual and group settings.

Prognosis

Most children with communication disorders experience a decrease in symptoms as they age. However, some adults with communication disorders continue to experience symptoms, depending on the etiology of the disorder. Early intervention is the best approach to ensure successful treatment outcomes for clients with communication disorders.

SPECIFIC LEARNING DISORDER

Description of the Disorder and Typical Client Characteristics

In the *DSM-5* specific learning disorder describes a category of clinically significant impairments that were previously characterized as learning disorders in the *DSM-IV-TR*. The following disorders are no longer used in the *DSM-5*: dyslexia (reading disorder), dyscalculia (mathematics disorder), and dysgraphia (disorder of written expression); instead, the APA recommends clinicians specify the type of learning disorder in the diagnosis (e.g., specific learning disorder, with impairment in mathematics).

The cause of specific learning disorder is unknown. Approximately 5–15% of school-age children, across cultures, have a learning disorder (i.e., math, reading, or writing), and it is estimated that 4% of adults have a learning disorder (APA, 2013). Specific learning disorder may occur as a result of neurodevelopmental disabilities or medical conditions, but many cases have no known cause.

2-5% of Population

5% of School-aged Children

Clients with specific learning disorder score significantly lower on standardized achievement tests, below the expected range based on their age, level of education, and measured intelligence level. In addition, clients with specific learning disorder may experience psychological disturbance as a result of the learning problem; a disturbance that may impair their academic or daily functioning. As a result, clients with specific learning disorder may struggle with self-esteem and self-worth, and they are twice as likely to drop out of school compared to students without a learning disorder. Many clients with conduct disorder or oppositional defiant disorder, ADHD, and some depressive disorders, also have specific learning disorder.

Counselor Considerations

Counselors treating clients with specific learning disorder should pay careful attention to the role of cultural factors in the treatment of the disorder. Standardized test results are required to diagnose specific learning disorder; however, high-stakes standardized academic tests have been criticized because certain populations of students tend to score lower on these types of assessments, regardless of ability levels. These populations include English language learners, students with disabilities, residents of low-income areas, and African and Hispanic American students (Martin, 2012; Pullin, 2005). Males are two to three times more likely to be diagnosed with a specific learning disorder, after controlling for factors such as race, socioeconomic status, and language as potential confounding factors (APA, 2013).

Treatment Models and Interventions

Specific learning disorder is typically addressed through special education and accommodations in mainstream educational settings. Should the child qualify as having a *learning disability*, he or she may have an Individualized Education Plan or a 504 plan that specifies special accommodations the school must provide to facilitate success. However, many counselors do work with children and adults who have a specific learning disorder, and they may address co-occurring disorders (e.g., depression or ADHD), and the struggles which relate to the learning disorder. Counselors who serve clients with specific learning disorder can incorporate self-esteem–building components along with consistent involvement from family members. As with other disorders that manifest during childhood, counselors' collaboration with parents, guardians, and teachers can increase chances for success in school and home environments.

SLD = no IEP support

GROUP COUNSELING   In the published literature on treatment for individuals with specific learning disorder, researchers often use the term *learning disability* (a legal term) to refer to clinically significant impairments in academic functioning. Group counseling is

Psychoed

one treatment method that has been used with clients with learning disabilities, primarily with children in school settings. For middle school students with learning disabilities, group counseling is beneficial for increasing students' knowledge about the disability, increasing self-advocacy skills, and revealing strengths and assets (Mishna, Muskat, & Wiener, 2010). In one nonrandomized pre-post comparison study, expressive-supportive group counseling was an effective mode of treatment for children ages 10 to 18 who had learning disabilities (Leichtentritt & Shechtman, 2010). The group therapy treatment addressed the social-emotional aspect of the disorder, and the study's findings indicated that the intervention helped address the children's adjustment and social competence. The expressive-supportive group counseling model included various creative expression mediums such as art therapy, bibliotherapy, therapeutic games, and photography over 13 weekly sessions.

CAREER COUNSELING   Research suggests that certain groups of adolescents with learning disabilities, particularly African and Hispanic American males from low socioeconomic status households, are at risk for a number of poor outcomes later in life, including high school dropout, unemployment, and incarceration (Williams, Brown, Greer, & Jenkins, 2011). College students with learning disabilities have reported struggling with career decision making, experiencing difficulty explaining the nature of their disability, and struggling when asked to share the impact of their learning disability on their future careers (Hitchings et al., 2010). Career counseling in high school, college, and through adulthood is one intervention that may help those with learning disabilities understand the disability, identify career and life goals, and learn to advocate for reasonable accommodations in work and school environments.

Prognosis

Specific learning disorder is enduring and irreversible. However, individuals can learn to decrease the impact of the disorder on their academic and life activities by incorporating coping skills and requesting reasonable accommodations in work or school environments. Counselors have an important role to play in empowering clients with the resources and skills they need to manage this disorder.

DEVELOPMENTAL COORDINATION DISORDER

Description of the Disorder and Typical Client Characteristics

Developmental coordination disorder (DCD) is often referred to as dyspraxia or "clumsy child syndrome" (Sugden, Kirby, & Dunford, 2008, p. 174), due to the coordination difficulties demonstrated by those diagnosed with the disorder. Children diagnosed with DCD demonstrate motor skills that are below their chronological age and that interfere with their daily living activities. Children with this disorder exhibit difficulties in balance, manual (i.e., finger) dexterity, agility, and locomotion (i.e., the ability to move from one place to another). These difficulties can be seen in areas such as self-care activities (e.g., dressing or bathing), schoolwork (e.g., handwriting), and other leisure activities (e.g., riding a bike, throwing a baseball). For children who have an intellectual disability, these difficulties must be more pronounced than what is normally associated with the intellectual disability diagnosis, in order for them to warrant receiving this diagnosis. In addition, DCD cannot be diagnosed as a result of a general medical condition, such as cerebral palsy (Peters & Henderson, 2008). DCD is often co-occurring in clients diagnosed with ADHD, specific learning disorder, and autism spectrum disorder (Sugden et al., 2008).

Children diagnosed with DCD may struggle with low self-esteem, difficulty with social skills, lower academic performance, and adolescent behavioral issues (Smits-Engelsman et al., 2012) secondary to the frustrations associated with not fitting in socially, and because of struggles with the tasks of daily living. Because of their difficulties with balance and coordination, games and sports are more difficult for children with DCD, thus making it harder for them to fit in and socialize during recess or other playtimes. The manual coordination problems often associated with this disorder slow down handwriting speed, causing these children to need additional time with schoolwork. DCD is usually diagnosed in childhood.

Counselor Considerations

Counselors typically work with clients with DCD as a secondary provider, addressing symptoms that occur secondary to the disorder, but not addressing the disorder's treatment per se. Assessment for DCD involves examining the history of a child's development and is performed by specialty providers. When working with this population, counselors will need to refer clients to health care providers specially trained to treat the physical aspects of this disorder. These providers include physical, occupational, and speech therapists. Counselors' primary role will be to address the psychological issues with which this population may struggle.

When selecting counseling strategies for use with clients diagnosed with DCD, a counselor should consider the following: interventions should be appropriate for the client's developmental level (e.g., child or adult), goals should involve a focus on tasks that are important to the client (e.g., increased functioning in daily living tasks, developing social skills), and the activities should enhance the quality of a client's life (Sugden, Chambers, & Utley, 2006). Providing structure to counseling sessions may ease clients' anxiety as clients who are frustrated based on coordination or social difficulties may appreciate knowing what to expect in a counseling session. This structure relieves clients' anxiety about whether they will encounter an activity they are unable to perform.

When working with children, counselors should include family members in treatment. Counselors should view parents as the experts on their child and involve the child and their parents in goal collaboration (Sugden et al., 2008). Creating goals for daily living activities and social integration with peers is essential to positive outcomes for children with DCD. Counselors should encourage parents to perform physical activities with their children, as children with DCD tend to become frustrated with sporting-type activities. This frustration can even cause obesity in this population secondary to inactivity (Zhu, Wu, & Cairney, 2011). Praise and encouragement in a counseling setting are integral to empowering children with DCD.

Treatment Models and Interventions

When working with this population, counselors will need to provide a referral to a physical health provider who can treat the physical aspects of this disorder. Physical, occupational, and speech therapists are trained to meet the varying needs of this population, and their involvement will be required. Randomized controlled trials have demonstrated efficacy for several interventions. These include aquatic therapy (Hillier, McIntyre, & Plummer, 2010), diet and nutrition adjustments (e.g., omega-3 and omega-5 fatty acid supplements; Richardson & Montgomery, 2005), and motor skills interventions (Pless & Carlsson, 2000). Counselors will find their role involves counseling related to the psychological factors associated with the DCD diagnosis, such as anxiety, self-esteem struggles, or life dissatisfaction.

There are no medications commonly prescribed for the treatment of DCD. Most often, medications may be prescribed for other symptoms that may be co-occurring or exacerbated by the frustration associated with DCD, such as depression or anxiety.

SPECIFIC SKILLS APPROACH (SSA)   SSA is normally performed by a physical or occupational therapist. SSA is based on the concept that clients can improve motor skills through the use of learning and physiological control processes. With repetition of correctly performed skills, clients' bodies learn how to respond and move in a more functional manner. For SSA, clients must be active participants in their therapy, practice their exercises out of their medical sessions, and take the appropriate time to develop each skill individually (Pless & Carlsson, 2000). Counselors can help this population develop behavioral plans that will ensure their success in following through on practicing their exercises.

SENSORY INTEGRATION   Sensory integration is a technique typically employed by occupational therapists (Pollack, 2009). The technique focuses on neurological components that affect clients' abilities to carry out purposeful tasks or movements. Occupational therapists who use sensory integration techniques engage a child in playful activity. Trampolines, balls, swings, and equipment suspended from the ceiling are all a part of a sensory integration experience. Children are encouraged to explore the equipment prior to being guided through activities with the therapist. All activities create an intense tactile, vestibular, and proprioceptive response (e.g., textures and fabrics, sense of balance, and perceiving objects in relation to the body). An occupational therapist uses sensory integration to enhance functioning within the nervous system in order to plan for and execute a desired behavior. This technique can be tailored to meet clients' individual needs and challenges, and it is also used as an intervention for other disorders, such as autism spectrum disorder (Pollack, 2009).

COGNITIVE BEHAVIORAL THERAPY (CBT)   A CBT, problem-solving approach may be helpful when working with a child with DCD, especially as related to the secondary symptoms of anxiety, depression, and self-esteem and/or social struggles. An intervention called Cognitive Intervention to Daily Occupational Performance (CO-OP) is a cognitive and verbal plan made by the counselor with a client, which may help him or her in performing a motor task (Smits-Engelsman et al., 2012).

The main strategy of the CO-OP process is summed up in the phrase, "Goal, Plan, Do, Check." This phrase assists a counselor in educating a child to recall specific steps when a child desires to perform a task, such as moving a piece on a board game (Smits-Engelsman et al., 2012). First, clients visualize the task they want to perform; this becomes their goal. Second, they work with the counselor to plan how to execute their movement. Next, they attempt to perform the desired activity. Finally, the counselor and child reflect on what made the activity successful or unsuccessful (Sugden, 2007). This technique uses the benefit of structure and routine to assist a child in skill development. The goal is for the child to utilize this strategy outside the counseling setting. Learning a task such as moving a piece on a board game will develop motor skills as well as social skills. Children who have confidence in their ability to play a board game are more likely to ask a peer to play with them. This process can be repeated and used with a variety of tasks with the goal of slowly developing a child's abilities.

Prognosis

Historically, it was believed that for children with this disorder, motor skills would organically improve as a child developed. Current research does not reflect this belief. Children who do not work on developing fine and gross motor skills will likely continue to struggle with activities involving balance, movement, and coordination. Interventions focused on motor skill improvement create a more optimistic outcome for those diagnosed with DCD.

Clients who do not receive intervention for factors associated with DCD (e.g., anxiety, low satisfaction with life, motor skills) were shown in one study to have negative outcomes, which included higher rates of criminal behavior, substance abuse, and psychiatric disorders (Barnhart, Davenport, Epps, & Nordquist, 2003). Children who receive interventions based on their psychosocial and motor skill needs have a better opportunity for a positive prognosis.

STEREOTYPIC MOVEMENT DISORDER

Description of the Disorder and Typical Client Characteristics

Stereotypic movement disorder (SMD) involves prolonged repetitive, patterned, or rhythmic movements or behaviors. These behaviors are able to be suppressed by distraction or outside stimuli. In the general population, the prevalence of SMD is unknown; however, rates of SMD are higher in clients diagnosed with an intellectual disability and autism spectrum disorder (Sadock, Sadock, & Ruiz, 2011). Repetitive movements are common in young children, as well as in children who have an intellectual disability, are visually or hearing impaired, or are diagnosed on the autism spectrum disorder. SMD is distinguished from normal repetitive movements by its intensity, peculiarity, or prolonged repetition. With SMD, the behaviors interfere with daily living tasks and may involve self-injurious behaviors. Typical stereotypical movement behaviors include hand flapping, pacing, spinning, body rocking, and/or hair twirling (Freeman, Soltanifar, & Baer, 2010). These behaviors are thought to be self-soothing to clients who have SMD, and as such, the behavior is self-reinforcing.

Counselor Considerations

Counselors working with clients diagnosed with SMD should recognize that they often have comorbid disorders. Counselors should work to treat clients' comorbidities (e.g., autism spectrum disorder, tic disorders) in addition to their repetitive behaviors. Clients who exhibit self-injurious behaviors may present with scratches, cuts, or bruises. Self-injurious behavior is more common in SMD clients also diagnosed with severe intellectual disability (Carey, Crocker, Elias, Feldman, & Coleman, 2009), and these types of behaviors should be addressed in clients' treatment plans. The type of self-injury associated with SMD is best described as compulsive and repetitive, meaning clients are not deliberately thinking about engaging in the behavior.

Treatment Models and Interventions

Behavior therapy is the most widely used therapeutic intervention with clients who have SMD. Habit reversal training is one type of intervention counselors may use with clients with SMD (Miller, Singer, Bridges, & Waranch, 2006). The first step in habit reversal training is to make clients aware of their behavior by asking them to perform the specific behavior. This technique raises awareness for clients of the dynamics of the behavior. Counselors then ask clients to replace the original behavior with an alternate behavior. Examples of alternate behaviors include sitting on their hands, holding on to an object, or placing their hands in their pockets. Alternate behaviors should be adaptive and not cause additional problems (e.g., nail biting could create new problems) for clients. The final habit reversal training concept involves social support to assist clients in maintaining progress. Counselors and family members should positively reinforce and encourage clients as they progress and reduce SMD behaviors (Crosby, Dehlin, Mitchell, & Twohig, 2012).

For clients who have SMD and engage in self-injurious behaviors, physical activities that are not harmful may be beneficial in reducing injurious behaviors. Creating opportunities for physical expression that is not harmful to clients may reduce self-injurious behaviors. Behavioral alternative techniques for younger children might include pulling apart building blocks. For older children and adolescents, ripping paper or magazines may be successful interventions to decrease self-injury.

There are currently no medications approved to treat SMD. However, medications may help control some of the symptoms associated with SMD. For example, medications may help with agitation and anxiety as these symptoms may fuel the movements. There is evidence that certain selective serotonin reuptake inhibitors (SSRIs) have success in reducing stereotypic movements (First & Tasman, 2011).

Prognosis

Stereotypic movement disorder tends to be persistent over a lifetime and is most commonly found in clients with autism spectrum disorder and in those who have an intellectual disability (Barry, Baird, Lascelles, Bunton, & Hedderly, 2011). Behavioral interventions and medications may control some of the behaviors and seem to show the most success (Singer, 2011). The general prognosis for SMD depends on the success of treating underlying factors and comorbidities.

TIC DISORDERS

Description of the Disorders and Typical Client Characteristics

In the *DSM-5*, tic disorders include Tourette's disorder, persistent (chronic) motor or vocal tic disorder, provisional tic disorder, other specified tic disorder, and unspecified tic disorder. Tic disorders are characterized by the presence of chronic phonic (e.g., noises through the nose, throat, or mouth) and motor (e.g., body movement) tics. Chronic tic disorders can be found in approximately 1% of the population, with the majority diagnosed in childhood (Franklin, Best, Wilson, Loew, & Compton, 2011). Clients express a need to complete a tic in order to relieve an inner urge. These tics appear as rapid, sudden, recurrent movements or sounds (APA, 2013), and may cause substantial disruption to family, social, and occupational functioning. Tics may be simple (e.g., one movement or sound) or complex (e.g., multiple movements, words, or partial phrases), and studies have shown clients are able to control most tics with training (Shprecher & Kurlan, 2009).

motor = body

Tourette's disorder begins in childhood, affecting 3–6 children per 1,000 (Scahill, Sukhodolsky, Williams, & Leckman, 2005), and involves the inclusion of both motor and vocal tics, though they do not have to occur simultaneously. Tics occur repeatedly throughout the day and the *DSM-5* specifies that the person must experience them for longer than one year to qualify for a tic disorder diagnosis. In order for a client to be diagnosed with Tourette's, the onset has to occur prior to age 18 and cannot be due to a general medical condition or substance use. Tics normally present in children starting at age five and become worse by 12 years of age. However, by late adolescence, up to 80% of children diagnosed with Tourette's have noticed a decline in symptoms (Sukholdolsky et al., 2009).

Chronic motor or vocal tic disorder is characterized by physical or verbal tics that occur several times each day and last for a minimum of one year. Clients diagnosed with chronic motor or vocal tic disorder will not have the presence of both types of tics, as in Tourette's. Rather, they will only demonstrate one or the other type of tic. In order to receive a diagnosis of a motor or vocal tic disorder, the tics must not originate from a medical condition or substance use. Tics begin during childhood, generally from age three to age eight, and tend to decline in severity as children mature.

Clients diagnosed with provisional tic disorder also experience motor or vocal tics only, not a combination of the two; however, the experience of tics does not have to reach the minimum of one year, as in chronic motor or vocal tic disorder (Plessen, 2013). Clients diagnosed with other specified tic disorder or unspecified tic disorder experience tic symptoms, but do not meet the criteria for any other type of tic disorder (Plessen, 2013). This may include tics lasting less than four weeks, or tics initiating in clients over the age of 18 (Walkup, Ferrão, Leckman, Stein, & Singer, 2010).

Counselor Considerations

Counselors working with clients diagnosed with tic disorders should be sure to address the co-occurring symptoms associated with this population. Psychoeducation, relaxation training, and physical activity are suggested initial treatments for this population. If tics have not subsided after the use of psychosocial treatments, medications may be utilized to address symptoms (Metzger, Wanderer, & Roessner, 2012). Counselors should also plan to work with medical professionals to develop a comprehensive treatment plan that takes into account medical treatments and interventions that may help the client reach his or her goals.

Treatment Models and Interventions

Behavior therapy may be effective with children diagnosed with Tourette's disorder (Piacentini et al., 2010). With children, therapy may be more effective if parents are provided with an opportunity to be involved with treatment. Parent management training (discussed in detail in Chapter 12 in the oppositional defiant disorder and conduct disorder treatment section) has shown short-term improvements for children who exhibit disruptive behavior symptoms associated with this disorder (Scahill et al., 2006). Disruptive and angry outbursts may be common due to frustrations associated with continued tics. Anger control training has demonstrated positive results in at least one randomized

[handwritten margin notes: ABA to teach age appropriate social communication operant / BT = classical operant conditioning]

controlled study (Sukholdolsky et al., 2009). Most importantly, psychoeducation may assist in alleviating clients' and families' anxieties and frustration with the disorder.

BEHAVIOR THERAPY (BT) BT has shown positive results in reducing the frequency of tics (Harris & Wu, 2010; Piacentini et al., 2010). One method of behavior therapy includes rewarding clients for tic suppression and discouraging disruptive tics. This intervention involves a counselor practicing with the client until the client is fatigued from suppressing tic symptoms (Shprecher & Kurlan, 2009). For example, the client is asked to suppress tic behaviors for a certain time period, 10- or 20-second intervals. If the client completes the tic suppression successfully, the client receives a behavioral or material reward. This may be an opportunity to play a video game for five minutes, or to read a new magazine. As suppression grows more successful, the time periods increase in length. Eventually, the reward system will be removed in hopes that the client will continue suppression on their own. Counselors working from a behavior therapy framework believe tics are semivoluntary actions, and thus clients are able to control some of their tic responses (Himle, Woods, & Bunaciu, 2008).

Habit reversal training (HRT) is another type of behavioral intervention used to alleviate the occurrence of tics. HRT tends to be most beneficial for clients with severely disruptive tics (Shprecher & Kurlan, 2009). HRT involves a counselor using psychoeducation regarding tics, negative reinforcement of tics, tic awareness and response, and finally, relapse prevention (Franklin et al., 2011). In using this HRT approach, clients are first challenged to develop their awareness of tic responses (i.e., when do they occur, for how long do they occur, what are noticeable patterns, what warning signs do I experience). Warning signs are then discussed (e.g., "I smack my lips when I feel they're getting dry"). Clients then explore in more detail how they know the tic is going to occur, and associated behaviors and feelings are discussed. The client then tries to control or suppress the using strategies they have typically tried.

Next, counselors focus clients on creating a new response to the tic, which is referred to as competing response work. For example, clients who smack their lips may find it useful to press their lips together and hold for five seconds when they feel the urge to tic. Replacing one activity with another can assist them in becoming both aware and working to suppress or replace current tics. Finally, counselors should encourage continued support from parents in order to motivate clients' suppression of tics (Feldman, Storch, & Murphy, 2011).

COGNITIVE BEHAVIORAL THERAPY (CBT) Counselors using cognitive behavioral treatments view tics as either positively reinforcing (e.g., receiving support from others) or negatively reinforcing (e.g., tension release; O'Connor et al., 2009). Clients have shown benefit from psychoeducation, relaxation exercises, and restructuring of negative thoughts. Effective intervention strategies include encouraging clients to concentrate on one activity at a time, eliminating as many distractions as possible, positive thinking, and working to restructure negative schema (O'Connor et al., 2009). For example, a client may decide that saying three sentences in a public place (i.e., school or work) without tics is important. Encouraging clients to focus on what message they would like to convey and eliminating inner and outer distractions is important to reduce feelings of frustration. Clients should stop themselves from thinking negatively and ignore the body language of others in the room. Counselors may advise clients to reassure themselves that they will perform the task successfully. Clients will then focus on practicing conveying a message. Counselors continue verbal and nonverbal support through encouraging words and head nodding. After the message is given by clients, counselors work to reduce the negative self-talk clients experienced during the activity.

The use of cognitive restructuring techniques is one method of reducing disruptive behaviors in this population. Counselors educate clients on the use of positive imagery, muscle relaxation, and breathing techniques to calm themselves during situations where they feel they may get angry. Counselors may ask clients to recall situations when they acted aggressively, then use cognitive restructuring of negative or faulty schemas to assign new meaning to their feelings or behaviors. Additionally, counselors may role-play to determine a more positive course of action for the future, using newly formed schemas. Clients may be asked to practice these anger-reducing techniques at home and journal in a one-page log regarding their progress (Sukhodolsky et al., 2009). Journals may be reviewed in session to determine if negative schemas were successfully restructured.

PSYCHOPHARMACOTHERAPY Tic management can be controlled with antidepressants and/or tranquilizers (Scahill et al., 2006). Benzodiazepines (i.e. Clonazepam) have shown moderate effects in relieving tic symptoms (Shprecher & Kurlan, 2009). Additionally, antipsychotics such as haloperidol and risperidone are often prescribed to treat symptoms of Tourette's disorder and persistent tic disorder (Dion, Annable, Sandor, & Chouinard, 2002).

Prognosis

Most clients diagnosed with tic disorders see a significant improvement in the experience of tics by adolescence or early adulthood (Sprecher & Kurlan, 2009). The majority of tic disorders will become benign as children mature (Plessen, 2013).

DESCRIPTION OF THE NEUROCOGNITIVE DISORDERS

The *DSM-5* includes the following neurocognitive disorders: delirium, major and mild neurocognitive disorders (APA, 2013). According to the *DSM-5* (APA, 2013), delirium involves a disturbance in one's attention (i.e., difficulties staying focused, sustaining attention, and shifting attention and awareness to what is going on in one's environment). To receive the delirium diagnosis, there also has to be evidence that the disturbance is caused by a physiological consequence of substance intoxication/withdrawal, another medical condition, or exposure to a toxin. These disturbances typically develop over a short amount of time (an hour to a few days), and typically fluctuate in severity over time, or the course of a day. Delirium must also involve a disturbance in cognition (e.g., disorientation, language perception, memory deficits).

Major and mild neurocognitive disorders involve cognitive decline from a prior level of functioning and impact a client's attention, executive functioning, learning and memory, language, perceptual-motor, or social cognitions (APA, 2013). According to the *DSM-5* criteria, these deficits must interfere with independence in everyday activities. Neurocognitive disorders are progressive disorders that impact clients' neurocognitive abilities. Neurocognitive disorders often include symptoms such as loss of judgment, memory loss, coordination, recognition, and speech and language difficulties (Bharucha et al., 2009).

COUNSELOR CONSIDERATIONS

Because delirium has firmly founded physiological foundations and significantly impacts one's orientation, psychosocial approaches (e.g., talk therapies) are not an appropriate treatment; clients are unable to benefit from this because of their disorientation. Instead, a counselor's role is to accurately identify and assess the delirium and make a referral for medical intervention so that the cause of the delirium can be identified and medical intervention can occur. Clients with delirium can present in a wide array of settings, and all counselors must be prepared for a client to, at some point, present with this disorder. Regardless of the setting in which a counselor works, all counselors should be familiar with and have easy access to at least one assessment procedure that can be used in assessing for client delirium.

Because clients with delirium are, by definition, disoriented, they are at risk for harming themselves and possibly others. As such, immediate intervention and referral should occur. Clients with delirium will need immediate medical attention, and counselors should ensure the client is transitioned into a safe setting with medical professionals.

When working with clients with either delirium or major or mild neurocognitive disorders, family and caregiver involvement is important. In the case of delirium, support-ive others can help support the client as he or she reorients. When working with those with major or mild neurocognitive disorders, caregivers and family will be helpful in pro-viding the counselors with information about the clients' symptoms and in ensuring the work done in counseling is transferred into the clients' living environments.

During the early stages of cognitive decline, behavioral strategies (e.g., making lists) can help support clients as they adapt to increasing memory loss; learned strategies can help them manage the symptoms of the disorder. Activities that are physically, mentally, and socially stimulating may also slow the progression of neurocognitive disorders (Wierenga & Bondi, 2011). Reminiscence therapy is one example of a psychosocial treatment approach that may benefit clients. Counselors can also play an important role in connecting clients with community resources that can support their current and future needs (e.g., Meals on Wheels programs, senior center supports and resources, transportation services).

PROGNOSIS

Delirium has a much better prognosis than major and mild neurocognitive disorders. Early identification and treatment of delirium can stop it from developing, and most importantly, halt any potential long-term effects associated with the disorder. While there is no treatment for major or mild neurocognitive disorder, mentally, physically, and socially stimulating activities and medical and psychological intervention may be able to prolong their onset or progression. The ability to delay onset or progression will vary and depends on the etiology of the disorder, and its severity.

DELIRIUM

Description of the Disorder and Typical Client Characteristics

Delirium involves a disturbance in one's attention, consciousness, language, thought processes, visuospatial abilities, orientation (i.e., awareness of one's surroundings), and memory, all of which contribute to the client appearing confused. Additional accompanying factors may include disturbed sleep, hallucinations, and restlessness or agitation (Cerejeira & Mukaetova-Ladinska, 2011). When diagnosing delirium, the following specifiers can be coded: *substance intoxication delirium, substance withdrawal delirium, medication-induced delirium, delirium due to another medical condition,* or *delirium due to multiple etiologies.*

Delirium is known to co-occur as a symptom in major or mild neurocognitive disorders, with the neurocognitive disorders' etiologies causing the onset of delirium (Ganguli et al., 2011). Delirium includes changes in behavior, emotions, attention, and cognitions, and is frequently thought to only affect the elderly; however, clients of any age may experience delirium (Cerejeira & Mukaetova-Ladinska, 2011).

Delirium is most common in older adults and frequently occurs secondary to physical health conditions, medication use, and medical procedures. However, substance-induced delirium may occur in younger populations of clients with the symptoms being similar to those experienced by the older populations (Grover et al., 2012). Counselors may mistakenly associate delirium symptoms with stereotypical traits of older adult clients (e.g., forgetfulness, confusion, or fatigue). It is important that counselors monitor their stereotypes of older adults so as to avoid missing possible delirium symptoms.

Research suggests that 12–39% of cases of delirium are a result of the direct or indirect effects of a client's medication (Alexander, 2009). Changes in an aging body's abilities' to metabolize drugs and the occurrence of disease (e.g., cancer) make it more difficult for older adults to metabolize medications. Some medications have a greater probability of causing delirium. Additionally, many health conditions may cause a client to experience delirium, including cardiac failure, stroke, infection, dehydration, and metabolic difficulties (Fong, Tulebaev, & Inouye, 2009). Sleep deprivation, dehydration, visual or hearing impairment, immobility, and newly introduced medications are all considered risk factors for delirium. Counselors working in substance abuse settings, nursing home environments, or hospitals may encounter delirium more often than counselors working in other settings. Disrupted brain functioning secondary to medical procedures, or the use of multiple prescription medications, increases the probability that one will develop delirium (Cerejeira & Mukaetova-Ladinska, 2011).

Phillips (2012) identified three subtypes of delirium. The first, hyperactive delirium, is perhaps the easiest subtype for a counselor to identify. Clients with hyperactive delirium exhibit markedly extreme behaviors including agitation, restlessness, as well as hallucinations or delusions. The second subtype, hypoactive delirium, may be more difficult to detect in older adults. A client experiencing hypoactive delirium will seem particularly lethargic and appear tired or exhausted. Changes in a client's appetite or social functioning may signal the onset of hypoactive delirium. The final subtype, mixed delirium, includes a mix of both hyperactive and hypoactive subtypes. A fluctuation from restlessness to lethargy, or a combination of exhaustion and agitation, may occur for a client experiencing mixed delirium.

The course of the disorder depends on early recognition of the onset and contributing and sustaining factors. Early recognition improves the prognosis for clients. Removing contributing factors (e.g., medications), and/or implementing certain medications (e.g., haloperidol) may be beneficial in reducing the length and severity of delirium (Cerejeira & Mukaetova-Ladinska, 2011).

Counselors can expect a variety of accompanying symptoms for clients diagnosed with delirium. Anxiety, confusion, and agitation are common. Working with medical staff to understand specific concerns, needs, and prognosis may be beneficial to counselors working with this population (Goldberg et al., 2012).

Counselor Considerations

It is especially important that counselors are able to accurately assess for, and identify, delirium. Deliriums can be difficult to identify and may mask as other mental and physical health disorders. Interviews with family members, a review of a client's medical history, or simple neurocognitive tests can be used to find hints that a client may have delirium. It is important that counselors working with people who have delirium work collaboratively with medical professionals trained in treating neurological disorders.

As mentioned, early detection and accurate assessment of delirium is critically important. One assessment tool commonly used to screen for delirium is the Mini-Mental Status Exam (MMSE; Folstein, Folstein, & McHugh, 1975). The MMSE can be used as a preliminary screening tool to assess for both delirium and major or minor neurocognitive disorder, and this assessment is readily available on the Internet. The MMSE consists of 11 weighted questions which assess five distinct areas: language, recall, attention and calculation, orientation, and registration (Folstein et al., 1975). Questions and tasks include, "What year is it?", asking clients to spell a five letter word backwards (e.g., earth), asking clients to recall three objects after you say them and later recall them, and having clients copy a figure placed in front of them. The inability to correctly complete these tasks could suggest a delirium or a neurocognitive disorder. A client scoring 23 or less out of 30 points will benefit from further assessment.

Another assessment tool used to assess for delirium is the Confusion Assessment Method (CAM; Inouye et al., 1990). This 12-question assessment tool examines areas of inattention, disorganized thinking, and altered layers of consciousness. Clients do not answer the questions directly; rather, the questions are used as reflection items for counselors. One example of a CAM item includes, "Did the patient have difficulty focusing attention?" Currently the CAM is the most widely used instrument for delirium detection (Cerejeira & Mukaetova-Ladinska, 2011).

For counselors working in an inpatient or hospital setting, coordinating care with medical staff is important in altering the course of delirium. It is important that counselors recognize and address elevated cognitive difficulties, increased confusion, and/or anxiety. Counselors concerned that delirium may be present in a client receiving counseling in outpatient clinic settings should immediately notify their supervisor and the client's emergency contact listed on intake paperwork. Transportation to a medical facility for further treatment should be coordinated immediately, and for safety reasons, the client should not be allowed to leave the setting on his or her own.

Treatment Models and Interventions

Early identification of delirium symptoms provides a high probability for complete recovery. Generally, if an underlying symptom is recognized, it can be treated accordingly. Delirium is most often confused with acute psychosis or neurocognitive disorders. It can be difficult to diagnose because it often co-occurs with preexisting neurocognitive disorders (Lundstrom, Stenvall, & Oloffson, 2012), and it may be difficult to differentiate from normal developmental issues in older adults. Recovery may take longer for older adults, and if the originating symptom is left unrecognized, permanent brain damage may occur.

Because delirium has biological foundations, traditional talk therapy approaches are not an appropriate treatment. A counselor's role is to accurately identify and assess the delirium and make a referral for medical intervention. If a counselor suspects a client is experiencing delirium during a counseling session, frequent eye contact is important, as is speaking clearly and simply. If clients are agitated, relaxation exercises may be used to help relax the client (Fong et al., 2009). In severe cases, clients may need to be restrained so they do not harm themselves or someone else. Clients who experience delirium tremors, related to alcohol or substance withdrawal, should receive immediate medical attention. After a client has received medical attention, a counselor can assist the client in maintaining orientation to his or her environment.

maintain orientation to client's environment

Concerned family members often initiate the counseling process for this population. Family involvement is a key component for successful recognition of early symptoms as well as intervention. Clients who have delirium cannot be expected to follow through with their own treatment, and they need supportive people involved to ensure they will follow through. Educating family regarding the symptoms and the reversibility of delirium may assist in providing holistic care to the client. Family members can also be involved in monitoring the client's symptoms and alerting the counselor and other providers to developing symptoms such as mood swings, rambling speech, restlessness at night, a high fever, or difficulty concentrating. Addressing a plan for treatment that includes appropriate referrals and conveying the importance of medical intervention is important to ensuring a positive treatment outcome.

As mentioned earlier, delirium can be a direct result of the use of medications and substances. It is important to be aware of what medications the client is taking. Family and friends can be a good resource in determining what substances or medications the client is using. In addition, medications may be prescribed for the treatment of delirium itself.

Antipsychotics, such as haloperidol, may be prescribed to reduce the duration and severity of delirium symptomology (Fong et al., 2009). Antipsychotics are the most commonly prescribed medications for the treatment of delirium. Physicians may address certain symptoms of delirium with benzodiazepines, such as lorazepam (Fong et al., 2009). Generally, benzodiazepines will be prescribed following poor reactions to antipsychotic medications (Fong et al., 2009).

Prognosis

Early recognition and treatment can reverse the harmful short- and long-term effects of delirium. Delirium is associated with increased length of hospital stay, greater health care costs, necessitated institutional care, and higher rates of death (Mattoo, Grover, & Gupta, 2010). Prevention of many cases of delirium can occur if warning signs and risk factors are recognized and treated early (Mattoo et al., 2010).

NEUROCOGNITIVE DISORDERS: MAJOR OR MILD

Description of the Disorders and Typical Client Characteristics

Neurocognitive disorders are progressive disorders that impact clients' neurocognitive abilities. Neurocognitive disorders often include symptoms such as memory loss; loss of judgment, coordination, and recognition; and speech and language difficulties (Bharucha et al., 2009). Major and mild neurocognitive disorders are diagnosed separately and differ mainly in terms of their severity, with the major classification requiring evidence of significant cognitive decline, and mild requiring only modest declines. Additionally, to qualify for the major classification, one must have substantial impairments in cognitive performance and the impairments must interfere with one's independence in everyday living. With the mild classification, the cognitive deficits do not interfere with the client's independent living capacity.

There are many forms of neurocognitive disorder, all with various physiological root-causes. The distinction between a major or mild classification involves the progression of symptoms. A client experiencing subtle personality changes due to the onset of vascular or semantic neurocognitive disorder would be classified as having a mild neurocognitive disorder. As the disorder progresses and symptoms become more severe, the client's classification would change to major neurocognitive disorder (Jeste et al., 2010). Using the *DSM-5* counselors can specify with both major or mild neurocognitive disorder whether the disorder is due to Alzheimer's disease, frontotemporal lobar degeneration, Lewy body disease, vascular disease, traumatic brain injury, substance/medication use, HIV infection, prion disease, Parkinson's disease, Huntington's disease, another medical condition, multiple etiologies, or if its etiology is unspecified.

Vascular neurocognitive disorder is a common form of this disorder. Vascular neurocognitive disorder may occur after blood flow to the brain is stopped or slowed. Risk factors for developing vascular neurocognitive disorder include smoking cigarettes, obesity, and stroke (Korczyn, Vakhapova, & Grinberg, 2012), all of which decrease blood flow. This lack of blood flow to certain areas of the body decreases the amount of cells in that area, causing them to die. Loss of blood flow may cause memory loss, confusion, or difficulty with speech. Clients with vascular neurocognitive disorder often experience accompanying depression.

Clients diagnosed with neurocognitive disorders, including neurocognitive disorder with Lewy bodies and Alzheimer's disease, experience gradual loss of nerve cells, which are essential to healthy neurological functioning (Caputo et al., 2008). Neurocognitive disorder with Lewy bodies is differentiated by cognitive decline, accompanied by three additional factors. These factors include rigidity of the body (e.g., symptoms similar to Parkinson's disease), hallucinations, and changes in attention (e.g., staring off into space). Neurocognitive disorder with Lewy bodies is difficult to diagnose as it has symptoms similar to Alzheimer's disease.

Alzheimer's disease is the most common cause of neurocognitive disorder. Alzheimer's is a degenerative disease, with those afflicted generally progressing through three stages (i.e., early, moderate, and severe). In the early stages of Alzheimer's disease, symptoms are often missed because of stereotypical beliefs about the elderly population (e.g., forgetfulness is to be expected, older adults are often confused and lethargic). Clients may demonstrate irritation if they are unable to perform a task, show unwillingness or disinterest in trying new activities, or exhibit poor judgment. Other symptoms include increased apathy, forgetfulness, or showing less consideration for others' feelings. Many times, family members who initially attributed these factors to the normal aging process will be able in hindsight to attribute these symptoms to the early stages of a neurocognitive disorder.

As those with Alzheimer's disease progress to the moderate stage, their functioning decreases and the symptoms typically become more recognizable to others. Characteristics of moderate neurocognitive decline include extreme confusion, inappropriate behavior, and/or poor hygiene. Forgetfulness becomes more pronounced and potentially dangerous during this stage. For example, a burner on the stove may be left ignited or a client may become disoriented and get lost when running errands. A client may forget to eat or may have trouble remembering the faces of loved ones.

A client in the severe stage of Alzheimer's disease will need constant care. This stage is marked by severe impacts on functioning. Aggressive behaviors are frequently demonstrated, with 68–90% of residents in nursing facilities who have Alzheimer's disease expressing aggressive behavior (Australian Institute of Health and Welfare [AIHW], 2004). Clients at this stage are often unable to recognize family members, may lack control over bodily functions, and will require assistance with all activities of daily living. Additionally, difficulties with using or understanding speech may occur during this stage of the disease (State Government of Victoria, 2013).

Counselor Considerations

Clients in the early stages of a neurocognitive disorder may seek counseling in an outpatient mental health setting. In these sessions, counselors should reduce session distractions such as noises (e.g., phones ringing, background music); clients will benefit from a relaxing environment.

It is important that counselors encourage family members' or caregivers' involvement in clients' treatment. The degenerative nature of this disorder will require others' supportive involvement. In addition, caregivers may need to provide transportation, as it may be unsafe for these clients to drive. Family members can also be an excellent source of information and provide data on the clients' behaviors.

Planning for the future with clients diagnosed with a neurocognitive disorder is an integral component of treatment planning, and again, family involvement in these conversations is important. It is critical to examine clients' social networks and to identify supports that can assist them in their transition through the disorder.

Counselors should regularly assess for escalating symptoms associated with this disorder. Counselors might ask about meals and daily living activities while noting hygiene and confusion. Additionally, asking about escalated agitation and aggression, and whether they are experiencing more instances of forgetfulness, may provide insight into the progression of clients' cognitive decline. Dramatic changes in functioning should be relayed to caregivers and family members. Clients in later stages are likely to be seen in medical facilities or nursing home settings, and they have needs outside the scope of traditional talk therapy or outpatient counseling. Counselors must adapt to these changes and modify clients' treatment plans according to changing needs.

Treatment Models and Interventions

When counseling clients with a neurocognitive disorder, counselors must examine each client's unique needs. Providing clients with behavioral strategies (e.g., how to engage in social activities, maintaining a "log" or schedule for mealtimes/activities) during earlier stages of cognitive decline can help them manage the disorder. Focusing on sobriety maintenance with clients experiencing substance-induced neurocognitive disorder may also help slow the disorder's progression.

Physically, mentally, and socially stimulating activities may slow the progression of neurocognitive disorders (Wierenga & Bondi, 2011). Counselors can connect clients with resources related to social activities (e.g., senior centers), adult day care centers, in-home services, and community fitness centers. These resources should be discussed, and when possible, presented visually to assist in clients' cognitive processing.

Clients diagnosed with a major neurocognitive disorder may not benefit from traditional talk therapy secondary to the symptoms associated with the progression of the disorder. The client's degree of cognitive impairment and capacity to remember and apply session material will need to be considered when selecting interventions. Additionally, because of the nature of this disorder, there is no treatment per se; however, psychosocial approaches may help to manage symptoms, and medication may help to manage associated symptoms and slow the development of the disorder.

COGNITIVE BEHAVIORAL THERAPY (CBT)   The diagnosis of a neurocognitive disorder increases the risk of anxiety and depression for a client. CBT may help clients who have mild cognitive impairment (Gibson, 2010). Utilizing CBT, a counselor would assist clients in examining the relationship between their current thoughts and subsequent behaviors. After this examination, collaboration on the goal-setting process can occur. Working in the "here and now" to identify cognitions may be helpful with this population. Sessions can be tape recorded for a client to review at a later time, secondary to the memory impairment that occurs with this disorder.

Working from a CBT approach, homework assignments might include the application of relaxation techniques when clients have negative cognitions, or the tracking of daily activities or thoughts in a log. Maintaining and enhancing current levels of socialization may also be beneficial with regard to cognitive functioning. A counselor working with a client with a neurocognitive disorder must be aware of the impact of cognitive decline. A client expressing increased frustration or confusion may not benefit from continued talk therapy, such as CBT, which requires an intact memory (Gibson, 2010).

BEHAVIOR THERAPY (BT)   Counselors working from a BT approach will use interventions such as relaxation training (e.g., breathing techniques, imagery) to reduce clients' feelings of anxiety or agitation (Kraus et al., 2008). Using a BT approach, counselors will place an emphasis on having clients identify behavior patterns that impact mood or functioning. For example, clients can be asked to describe and document their mood on a scale from 1 to 10 to compare mood changes throughout the day as related to behavioral experiences, and thus recognize patterns. Another intervention that may decrease negative mood symptoms for clients with a neurocognitive disorder is to use pleasant event situations. Pleasant event situations involve a client identifying experiences and increasing their frequency so as to enhance their emotional state. For example, a client might identify that a quiet activity such as bird watching helps him or her to feel more relaxed when anxious. Some clients may prefer a more physical pleasant event such as going for a walk, or a more interactive event such as engaging in conversation with a friend. The integration of even 2–3 pleasant events a week for nursing home residents with a major neurocognitive disorder was shown to reduce depression and agitation in one study (Lichtenburg et al., 2005). Relatedly, behavioral activation therapy (which is discussed in more detail in Chapter 4), an approach that focuses on actively engaging in activities, has been utilized with this population and has been shown to decrease somatic symptomology and enhance a positive mood state (Kraus et al., 2008).

REMINISCENCE THERAPY   Clients may enjoy reliving memories such as stories or events from their lifetime, and this can have therapeutic value. This approach, reminiscence therapy, is often used with clients who have neurocognitive disorders (Woods, Spector, Jones, Orrell, & Davies, 2005). Using this approach, a counselor can ask clients or caregivers to bring in items representing clients' fond memories. These items may include photographs, family heirlooms, or other things that are important to the client. Clients can choose an item, hold it, and talk about their memories with a counselor. Clients may struggle to remember the importance of the item. Counselors should ask questions about the object itself, such as "What does it feel like?" or, "What other objects does it remind you of?"

Reminiscence therapy facilitates a number of benefits for clients with neurocognitive disorders. Clients are able to communicate and interact with others, evaluate their lives, and begin to prepare for death. Reminiscence therapy has been shown to increase self-esteem, enhance positive mood states, and improve communication skills for clients with neurocognitive disorders. Mental health providers using this intervention with clients have seen an increase in their self-worth, individuality, and identity (Dempsey et al., 2012). One randomized controlled study on the effects of cognitive stimulation techniques, such as reminiscence therapy, demonstrated significant improvement in cognitions and quality of life. This intervention is both cost-effective and beneficial for clients with neurocognitive disorders (Aguirre et al., 2010).

CREATIVE TOOLBOX 13.2   Memory Basket

Meredith Rausch, MS

Activity Overview

This reminiscence therapy activity involves clients gathering together items and mementos that carry personal meaning and/or emotion, and reviewing them with friends, family, or the counselor.

Treatment Goal(s) of Activity

The primary goal of the memory basket activity is to reduce anxiety and depressive symptoms in clients with a mild or major neurocognitive disorder. A secondary goal is to increase clients' communication and build interpersonal relationships. Reminiscence serves to increase communication and enhance interpersonal relationships; assist clients in dealing with grief, loss, and depression; and support life review and reintegration of important events.

Directions

Clients are invited to gather together items and mementos that carry personal meaning and/or emotion. Items can be photographs, trinkets, family heirlooms, music, and/or other household or familiar items. Once or twice a week, the collection is brought out for conversation with friends, family, or a counselor. Clients select items and discuss the memory or importance of each item. Family or caregiver assistance may be required for this activity. Asking family members or caregivers to bring in items that are familiar or memorable to the client will assist in the creation of the memory basket. Placing the items in the basket and allowing the client to choose each item to discuss is an important aspect of this activity. Counselors should encourage discussion about the memories associated with each item and ask questions about texture, smell, colors, or sounds of the item if the client struggles to remember the item's importance.

Process Questions

1. What do you remember about this item?
2. Where do you normally keep it in your home?
3. Who gave this to you?
4. What emotion comes to mind when you hold this?
5. What does that item feel like? Is it . . . (e.g., heavy, light, soft, hard)?
6. Would you like to tell a friend about this item?

FAMILY/CAREGIVER INVOLVEMENT   Whatever approach to treatment is used, a focus on families and caregivers is important when working with clients who have neurocognitive disorders. Providing psychoeducation and addressing issues relative to caregiving, such as guilt, depression, and frustrations, are necessary to assist family members through the caregiving process. In high-conflict families, involving an outside caregiver or visiting nurse instead of family members may be a better choice (Robinson et al., 2011). It is also helpful to involve caregivers in any treatment interventions that are used with the client. For example, if behavior therapy skills such as memory techniques are taught to clients, soliciting a caregiver in the application of this technique may ensure greater success.

Clients diagnosed with a neurocognitive disorder will eventually need to have family members perform decision-making tasks for their benefit. When counseling this population, it is important to work with clients to convey and communicate their wishes for their future. Creating a detailed plan with a client prior to worsening cognitive symptoms can allow them to think through the process. Considerations such as, "Which family member(s) would I like to make decisions for me?" as well as, "If a certain situation occurs, what would I like to have decided?" are important. Planning ahead with clients provides them with a feeling of control over their future and facilitates discussions with family members during this transitional time (Elliott, Gessert, & Peden-McAlpine, 2009).

Because of the increased need for assistance from family members, caregivers are likely to feel fatigued and need respite, thus supports may need to be provided for them; healthy caregivers are best able to support the client and his or her treatment goals. Counselors can provide information on community peer support groups. Providing families with a list of reliable and valid websites can assist them in understanding neurocognitive disorders (Cook, Cook, & Hutchinson, 2012). Websites including basic educational information, personal stories from patients, and links to service providers, may be of additional comfort and assistance to family members and caregivers.

PSYCHOPHARMACOTHERAPY   Medication can be an important method of treatment for clients with neurocognitive disorders (Gibson, 2010). Anticonvulsant, antidepressant, antipsychotic, and benzodiazepine prescriptions are frequently utilized to treat symptoms associated with neurocognitive disorders. Medication should be monitored by a physician for clients living at home and may need to be administered by a caregiver to monitor and regulate efficacy (Rhee, Csernansky, Emanuel, Chang, & Shega, 2011).

Cholinesterase inhibitors such as donepezil (e.g., Aricept), rivastigmine (e.g., Excelon), memantine (e.g., Namenda), and galantamine (e.g., Razadyne) have contributed to increases in functioning and cognitive improvements for some people with this disorder. However, those who take these medications still experience symptom escalations, and eventual decline as the disorder progresses.

Prognosis

Clients participating in mentally, physically, and socially stimulating activities may be able to prolong the onset or progression of a neurocognitive disorder (Luppa, Luck, Brahler, Konig, & Riedel-Heller, 2008). The ability to delay onset or progression varies individually.

Within the first year of a neurocognitive disorder diagnosis, 20% of patients are institutionalized. After five years, the number rises to 50%; after eight years, 90% of patients will need secure care (Luppa et al., 2008). Many times, the increasing need for intensive care for this population creates a great deal of stress on their at-home caregiver. Initially, many clients receive care from a family member; however, the majority of clients are transferred to a nursing home or other care facility to accommodate the growing needs associated with escalating cognitive decline. Progression may be slowed, but cognitive decline is inevitable. Pneumonia and heart disease are the leading causes of death in those with neurocognitive disorder, possibly a reflection of lack of proper feeding and self-management of care during later stages of cognitive decline (Brunnstrom & Englund, 2009).

TREATMENT PLAN FOR MELINDA

The beginning of this chapter introduced readers to Melinda, a 27-year-old Caucasian female who struggles with adult ADHD symptoms, as well as anxiety secondary to starting graduate school and juggling multiple responsibilities. In order to provide Melinda with appropriate evidence-based treatment, an effective counselor must consider multiple factors. The following I CAN START acronym, listed below, provides a conceptual framework and outlines treatment considerations that may be helpful in treating Melinda's presenting symptoms.

C = Contextual Assessment

Melinda has a cultural value of hard work. She feels life is tougher for females, but she is determined to "show everyone" she can "do it." Both her mother and father have bachelor's degrees; she feels confident in her ability to earn her graduate degree. Melinda's parents are married and she has a healthy sense of attachment to others. Developmentally, she is attempting to complete graduate school so she can begin to settle into a stable career. She lived with her parents or lived at college until she was 25, and at 27, she is developing the life skills associated with independent living. More recently, she began graduate school and is struggling to manage going to school full-time while working. She reports that she is a sporadically practicing Lutheran (attends church services 1–2 times per month—if she wakes up on time), but despite her difficulties in attending church, she reports clear and solid spiritual and religious beliefs.

A = Assessment and Diagnosis

Diagnosis = Attention-Deficit/Hyperactivity Disorder (Combined Type) 314.01 (F90.2);

Adjustment Disorder with anxious features 309.24 (F43.22).

The Conner's Adult ADHD Rating Scales (CAARS; Conners, 1998) will be used to substantiate that Melinda meets the criteria required to be diagnosed with ADHD.

N = Necessary Level of Care

Outpatient, individual counseling (once per week)

Outpatient, group counseling (time management; once per week)

S = Strength-Based Lens

Self: Melinda is vivacious and energetic. She has multiple outside interests and enjoys being creative, learning, and interacting with others. Melinda is insightful and resourceful and has tried several methods to improve her organizational skills and memory. She continues to be relatively successful and function at a high level despite her struggles and frustrations.

Family: Melinda sees family 2–3 times per month and lives in the same community as her parents. She speaks with her older sister on the phone 1–2 times per week and enjoys having dinner with her sister a few times each month. Her family members are willing to support her in her efforts to create change, and they are positive social supports.

Community: Melinda has several friends, though none she would consider her "best" friend. She enjoys attending church, although her attendance is sporadic. She reports that she knows and trusts a number of people at her church. She participates in a study group at school and enjoys her coworkers. She is not currently dating, but would enjoy entering into another relationship at the right time.

T = Treatment Approach

Cognitive Behavioral Therapy (CBT)

A = Aim and Objectives of Treatment (6-month objectives)

Melinda will learn organization skills and strategies she can use to help her be successful in paying her bills on time, and in preventing the loss of important items →

- *Melinda will pay her monthly bills on time.* To help her with this she will:
  - Organize a spot in her apartment for paying and organizing bills and paying them on time.
  - List bills on a monthly spreadsheet and check them off as she pays them.
  - Save her bills and receipts in a crate in a specified location.
  - Begin to explore automatic electronic bill payment.
  - Solicit her parents' and sister's help in developing additional strategies to help her be successful at this task.

- *Melinda will learn and use organizational skills to help prevent her from losing her items.* To help her with this she will:
  - Develop an organizational system that helps her locate her important items.
  - Identify a set place where she will keep her phone, her car keys, and her license and credit card.
  - Place these items back in the identified places 90% of the time.
  - Learn and practice self-mediating skills.

Melinda will learn time management skills that can help her declutter her schedule and complete school projects →
- *Melinda will declutter her schedule.* To help her with this she will:
  - Learn basic time management skills and apply these successfully, demonstrated by removing two unnecessary activities from her schedule so that she will have more time to focus on being organized and successful.
- *Melinda will punctually complete all school projects.* To help her with this she will:
  - Learn basic time management skills and apply these successfully, demonstrated by listing all major projects on a spreadsheet and checking them off as they are completed. Melinda will reward herself for all completed projects with a movie night with her sister each weekend.

Melinda will increase her sense of self-efficacy → Melinda will replace negative schemas with positive schemas and will attempt to use positive self-talk, especially as related to her ADHD symptoms, 75% of the time.

Melinda will increase her anxiety-management skills → Melinda will practice her relaxation and meditation skills at least 2 times per day for 5 minutes.

Melinda will increase her attentiveness skills → Melinda will apply mindfulness skills at least 1 time per day for 5 minutes. Melinda will learn and practice attention-building exercises, and she will apply these when talking with her family members, coworkers, and peers at least 3 times per week.

R = Research-Based Interventions *(based on CBT)*

Counselor will utilize cognitive restructuring techniques with Melinda.

Counselor will assign appropriate homework assignments and review strategies and progress of each assignment with Melinda.

Counselor will assist Melinda in the development and application of the following skills:
- Mindfulness and attentiveness
- Self-efficacy and positive schemas
- Behavioral self-mediating/regulation skills

T = Therapeutic Support Services

Referral to a psychiatrist for consultation regarding ADHD medication

Participation in a campus time management counseling group

Weekly individual counseling

References

Aguirre, E., Spector, A., Hoe, J., Russell, I. T., Knapp, M., Woods, R. T., . . . Orrell, M. (2010). Maintenance cognitive stimulation therapy (CST) for dementia: A single-blind, multi centre, randomized control trial of maintenance CST vs. CST for dementia. *Trials, 11*(46).

Alexander, E. (2009). Delirium in the intensive care unit: Medications as risk factors. *Critical Care Nurse, 29*, 85–87.

American Psychiatric Association (APA). (2013). *Diagnostic and statistical manual of mental disorders* (5th ed.). Washington: Author.

Australian Institute of Health and Welfare (AIHW). (2004). *The impact of dementia on the health and aged care systems.* AIHW Cat. No. Age 37, AIHW, Canberra.

Bailey, R. K., & Owens, D. L. (2005). Overcoming challenges in the diagnosis and treatment of Attention-Deficit/Hyperactivity Disorder in African Americans. *Journal of the National Medical Association, 97,* S5–S10.

Barnhart, R. C., Davenport, M. J., Epps, S. B., & Nordquist, V. M. (2003). Developmental coordination disorder. *Physical Therapy, 83,* 722–731.

Barry, S., Baird, G., Lascelles, K., Bunton, B., & Hedderly, T. (2011). Neurodevelopmental movement disorders—an update on childhood motor stereotypes. *Developmental Medicine and Child Neurology, 53,* 979–985.

Beilby, J. M., Byrnes, M. L., & Yaruss, J. S. (2012). Acceptance and commitment therapy for adults who stutter: Psychosocial adjustment and speech fluency. *Journal of Fluency Disorders, 37,* 289–299.

Bharucha, A., Anand, V., Forlizzi, J., Dew, M. A., Reynolds, C. F., Stevens, S., . . . Wactlar, H. (2009). Intelligent assistive technology applications to dementia care: Current capabilities, limitations, and future challenges. *American Journal of Geriatric Psychiatry, 17,* 88–104.

Biederman J., Mick, E., Faraone, S. V., Braaten, E., Doyle, A., Spencer, T., . . . Johnson, M. A. (2002). Influence of gender on attention deficit hyperactivity disorder in children referred to a psychiatric clinic. *American Journal of Psychiatry, 159,* 36–42.

Boutot, E., & Hume, K. (2012). Beyond time out and table time: Today's applied behavior analysis for students with autism. *Education and Training in Autism and Developmental Disabilities, 47,* 23–38.

Brunnstrom, H. R., & Englund, E. M. (2009). Cause of death in patients with dementia disorders. *European Journal of Neurology, 16,* 488–492.

Caputo, M., Monastero, R., Mariani, E., Santucci, A., Mangialasche, F., Camarda, R., . . . Mecocci, P. (2008). Neuropsychiatric symptoms in 921 elderly subjects with dementia: A comparison between vascular and neurodegenerative types. *Acta Psychiatrica Scandinavica, 117,* 455–464.

Carey, W. B., Crocker, A. C., Elias, E. R., Feldman, H. M., & Coleman, W. L. (2009). *Developmental-behavioral pediatrics: Expert consult-online and print.* Philadelphia, PA: Saunders Elsevier.

Casenhiser, D. M., Shanker, S. G., & Stieben, J. (2013). Learning through interaction in children with autism: Preliminary data from a social-communication-based intervention. *Autism, 17*(2), 220–241.

Centers for Disease Control and Prevention (CDC). (2012a). *Vaccine safety: Concerns about autism.* Retrieved March 18, 2013 from: http://www.cdc.gov/vaccinesafety/concerns/autism/index.html

Centers for Disease Control and Prevention (CDC). (2012b). *Prevalence of Autism Spectrum Disorders—Autism and Developmental Disabilities Monitoring Network, 14 Sites, United States, 2008.* MMWR 2012; 61(SS03): 1–19. Retrieved March 18, 2013 from: http://www.cdc.gov/mmwr/preview/mmwrhtml/ss6103a1.htm?s_cid=ss6103a1_w

Centers for Disease Control and Prevention (CDC). (2013). *Autism spectrum disorders (ASDs).* Retrieved from: http://www.cdc.gov/ncbddd/autism/treatment.html

Cerejeira, J., & Mukaetova-Ladinska, E. B. (2011). A clinical update on delirium: From early recognition to effective management. *Nursing Research and Practice, 875196.* doi: 10.1155/2011/875196

Conners, C. K. (1998). Rating scales in attention-deficit/hyperactivity disorder: Use in assessment and treatment monitoring. *Journal of Clinical Psychiatry, 59,* 24–30.

Cook, M., Cook, G., & Hutchinson, F. (2012). How to use Web-based information to support people with dementia. *Nursing Older People, 24,* 14–20.

Crosby, J. M., Dehlin, J. P., Mitchell, P. R., & Twohig, M. P. (2012). Acceptance and commitment therapy and habit reversal training for the treatment of trichotillomania. *Cognitive and Behavioral Practice, 19,* 595–605.

Deb, S., & Unwin, G. L. (2007). Psychotropic medication for behaviour problems in people with intellectual disability: A review of the current literature. *Current Opinion in Psychiatry, 20,* 461–466.

Dempsey, L., Murphy, K., Cooney, A., Casey, D., O'Shea, E., Devane, D., . . . Hunter, A. (2012). Reminiscence in dementia: A concept analysis. *Dementia.* Advance online publication.

Dion, Y., Annable, L., Sandor, P., & Chouinard, G. (2002). Risperidone in the treatment of Tourette syndrome: A double-blind, placebo-controlled trial. *Journal of Clinical Psychopharmacology, 22,* 31–39.

Eldevik, S., Hastings, R. P., Hughes, J. C., Jahr, E., Eikeseth, S., & Cross, S. (2009). *Journal of Clinical Child & Adolescent Psychology, 38*, 439–450.

Elliott, B. A., Gessert, C. E., & Peden-McAlpine, C. (2009). Family decision-making in advanced dementia: Narrative and ethics. *Scandanavian Journal of Caring Sciences, 23*, 251–258.

Emilsson, B., Gudjonsson, G., Sigurdsson, J. F., Baldursson, G., Einarsson, E., Olafsdottir, H., . . . Young, S. (2011). Cognitive behaviour therapy in medication-treated adults with ADHD and persistent symptoms: A randomized controlled trial. *BioMed Central Psychiatry, 11*, 1–10.

Feldman, M. A., Storch, E. A., & Murphy, T. K. (2011). Application of habit reversal training for the treatment of tics in early childhood. *Clinical Case Studies, 10*, 173–183.

First, M. B., & Tasman, A. (2011). *Clinical guide to the diagnosis and treatment of mental disorders* (2nd ed.). West Sussex, UK: John Wiley & Sons.

Folstein, M. F., Folstein, S. E., & McHugh, P. R. (1975). "Mini-mental state." A practical method for grading the cognitive state of patients for the clinician. *Journal of Psychiatric Research, 12*, 189–198.

Fong, T. G., Tulebaev, S. R., & Inouye, S. K. (2009). Delirium in elderly patients: Diagnosis, prevention and treatment. *Nature Reviews Neurology, 5*, 210–220.

Franklin, M. E., Best, S. H., Wilson, M. A., Loew, B., & Compton, S. N. (2011). Habit reversal training and acceptance and commitment therapy for Tourette Syndrome: A pilot project. *Journal of Developmental and Physical Disabilities, 23*, 43–60.

Freeman, R. D., Soltanifar, A., & Baer, S. (2010). Stereotypic movement disorder: Easily missed. *Developmental Medicine & Child Neurology, 52*(8), 733–738.

Ganguli, M., Blacker, D., Blazer, D. G., Grant, I., Jeste, D. V., Paulson, J. S., . . . Sachdev, P. S. (2011). Classification of neurocognitive disorders in DSM-5: A work in progress. *American Journal of Geriatric Psychiatry, 19*, 205–210.

Gibson, J. (2010). Cognitive behaviour therapy and the person with dementia. *Mental Health Practice, 14*, 20–23.

Goldberg, S. E., Whittamore, K. H., Harwood, R. H., Bradshaw, L. E., Gladman, J. R. F., & Jones, K. G. (2012). The prevalence of mental health problems among older adults admitted as an emergency to a general hospital. *Age & Ageing, 41*, 80–86.

Greenspan, S. I., & Wieder, S. (2009). *Engaging autism: Using the floortime approach to help children relate, communicate, and think*. Philadelphia, PA: Da Capo Press.

Grover, S., Kate, N., Malhotra, S., Chakrabarti, S., Mattoo, S. K., & Avasthi, A. (2012). Symptom profile of delirium in children and adolescent—does it differ from adults and elderly? *General Hospital Psychiatry, 34*, 626–632.

Harris, E., & Wu, S. W. (2010). Children with tic disorders: How to match treatment with symptoms. *Current Psychiatry, 9*, 29–36.

Hebebrand J., Dempfle, A., Saar, K., Thiele, H., Herpertz-Dahlmann, B., Linder, M., . . . Konrad, K. (2006). A genome-wide scan for attention-deficit/hyperactivity disorder in 155 German sib-pairs. *Molecular Psychiatry, 11*, 196–205.

Hillier, S., McIntyre, A., & Plummer, L. (2010). Aquatic physical therapy for children with developmental coordination disorder: A pilot randomized controlled trial. *Physical & Occupational Therapy in Pediatrics, 30*, 111–124.

Himle, M. B., Woods, D. W., & Bunaciu, L. (2008). Evaluating the role of contingency in differentially reinforced tic suppression. *Journal of Applied Behavior Analysis, 41*, 285–289.

Hitchings, W. E., Johnson, K. K., Luzzo, D. A., Retish, P., Hinz, C., & Hake, J. (2010). Identifying the career development needs of community college student with and without learning disabilities. *Journal of Applied Research in the Community College, 18*, 22–29.

Inouye, S. K., van Dyck, C. H., Alessi, C. A., Balkin, S., Siegal, A. P., & Horwitz, R. I. (1990). Clarifying confusion: The confusion assessment method. A new method for detection of delirium. *Annals of Internal Medicine, 113*, 941–948.

Jeste, D., Blacker, D., Blazer, D., Ganguli, M., Grant, I., Paulsen, J., . . . Sachdev, P. (2010). Neurocognitive disorders: A proposal from the DSM-5 neurocognitive disorders work group. *American Psychiatric Association, 1*–17.

Koegel, R. L., & Koegel, L. K. (2006). *Pivotal response treatment for autism: Communication, social, & academic development*. Baltimore, MD: Paul H. Brookes Publishing.

Kooij, J. J. S. (2013). Adult ADHD: *Diagnostic assessment and treatment* (3rd ed.). London, England: Springer-Verlag.

Korczyn, A. D., Vakhapova, V., & Grinberg, L. T. (2012). Vascular dementia. *Journal of the Neurological Sciences, 322*(1/2), 17–19.

Kraus, C. A., Seignourel, P., Balasubramanyam, V., Snow, A. L., Wilson, N. L., Kunik, M. E., . . . Stanley, M. A. (2008). Cognitive-behavioral treatment for anxiety in patients with dementia. *Journal of Psychiatric Practice, 14*, 186–192.

Leahy, M. M., O'Dwyer, M., & Ryan, F. (2012). Witnessing stories: Definitional ceremonies in narrative therapy with adults who stutter. *Journal of Fluency Disorders, 37*, 234–241.

Leichtentritt, J., & Shechtman, Z. (2010). Children with and without learning disabilities: A comparison of processes and outcomes following group counseling. *Journal of Learning Disabilities, 43*, 169–179.

Lichtenburg, P. A., Kemp-Havican, J., MacNeill, S. E., & Johnson, A. S. (2005). Pilot study of behavioral treatment in dementia care units. *The Gerontologist, 45*(3), 406–410.

Lofthouse, N. L., Arnold, L. E., Hersch, S., Hurt, E., & DeBeus, R. (2011). A review of neurofeedback treatment for pediatric ADHD. *Journal of Attention Disorders, 16*, 351–372.

Lovaas, O. I. (1987). Behavioral treatment and normal educational and intellectual functioning in young autistic children. *Journal of Consulting and Clinical Psychology, 55*, 3–9.

Lundstrom, M., Stenvall, M., & Oloffson, B. (2012). Symptom profile of postoperative delirium in patients with and without dementia. *Journal of Geriatric Psychiatry & Neurology, 25*, 162–169.

Luppa, M., Luck, T., Brahler, E., Konig, H. H., & Riedel-Heller, S. G. (2008). Prediction of institutionalization in dementia. A systematic review. *Dementia and Geriatric Cognitive Disorders, 29*, 164–175.

Martin, P. C. (2012). Misuse of high-stakes test scores for evaluative purposes: Neglecting the reality of schools and students. *Current Issues in Education, 15*, 1–11.

Matson, J. L., Turygin, N. C., Beighley, J., Rieske, R., Tureck, K., & Matson, M. L. (2012b). Applied Behavior Analysis in Autism Spectrum Disorders: Recent developments, strengths, and pitfalls. *Research in Autism Spectrum Disorders, 6*, 144–150.

Mattoo, S. K., Grover, S., & Gupta, N. (2010). Delirium in general practice. *Indian Journal of Medical Research, 131*, 387–398.

Menzies, R. G., O'Brian, S., Onslow, M., Packman, A., St Clare, T., & Block., S. (2008). An experimental clinical trial of a cognitive-behavior therapy package for chronic stuttering. *Journal of Speech, Language, and Hearing Research, 51*, 1451–1464.

Menzies, R. G., Onslow, M., Packman, A., & O'Brian, S. (2009). Cognitive behavior therapy for adults who stutter: A tutorial for speech-language pathologists. *Journal of Fluency Disorders, 34*, 187–200.

Mesibov, G. B., Shea, V., & Schopler, E. (2004). *The TEACCH approach to Autism Spectrum Disorders: Issues in clinical child psychology*. New York, NY: Springer.

Metzger, H., Wanderer, S., & Roessner, V. (2012). Tic disorders. In J. M. Ray (Ed.), *IACAPAP e-textbook of child and adolescent mental health*. Geneva, Switzerland: International Association for Child and Adolescent Psychiatry and Allied Professions.

Mick E., & Faraone, S.V. (2008). Genetics of attention deficit hyperactivity disorder. *Child and Adolescent Psychiatry, 17*, 261–284.

Miller, J. M., Singer, H. S., Bridges, D. D., & Waranch, H. R. (2006). Behavioral therapy for treatment of stereotypic movements in nonautistic children. *Journal of Child Neurology, 21*, 119–125.

Mishna, F., Muskat, B., & Wiener, J. (2010). "I'm not lazy; it's just that I learn differently": Development and implementation of a manualized school-based group for students with learning disabilities. *Social Works with Groups, 33*, 139–159.

O'Connor, K. P., Laverdure, A., Taillon, A., Stip, E., Borgeat, F., & Lavoie, M. (2009). Cognitive behavioral management of Tourette's syndrome and chronic tic disorder in medicated and unmedicated samples. *Behaviour Research and Therapy, 47*, 1090–1095.

Pajareya, L., & Nopmaneejumruslers, K. (2011). A pilot randomized controlled trial of DIR/Floortime™ parent training intervention for pre-school children with autistic spectrum disorders. *Autism, 15*, 1–15.

Panerai, S., Ferrante, L., & Zingale, M. (2002). Benefits of the TEACCH programme as compared with a non-specific approach. *Journal of Intellectual Disability Research, 46*, 318–327.

Paykina, N., Greenhill, L. I., & Gorman, J., M. (2007). Pharmacological treatments for attention-deficit/hyperactive disorder. In P. E. Nathan & J. M. Gorman (Eds.), *A guide to treatments that work* (pp. 20–70) New York, NY: Oxford.

Peters, J. M., & Henderson, S. E. (2008). Understanding coordination disorder (DCD) and its impact on families: The contribution of single case studies. *International Journal of Disability, Development and Education, 55*, 97–111.

Phillips, L. A. (2012). Delirium in geriatric patients: Identification and prevention. *MEDSURG Nursing, 22*, 9–12.

Piacentini, J., Woods, D. W., Scahill, L., Wilhelm, S., Peterson, A. L., Chang, S., . . . Walkup, J. T. (2010). Behavior therapy for children with Tourette Disorder: A randomized controlled trial. *JAMA: The Journal of the American Medical Association, 303*, 1929–1937.

Pless, M., & Carlsson, M. (2000). Effects of motor skill intervention on developmental coordination disorder: A meta-analysis. *Adapted Physical Activity Quarterly, 17*, 381–401.

Plessen, K. (2013). Tic disorders and Tourette's syndrome. *European Child & Adolescent Psychiatry, 22*, 55–60.

Pollack, N. (2009). Sensory integration: A review of the current state of the evidence. *Occupational Therapy Now, 11*(5), 6–10.

Pullin, D. (2005). When one size does not fit all—the special challenges of accountability testing for students with disabilities. *Yearbook of the National Society for the Study of Education, 104*, 199–222.

Reichow, B., Barton, E. E., Boyd, B. A., & Hume, K. (2012). Early intensive behavioral intervention (EIBI) for young children with autism spectrum disorders (ASD). *Cochrane Database of Systematic Reviews, 10*.

Rhee, Y., Csernansky, J. G., Emanuel, L. L., Chang, C., & Shega, J. W. (2011). Psychotropic medication burden and factors associated with antipsychotic use: An analysis of a population-based sample of community-dwelling older persons with dementia. *Journal of the American Geriatrics Society, 59,* 2100–2107.

Richardson, A. J., & Montgomery, P. (2005). The Oxford-Durham study: A randomized, controlled trial of dietary supplementation with fatty acids in children with developmental coordination disorder. *Pediatrics, 115,* 1360–1366.

Robinson, C. M., Paukert, A., Kraus-Schuman, C. A., Snow, A. L., Kunik, M. E., Wilson, N. L., . . . Stanley, M. A. (2011). The involvement of multiple caregivers in cognitive-behavior therapy for anxiety in persons with dementia. *Aging and Mental Health, 15,* 291–298.

Rogers, S. J., & Dawson, G. (2009). *Play and engagement in early Autism: The Early Start Denver Model. Volume I: The treatment.* New York, NY: Guilford.

Roid, G. H. (2003). *Stanford-Binet Intelligence Scales, Fifth Edition: Technical manual.* Itasca, IL: Riverside.

Sadock, B. J., Sadock, V. A., & Ruiz, P. (2011). *Kaplan and Sadock's study guide and self-examination review in psychiatry* (9th ed.). Philadelphia, PA: Lippincott, Williams, & Wilkins.

Scahill, L., Erenberg, G., Berlin, C. M., Budman, C., Coffey, B. J., Jankovic, J., . . . Walkup, J. (2006). Contemporary assessment and pharmacotherapy of Tourette syndrome. *NeuroRx, 3,* 192–206.

Scahill, L., Sukhodolsky, D. G., Williams, S. K., & Leckman, J. F. (2005). Public health significance of tic disorders in children and adolescents. *Advanced Neurology, 96,* 240–248.

Shprecher, D., & Kurlan, R. (2009). The management of tics. *Movement Disorders, 1,* 15–24.

Singer, H. S. (2011). Stereotypic movement disorders. *Handbook of Clinical Neurology, 100,* 631–639.

Smits-Engelsman, B. C., Blank, R., van der Kaay, A. C., Mosterd-van der Meijs, R., Vlugt-van den Brand, E., Polatajko, H. J., . . . Wilson, P. H. (2012). Efficacy of interventions to improve motor performance in children with developmental coordination disorder: A combined systematic review and meta-analysis. *Developmental Medicine & Child Neurology, 55,* 229–237.

State Government of Victoria. (2013). *Dementia, through all its stages.* Better Health Channel. Retrieved from: http://www.betterhealth.vic.gov.au/bhcv2/bhcarticles.nsf/pages/Dementia_through_all_its_stages

Sturmey, P. (2012). Treatment of psychopathology in people with intellectual and other disabilities. *The Canadian Journal of Psychiatry, 57,* 593–600.

Sugden, D. A. (2007). Current approaches to intervention in children with developmental coordination disorder. *Developmental Medicine & Child Neurology, 49,* 467–471.

Sugden, D. A., Chambers, M., & Utley, A. (2006). *Leeds consensus statement.* Retrieved from: http://www.dcd-uk.org/consensus.html

Sugden, D., Kirby, A., & Dunford, C. (2008). Issues surrounding children with developmental coordination disorder. *International Journal of Disability, Development and Education, 55,* 173–187.

Sukhodolsky, D. G., Vitulano, L. A., Carroll, D. H., McGuire, J., Leckman, J. F., & Scahill, L. (2009). Randomized trial of anger control training for adolescents with Tourette's Syndrome and disruptive behavior. *Journal of the American Academy for Child Adolescent Psychiatry, 48,* 413–421.

Üçok, A., & Gaebel, W. (2008). Side effects of atypical antipsychotics: A brief overview. *World Psychiatry, 7,* 58–62.

Van Bourgondien, M. E., Reichle, N. C., & Schopler, E. (2003). Effects of a model treatment program. *Journal of Autism and Developmental Disabilities, 33,* 131–140.

Virta, M., Salakari, A., Antila, M., Chydenius, E., Partinen, M., Kaski, M., . . . Iivanainen, M. (2010). Short cognitive behavioural therapy and cognitive training for adults with ADHD—a randomized controlled pilot study. *Neuropsychiatric Disease and Treatment, 7*(Suppl 6), 443–453.

Virués-Ortega J. (2010). Applied behavior analytic intervention for autism in early childhood: Meta-analysis, meta-regression and dose-response meta-analysis of multiple outcomes. *Clinical Psychology Review, 30,* 387–399.

Walkup, J. T., Ferrão, Y., Leckman, J. F., Stein, D. J., & Singer, H. (2010). Tic disorders: Some key issues for DSM-V. *Depression and Anxiety, 27,* 600–610.

Wechsler, D. (2004). *The Wechsler intelligence scale for children—fourth edition.* London, England: Pearson Assessment.

Wierenga, C. E., & Bondi, M. W. (2011). Dementia and Alzheimer's disease: What we know now. *Journal of the American Society on Aging, 35,* 37–45.

Williams, N. F., Brown, S., Greer, C., & Jenkins, F. D. (2011). Academic failure, unemployment, and incarceration: Poor outcomes for transition school-aged youth with learning disabilities and emotional and behavioral disorders. *Rehabilitation Counselors and Educators Journal, 4,* 3–8.

Woods, B., Spector, A. E., Jones, C. A., Orrell, M., & Davies, S. P. (2005). Reminiscence therapy for dementia. *Cochrane Database of Systematic Reviews, 18*(2), Art. No.: CD001120.

Young, S., & Ross, R. R. (2007). *R&R2ADHD for youths and adults: A pro-social training program.* Ottawa, Canada: Cognitive Centre of Canada.

Zhu, Y., Wu, S. K., & Cairney, J. (2011). Obesity and motor coordination in Taiwanese children with and without developmental coordination disorder. *Research in Developmental Disabilities: A Multidisciplinary Journal, 32,* 801–807.

[Handwritten annotations: Phase oriented approach | mind-body disorders | CBT | antianxiety meds | ↑ seratonin | DID is often the result of trauma | IAD used to be called hypochondria | Factitious disorder - difficult to id + monitor - affects .5% of pop - more common in females | PT-AMD new DSM diagnosis | Somatic symptoms · can be caused by emotional diff · can be faked · can be made worse by mh difficulties]

Dissociative Disorders and Somatic Symptom and Related Disorders

CASSANDRA G. PUSATERI, LASHAUNA M. DEAN, AND MATTHEW J. PAYLO

CASE STUDY: STEPHANIE

Stephanie is an easy-going, 25-year-old single Caucasian female who has lived in the Northeast her entire life, and recently graduated from college. A proficient and prolific skier, she recently decided to move to Colorado to follow her lifelong dream of becoming a professional ski instructor. Although Stephanie has been skiing her entire life and was previously employed as a seasonal ski instructor at a number of smaller resorts in the Northeast, pushing this dream to the next level felt new and scary to her. She informed her father and mother of her decision and packed her bags to head west.

Her family was less than supportive of her decision. She has always had a tumultuous relationship with her parents, and they often told her that she was "impulsive" and "irrational." In their eyes, she has consistently underperformed and underachieved, never measuring up to her true potential. For example, she never seemed to meet their expectations for her academic career, yet she was on the honor roll throughout high school and was on the dean's list numerous times in college. Her parents have always believed that she never tried hard enough, never put enough time into her studies, and focused on things that "really did not matter." Although she was very popular and valued friends, socializing, and being involved in extracurricular activities, her parents believed she lacked direction and focus, and that her friends were a bad influence on her.

Her father, a respected attorney in the local community, has always wanted Stephanie to become a traditional career professional. He would state that he wanted what he thought was "best for her," and this involves her holding a prestigious position in the community. He believes that skiing is "just a hobby," not a sustainable profession. He frequently lectures Stephanie about this distinction. Stephanie has historically found it difficult to communicate openly and honestly with her father, and she uses humor to avoid having open, honest conversations.

Stephanie has always been a bit of a thrill seeker. She is fearless and she engages in outdoor activities (e.g., water skiing, sailing, hiking, mountain biking, sky diving). She is adventurous and thrives on new experiences.

During her drive to Colorado, she felt her throat constricting and began to have trouble breathing. Just outside of Chicago she noticed she was struggling to breath and decided to stop. Concurrently, she felt a sharp, persistent pain in the right side of her neck that seemed to radiate into her trapezius muscle. Stephanie did not have health insurance at the time, and she did not know what to do. She called her family and then decided to leave her car outside of Chicago and fly home. Once home, she was seen by multiple physicians and specialists. All tests and workups were inconclusive. Even so, Stephanie perseverated on the pain in her neck, often spending an excessive amount of time talking about her pain, thinking about her pain, and even avoiding others because of embarrassment about her pain and her return home.

It has now been over a year and she still reports excessive pain in her neck. In an attempt to treat her neck pain, multiple medications have been prescribed, yet none have been successful. Currently Stephanie is living in her parents' home and appears to have returned to her college lifestyle (e.g., staying out late at night and sleeping late in the mornings). She has experienced considerable weight gain over the past year, and due to her neck pain, she no longer engages in outdoor activities. Stephanie is very concerned about her future and is unsure if she should go back to school or select a new career path. She seeks a mental health consultation after numerous suggestions from her pain management specialist.

DESCRIPTION OF THE DISSOCIATIVE DISORDERS

Dissociative identity disorder, dissociative amnesia, and depersonalization/derealization disorder all share a common goal of protecting one from particularly painful experiences. One way to protect from psychological trauma (i.e., threats to one's cognitive, emotional, and behavioral well-being) is to distance oneself from the threat (Cloitre, Petkova, Wang, & Lu, 2012). Therefore, it is not surprising that the occurrence of childhood trauma (e.g., sexual, physical, and emotional abuse) and repeated traumas are believed to be a common precursor to dissociative symptomology (American Psychiatric Association [APA], 2013).

Dissociative disorders can be found among individuals of any socioeconomic status (Stein et al., 2013). However, people with these disorders may have difficulty securing and maintaining employment, placing them in a lower socioeconomic bracket with limited access to insurance. Moreover, those with dissociative disorders may have difficulty with interpersonal relationships due to previous trauma and/or current symptomology. The prevalence of dissociative disorders is reported to be rather low and will be explored in more detail in the sections specific to the individual disorders. Because of their low prevalence, counselors will rarely have the opportunity to work with people with these disorders.

COUNSELOR CONSIDERATIONS

A strong therapeutic alliance is the cornerstone of effective dissemination of mental health services to clients with dissociative disorders. The client may feel shame and embarrassment in regard to his or her dissociative symptomology and/or previous trauma experiences (APA, 2013). Therefore, it is critical that counselors demonstrate the core conditions of empathy, unconditional positive regard, and genuineness. By exhibiting these qualities, a safe environment is cultivated (Gentile, Dillon, & Gillig, 2013). Also, given that individuals with dissociative disorders are at risk for suicide (APA, 2013), a strong therapeutic alliance allows for more accurate assessments of suicidal ideation and intent and the appropriate provision of necessary services.

Given their shared symptomology with other psychological disorders, counselors are also charged with the responsibility of accurately diagnosing dissociative disorders (APA, 2013; Gentile et al., 2013; Stein et al., 2013). Dissociative symptoms can be present in other disorders related to trauma or stress (i.e., PTSD, acute stress disorder), yet the person may not have a dissociative disorder diagnosis. In fact, the *DSM-5* includes a new specification for PTSD entitled "with dissociative symptoms" (American Psychiatric Association [APA], 2013, p. 272). Likewise, trauma- or stress-related symptomology may be present in dissociative disorders but, the person may not qualify as having a trauma- and stressor-related diagnosis. Finally, many clients with these disorders meet the criteria for one or more psychological disorders. Therefore, it is of the utmost importance that counselors consult the *DSM-5* and other mental health and medical professionals, when appropriate, to ensure the accurate diagnosis of dissociative disorders.

There are several assessments that can aid in the task of diagnosing dissociative disorders. The Dissociative Experiences Scale (Bernstein & Putnam, 1986) measures common experiences related to dissociation (Olsen, Clapp, Parra, & Beck, 2013). The Peritraumatic Dissociative Experiences Questionnaire (Marmar, Weiss, & Metzler, 1997) measures altered awareness and derealization during traumatic experiences (Bryant et al., 2009). The Multidimensional Inventory of Dissociation (Dell, 2006) can be used to assess for dissociative phenomena (e.g., gaps in long-term memory), as well as current functioning (Dell, 2013). Medical assessments may also be used to rule out organic causes of symptomology (Woo, 2010).

PROGNOSIS

The prognosis of all dissociative disorders depends on each client's circumstances. Once a client begins treatment, the quality of the therapeutic alliance and suitability of utilized techniques and interventions can influence successful treatment of the disorder. Research suggests that individuals diagnosed with dissociative disorders are inclined to seek treatment (Stein et al., 2013), which suggests that decreased personal motivation to seek mental health services may be less of a concern. Among the disorders outlined in this chapter, the duration of dissociative symptoms vary. If provided appropriate treatment, symptom resolution could range from days to years.

DISSOCIATIVE IDENTITY DISORDER

Description of the Disorder and Typical Client Characteristics

A client diagnosed with dissociative identity disorder (DID) described her experience as follows: "If you smash anything hard enough, enough times, it will smash into pieces. I guess that's what happened to me" (Rothschild, 2009, p. 178). Formerly known as multiple personality disorder, DID is descriptive of an individual who has two or more separate personalities and episodic amnesia related to the personalities' dominance at different times (APA, 2013; Pais, 2009). Trauma during childhood, predominantly sexual abuse, is believed to be a common precursor to DID, with the etiological concept being that the mind creates different personalities to protect the individual from psychological injury (Gillig, 2009; Pais, 2009). Awareness of the other personalities and their behaviors varies among those with DID (Rothschild, 2009). Throughout this section, the distinct personalities developed in this disorder will be referred to as *alters,* given the common use of this term in the DID literature (see Gentile et al., 2013; Gillig, 2009; Rothschild, 2009).

Although each client is unique in regard to his or her presentation, typically, switching between alters is indicated by "trancelike behavior, eye blinking, eye rolling, and changes in posture" (Gentile et al., 2013, p. 24) and is precipitated by stressors (APA, 2013). Alters can differ depending on the purpose they serve. For example, a client who is female may have a male alter whose purpose is to protect the client when threatened. A client with DID often has strained familial relationships related to previous childhood trauma and/or current symptomology, and may have minimal social support. Clients with DID also generally have difficulty maintaining employment. DID is a rare diagnosis with prevalence reported to be 1.5% among adults, with males and females having similar prevalence rates (APA, 2013).

Counselor Considerations

Accurate assessment is especially important with DID. Clients with DID may present with comorbid psychological disorders (APA, 2013), and/or may seek services for other psychological concerns (Gillig, 2009). Therefore, it is important that counselors determine whether symptomology presented in counseling is due to DID or is better accounted for by another disorder. For instance, Gentile et al. (2013) recommend ruling out "hypnotic states, seizure activity with personality change, psychosis with ego fragmentation, and rapid cycling bipolar disorder" when assessing DID-related symptoms (p. 24).

Given that over half of outpatient clients with DID have attempted suicide, the next important consideration is assessing suicide risk (APA, 2013; Gillig, 2009). However, it is also important for counselors to remember that assessing for suicide can be complicated by the characteristics of the disorder. For example, an accurate assessment may be difficult if the alters have varying degrees of suicidal ideation and risk, and various alters may not be accessible during a counselor-generated suicide assessment.

The next important consideration is the possible risky behavior of a person's alters. Sexual promiscuity and criminal behavior are examples of high-risk behaviors that may occur when different alters are present (Gillig, 2009; Ross, 2008). Any high-risk behavior of the alters can present legal and ethical dilemmas for counselors. For example, an alter could report to a counselor that he or she plans to harm a family member or close friend. The host may not be aware of this plan and fervently deny any ideation to harm someone close to him or her. However, the risk remains as the alter could dominate and fulfill the plan. The counselor would then be required to take necessary steps to keep the client and identified party safe from harm. Therefore, it is important for the counselor to consider the potential actions of each alter and take steps during the counseling sessions to ensure the safety of the client and those around him or her.

Another consideration is the controversy around the validity of DID (Harper, 2011). There are mental health professionals who believe DID exists, others who reject its presence, and still others who fall between the two opposing viewpoints. Because of these mixed opinions, DID can be either under- or overdiagnosed, making service provision, especially referrals for additional services, difficult (Gentile et al., 2013; Gillig, 2009). Therefore, as previously mentioned, accurate diagnosis and appropriate treatment are imperative (Pais, 2009). Although the controversy around DID is an important consideration, counselors should approach each client without judgment as rejection of a client's perceived symptoms could damage the therapeutic alliance and therefore negatively affect the therapeutic process.

Culture and the symptomology of DID is another counselor consideration when working with those who have DID. There are cultures whose religious/spiritual ideas support "possession" and "nonepileptic seizures"; these are not only considered normal, but are desired (APA, 2013, p. 295). An example of this would be the practice of speaking in tongues. According to some religions, after demonstrating faith and being cleansed by the death of Jesus Christ, one is a vessel to be used by the Holy Spirit to communicate in languages and speak in tongues that are unknown to the person (Church of God, 2013; King, n.d.). This possession provides evidence of one's faith. As this example demonstrates, it is important to consider a client's cultural identity and accompanying perceptions and experiences when providing a diagnosis of DID. More specifically, a counselor should determine if the client's symptomology causes distress and therefore is better accounted for by a diagnosis of DID, or if it is considered acceptable within the cultural context.

Finally, the inclusion of family members can be helpful during the therapeutic process with those who have DID (Pais, 2009). Family members can share their experiences with each alter, provide information about periods of time the client does not remember, and offer additional emotional support. Counselors can also use psychoeducation to cultivate a better understanding of DID and help the family unit develop plans to keep all members safe (Pais, 2009).

Treatment Models and Interventions

In the literature, there are no randomized controlled studies that support the use of psychosocial treatments when providing mental health services to clients diagnosed with DID. The literature does contain a number of case studies which suggest effectiveness in using different treatments. Overall, the literature suggests that the treatment of DID should be intensive and will likely require years of treatment by a skilled professional. Because of the trauma associated with DID, trauma-focused treatment will be an important aspect of treatment. In this section, general theoretical considerations when treating those with DID will be presented.

There is general consensus within the field of counseling that even though there are no evidence-based approaches for treating individuals with DID, counselors should consider assuming a phase-oriented treatment approach to working with these individuals

(International Society for the Study of Trauma and Dissociation, 2011; see the International Society for the Study of Trauma and Dissociation's website for a free, downloadable document that details guidelines for treating DID in adults). The assumptions of this approach are that abuse caused this disorder, protective alter identities shield individuals from traumatic memories, and integration of these identities is the paramount treatment goal.

This phase-oriented approach involves (a) establishing safety and skills training (e.g., emotional awareness and regulation, tolerance of distress), which aids in the stabilization and symptom reduction of the individual; (b) confronting incongruencies of memories and seeking integration of those traumatic memories; and (c) working toward identity integration of the multiple alters (e.g., components, identities) of the individual.

This phase-oriented approach works well with insight-oriented therapies, dialectical behavioral therapy, acceptance and commitment therapy, and cognitive behavioral therapy (International Society for the Study of Trauma and Dissociation, 2011). A CBT approach enables clients to find effective coping strategies and increase their problem-solving skills, and aids them in confronting their cognitive distortions (Gillig, 2009). The tactical-integration model (Fine, 1999) is the most well-known CBT model for treating DID (Harper, 2011). In this model, a phasic design is used to initially develop a strong therapeutic relationship, implement cognitive restructuring, integrate the alters to accomplish specific tasks, and, when the client is ready, prepare him or her for using these skills outside of the therapeutic environment (Fine, 1999).

The primary goal when providing mental health services to clients with DID is the integration of the alter identities; therefore, integration is a common component of all proposed DID treatments. However, there has been some disagreement on the meaning of integration. Integration can refer either to the blending of alter identities and/or the recognition and increased self-awareness of the alter identities. The client is asked to fully acknowledge each alter, its purpose, desires, and/or emotions. The hope is that the alters will begin to cooperate instead of fight for control.

Counselors need to facilitate clients' awareness of these alter identities and the roles and importance of these identities. This can sometimes be done through the use of hypnosis. Specialized training is required to use hypnosis.

Counselors will also need to help clients process, tolerate, and integrate past traumatic experiences. In this sense, DID treatment has a trauma focus. This trauma focus may require the counselor to aid the client in reframing traumatic experiences and countering irrational guilt and shame associated with the trauma. The trauma treatments discussed in Chapter 7 may be helpful to this end. The later stages of DID treatment allow clients to synthesize their past traumatic experiences. With a more coherent sense of their histories, clients can begin to fully integrate their identity.

In the literature, there are no randomized controlled studies that support the use of medications in treating clients diagnosed with DID. However, given the likelihood of comorbidity with other disorders (APA, 2013), many clients who are diagnosed with DID are prescribed medications to treat comorbid disorders. Depressive and trauma- and stressor-related disorders are often diagnosed concurrently with DID (APA, 2013), the symptomology of which may be treated using medications. For example, if a client is diagnosed with DID and major depressive disorder, the client may be prescribed medication to manage the depressive symptoms, thereby allowing for more effective treatment of the dissociative symptomology.

Counselors working with clients who have been prescribed medications should incorporate medication management into the client's treatment plan. Because of the memory lapses associated with this disorder, many clients diagnosed with DID may have difficulty taking their medication as prescribed.

Prognosis

Because of the paucity of research on DID, it is difficult to predict the course and prognosis of this disorder. Treatment is often lengthy and some characteristics have been associated with a poorer prognosis. These characteristics include self-destructive behaviors, poor attachments, fewer healthy, supportive relationships, an inability to form a therapeutic relationship, a lack of internal and external resources (i.e., awareness, coping skills, support), and a lack of overall motivation to make changes (Baars et al., 2010).

DISSOCIATIVE AMNESIA

Description of the Disorder and Typical Client Characteristics

Dissociative amnesia is characterized as the inability of an individual to remember information about his or her life experiences (APA, 2013). Dissociative amnesia is related to emotional and/or cognitive stress and does not have organic causes (Woo, 2010). Dissociative amnesia can range from the inability to remember information during a specific period of time or related to a specific event, to the inability to remember the entirety of one's past. Unique to dissociative amnesia, as compared to the other *DSM-5* dissociative disorders, is the presence or absence of dissociative fugue (i.e., traveling or wandering that is associated with the amnesia). Severe trauma typically precedes dissociative amnesia and it is associated with a history of severe physical and sexual childhood abuse and/or exposure to interpersonal violence as an adult. The impact of the disorder on everyday functioning can vary depending on the severity of the amnesia (APA, 2013).

Although each client is unique in regard to clinical presentation, certain characteristics are common among clients with dissociative amnesia. They typically have little social support available to them, which can be related to the previous traumas or to the amnesia itself. They are typically troubled by their inability to remember certain events and/or distressed by memories as they return. Employment and ability to perform activities of daily living will vary among clients with dissociative amnesia. Essentially, the presentation of a client with dissociative amnesia will depend on the severity of the symptomology. Like DID, the prevalence of dissociative amnesia is rare with prevalence rates of 1.8% among adults, accounting for 1% of males and 2.6% of females (APA, 2013).

Counselor Considerations

There are four primary considerations when providing counseling services to clients with dissociative amnesia. The first consideration is the risk for suicide. The risk for suicide is high among individuals diagnosed with dissociative amnesia (APA, 2013). As stated previously, an inability to remember can be distressing as can the return of particularly painful memories of occurrences during the amnesia. Therefore, it is important that assessments for suicidal ideation and intent be performed regularly during the therapeutic process as the risk for suicide can fluctuate. Counselors should be prepared for the possibility that clients may need to be admitted to a secure care facility and/or they will require regular suicide assessments.

The second consideration is the difficulty associated with the assessment of dissociative amnesia. An initial assessment may be complicated by the client's inability to remember aspects of his or her past. Additionally, there are several psychological disorders, including other dissociative disorders, which manifest with symptomology similar to dissociative amnesia. Amnesia can also be related to substance use or have organic causes (Woo, 2010). Therefore, other psychological disorders and organic causes should be ruled out before making a definitive diagnosis of dissociative amnesia (Woo, 2010). Furthermore, a client may not be aware of the dissociative amnesia. Therefore, the disorder may go undiagnosed for a time before the symptoms are identified. All of these factors indicate the need for accurate assessment and diagnosis of this disorder.

The third consideration is the intersection between culture and the symptomology of dissociative amnesia. People from diverse cultures have unique experiences related to dissociative experiences. For example, among some women from Puerto Rico and the Caribbean and some other Hispanic groups, *ataque de nervios* (attack of nerves) is considered a normal "nonpossession trance . . . following exposure to stressful events" (Somer, 2006, p. 217). *Ataque de nervios* is a culturally accepted way to distance the self from traumatic events and can manifest in several behaviors, one of which is amnesia (Lewis-Fernandez et al., 2010; Somer, 2006). Counselors will need to determine whether a client meets the full diagnostic criteria for dissociative amnesia, or is simply engaged in a culturally accepted practice.

Finally, clients diagnosed with dissociative amnesia have the capacity to commit criminal acts without recollection of the event. Situations such as this could present legal and ethical dilemmas for counselors. Although the propensity for criminal behavior should not be generalized to every client, it is the counselor's responsibility to gather an adequate amount of background information to ensure the safety of the client as well as those around him or her. If the counselor is aware of previous harmful behavior to self or others and does not put safeguards in place, he or she could be held legally liable.

Treatment Models and Interventions

There is a dearth of literature available on dissociative amnesia and effective treatment modalities (Woo, 2010). Few empirically-based studies could be found in the literature.

There is no literature available to suggest that medications are an effective form of treatment for dissociative amnesia per se. However, given the likelihood of comorbidity (APA, 2013), many clients who are diagnosed with dissociative amnesia are prescribed medications to treat comorbid disorders. Persistent depressive disorder and major depressive disorder, among others, are often diagnosed concurrently with dissociative amnesia (APA, 2013), and these disorders are often treated using medications.

SEQUENTIAL TREATMENT—SYMPTOM REGULATION AND NARRATIVE THERAPY Sequential treatment may be useful in treating dissociative amnesia as well as depersonalization/derealization disorder (Cloitre et al., 2012). A randomized controlled trial was conducted using a sample of women with a primary diagnosis of PTSD and a history of childhood physical and/or sexual abuse (Cloitre et al., 2012). The results indicated that those participants with high levels of dissociative symptomology related to dissociative amnesia and depersonalization/derealization improved—during and after treatment—when a sequential treatment model included symptom regulation and narrative therapy (White & Epston, 1990).

This approach involves counselors assisting clients in becoming increasingly aware of their emotional states, especially as related to life stressors and previous traumatic experiences (Cloitre et al., 2012). For example, counselors assist clients with identifying emotionally triggering experiences, labeling the emotions, describing any physiological changes, and recognizing any resulting behaviors. Next, counselors use psychoeducation to assist clients with learning and integrating coping strategies to manage these emotions and stressors. For example, counselors could teach clients the use of deep breathing and guided imagery to regulate emotions. Finally, narrative storytelling is used to engage cognitive and emotional processes. For example, schemas (or cognitions) may be rooted in the trauma linked to the dissociative amnesia and may emerge when the client begins to share his or her narrative. Therefore, counselors assist clients with identifying these schemas and slowly creating, or writing, a new narrative.

MINDFULNESS-BASED THERAPY (MBT) The use of MBT with attention to acceptance and commitment therapy (ACT; Hayes, Strosahl, & Wilson, 2012) concepts may be effective in the treatment of dissociative amnesia (Baslet & Hill, 2011). In one case study, this treatment approach resulted in the recovery of much of a client's memory during, and one month after, hospitalization (Baslet & Hill, 2011). This approach aims to reduce the pressure for the client to remember, and to encourage awareness and acceptance of the client's emotional and physical experiences as they naturally emerge.

MBT and ACT approaches can be used in both group and individual counseling sessions (Baslet & Hill, 2011). These activities can be incorporated into group counseling and can focus on identifying life goals, acknowledging productive behaviors, and promoting the understanding and integration of mindfulness in clients' lives. An example would be asking clients to write *personal mission statements* representing their ambitions and values as well as behaviors that will help them reach their goals (Baslet & Hill, 2011). Other examples include using psychoeducation and meditation to increase mindfulness inside and outside the counseling setting. The intention behind these activities is to shift clients' focus to actions that can be taken to reach their goals and promote a positive, nonjudgmental perspective of themselves and their future (Baslet & Hill, 2011).

In applying MBT, activities used during individual counseling sessions can pertain to reflection on various aspects of the client's past, present, or future. For example, a client could be asked to draw his or her perception of any interpersonal relationships inside the past and the present. The counselor could then note any significant aspects of the drawings as well as any patterns or themes. The counselor's involvement in this process is key as it reduces pressure for the client to remember content previously discussed. Journaling is another example, as it provides the client the freedom to record any reflections that occur between or during sessions. The objective of these activities is not to analyze the content, but rather acknowledge the shift in the client's perspective with the overall goal being the natural emergence of memories (Baslet & Hill, 2011).

CREATIVE TOOLBOX ACTIVITY 14.1   Portrait of Self-Awareness

Cassandra Pusateri, PhD, NCC

Activity Overview

The Portrait of Self-Awareness is a creative intervention designed to increase mindfulness among clients diagnosed with dissociative disorders. This activity includes the use of an art-based medium (e.g., paint, colored pencils, crayons) to create an unrestricted space for clients to explore their current emotional, physiological, and cognitive experiences. Through participation in this activity, clients gain an increased awareness of self, and counselors are provided with valuable insight into the world of their clients.

Treatment Goal(s) of Activity

The primary goals of the Portrait of Self-Awareness are to (a) increase awareness of physiological and emotional experiences as well as emerging cognitions; (b) promote acceptance of these experiences and cognitions without judgment; and (c) ultimately encourage mindfulness inside and outside the counseling environment.

Directions

1. Gather necessary materials for the activity, including at least two art-based media (e.g., paint, crayons, markers) and two to three pieces of blank paper.
2. Ask the client to identify his or her prominent in-the-moment emotional experience. It is important that the client focuses on his or her present emotional experience.
3. Ask the client to use the art-based media to depict this emotional experience. Many clients will ask what they "should" be depicting. It is important to encourage the free and natural expression of the client's experience(s).
4. As the client is artfully depicting his or her emotional experience, periodically ask the client to identify any physiological sensations, emotional experiences, or cognitions that naturally emerge. If the client attempts to judge these, reinforce the nonjudgmental acceptance of these experiences.
5. When appropriate, ask questions to assist the client with the artful depiction. For example, "As you experience new physiological or emotional sensations or cognitions, would your artwork change?" Additionally, note any patterns or themes present during the client's artful depiction and/or verbal description.
6. After the artwork is completed, encourage the client to reflect on the experience in session and/or through journaling outside the session. Additionally, share with the client any insights you gained through the activity.

Process Questions

1. What stands out for you as you reflect on this activity?
2. What was it like to allow your emotions and thoughts to flow freely?
3. Did you have difficulty accepting your experiences without judgment?
4. Were there any physiological sensations or cognitions that stood out for you?
5. How might your judgment of these experiences affect your everyday life?
6. If these experiences emerge in the future, how might you welcome them?

Prognosis

Although the return of memory can be rather quick in most cases (Woo, 2010), the prognosis of dissociative amnesia appears to be specific to the severity of the disorder. Removal of the source of, or triggers to, trauma may result in immediate restoration of memory (APA, 2013). Conversely, an individual who fails to remember most of his or her past might require more time, which could result in the gradual return of memories. Regardless, in advance, clients should be prepared for a return of memory, as these memories may be particularly distressing.

DEPERSONALIZATION/DEREALIZATION DISORDER

Description of the Disorder and Typical Client Characteristics

Depersonalization/derealization disorder is characterized by consistent episodes of depersonalization and/or derealization. Depersonalization involves the perception that one is an observer of his or her physical, emotional, and cognitive experiences (APA, 2013). For example, a client may feel as though he is an actor in a play about his life (Aliyev & Aliyev, 2011). Derealization involves experiencing the world and everything in it as though it is distorted or unreal (APA, 2013). For example, a client may perceive her environment as familiar, but experience it differently than once remembered. According to the *DSM-5* criteria for this disorder, this population remains connected with reality despite their symptoms of depersonalization and derealization.

Prior to the onset of symptomology, people may have experienced a traumatic or stressful event (APA, 2013). Severe stress during childhood (e.g., emotional abuse or neglect, physical abuse) is believed to be a common precursor to the emergence of depersonalization and/or derealization (APA, 2013). Depersonalization/derealization is conceptualized as a way for an individual to protect himself or herself from traumatic or extremely stressful memories or stressful experiences in the present.

Depersonalization/derealization disorder typically manifests between 16 and 23 years of age (Hollander, 2009). It is believed that the experiences of depersonalization and/or derealization are fairly common. However, a much smaller proportion of the population meets the *DSM-5* criteria for depersonalization/derealization disorder. Like dissociate identity disorder and dissociative amnesia, the prevalence of depersonalization/derealization disorder is rare, with an average prevalence rate of 2%, with males and females equally represented (APA, 2013). Clients with depersonalization/derealization disorder may present in counseling with a flat affect. The emotional and physical numbing that many experience can prove to be a barrier to the development and cultivation of interpersonal relationships, resulting in strained or limited social support and a history of unemployment (APA, 2013).

Counselor Considerations

Cultural and religious issues should be considered when diagnosing and treating depersonalization and/or derealization disorder (APA, 2013). For example, some who ascribe to the Wiccan belief system may seek an experience where he or she "finds himself or herself seeming to stand or hover in a corner of the room, looking down on his or her physical body . . . with complete visual [and often auditory] awareness" (Farrar & Farrar,

1984, p. 213). In another example, those who practice Hasidic Judaism believe in achieving an increased awareness of God through depersonalization (Somer, 2006). The spiritual experiences described here could be identified by a counselor as depersonalization. Therefore, before a diagnosis is made or an intervention is initiated, the client's cultural context and any intersection between that context and his or her symptomology should be explored.

The next consideration is the difficulty associated with diagnosing depersonalization/derealization disorder. There are several other psychological disorders that share similar symptomology (APA, 2013). For example, experiences of depersonalization and/or derealization are considered symptoms and a specifier of PTSD in the *DSM-5* (APA, 2013). Additionally, counselors should consider ruling out panic disorder given the similarity between the underlying symptoms (Hollander, 2009). Finally, various drugs can cause symptoms of depersonalization/derealization (APA, 2013). Therefore, it is crucial that counselors take appropriate measures to determine which diagnosis best accounts for the client's symptomology and then move forward accordingly.

The final consideration is associated with the intersection between the client's symptomology and the therapeutic alliance and process. As previously mentioned, clients with depersonalization/derealization disorder can present with an extremely flat affect and/or emotional and physical numbing (APA, 2013). Not only could these factors create barriers to the establishment of rapport and trust, these symptoms could also affect the development of and progress toward therapeutic goals. Additionally, a continual focus on previous trauma or intense emotional experiences may lead to increased occurrences of depersonalization/derealization during counseling sessions and/or a client's premature termination of counseling. Therefore, counselors are encouraged to enter the therapeutic process with caution and awareness of the many factors that could affect therapeutic outcomes.

Treatment Models and Interventions

There is a limited body of research addressing the treatment of depersonalization/derealization disorder. Two randomized controlled trials (Aliyev & Aliyev, 2011; Cloitre et al., 2012) and one controlled treatment trial (Nuller, Morozova, Kushnir, & Hamper, 2001) demonstrated the efficacy of psychopharmacological and sequential treatment modalities with this population. The psychosocial treatment of this disorder includes multiple therapeutic approaches as opposed to one stand-alone approach. For example, each includes a component of symptom regulation in conjunction with other interventions, which speaks to the potential effect of symptomology on the therapeutic process (Cloitre et al., 2012; Hollander, 2009). Therefore, counselors should focus on symptom regulation before beginning other interventions.

SEQUENTIAL TREATMENT—SYMPTOM REGULATION AND NARRATIVE THERAPY The results of a randomized controlled trial indicate that participants with high levels of dissociative symptomology related to dissociative amnesia and depersonalization/derealization improved during and after treatment when a sequential treatment model including symptom regulation and narrative therapy was used (Cloitre et al., 2012). Please see the previous treatment section (on dissociative amnesia disorder) for a more detailed description of this intervention.

EYE CLOSURE, EYE MOVEMENTS Eye Closure, Eye Movements (ECEM; Hollander, 2009) has been suggested as an effective intervention in the treatment of depersonalization/ derealization disorder. ECEM incorporates hypnosis and eye movements similar to those used in Eye Movement Desensitization and Reprocessing (Shapiro, 2001; See the PTSD treatment section in Chapter 7 for more information). Hypnosis is used to regulate the client's breathing, as many with depersonalization/derealization disorder tend to hold their breath. Once breathing is stabilized, clients are encouraged to become increasingly aware of self (e.g., physiological sensations, thoughts, emotions) with the objective of reducing and eventually eliminating psychological distancing. Then, eye movements are used to reprocess triggers to, and any fears associated with, the symptomology of this disorder. These eye movements can be achieved by moving the eyes from side to side or bilaterally with or without the assistance of the counselor (Hollander, 2009).

More specifically, ECEM includes five stages: (a) an intake assessment; (b) bringing the client's awareness to the most recent episode of depersonalization and/or derealization and then using hypnosis to regulate the client's breathing; (c) enhancing the client's awareness of himself or herself (e.g., senses, cognitions, memories); (d) identifying triggers and reprocessing using eye movements; and (e) reprocessing any fears associated with future depersonalization and/or derealization (Hollander, 2009). Specialized training is required for the competent use of hypnosis and eye movements in the treatment of this disorder.

PSYCHOPHARMACOTHERAPY There is limited research to suggest that medications are useful in the treatment of depersonalization/derealization disorder. Nonetheless, some research has shown lamotrigine, also known as Lamictal, and naloxone, also known as Narcan, can be effective in the treatment of depersonalization/derealization disorder (Aliyev & Aliyev, 2011; Nuller et al., 2001).

Traditionally used to prevent mood swings among individuals diagnosed with bipolar disorder, lamotrigine has several possible side effects, including "rash, blurred or double vision, fever, nausea, vomiting, dizziness, headache, tremor, abdominal pain, lack of coordination, back pain, sleepiness, tiredness, trouble sleeping, dry mouth" (*PDR Consumer Guide to Prescription Drugs*; Physicians' Desk Reference, 2011, p. 265). Additionally, and most importantly, lamotrigine may result in an increase in suicidal ideation (Physicians' Desk Reference, 2011), and counselors must regularly assess for changes in mood and subsequent increased suicidal ideation, and act accordingly.

Naloxone is an opioid antagonist and is traditionally used to reverse the effects of opioids. Naloxone is given by a health care provider in the form of an injection (U.S. National Library of Medicine [NLM] & National Institutes of Health [NIH], 2013). The side effects of naloxone may include "pain, burning, or redness at the injection site; nausea; vomiting; uncontrollable shaking of a part of your body; pain, burning, numbness, or tingling in the hands or feet; sweating; hot flashes or flushing" (NLM & NIH, 2013, para. 6). If an individual consistently takes opioid medications, he or she may experience withdrawal symptoms when treated with naloxone (NLM & NIH, 2013). Therefore, it is imperative that counselors be familiar with the withdrawal symptoms and provide additional services as needed.

Depressive and anxiety disorders—among others—are often diagnosed concurrently with depersonalization/derealization disorder (APA, 2013). Given the likelihood of comorbidity (APA, 2013), many clients who are diagnosed with depersonalization/derealization disorder are prescribed medications to treat comorbid disorders.

Prognosis

The duration of depersonalization/derealization disorder can range from hours or days to months and years. Clients with this disorder tend to take extreme measures to avoid harm. Episodes of depersonalization and derealization can be brought on by environmental factors related to setting and stress, the severity of the symptomology of comorbid disorders, and inappropriate amounts of sleep (APA, 2013). Therefore, psychoeducation about the disorder, identification of potential triggers, and exploration of effective coping strategies may assist in the reduction of symptomology and ultimately improve the client's prognosis. Overall, the resolution of depersonalization/derealization disorder is highly dependent on the individual's circumstances and can take varying amounts of time to remit.

DESCRIPTION OF THE SOMATIC SYMPTOM AND RELATED DISORDERS

The Greek origin of the word *somatic is of the body,* providing an appropriate and accurate label for a set of disorders relating specifically to physiological symptoms. Somatic symptom and related disorders involve physical health concerns that cannot be explained organically and/or is inconsistent with preexisting medical diagnoses (APA, 2013).

> *mind– body connection is real*

Somatic symptom disorder, illness anxiety disorder, conversion disorder, psychological factors affecting other medical conditions, and factitious disorder are included in this diagnostic category. These disorders are relatively uncommon among the general population; however, they are seen with some frequency in medical settings (APA, 2013). Because of the physical complaints associated with these disorders, most clients initially seek care through physicians, but are eventually referred to mental health professionals secondary to no medical issues being indicated. People with disorders in this category are often resistant to psychological interventions because the physiological nature of their symptoms leads them to believe that a medical explanation is warranted. A key characteristic in clients with somatic disorders is *doctor shopping* or persistently seeking medical treatment from a variety of physicians in order to obtain a medical diagnosis. By the time a client with this disorder reaches a counselor's office, he or she has likely visited multiple physicians, and physical health problems have been ruled out as the cause of their perceived illness or symptoms.

> *↓ drops during stress*
>
> *meds can ↑ seroton*

COUNSELOR CONSIDERATIONS

Given the nature of the symptomology, there are unique considerations for counselors providing services to clients with somatic symptom and related disorders. The importance of building a strong therapeutic alliance with clients cannot be overstated. Clients diagnosed with these disorders can feel misunderstood and invalidated by others (Hart & Bjorgvinsson, 2010), and therefore may enter the therapeutic relationship with an inherent lack of trust in counseling. Counselors can use counseling microskills and the tenets of person centered therapy (i.e., empathy, unconditional positive regard, and genuineness) to build rapport and trust. Focusing on better understanding a client's experience rather than attempting to prove or disprove his or her symptoms opens the gateway for positive therapeutic outcomes.

Comorbidity with other psychological disorders like depression and anxiety is common among clients diagnosed with somatic symptom and related disorders (Nickel, Ademmer, & Egle, 2010). Therefore, counselors should be intentional and thorough in their assessments. Linking a client's symptomology with the most appropriate mental disorder is essential in determining the best course of treatment.

PROGNOSIS

The prognosis for somatic symptom and related disorders largely depends on adequate clinical recognition of the problem, and to this end, a thorough evaluation and assessment are important. Dynamic assessment that is multidimensional in nature is required to accurately diagnose and treat, and should involve detailed interviewing focused on the biological, psychosocial, and psychological aspects of a client's history. Also, any assessment and plan for treatment should be holistic in nature, involving all service providers and supports (e.g., primary care physician, psychiatrist, neurologist, family members, and any other social support people).

Some disorders in this category have a better prognosis than others due to symptom severity and/or established links between symptomology and other comorbid psychological disorders. Clients diagnosed with illness anxiety disorder have more positive treatment outcomes than conversion disorder. Counseling interventions that focus on educating clients about their condition, addressing cognitions which support the disorder, and helping clients find healthier ways to express their emotions have been associated with symptom reduction and positive outcomes.

SOMATIC SYMPTOM DISORDER

Description of the Disorder and Typical Client Characteristics

Somatic symptom disorder (SSD) is characterized by physiological complaints that may or may not have an organic explanation. These complaints are typically accompanied by thoughts, feelings, and behaviors that are excessive or disproportionate to the illness, persist for at least six months, and cause disruption in daily functioning (APA, 2013). As counselors do not have the competence to treat physical health issues, they must rely on medical providers' judgment in determining what client experiences are disproportionate to the illness.

Although the most common physical complaints are related to pain, somatic symptoms can also involve dizziness, fatigue, gastrointestinal complaints, and sexual dysfunction (Sattel et al., 2012). The prevalence of this disorder has been estimated to be 5–7% in the general population (APA, 2013) and up to 22% in medical settings (Schade, Torres, & Beyebach, 2011), with women being diagnosed with SSD at higher rates.

Counselor Considerations

People with SSD are often referred to medical specialists and seek multiple opinions from various health care providers (Nickel, Ademmer, & Egle, 2010). As such, clients with SSD have typically seen numerous health care providers and may become frustrated with repeatedly explaining their symptoms to new professionals. Research has found positive treatment outcomes for clients when their symptoms are validated and when the health care professional has communicated empathy and understanding to clients suffering with SSD (Sharma & Manjula, 2013). As such, strong therapeutic relationship is critically important when working with clients diagnosed with SSD.

Clients may believe that the use of psychosocial treatments implies that their symptoms are not valid. The focus of counseling should not be on confronting the client's symptoms as purely somatic, but rather using advanced empathy and genuineness to encourage the client to open up about his or her feelings and experiences. Those with SSD often lack insight and struggle to identify their emotions, and instead fixate on their bodily sensations (Nickel et al., 2010). Therefore, an important goal of treatment is to help clients identify and connect with their emotional experiences and how they relate to their somatic concerns.

Focusing on health complaints can cause an unhealthy cycle of behaviors that then feed back into the disorder. Individuals with SSD may, over time, begin to withdraw from work, relationships, and other common activities. This then leads to more psychosocial problems such as unemployment, financial instability, lack of supportive relationships, and mounting medical bills. Therefore, it is helpful for counselors to help clients identify and build support systems and use healthier, prosocial coping skills in their social interactions. For example, a treatment goal might be to reduce the number of complaints made about physical symptoms to a client's support system each week.

The comorbidity rates of SSD are relatively high with as many as 80% of clients also meeting the criteria for a depression or anxiety diagnosis (Nickel et al., 2010). This presents counselors with the additional challenge of ferreting out somatic symptoms from symptomology related to other psychological disorders. A detailed assessment should be conducted including questions that inquire about a variety of physical and emotional issues. The assessment should explore suicidal history and key areas of functioning (e.g., occupational and/or academic trends and social relationships and interactions).

In addition, culture should be considered before diagnosis and treatment decisions are made, as people from different cultures often somaticize psychological reactions. For example, Asian women of Korean and Japanese decent more often report somatic symptoms when experiencing depression or psychosocial distress (Arnault & Kim, 2008). Similarly, people of Chinese descent often defer to somatic symptoms when experiencing depression, and this somatization is often connected to difficulty in identifying and expressing emotions (Ryder et al., 2008).

Voices from the Trenches 14.1: In the Pearson etext, click here to listen to a discussion of important considerations when working with people who have somatic symptoms disorders.

Treatment Models and Interventions

Clients with this disorder are often frustrated by the medical care they have received and can be defensive and resistant to explaining their symptoms to new professionals. Clients' relationships with primary care physicians and specialists are often strained because of clients' determination to find a medical explanation for their symptoms (Woolfolk & Allen, 2012). Treatment depends on what aspects of the disorder are being addressed. Psychodynamic therapy is suggested as helpful in addressing early unresolved life issues that relate to somatic complaints. Cognitive behavioral therapy has been used to address the role dysfunctional thoughts and beliefs play in the manifestation of behavioral symptoms. Additionally, affective-cognitive behavioral therapy, which emphasizes the role that emotions as well as cognitions play in SSD, has been used with some success. Lastly, the use of psychotropic medications has been found to be helpful in treating this disorder.

BRIEF PSYCHODYNAMIC THERAPY Short-term or brief forms of psychodynamic therapy can be helpful in treating SSD. Psychodynamic therapy posits that many of the clients' somatic complaints are rooted in unresolved early life experiences, and that those experiences will play out in the relationship between the counselor and the client (Nickel et al., 2010). Unresolved childhood traumas are common among individuals with SSD. These traumas might include sexual and physical abuse, death of a parent during childhood, and/or emotional neglect (Nickel et al., 2010). The results of a meta-analysis suggest that clients treated using these brief psychodynamic approaches have experienced a reduction of physical and emotional distressing symptoms, enhanced psychosocial functioning, and have increased their "awareness of unconscious processes and emotional experiencing" (Abbass, Kisely, & Kroenke, 2009, p. 271).

Brief psychodynamic therapy begins with a biopsychosocial evaluation that may span one to two sessions. Next, the counselor works with clients to identify the connection between their somatic symptoms and past unconscious or unresolved conflicts (Nickel et al., 2010). Once unresolved issues are processed, the counselor may provide psychoeducation regarding the client's somatic complaints, and identify a plan that takes the client away from his or her pursuit and/or reliance on medical interventions.

Clinical Toolbox 14.1: In the Pearson etext, click here to read about an activity that can be used to help clients deal take control of somatic symptoms.

COGNITIVE BEHAVIORAL THERAPY (CBT) Several randomized controlled trials and a number of noncontrolled research studies have demonstrated CBT to be effective in reducing somatic complaints (Sharma & Manjula, 2013). The use of CBT in the treatment of SSD includes reframing previously negative, defeatist thoughts into more functional cognitions (Woolfolk & Allen, 2012). Counselors using CBT initially help clients identify their dysfunctional thoughts and then explore evidence that either supports or disproves those beliefs. For example, a client with SSD may hold the belief that if he or she seeks the medical consultation of numerous physicians, eventually a medical diagnosis will be obtained. A cognitive behavioral therapist would work with the client to examine evidence that supports or disproves his or her dysfunctional belief. This change could occur through a talk therapy conversation or by co-constructing a list that offers clients an additional visual cue which depicts how their beliefs are not functional (Woolfolk & Allen, 2012). Counselors then help clients conduct behavioral experiments with the goal of helping them to reengage in activities they previously enjoyed prior to the onset of the disorder. The activities may include adaptive living or leisure activities. Clients with SSD often stop engaging in previously helpful activities because they believe it will exacerbate their somatic symptoms. Therefore, a homework assignment for a client with complaints about pain, who previously stopped exercising, would be to walk around the neighborhood for 10 minutes and then journal about any emerging thoughts and/or feelings.

Clinical Toolbox 14.2: In the Pearson etext, click here to read about an activity that can be used to help clients change their cognitions that support somatic symptoms.

AFFECTIVE-COGNITIVE BEHAVIORAL THERAPY (A-CBT) Traditional CBT tends to focus on targeting cognitions as a primary source of change and places a less direct emphasis on emotions per se. A-CBT integrates the exploration of the client's emotions, teaching relaxation and stress management strategies and helping clients identify distressing thoughts (Woolfolk & Allen, 2010). Several randomized controlled trials suggest A-CBT to be effective in reducing somatic complaints (Woolfolk & Allen, 2010). The goal of A-CBT is to have clients focus less on their symptoms and instead focus on becoming more aware of their emotions and associated cognitions as related to their symptoms. For example, a counselor can utilize a thought and feeling record that asks the client to describe when his or her physical symptoms are more or less severe, specifically paying attention to the interplay of his or her emotional and cognitive cues (Woolfolk & Allen, 2010).

Clinical Toolbox 14.3: In the Pearson etext, click here to view a worksheet that clients can use to record their somatic thoughts, feelings, behavior, and perceived physical symptoms.

In A-CBT, the counselor helps clients label their experiences, make distinctions between their cognitions and emotions, and eventually question their emotions that coincide with the cognition. For example, say a client recounts an event when he or she was asked to go hiking, but the client did not go because of fears of somatic discomfort. In this scenario, the counselor could have the client recount or act out the event, occasionally asking the client to verbally insert the statement, "I cannot do this because I know it will hurt" as he or she recounts the story. In the moment of the inserted statement, the counselor would ask the client to identify the feelings that emerge when he or she hears these statements. The intention is to increase clients' self-awareness of their thoughts and emotions. These distinctions between thoughts and emotions are required before clients can dispute cognitions or even participate in cognitive restructuring. A-CBT involves enhancing clients' awareness of their thoughts and emotions, cognitively restructuring maladaptive thinking, addressing illness-related behaviors (e.g., being in the *sick role*), and developing clients' communication and assertiveness skills (Woolfolk & Allen, 2010).

CREATIVE TOOLBOX ACTIVITY 14.2   Know Your Warning Signs

William B. McKibben, MS, LPCA, NCC

Activity Overview

In this activity clients color in areas of a blank outline of a body, and indicate where they feel distress, pain, or discomfort. The intent of the activity is to develop one's awareness of bodily sensations. Clients learn to recognize bodily sensations and to effectively intervene in the moment, thus preventing escalation of distress. This activity can be used to address a variety of concerns, including somatic concerns, anxiety or mood symptoms.

Treatment Goal(s) of Activity

This activity allows the counselor to collaborate with the client to identify any automatic thoughts or irrational beliefs that may be attached to various bodily sensations, and to intervene using cognitive behavioral interventions. The activity also allows the client to develop, practice, and use coping skills in the moment when perceiving illness or pain in the body. The primary goals of this activity are to (a) help clients recognize bodily sensations; (b) teach clients how to apply effective coping skills upon recognition of bodily sensations; and (c) teach clients to engage with emotions.

Directions

1. Either print or draw a blank outline of a human body on a piece of paper and give it to the client along with crayons, colored pencils, and/or paints.
2. Ask the client to close his or her eyes for a moment and think of times when he or she feels bodily pain or illness.
3. Ask the client to take a few minutes to color the areas on the body outline where he or she feels pain or illness in his or her body. Invite the client to select and use colors or textures that best fit the sensations or experiences.
4. When the client is finished, ask him or her to share what the shaded areas represent. Some clients may color in certain areas, some may draw shapes, and some may write/label areas—process what these mean to the client.

Process Questions

1. What was this exercise like for you?
2. When you notice [*identified sensation*] in your body, what is typically going on around you? How often do you notice [*identified sensation*]?
3. When you feel [*identified sensation*] in your body, what is the first thought that enters your mind? What happens when that thought pops into your head?
4. Are you feeling any of these sensations right now? If yes, how intense are they on a scale of 1–10, with 1 being not intense at all, and 10 being the most intense you have ever felt? What are you thinking right now about the sensations you are experiencing?
5. When you experience these sensations, to what are you reacting? [Is the client reacting to the sensation, or to the thought about the sensation?]
6. What are some things you can do in the moment to address [*identified sensation*]?

PSYCHOPHARMACOTHERAPY The literature on the effectiveness of medication in the treatment of SSD is divided, with some studies reporting effective treatment outcomes and others finding no lasting results related to medication use (Guglielmo, Martinotti, & Janiri, 2012). Selective serotonin reuptake inhibitors (SSRIs) and other types of antidepressants can provide temporary relief for clients with somatic symptoms. However, some clients, often those with the most severe complaints, do not respond to the use of medication (Guglielmo et al., 2012). CBT may enhance the effectiveness of medications used to treat this disorder (Guglielmo et al., 2012).

The study of the effectiveness of pharmacological interventions is complicated by the high incidence of comorbidity that somatic symptom disorders have with anxiety and depression. Generalized anxiety disorder and somatic symptoms often go hand-in-hand. In one placebo-controlled clinical trial, it was found that somatic symptoms, as well as generalized anxiety, were reduced in participants who received duloxetine (i.e., Cymbalta), and venlafaxine (i.e., Effexor). A trend in this and many other studies is that once the primary diagnosis (usually depression or anxiety) is treated, somatic symptoms usually decrease as well (Nicolini et al., 2009).

Prognosis

Clients' perceptions that their struggles are rooted in medical issues often precludes their seeking psychosocial treatments, and can contribute to their being resistant to psychological interventions. A high percentage of clients with SSD are not adequately assessed and therefore continue to doctor shop and avoid seeking mental health care. Additionally, SSD is highly comorbid with depression and anxiety, and treatment gains may not be seen until the depression and anxiety symptoms are first managed. Because of the comorbidity, the depression and/or anxiety must be treated first or simultaneously with the somatic complaints in order to see progress in the somatic complaints, thus making treatment long-term in nature. The course of SSD is also varied with some people experiencing symptoms that ebb and flow over time and others having persistent symptoms throughout their lifetimes (Woolfolk & Allen, 2012).

ILLNESS ANXIETY DISORDER

Description of the Disorder and Typical Client Characteristics

Illness anxiety disorder (IAD), formerly referred to in the *DSM-IV-TR* as hypochondriasis, involves a fixation on acquisition of a serious illness (APA, 2013). Those with this disorder may be easily triggered by normal bodily sensations such as vibrations, palpitations, or any other typical body noise, thus leading them to excessively check their bodies and to repeatedly seek medical help (Hart & Bjorgvinsson, 2010). According to the *DSM-5*, the preoccupation must have been present for at least six months and involve either care-seeking or care-avoidant behaviors. Individuals who are care-seeking will attempt to obtain medical treatment for the symptoms, and individuals who are care-avoidant will evade any type of medical treatment because of their worry that a feared medical diagnosis will be confirmed (APA, 2013). IAD is estimated to occur in 1–10% of community-based samples (APA, 2013), and men and women have equal representation among those diagnosed with the disorder (Woolfolk & Allen, 2012). Most cases of IAD are initially identified in medical settings, and they are then referred for a psychological evaluation and psychosocial treatment.

Counselor Considerations

People with IAD often become involved in a cycle of anxiety that serves to perpetuate and exacerbate their symptoms. For example, individuals with IAD often consult multiple physicians about their symptoms, which then results in referrals to specialists for further assessment, thereby increasing the anxiety that a medical diagnosis will be made (Hart & Bjorgvinsson, 2010). Additionally, this population often researches their symptoms online and finds a bevy of possible medical explanations, which typically results in increased anxiety.

Clients often seek validation of their symptoms and experiences from primary care physicians (Hart & Bjorgvinsson, 2010). This often results in physicians becoming despondent and frustrated with repetitive rejected attempts to help the client (Noyes, Longley, Langbehn, Stuart, & Kukoyi, 2010). People with this disorder may also seek validation from others and also come to feel invalidated by their family members and friends (Hart & Bjorgvinsson, 2010). They often spend enormous amounts of time attempting to make others understand the nature of their bodily complaints, leading to feelings of exasperation, invalidation, and isolation. As such, in the first few sessions, the counselor should work on building rapport and validating the client's experience, avoiding discussion or placing a focus on specific perceived physical symptoms. Counselors should listen objectively to the client's history and story without trying to prove or disprove the symptoms as real or not. Because of ruptured or strained relationships, counselors may also need to help this population develop the skills necessary to enhance their relationships.

Treatment Models and Interventions

Once a counselor has established a solid therapeutic relationship, the counselor can begin to help the client challenge his or her focus on illness. Counselors need to be careful to not challenge the client's beliefs too harshly, as this will destroy therapeutic rapport. CBT's focus on addressing underlying anxiety makes it an effective treatment for IAD (Sørensen, Birket-Smith, Wattar, Buemann, & Salkovskis, 2011). CBT has also been expanded to include mindfulness interventions, which attempt to pull the client's attention away from the somatic complaints. In addition, the use of certain medications are effective in the short-term treatment of IAD.

COGNITIVE BEHAVIORAL THERAPY (CBT) In one randomized controlled trial, CBT was an effective treatment for IAD at baseline and at a 6-month follow-up (Sørensen et al., 2011). In a group setting, CBT was also effective in treating IAD, with the added benefit of cost-effectiveness (Hedman et al., 2010). The use of CBT in the treatment of IAD involves: (a) identifying and articulating a clear picture of the health-related anxiety, which includes increasing insight into the emotional, cognitive, and behavioral aspects of the anxiety; (b) conducting behavioral experiments that challenge the client's previously accepted maladaptive beliefs; (c) a psychoeducational component that serves to educate the client about the illnesses and strategies for stress management; and (d) behavioral exposure to illness thoughts, pictures, and/or information with the goal of desensitizing the client to previous triggers of his or her illness anxiety. Typically, CBT for use with this disorder lasts between 6 and 12 sessions, but it can extend to more sessions as needed.

Clinical Toolbox 14.4: In the Pearson etext, click here to view a video demonstration of the use of CBT techniques with a client with illness anxiety disorder.

MINDFULNESS-BASED THERAPY (MBT)   Several studies have investigated treatment approaches that integrate MBT with CBT, or mindfulness-based cognitive therapy (MBCT), and found favorable treatment outcomes (Williams, McManus, Muse, & Williams, 2011). MBT differs from traditional CBT in that it does not challenge the client's beliefs, but instead focuses on training him or her to control attention to anxiety-producing thoughts. Typical MBCT involves helping clients gain awareness of their cycle of anxiety through mindfulness meditation and mindful breathing. During these activities, clients are asked to tune in to their body and conduct a body scan. In this intervention, clients focus their attention on their own bodily cues and notice how their physical symptoms increase as they focus more attention on them. Next, clients are taught to refocus their attention away from previously distressing thoughts with the goal of avoiding the accompanying cycle of anxiety. MBCT places an emphasis on education and encourages clients to practice what they are learning outside of counseling (Lovas & Barsky, 2010). Additionally, it also helps clients gain an overall awareness of their personal anxiety patterns (Williams et al., 2011).

PSYCHOPHARMACOTHERAPY   The use of medications has demonstrated success in treating IAD (Hart & Bjorgvinsson, 2010; Schweitzer, Zafar, Pavlicova, & Fallon, 2011). Some research suggests that clients with IAD who are treated with selective serotonin reuptake inhibitors (SSRIs) achieve significant periods of remission from their symptoms; more research is warranted on the efficacy of SSRIs with this population (Schweitzer et al., 2011). However, counselors should be aware that the use of medications to treat IAD can have unintended side effects, which could increase a client's health-related anxiety.

Fluoxetine and clomipramine have also been found to be effective in reducing illness-related anxiety (Margariños, Zafar, Nissenson, & Blanco, 2002). Fluoxetine and clomipramine are both also used to treat depression and obsessive-compulsive disorders. Additionally, imipramine, also traditionally used to treat depression, was found to be effective in treating IAD that was comorbid with depression (Margariños et al., 2002).

Prognosis

Several studies indicate positive therapeutic outcomes for clients diagnosed with IAD (Hedman et al., 2010; Sørensen et al., 2011; Williams et al., 2011). Treatment interventions that target underlying anxiety and empowering clients to take control of their symptoms may be the most effective in treating IAD (Hedman et al., 2010; Sørensen et al., 2011; Williams et al., 2011). However, as mentioned, accurate identification of the disorder can be a barrier to treatment, as many individuals with IAD are seen in medical settings.

CONVERSION DISORDER (FUNCTIONAL NEUROLOGICAL SYMPTOM DISORDER)

Description of the Disorder and Typical Client Characteristics

Unlike other somatic symptom and related disorders, clients diagnosed with conversion disorder (CD) exhibit actual neurologically based symptoms (e.g., seizures, altered motor function, abnormal movements, difficulties with speech and/or swallowing, and problems with sensory functions; Erten, Yenilmez, Fistikci, & Saatcioglu, 2013). CD can present as deficits in motor activity (e.g., impaired walking, lack of coordination and balance, tremors, paralysis of a limb or body, speech impairment), or as a deficit in the client's senses (e.g., impaired hearing, impaired vision, loss of sense of touch). However, these symptoms are not caused by an organic disease or a psychological disorder, and they can be acute or persistent (APA, 2013).

Many people who have conversion disorder experience a psychological stressor as the precursor to symptomology, with most experiencing at least one major stressor prior to the onset of symptoms (Erten et al., 2013). Psychological stressors can include childhood physical and sexual trauma, the ending of significant relationships, death, and interpersonal relationship problems, among others (APA, 2013; Maqsood, Akram, & Ali, 2010).

CD requires assessment by a physician, and its population prevalence is unclear (APA, 2013). However, the prevalence is higher in women than men (APA, 2013).

Changes resembling those found in CD are common in some culturally sanctioned rituals, and counselors should rule out that the symptoms are not explained better by a cultural context (APA, 2013). Diagnostically, CD and factitious disorder have several key criteria in common. However, a main distinction between the two disorders is that clients with CD do not appear to have conscious control over their symptoms.

Counselor Considerations

As is true with the other somatic disorders, clients with CD do not typically seek counseling services because they perceive their experiences are due to a medical disorder. Clients can also be resistant to considering a psychological explanation for their medical challenges and therefore seek medical solutions.

Counselors should avoid judging whether or not clients are actively producing or controlling their symptoms. Instead, counselors should focus on well-rounded assessment procedures that include further analysis of biopsychosocial influences.

Some research suggests that those who have CD often have maladaptive personality traits and temperaments (APA, 2013; Erten et al., 2013). Individuals diagnosed with CD "have a fear of uncertainty, pessimistic thoughts, are shy and expect problems to arise . . . self-defeating . . . more impulsive, harm avoidant, and sensitive" (Erten at al., 2013, p. 369). When addressing CD in counseling, the goal of counseling should not be to change maladaptive personality traits per se, but to explore adaptive ways of coping with life stressors (Goldstein et al., 2010). For example, counseling could focus on identifying faulty beliefs, developing healthier ways to express emotions, and replacing negative thoughts with affirmative and empowering cognitions.

Several studies support a prevalence of life stressors as an antecedent to the onset of CD. Furthermore, these life stressors have been linked to an increase in symptom severity and the introduction of new symptoms (Maqsood et al., 2010). The therapeutic relationship and process offers clients with CD a safe place to explore childhood trauma or any other key life stressors that may have contributed to the development or maintenance of CD.

Treatment Models and Interventions

Because CD is mostly treated in medical settings, such as neurology clinics, the disorder is rarely encountered among counselors. When counselors do work with clients who have this disorder, it is generally because they have been diagnosed and referred by a medical professional for psychosocial treatment. Treatment is further complicated by the manifestation of real neurological symptoms. Therefore, good communication between the treatment team members (e.g., the client's primary physician, neurologist, and mental health provider) is strongly recommended. Additionally, assessment should focus on the biological, psychological, and social aspects of the client's life (Stone, Vuilleumier, & Friedman, 2010).

Literature about the effective use of psychotropic medications in the treatment of CD is sparse. No randomized controlled studies which suggest the use of psychotropic as a stand-alone therapy could be found in the literature, suggesting that medications are not, at this time, an appropriate treatment intervention.

PSYCHOEDUCATION Psychoeducation with CD involves educating clients about the various aspects of CD including some of the typical symptoms, origins, and treatments. Psychoeducation typically includes providing information on the alternative origins of the symptoms (e.g., stress, psychological or environmental stressors); a plan for the management of symptoms; and ways to control symptoms and prevent them from escalating (Baxter et al., 2012). Psychoeducation can improve an understanding of the condition, and research suggests that it may decrease symptoms (Baxter et al., 2012). When providing psychoeducation, it is important that it be a collaborative process between the client, the medical treatment team, and the counselor. The client must come to understand the nonmedically based diagnosis and be willing to address the psychological origins of his or her symptoms. When using psychoeducation, counselors can help clients understand their diagnosis, teach them ways to control and cope with their illness, and helping them construct a plan of action to move forward (Baxter et al., 2012).

MINDFULNESS-BASED THERAPY (MBT) Counselors utilizing MBT encourage clients to (a) separate the self from overstimulating physical environments and maintain a focus on the here and now; (b) focus on living more fully and healthily rather than eliminating symptoms; and (c) reengage in activities, even if physical discomfort was experienced (Baslet & Hill, 2011). By learning to focus on their moment-to-moment interactions instead of their physical symptoms, clients can begin to alleviate the symptoms associated with CD (Baslet & Hill, 2011). Similar to other forms of therapy, MBT begins with psychoeducation as well as stress-management training, prior to mindfulness-based strategies being taught. Initial sessions involve teaching clients mindful meditation, how to focus on the here-and-now, and the principle that thoughts and body sensations cannot be controlled, but actions can be controlled (Baslet & Hill, 2011). Next, the counselor works with clients to shift their focus from obsessive thoughts about their physical complaints to present-moment productivity. For example, in session, if a client complains about memory loss, the counselor could continuously redirect the client's focus to the present by utilizing activities such as drawing and writing activities. A mindfulness perspective aids the client in focusing on his or her experiences (e.g., related to the drawing and writing activities), recounting or over-analyzing the memory loss. The client can then pay attention to his or her moment-by-moment emotions and what he or she was experiencing through his or her senses in the drawing and writing activities. The client can eventually shift from concerns that he or she could not remember past events to being present focused (Baslet & Hill, 2011).

COGNITIVE BEHAVIORAL THERAPY (CBT)   CBT may be effective in treating CD (Goldstein et al., 2010). This treatment focuses on clients' interpretation of the behavioral, emotional, and cognitive responses to their experience. The counselor aids clients in replacing their negative thoughts and beliefs with more positive, affirming cognitions. An important aspect of this approach is clients learning to reengage in activities they have terminated because of the disorder (Goldstein et al., 2010).

In applying this approach, the counselor could ask the client to recall the cognitions and behaviors he or she commonly experiences at the cusp of the altered voluntary motor or sensory function (i.e., an inability to move parts of the body and/or use senses normally). The counselor can then work with the client to identify what distressing thoughts and behaviors are experienced. Once those cognitions and behaviors are identified, the counselor can aid the client in identifying the underlying core beliefs and evaluating the evidence that supports or refutes the maladaptive thoughts and behaviors (Goldstein et al., 2010).

Prognosis

Positive outcomes for clients diagnosed with CD are associated with an acute onset of symptoms (Woolfolk & Allen, 2012). Long-term remission of CD has been seen when symptoms are brief in duration and less severe. Prognosis is complicated by comorbidity with other psychological disorders, including other somatic symptom and related disorders. Although the assessment and diagnosis of CD is difficult (Nicholson, Stone, & Kanaan, 2011), various counseling techniques have demonstrated success in reducing symptomology. However, to facilitate successful outcomes, any therapeutic intervention should involve a treatment team approach.

PSYCHOLOGICAL FACTORS AFFECTING OTHER MEDICAL CONDITIONS

Description of the Disorder and Typical Client Characteristics

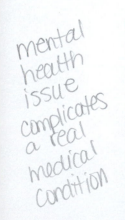

Psychological factors affecting other medical conditions (PFAMC) is a new disorder in the *DSM-5*. PFAMC replaced the previous related *DSM-IV-TR* diagnosis "Other conditions that may be a focus of clinical attention" (APA, 2000, p. 731). PFAMC is different from the other somatic symptom and related disorders in that an actual medical condition exists, but is complicated by psychological and/or behavioral factors. For example, a client's asthma may be exasperated by anxiety (APA, 2013). Those with this disorder may present with poor psychosocial interaction, maladaptive coping skills, life stressors or trauma, and/or a rejection of symptoms leading to noncompliance with medical advice. The prevalence of this disorder is unknown.

mental health issue complicates a real medical condition

Counselor Considerations

PFAMC can be confused with other diagnosable mental health disorders. Counselors are encouraged to exercise caution when determining whether the psychological factors or their effect on the medical condition are of key importance, and medical professionals will need to be consulted to make these determinations.

A diagnosis commonly mistaken for PFAMC is adjustment disorder. The hallmark of adjustment disorder is that the onset of symptoms developed in response to a stressor, such as the development of a medical condition. In contrast, an already existing medical condition is aggravated by psychological factors in PFAMC. For example, a client may experience severe anxiety following a diagnosis of cancer and would therefore be diagnosed with adjustment disorder. However, if a client's hypertension worsens after becoming severely distressed, he or she would be diagnosed with PFAMC.

As with any psychological distress, counselors will need to use basic counseling microskills and empathic understanding to help clients work on alleviating some of the psychological triggers or factors exacerbating their symptoms. Counselors should be aware of the medical condition and take time to research all of the related symptoms and treatments. Additionally, the presence of an actual medical condition is a key distinction from other somatic symptom and related disorders, and these considerations should be incorporated into counseling.

Treatment Models and Interventions

As this is a new psychological disorder in the *DSM* system, randomized controlled studies have not been conducted and little is known about the effectiveness of treatments.

PSYCHOEDUCATION   The goal of psychoeducation is to increase the client's awareness of, and provide helpful information about PFAMC. Clients with PFAMC may be lacking awareness about how psychological responses can worsen their medical conditions. Psychoeducation can involve discussing how the medical condition is specifically affected by psychological distress, developing a plan for managing the distress, and identifying and learning healthier coping strategies (Baxter et al., 2012). Again, counselors need to be aware of their appropriate scope of practice when providing education, and they must consult and refer clients to medical professionals as appropriate.

COGNITIVE BEHAVIORAL THERAPY (CBT)   Many of the principles and interventions used in CBT can be applied to treat PFAMC (Woolfolk & Allen, 2012). For example, when aiming to decrease unhealthy thoughts and reduce physiological responses, thought records can be used to help clients identify and change activating cognitions and behaviors. Additionally, relaxation and stress management training can be used to assist clients with learning effective coping strategies (Goldstein et al., 2010; Woolfolk & Allen, 2012).

PSYCHOPHARMACOTHERAPY   The use of antidepressant and antianxiety medications may be effective in relieving the psychological distress associated with this disorder (Somashekar, Jainer, & Wuntakal, 2013). Many of the underlying complications of this disorder are psychologically based, and therefore, may respond well to a combination of psychosocial treatments and psychopharmacotherapy. Any medication chosen should be examined carefully for potential side effects, as they may exacerbate the psychological and/or medical symptoms.

Prognosis

The prognosis of PFAMC will be contingent on adequate treatment of the psychological factors. However, as with the other somatic symptom disorders, various forms of treatment have been found to have positive outcomes for clients. Because this disorder is comorbid with a wide variety of psychological disorders, the first barrier to positive outcomes for clients will be accurate diagnosis and assessment. Treatment will then need to be focused on helping the client find healthier ways of managing his or her health-related distress.

FACTITIOUS DISORDER

Description of the Disorder and Typical Client Characteristics

Factitious disorder (FD) is one of the most difficult disorders to identify and monitor. FD contains two subtypes, factitious disorder imposed on self and factitious disorder imposed on another (formally referred to as factitious disorder by proxy in the *DSM-IV-TR*). In factitious disorder imposed on self, physical and/or psychological symptoms are feigned with no obvious personal external gains or rewards to the individual. In factitious disorder imposed on another, an individual falsifies physical and/or psychological symptoms in a third party (e.g., a child) with no obvious external rewards or gains. Factitious disorder imposed on another most commonly involves a caregiver feigning symptoms in order to gain "attention for being a devoted parent of a child who is constantly sick" and "deceiving and manipulating physicians and other medical staff who are usually respected for their knowledge and influence" (Frye & Feldman, 2012, p. 50). In either category, symptoms can occur in the midst of a single episode or recurrent episodes (APA, 2013).

The key motivation for feigning FD symptoms is to play the "sick role" and gain the attention of medical personnel, thereby meeting a "psychological need" (Kanaan & Wessely, 2010, p. 70) of which the person is not typically conscious or aware. Clients with FD do not seek external rewards such as money or housing as a result of the illness. Instead, they appear to fake illness in order to replicate relationships they cannot normally acquire in their social environments, or to get out of undesirable situations (e.g., tumultuous relationships and stressful work conditions; IsHak et al., 2010). This can lead to intense and often unhealthy relationships with medical staff, and strained interpersonal relationships. In FD by proxy, the caregiver often increases the symptom severity if the medical staff is not interested in the child, which can lead to child abuse and maltreatment (Criddle, 2010).

According to several case studies, those with FD initially present with patterns of repetitive hospital and emergency room visits, inconsistencies in their medical and/or psychological symptomology, a history of unemployment or inability to maintain continuous employment, doctor shopping or frequently changing medical and psychological staff, and noncompliance with treatment recommendations. Additionally, women are more likely to be diagnosed with FD than men, and individuals with FD sometimes have a background of working in health care–related fields (Sansone & Sansone, 2012). The prevalence of FD is largely unknown, but is estimated to be between 0.5% in the general population and up to 8% for individuals hospitalized in psychiatric units (APA, 2013; IsHak et al., 2010). The incidence of FD by proxy is even more unclear, with estimates suggesting that from 2 in 100,000 to 1 in 1,000,000 children are affected (Criddle, 2010).

Counselor Considerations

Because FD, by definition, involves deception, it can be extremely difficult to identify and diagnose. Further complicating accurate detection is that an individual may actually have a medical condition or psychological diagnosis, but may be exaggerating, intensifying, or causing new injuries to add to the severity of the preexisting condition (Hagglund, 2009). Additionally, a client may appear to have symptoms of a medical disorder when none exists. For example, a client may initially be treated for Crohn's disease, yet after numerous emergency room admissions and complaints of depression, be hospitalized for a psychological evaluation. During this hospitalization, it might be revealed that the client is actually inserting a toothbrush in her or his rectum at night in order to simulate symptoms of Crohn's disease (IsHak et al., 2010).

Most cases of FD are discovered in primary care settings. However, discovery of FD is difficult due to the incidence of doctor shopping associated with the disorder; if they do not receive the desired attention or outcomes, they often immediately discharge themselves from the medical facility and seek another physician (Criddle, 2010). Therefore, counselors are rarely in a position to be the first to identify this disorder.

Further complicating diagnosis in FD by proxy is the role that medical professionals unwittingly take in reinforcing the outcomes the person seeks (i.e., emotional connection, validation), thus furthering the maltreatment of the child. Medical professionals may be deceived because of the caregiver's adeptness at deception and feigning symptoms, fear of litigation on the physician's part, broken and inaccurate medical records, and the presentation of the caregiver as caring and warm (Criddle, 2010).

When FD is the source of treatment, it is often dually diagnosed with another somatic symptom and related disorder. A connection between FD and personality and depressive disorders has been demonstrated in the literature, with some literature positing a psychoanalytical link between parental attachment and unresolved abandonment issues (Hagglund, 2009). Cases of FD by proxy may be encountered in a school setting and present as the caregiver requesting services for the student that are not needed (Frye & Feldman, 2012). These services typically include costly evaluations by the school psychologist to determine if physical or mental disabilities are present.

Counselors should be aware of the seriousness of child abuse by proxy in FD. In these cases, symptoms may start off mild, with the caregiver feigning symptoms not experienced by the child. However, if the caregiver does not receive the attention he or she is seeking, he or she may start to tamper with lab specimens or even medical records (Criddle, 2010). At its most severe, caregivers may resort to inducing an illness in the child by poisoning, suffocation, breaking bones, putting foreign bodies in their child, and reinfecting wounds or needle sites (Criddle, 2010). In working with someone with FD by proxy, counselors should ensure that the person with FD is separated from the person being harmed (Criddle, 2010). In the case of suspected child abuse, counselors are urged to report their suspicions to the primary physician and the appropriate child welfare agency. It is also important that counselors carefully detail and document factual observations.

The dilemma faced by many professionals working with FD is whether or not confrontation is necessary or helpful. Several recommendations highlight the need to focus on the motivations for feigning symptoms rather than on the symptoms themselves (IsHak et al., 2010; Kozlowska, Foley, & Savage, 2012). When individuals with FD are confronted, therapeutic rapport can be irreversibly damaged and an increased risk for suicide and/or self-harm sometimes emerges. Instead, counselors are encouraged to "view the symptoms as part of an unconscious process rather than telling the patient that the problem is *all in your head*" (Sharma & Manjula, 2013, p. 118). Counselors should note that people with FD may be resistant to recommendations that risk exposure of the feigned symptoms (e.g., psychological evaluations or medical assessments). It may also be helpful to direct the client's focus away from the actual physical symptoms and to explore themes of abandonment, rejection, and social inadequacy.

Treatment Models and Interventions

Because of the previously mentioned difficulties in determining this disorder's presence, and because of the secretive nature of this disorder, there are no clear guidelines in the literature for treating FD (Sansone & Sansone, 2012). Counselors are encouraged to assist the client with identifying the onset of symptomology and any relevant biopsychosocial events that occurred during that time. Taking a nonblaming stance and focusing on collaboration with the client is essential (Kozlowska et al., 2012).

The starting point for the treatment of FD is accurate diagnosis (Sansone & Sansone, 2012), yet accurate diagnosis of FD can take several years because of doctor shopping, physicians' fears of malpractice lawsuits, the possibility of actual medical pathology, and inconsistent medical histories. Factitious disorder by proxy often involves deep-rooted psychological issues on the part of the caregiver that should be met with empathy (Clarke & Skokauskas, 2010).

Family members or significant others can provide crucial information about the medical and psychosocial history of the client; information that can be incorporated into the therapeutic process (IsHak et al., 2010; Koslowska et al., 2012). Family therapy can be utilized to "untangle and understand the process of how the family arrived at their current position, and to identity what factors trigger and perpetuate the family's pattern of functioning" (Kozlowska et al., 2012, p. 571).

Kozlowska et al. (2012) described a family systems–oriented treatment approach that was helpful in treating this disorder in a school-age child. First, a clinical assessment was performed to understand the client's and family's history and to ascertain a full medical history. Then, assessments were used to better understand attachment styles and levels of emotional and psychological functioning. This assessment provided the family with insight into the maladaptive functioning that might have encouraged the feigning of symptoms. Lastly, interventions focused on problem solving and empowerment were utilized to assist the family with taking responsibility for the solution and decreasing their reliance on medical staff. The treatment was successful for the client, as her symptoms disappeared and she was able to return to regular school activities (Kozlowska et al., 2012).

Prognosis

Because of the difficulty associated with detecting and tracking the disorder, the prognosis of FD is unclear. FD by proxy should be viewed as a potentially life-threatening disorder with high recidivism rates; the prognosis is poor if a child victim is left with an untreated caregiver with FD (Criddle, 2010). Those with FD often cycle through medical facilities for several years, accumulating high medical bills and receiving expensive procedures. The counselor should avoid confronting and blaming the client, and instead focus on the deep-rooted psychological origins of the behaviors. With proper treatment and the use of an interdisciplinary team, individuals with FD can develop healthier ways of expressing their psychological distress and getting their needs met.

TREATMENT PLAN FOR STEPHANIE

This chapter began with a discussion of Stephanie, a 25-year-old single Caucasian female with persistent, unexplained neck pain. Stephanie meets the criteria for somatic symptom disorder. A counselor must consider a number of factors before moving ahead with a strength-based treatment approach. The following I CAN START conceptual framework outlines treatment considerations that may be helpful in working with Stephanie.

C = Contextual Assessment

Stephanie is a young college-educated adult female. She is currently unemployed and living in her parents' home. Within their home, she is safe and comfortable; all her basic needs are being met. Because Stephanie's family is from a high socioeconomic status, she has a number of opportunities and privileges. She reports no religious beliefs or foundations that can be included in her treatment plan. She is traversing varied developmental issues. She is struggling with determining her career direction and focus, and with establishing her needs and wants apart from her parents.

A = Assessment and Diagnosis

Diagnosis = Somatic Symptom Disorder (with predominant pain, persistent, moderate) 300.82 (F45.1).
To aid in her career development, Stephanie will complete two career development assessment measures. While she has health symptoms, she has received multiple medical evaluations from numerous physician specialists.

N = Necessary Level of Care

Outpatient, individual counseling (once per week)

S = Strength-Based Lens

Self: Stephanie is an easygoing, worldly, active, curious, and sociable young woman. She is intelligent and has done well academically. Stephanie is charismatic, extremely likable, and seems to make friends very easily. She has a strong social support system. She used to enjoy being outdoors and engaging in physical activities (e.g., skiing, biking, swimming). Despite her somatic concerns, she enjoys good health, and does not, upon initial assessment, have any co-occurring mental disorders (which is unusual for someone diagnosed with this disorder given the high co-occurrence of anxiety and depressive disorders).

Family: Stephanie's parents are loving and supportive. They have provided her with a place to live and they meet all of her basic needs. She cares about her mother and father and appears to have a solid relationship with them, although her father desires that she seek further education to enable her to enter a professional occupation. Her family supports her decision to enter counseling.

Community: Stephanie lives in a safe and supportive community. She appears to be very social and she still has a number of friends within the community. Her family's social status also provides her with access to a number of opportunities and resources in the community. In the past, she was more involved in the local community by teaching young children how to ski. She still possesses the desire to help others in the community learn and succeed.

T = Treatment Approach

Affective-Cognitive Behavioral Therapy (A-CBT)

A = Aim and Objectives of Treatment (3-month objectives)

Stephanie will become better aware of how her thoughts impact her emotions, behaviors, and perception of pain → Stephanie will utilize a thought and feelings record five times a week to document the interplay between her thoughts, feelings, behaviors, and perceived levels of pain.

Stephanie will learn to apply cognitive skills to challenge her negative somatic-related thoughts → Stephanie will identify and learn two thought changing skills (e.g., thought stopping, cognitive restructuring) to help her examine how these thought patterns are impacting her emotions and subsequent actions; she will apply these cognitive skills and challenge her negative thoughts (thus altering her emotions and actions) 80% of the time.

Stephanie will learn to communicate her thoughts, feelings, and needs in appropriate, assertive ways → Stephanie will learn how to assertively express her thoughts and feelings directly with family members (e.g., father) and friends, and she will do this at least five times a week.

Stephanie will not let her fear of physical activity get in the way of her engaging in activities she enjoys → Stephanie will learn two relaxation (e.g., stress management techniques) that she can use to help her tolerate her perceptions of pain/physical discomfort, and she will use these techniques 75% of the time so as to participate in activities she once enjoyed. Additionally, Stephanie will create a hierarchy of stimuli that she perceives cause her discomfort (e.g., physical activities around the house, to a relaxed swim in the pool, moving to the more strenuous outdoor activities she enjoys such as skiing). She will gradually resist the desire to avoid these activities, moving to a place where she engages in the activities she wants to engage in 75% of the time.

Stephanie will develop career plans and communicate these to her family → Stephanie will select and read one book on choosing a career path. She will reflect weekly on this connection by journaling and then evaluating the pros and cons of each potential schooling or career option. She will also complete 2 career assessments and review the results with her counselor. She will develop a plan for her career development, and she will convey this plan to her family.

R = Research-Based Interventions (based on A-CBT)

Counselor will help Stephanie develop and apply the following skills:

- Increase awareness of cognitions and how they impact emotions, actions/behaviors, and pain perceptions
- Challenge negative thoughts that contribute to the maintenance of the behavioral avoidance cycle
- Tolerate physical symptoms through relaxation and stress management strategies
- Engage in behavioral experiments to connect with previously enjoyed activities
- Develop her ability to communicate her thoughts and feelings in appropriate, assertive ways

T = Therapeutic Support Services

Continued pain management consultation with a physician

Weekly individual counseling

Medical evaluation for the integration of holistic wellness techniques such as exercise, diet, and nutrition

References

Abbass, A., Kisely, S., & Kroenke, K. (2009). Short-term psychodynamic psychotherapy for somatic disorders. *Psychotherapy and Psychosomatics, 78*, 265–274.

Aliyev, N. A., & Aliyev, Z. N. (2011). Lamotrigine in the immediate treatment of outpatients with depersonalization disorder without psychiatric comorbidity: Randomized, double-blind, placebo-controlled study. *Journal of Clinical Psychopharmacology, 31*, 61–65.

Arnault, D. S., & Kim, O. (2008). Is there an Asian idiom of distress? Somatic symptoms in female Japanese and Korean students. *Archives of Psychiatric Nursing, 22*, 27–38.

American Psychiatric Association (APA). (2013). *Diagnostic and statistical manual of mental disorders* (5th ed.; DSM-5). Washington, DC: Author.

Baars, E. W., van der Hart, O., Nijenhuis, E. R., Chu, J. A., Glas, G., & Draijer, N. (2010). Predicting stabilizing treatment outcomes for complex posttraumatic stress disorder and dissociative identity disorder: An expertise-based prognostic model. *Journal of Trauma and Dissociation, 12*, 67–87.

Baslet, G., & Hill, J. (2011). Case report: Brief mindfulness-based psychotherapeutic interview during inpatient hospitalization in a patient with conversion and dissociation. *Clinical Case Studies, 10*, 95–109.

Baxter, S., Mayor, R., Baird, W., Brown, R., Cock, H., Howlett, S., . . . Reuber, M. (2012). Understanding patient perceptions following a psycho-educational intervention for psychogenic non-epileptic seizures. *Epilepsy and Behavior, 23*, 487–493.

Bernstein, E., & Putnam, F. W. (1986). Development, reliability and validity of a dissociation scale. *The Journal of Nervous and Mental Disease, 174*, 727–735.

Bryant, R. A., Brooks, R., Silove, D., Creamer, M., O'Donnell, M., McFarlane, A. C., . . . Marmar, C. R. (2009). The latent structure of the Peritraumatic Dissociative Experiences Questionnaire. *Journal of Traumatic Stress, 22*, 69–73.

Church of God. (2013). *Beliefs: Church of God is . . .* Retrieved from: http://www.churchofgod.org

Clarke, C. & Skokauskas, N. (2010). Pediatric symptom falsification ("Munchausen syndrome by proxy") psychiatric manifestations. *British Journal of Medical Practitioners, 3*, 39–42.

Cloitre, M., Petkova, E., Wang, J., & Lu, F. (2012). An examination of the influence of a sequential treatment on the course and impact of dissociation among women with PTSD related to childhood abuse. *Depression and Anxiety, 29*, 709–717.

Criddle, L. (2010). Monsters in the closet: Munchausen syndrome by proxy. *Critical Care Nurse, 30*, 46–54.

Dell, P. F. (2006). Multidimensional Inventory of Dissociation (MID): A comprehensive measure of pathological dissociation. *Journal of Trauma and Dissociation, 7*, 77–106.

Dell, P. F. (2013). Three dimensions of dissociative amnesia. *Journal of Trauma and Dissociation, 14*, 25–39.

Erten, E., Yenilmez, Y., Fistikci, N., & Saatcioglu, O. (2013). The relationship between temperament and character in conversion disorder and comorbid depression. *Comprehensive Psychiatry, 55*, 354–361.

Farrar, J., & Farrar, S. (1984). *A witches' bible: The complete witches' handbook*. Blaine, WA: Phoenix Publishing.

Fine, C. G. (1999). The tactical-integration model for the treatment of dissociative identity disorder and allied dissociative disorders. *American Journal of Psychotherapy, 53*, 361– 376.

Frye, E. M., & Feldman, M.D. (2012). Factitious disorder by proxy in educational settings: A review. *Educational Psychology Review, 24*, 47–61.

Gentile, J. P., Dillon, K. S., & Gillig, P. M. (2013). Psychotherapy and pharmacotherapy for patients with dissociative identity disorder. *Innovations in Clinical Neuroscience, 10*, 22–29.

Gillig, P. M. (2009). Dissociative identity disorder: A controversial diagnosis. *Psychiatry, 6*, 24–29.

Goldstein, L., Chalder, T., Chigwedere, C., Khondoker, M., Moriarty, J., Toone, B., & . . . Mellers, J. (2010). Cognitive-behavioral therapy for psychogenic nonepileptic seizures: A pilot RCT. *Neurology, 74*, 1986–1994.

Guglielmo, R., Martinotti, G., & Janiri, L. (2012). Gabapentin as add-on treatment for somatoform disorder: A case report. *Clinical Neuropharmacology, 35*, 45–46.

Hagglund, L. A. (2009). Challenges in the treatment of factitious disorder: A case study. *Archives of Psychiatric Nursing, 23*, 58–64.

Harper, S. (2011). An examination of structural dissociation of the personality and the implications for cognitive behavioural therapy. *The Cognitive Behaviour Therapist, 4*, 53–67.

Hart, J., & Bjorgvinsson, T. (2010). Health anxiety and hypochondriasis: Description and treatment issues highlighted through a case illustration. *Bulletin of the Menninger Clinic, 74*, 122–140.

Hayes, S. C., Strosahl, K. D., & Wilson, K. G. (2012). *Acceptance and commitment therapy: The process and practice of mindful change*. New York, NY: Guilford.

Hedman, E., Ljotsson, B., Andersson, E., Ruck, C., Andersson, G., & Lindefors, N. (2010). Effectiveness and cost offset analysis of group CBT for hypochondriasis delivered in a psychiatric setting: An open trail. *Cognitive Behavior Therapy, 39*, 239–250.

Hollander, H. E. (2009). ECEM (Eye Closure, Eye Movements): Application to depersonalization disorder. *American Journal of Clinical Hypnosis, 52*, 95–109.

International Society for the Study of Trauma and Dissociation. (2011). [Chu, J. A., Dell, P. F., Van der Hart, O., Cardeña, E., Barach, P. M., Somer, E., . . . Twombly, J.]. Guidelines for treating dissociative identity disorder in adults, third revision. *Journal of Trauma & Dissociation, 12*, 115–187.

IsHak, W. W., Rasyidi, E., Saah, T., Vasa, M., Ettekal, A., & Fan, A. (2010). Factitious disorder case series with variations of psychological and physical symptoms. *Primary Psychiatry, 17*, 40–43.

Kanaan, R. A., & Wessely, S. C. (2010). The origins of factitious disorder. *History of the Human Sciences, 23*, 68–85.

King, J. H. (n.d.). *Who we are: Our beliefs*. Retrieved from: http://www.iphc.org

Kozlowska, K., Foley, S., & Savage, B. (2012). Fabricated illness: Working within the family system to find a pathway to health. *Family Process, 51*, 570–587.

Lewis-Fernandez, R., Gorritz, M., Raggio, G. A., Pelaez, C., Chen, H., & Guarnaccia, P. J. (2010). Association of trauma-related disorders and dissociation with four idioms of distress among Latino psychiatric outpatients. *Culture, Medicine, and Psychiatry, 34*, 219–243.

Lovas, D. A., & Barsky, A. J. (2010). Mindfulness-based cognitive therapy for hypochondriasis, or severe health anxiety: A pilot study. *Journal of Anxiety Disorder, 24*, 931–935.

Magariños, M., Zafar, U., Nissenson, K., & Blanco, C. (2002). Epidemiology and treatment of hypochondriasis. *CNS Drugs, 16*(1), 9–22.

Maqsood, N., Akram, B., & Ali, W. (2010). Patients with conversion disorder: Psycho-social stressors and life events. *Professional Medical Journal, 17*, 715–720.

Marmar, C. R., Weiss, D. S., & Metzler, T. J. (1997). The Peritraumatic Dissociative Experiences Questionnaire. In J. P. Wilson & T. M. Keane (Eds.), *Assessing psychological trauma and PTSD* (pp. 412–428). New York, NY: Guilford.

Nicholson, T. R., Stone, J., & Kanaan, R. A. (2011). Conversion disorder: A problematic diagnosis. *Journal of Neurology, Neurosurgery, and Psychiatry, 82*, 1267–1273.

Nickel, R., Ademmer, K., & Egle, U. T. (2010). Manualized psychodynamic-interactional group therapy for the treatment of somatoform pain disorders. *Bulletin of the Menninger Clinic, 74*, 219–237.

Nicolini, H., Bakish, D., Duenas, H., Spann, M., Erickson, J., Hallberg, C., . . . Russell, J. M. (2009). Improvement of psychic and somatic symptoms in adult patients with generalized anxiety disorder: Examination from a duloxetine, venlafaxine extended-release and placebo-controlled trial. *Psychological Medicine, 39*, 267–276.

Noyes, R., Longley, S. L., Langbehn, D. R., Stuart, S. P., & Kukoyi, O. A. (2010). Hypochondriacal symptoms associated with a less therapeutic physician-patient relationship. *Psychiatry, 73,* 57–69.

Nuller, Y. L., Morozova, M. G., Kushnir, O. N., & Hamper, N. (2001). Effect of naloxone therapy on depersonalization: A pilot study. *Journal of Psychopharmacology, 15,* 93–95.

Olsen, S. A., Clapp, J. D., Parra, G. R., & Beck, J. G. (2013). Factor structure of the Dissociative Experiences Scale: A examination across sexual assault status. *Journal of Psychopathology and Behavioral Assessment.* Online First Articles. Retrieved from: http://link.springer.com/article/10.1007/s10862-013-9347-4/fulltext.html

Pais, S. (2009). A systemic approach to the treatment of dissociative identity disorder. *Journal of Family Psychotherapy, 20,* 72–88.

Physicians' Desk Reference. (2011). *PDR consumer guide to prescription drugs.* Montvale, NJ: PDR Network, LLC.

Ross, C. A. (2008). Case report: A convicted sex offender with dissociative identity disorder. *Journal of Trauma and Dissociation, 9,* 551–562.

Rothschild, D. (2009). On becoming one-self: Reflections on the concept of integration as seen through a case of dissociative identity disorder. *Psychoanalytic Dialogues, 19,* 175–187.

Ryder, A. G., Yang, J., Zhu, X., Yao, S., Yi, J., Heine, S. J., . . . Bagby, R. M. (2008). The cultural shaping of depression: Somatic symptoms in China, psychological symptoms in North America? *Journal of Abnormal Psychology, 117*(2), 200–313.

Sansone, R. A., & Sansone, L. A. (2012). Medically self-sabotaging behavior and its relationship with borderline personality. *Primary Care Reports, 18,* 37–47.

Sattel, H., Lahmann, C., Gündel, H., Guthrie, E., Kruse, J., Noll-Hussong, M., . . . Henningsen, P. (2012). Brief psychodynamic interpersonal psychotherapy for patients with multisomatoform disorder: Randomised controlled trial. *The British Journal of Psychiatry: The Journal of Mental Science, 200,* 60–67.

Schade, N., Torres, P., & Beyebach, M. (2011). Cost-efficiency of a brief family intervention for somatoform patients in primary care. *Families, Systems, and Health, 29,* 197–205.

Schweitzer, P. J., Zafar, U., Pavlicova, M., & Fallon, B. A. (2011). Long-term follow-up of hypochondriasis after selective serotonin reuptake inhibitor treatment. *Journal of Clinical Psychopharmacology, 31,* 365–368.

Shapiro, F. (2001). *Eye movement desensitization and reprocessing: Basic principles, protocols, and procedures* (2nd ed.). New York, NY: Guilford.

Sharma, M. P., & Manjula, M. (2013). Behavioural and psychological management of somatic symptom disorders: An overview. *International Review of Psychiatry, 25,* 116–124.

Somashekar, B., Jainer, A., & Wuntakal, B. (2013). Psychopharmacotherapy of somatic symptoms disorders. *International Review of Psychiatry, 25,* 107–115.

Somer, E. (2006). Culture-bound dissociation: A comparative analysis. *Psychiatric Clinics of North America, 29,* 213–226.

Sørensen P., Birket-Smith, M., Wattar, U., Buemann, I., & Salkovskis, P. (2011). A randomized clinical trial of cognitive behavioural therapy versus short-term psychodynamic psychotherapy versus no intervention for patients with hypochondriasis. *Psychological Medicine, 41,* 431–441.

Stein, D. J., Koenen, K. C., Friedman, M. J., Hill, E., McLaughlin, K. A., Petukhova, M., . . . Kessler, R. C. (2013). Dissociation in posttraumatic stress disorder: Evidence from the World Mental Health surveys. *Biological Psychiatry, 73,* 302–312.

Stone, J., Vuilleumier, P., & Friedman, J. H. (2010). Conversion disorder: Separating the "how" from the "why." *Neurology, 74,* 190–191.

U.S. National Library of Medicine (NLM) & National Institutes of Health (NIH). (2013). *MedlinePlus: Naloxone injection.* Retrieved from: http://www.nlm.nih.gov/medlineplus/

White, M., & Epston, D. (1990). *Narrative means to a therapeutic ends.* New York, NY: W. W. Norton.

Williams, M. J., McManus, F., Muse, K., & Williams, J. M. (2011). Mindfulness-based cognitive therapy for severe health anxiety (hypochondriasis): An interpretative phenomenological analysis of patients' experiences. *British Journal of Clinical Psychology, 50,* 379–397.

Woo, D. (2010). A case of dissociative amnesia in an older woman. *Clinical Geriatrics, 18,* 7–10.

Woolfolk, R. L., & Allen, L. A. (2010). Affective-cognitive behavioral therapy for somatization disorder. *Journal of Cognitive Psychotherapy: An International Quarterly, 24,* 116–131.

Woolfolk, R. L., & Allen, L. A. (2012). Cognitive behavioral therapy for somatoform disorders. In I. R. De Oliveira (Ed.), *Standard and innovative strategies in cognitive behavior therapy* (pp. 118–144). Croatia: InTech.

Sexual desire disorder
affect men + women
have not been extensively researched, especially in men
responsive to meds

Sleep-Wake Disorders, Sexual Dysfunctions, Paraphilic Disorders, and Gender Dysphoria

ED
caused by
meds,
mental health
responsive to couple's therapy

Paraphilias
problem when
behaviors cause
distress to
self or others

GDD-(GID)
emotional
difficulties
as result of
gender issues
often related
to judgement
and stigma

Matthew J. Paylo, Victoria E. Kress, and Brandy L. Kelly Gilea

CASE STUDY: MR. JONES

Mr. Jones, a 65-year-old Caucasian man, self-refers to counseling with a complaint of severe sleep disturbance that affects his daytime functioning. Mr. Jones has three adult children and a wife of 42 years with whom he has a good relationship. He first experienced insomnia approximately five years ago when the small business he owns ran into financial difficulties. Within a year his business stabilized, but he found his sleep problems continued.

Over the years, he has been prescribed a number of medications by his primary care physician. He has taken temazepam (i.e., Restoril), zolpidem (i.e., Ambien), as well as antidepressants such as trazodone and amitriptyline (i.e., Elavil). While some preliminary benefit was derived from these medications, Mr. Jones gave up on each one after several weeks because of their side effects and his perception that they were not effective.

Mr. Jones's sleep difficulties have had a serious impact on his functioning. He finds that he feels tired and irritable most days, especially when the night before was a sleepless night. He used to walk with his friends every morning, but has stopped because of his fatigue. He is finding that his difficulties focusing and the irritability he experiences secondary to a bad night's sleep keep him from engaging with his friends and family as much as he used to. He has also taken to drinking a pot of coffee a day to keep himself awake. He finds he is making more mistakes in his business and reports his head often feels foggy from the lack of sleep. When he is at work, he often lays his head on his desk and takes short naps.

In terms of his sleep patterns, Mr. Jones notes that he lies down to go to bed at about 10 p.m. Sometimes he falls asleep in less than 10 minutes, but other times it takes him "hours" to fall asleep. He awakens at least three times per night, and at least one of these awakenings lasts 2–3 hours. During these times when he is awake at night, he reports he stares at the clock and becomes frustrated as he thinks things like, "I'll never get to sleep and tomorrow I will feel horrible all day," and "The more time that goes by and I am awake, the worse I will feel tomorrow." These thoughts make him feel anxious and make it even more difficult for him to fall asleep. During these extended time periods when he cannot go back to sleep, he will often get up and work on his business's paper-work. He finds he then falls asleep about 5:30–6:00 a.m., only to fall into a deep sleep until 8 or 9 a.m., at which point he is late for work.

Mr. Jones denies any symptoms of depression, anxiety, or any other mental disorder. He reports some stress related to managing the bookkeeping tasks associated with owning a business. His physician has put him through medical examinations and sent him to a sleep lab for an examination and a sleep study, and no physical abnormalities were found.

SLEEP-WAKE DISORDERS, SEXUAL DYSFUNCTIONS, PARAPHILIC DISORDERS, AND GENDER DYSPHORIA

In this chapter, the sleep-wake disorders, sexual dysfunctions, paraphilic disorders, and gender dysphoria addressed in the *DSM-5* (American Psychiatric Association [APA], 2013) will be explored. Because there are multiple disorders associated with these diagnostic categories, and because these disorders are less frequently the primary focus in counseling, this chapter's structure deviates from that of prior chapters. Instead of individually detailing each specific disorder as was done in prior chapters, the disorders' categories will be summarized and a generalized overview of treatment approaches will be provided. As in the previous chapters, a description of the disorder category and typical client characteristics will first be discussed, followed by counselor considerations and treatment models and interventions.

SLEEP-WAKE DISORDERS

Description of the Disorder and Typical Client Characteristics

Sleep-wake disorders are relatively common, affecting almost 10% of the general population (Ram, Seirawan, Kumar, & Clark, 2010). The most prevalent of these sleep-wake disorders are insomnia, sleep apnea, and restless leg syndrome (Ram et al., 2010). While sleep disturbance can stem from another mental disorder, a general medical condition, or be induced by a substance, the sleep disorders outlined in this section are primary diagnoses, and not symptoms of other disorders or conditions.

In the *DSM-5*, sleep-wake disorders are divided into categories that are based on the type of sleep disturbance: (a) insomnia or the difficult of initiating, maintaining, or returning to sleep; (b) hypersomnia or excessive sleepiness disorders (i.e., hypersomnolence and narcolepsy); (c) breathing-related sleep disorders; (d) circadian rhythm sleep-wake disorder; and (e) parasomnia, or abnormal behaviors or events which occur between wakefulness and sleep (APA, 2013). The following is a brief definition of each disorder category.

- *Insomnia disorder* involves difficulty in initiating, maintaining, or returning to sleep. Most common of all sleep-wake disorders, insomnia is often associated with anxiety, somatized or muscular tension, and stress or life changes (Sadock & Sadock, 2007).
- Hypersomnia involves disorders of excessive sleepiness. *Hypersomnolence disorder* is identified as excessive sleepiness despite adequate nighttime sleep. People with these disorders typically have difficulties waking up, staying awake during daytime hours, or feeling their sleep was restorative, even if they have prolonged periods of sleep. *Narcolepsy* is conceptualized as a need for excessive sleep as seen by involuntarily lapsing into REM sleep during daytime hours. These involuntary lapses often occur during inappropriate times (e.g., when eating, driving, or engaged in sexual activity; Sadock & Sadock, 2007).
- Breathing-related sleep disorders involve abnormal respiration during sleep (e.g., snoring, gasping) and consist of the following disorders: obstructive sleep apnea hypopnea, central sleep apnea, and sleep-related hypoventilation. *Obstructive sleep apnea hypopnea* involves exhibiting abnormal respiration during sleep, with the person consequently feeling fatigued and unrefreshed upon awaking. Essentially, the throat muscles relax and the airway is blocked or airflow is slowed, thus creating a condition where the person stops and starts breathing throughout the sleep cycle. Often this process takes up to 10 seconds, and then begins again with another arousal. This condition more often affects obese, middle-aged people (Sadock & Sadock, 2007). *Central sleep apnea* involves abnormal respirations during sleep, as seen by the stopping and restarting of breathing. Unlike obstructive sleep apnea, central sleep apnea is caused by the brain's inability to send proper signals to the muscles involved in breathing functions. This type of sleep apnea is rare and less common than obstructive sleep apnea. *Sleep-related hypoventilation* involves decreased respiration during sleep, which elevates carbon monoxide levels (APA, 2013).
- *Circadian rhythm sleep-wake disorder* involves a mismatching of one's internal clock (i.e., endogenous circadian sleep-wake system) and one's lifestyle. This sleep disturbance interferes with an individual's ability to function and be alert (because of sleepiness or insomnia) secondary to the mismatch of his or her sleep-wake system.
- Parasomnias, or abnormal behaviors or events that occur between wakefulness and sleep, consist of non-rapid eye movement sleep arousal disorder, nightmare disorder, rapid eye movement sleep behavior disorder, and restless leg syndrome. *Non-rapid eye movement sleep arousal disorder* involves frequently awaking during the beginning three stages of sleep and is accompanied by either a sense of terror (i.e., sleep terrors) or engaging in walking or other activities without exiting the sleep cycle (i.e., sleepwalking). *Nightmare disorder* involves frequently awakening during sleep because of intense, frightening dreams. These dreams cause significant discomfort and distress. *Rapid eye movement sleep behavior disorder* involves frequently making vocalizations or movements during REM sleep. *Restless leg syndrome* is characterized by a desire to move one's legs due to unpleasant, uncomfortable sensations in the legs, which usually occur when sitting or lying down. These repetitive patterns of behavior (i.e., getting up to move around to relieve the sensations secondary to discomfort) can lead to general restlessness, which in turn disrupts sleep.

Counselor Considerations

Sleep disturbances are often a symptom of another mental health concern. Counselors should remember though that sleep symptoms are not always a related to another disorder, and they may in fact be a symptom of a primary sleep disorder (Sadock & Sadock, 2007).

Although counselors can usually diagnose most sleep-wake disorders through the use of traditional clinical interviews, more complicated sleep-wake disorders (i.e., sleep apnea, REM sleep behavior disorders, intractable insomnia) will require counselors to make a referral to a sleep disorder center or to a sleep disorder specialist (e.g., a physician certified in sleep medicine). The benefits of referring clients with more chronic, severe sleep-wake disorders to these centers are the use of laboratory examinations, which include all-night polysomnography (e.g., records of EEG activity). These centers provide a number of laboratory examinations that allow for the accurate diagnosis and treatment of many sleep-wake disorders within a controlled, safe environment.

Treatment Models and Interventions

Sleep patterns and sleep requirements change throughout the life span and affect people in different ways. When sleep disturbances occur, daytime consequences such as sleepiness, fatigue, and insomnia plague one's ability to be alert and function optimally. Generally, cognitive behavioral therapy, behavior therapy, medications, oral applications (i.e., a mouth guard that repositions the lower jaw and tongue during sleep and allows for more open airways and less obstructions in breathing), and ventilators are used to address sleep disturbances (Moul, Morin, Buysse, Reynolds, & Kupfer, 2007; Riemann & Perlis, 2009). Emerging approaches for treating each sleep-wake disorder category (i.e., insomnia, hypersomnia, breathing-related, and parasomnias) will be briefly presented.

INSOMNIA   Insomnia occurs in up to one-third of adults and is more commonly reported in females (APA, 2013). In women, the first onset of insomnia is frequently associated with the birth of a child or menopause (APA, 2013). Numerous randomized controlled trials suggest the effectiveness of medications, cognitive behavioral therapy, and behavior therapy interventions in the treatment of insomnia (Gellis, Arigo, & Elliott, 2013; Jernelov et al., 2012). While clients often utilize sleep medication as a first resort in the management of insomnia, medication (i.e., sedative-hypnotics, benzodiazepines) only provides short-term relief and does not always remain effective in the long-term (Riemann & Perlis, 2009). As such, psychosocial therapies are an important adjunct to the use of medications. Additionally, the long-term side effects and consequences of these medications are not fully understood.

Cognitive behavioral therapy and behavioral interventions appear to be the most effective psychosocial approaches in treating insomnia, and treatment gains are often maintained (Riemann & Perlis, 2009). Although there are differences among the CBT approaches, most of these approaches involve psychoeducation and the establishment of sleep hygiene rules, relaxation techniques, sleep restrictions, and cognitive techniques. Examples of good sleep hygiene rules are: clients only going to bed when tired; only using the bedroom for appropriate bedroom-related activities; regulating the bedroom environment (e.g., light, temperature, noise); and leaving the bedroom if they are unable to fall asleep after 15 minutes, and returning only when tired. The use of relaxation techniques such as progressive muscle relaxation (i.e., the gradual tensing and then relaxing of major muscle groups) allows the client to feel the difference between tense and relaxed muscles, while effectively loosening and soothing muscles, and can aid in relaxation and sleep.

Sleep restriction is another technique often utilized when teaching clients good sleep hygiene. Sleep restriction involves clients only sleeping during one consistent time period a day, and not napping.

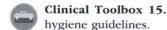 **Clinical Toolbox 15.1:** In the Pearson etext, click here to read good sleep hygiene guidelines.

Secondary to difficulties falling or staying asleep, clients often perseverate and worry about their sleep struggles, and this contributes to insomnia. As such, cognitive thought stopping can also be helpful in encouraging sleep. By confronting and challenging their thoughts, thought stopping can aid a client in breaking the cycle of excessive sleep-related worry. Clients can be invited to role-play cognitive techniques in sessions and then practice them outside of sessions to diminish the impacts of this excessive worry about sleeping and the inability to clear their mind before sleep (Sadock & Sadock, 2007).

 Clinical Toolbox 15.2: In the Pearson etext, click here to watch a psychoeducational/behavioral intervention that can be used in treating insomnia.

CREATIVE TOOLBOX ACTIVITY 15.1   Sleep Hygiene Collage

Victoria E. Kress, PhD, LPCC-S, NCC

Activity Overview

After the client is provided with psychoeducation about good sleep hygiene, he or she is invited to develop a collage that reinforces the learned sleep hygiene concepts (e.g., only go to bed when tired, no taking naps). This activity can be useful with clients who struggle with a variety of sleep disorders (e.g., insomnia, hypersomnia, sleep apnea), or with disorders in which sleep disturbance is a symptom (e.g., depression, bipolar).

Treatment Goal(s) of Activity

Sleep hygiene and psychoeducation are grounded in a cognitive behavioral therapy approach to treating sleep difficulties. The goal of this activity is to help clients learn and apply the concepts of good sleep hygiene, which are demonstrated to be effective in addressing sleep difficulties.

Directions

1. Provide the client with psychoeducation on the basic concepts of good sleep hygiene (see Clinical Toolbox 15.1 as an example resource).
2. Give the client a sheet of paper (with a line down the center) and an assortment of magazines and invite him or her to develop a collage.
3. Instruct the client to cut out and adhere to one side of the paper words and images of things the client does that are NOT consistent with good sleep hygiene.
4. Instruct the client to cut out and adhere to the other side of the paper words and images that ARE consistent with good sleep hygiene.
5. Upon completion and even during the activity, process the sleep hygiene concepts learned and apply them to the client's unique struggles.

Process Questions

1. With regard to the sleep hygiene concepts you learned about today, what are the areas and behaviors where you most struggle?
2. What things are you doing well with regard to sleep hygiene?
3. What are five things you can start doing today to enhance your sleep hygiene?
4. What barriers do you think you will have with regard to improving your sleep hygiene?
5. What supports or resources do you need to pull on to help you achieve better sleep hygiene?

too much

HYPERSOMNIA   Hypersomnia, or disorders of excessive sleepiness such as hypersomnolence and narcolepsy, warrant a medical evaluation and consultation. Psychopharmacotherapy is the standard of care for these disorders, and typically includes the use of stimulants (e.g., amphetamines) and other pharmacological treatments (e.g., antidepressants; Conroy, Novick, & Swanson, 2012). The stimulant medication mazindol may be effective in reducing symptoms, especially in cases of drug-resistant hypersomnia (Nittur et al., 2013). Modafinil is also commonly used to treat hypersomnia and promote daytime wakefulness (Lavault et al., 2011). Although considered more of an adjunct treatment, behavior therapy (e.g., sleep education, sleep hygiene) is often utilized in the management of these disorders and complements psychopharmacotherapy interventions (Billiard et al., 2006; Conroy et al., 2012).

> **Clinical Toolbox 15.3:** In the Pearson etext, click here to read about an activity that can be used to help clients initiate sleep.

In particular, clients with narcolepsy benefit from going to bed and waking at the same time each day, as well as having scheduled naps structured throughout their daytime hours (e.g., either one long nap midday or multiple naps spaced out equally throughout the day; Billiard et al., 2006).

BREATHING-RELATED SLEEP DISORDERS   Breathing-related sleep disorders involve abnormal respiration during sleep (e.g., snoring, gasping) and includes the following disorders: obstructive sleep apnea hypopnea, central sleep apnea, and sleep-related hypoventilation. Cultural factors can be relevant in the diagnosis of breathing-related sleep disorders. Females may underreport snoring and are more likely to suffer from symptoms of fatigue than sleepiness (APA, 2013). Those of Asian ancestry may also be at a higher risk of developing obstructive sleep apnea hypopnea (APA, 2013).

Sleep apnea, or the cessation of breathing for short periods of time during sleep, is the most common breathing-related sleep disorder. In the case of *obstructive sleep apnea hypopnea* (i.e., collapsing of the pharyngeal airway with decreased airflow), treatment consists of behavioral interventions (e.g., sleep hygiene), reducing alcohol consumption and smoking, weight loss and dieting, utilizing oral applications and continuous positive airway pressure (CPAP), and using oral surgery procedures (i.e., maxillomandibular advancement [MMA]) when warranted (Azagra-Calero, Espinar-Escalona, Barrera-Mora, Liamas-Carreras, & Solano-Reina, 2012). CPAP, an effective treatment for sleep apnea, involves using a mask that fits directly over one's nose or nose and mouth, and regulates breathing and airflow.

A more invasive intervention, maxillomandibular advancement (MMA), is a surgical procedure that involves moving a person's jaw and stretching the tongue away from the pharynx. MMA is the most evidence-based treatment for obstructive sleep apnea hypopnea, boasting extremely high success rates (i.e., 75–100%) and substantial accompanying improvements in quality of life (Azagra-Calero et al., 2012; Holty & Guilleminault, 2010).

Central sleep apnea (i.e., the decreased communication between the brain and respiratory muscles) treatments include continuous positive airway pressure (CPAP) machines, respiratory stimulants (i.e., theophylline, acetazolamide), and the use of nonbenzodiazepine hypnotics (Quadri, Drake, & Hudgel, 2009).

Sleep-related hypoventilation is a new *DSM-5* sleep disorder diagnosis (APA, 2013), and treatment focuses on increasing one's ventilation. The most evidence-based treatment approach consists of noninvasive ventilation or positive pressure ventilation (Becker, 2006). Positive pressure ventilation is substantially less intrusive than invasive ventilation in that it does not typically negatively influence daily activity and function, has less risk of infection, and intermittent treatment is possible (Becker, 2006). A thorough substance use assessment is necessary, as alcohol, opioids, and central nervous system depressants can reduce ventilatory drive and contribute to breathing-related sleep symptoms (APA, 2013).

CIRCADIAN RHYTHM SLEEP-WAKE DISORDER *Circadian rhythm sleep-wake disorder* (i.e., the mismatch between external and internal sleep-wake systems) can be treated using behavior modification techniques. The counselor essentially aims to assist clients in stabilizing their sleep patterns. Whether dealing with difficulties with shift work or delayed or advanced sleep phase, those with this disorder need assistance in sleep stability. Treatment may include the following interventions: psychoeducation, light therapy (i.e., increasing melatonin), avoiding or reducing alcohol and caffeine, and establishing specific sleep hygiene rules (Yang & Ebben, 2008). For example, with clients who suffer from delayed phase type (e.g., colloquially referred to as "night owls"), a counselor can assist the client in progressively scheduling earlier and earlier bedtimes, while recommending bright light exposure during early normal wake times (i.e., 6–7 a.m.). Clients can also be encouraged to maintain strict bedroom rules (i.e., utilizing the bedroom just for bedroom activities) and control the environment by keeping blinds in the bedroom consistently open to aid in the rematching of their internal and external sleep-wake systems.

PARASOMNIAS Parasomnias are the abnormal behaviors or events that occur between wakefulness and sleep. These disorders consist of non-rapid eye movement sleep arousal disorders, nightmare disorder, rapid eye movement sleep behavior disorder, and restless leg syndrome.

Those with *non-rapid eye movement sleep arousal disorders* engage in a variety of behaviors during these altered states. The *DSM-5* specifies sleepwalking and/or the occurrence of sleep terrors as the two primary behaviors in which one engages during the incomplete awakening from sleep. Also, sleepwalking with sleep-related eating or sleep-related sexual behavior (sexsomnia) can be coded, as can a sleep terror type. Sleepwalking activity occurs more in females during childhood, but more frequently in males during adulthood (APA, 2013).

There is limited research and evidence-based practices suggestions for the treatment of non-rapid eye movement sleep arousal disorders. These disorders are more common in children, although they can also be diagnosed in adults. In children, these disorders are often associated with changes in the family structure (i.e., divorce, separation, death of parent), changes in place of residence, or family discord (Talarczyk, 2011). Some limited, preliminary evidence suggests that children with these disorders benefit from a family therapy approach aimed at increasing parental availability and emotional connection with the child, thus increasing the child's sense of security and comfort (Talarczyk, 2011). In adults, sleep deprivation, co-occurring disorders (i.e., depression and anxiety), changes in schedule, increased levels of stress, and substance use can increase sleep arousal (i.e., walking and terrors). Interventions that either reduce deep sleep (e.g., slow wave phases of sleep consisting of 3 and 4 non-rapid eye movement sleep) such as the use of benzodiazepines (i.e., clonazepam), behavioral changes (i.e., waking before the sleep events occur), or counseling to address stress and other co-occurring disorders are the current treatments of choice (Szelenberger, Niemcewicz, & Dabrowska, 2005). Medications may also cause behaviors that appear to be similar to those of non-rapid eye movement sleep arousal disorders. Also, the use of, or withdrawal from, substances or medications such as benzodiazepines, nonbenzodiazepines, sedative-hypnotics, opioids, cocaine, nicotine, antipsychotics, tricyclic antidepressants, and chloral hydrate may cause the sleep experiences associated with this disorder (APA, 2013).

While more prevalent in children, *nightmare disorder* impairs one's quality of life by disturbing sleep and creating sleep avoidance and sleep deprivation. Women report more frequent nightmares than men, and the content of nightmares varies with gender (APA, 2013). Men are more likely to have nightmares about war and violence, while women are more likely to experience nightmares about harassment or loss of a loved one (APA, 2013). The most evidence-based approaches for treating nightmare disorder consist of psychopharmacotherapy (i.e., prazosin, clonidine) and cognitive behavioral therapy utilizing behavioral interventions (Aurora et al., 2010). Since most medication studies have only explored the treatment of PTSD-related nightmares, the use of medication in treating nightmare disorder is currently not supported by research. The importance and meaning of nightmares in a client's cultural context should be explored to facilitate counselor sensitivity (APA, 2013).

The use of CBT with behavioral interventions is indicated as a best practice intervention for either type of nightmare disorder (Aurora et al., 2010). A major component of this type of treatment involves image rehearsal therapy. Image rehearsal therapy involves clients recalling their nightmares, writing them down, and altering the themes, the ending, or any part of the nightmare to make it more positive. Next, the new dream scenario is rehearsed so that when clients have this dream again, they can dispute the unwanted aspects of the dream (Aurora et al., 2010). The aim of this approach is to help clients make a cognitive shift such that they actually refute the dream's viability or relevance. This technique is practiced during wake time for 15 to 20 minutes a day.

Lucid dreaming therapy is a CBT intervention similar to image rehearsal therapy. Where it differs is in that the disputing of the dream's unwanted material is attempted not after the dream has occurred, but within the dream. Another approach to treating nightmare disorder consists of exposure, relaxation, and rescripting therapy (ERRT; Aurora et al., 2010). ERRT involves addressing anxiety through education, progressive muscle relaxation, sleep hygiene, and rescripting nightmares (or exposure). This is done through the rewriting of the dream and exposure homework assignments, aiming to desensitize the content of the dream by continual exposure to the dream, themes, and associated material.

Rapid eye movement sleep behavior disorders (i.e., vocalization or complex behaviors during rapid eye movement [REM] stages of sleep) are more common in adults than children, and can be a precursor for a more severe neurological condition (e.g., Parkinson's disease; Erman, 2008); therefore, a medical evaluation is always warranted. Normal REM sleep is characterized by muscle atonia (i.e., complete loss of muscle tone, paralysis), yet individuals with this disorder can exhibit complex, purposeful behaviors such as talking, kicking, screaming, grabbing, and punching. Additionally, dreaming is common during the REM stages of sleep, and most people with this disorder act out their dreams. This can present considerable difficulties because of the risk of physical harm to one's self or others. For example, people may act out sporting events, fend off attackers, or even yell or become aggressive with others. Medications (i.e., melatonin, clonazepam) are currently the only treatment option for those with rapid eye movement sleep behavior disorder (Erman, 2008).

Restless leg syndrome (RLS) is a neurological disorder associated with extreme sensations in the legs that worsen during rest or sleep. Typically, one most move their legs in order to obtain relief. The symtoms tend to become worse in the evenings (APA, 2013). RLS is often associated with iron deficiency, renal failure, and pregnancy, and is more common in women (APA, 2013). In milder cases, clients suffering from RLS can achieve relief by engaging in self-directed activities (e.g., reading a book, hot or cold massage, stretching, exercise, rubbing legs) when sensations begin (Byrne, Sinha, & Chaudhuri, 2006). In more severe cases, medications, or more specifically, the use of low-dose dopamine agonists (i.e., pramipexole, ropinirole) are considered the treatment of choice (Aurora et al., 2012; Moul et al., 2007). All clients who present with RLS should have their serum ferritin level (i.e., a measure of the stored iron within the human body) tested; in some cases, an iron deficit can be the cause of RLS and this can easily be treated with iron replacement (Moul et al., 2007). Additionally, the use of anticonvulsants (i.e., gabapentin and carbamazepine) and opioids (i.e., oxycodone, codeine) should only be considered if low-dose dopamine agonists or iron replacement is unwarranted or unsuccessful (Moul et al., 2007).

Prognosis

The prognosis for sleep-wake disorders varies by disorder. Some disorders with a more neurological etiology (i.e., restless leg syndrome, rapid eye movement sleep behavior disorders) appear to respond well to medications, while others with a more psychological etiology (i.e., sleep terrors, sleepwalking) respond to a combination of medication and counseling. Generally, behavior therapy, cognitive behavioral therapy, psychopharmacotherapy, oral applications, continuous positive airway pressure (CPAP) machines, and ventilators are effective in the treatment of sleep-wake disorders (Moul et al., 2007; Reinmann & Perlis, 2009).

SEXUAL DYSFUNCTIONS

Description of the Disorder and Typical Client Characteristics

Landmark nationwide research studies over the past few decades (e.g., DeRogatis & Burnett, 2008; Feldman, Goldstein, Hatzichristou, Krane, & McKinlay, 1994; Laumann, Paik, & Rosen, 1999) have revealed that sexual dysfunction, affecting between 30–50% of people (lifetime prevalence rates), is more prevalent than anxiety, depressive disorders, or substance use disorders. These sexual dysfunctions (e.g., related to sexual desire, excitement, orgasm, resolution) can be considered either chronic (i.e., lifelong) or acquired, and can occur during all sexual activities (i.e., generalized), or just in the context of certain situations. Sexual dysfunctions frequently occur with other mental disorders (i.e., depressive disorders, anxiety disorders, and personality disorders) and can lead to and exacerbate relationship issues (Sadock & Sadock, 2007).

Sexual dysfunction involves a disturbance in sexual functioning and sexual desire, which causes considerable distress and difficulties in personal relationships. Simplistically, these disorders inhibit or restrict individuals' ability to participate in a sexual relationship in the way they desire. The *DSM-5* (APA, 2013) includes the following sexual dysfunctions disorders: delayed ejaculation, erectile disorder, female orgasmic disorder, female sexual interest/arousal disorder, genito-pelvic pain/penetration disorder, male hypoactive sexual desire disorder, and premature (early) ejaculation. What follows are brief summaries of these sexual dysfunction disorders.

- *Delayed ejaculation* is characterized by an inability, or significantly delayed ability, to ejaculate in sexual activities most of the time (e.g., 75% or greater).
- *Erectile disorder* is conceptualized as an inability to obtain or maintain an erection during sexual activity most of the time (e.g., 75% or greater).
- *Female orgasmic disorder* is identified as an inability, reduced intensity, or significant delayed ability to orgasm during sexual activity most of the time (e.g., 75% or greater).
- *Female sexual interest/arousal disorder* involves a reduced interest in sexual interaction and a lack of arousal as displayed by a reduced interest, initiation, excitement, and arousal in sexual activity most of the time (e.g., 75% or greater).
- *Genito-pelvic pain/penetration disorder* involves persistent difficulty with either vaginal penetration during intercourse (e.g., tensing or tightening), or an increased sense of vaginal pain during intercourse, which occurs over a 6-month period of time.
- *Male hypoactive sexual desire disorder* involves deficient or reduced desire for sexual activity over a 6-month period of time.
- *Premature ejaculation* involves a persistent, unwanted pattern of ejaculating within 1 minute of vaginal penetration most of the time (e.g., 75% or greater) over a 6-month period of time.

As is true with all disorders, the client has to experience clinically significant distress to receive one of these diagnoses. Many people who experience sexual dysfunction do not perceive that it is an issue or problem (DeRogatis & Burnett, 2008). Issues such as body image, attraction to one's partner, boredom in sexual routine, and co-occurring mental health disorders (i.e., depression or substance use) confound the issues associated with sexual dysfunction, making sexual dysfunctions complicated to assess and treat. Expectations and attitudes about experiencing sexual pleasure are often related to culture, and these cultural factors must also be considered when diagnosing and treating these disorders (APA, 2013).

By definition, clients who have sexual disorders experience some type of distress or anxiety associated with the sexual dysfunction. This anxiety is often connected and overlapping with issues of intimacy and attachment, all of which exacerbate the sexual dysfunction (Stephenson & Meston, 2010). Performance anxiety, or the critical self-evaluation of one's performance in the moment, can add to one's anxiety and increase sexual dysfunction (Sadock & Sadock, 2007). Negative self-talk feeds anxiety during sexual interactions and is typically rooted in past perceived failures; the person thinks that present and future self-perceived sexual failures are inevitable. Sometimes these dysfunctions are tied to misinformation about sexual arousal and functioning (e.g., a woman speculating it is taking her longer than she thinks it should to reach orgasm, or a woman erroneously speculating that she should be able to achieve orgasm through penile penetration alone). Education and information on normal sexual functioning can help to alleviate some of this anxiety and lead to the resolution of perceived sexual dysfunction. Counselors also need to consider that people's sexual activity may decline with age due to diminished desire and a possible increase in physical health issues (Lindau et al., 2007).

Counselor Considerations

Because the topic of sex can cause clients to feel embarrassed or even ashamed, counselors should take extra care to empathically engage with clients around their struggles. Perceptions of being dysfunctional may make clients especially vulnerable to disclosure and open discourse about their experiences. Many people have never openly talked about their sexual fantasies, behaviors, functioning, and expectations, and doing so can be exceptionally uncomfortable. Those who have experienced sexual victimization and struggle with shame may especially struggle with processing sexual dysfunctions.

Treating clients with sexual dysfunctions can be difficult for counselors who experience discomfort with the topic of sexuality. It is important that counselors feel comfortable with their own sexuality and understand their attitudes and biases toward sexuality. Counselors who feel uncomfortable with the topic of sex may minimize or miss vital information about the onset, course, and impairment of the dysfunction.

Countertransference is another issue that counselors need to be aware of when treating sexual dysfunction disorders. Because of the intimacy of the subject matter, counselors are more susceptible to countertransference and should utilize supervision to identify, normalize, interpret, and diffuse these reactions so that their own reactions to the material will not inhibit the counseling process. Additionally, counselors should be well versed in couples therapy and a systems way of thinking as sexuality occurs in a context. These disorders affect the partner system and even if the client is seen in individual counseling, counselors must understand how these disorders are experienced and are maintained within interpersonal relationships.

Counselors can conceptualize a client's sexual dysfunction in context by considering the following influences: (a) biological (e.g., age, medication, hormonal); (b) psychological (e.g., mental health, sexual knowledge, experience, attitudes); and (c) social (e.g., partner's health, partner's availability, conditions of sex; Wincze, Bach, & Barlow, 2008). Once a counselor has a comprehensive understanding of these influences, he or she can begin to understand the sexual dysfunction within the client's context and lived experience.

Sexual desire and functioning may also vary with age (APA, 2013), and these developmental changes should be considered when diagnosing and treating these disorders. Additionally, counselors need to screen for substance use and consult with a medical professional when it is indicated because some substances and medications can actually induce sexual dysfunction (i.e., *substance/medication-induced sexual dysfunction*). Many medications and substances may have adverse sexual side effects including, but not limited to, antipsychotics, antidepressants (e.g., SSRIs), lithium, antihistamines, anticholinergics, alcohol, and opioids (Sadock & Sadock, 2007). The side effects of psychotropic medication, especially sexual dysfunction, are a major cause of client discontinuation of medication (Preston, O'Neal, & Talaga, 2013) and can complicate the treatment of comorbid psychological and medical conditions. Helping clients to develop adaptive solutions to their sexual struggles may help them comply with the medication recommendations made by their physicians.

Sex therapy is a specific approach to treating sexual dysfunction. This approach sees the couple as the object of treatment and focuses directly on the behavior involved in the sexual dysfunction; therefore not all couples are willing, or appropriate, for this type of treatment. Some components that affect the outcomes of couples' sexual treatment are (a) the quality and strength of the couple's relationship, (b) the motivation for treatment of both partners, (c) the lack of impairing mental illnesses, (d) the level of attraction between the partners, and (e) the initial compliance with the treatment program as observed through the completion of homework assignments (Hawton, 1995). Sex therapy tends to be short-term, behavioral, and sensate focused (e.g., uses sensory awareness exercises to increase intimacy). For example, during intercourse, couples are asked to stop and use sensate-focused exercises to heighten their awareness to each other's erogenous zones, receiving pleasure without penetration.

Treatment Models and Interventions

Historically, sexual dysfunction disorders were treated using psychodynamic, behavioral, or cognitive behavioral approaches. Randomized controlled trials of psychosocial approaches for use in treating sexual disorders are limited. With the more recent medicalization of sexual dysfunction disorders, treatment approaches have been heavily influenced by the development and use of various medications (Duterte, Segraves, & Althof, 2007; Wincze et al., 2008). Medications have demonstrated success in treating erectile dysfunction (Duterte et al., 2007). Emerging approaches for treating each sexual dysfunction will be presented in the following section.

SEXUAL DESIRE DISORDERS (FEMALE SEXUAL INTEREST/AROUSAL DISORDER AND MALE HYPOACTIVE SEXUAL DESIRE DISORDER) Levels of sexual desire vary with age, and men typically report higher intensity and frequency of desire than women (APA, 2013). There is minimal research on men with hypoactive sexual desire disorder, and most research has involved females who have this disorder. Higher prevalence rates of low sexual desire in men and women are reported in East Asian cultures, and this may be associated with cultural attitudes of guilt or shame related to sex (APA, 2013). Behavior therapy and cognitive behavioral therapy have been modestly helpful in treating hypoactive sexual desire disorders, yet often the gains are not maintained over a 3-year period (Duterte et al., 2007).

In females with arousal issues, the drug bupropion (e.g., Wellbutrin or Zyban) has had some modest effects in terms of enhancing arousal symptoms, yet the effectiveness of this medication is still unclear. The drug may be useful in that it decreases depressive symptoms, thus altering arousal (Duterte et al., 2007). Bupropion is sometimes used as an adjunct medication to treat sexual side effects caused by SSRI medication (Preston et al., 2013). Although no pharmacotherapy has been established in the literature as being an evidence-based approach to treating hypoactive sexual desire disorder, researchers are exploring the use of medication in altering androgen and testosterone levels as a means of increasing libido (Duterte et al., 2007).

ERECTILE DYSFUNCTION   Reports of erectile dysfunction vary across cultures; cultural differences in expectations and definition of this condition may account for these discrepancies (APA, 2013). Psychosocial approaches (i.e., behavior, cognitive behavioral, and interpersonal therapies) have been used in treating lifelong and acquired erectile dysfunction, yet relapse has plagued this form of treatment (Duterte et al., 2007). Most of the studied approaches have utilized a couples or group therapy format ranging between 4 to 20 meetings. These sessions typically focus on addressing communication issues, irrational thoughts, reducing anxiety through progressive relaxation, and discussing the specific sexual dysfunctions.

Sex-focused therapy involves directly focusing on sex and may include talking about sexual functioning, sexual feelings, and exploring intimacy. Specialized training should be sought before counselors engage in sex-focused therapy with clients. Sex-focused therapy is a form of talk therapy and never involves sexual contact with a client.

The most evidence-based approach to treating erectile dysfunctions involves a combination of group therapy and pharmacotherapy (e.g., sildenafil [Viagra], tadalafil [Cialis]; Melnik, Soares, & Nasselo, 2007). Sildenafil (i.e., Viagra) is an example of one of the FDA-approved medications for treating erectile dysfunction. Viagra allows a man to achieve a natural erection given adequate stimulation. It reaches a maximum plasma level (i.e., it effectively works) after one hour, and the half-life (i.e., the amount of time that it works most effectively) is between 3 to 5 hours (Duterte et al., 2007). Cialis begins to take effect a bit faster (within about 15 minutes), and the effects last much longer (up to 36 hours in some cases).

In cases in which erectile dysfunction is attributed to SSRI use, adjunct treatment with bupropion (i.e., Wellbutrin) and sildenafil (i.e., Viagra) may alleviate symptoms (Preston et al., 2013). Those with heart conditions need to utilize sildenafil cautiously, and only under the supervision of a physician.

Other more invasive interventions performed by a urologist such as vacuum tumescence devices, transurethral systems, intraurethral semisolid pellets of prostaglandin E1, and intracorporeal injection therapy with alprostadil are utilized less frequently and are only utilized in severe cases (Hatzimouratidis et al., 2010).

PREMATURE EJACULATION   Historically, premature ejaculation has been treated with behavioral techniques such as the *stop-start* technique and the *squeeze* technique (Duterte et al.,

CREATIVE TOOLBOX ACTIVITY 15.2   Tune In: Mindfulness Meditation for Erectile Disorder

Varunee Faii Sangganjanavanich, PhD, LPCC-S, NCC, ACS

Activity Overview

Mindfulness meditation can be used to help clients who experience erectile disorder. Mindfulness meditation allows clients to better pay attention to their surroundings and inner experiences (e.g., thoughts, feelings). Using this activity, clients learn how to use mindfulness to manage erectile disorder.

Treatment Goal(s) of Activity

Mindfulness meditation can help clients become better tuned in to their surroundings (e.g., knowing what surrounds them and what brings/does not bring them a sense of pleasure) and more connected to the thoughts and/or feelings that contribute to their erectile dysfunction. The goals of this activity are to help clients (a) increase their awareness of their surroundings and environment; (b) learn to observe their thoughts and/or feelings; and (c) be aware of how their thoughts and/or feelings may impact their sexual experience.

Directions

1. Briefly explain mindfulness meditation, including its process and benefits.
2. Inform the client that he will be, engaging in mindfulness meditation for 10–15 minutes. The duration of the activity can be increased if the client has prior meditation experience.
3. Allow the client to choose the option of meditating with or without listening to soft music. If the client chooses the music option, the counselor begins to play the music. Regardless of these two options, the counselor should prepare to be quiet and reduce body movement.
4. Instruct the client to sit in a comfortable position, close his eyes, and to consider a recent experience in which he struggled with erectile dysfunction. Invite the client to let his mind flow from one thought/feeling to another, as he connects with this experience.

Process Questions

1. What was the experience like for you?
2. What was the thought and/or feeling that first entered your mind?
3. What other thoughts and/or feelings emerged during your meditation?
4. Based on those thoughts and/or feelings, which one is the most difficult to deal with? Why? How did you deal with it?
5. How do you think this line of thought and/or feelings may impact your sexual experience?
6. How can you use your awareness of your thoughts and feelings to improve your sexual experience?

2007). The stop-start technique involves the client identifying when he or she is experiencing mid-level excitement during sexual intercourse. At this time, the client then stops and waits for the excitement level to decrease minimally before continuing. This technique requires practice and should be implemented gradually (i.e., clients are instructed to practice with self-stimulation, then partner hand stimulation, slow movement intercourse, and then stop-start thrusting intercourse). The squeeze technique consists of squeezing near the top of the penis (shaft) between the thumb and forefinger. This often causes a reduction in the erection, which aids in the prevention of premature ejaculation. This technique requires significant practice to implement effectively.

Additionally, a number of large-scale studies have highlighted that medications (e.g., SSRIs, clomipramine) are effective in delaying ejaculation (Duterte et al., 2007). SSRIs, specifically paroxetine, sertraline, and fluoxetine, are successful in treating premature ejaculation, and full effects usually appear within two weeks of beginning medication (Hatzimouratidis et al., 2010). Topical creams and sprays (e.g., prilocaine-lidocaine) are effective in improving ejaculatory latency, control, and sexual satisfaction of men with premature ejaculation, and are currently the treatment of choice for premature ejaculation (Carson & Wyllie, 2010).

Premature ejaculation is reported across cultures, but it appears to be more common in men of Asian descent than in men living in Australia, Europe, or the United States (APA, 2013). Prevalence rates are difficult to estimate due to the difficulty of defining this disorder, as well as the influence of stigma surrounding this condition.

ORGASMIC DISORDERS (FEMALE ORGASMIC DISORDER AND DELAYED EJACULATION)

Female orgasmic disorder is significantly more common than delayed ejaculation (Duterte et al., 2007). For female orgasmic disorder, the prevailing treatment is either a training program in self-stimulation (i.e., masturbating) or couples counseling. Self-stimulation training involves first exposing clients to videos and written material on specific techniques utilized in self-stimulation (Duterte et al., 2007). Clients who participate in these programs often find that while orgasms are eventually reached individually and with self-stimulation, they are more elusive in the context of partner encounters (e.g., intercourse).

In men, there are no evidenced-based approaches to treating delayed ejaculation (Duterte et al., 2007). A prevailing approach to treating delayed ejaculation, as well as female orgasmic disorder, is to engage the client and his partner in couples counseling. The focus of this treatment is on the fundamentals of sexual responsiveness and increasing the couple's communication skills in an attempt to promote enhanced sexual communication and stimulation. Couples are typically asked to stop engaging in intercourse during this portion of treatment and are often asked to complete homework assignments that seek to enhance intimacy, their awareness of each other's erogenous zones, reduced performance anxiety, and a greater focus on providing pleasure through other types of stimulation and activities. Eventually, once an increase in intimacy and awareness is achieved, intercourse is reintroduced. More research on evidence-based practices to treat these orgasmic disorders is warranted.

Sociocultural factors may influence the development of female orgasmic disorder, as well as the levels of associated distress. Cultural expectations and attitudes about sex may impact one's ability to experience sexual pleasure (APA, 2013). There is also great variation in the importance that women attribute to achieving orgasm to overall sexual satisfaction (APA, 2013). As such, levels of distress due to failure to experience orgasm vary as well. Finally, a lack of knowledge about normal female sexual functioning can cause some women to think they have a sexual dysfunction, when in reality, they function normally.

GENITO-PELVIC PAIN/PENETRATION DISORDER Women with genito-pelvic pain disorder feel pain with vaginal penetration, which results in intense anxiety and sexual avoidance behaviors. The typical treatment approach for penetration disorder is behavioral in nature and consists of: (a) suspending attempts at intercourse; (b) in vivo gradual self-insertion of dilators of increasing sizes; (c) systematic desensitization; (d) kegel exercises (i.e., contracting and relaxing pelvic floor muscles); and (e) processing the emotions, thoughts, and fears which surround sexual encounters (Duterte et al., 2007). A number of additional issues may underlie this disorder such as anxiety, trauma (e.g., sexual, physical abuse), and relationship issues. Counselors should assess and explore these areas when it is warranted. Additionally, inadequate sexual education and religious orthodoxy may be associated with the development of these symptoms, but the literature is not conclusive (APA, 2013). Currently, no pharmacotherapy options are available for penetration disorder.

Prognosis

Prognosis varies with each sexual dysfunction and is often based on whether the dysfunction is chronic or situational. One's prognosis is confounded by other issues such as body image, attraction to one's partner, boredom in sexual routine, and other mental health disorders (e.g., depression or substance use), and relapse is fairly common with all sexual dysfunction disorders. Counselors need to communicate realistic expectations for treating these dysfunctions, making sure they convey that while improvements are definitely possible, so is relapse. Relapse prevention plans should be put into place as a part of the therapeutic process.

PARAPHILIC DISORDERS *— Generally resistant to treatment*

Description of the Disorder and Typical Client Characteristics

Paraphilic disorders appear to be rare (Sadock & Sadock, 2007), but the true prevalence rates of these disorders are unclear because of the shame associated with disclosure (APA, 2013). Paraphilic disorders are more common in males than females; however, data on the occurrence of these disorders in females is limited (APA, 2013). At the root of paraphilias are arousing sexual urges, thoughts, fantasies, or behaviors that are atypical, often begin in adolescence, and are more common in males than females (Beech & Harkins, 2012). Those with paraphilic disorders often have multiple paraphilia and are unaware of the impact of these disorders, usually only seeking treatment at the urging of a friend or family member or as a legal consequence of their behaviors.

Diagnosed when functioning inhibited harm to self or others

Paraphilic disorders consist of three essential elements: (a) a deviant, abnormal mode of sexual gratification (i.e., sexually deviant urge, fantasy, thought or behavior); (b) a consistent pattern (i.e., occurring for at least 6 months) of deviant, abnormal arousal and urges; and (c) the deviant, abnormal urges, thoughts, and behaviors cause significant impairment and distress (First & Halon, 2008). Although there are hundreds of different kinds of categories of paraphilia, the *DSM-5* (APA, 2013) outlines the eight most common categories. These consist of the following: voyeuristic disorder, exhibitionistic disorder, frotteuristic disorder, sexual masochism disorder, sexual sadism disorder, pedophilic disorder, fetishistic disorder, and transvestic disorder. The category that covers any additional paraphilia is other specified paraphilic disorder. What follows is a brief summary of each paraphilia:

- *Voyeuristic disorder* involves acting on the urge to observe an unsuspecting person either nude or disrobing, or an unsuspecting person engaged in sexual behavior.
- *Exhibitionistic disorder* involves acting on the urge to expose one's genitals to an unsuspecting person.
- *Frotteuristic disorder* involves acting on the urge to rub against or touch a person without his or her consent.
- *Sexual masochism disorder* involves being sexually aroused by being sexually humiliated, beaten, bound, and made to suffer during sexual activity.
- *Sexual sadism disorder* involves being aroused by observing another being physically or psychologically made to suffer; the person may or may not have acted on these urges with a nonconsenting person.
- *Pedophilic disorder* involves fantasizing, having urges, or acting on arousal urges to engage children (i.e., under 13 years old) in sexual activity.
- *Fetishistic disorder* involves fantasizing, having urges, or seeking sexual arousal from nonliving objects, or being hyperfocused and sexually aroused by nongenital body parts.
- *Transvestic disorder* involves fantasizing, becoming aroused, having urges, or acting on urges related to cross-dressing.
- *Other specified paraphilic disorder* involves having fantasies, urges, or acting on arousal urges that do not fit into any of the other mentioned categories. For example, one might be sexually aroused by animals (*zoophilia*), urine (*urophilia*), feces (*coprophilia*), corpses (*necrophilia*), and other nonsexual objects and activities.

Some of these paraphilia involve illegal activities (i.e., pedophilia, voyeurism, exhibitionism, frotteurism), while others may involve consent (i.e., sexual masochism), or are not illegal at all (i.e., transvestic fetishism). Legally, any time an individual forces another to engage in a sexual act, or because of one's position he or she is unable to give consent in a sexual act (e.g., such as a child), it is considered a sexual offense. In some cases and scenarios, clients' behaviors could lead to legal involvement and serious victimization of others; any ethics-related issues need to be considered in providing comprehensive treatment.

A person's impulse control or ability to control their sexual urges, thoughts, fantasies, or behaviors is an important aspect of assessment. At a milder level on the spectrum, one can have these arousing urges, but be able to refrain from acting on them, especially if they involve the victimization of another. On the other end of the spectrum, people may have similar urges, and, having limited impulse control, act on them. These disorders mirror impulse control disorder dynamics in that there is often a cycle of increasing tension that builds until release (i.e., acting on the paraphilic urges), which is then often followed by feelings of remorse and guilt. Eventually, tension builds again and the cycle starts over. Because of the similarities of the paraphilic disorders and treatments, they will be considered as a class of disorders and discussed as a whole in the counselor considerations and treatment sections that follow.

Counselor Considerations

People with paraphilic disorders do not often enter treatment to address these issues. Rather, they more typically seek treatment for co-occurring disorders. People often associate the paraphilia with pleasure, and they may only enter treatment because of the negative consequences of their behaviors (e.g., pressure from a partner, legal consequences). There-fore, the client's motivation to change is always an important consideration, especially if the client is mandated for treatment by the legal system.

As mentioned previously in the sexual dysfunction section, counselors are often susceptible to countertransference when working with clients with sexual-related disor-ders. Because of the intimacy of the subject matter and the atypical desires and fantasies of this population, counselors should utilize supervision and consultation to identify, interpret, and diffuse so that their own reactions and beliefs do not inhibit the counseling process. Counselors who have difficulties managing their personal reactions to clients' sexual arousals and desires run the risk of undermining the therapeutic relationship and creating more distress and guilt within the client.

Additionally, it is important for counselors to assess cultural considerations as related to the client's sexual behavior. Variations in cross-culturally normative sexual behaviors may account for perceived deviations from the majority culture's norms (APA, 2013).

Treatment Models and Interventions

There is little research that can be used to inform treatment with those with para-philias. Evidence-based research for the treatment of these disorders is sparse, but there is some limited support suggesting that cognitive behavioral therapy and behav-ior therapy used and in conjunction with pharmacotherapy may be useful (Beech & Harkins, 2012).

BEHAVIOR THERAPY (BT)   BT is based on the idea that all behaviors are learned and rein-forced, thus maintained. In treating paraphilic disorders, counselors aid clients in learning behavioral principles that are then used to change their existent behaviors and create new, more socially acceptable sexual responses and behaviors. BT interventions consist of aversion therapy, covert sensitization (or extinction), and orgasmic reconditioning, which are often complemented by psychoeducation, assertiveness training, and social skills training (Beech & Harkins, 2012).

Aversion therapy (i.e., the simultaneous exposure of the stimulus with some level of discomfort) can take many forms in the treatment of paraphilic disorders including pairing the deviant desire (e.g., urge) with a level of discomfort, which may include olfactory (e.g., feces, rotting eggs) or ammonia (e.g., ammonia salts) smells. Similarly, covert sensi-tization is the pairing of deviant desires and fantasies with imagined unpleasant outcomes (e.g., imagined sickness, humiliation, or imprisonment). Conversely, covert extinction is when the deviant desire or fantasy is imagined without the desired reinforcing positive feeling or reaction that typically accompanies the act.

Additionally, orgasmic reconditioning is another behavioral technique utilized in the treatment of paraphilic disorders. Clients are instructed to masturbate to their deviant desire until they become close to orgasm. At this point, clients are then asked to alter their thinking to a nondeviant desire or fantasy. The intention is that this new desire or fantasy will begin to be paired with an orgasm. An alternative to this approach can include directing clients to masturbate solely to this nondeviant desire. These approaches have not been rigorously studied through the use of RCTs and require more research support before they can be suggested as a best practice.

Clinical Toolbox 15.4: In the Pearson etext, click here to read about a treatment activity that can be used when working with clients who have exhibitionistic disorder.

COGNITIVE BEHAVIORAL THERAPY (CBT)   CBT is the most frequently utilized approach to treating paraphilic disorders. This may be due to the versatility of the approach in not only addressing clients' cognitive distortions (i.e., deviant thoughts, desires), but also the connection between the deviant cognitions and the deviant behaviors (Beech & Harkins, 2012). The central aims of CBT are to increase clients' awareness of their deviant cognitions and their covert and overt behaviors, and eventually to empower clients to incorporate their own policing strategies (i.e., self-management skills) to identify and plan for triggers and relapse situations. Counselors address cognition as well as clients' behaviors, not only utilizing the behavioral techniques previously mentioned, but also utilizing skills training (e.g., behavioral rehearsal), modeling, and relapse prevention (Beech & Harkins, 2012). Treatment consists of increasing awareness (e.g., identify triggers and areas of stress), aversion therapy, thought stopping, cognitive restructuring, orgasm reconditioning, and increasing empathy with victims. CBT approaches need further research to validate their effectiveness.

PSYCHOPHARMACOTHERAPY   Medication is sometimes used to treat paraphilias, but psychosocial approaches should be used in conjunction with psychopharmacotherapy. Medication use typically includes antiandrogenic, serotonergic, and estrogen drugs (Guay, 2009).

Antiandrogenic drugs (e.g., medroxyprogesterone) lower testosterone levels and may decrease sexual interest and performance (Beech & Harkins, 2012), but this treatment approach is an emerging treatment option for managing more severe paraphilias and situations. Because of ethical and pragmatic difficulties related to the use of these drugs, there are no large-scale studies on the utilization of antiandrogenic drugs. However, some case reports have highlighted the effectiveness and promise of this treatment (Beech & Harkins, 2012).

SSRIs and tricyclic antidepressants hold promise in treating the deviant desires and arousal urges of those diagnosed with paraphilic disorders (Beech & Harkins, 2012). Although it is early in the process of validation, SSRIs appear to be promising when utilized in conjunction with CBT and can decrease clients' deviant desires, behaviors, and the obsessions connected with compulsions. Further research and validation of the treatment of SSRIs in treating paraphilias is needed (Beech & Harkins, 2012). In cases in which SSRIs are not producing results, clients may benefit from switching to a tricyclic antidepressant, or vice versa (Guay, 2009).

Prognosis

People with paraphilic disorders tend to have rigid cognitions and behaviors that are resistant to many forms of treatment. These behaviors tend to be more pervasive in times of stress and uncertainty; therefore, the overall prognosis for the paraphilia-related behaviors is not favorable. Even if gains have been made through treatment, relapse is common (Beech & Harkins, 2012).

GENDER DYSPHORIA

Description of the Disorder and Typical Client Characteristics

Few studies exist that explore the prevalence of gender dysphoria (formally known as gender identity disorder in the *DSM-IV-TR*), yet most contend that it is rare (i.e., less than 1% of the general population) and more prevalent in males than females (Korte et al., 2008; Sadock & Sadock, 2007). Gender dysphoria occurs in many countries and cultures, even in those cultures with more than male and female gender classification categories (APA, 2013).

Many professionals believe that gender dysphoria should not even be considered a mental disorder, on the basis that even though gender dsyphoria is rare, it is not unhealthy or abnormal. At the root of the controversy is the debate over the origin of the disorder. Two dichotomous theories exist in this debate, with one contending that gender dysphoria is biologically based, and the other contending that gender dysphoria is a conditioned response (which suggests it can be changed). Most people believe that gender dysphoria is likely the result of a "complex biopsychosocial interaction" (Korte et al., 2008, p. 834).

Essentially, gender dysphoria involves feelings of discomfort associated with the incongruence between one's biological sex and one's experienced or expressed gender (APA, 2013). While at birth most people are assigned a biological sex (e.g., male or female), experienced or expressed gender is how the person identifies himself or herself in relation to gender. People with gender dysphoria have a strong, enduring pattern of identifying with the opposite gender, while concurrently feeling a strong discomfort with their assigned gender. These concerns and discomfort are so persistent that these gender identity uncertainties become one of the most important, pressing aspects of their lives.

According to the *DSM-5* (APA, 2013), gender dysphoria can occur either in children, or in adolescents and adults. In children, this desire to become the preferred sex may be seen through their behaviors (e.g., a strong preference for cross-gender dress, roles, and activities; rejection of typically assigned gender activities), and may or may not be verbalized. This verbalization in children reflects a child's ability to have insight into his or her experience, but it is not required for a diagnosis of gender dysphoria. In adolescent and adults, desires to become the preferred sex are verbalized and expressed as a wish to change their current sex characteristics and adopt the preferred sex's characteristics.

Counselor Considerations

As previously mentioned, counselors' comfort level discussing sexual issues can affect clients' willingness and ability to disclose important relevant experiences, thoughts, and feelings. More than with most other disorders discussed in this text, gender dysphoria and its related considerations (e.g., gender reassignment surgery) can be personally triggering for counselors. Therefore, it is critical that counselors are aware of their personal opinions, values, and biases when working with this population. If counselors are not comfortable taking a flexible approach with this population and/or they lack the requisite skill to work with gender dysphoria-related issues in treatment, they should seek consultation and supervision and make appropriate referrals as needed.

If counselors work with this population, they need to be mindful of the therapeutic relationship. If a counselor is going to be helpful, he or she needs to build a sense of trust and acceptance. It is essential that a counselor assume a nonjudgmental stance when exploring a client's gender struggles, dysphoria, and identity. Without these basic therapeutic elements (i.e., acceptance, empathy, nonjudgmental stance) clients will not be able to progress in treatment.

Counselors need to consider that many clients with gender dysphoria are not interested in changing their feelings and emotions, but are interested in making their physical body match their perceived images of themselves. Therefore the goals of counseling include being supportive and providing education on the range of options available to clients. Additionally, counselors may aid in helping clients identify and alleviate areas of conflict and stress that undermine and exacerbate their gender dysphoria.

A differentiation must be made between symptoms of gender dysphoria and nonconformity to cultural gender stereotypes. Atypical expressions of gender alone are not indicative of gender dysphoria, and criteria for impairment and distress must be met to receive a gender dysphoria diagnosis (APA, 2013). High levels of anxiety and distress (related to their gender) are characteristic of those experiencing gender dysphoria in Western and non-Western cultures, even in those with accepting attitudes toward variations in gender expression (APA, 2013).

One final consideration in treating those with gender dysphoria relates to clients who are seeking a mental health consultation for determining the readiness of hormonal and surgical treatments. Counselors, regardless of their position on these treatments, need to be mindful of just evaluating the client's readiness, which can include: (a) relevant history and development of the individual's gender identity, (b) other psychiatric diagnoses if any are present, and (c) the adherence to the Harry Benjamin International Gender Dysphoria Association Standards of Care when providing a rationale for this type of treatment (Meyer et al., 2001).

Treatment Models and Interventions

No randomized controlled trials have been conducted on the treatment of gender dysphoria (Korte et al., 2008). The Harry Benjamin International Gender Dysphoria Association, a group of multidiscipline professionals advocating for the appropriate treatment for those with gender dysphoria, has been critical of the psychiatric community's approach to this population, and has proposed a set of best practices or standards of care (Meyer et al., 2001). According to this group, counseling should consist of adequate assessments, supportive counseling, real-life experience as the preferred sex, and the possible referral and use of hormonal and surgical therapies (Meyer et al., 2001). A brief description of each component is provided.

SUPPORTIVE COUNSELING   Counseling should focus on the relevant gender issues and any symptoms related to anxiety, depression, discomfort, and self-esteem. Often this is accomplished by the counselor assuming an insight-oriented and supportive approach to counseling. The treatment process usually progresses through the following stages: (a) identification, recognition, and acceptance of the client with gender dysphoria; (b) assessment and evaluation of the client's gender identity, along with any emotional and behavioral problems, as well as any relevant struggles within the client's context and environment; and, (c) evaluation of any comorbid problems such as depression, anxiety, discomfort, and issues with self-esteem (Meyer et al., 2001).

In supportive counseling, family relationships and relationship struggles involving intimacy and work/school–related issues may also arise. Counselors also need to educate clients on their options in dealing with, and possibly altering, their current sex through the use of more intrusive interventions such as hormonal and surgical therapy. This process is generally referred to as gender reassignment. Counselors should aid clients in the evaluation of the advantages and disadvantages of physical interventions. Although many people do not pursue gender reassignment, those who do usually find the process to be extremely slow and laden with obstacles; therefore, counselors can be supportive of clients throughout this difficult time, aiding them in dealing with their frustration and navigating these numerous hurdles. As clients progress through different stages of their gender identity development process, counseling may be more or less warranted depending on their level of discomfort, frustration, anxiety, and stress.

Voices from the Trenches 15.1: In the Pearson etext, click here to view a discussion of relevant considerations when working with clients who experience gender dysphoria.

REAL-LIFE EXPERIENCES   Real-life experience, which typically occurs before hormonal therapy begins, involves fully adopting the preferred gender identity in real-life settings (Meyer et al., 2001). This change to presenting as the preferred sex can have significant effects on a client's professional, educational, social, and family life and should only be pursued if clients are fully aware of possible consequences. Often the consequences of their change in gender presentation are unforeseen, but may not be all negative. For example, while some may experience an increase in interpersonal difficulties and possible issues with unresponsive family members, many may experience a decrease in internal discomfort. They may also find that supportive and reassuring allies emerge. Counselors need to be mindful that while they can discuss with the client the idea of living as the preferred sex, this decision and the implementation of this decision need to be the client's responsibility, and the client needs to be comfortable with that decision.

GENDER REASSIGNMENT OR PHYSICAL INTERVENTIONS (I.E., SURGERY OR HORMONAL THERAPY)   These interventions can be divided into three categories: (a) interventions that are reversible and involve the use of certain medication that suppress estrogen or testosterone (e.g., medroxyprogesterone); (b) interventions that are only partially reversible and include the introduction of hormonal interventions (e.g., use of estrogen or testosterone); or (c) interventions that are not reversible and involve surgery (e.g., penectomy, neophallus; Meyer et al., 2001). These interventions involving physiological changes tend to be applied in a progressive way, allowing clients time to more deeply settle into and explore their gender identity, and time to start to present as their preferred sex. Hormone replacement medication may stimulate the development of secondary sex characteristics, such as the development of facial hair or breasts and the distribution of body fat. It has been recommended that no irreversible intervention should be carried out until the client reaches adulthood or until an adolescent has had at least two years of real-life experience in the sex in which the adolescent identifies (Meyer et al., 2001). Even though these interventions can be costly and may not deliver exactly the result the client had hoped for most people who undergo the differing levels of gender reassignment (i.e., surgery or hormonal treatment) perceive their reassignment favorably, and most report stable or improved life circumstances related to their work, relationships, and sex life after the interventions (Johansson, Sundbom, Hojerback, & Bodlund, 2010).

Prognosis

As stated previously, because of the limited research on the treatment of those with gender dysphoria, the prognosis is difficult to predict. To complicate matters, not everyone with gender identity uniquenesses experiences gender dysphoria or seeks gender reassignment. Although many people report a more stable or improved life circumstance after gender reassignment (Johansson et al., 2010), more research, especially studies that investigate the longitudinal or long-term effects of such interventions, need to be conducted.

TREATMENT PLAN FOR MR. JONES

This chapter began with a discussion of Mr. Jones, a 65-year old Caucasian male who is experiencing severe sleep difficulties. The following I CAN START conceptual framework outlines treatment considerations that may be helpful in working with Mr. Jones.

C = Contextual Assessment

Mr. Jones is not involved in any religious organizations. In terms of his culture, he is from a working-class, lower socioeconomic status family, and he has a strong work ethic, which has supported the success of his small business. He has financial resources and all of his basic needs are met. Developmentally, he is at Erikson's stage of generativity versus stagnation. He has a strong sense of generativity and he feels good about what he has accomplished in terms of his family, career, and social/community involvement (in the Kiwanis Club and with his friends).

A = Assessment and Diagnosis

Diagnosis = Insomnia Disorder (persistent) 780.52 (G47.00)

N = Necessary Level of Care

Outpatient, individual counseling (once per week)

S = Strength-Based Lens

Self: Mr. Jones has a strong work ethic and a good sense of efficacy; he knows what he wants and he works hard to get it. He is also intelligent and resourceful, as demonstrated by his starting and sustaining a small business.

Family: Mr. Jones has a supportive wife and regular contact with his three children, who live in his community.

Community: Mr. Jones is active and involved in the Kiwanis Club. He has a group of lifelong friends with whom he socializes and walks with on a regular basis. He lives in a safe community and has access to health care resources.

T = Treatment Approach

Cognitive Behavioral Therapy

A = Aim and Objectives of Treatment (3-month objectives)

Mr. Jones will learn how to use meditation to help him fall asleep initially, and as his sleep is interrupted throughout the night → Mr. Jones will learn meditation skills and use these 90% of the time to help him fall asleep or reinstate his sleep.

Mr. Jones will learn about proper sleep hygiene and will apply these concepts to improve his sleep → Mr. Jones will process sleep hygiene issues with his counselor, create a sleep hygiene collage (see Creative Toolbox 15.1), and apply these concepts 90% of the time.

Mr. Jones will learn how to use thought-stopping techniques to help him fall asleep, and upon nighttime wakening, to fall back asleep → Mr. Jones will learn two different thought-stopping techniques he can use to enhance intrusive thoughts that occur in relation to his sleep, and he will use these skills 90% of the time.

R = Research-Based Interventions (Cognitive Behavioral Therapy)

Counselor will help Mr. Jones:

- Develop an understanding of good sleep hygiene and help him develop the skills necessary to implement and apply this information
- Learn relaxation techniques (e.g., meditation) that can help him fall asleep and stay asleep
- Learn cognitive thought stopping as a skill to help alleviate his anxiety when he has trouble falling asleep

T = Therapeutic Support Services

Weekly individual therapy

Should treatment not progress, a possible referral to a psychiatrist for an additional attempt at pharmacotherapy may be warranted.

References

American Psychiatric Association (APA). (2013). *Diagnostic and statistical manual of mental disorders* (5th ed.; *DSM-5*). Washington, DC: Author.

Aurora, R. N., Kristo, D. A., Bista, S. R., Rowley, J. A., Zak, R. S., Casey, K. R., . . . Rosenberg, R. S. (2012). The treatment of restless leg syndrome and periodic limb movement disorders in adults—An update for 2012: Practice parameters with evidence-based systematic review and meta-analyses. *Sleep, 35,* 1039–1062.

Aurora, R. N., Zak, R. S., Auerbach, S. H., Casey, K. R., Chowdhuri, S., Karippot, A. K., . . . Morgenthaler, T. I. (2010). Best practices guide for the treatment of nightmare disorder in adults. *Journal of Clinical Sleep Medicine, 6,* 389–401.

Azagra-Calero, E., Espinar-Escalona, E., Barrera-Mora, J., Liamas-Carreras, J., & Solano-Reina, E. (2012). Obstructive sleep apnea syndrome (OSAS): Review of the literature. *Oral Medication and Pathology, 17,* 925–929.

Becker, H. F. (2006). Central sleep related breathing disorders: Diagnostic and therapeutic features. *GMS Current Topics in Otorhinolarynogology: Head and Neck Surgery, 5.* Retrieved from: http://www.egms.de/static/en/journals/cto/2006-5/cto000034.shtml

Beech, A. R., & Harkins, L. (2012). DSM-IV paraphilia: Descriptions, demographics and treatment interventions. *Aggression and Violent Behaviors, 17,* 527–539.

Billiard, M., Bassetti, C., Dauvilliers, Y., Dolenc-Groselj, L., Lammers, G. J., Mayer, G., . . . & Sonka, K. (2006). EFNS guidelines on management of narcolepsy. *European Journal of Neurology, 13*(10), 1035–1048.

Byrne, R., Sinha, S., & Chaudhuri, K. R. (2006). Restless leg syndrome: Diagnosis and review of management options. *Neuropsychiatric Disease and Treatment, 2,* 155–164.

Carson, C., & Wyllie, M. (2010). Improved ejaculatory latency, control and sexual satisfaction when PSD502 is applied topically to men with premature ejaculation: Results of a phase III, double-blind, placebo-controlled study. *Journal of Sexual Medicine, 7,* 3179–3189.

Conroy, D. A., Novick, D. M., & Swanson, L. M. (2012). Behavioral management of hypersomnia. *Sleep Medicine Clinics, 7,* 325–331.

DeRogatis, L. R., & Burnett, A. L. (2008). The epidemiology of sexual dysfunctions. *Journal of Sexual Medicine, 5,* 289–300.

Duterte, E., Segraves, T., & Althof, S. (2007). Psychotherapy and pharmacotherapy for sexual dysfunction. In P. E. Nathan & J. M. Gorman (Eds.), *A guide to treatments that work* (pp. 531–560) New York, NY: Oxford.

Erman, M. (2008). Parasomnias: Rapid eye movement sleep behavior disorder. *Primary Psychiatry, 15,* 32–34.

Feldman, H. A., Goldstein, I., Hatzichristou, D. G., Krane, R. J., & McKinlay, J. B. (1994). Impotence and its medical and psychological correlates: Results of the Massachusetts Male Aging Study. *Journal of Urology, 151,* 54–61.

First, M. B., & Halon, R. L. (2008). Use of DSM paraphilia diagnosis in sexually violent predators commitment cases. *The Journal of the American Academy of Psychiatry and the Law, 36,* 443–454.

Gellis, L. A., Arigo, D., & Elliott, J. C. (2013). Cognitive refocusing treatment for insomnia: A randomized controlled trial in university students. *Behavior Therapy, 44,* 100–110.

Guay, D. R. (2009). Drug treatment of paraphilic and nonparaphilic sexual disorders. *Clinical Therapeutics, 31*(1), 1–31.

Hatzimouratidis, K., Amar, E., Eardley, I., Guiliano, F., Hatzichristou, D., Montorsi, F., . . . Wespes, E. (2010). Guidelines on male sexual dysfunction: erectile dysfunction and premature ejaculation. *European Urology, 57,* 804–814.

Hawton, K. (1995). Treatment of sexual dysfunction by sex therapy and other approaches. *British Journal of Psychiatry, 161,* 307–314.

Holty, J. C., & Guilleminault, C. (2010). Maxillomandibular advancement for treatment of obstructive sleep apnea: A systematic review and meta-analysis. *Sleep Medicine, 14,* 287–297.

Jernelov, S. Lekander, M., Blom, K., Rydh, B., Ljotsson, B., Axelsson, J., . . . Kaldo, V. (2012). Efficacy of a behavioral self-help treatment with or without therapist guidance for comorbid and primary insomnia: A randomized controlled trial. *BMC Psychiatry, 12.* Retrieved from: http://www.biomedcentral.com/1471-244X/12/5.

Johansson, A., Sundbom, E., Hojerback, T., & Bodlund, O. (2010). A five-year follow-up study of Swedish adults with gender identity disorder. *Archives of Sexual Behaviors, 39,* 1429–1437.

Korte, A., Goecker, D., Krude, H., Lehmkuhl, U., Gruters-Kieslich, A., & Beier, K. M. (2008). Gender identity disorders in children and adolescence: Currently debated concepts and treatment strategies. *Deutsches Arzteblatt International, 105,* 834–841.

Laumann, E. O., Paik, A., & Rosen, R. C. (1999). Sexual dysfunction in the United States. *Journal of the American Medical Association, 281,* 537–544.

Lavault, S., Dauvilliers, Y., Drouot, X., Leu-Semenescu, S., Golmard, J., Lecendreux, M., . . . Arnulf, I. (2011). Benefit and risk of modafinil in idiopathic hypersomnia vs. narcolepsy with cataplexy. *Sleep Medicine, 12*(6), 550–556.

Lindau, S. T., Schumm, L. P., Laumann, E. O., Levinson, W., O'Muirchertaigh, C. A., & Waite, L. J. (2007). A study of sexuality and health among older adults in the United States. *New England Journal of Medicine, 357,* 762–774.

Melnik, T., Soares, B. G., & Nasselo, A. G. (2007). Psychosocial interventions for erectile dysfunction. *The Cochrane Library, 3.* Retrieved from: http://www.ncbi.nlm.nih.gov/pubmed/17636774

Meyer, W., Bockting, W. O., Cohen-Kettenis, P. C., Coleman, E., DiCeglie, D., Devor, H., . . . Wheeler, C. C. (2001). *Harry Benjamin international gender dysphoria association's standards of care for gender identity disorders* (6th ed.). Dusseldorf: Symposium Publishing.

Moul, D. E., Morin, C. M., Buysse, D. J., Reynolds, C. F., & Kupfer, D. J. (2007). Treatment of insomnia and restless leg syndrome. In P. E. Nathan & J. M. Gorman (Eds.), *A guide to treatments that work* (pp. 611–640) New York, NY: Oxford.

Nittur, N., Konofal, E., Dauvilliers, Y., Franco, P., Leu-Semenescu, S., Cock, V., & . . . Arnulf, I. (2013). Mazindol in narcolepsy and idiopathic and symptomatic hypersomnia refractory to stimulants: a long-term chart review. *Sleep Medicine, 14*(1), 30–36.

Preston, J. D., O'Neal, J. H., & Talaga, M. C. (2013). *Handbook of clinical psychopharmacology for therapists* (7th ed.). Oakland, CA: New Harbinger.

Quadri, S., Drake, C., & Hudgel, D. W. (2009). Improvement of idiopathic central sleep apnea with zolpidem. *Journal of Clinical Sleep Medicine, 5,* 122–129.

Ram, S., Seirawan, H., Kumar, S. K. S., & Clark, G. T. (2010). Prevalence and impact of sleep disorders and sleep habits in the United States. *Sleep Breath, 14,* 63–70.

Riemann, D., & Perlis, M. L. (2009). The treatments of chronic insomnia: A review of benzodiazepine receptor agonist and psychological and behavioral therapies. *Sleep Medicine Reviews, 13,* 205–214.

Sadock, B. J., & Sadock, V. A. (2007). *Kaplan and Sadock's synopsis of psychiatry: Behavioral sciences/ clinical psychiatry* (10th ed.). Philadelphia, PA: Lippincott Williams & Wilkins.

Stephenson, K. R., & Meston, C. M. (2010). When are sexual difficulties distressing for women? The selective protective value of intimate relationships. *Journal of Sexual Medicine, 7,* 3683–3694.

Szelenberger, W., Niemcewicz, S., & Dabrowska, A. J. (2005). Sleepwalking and night terrors: Psychopathological and psychophysiological correlates. *International Review of Psychiatry, 17,* 263–270.

Talarczyk, M. (2011). The authorial model of the therapy used in night terrors and sleep disorders in children. *Archives of Psychiatry and Psychotherapy, 2,* 45–51.

Wincze, J. P., Bach, A. K., & Barlow, D. H. (2008). Sexual dysfunction. In D. H. Barlow (Ed.), *Clinical handbook of psychological disorders: A step-by-step treatment manual* (4th ed., pp. 615–661). New York, NY: Guilford.

Yang, C., & Ebben, M. R. (2008). Behavioral therapy, sleep hygiene, and psychotherapy. In S. R. Pandi-Perumal, J. C. Verster, J. M. Monti, M. Lader, & S. Z. Langer (Eds.), *Sleep disorders: Diagnostics and therapeutics* (pp. 115–123). New York, NY: Informa Healthcare.

NAME INDEX

SUBJECT INDEX